AF541196

DEMOGRAPHIC TRANSITION
An Asian Perspective

DEMOGRAPHIC TRANSITION
An Asian Perspective

Edited by
Rajiv Balakrishnan

in association with
COUNCIL FOR SOCIAL DEVELOPMENT, New Delhi

KONARK PUBLISHERS PVT LTD

KONARK PUBLISHERS PVT LTD
206, First Floor, Peacock Lane,
Shahpur Jat, New Delhi-110049
Phone: (0-11) 41055065, 65254972
e-mail: konarkpublishers@hotmail.com

Copyright © Council for Social Development, New Delhi, 2011

All rights reserved. No part of this book may be reproduced or utilised in any form or by any means, electronic or mechanical, including photocopying, recording, or by any information storage and retrieval system, without prior permission in writing from the publishers.

Cataloging in Publication Data—DK
Courtesy: D.K. Agencies (P) Ltd. <docinfo@dkagencies.com>

Demographic transition : an Asian perspective / edited by **Rajiv Balakrishnan**.
p. cm.
Papers presented at a seminar organised by the Council for Social Development.
Includes bibliographical references and index.
ISBN 8122007864

1. Demographic transition—Asia—Congresses. 2. Demographic transition—India—Congresses. 3. Population aging—Asia—Congresses. 4. Population aging—India—Congresses. I. Balakrishnan, Rajiv. II. Council for Social Development (India)

DDC 304.62095 22

Typeset by The Laser Printers, New Delhi-110027, and printed at ASK Advertising Aids Pvt Ltd, Okhla, New Delhi

In memory of my late parents
Arangil Balakrishnan and Seetha Balakrishnan

Foreword

Developing countries the world over are at various stages of 'demographic transition', i.e. transition from high to low mortality and fertility. Falling mortality and the lag in fertility decline have resulted in a dramatic change in the population growth in these countries. This places heavy demands on governments to ensure that the basic needs of an ever growing population are met. While it is true that the increase in the number of births eventually will contribute to a growing workforce and yield a 'demographic dividend', the quality of the workforce in less developed country settings, in terms of how well nourished, healthy and educated it is, continues to be a major obstacle to development. The benefits of the 'demographic dividend' can only be reaped if the obstacle is overcome. Thus a good part of the challenges thrown up by the demographic transition lies in factors unrelated to population growth, such as the efficacy of government interventions, and the extent to which development is inclusive and participatory. Nonetheless efforts to contain population growth too are important, because it makes the task of governments that much easier.

It is against this backdrop that the book addresses some of the key demographic challenges before the nation. In doing so, it not only comprehensively highlights demographic trajectories but factors in a whole host of related variables as well, such as women's reproductive health, which in turn leads us on to issues of women's autonomy with respect to decisions about the reproductive burdens they will have to bear, the role of education and the mass media in precipitating a shift to the small family norm, decentralisation to facilitate a more effective delivery of health and family planning services, and so on. This kind of focus places this volume firmly in the domain of social development.

While the problem of overpopulation has been with us for some time, and the phenomenon of persisting high birth rates, which is at its root, continues to prevail in parts of the country, more recently, a new demographic challenge has come upon the scene, namely, that of population ageing, which occurs when longevity goes up due to mortality decline and the young-age population shrinks relatively to the elderly population due to a fall in the birth rate. The fact that India is among the countries of the world where population ageing is taking place at a relatively low level of resources has implications for the burden of elderly care, which, as the data in this book suggests, is likely to be of staggering proportions in the years to come. There is, however, some cause for hope, because the family in India continues to remain a stable institution for the care of the elderly. At the same time, the book draws attention to other approaches, such as low-cost institutional care for the elderly as a complement and supplement to family support. The volume also gives us demographic insights into that tragic phenomenon associated with the demographic transition, namely, the growing incidence of female foeticide.

The book is structured around a seminar organised by the Council for Social Development with the objective of elucidating and expanding upon the issues related to demographic transition. The concerns that are raised demand challenging responses. It is my hope that the volume would be of use to the community of development professionals and policy planners. It should also serve as useful introductory material to students who have opted for various fields of development studies.

I take this opportunity to commend and thank Dr. Rajiv Balakrishnan for bringing out this very important and timely volume. The issues deliberated here are ones which the Council for Social Development is deeply concerned with and endeavours to bring to public discourse. Dr. Balakrishnan has drawn upon his own contribution and those of other renowned scholars to bring clarity and depth to the topic.

Muchkund Dubey
President
Council for Social Development, New Delhi.

Preface

This book is an outcome of a seminar I organised for the Council for Social Development on the theme *Demographic Transition in South Asia: Contours, Contexts, Constraints & Consequences*. Prof. Muchkund Dubey, President of the Council, was a key motivator in getting the seminar and the book to be structured around it off the ground.

The volume stitches together a vast canvas, going back to India's colonial past, to a time when mortality rates began to fall even as poverty was rampant and epidemiological conditions abysmal. Two authors in this volume contribute to our understanding of this period of demographic history—Tim Dyson and Gopinath Ravindran. While Dyson shows how historical factors can explain the demographic similarities between southern and eastern India on the one hand and South East Asia on the other, Gopinath shows how ecological factors have shaped regional demographic trajectories within Madras presidency. Both show how demographic history can be a lens that facilitates a better understanding of the present.

Together with the contributions of these authors and the profile of demographic history in Chapter 1, we see how the decline in mortality owed not to improvements in health and resistance to disease, or in extensive public health interventions, but in factors like disease surveillance, which allowed the spread of epidemics to be nipped in the bud, to famine relief measures, facilitated by the spread of rail and road links, to immunities acquired by people long subject to debilitating diseases, to government sponsored immunisation programmes and the like. The reduction of rainfall variability, which reduced severe food shortfalls while not improving living conditions substantially also has been identified as a factor acting to contain death. All these go to underscore the need to work for a more equitable social order and the comprehensive health care envisaged by the Bhore Commission.

Another key feature of this book, apart from the depth of historical material that it taps, is the comprehensive profiling of demographic indicators for the subcontinent and its regions for over a century-long period, by M.K. Premi. This shows, among other things, that the south Indian States of Kerala and

Tamil Nadu have been at the forefront of the transition from high to low fertility and mortality. K.C. Zachariah and S. Irudaya Rajan, in their contribution to this volume, focus specifically on these two States.

Of the key themes thrown up by the subcontinent's demography, one is that of persisting high fertility, which continues in parts of the country to this day. Tulsi Patel, a sociologist, adds to our understanding of the factors at work to keep fertility high, and also the factors that come into play to curtail child-bearing. We note also that the circumstances that have made inroads into high fertility are many including decline in infant mortality, urbanisation, the spread of schooling (which increases 'child costs'), aspirations for children, even among illiterate mothers, the role of the mass media, the demonstration effect, and the family planning programme. The last of these - the family planning programme, had long been geared to government-set targets for 'couple protection', but new policy winds began to blow in the mid nineties. Targets were abolished, and the emphasis began to shift to programme management to deliver reproductive and health services to those wanting them. Nirmala Murthy, looks at issues in this area. She finds that the programme has begun to be better geared to catering to reproductive health, and that the effectiveness of contraceptive use may even have gone up as a consequence.

Much of the problem of reproductive health, however, lies with the health seekers themselves, their powerlessness, and the culture of silence that prevents them from being more demanding, as is suggested by Komila Parthi on the reproductive and mental health of women in Punjab, a State that has seen steep fertility declines. Complementing Parthi's study, the chapter by Carol Vlassoff and her colleagues—which is based on micro data from Gujarat affirms how, within the family, women's health concerns are neglected relative to men's. Chapters on related themes include a theoretical one on issues pertaining to neglect of females with respect to allocation of food, by John Hoddinott, and this author's (Rajiv Balakrishnan's) contribution, which aims to throw light on these sorts of concerns specifically with respect to the neglect of female children, the premature death of girls, and female infanticide, in an overarching context of demographic transition.

That fertility decline impacts the FMR is one consequence of the demographic transition. Another is the phenomenon of the greying of population, which occurs when falling mortality and fertility trigger changes in the age structure and foster an explosion of the proportion of the elderly. Statistical projections paint an alarming picture. Irudaya Rajan and Sabu Aliyar show, the onerous care-burden on the young that ageing will impose in the future, in an Indian State namely Kerala where longevity increases and mortality declines have been the steepest. Significantly, Rajan and Aliyar find that family support for the elderly is extensive going by the criterion of co-residence. Extensive family support for the elderly in Asian settings is shown also by primary data in the chapters by John Knodel and Chanpen Saengtienchai (for Thailand) and John C. Caldwell, P.H. Reddy and Pat Caldwell (for South India). It is indicated further in national level data sets reported upon for India and China by Rajagopal Dhar Chakrabarti. Mussaddeq Chowdhury and Jeffrey Nugent, stress that the State should provide types of elderly support that would supplement and intensify family-based care and not be a substitute for it. At the same time, it is noteworthy that even relatively small percentages of elderly with no access to familial support, given the large population, would throw up care challenges that the State needs to gear itself up to.

Also salient is the fact that ageing in the less developed countries is taking place in a context of widespread poverty and at a low level of resources in contrast to the experience of the west. Consequently, the fact that familial support is extensive doesn't mean that the elderly necessarily receive sufficient care. This—a major concern that the problem of ageing presents to the less developed countries—only goes to reiterate the need for making the structure of opportunity widely participatory, so that the demographic dividend, which is going to be with us for some time, can be reaped to its fullest extent and the care burden of the elderly made more manageable. Strategies by which the elderly are helped to lead a productive life also are important. Finally, low cost medical domiciliary and institutional care have the potential to emerge as a viable support system to complement and supplement family-based care. The book concludes on this optimistic note - the last chapter, by P. Thulasi Bai, a retired civil surgeon, shows how it is possible, even in a situation of a paucity of resources, to provide critical and specialised low-cost medical inputs which can improve the quality of their lives, to the point of even restoring them to productive work, and create conditions by which they can die in peace and dignity.

Overall, the book has sought to present an integrated picture, to tell the as yet unfolding story of demographic transition in an Asian perspective. In telling the story, I have many people to acknowledge. Many manuscripts were commissioned particularly for this volume and I am grateful to the many eminent scholars and population professionals who took time off to make very valuable contributions. They were also extremely patient with me and painstakingly responded to my many editorial requests.

I thank the Council for permission to use contributions from a special issue of their journal, *Social Change* (which I guest edited), and which had as its theme *The Family in Historical and Contemporary Times.* For motivating me to bring out this special issue, I am deeply indebted to the late Prof. Amar

Kumar Singh, erstwhile Chairman of the Council for Social Development, former Vice Chancellor of Ranchi University, and, for long, Honorary Editor of *Social Change*.

Another major influence that has gone into shaping this book is the CSD's teaching programme for Indian Foreign Service probationers. Prof. Muchkund Dubey, on whose initiative the programme began, asked me to lecture on the demographic transition. My goal then was, and continues to be, to communicate the key themes in simple and lucid fashion.

My colleagues at the Council of Social Development who contributed to administrative and library facilitation were Mr. R.S. Somi, Finance & Administrative Officer, CSD, who I thank for his continuous support, and Ms. Gurmeet Kaur, Librarian, who took considerable pains to procure the research materials I needed to stitch the book together.

I acknowledge my teacher, Prof. M.K. Premi, who mentored me in the discipline of demography at the Jawaharlal Nehru University when I studied for my PhD in Population Studies. I thank him also for being so good as to contribute two papers to the collection, which immensely add to its value.

My close family and friends were a constant support to me during the ups and downs of the production of this book. My sister and brother-in-law, Meera and Amit, were there for me, as always, leaving no stone unturned to help me tide over difficult times. My uncle and aunt, Lt. Col. A. Vijaya Raghavan and Sita Vijaya Raghavan, created a very supportive atmosphere for me in Chennai. In particular, I would like to mention my indebtedness to my late parents who would have been very happy at the fruition of my fourth book on development and related issues.

My aim in this book has been to give the reader a sense of both the broader canvas as well as findings from studies on specific themes. It is my sincere hope that the tome will advance, for its readers, demography's depths, intricacies and nuances.

Rajiv Balakrishnan

About the Contributors

Rajiv Balakrishnan is a demographer and development specialist. He holds a PhD in Population Studies and a Masters in Sociology from the Jawaharlal Nehru University, and a Bachelors degree in Economics from the University of Madras. He was at the East-West Population Institute in Honolulu on a one-year doctoral fellowship from 1987 to 1988. He served on the faculty of Council for Social Development (CSD), New Delhi, for fifteen years, during which time he engaged in research and developed and taught curricula on demography as well as (for the Council's annual research methods course) on 'Hypotheses and perceptual shifts'. He also guest edited three special issues of the CSD's journal, *Social Change*, and subsequently, for three years, served as the journal's Joint Editor. Dr. Balakrishnan has published in journals like the *Indian Social Science Review, Sociological Bulletin, Economic & Political Weekly, Social Change,* and *Social Action.* He is the principal author of three previous edited books brought out by the CSD on social development issues, namely (i) *Jharkhand Matters : Essays in Ethnicity, Regionalism and Development* (ii) *Participatory Pathways—Case Studies of People's Participation in Development Initiatives* and (iii) Rajiv Balakrishnan and Muchkund Dubey, eds *Social Development in India : Paths Tread and the Road Ahead.* He can be contacted at <rajiv.bala@yahoo.in> His website address is http://sites.google.com/site/rajivbalak/

Tim Dyson is Professor of Population Studies in the Development Studies Institute at the London School of Economics. He has held visiting positions at the Australian National University in Canberra, the International Institute of Population Sciences in Mumbai, and the American University of Beirut. He was elected as a Fellow of the British Academy in 2001. His main areas of research are on population and development, demographic time series, world food prospects, global warming and climate change, and the past, present and future population of the Indian subcontinent. His recent papers include: 'HIV/AIDS and urbanization', *Population and Development*

Review 29(3):427-42, September 2003; 'On development, demography and climate change: The end of the world as we know it?' *Population and Environment* 27(2):117-49, November 2005; and 'New evidence on child mortality in Iraq', *Economic and Political Weekly* Vol. XLIV, No 2, January 10, 2009. He is co-editor with Cormac Ó Gráda of *Famine Demography* published by Oxford University Press in 2002; and with Robert Cassen and Leela Visaria he is co-editor of and contributor to *Twenty-First Century India: Population, Economy, Human Development, and the Environment* also published by Oxford University Press in 2004.

Ravindran Gopinath is Head of the Department of History & Culture, Faculty of Humanities and Languages, Jamia Millia Islamia, New Delhi.

Tulsi Patel is Professor of Sociology at Department of Sociology, Delhi School of Economics, University of Delhi. She previously taught at Jamia Millia Islamia, New Delhi, and at Miranda House, University of Delhi. She was Chair, India Studies, at South Asia Institute, University of Heidelberg, Germany in 2005-06, was an honorary Research Associate at the University of Manchester (2001-2004), and has undertaken academic assignments and fellowships at the London School of Economics, Royal Holloway College, London (1996-97). She is on the advisory board of various academic journals and is the Secretary, Indian Sociological Society. She has published articles in national and international journals. Her books include *Fertility Behaviour: Population and society in a Rajasthan Village* (1994, 2nd edition 2006, Oxford University Press), and edited volumes on *Sex Selective abortion in India* (2007, Sage Publications), The *Family in India* (2005, Sage Publications) and with B. S. Baviskar, *Understanding Indian Society: Past and Present* (2010, Orient Blackswan).

Mahendra K. Premi, formerly Professor of Demography at the Jawaharlal Nehru University, received his doctorate from the University of Chicago in 1968. He is the author of several books, including two that were published by the East-West Center, Honolulu, Hawaii, where he had been a Visiting Fellow. His books include *India's Population: Heading Towards a Billion*, *Social Demography: A Systematic Exposition*, and *Population of India in the New Millennium: Census 2001*. Prof. Premi was President of the Indian Association for the Study of Population for four years, and has been connected with the census organisation for four decades.

K.C. Zachariah is currently Honorary Professor at the Centre for Development Studies, Thiruvananthapuram, Kerala. He has over five decades of research experience and has worked extensively on fertility, mortality and migration. He has served as United Nations Expert at the Cairo Demographic Centre,

Deputy Director of the International Institute for Population Sciences, Mumbai and Principal Demographer at the World Bank. Recently, he worked extensively on international migration and coordinated five large-scale migration surveys (1998, 2003, 2007, 2008, 2009) in Kerala along with S Irudaya Rajan.

S. Irudaya Rajan is Chair Professor, Ministry of Overseas Indian Affairs (MOIA) Research Unit on International Migration at the Centre for Development Studies, Thiruvananthapuram, Kerala. He has more than two decades of research experience in Kerala; has coordinated five major migration surveys (1998, 2003, 2007, 2008 and 2009) in Kerala (with Professor K C Zachariah) and has published books and articles on social, economic and demographic implications on international migration. He is member of the National Migration Policy drafting group appointed by the MOIA. He is editor of the Annual Series *India Migration Report* brought out by Routledge.

Nirmala Murthy is presently the President of the Foundation for Research in Health Systems, Ahmedabad. She holds a doctor of science degree from Harvard University and has been in the field of health for about four decades. She has had a rich experience of teaching and research at MIT, Cambridge, Harvard School of Public Health, Boston and the Indian Institute of Management, Ahmedabad.

Komila Parthi holds a doctoral degree in Psychology. Issues related to Women and Children, Psychosocial Development, Health and Applied Counseling are her special research interests

Carol Vlassoff received her PhD in Economics and Demography from the University of Pune, India, in 1977. Thereafter, she held key positions in Canada's two major development organisations, the International Development Research Centre (IDRC) and the Canadian International Development Agency (CIDA). Dr Vlassoff worked for 17 years with the World Health Organization, in Geneva, Surinam and Washington, D.C. She is now Adjunct Professor at the University of Ottawa in the Department of Community Medicine and Epidemiology and continues to pursue research in rural Maharashtra.

Shobha Rao is currently Head of the Biometry and Nutrition Group at Agharkar Research Institute, Pune. Her work on leprosy for the first time highlighted gender issues with respect to the disease and demonstrated its long term consequences. Dr. Rao has vast research experience in the field of community nutrition and health. She has published over 70 research papers in national and international journals. She has published 6 books and contributed chapters to 7 books. Soon after completion of a Ph.D., she was on tenure as a Visiting Research Fellow in the School of Public Health at the University of California, Berkeley, USA. During 1988-1991, she was Member, Steering Committee of World Health Organisation, Geneva. Her contribution to science has been acknowledged by the Government of India through a national award for the year 2005, given by the Department of Science and Technology.

Varsha Garole has obtained her Ph.D. in Biometry and Nutrition and is mainly responsible for the collection of the data on leprosy patients through detailed questionnaires and documenting case studies.

Neelima Karandikar has Master´s in Social Work and was mainly involved in data collection on leprosy patients using both structured questionnaires and documenting case studies in the project. She was responsible for data entry and helped in data analysis.

Mandana Azar was a member of the project staff involved with data collection for the co-authored chapter 10.

Asawari Kanade is a scientist at the Biometry and Nutrition Group of Agharkar Research Institute, Pune and is working in community nutrition. She has expertise in handling longitudinal data and is mainly involved in the statistical analysis of the data.

John Hoddinott is Deputy Director of the Poverty, Health and Nutrition Division of the International Food Policy Research Institute, Washington D.C.

Sabu Aliyar is a demographer affiliated to Centre for Development Studies, Thiruvananthapuram, Kerala. He is an inaugural recipient of the Canada-HOPE fellowship given to three scientists in the developing countries by the Government of Canada through its Canadian Institute of Health Research, and is a Research Fellow at Acadia University, Canada. Dr. Aliyar has been involved widely on international researches and has co-authored with noted demographers and scientists. He is a recipient of several international scholarships - IUSSP, Max-Planck Institute of Demographic Research, Germany and Asian Meta Centre, Singapore.

John C. Caldwell is Adjunct Professor, the Australian Demographic and Social Research Institute, College of Arts and Social Sciences, Australian National University, Canberra, Australia. He is an eminent demographer and has worked extensively on fertility and health transition.

P.H. Reddy is formerly director of the Population Research Centre, Bangalore. He has written widely on south Indian demography in collaboration with John C. Caldwell and Pat Caldwell.

Pat Caldwell has extensively co-authored on south Indian demography with John C. Caldwell and P.H. Reddy.

Professor John Knodel, PhD is Professor Emeritus at the University of Michigan. He has conducted collaborative research in Southeast Asia for nearly four decades, in Thailand, Cambodia and Vietnam. His recent research focuses on three main topics: 1) the well-being of older persons especially in the context of the family and in relation to gender and aging 2) the impact of the AIDS epidemic on older age parents whose adult children have AIDS and the parents' contribution to AIDS care giving and assistance with treatment (ART) adherence, and 3) the impact of migration of adult children on the well-being of older age parents who remain in rural areas. His research has involved collaborations with the College of Populations Studies and Faculty of Nursing at Chulalongkorn University in Bangkok, the Institute of Sociology in Hanoi, and the Cooperation Committee for Cambodia.

Chanpen Saengtienchai (MA. in demography, 1984, Australian National University) is former senior researcher at Institute of Population Studies, Chulalongkorn University, Thailand. She has been working in the area of ageing since 1986. Her interest centres on issues related to aging, includes psychological well-being and religion of older persons, and the impacts of HIV/AIDS and migration on older parents. She is currently collaborating with researchers from the US , Thailand and Cambodia on these topics.

Rajagopal Dhar Chakraborti is Head of the Department of South & Southeast Asian Studies and Professor of Economics and Demography at Calcutta University, India. He is also International Faculty, United Nations International Institute on Ageing (INIA), Malta.

Mussaddeq Chowdhury is Associate Professor of Economics, University of Redlands, United States. He holds a PhD from the University of Southern California.

Jeffrey B. Nugent is Professor of Economics at the University of Southern California where he teaches Development Economics. As a researcher in this field, he has worked on a wide variety of issues, problems and analytical techniques and in - and on, a variety of countries from Latin America, Africa, South and East Asia, and especially the Middle East and North Africa. In recent years, much of this work has focused on trade, foreign investment, labor markets and income distribution issues, including both household and firm behavior. Much of this work makes use of new institutional economics, political economy and econometric perspectives, emphasising the role of institutional considerations including transaction costs and contract enforcement. He has served on the Board of the Cairo-based Economic Research Forum, the Middle East Economic Association (for which he served as Executive Secretary for four years and President for three), and the Western Economic Association International, and serves on the editorial boards of eight scholarly journals. He also serves as a Research Fellow of IZA.

P. Thulasibai, a retired civil surgeon, is the President of the Santhitheeram Charitable Trust. She does humanitarian work for the Santhiheeram Hospice, which has been set up (on the outskirts of Trissur City, Kerala) under the aegis of the trust to provide critical care for the ailing elderly who do not have anywhere else to go.

Contents

Part IV
INDIA'S DEMOGRAPHIC TRAJECTORIES

Part V
FAMILY PLANNING AND REPRODUCTIVE HEALTH

Part VI
GENDER AND THE FEMALE-MALE RATIO

PART VII
GREYING IN THE LESS DEVELOPED WORLD

Part I

INTRODUCTION

Chapter 1

Demographic Transition: Trajectories, Triggers and Tailspins

Rajiv Balakrishnan

In the decades following World War I (1921 to 1951), mortality in the Indian subcontinent fell to levels unparalleled in the region's demographic history (Figures 1 and 2). This triggered off a phenomenal population growth of 2.5% per annum. The earlier half century, from around the first British Indian Census of 1872, was, by comparison, a period of rising death tolls, which rose to unprecedented heights at the time of the Great Influenza Epidemic of 1918-19. Life expectancy declined sharply—by 20%, since the 1890s. The period of rising mortality preceding 1921 occurred, ironically, a time when 'western policy seemed to have established the basis for better health and longevity'. The Indian Medical Service had expanded its activities, famine relief was systematised, railways and road links—which made possible the transport of food relief and played a critical role in famine management—were built, and irrigation systems, allowing for an increase in food production, set up. Moreover, malnourishment, which along with poor sanitation, created conditions conducive to disease and death, was on the decline. The period was one in which food was more available and real wages rose—notwithstanding the social dislocations that saw cultivators lose their land to money-lenders

Note: This chapter draws on the following writings of the author: (i) CSD working paper 001/3, titled 'The Social Context of the Family Planning Programme: Evidence of 1990s Survey Data from Uttar Pradesh', (ii) 'Fertility and the Value of children in Three Asian Countries: A Review of Salient Themes', *Social Change* 26(2): 74-86, (iii) 'Faces of the Family: Past and Present', *Social Change* 26(2): 3-9, (iv) 'A Note on Ageing and the Elderly in the Less Developed World', *Social Change* 29(1&2): 207-210.

and indigenous artisans being hard put to market their products in the face of competition from foreign goods, or, in urban areas, the growing inflation that cut into the wages of coolies (Klein 1989: 389-390, 394-396, 403).

While low living standards, lack of medical care, malnutrition and insanitation due to overcrowding and reduced resistance to disease, were long-term underlying causes of the heavy toll of mortality in the 19th century, there was no *deterioration* in conditions that could account for unusually high death rates in the 1872-1921 period (Klein 1989: 393-394). Famines did take a terrible

FIGURE 1: Death Rates, British India, 1881-1921

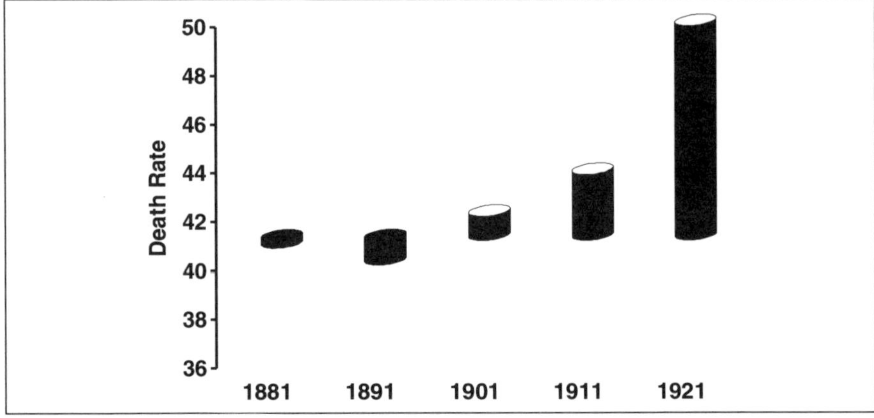

Note: Figure generated from actuarial estimates by G.F. Hardy, cited in Klein 1989: 390.

FIGURE 2: Death Rates, India, 1921-1971

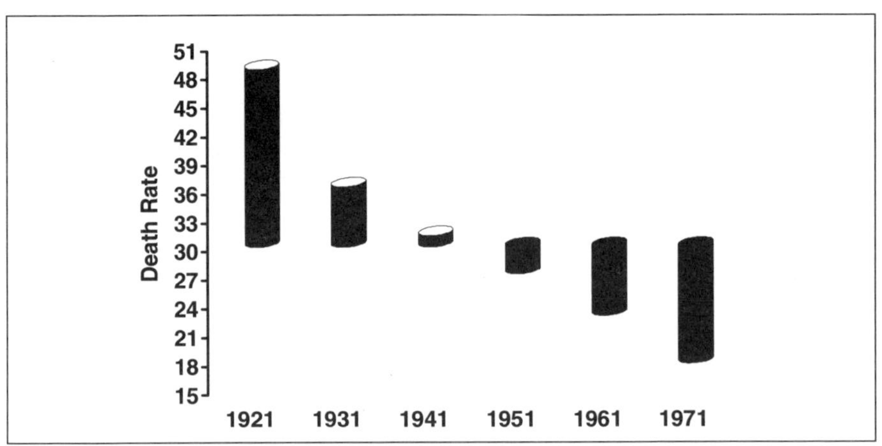

Source: Figure generated from data calculated by Kingsley Davis by the reverse survival method (Davis 1951: 36). Cited in Klein 1989: 390.

toll—of over 14 million lives in this period, but they were much less deadly than the famines of the early and mid 19th century, thanks to relief measures made possible by modern means of transport and the development of labour markets. Famine deaths, in fact, were far greater *prior to* 1872. We see also that the proportion of famine deaths fell drastically between 1872/81 and 1911-21, with disease mortality increasing far more rapidly than average mortality (Figure 3). In this period of rising disease mortality, plague claimed more than 12 million lives (accounting for 95% of the world's plague pandemic mortality), while over 17 million were felled by the killer influenza epidemic of 1918-1919 (Klein 1989: 396-398). Yet, famine, plague, and influenza together accounted for less than 10% of the deaths in the 1872-1921 half century. Most of the deaths in this period were caused by a host of other diseases—malaria, pneumonia and respiratory diseases, TB and typhoid, cholera, measles, puerperal fever and small pox were identified as major killers. Diphtheria, tetanus, *kala azar*, hepatitis, scarlet fever, syphilis, encephalitis, enteric fever, typhus and backwater fever were among the mortality's lesser messengers. Malaria, pneumonia and related respiratory diseases, TB and diarrhoea were the deadliest killers, each responsible for a greater number of fatalities than famine, the plague and influenza combined. Malaria, as per the cause of mortality statistics of Indian Medical Service, was estimated to cause a million deaths every year (Klein 1989: 398, 399).

Thus, 1872-1921 'crescendo of death' can be explained neither in terms of famine and increasing malnutrition, nor by the 'misfortune' hypothesis that assigns salience to the wildfire spread of epidemic disease like plague and influenza. What then explains the surge in lethal disease mortality at this point in history? Was it caused by new disease vectors that the colonial encounter inducted into a subcontinent hitherto not exposed to microbes from afar and hence bereft of acquired immunities to microbe invaders from across the seas? The historical evidence discounts such a possibility, as the subcontinent's killer diseases were largely indigenous. In contrast to the Indian experience, in America, Australia, Tasmania and Polynesia, the indigenes, previously isolated from foreign contact, were defenseless against the onslaught of new diseases from the Old World. India's contacts by land and sea, as also, the Mongol invasions, had exposed the region to Eurasian disease long before the colonial presence. There are indications also that some of the 'European' diseases themselves may have had Indian origins. Thus, the Black Death bacillus which decimated 30% of Europe in the 14th Century may have originated in plague-ridden parts of India, while the plague itself, which is thought to have entered India from China via Bombay in 1896, too may have had earlier roots in India (Klein 1989: 399-401).

The mortality crescendo of 1872-1921 *can*, nonetheless be attributed to a

FIGURE 3: Mortality and Disease Mortality Increases, 1872/81 to 1911/21

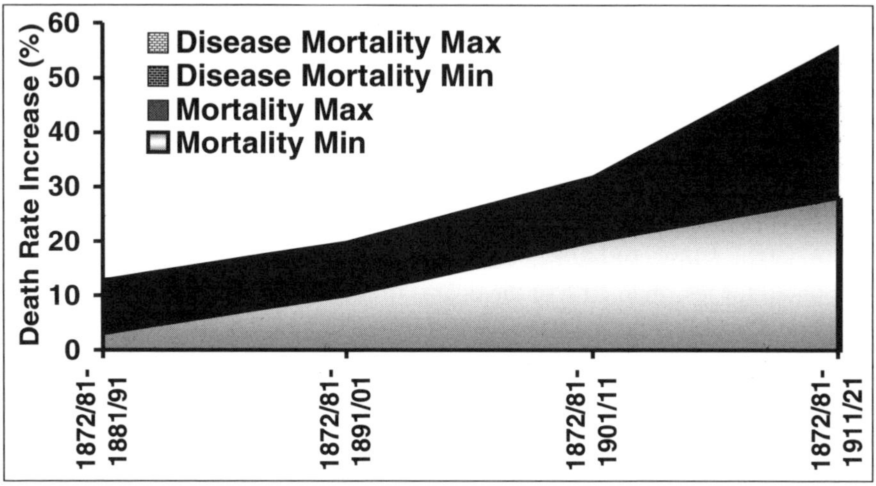

Source: Data compiled in Klein 1989: 392.

'foreign hand', in so far as the spread of disease in India operated largely via factors related to activities of the colonial power. In earlier times, in the context of limited trade and low levels of mobility, diseases had been contained in the context of acquired immunity, natural selection, and disease-host accommodation. Thus, malaria zones in the Himalayan terai were deadly for migrants and travelers, but not for the locals. This state of affairs had largely prevailed, though periodically the balance was disturbed by foreign contact, migration, and new disease strains. In the colonial period, however, the diffusion of trade and human mobility upset the earlier ecological balance. Economic development led to displacement, causing movement of migrants seeking new employment in cities, development projects, or plantations. Famines pushed people in distress to relief works. The phenomenal growth of human mobility during this period is evidenced by the fact that railway trips increased from 19 million per annum in 1872 to 535 million per annum in 1921. As a consequence of the rapid multiplication of people on the move, microbes got spread far and wide, with the result that people who did not have the acquired immunity of the original locale inhabitants became fatally susceptible. TB, which became endemic in regions of urban congestion and poverty, spread to rural areas. Modernisation led to the spread of disease through trade as well. Thus, the plague flea and the microbes X. cheopis and P. pasteurella were transported throughout India due to a massive trade in grain (Klein 1990: 401-403).

Further, The colonial government's activities in India caused stagnation of water flows, which fostered diseases like cholera and typhoid (Klein 1990: 403). Let us now look at this aspect a little closer, by focusing on cholera mortality in India, which peaked in the late 19th century (1887-96) (Klein 1994: 493-494). While malnutrition has been identified as a major factor in susceptibility to the disease, the peak in cholera deaths (as Figure 4 shows), occurred in 1887-1896, a decade that was *less* ravaged by famine mortality than the ones that preceded and succeeded it (Klein 1994: 494-495). Moreover, living standards evidently were on an *upward* course in the period of rising death rates, while, between the world wars, when mortality (including cholera mortality) began its sustained decline, food availability fell (Klein 1990: 34; Klein 1994: 493-494). It is true that since antiquity, conditions in India have been conducive to the proliferation of the water borne cholera bacilli. The monsoons and the irrigation-oriented economy of the Indus Valley Civilisation provided breeding grounds, while the movement of peoples, through pilgrimages, caravan trade and imperial wars, potentially could spread infection from contaminated water bodies. Cholera however became endemic in central India, Punjab and other areas only after the mid-nineteenth century. Modern transport such as the Railways were thought to spread the disease from its 'endemic haunts' in the late 19th century, for instance, in the eastern United Provinces and the sub-continent's southern tip. Moreover, '... the cholera deity reached into new regions and, acculturating, it made numerous new nests from where it propagated infection locally'. The epidemics, it is argued, were too widespread to be explained solely in terms of its spread from a few endemic locales (Klein 1994: 496-497).

Factors that contributed to the bacilli's spread include its longevity in water and the greater susceptibility of malnourished people (of which they were many). Also critical was cholera's dissemination through *carriers* who were either not themselves infected or suffered milder infections—and hence did not die. Finally, as we have already noted, modern transport increased the flow of people, for instance to festivals and fairs, with the growth of commerce too a contributory factor, as was labour mobility in response to new opportunities. On the other hand, water resources remained underdeveloped, with the result that labourers, pilgrims, traders, and market bound farmers, forced to use polluted water bodies, got infected. Finally, the growth of commercial towns led to crowding in slums, but no commensurate improvement in sanitation, with the result that underground seepage created '... among the world's worst water supplies'. Under normal environmental conditions, the cholera bacillus, in a relatively benign fashion, either found a healthy host in which to reside, or fostered 'at least a smoldering infection' of the shape and size of cholerine or choleric diarrhea. When water bodies got heavily polluted, however, and '... susceptible multitudes descended on scarce [water] supplies', particularly when the resistance of the victims was already low on account of arduous journeys, lethal infections set in (Klein 1994: 497,499-500,502,505,507). In environmentally degraded—but not intensely polluted locales, the cholera bacillus fostered a 'smoldering infection' of cholerine or choleric diarrhoea. When water bodies got intensely polluted, however, many were infected with cholera gravis and not merely diarrhoea, setting the stage for the spread of lethal infections (Klein 1994: 500).

It was the religious fairs and festivals as hubs of cholera that attracted the most attention by medical authorities, to the neglect of 'secondary foci'. The 'grim spectacle' of pilgrims fleeing from sites of cholera infections was compelling, more so as there were some 20 to 50 million pilgrims peregrinating every year. Furthermore, pandemics sometimes did have their source in great festivals. The locales of these festivals became environmental disasters, due to overcrowding and pressure on water resources—tanks, cesspools, small rivers, and the like, which got polluted with sewage and filth. Devotees who thronged sacred tanks bathed, washed clothes, and rinsed their mouths there. Sacred pools with contaminated stagnant water were sites of spiritual purification. When pilgrims at a great festival were stricken by the dreaded disease, it led to a 'desperate, panicky flight', a process that spread the disease to distant places. Notably, the pilgrims got infected also from water bodies *en route*. These were used for defecation and drinking, and became nodal points for the spread of the disease, infecting itinerant villagers, merchants, pilgrims, mendicants, etc.

FIGURE 4: Cholera Mortality, British India and India-Pakistan, 1877-1954

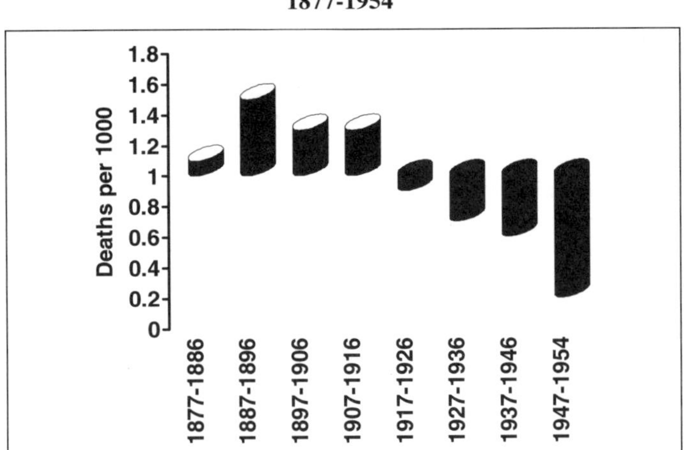

Data Source: Klein, Ira. 1994. 'Imperialism, ecology and disease: Cholera in India, 1850-1950'. *Indian Economic & Social History Review*. 31(4): 492.

Nodal points, in general, were however ignored, and health officials focused on containing the disease at their supposed 'staging points'. Thus, at Hardwar in 1891, they established pilgrim camps along the fast flowing waters of the Ganges, connected the stagnant Bhim Goda pool, used for sacred purposes, to the Ganges River, organised vaccination, sanitary patrols etc. (Klein 1994: 500, 503-505).

The focus on pilgrimage sites in the fight against cholera was bolstered by the widespread epidemic of 1865, which occurred in the wake of the Mahadeo festival. The festival was banned in 1867, and when epidemics broke out in the following years, the belief in the supposed centrality of pilgrim traffic in the spread of cholera came to be questioned, and the role of railway transport in the dissemination of the disease came to be better understood. In the great post-Mutiny 'railroad building era', designed to serve the needs of internal and international commerce, the railways had became purveyors of disease and death. Construction gangs employed in track construction, lived in unsanitary and crowded work sites, and when cholera struck, workers fleeing the area became the bacilli's unwitting collaborators. A similar scenario was played out in roads that served to link up rail routes. In late 1860s, the Great Indian Peninsular Railway extended east from Bombay up to Nagpur, and was connected to Jubblepur, the terminus of the railway line from Calcutta, via the Nagpur highway, which became critical to travel across the subcontinent, and also served to maintain postal communication between Bengal Presidency and Europe. Given the importance of the Nagpur highway, intensive road building activities were undertaken, but sanitary conditions at the work sites at which construction workers had to camp was abysmal. Water supplies were far from adequate, '... which made the whole region a potential cholera death trap'. Well digging was made problematic by rocky sub strata, water bodies like tanks were hard to come by, and streams ran dry in the summer months, all of which was compounded by the vagaries of the monsoon. Intensified pollution of scarce water bodies caused by the failure of the monsoon in 1868-69 raised infection risks and led to widespread outbreaks of cholera. With the lack of rains affecting agricultural output, cholera-synergistic malnutrition and starvation too were unleashed (Klein 1994: 506-509).

Transport—as we have seen, a key factor in the dissemination of the disease—got amplified by growing commerce. This is illustrated by the case of Bhandara, a 4000 square mile 'lake region of Nagpur', replete with tanks and artificial reservoirs that were created to grow superior quality rice and sugarcane in conditions of scarce rainfall. Soon, the roads from Bhandara to the markets of Nagpur and Kamthi were congested with grain carts, and the meager water bodies on the route got polluted. Carters, labour gangs, travelers, were all at risk. Life support resources continued to lag behind the development of rail and roadways, into the 20th century. Pleas for sanitary improvements by health officials were not heeded by railway managers, and though a few efforts were made to improve sanitary conditions by digging wells, the work was slow and worker availability poor. In this scenario, '... water remained scarce, and banning contaminated sources was as effective as outlawing thirst' (Klein 1994: 509-510).

Development-related activities in the late colonial period caused ecological decay also as a consequence of colonial government's management of waterways, as the case of Bengal strikingly illustrates. In the pre-colonial past, when, in the dry season, rivers ebbed and became stagnant pools, their waters, used for cremation, cooking, bathing, defecation, etc, got badly polluted—but the monsoons revived the rivers; waste and microbes were speedily dispersed and pathogens chemically neutralised, with the result that the waters regained their purity and were reasonably safe for consumption. Moreover, the rain-swollen waters of the rivers carried fertile silt through streams and irrigation channels and so brought these nutrient-rich deposits to the rice fields. Colonial development led to clogging of these water systems. Due to the proliferation of petty dams, rivers became silted, soils got deprived of nutrients, sanitation and drainage suffered. Corpses, traditionally disposed off in the waters by those too poor to cremate them, decomposed in sluggish waters. The waters got polluted also by human excreta, pollutants from the washing of soiled clothes, etc. Ecological decay was rampant, and cholera bacilli multiplied in polluted waters (Klein 1994: 511-513).

In explaining the eventual decline of cholera, one noteworthy factor is that its devastation was greatest in locales it had not previously struck, which suggests that survivors—either healthy carriers, or those who suffered milder infections (choleric diarrhoea or cholerine) developed and passed on immunities to their offspring. Yet, acquired immunity can only be a partial explanation, as in Bengal, cholera's 'most infamous lair', the disease was prevalent throughout the 19th century. So, there had to be other factors at work. One of these was famine—given the synergy between malnutrition and cholera, conditions of famine were propitious to the spread of the disease. The record shows that cholera mortality scaled peaks in famine years, for instance, in 1877, in Madras, when the death toll from cholera was 357,000, and in 1900—the year of the highest annual cholera mortality for India as a whole—when cholera claimed 346,000 lives in Bengal and 165,000 more in Bombay. Yet, the link with famine was not clear-cut. Thus, the late 19th century peaks of cholera mortality occurred in the absence of famine. Further, while famines declined from 1900, cholera mortality fell only much later, from the 1920s (Klein 1994: 515-517). This attests to the salience of development-related factors in the spread of the disease.

The dramatic decline in the death rate—as much as 60% between the world wars was substantially due to the demise of influenza, but if the 17 million deaths caused by the Influenza Epidemic are excluded, the decline in mortality was still a staggering 30%. Mortality plummeted at a time of stagnating per capita income, while, in the (preceding) years of rising mortality (1872-1921), per capita income had grown significantly. The inter-war years, it is noteworthy, were a time when unemployment grew rampant, following an industrial recession, which also affected agriculture. In the Indian context, 'Poverty was a continuum through the period that mortality began its remarkable descent' (Klein 1990: 33-39). It was a time when per capita food availability fell, and nutritional data collected by the then government identified abysmal nutritional deficiencies as contributing to morbidity and mortality. In Europe, by comparison, increases in food availability were a critical factor in mortality decline. In India, as noted, per capita food availability fell. Moreover, nutritional data collected by the government during this time showed abysmal deficiencies, which were identified as contributing to morbidity and mortality (Klein 1990: 33-39).

If mortality decline in India occurred when food availability reduced, was the fall in the death rate due to improvements in factors related to sanitation and environment? Typical environmental conditions in the village left much to be desired. Dwellings were ill-ventilated, overcrowded and leaky, farm animals were often kept on the premises, pits adjacent to the dwellings—dug to store human wastes, were a breeding ground for mosquitoes, and compost heaps, where cow dung and other organic matter decomposed, attracted rodents and vermin. Moreover, given the lack of proper sanitation, villagers relieved themselves in fields or ponds, creating conditions conducive to the spread of diseases such as cholera, typhoid fever, dysentery, and hookworm diseases. Between the wars, when mortality fell, the risks from stagnant and polluted water actually increased due to the construction of canals, irrigation dams, etc. In urban areas too, environmental conditions were very poor, and showed no improvement throughout the colonial period. Towns and the 'great' port cities were home to crowded slums lacking proper sanitation, rendered so by inadequate suburban transport and low working class salaries. Overall, a sad story of a colonial government narrowly focused on material progress, to the neglect of ecological and health consequences (Klein 1990: 39-42, 63).

Nonetheless, one must give the colonial government credit where it is due—the stalwart efforts of the Indian Medical Service (IMS) in fighting disease merit laudable mention. After WW I, the IMS, armed with new cadres of sub-assistant surgeons and hospital assistants, and through its Municipal Health Officers, who were appointed to many new towns, undertook a variety of health measures. Dispensary treatments before WW II were double those before WW I, with millions receiving medical attention for deadly diseases like malaria, diarrhoea and dysentery, and TB. Malaria treatments totaled 13 million per year before WW II, more than twice the figure for the period before WW I. In this period of 20 million annual vaccinations for small pox, over four million were vaccinated every year for cholera. The efforts of the IMS, alas, were a mere drop in the ocean. Safe water supplies provided protection from cholera to a miniscule percentage of the population. As for the cholera vaccine, it offered only short-term protection for a few months, and was usually administered only after an outbreak. Smallpox vaccination was limited too, because the vaccinators were too few to ensure that the entire population was covered. Even if these efforts had been more successful, it is noteworthy, they would have merely scratched the surface. Cholera's decline appears to be related to factors other than safe water supplies, which secured protection only for a few protected urban enclaves. Significantly, famines, which weakened resistance and increased susceptibility to disease, were on the wane (Klein 1990: 45, 47-48).

As for malaria, the campaign to eradicate it floundered, notwithstanding a few showcase successes in Delhi, the Damodar coalfields, and in West Bengal (in Jangipur and Meenglas), where mosquito breeding was stemmed. The limits to the onslaught on malaria became evident in Mian Mir, where a major campaign against mosquito breeding was launched. Millions of mosquito larvae were decimated, but mosquitoes surprised the specialists by their ability to breed in both running as well as stagnant water. Moreover, the half-mile flight range of the mosquito meant that it could breed in surrounding areas and then fly into the village locale to wreck havoc. The realisation dawned that mosquitoes could not be eliminated without proper environmental management, not only in the rainfall abundant 'wet' regions, but also in the 'dry' areas, where development works in the forms of tanks, irrigation canals, and dams provided artificially created havens for mosquito larvae. In towns, proper drainage was seen as the key to fighting the mosquito menace, but again, ground realities were difficult to tackle. Acknowledging defeat, the Health Commissioners sought to promote quinine as a prophylaxis, but though the medicine was distributed to millions annually—a one hundred per cent increase over the pre WWI period, succor reached only a fraction of the 100 million malaria victims in India (Klein 1990: 48-50).

Tuberculosis, the 'white plague', another formidable antagonist the IMS was pitted against—a highly contagious disease—came into its own in crowded areas where living conditions were sub-standard. Commercial development in India, the IMS believed, was creating conditions of overcrowding and environmental decay, thus giving free reign to the dreaded disease, which flourished in overcrowded urban centres. In rural areas, though overcrowding and poor ventilation were not so severe, low incomes and primitive living conditions made villagers susceptible to infection from migrants, and tuberculosis as a killer in village India was second only to cholera. At the national level, the disease claimed 1.5 million lives annually. IMS doctors identified the major efforts needed in providing better housing and less overcrowding, upliftment of the poor and popular education. The radical reform advocated by the IMS was crippled by lack of political support and a deficiency of funds (Klein 1990: 50-51).

Many of the post WW I activities of the IMS, such as nutritional programmes, midwife training, malaria control and comprehensive health plans were very limited in scope, affecting a very small percentage of the population. Thus, though the 30 percent of births in urban South India attended by trained midwives could be claimed as a success, this was only a minor percentage of all deliveries in a predominantly rural region. The figure for all India was a mere 2%. The IMS, for its part, was remarkably candid in assessing its own activities, overtly acknowledging failure in its efforts to contain disease and mortality. Thus, with commendable integrity, it refused to take credit for the fall in infant mortality, given that the most persistent declines occurred in regions where there were practically no child welfare schemes in place. Similarly, there was no indication that the waning of the Great Influenza epidemic had anything to do with government efforts, which were limited to sympathy and the distribution of free blankets. That deadly killer, the plague, too suffered terrible reverses after WW I, but no authority came forward to attribute it to public health activities (Klein 1990:47-48).

If India's mortality decline in the inter-war years does not lie in improved nutrition, better sanitation, the spread of medical services, or the impact of public health then, according to Klein, we must revert to the immunology explanation. Malevolent microbes, Klein (1990: 52-63) contends stimulated immunological defense systems which eventually triggered mortality decline. The least immune succumbed, but survivors passed on immunities to their progeny. As resistance to disease depends on nutrition, social factors were important too. The depredations of disease fell more heavily on the poor, who, because of malnutrition, were not able to develop immunological robustness. Immunological defense, it is also noteworthy, was strain specific, with immunities for different diseases were acquired over separate periods of time, long before the 'crescendo of mortality' in the early 20th century. Thus, at the time malaria lost out to acquired immunity, the raging plague and influenza epidemics grabbed the limelight. It was acquired immunity also that brought the dreaded plague to its knees after World War I; both humans and rodents developed powerful immunities, which were passed on to progeny by survivors (Klein 1990:52,54-56,61).

In another take on declining mortality in India post 1921, Guha (2001) attributes it to an improvement in immunity levels due to a decline in the *variability* of nutrition. In the 1920s and the 1930s, in India, 'the bulk of the population' was above the lower limit of the range of 'moderate' malnutrition. By contrast, prior to 1921, 'at least a significant minority' had fallen below the range, and a weakened populace was more susceptible to disease. This difference between life and death was a difference between moderate malnutrition, which does not enhance the death rate, and severe, debilitating malnutrition, which trebles it. It is true that malnutrition can deny the parasite the sustenance it needs, and so inhibit the outbreak of the disease, in other words, in can be disease-antagonistic. What then caused nutrition levels to improve? Guha cites evidence to show that a decline in weather-related variability in agricultural output was the key factor at work. While public health measures could have helped contain disease outbreaks, '... the Indian population in the second quarter of the twentieth century lived longer because the weather gods enabled it to maintain a stable level of moderate malnutrition rather than alternately plunge between adequate nutrition and severe malnutrition as it was doing earlier' (Guha 2001: 84-86).

Another analyst (Arnold 1989) emphasises the colonial government's system for monitoring and surveillance of disease which could have, along with public health measures, nipped mortality in the bud by *averting* disease outbreaks. The data from this system were extensively used, allowing surges in specific disease at a particular time and place to be anticipated (Dyson and Das Gupta 2001: 80). Arnold, in his (1989) paper on cholera, notes that the vital registration system, set up and operationalised in the late 1860s and 1870s, at a time when confusion about the disease and its transmission was prevalent, made it possible to predict the likely timing and locale of epidemic outbreaks. In this context, it is noteworthy that notwithstanding the colonial regieme's raison d'etre of wealth extraction, public health measures had indeed been put in place. Other steps were taken as well. One such was an early warning system in the form of special postcards to be sent by the village chowkidar to the nearest health officer the moment cholera was detected. In the context of pilgrimage as a source of cholera dissemination, pilgrims were monitored to see if they were carrying the disease. By the early decades of the 20th century, Arnold argues, western medicine and sanitation gained in credence and popularity, while public health funds were allocated to elected officials of local bodies under the Government of India Act of 1919 further promoted the control of cholera. Facilities for small towns were hamstrung by funds constraints, but in the big cities like Calcutta and Madras, piped water and sewage had a strong impact. Arnold is of the view that improved sanitation, medical intervention, piped water, medical surveillance at fairs and festivals, inoculation, the vital registration system, all acted in concert to break the epidemiological back of cholera mortality, at the same time leaving unsolved the basic problems of poverty and ill health (Arnold 1989: 274, 275, 276, 277, 278, 279).

As we have seen, of increasing immunity and public health measures need not be seen as mutually exclusive. Both have been factors at work. Notably, also, in the work of Klein (1989, 1990, 1994), Arnold (1989) and Guha (2001), the mortality decline that set in after 1921 in the subcontinent was seen to occur even as poverty and malnutrition were pervasive and nutritional deficiencies widespread. After Independence, other factors assumed importance—better protection of water sources in towns, coupled with urbanisation, better nutrition, medicine and even living conditions (Klein 1994: 517). Klein (1989, 1990, 1994) and Arnold (1989) also underscore another salient factor, namely, the fact that famines, which weakened resistance to disease, had been on the wane.

South Asia's history of periodically recurring famines goes back to antiquity, but gauging the impacts of famine's ravages, for instance, in terms of mortality rates or disease susceptibility, was made possible only after the setting up of demographic data gathering systems after the 1860s. Since then, the first 'major' famine (as opposed to a 'local' one) occurred in 1876-78, striking southern, central and western India with particular intensity. Then, a decade later, two famines—the famines of 1896-97 and 1899-1900, raged through 'much of the subcontinent', one on the heels of the other. In all these famines, the failure of the monsoon winds—harbingers of rain-bearing clouds, typically from June to October, resulted in drought, a 'principal proximate cause' of the agricultural failure, resulting in food scarcities that led to hoarding and spiraling prices. These agricultural crises also engendered unemployment, creating entitlement failures among field labourers and rural artisans, who had to migrate hither and thither in search of jobs (Dyson 1991a: 6).

Focusing on the late 19th century famines, Dyson (1991a:7-8) selects three locales—Madras Presidency to study the 1876-78 famine, and to study the 1896-97 and the 1899-1900 famines, Central Provinces and Bombay Presidency respectively. The famine of 1876-1878, the data for Madras suggest, had its beginnings in 1875, on account of the deficiency of the Southwest monsoon, which normally brings in the rains in June-October. In the succeeding year, 1876, the rains never came, and food prices spiralled upward, mirroring drought-induced crop failure. This was a time also of rising mortality, which peaked in January 1877. Correspondingly, the conception rate, computed by reverse surviving annual registered births, was below its normal levels through the famine months—mechanisms such as reduced coital frequency, postponement of marriage, decline in fecundity, and spousal separation at a time of famine-time migration of male wage seekers, have typically been implicated in this process. Finally, with the arrival of the monsoon in late 1887, things began to get back to normal; agriculture revived and labourers resumed work on the fields. However, mortality in this period of resumed rainfall rose to an even higher crescendo, before it dramatically declined the following year (1878). Thus the mortality trajectory was doubled-peaked, or forked. This evidently, was a result of two major epidemics. The first peak, in January 1877 (before the rains), was related to cholera, which typically spread when water bodies stagnated, and were easily polluted by defecation, bathing, etc. If cholera deaths are subtracted from the overall CDR, the January 1877 peak practically disappears, and we are left with the second peak, coinciding with the rains towards the latter half of 1877. Rains are associated with a number of diseases, particularly, in the 19th century context, malaria. The fact that 62% of deaths in the last half of 1877 were classified as 'fevers'—suggestive of malarial mortality, is therefore salient. By the end of 1877, when mortality fell, food consumption may have been improving, though prices, while on a declining trajectory, continued to remain high and the conception rate remained suppressed (Dyson 1991a: 13, 14).

The next major famines occurred in the last decade of the 19th century. Rainfall inadequacy, poor harvests, and rising prices in 1894-1895 were precursors of the famine of 1896-1897. Things took a turn for the worse when the rains abruptly ceased in August 1896, leading to a sharp rise in the CDR (Crude Death Rate) in the last quarter of that year. Through all this time, from 1894 to 1896, a price rise occurred, while correspondingly, the conception rate fell—the typical pattern we have seen for Madras, in the 1876-1878 famine years. The arrival of rains in mid-1897 made possible the resumption of cultivation, but the rains created conditions conducive to outbreaks of malaria, with the death rate peak from May to December 1897, significantly owing to malaria's depredations. Following this, the CDR plunged, as did prices, while conceptions correspondingly increased. Another catastrophe was, however, ominously waiting in the wings—the failure of the monsoon in 1899. Again, prices rose, and conceptions declined. As in the case of the Madras famine, the peaking of the death rate occurred only much later—in August-September 1900, when the rains resumed, with malaria a significantly contributory to the death toll (Dyson 1991a: 15-16).

In Bombay Presidency, rainfall failures in 1896 and 1899 were the famine triggers, with the conception rate, an indicator of famine distress, declining far more severely in the famine years 1899-1900 as compared to the earlier famine year of 1897. Despite the modest death rate rise in 1897, conceptions did fall off sharply, indicating famine distress. In early 1900, the death rate peaked, first in early 1900, with cholera contributing to it substantially. A second peak occurred in late 1900, to which malaria appears to have a considerable claim (Dyson 1991a: 17).

A number of common characteristics can be discerned from these famines of the late 19th century. Firstly, the conception rate, a sensitive indicator of famine distress, closely parallels the price level in the initial phase of rising prices, even before mortality has begun to peak. Famine distress subsequently gets accentuated by rising mortality and morbidity. Mortality from cholera is at its worst in the initial phase of the famine, when itinerants in search of livelihood create conditions of overcrowding at relief centres, leading to overuse and pollution of water bodies. We see also, examining our three major famines, that mortality rises to a crescendo with the resumption of rains, when malaria's malevolence is unleashed. This may have been due to accumulation of water in which mosquitoes could breed, in turn caused by the extraordinary clogging of drains that had not been flushed out for a long time on account of the failure of the previous monsoon. Another likely factor at work is that failure of a previous monsoon, by reducing exposure to malaria, had reduced resistance levels. Migrants returning home after their wandering in the famine years could also have brought with them strains of malaria to which the local populace did not have immunity. Finally, improvement of nutritional levels (due to the resumption of agricultural employment made possible by the rains) can increase the malaria parasite's ability to multiply in the human body. (Dyson 1991a: 18, 22, 24). 'Decent' nutrition was a source of 'high resistance or slight susceptibility' normal to Europeans, but in the case of malnourished Indians, even fasting for a few days made them susceptible to the disease (Dyson 1994:497). A population weakened by famine was easy prey. Though the victims began to gain strength when food availability increased, they were still quite weak, and at this critical juncture, the parasites in their bodies grew stronger due to the improved nutrition in their hosts.

We have seen how a synergy operated between disease-mortality and the incidence of famine. Arnold (1989) presents some striking statistics on this aspect with respect to the cholera epidemic that struck Madras Presidency in the 1870s. While in 1873 and 1874, cholera deaths numbered a mere 840 and 313 respectively, in 1874, the figure had risen dramatically to 94,546. It rose further to 94,564 in 1875, 148,193 in 1876, and 357,430 in 1877 (12.24 per thousand of population). The falling year, 1878, cholera mortality fell to 47,167, before eventually dropping to 613 in 1880. The onset of the epidemic had preceded the famine of 1876, which struck the 'Ceded Districts' in dry interior of the Presidency, namely, Bellary, Kurnool and Cuddapah, and the epidemic faded away before the famine was over. However, in 1877, the ten major famine districts had a cholera mortality rate of 18 per thousand, as against 11.1 per thousand in the five districts where famine would strike later, and 4.6 per thousand in the non-famine districts. As noted earlier, the migration of the famine-affected to relief centres or cities was an important factor in the famine-cholera synergy. The overuse of water sources in these locales created conditions conducive to the disease (Arnold 1989:267-268).

Notably, cholera assumed epidemic proportions *also* outside of the Ceded districts, which were *not* famine afflicted, for instance, Thanjavur, an agriculturally prosperous district, its irrigation canals fed by the Cauvery. Famine in neighbouring areas led to an influx of refugees, which was a factor in the high incidence of Cholera mortality in Thanjavur. In Thanjavur, it was the abundance rather than the scarcity of water that was the key factor at work. That led to a high density of settlement, which, coupled with the use of water flows from the Cauvery a variety of purposes—washing, drinking, cooking, defecating, created conditions conducive for the spread of epidemic. This was compounded by the denial to dalits of access water sources like tanks and wells. As can be expected, the incidence of cholera was noticeably lower in the upland *talukas*. In the dry districts, monsoon-swollen rivers brought death in their wake from polluted sources upstream (Arnold 1989:269-270). Under normal conditions, augmented river flows should have increased the health of the eco system, as we have earlier noted (Klein 1994: 500), but the density of population on the riverbank and intensified water use were special factors. Another salient factor at work (Arnold 1989: 270, 271-273) were cyclones from the Bay of Bengal that brought periodic flooding in their wake and contaminated water supplies. Once the disease struck, migrant labourers and afflicted pilgrims carried the disease far and wide when they fled the epidemic areas

So far, we have sketched out various aspects of the demographic regieme in the Indian subcontinent prior to Indian independence. We now step back a little, and broaden the canvas, to include demographic processes not only in South Asia, but to a region extending to South-East Asia as well. This leads us to the first of the contributed papers—Chapter 2 (the chapter following the introduction), titled *Aspects of the Population History of South Asia in Southeast Asian Perspective*, by Tim Dyson. Dyson draws attention to a geographical divide within the Indian peninsula, roughly marked out by the Vindhya and Satpura ranges in central India, where the cultural regions of West Asia and South East Asia meet. To the north and west of these hill ranges are parts of India characterised by high rates of fertility and mortality, and marked excess female mortality. The southern and eastern parts of India, present a contrasting picture with respect to these factors.

Like southern and eastern India, Southeast Asia, is likely to have had modest levels of fertility prior to the fertility transition in the middle of the 20th century. Secondly, like the southern and eastern parts of India, Southeast Asia has had a relatively successful record of mortality reduction. Moreover, the fertility decline in both Southeast Asia and southern and eastern India have been relatively speedy. Underlying these similarities are 'fundamental socio-cultural commonalities' between southern and eastern India on the one hand, and Southeast Asia, on the other. The relatively favourable position of females in society, which has an important bearing on their say in decisions on childcare and the curtailing of fertility, is a key factor. Rice based agriculture—which favours women's work force participation and fosters women's autonomy, and women's status as shaped by kinship systems, are related considerations.

Also of salience to the demography of South and South East Asia are the ancient cultural exchanges between the 2nd and 14th centuries BP (Before the Present), in the form of 'Indianisation', or the diffusion of Indian culture from the predominantly Dravidian areas of southern and eastern parts of the sub-continent, which probably was facilitated by the initial socio-cultural similarities between these regions and South East Asia. Indianisation, though it incorporated elements of the Aryan Sanskritic culture of the north and northwestern parts of the sub-continent, spread to South East Asia via the Dravidian civilisations in the south and east. Merchants, scholars and priests were the carriers of this cultural heritage of language, religion, art and administration to South-East Asia, leading, in the initial stages, to the transplantation of court cultures in the region. Cultural transfers at a more popular level occurred with the spread of Buddhism, due to which pilgrimages to India and Sri Lanka from South East Asia become common.

Colonialism, which ushered in a new phase of interactions between South and South-East Asia, followed an eastern projection of trade in cotton, cotton cloth and opium. Its foothold in South Asia and the resources of the subcontinent bolstered the British Empire's hegemony in South East Asia. In this context, indentured labour migrated to the plantations of South East Asia, where it was difficult to recruit locals. Indian labourer, mostly Tamil in origin, migrated mostly to Burma, Malaysia, Singapore and Sri Lanka. Singapore, Malaysia and Fiji, where Indians became a significant proportion of the population, were other destinations. The non-Tamils in these migrant flows were mostly from other southern regions of India, namely, Andhra Pradesh and Kerala. In a century from the 1830s, about 30 million labourers migrated out to South East Asia, of which the net outflow was in the region of about 6 million labourers. In the context of India's vast population, the net losses were small. At the same time, transfers of population *into* India also occurred extensively, as is shown by the number of persons reporting foreign languages as their mother tongues between 1881 and 1931.

Citing data compiled for Malaysia, Dyson indicates that in 1921, the death rate for Indian labourers on the agricultural estates was phenomenally high as compared to the corresponding rate for the Malays (37.2 per thousand as against 25.4 per thousand). By 1947, due to improvements in the health of estate workers, the Indian death rate dropped dramatically to 15.8 per thousand, while the rate for the Malays dropped only marginally to 24.3. Subsequently, after Malaysian Independence in 1957, the decline was more for Malays. By 1976-84, the death rate stood at 5.3 for Malays and 7.3 for Indians. Dyson's compilation of comparable data for Sri Lanka shows a similar pattern. For Tamils, the death rate on the estates dropped from 35.4 to 18.2 between 1921 and the year of Sri Lankan Independence (1947), with the corresponding figures for Sri Lanka as a whole declining at a relatively modest pace, from 31.2 to 20.4. Thereafter, further declines occurred more speedily for the general population. In 1976-84, the crude death rate for Tamils stood at 14.8, while for the general population, it had dropped to a mere 7.7. On a cautionary note, Dyson observes that 'Tamils' include Sri Lankan Tamils, who constituted half the Tamil population, but goes on to add that the rates for both Tamil groups were broadly comparable.

The increase in human mobility in the colonial era is likely to have made disease transfers more frequent, Dyson argues, sketching out the findings of various studies. Cholera, plague and influenza are notable in this context. To consider first, the case of cholera, prior to the 19th century, it had sometimes spread within India and to South East Asia. The first pandemic began in 1817, and by 1822, it spread to South East Asia, China and Japan. Trade and military movements set in place by the British are likely to have been triggers. Of the many factors that led to the containment of the disease, the epidemiological surveillance via the vital registration system that the colonial power established in India, Dyson opines, was arguably the most important. This occurred against the backdrop of the collaboration between the major European powers in the 18th century to control the spread of diseases from Asia and Africa. Plague, another disease that ravaged the subcontinent in the colonial period, particularly in Bombay Presidency and rural Punjab, reached India through the entry point of the city of Bombay in 1896 from British controlled Hong Kong, via steamship. The southern and eastern parts of the subcontinent were not much affected, with the exception of the ports of Calcutta and Madras. It seems significant also that Southeast Asia too was not very badly affected, perhaps due to similarities of climatic conditions in these regions.

The third of the killer diseases, influenza, occurred in two major waves, of which the first spread from Europe to Egypt, to the seaports of Karachi, Bombay, Colombo, Rangoon, Singapore and Shanghai. The second wave, within India, began in Bombay and spread to other parts of the country, though there are indications that it was also introduced independently in the east of the subcontinent from Rangoon. While roughly half the population throughout India were afflicted with the disease, the fatality rate was relatively low in south and eastern India, including Bengal, Assam, and Burma. In Sri Lanka too, the fatality rate was low, with the disease killing only 1 percent of the population. In the northern and western regions of South Asia, by comparison, the fatality rate was as high as 10%. Evidently, influenza mortality was low in regions with a narrow temperature range, perhaps because the pneumonic complications associated with the disease, more likely to occur in regions where the difference between day and night temperatures was high, was the killer factor. By this reckoning, South East Asia should have been spared, which is borne out by the data for Burma. Sri Lanka too fits into this explanatory framework.

Smallpox, another fatal disease, with case fatality rates of 20%-30% in unprotected populations, affected nearly everyone in India by the beginning of the 19th century. The smallpox vaccine, discovered by Edward Jenner in 1796, reached Calcutta by 1802 via Colombo and Madras. Vaccination spread slowly in both India and South East Asia throughout the first half of the 19th century. By the 1870s, vaccination spread in a big way, leading to declines in smallpox mortality, from 10% of all deaths in the 1870s to a minor cause of death by the end of the century. *This is likely to have been a significant factor in the unprecedented population growth that occurred in South Asia, at a time of malarial epidemics and the devastating famines in the last three decades of the nineteenth century.* A case for a similar scenario in South East Asia is likely, Dyson contends. In this context of mortality decline, fast population growth could be expected, though, Dyson notes, according to some scholars, it was fertility rise that led to faster population growth in the 19th century. Malaria, yet another killer disease in India, began to decline in 1918, and contributed significantly to total mortality decline in South Asia as a whole.

Notably, throughout the littoral zone of the Bay of Bengal—most of Sri Lanka, southern and eastern India, Bangladesh, and a large part of the coastal strip reaching down to Burma, population growth was at a high level. This was a region that, in the typology of Geddes, was a region of ‘High Natural Increase’ / ‘Variable Natural Increase’ (both indicating a high population growth rate). Vital registration data showed that there was little annual variation in death rates in this region. That these were non-malaria epidemic areas, Dyson believes, was significant. Even the relatively low fertility rates here were sufficient to produce high rates of natural increase. In contrast to eastern and southern India, the malaria-ravaged Gangetic plain and West Bengal were regions of ‘Stagnation’ in Geddes’ classification. Here high rates of mortality meant that population growth rates stagnated. Western and Northwestern India, generally dry areas but with potential for malarial epidemics and famines, were regions of ‘Recurrent Crisis’, where mortality variability is high, and demographic growth lurches forward in the short run only to be interrupted by epidemic malaria, famines, or other diseases.

Like Dyson's paper, the third chapter in this volume—*Contextualising Long-Run Demographic Change in Southern India* by Gopinath Ravindran, draws on the historical canvas, focusing specifically on demographic trajectories in the southern part of the subcontinent—in Madras Presidency. Ravindran's study districts include coastal districts in the west (South Kanara and Malabar) and in the east (Tanjore), which were 'non-famine' districts, as also, the districts in the Deccan—Bellary, Anantpur and Kurnool, which were the 'driest of the dry districts'. A third category comprises the dry non-coastal districts in the south of the Presidency—Salem, Coimbatore and Madura, which were less arid than the districts of the Deccan. Overall, the dry districts were subject to greater uncertainty in terms of rainfall and the volatility of food prices, as well as a higher level of revenue remissions—a variable indicating the extent of crop failure and risk. In contrast to the 'dry' districts, in the 'wet' regions, where the landholding pattern was inegalitarian, historical developments fostered the resistance and eventually, the empowerment of subaltern groups by way of growing state intervention. The dry regions, on the other hand, had neither a tradition of egalitarianism nor a history of popular movements.

In sketching the demography of the dry Deccan, Ravindran points out that mortality repeatedly peaked in 1891-92 and 1896-97. The root causes were: monsoon and crop failure, and epidemics that took their toll on a population debilitated by hunger. The 1892 peak brought down fertility sharply, due to the impact of dearth in lowering fecundity. Also contributing to the mortality peaks was another factor, first evidenced in 1896—the merchant, who emerged on the scene to purchase grain for sale in famine-ravaged Bombay and the North West provinces. This, in the context of the commercialisation that had proceeded apace in the Deccan, led to food shortages and rising prices. With the monsoon not doing too well, prices remained high. To add fuel to the fire, evil times were prophesised by astrologers. This, together with the situation of dearth, led to the postponement of marriages and a fall in the birth rate. Further, dearth reduced the birth rate by depressing fecundity. The birth rate fell also because fertility was held in check by the high incidence of widowhood, an offshoot of peaking mortality. Lending credence to these indications of mortality determining the level of fertility in the dry zone is Ravindran's finding that 'mortality lagged by four years significantly Granger-caused fertility in the dry districts'. Over time, the mortality variable determined fertility in both the wet and dry districts, but was a far more powerful explanatory in the dry districts. In the dry districts mortality increases pushed down fertility, while in the wet districts, it pushed fertility up, plausibly due to the replacement effect (replacement of dead children) or the insurance effect (having more children to offset the risk of child loss). Prices were related inversely to fertility in both wet and dry districts, during a period that overlapped with the Depression.

Unlike in the dry areas, where famine stalked the land, in the 'wet' districts of this study—comprising Malabar, Tanjore and South Kanara, diseases like cholera, smallpox, dysentery and diarrhoea were the major killers. Price hikes in the high mortality years suggest also that scarcity of the means of sustenance worked in combination with disease as purveyors of death. However, years of excess mortality were comparatively few, so that the possible impact of mortality on reducing fecundity is far less. The lower mortality in the wet regions should have increased the risk of conception, and thus kept fertility on the high side. However, in the conditions prevailing in southern India till the 1960s, there was one *other* factor that was salient in determining fertility, namely, nuptiality, which too has a critical bearing on the risk of conception. The higher mean age at marriage in Madras Presidency had slowed down the reproduction rate, and also, by slowing down the rate at which the next generation (their children) entered the reproductive ages. The proportion married was related also to spinsterhood and widowhood. The wet regions in general, and Malabar in particular, had a high incidence of spinsterhood. The low proportion of married women in Malabar, which, combined with the high incidence of widowhood, acted to keep Malabar's fertility (CWR) at a very low level, can be explained by sociological and cultural factors like matrilineal inheritance among the dominant Nayar caste, restrictions on Nambudri men's marriage, and the easy dissolution of marriage. As for widowhood, it was high in the wet districts, as it was in the high mortality Deccan. This, the author contends, can be attributed to the hold of high Hinduism in moderate mortality Malabar, South Kanara and Tanjore, and its proscriptions of widow remarriage. In the famine prone interior districts of Madura and Salem, widowhood levels were low, perhaps because high Hinduism had a weak foothold in the rural areas of this region, the author argues. Widowhood however was not as important a determinant of fertility as marriage—using data pooled for all the districts of the Presidency, Ravindran found that the correlation coefficients between the CWR on the one hand and the proportions married and widowed on other worked out to .300 and -.249 respectively.

Fertility, as shown by Child Women Ratios (CWRs), was far higher for the dry districts, except for the early 1880s, when the CWRs for the dry regions had plummeted on account of the after shocks of the severe famine of 1876-1878. However, the MCWR (Marital Child Woman Ratio) values were higher in wet regions, which had relatively low proportions married. In other words, while fewer women were married and hence exposed to the risk of conception, those that were married had higher fertility. *Overall fertility*, as measured by the CWR, was higher for the dry regions as compared to the wet regions, which suggests that, in the wet regions, delayed marriage and widowhood were important factors in keeping the birth rate low. It is noteworthy also that it was in the wet regions, the region of high MCWR, that we see indications of a strong MCWR decline, suggesting that the natural fertility regime had begun to crumble. In the dry districts, there was not much change in the CWR, and the MCWR declined only marginally.

What was it that led to the decline of mortality in the wet regions? Till the second decade of the twentieth century, a 'deadly triad of monsoon failure, profit driven market forces and diseases' acted to reduce life expectancy. Agricultural output and rainfall variation show a declining trend from the nineteen twenties to the nineteen forties, and this, Ravindran believes, is 'the most plausible explanation for the conundrum of Indian mortality decline', which broke the 'lethal concatenation' of monsoon failure, rising prices and disease. Social processes add to the picture, the author argues. Commercialisation and caste-class movements in the wet regions fostered precocious popular movements against oppression and exploitation. In areas where such traditions of political participation had evolved, State sponsored welfare schemes to improve health and demographic conditions were more successful. At the same time, traditional factors too operated to determine demographic outcomes. For instance, the 'social availability of non-marriage', popularised by its prevalence among the dominant Nayar caste, helped contain fertility. The incidence of widowhood and proscriptions on widow remarriage too operated to keep fertility in check.

Our third chapter thus shows, in the drought prone areas, a typical pattern of mortality crises operating to depress the conception rate and restrain population growth in the colonial period. This means that ecological factors were important in determining demographic trajectories in the region, suggesting thereby that public health intervention did not occur on a scale that would have acted as a counterweight to the depredations of mortality. By comparing this to the situation in the wet regions, Chapter 3 suggests a diversity of demographic trajectories, within Madras Presidency. It is also noteworthy that in the wet regions, where inegalitarian land holdings were at the root of resistance and empowerment of subaltern groups, the stage was set for democratisation processes that, at a later point in time, increased the effectiveness of state delivery of services. According to one study (Caldwell 1986), radicalism and egalitarianism were critical factors in the route to low mortality in the south Indian State of Kerala, which is represented in the wet districts. The dry Deccan, which did not have such a history, lagged behind. Thus, Ravindran's paper, like chapter 2, shows us links between the past and the present.

Let us now briefly look at some of the demographic trajectories in other parts of the sub-continent. We first look at the demography of the former British-Indian province of Berar, comprising Akola, Amraoti, Buldana and Yeomatal districts of Independent India's Maharashtra State. Drawing on vital registration data for the region for the years between 1881 and 1981, Dyson (1989) reconstructs a century of demographic history. The first four of these decades (1881-1921) were witness to major mortality peaks, during which time, as per annual data on birth and death rates, the Crude Death Rate (CDR) exceeded 50 per 1000 in as many as four years, and remained above the Crude Birth Rate (CBR) in as many as 12 years. Taken together, the worst mortality decade, with mortality disasters coming one on the heels of the other, was the decade of the 1890s. The CDR exceeded the CBR in five of the years of the decade, resulting in a 5% population loss, despite in-migration. Twice in the decade, life expectation at birth dropped to 15-20 years, for instance. In the years of great disasters, for instance, the famine of 1900 and the influenza epidemic of 1918, the expectation of life at birth was less than 10 years. Epidemic diseases and food shortage acted synergistically to decimate the population during these crises. Yet, there were years when no famine or epidemic loomed, when rainfall was good and prices fell. In 1898, one such year, the life expectancy at birth was in the region of 36 to 38 years. Over the entire century (1881-91 to 1971-81), population growth was negative or near zero only in 1891-1900 and 1911-20, primarily due to the killer famine of 1900 and the Great Influenza Epidemic of 1918. The decades immediately preceding the decades of famine and influenza—the decades of 1881-1990, and 1901-1910 were free of major disasters and the CRNI, or Crude Rate of Natural Increase (Crude Birth Rate minus Crude Death Rate) was of the magnitudes of 0.49 and 0.81 respectively (Dyson 1989: 150, 162, 181, 182).

After a near stationary CRNI of 0.01 in the decade of the Great Influenza Epidemic (1911-1920), the CRNI rose to 1.04 in 1921-1930, the decade of the agriculturally prosperous nineteen twenties in this cotton growing region, when world cotton prices were favourable. In the decade *preceding* the influenza decade, that is, the 1901-1910 decade, described as a decade of 'monotonous prosperity', the CRNI was as high as 0.81 Apparently, favourable conditions had led to higher levels of widow remarriage, and higher fertility. Conversely, in difficult times, when famine loomed large, mechanisms like separation of spouses due to distress migration of job seeking men, delays in onset of cohabitation, and reduced coital frequency operated to keep fertility low (Dyson 1989:162, 184-185). The CRNI stagnated at 0.70 in 1931-1940 and 0.63 in 1941-1950. While there were advances on some fronts, like famine control, with respect to other causes of death, such as TB, mortality is liable to have gained ground. Consequently, on an average, life expectancy in the nineteen twenties, thirties and forties, were at around the level that it was in the 1880s. Mortality's definitive downward trend in Berar occurred around the mid nineteen forties, significantly, after the transfer of power. Anti-malaria measures were one significant factor, which resulted, in some regions, in a 60%-75% drop in hospital attendance (Dyson 1989: 162,183, 184).

For a more complete the picture, we need to look at population growth before population statistics began to be collected by the colonial government in the late 19th century. Hence, it is useful here to refer to a study by Commander (1989) of the demographic history of a north Indian locale—the Doab, between the seventeenth and eighteenth century. The Doab, an alluvial plain lying between the Jamuna and Ganga, initially part of the North Western provinces, was subsequently incorporated in the United Provinces and is today part of the north Indian state of Uttar Pradesh. Prior to 1872, when the first British Indian census was held, there was little known about the demography of this region. The north India of the time was primarily rural, notwithstanding handloom production and a range of small-scale industries, which accounted for a small share of the labour force (Commander 1989: 49-50).

Labour scarcity was the main constraint on production in the Doab, with irrigated, better quality agricultural land drawing labour away from the predominantly rain fed regions, where agriculture was precarious (Commander 1989: 50). At the same time, protection against military depredations, for instance, of the kind that was provided by Raja Ramdayal Singh in the region of Landhaura in the Sharanpur district in the upper Doab, led to massive expansion of cultivation and population growth between 1807 and 1891 (Commander 1989: 51). Other evidences also point to rapid population growth in the Upper Doab in the first half-century of the 1800s, accompanied by growth in agricultural production. In the Mat, Jalesar and Noh Jil pargannas of Mathura, population grew at between 42% and 48% between 1834 and 1872. In Bareilly, another sample-surveyed locale, population density doubled between 1828 and 1872. Commander conjectures that the process may begun as early as the 18th century (Commander 1989: 53). According to one 1807 report, cultivation in Upper Doab, was at a lower level as compared to a hundred years earlier. Moreover, districts of this region for which early non-census data are available, namely, Meerut, Muzaffarnagar and Saharanpur, do indicate a level of population that was relatively high compared to what was earlier the case (Commander 1989: 51). In parts of the Doab at least, the population increases may have been boosted by in-migration (Commander 1989: 53).

By 1800, population density in the Doab had risen to as many as 800 people per square mile. A young population structure, with a large proportion of women in the childbearing ages, early age at marriage, and high fertility, were conducive to rapid growth of population, and adverse conditions like dearth and famines were not strong enough to dampen the potential for population growth (Commander 1989: 57-58). Even at the end of the sixteenth century, the Doab, which was a centre of the Mughals, had high levels of cultivation and population density. In 1595, cultivation in the Doab was over 70% of the area cultivated by 1909-1910. The capacity to increase productivity, through increase of area under the plough and also better irrigation facilities, provided a spurt to population growth (Commander 1989: 57). Between 1815 and the eighteen sixties, cultivation expanded considerably. From 51% in 1815, the area under cultivation shot up to 62% in 1875-80. In 1807-1880, output of all crops increased eightfold, with the net cropped area increasing threefold during this period. Correspondingly, population too was on a growth trajectory, having, in the Upper Doab, quadrupled between 1807 to 1880. In neighbouring Muzaffarnagar, population growth had led to a subdivision of holdings to a point where per capita food output was falling and increased productivity had become a prerequisite for sustaining a growing population (Commander 1989: 59-60).

Two major famines ravaged the Doab in the pre-1870 period—the famines of 1837-38 and 1860-61. Famine not only led to sharp falls in agricultural output, but also led to a decline in the area sown for the next harvest, decline in the level of employment, and rising prices. Those who had stocks or sufficient grain gained from the price rise, while those who did not had to resort to distress sales of landholding rights. In earlier times, one response to evade revenue payments was to migrate away, but with land having become scarce, this was no longer an option for those affected by the famine of 1837-38. However, precisely because desertion or migration had ceased to be an option by this time, money-lenders and those making grain advances had reason to be less worried about having to suffer the consequences of default. By 1840 a more organised system of food and work distribution had been set in place to deal with famine dislocations. When the famine of 1860-61 struck, leading to the collapse of the labour demand and the market for non-food items, agricultural labourers, petty producers, artisans, and the urban poor were hit. Still, mortality was contained due to improved transportation of grain, famine relief measures, and growth in irrigated area. In this context, excess mortality and relatively low demographic growth rates *post* 1880 were not invariably fostered by dearth; they became to be increasingly associated with '... several powerful epidemic-induced crises that culminated in the extraordinary influenza outbreak of 1918-19'. The impact of these epidemics was however strongest in the more backward parts of the Doab and among the poorer classes of society (Commander 1989: 66-68).

We have been somewhat erratic in our peregrinations through time. Our case study of Berar had shown a typically checkered growth in the decades preceding 1921, which is shown also by the sub-continent level data in Chapter 5. However, Commander's (1989) study suggests that in a longer-term perspective, this phase was separate from rapid population growth of earlier centuries in areas where agriculture was booming and cultivated area was hugely expanding. In the Doab, agricultural expansion was an important factor in ensuring that high fertility translated into high population growth. Yet, in the Doab as well as in Berar, one common factor was that fertility remained high. Notwithstanding disease and famine mortality, fertility rates in Berar remained at a moderately high level, though, in the immediate post famine years, it declined steeply. As we have earlier noted in studies from different parts of the subcontinent—Bombay and Madras Presidencies and the Central Provinces, apart from high mortality and morbidity acting to depress birth rates, the separation of spouses due to distress migration in times of famine, reduced coital frequency and delays in the onset of cohabitation were likely factors in depressing the fertility level. However, when famines began to wane, the conception rate rose (Dyson 1991a, Dyson 1991b). In the Berar study, looking at decadal variations, a principal factor in the inverse correlation that obtained between birth and death rates was the loss of fertility to widowhood. When mortality declined, concomitant to improvements in subsistence, for instance, during 1901-1911, fertility regained ground. Overall, throughout the one hundred years under study, the Total Fertility Rate (TFR) stayed mostly within levels of 5 to 6 live births per woman (Dyson 1989:184-186).

So far, we have not tried to probe this phenomenon of persisting high fertility. Let us now do so. To begin with, we look at a reconstruction of the demographic history of Ludhiana district, Punjab, from 1881 to 1991, by Dyson and Das Gupta (2001). The authors find a high degree of annual variation in the death rate till about 1920. In the decade 1881-1901, famines and malarial epidemics acted to create mortality peaks. The next decade, starting from the famine year of 1900, saw mortality shoot up on account of plague. In the peak year, 1902, a tenth of the population had been decimated, with life expectation at 10 and 5 years for males and females respectively. The plague was the last straw on the camel's back, coming as it did on the heels of the famine of 1989 and malaria, cholera and other fevers of 1900. Weakened by famine and disease, the population of the region was succumbed to the plague epidemic, which struck in 1901 and assumed epidemic proportions by 1902. The Crude Death Rate shot up by 73% over the previous decade, touching a high of 108 in 1902. Earlier, we noted how, in the famine years, fertility declined, and subsequently, the conception rate began to pick up as famine conditions disappeared (Dyson 1991a, 1991b). Looking at the 'decade of grim death' as a whole (1881-1901) the CBR declined only very slightly in Ludhiana, with the TFR registering a marginal fall, from 6.25 in the previous decade to 6.0. (Dyson and Das Gupta 2001: 88, 93). Notwithstanding the scale of the devastations wrought by the plague—and by other catastrophes, for instance, the famine of 1884, and of the disastrous decade of the 1890s, rejuvenation and revival occurred quickly.

The TFR, 5.8 in 1884, fell to 4.8 in 1885, and then quickly rose back to 5.8 the following year. Turning to the plague years, we find that the TFR fell briefly from 6.6 in 1900 to 5.1 in 1901, then sprang jumped to 6.5 in 1903 (Dyson and Das Gupta 2001: 94). Here again we have evidence of persisting high fertility, which the depredations of mortality are not able to entirely contain.

Apart from the issue of persisting high fertility, the Ludhiana study also shows that a key factor that led to fertility decline in this region was the decline in mortality variation. In a situation of unpredictable mortality peaks, the 'insurance motive for childbearing', by which parents have a greater number of children than they desire so as to insure against child loss, becomes salient. Conversely, when mortality becomes more predictable, the 'insurance motive for childbearing' declines. In Ludhiana, Dyson and Das Gupta show, this had happened by the 1911 to 1921 decade. This was so despite the major mortality disaster that occurred in 1918, when the influenza epidemic wiped out a tenth of the population, and the expectation of life at birth dropped to 10 and 7 years for males and females respectively. In this decade, the CDR rose from 30 to 105, while the IMR increased from 234 to 313. Still, the decade 1911 to 1921 did register mortality decline, with a life expectancy of 30 for most of the years of the decade. Moreover, if the year 1918 is excluded, the *mortality variation* in 1911-1920 is starkly below that of previous decades (Dyson and Das Gupta 2001: 94).

After 1920, mortality fluctuations evened out, with death rates remaining steady till about 1940, following which they declined steeply. It is noteworthy also that the 1920s to 1940s was a period of mortality decline for both adults and infants, with the average decline of the CDR of the magnitude of 31% and the corresponding figure for the IMR at 28%. The nineteen forties and nineteen fifties were periods of especially rapid gains in life expectancy, more sharp than what occurred in the sixties and seventies (Dyson and Das Gupta 2001: 87—table 5.3, 88—Figure 5.1, 92, 95). The nineteen forties mark another demographic milestone in Ludhiana, for it was in this time that fertility decline began, which was relatively early by Indian standards and also by developing countries standards. It is noteworthy that much of the decline occurred before the spread of modern contraceptives (Dyson and Das Gupta 2001: 96-97, 100). Agricultural prosperity in Ludhiana was critical to keeping mortality levels low, as a comparison between this part of the subcontinent and Berar shows. The vital registration system, which was extensively used to chart the course of disease, was of course important, as was the evening out of mortality fluctuations—another critical factor, according to Dyson and Das Gupta (2001: 98), one that was facilitated by the role of railways in food grain transportation and famine relief. Moreover, irrigation projects and the efforts to increase marketable produce gave a boost to agriculture and helped contain famine.

This in turn helped limit epidemics, which tended to strike famine-weakened populations. The decline of mortality fluctuations was important in creating a stability of expectations, and reducing the 'insurance' motive for childbearing (Dyson and Das Gupta 2001: 80, 93, 98-99).

Obviously, the fact that the insurance motive for childbearing operates in the first place implies that some norm of family size is operating. Thus, when mortality is more predictable, couples feel confident that they need to have fewer children to attain the norm. It is this that, as we have seen, led to the decline of fertility in Ludhiana. But what is it that shapes family-size norms that serve to keep fertility high? The crux of the matter is that children serve a variety of functions that are extremely valuable to the household. It is worth noting here that in China, resistance to the vigorously pursued 1970s family planning policy had been quite extreme, and the effort to restrict births far from universally successful, especially in rural areas. As per to the system of leasing out land to farmers in rural areas, families were assigned land in proportion to their size. Family labour was important, hence the view that there are 'three benefits from a son's marrying early: the daughter-in-law, the grandchildren, and the land' (Attane 2002). In a like vein, in village Manupur, Ludhiana district, Punjab—one of the villages of a Rockefeller Foundation birth control programme, Mamdani (1973) argues that the villagers were quite rational in choosing to have large families. He shows how, at a low level of technology, hired labour was uneconomical and family labour vital to the economic viability of farm households. Crop sharing arrangements whereby households contracted to harvest a piece of land also provided a rationale for many children in the family, as did the seasonal shortages of wage labour in the low technology agriculture of Manupur, at the time of harvest, weeding and sowing, all typically labour intensive activities (Mamdani, 1973: 76-77, 94-95). Not just family labour, but the labour of children was important. Children were engaged in a range of tedious tasks; more particularly, they grazed and cared for cattle, and collected animal waste for manure (Mamdani, 1973: 99, 100, 131). Offspring were a source of security for aged parents, and of help in emergencies like monsoon floods. They also facilitated the diversification of family income—many families in Manupur had educated one son for this reason. Finally, children contributed to the family's strength of numbers. They provided security in disputes over land encroachment by neighbouring cultivators, and were a source of strength in factional fights (Mamdani 1973: 44, 132-134, 136-37).

In their restudy of Manupur, Nag and Kak (1984) report that the sweep of the green revolution meant that fallow land, originally used for cattle grazing, increasingly came under the plough. This led to a decline in the demand for child labour, since cattle grazing and the collection of cow dung from the field have traditionally been the work of children (Nag and Kak 1984: 670, 673). Moreover, the use of chemical weed killers had obviated the need to employ children for de-weeding operations (Nag and Kak 1984: 670). A general social context of institutional change militated against child labour as well. In Manupur, the market economy had grown to the detriment of the *jajmani* system under which the harijans and service-providing castes were traditionally obligated to serve the land owning Jets in return for a share of the crops produced. So onerous were the terms of the traditional arrangement for the laborers and providers of services that the lower castes had to rely not only on the labour of adult males but on that of womenfolk and children as well. With the eclipse of the *jajmani* system and the growing salience of wage transactions in the market, the labour of children waned (Nag and Kak 1984: 670, 675). Nonetheless, the labour value of children continued to persist. School enrolment had increased in the area and children were in school six hours a day—but while the workload of children declined overall, they still did 'plenty of work' in their households. Though grazing grounds had disappeared, many households owned cattle, and tending them was the prime responsibility of children. Children gathered fodder in the field and converted it into cattle feed with the use chaff cutters. They helped their parents milk and wash cattle. On holidays, Jat boys would work 7-8 hours helping their parents in the field. Children of the poor castes spent hours collecting firewood and transporting it over long distances, and girls of all castes helped their mothers in the preparation of food, washing of clothes, cleaning of utensils, carrying water from the pump or well, and making cow dung cakes for use as fuel. They also cared for siblings, as did boys, and spent a lot of time making colourful mats that were sold or used as dowries (Nag and Kak, 1984: 669-670, 676).

In a more recent study of another north Indian village (village Mogra), Patel (1994) documents how, where there is little mechanisation, children contribute significantly to the household economy. After they reach the age of 10, children graze cattle and take them to the village pond for watering; they collect dung, twigs and firewood, and fetch water from the pond or well. 10-12 year old girls cook the evening meal, especially in the peak agricultural season, and milk, feed and tether cows. They do light tasks in the field like de-weeding. Young children with slingshots are engaged in scaring birds away from the fields; this is a time consuming task, for which hired labour is uneconomical. Boys take up male tasks by the time they are 15-16 years old. 12 year old girls have learnt how to remove stones from grain, grind grain in a hand mill, clean the cattle shed, and make dung cakes. They are encouraged also to acquire skills such as embroidery, bead work, cloth repair, the use of rags to make beds and to learn how to make stands for water pitchers. They help in house repair, and smear the walls and ground with dung paste. By the time a girl is ten years old, she has learnt all the female tasks. Children also learn traditional crafts like tailoring, carpentry, smithy and pottery. 6-7 year olds help their parents in numerous chores in the cattle shed and field and in the care of siblings. 5-10 year olds are involved in tasks like baby-sitting and running errands, which frees the household's elders for more productive work (Patel, 1994: 38-45). Children can also be an investment in the diversification of income sources (Patel 1994: 96). In sum, offspring are needed to sustain the household's resource base, provide it protection, contribute to its division of labour and its social networks, and relieve the elderly of their burdens. A household not blessed with children is reduced to a pitiful state and barrenness is a dreaded curse (Patel, 1994: 78-84, 89, 98-103, 154-55).

Another analyst, Cain (1978), in a study of rural Bangladesh, reports that *pardah* and constraints to women's involvement in productive activity meant that males played an important role in sustaining the household's resource base. More specifically, the labour of sons and their experience in managing agricultural operations was vital during periods of crisis such as floods or the death of the patriarch, at which time mature sons in the household could avert distress land sales. A greater number of male earners in the household also meant more opportunities for income diversification. This helped in times of weather-related disasters that potentially undermine agricultural yields. Frequent disputes over that vital asset in this agrarian society—land, and the absence of efficient dispute settlement mechanisms meant also that widows, bereft of the protection of mature sons, were vulnerable to the risk of property loss. In rural Bangladesh, sons thus played a crucial role in coping with and mitigating the consequences of weather induced disasters, widowhood, and the general environment of lawlessness and insecurity of property rights. One source of security, which Cain's path breaking analysis alludes to but does not go on to develop, are networks of extended kin, which can be as a source of help in emergencies. Cain does however indicate that in the Bangladesh setting, in contrast to the Indian villages of his sample, distress land sales were largely between brothers or patrykin. This suggests that these categories of kinfolk in Bangladesh functioned poorly as sources of mutual aid in troubled times (Cain 1981: 461). The role of relatives in providing assistance in times of distress can however be crucial. Thus, data from a sample of drought prone Indian villages attest to consumption smoothing arrangements whereby shortages that a household in a patrilocal setting is prone to as a consequence of crop failure are compensated by transfers from an affinal household located elsewhere and not similarly affected by local agricultural conditions. Commitments hinging on the kinship links between the households which enter into these implicit contracts, it is argued, makes the arrangement work, and makes it work in circumstances where enforcing and monitoring agreements between parties bound only by the letter of the law is not feasible (Rosensweig 1988; Rosenzweig and Stark 1989). This evidence of the role of the family in mitigating risks also underscores the salience of ties of marital kinship and underscores the value of daughters. Such a role for daughters is in fact explicitly recognised, in that daughters are perceived to be useful in augmenting a household's network of kinship relationships via affinal alliance (Patel 1994: 103).

Adding to our understanding of the value of children is Chapter 4—*Fertility and Family Planning in Rural India: Anthropological and Ethnographic Perspectives*, in which Tulsi Patel sifts through two village level-demographic ethnographies to give indications of the value of children in the lives of villagers. One of these two studies, which she herself had carried out in village Mogra, illustrates how fertility behaviour is sustained by values, calibrated both through the 'rule book' and through the individual, couple, family and society. Even young children are aware of the importance of the optimum number and sex composition of offspring, Patel says.

The author sketches out a number of case studies to show how motherhood bestows honour and cements the marital tie. In one instance, a woman was threatened by her husband when she did not bear a child after seven years of marriage. In another, a wife of the village accountant, who had not borne a child even after twelve years of marriage, feared that her husband would marry again. That this is liable to happen is shown by a third example, in which a woman named Labu, after failing to bear a child after several years of marriage, acquiesced to her husband's decision to take another wife. The second wife, Kanwari, was blind, but bore three sons. It was Kanwari who had greater authority in the family, despite being a junior wife. Other cases include that of Cuki, who gave birth to a son, an event that silenced the carping of her husband's sisters and his brother's wives. In the case of Anadi, who gave birth of a daughter, the stigma of barrenness was removed. Both Cuki and Anadi gained in self-esteem.

Patel brings out other societal aspects of childbearing by citing the plight of Rajuji, a man in his late sixties. Of Rajuji three wives, two died without giving him a son. The second gave him a daughter, who was married off. His third and current wife bore him a girl, who was two years old now. Patel spotted him carrying this girl with one arm, walking to the village pond to fetch water and herding cattle to water them. On her asking him if any girl or boy from his lineage—his immediate neighbours, would not help him, he replied: 'Even friends and relatives cease to exist when needed by a lonely person'. Thus, social networks 'operate on the principle of implicit reciprocity'.

Sons can be important also in the context of property and inheritance, as is brought home by the case of Pemji, a shepherd in his forties with only two surviving daughters. Pemji was heavily in debt due to his and his wife's illness, and wanted to sell off part of his land to repay his debts, but the land was in his father's name, and required that Pemji and his elder brother to act jointly in the matter, which was proving problematic. The elder brother, who had three sons, knew that in time the land would belong to him and his sons. If Pemji had even one son, he may not have been indebted or felt the need to dispose off the land.

Other case studies by Patel show how the dread of child loss, especially the death of sons, is a strong argument against sterilisation. In the case of Sugan, a woman in her late twenties, on the other hand, it was a matter of convincing the husband and mother in law of the desirability of sterilisation. Sugan eventually convinced them by arguing that if they had a fourth son, it would lead to further subdivision of land and make each son's inheritance very small, while, if the child turned out to be a daughter, the dowry expenses would be difficult to meet. In this context, it is noteworthy also, as Patel points out, citing anthropological literature, that the family planning establishment itself exerts a moral pressure to adopt contraception. The officials who visit households tend to have a higher status in society, and their pressures and that of the establishment build up to a point build where the prospective client succumbs. Thus, Chapter 4 not only shows the value of having many children, but also shows that after a point children can be burdensome, which suggests notions of optimal number of offspring.

The second ethnographic profile Patel discusses in Chapter 4 is a study of Gopalpalli, a village in the East Godavari district of Andhra Pradesh, studied by Minna Saavala. Specifically, the theme explored through this study is that of what constitutes an ethnographic rationale for curtailing childbearing. The children of the village are nurtured in conditions of food scarcity, and a constant refrain that is heard is the difficulty of nourishing children. What 'nourish' means in this context, is brought out by Pentamma, one village woman who said that those who had money could have many children, but asked how the poor could fill the bellies of many offspring. Having fewer children, in this context, was a matter of dignity and respectability, since feeding and clothing fewer children was easier. Apart from this are the connotations that attach to nurturing a child through a process of affectionate feeding by the mother, whereby personhood is conferred. A child properly fed is given love and affection and socially connected. In this context, to say that it is difficult to 'nourish' a child implies that ' ... it is difficult to build up their personhood through prestigious foodstuffs'. Perhaps this could have been a factor in restraining fertility in the past, during periods of famines and dearth, along with the other factors like postponement of marriages in hard times, widowhood, spousal separation caused by the famine-spurred migration of males wandering about to seek wages and the means of sustenance.

We have seen also how mortality decline weakens the insurance motive for childbearing and sets the stage for fertility decline. In more recent times, factors related to modernisation have acted to reduce fertility, for instance, as Nag and Kak have shown—via a reduction of the demand for child labour. Other factors at work in Manupur, according to Nag and Kak, include the fact that the commercialisation of agriculture and the emergence of modern credit systems had fostered the conviction that schooling was necessary to comprehend and grapple with the new world (Nag and Kak 1984: 673, 675). The demand for schooling was additionally fueled by growing opportunities in the non-agricultural sector for which schooling attainment was a requirement (Nag and Kak 1984: 676). This has been reported also from a drought prone south Indian locale where schooling was seen as a route to the non-farm sector and as an escape from the insecurity of dependence on agriculture. In this south Indian setting, daughters were educated so as to make them better wives to husbands in non-farm employment. They were sent to school also because it was felt that as educated mothers, they would be better at child rearing; and because it was felt that education would help them find better jobs (Caldwell, Reddy and Caldwell 1985: 33, 38-39). Moreover, education for girls meant a reduction of the dowries parents have to pay when their daughters marry (Nag and Kak 1984: 675, Hatti and Olsson 1983: 12-13) Less pragmatic considerations come into play as well. Thus, schooling is desired for its own sake, as a source of gentility and betterment (Caldwell, Reddy and Caldwell 1985: 36-37).

With the spread of schooling, children become increasingly expensive. Schooling is critical in fueling child costs, as minimum standards of clothing, food and health are expected of school going children, with peer pressures and expectations from teachers coming into play (Caldwell, Reddy and Caldwell 1982: 716). Expenditures on clothing and textbooks can be quite burdensome for the poor (Nag and Kak 1984: 676), and educating a child for white collar employment can mean additional costs to be incurred on bribes that must be paid before a job can be secured (Caldwell, Reddy and Caldwell 1982: 718). With schooling expenditures a drain on the family coffers, parents are motivated to have fewer children. Indicating this, over 50% of sterilised couples interviewed in a survey in south India said that the costs of educating and finding jobs for children had motivated them to curtail the size of their families (Caldwell, Reddy and Caldwell 1985: 45). Other, more recent studies, reporting on developments in Tamil Nadu, identify factors like poverty and rising material aspirations as acting to reduce fertility, together with political support for family planning and an efficient family planning programme (Visaria 2004: 67).

There is also another route through which schooling can boost child cost—

through the impact it has on the child when he or she becomes a parent. Mueller found in a study in Taiwan that sensitivity to child cost was a positive function of husband's schooling and to a lesser extent, of mother's schooling. She argues that this reflects schooling aspirations for children and among educated parents (Mueller 1972: 394). On the other hand, aspirations for children among the uneducated too can limit fertility, as studies by Bhat (2002) and McNay *et al.* (2003) suggest. This, however, is only part of the story. In a State level analysis, Jain (1985) finds that adult female literacy impacts on fertility mainly because it reduces infant mortality, which in turn leads to fertility decline on account of growing confidence in child survival. The phenomenon depends on *people's perceptions* of child mortality, which one study in Bangladesh found 'were not different from the conclusions drawn on the basis of more objective or scientific analysis' (Amin and Basu 2004: 5)

In Manupur, where, as we have seen, factors emerged to contain fertility, a shift in attitudes towards children had occurred; earlier, a large number of children were desired, but that is no longer the case (Nag and Kak 1984). The preference for 'small' families is now overwhelming, according to a national survey in which 85% of respondents in rural areas said that it is advantageous to have 'few' children (NCAER 1984). Increasing child expenses are integral to the picture in that as the perception that children are 'costly' gains currency, parents more and more deem it advantageous to have smaller families. The phenomenon, can be traced to the spread of schooling and related expenses; and to growing perceptions of child costs relative to the costs of 'other commodities'.

To recapitulate the ground we have covered so far—we started off by investigating the mortality transition in the subcontinent and concluded that it occurred without any improvement in living standards. Then we broadened our canvas to cover South East Asia as well, and found similarities between south and east India and South East Asia, with northwest India presenting a contrast. We also explored demographic trajectories in specific regions—Bombay and Madras Presidencies, and the Central Provinces. Within Madras Presidency, we found regional variations in demographic trajectories, attributable to ecological factors. We went on to explore demographic transitions in Berar and Ludhiana, which underscored the evidence of persisting high fertility. In Berar, the evidence suggested that high mortality was acting to depress fertility by sustaining a high incidence of widowhood, a theme we also encountered in Chapter 3, on demographic trajectories in Madras Presidency. Drawing on the Ludhiana study, we identified the insurance motive for childbearing as a key factor operating to keep fertility high. We then went on in Chapter 4, to investigate the ethnographic underpinning of high fertility, and also, of optimal fertility. We now come to Chapter 5, in which M.K. Premi provides a meticulous and comprehensive statistical profile of demographic trajectories in the subcontinent, while also giving indications of the factors that are likely to be at the root of regional differentials.

Chapter 5 begins by dividing India's population growth since 1891 into four parts. 1921 is the year of the Great Divide, which demarcates a period of chequered population growth from one in which growth was moderately increasing (1921-1951). Following this came a period of rapid growth (1951-1981). After 1981, there have been definite indications of the earlier rapid growth slowing down. The chequered growth till 1921 was because of famines and plagues during the 30 or so preceding years, which periodically decimated the population. Both the 1891-1901 and the 1901-1911 census decades saw many famines, notably, a severe one in 1907 in parts of Uttar Pradesh. Plague struck the Bengal and Bombay presidencies, and both plague and malaria were widespread in Punjab and Uttar Pradesh. However, since famines struck less often and for shorter periods in 1901-1911, population grew appreciably between 1891-1901 and 1901-1911. In the 1911 to 1920 decade, the Great Influenza Epidemic wiped out an estimated 7% of the population, and the growth rate dropped precipitously in the 1901-1911 to 1911-1921 period. Subsequently, with the major mortality factors brought under control, the country witnessed a gradual rise in population growth. After Independence in 1947, the drop in the death rate became more pronounced, resulting in a doubling of the population in 34 years, from 347.5 million in 1947 to 683 million in 1981. Then, around the beginning of the 1970s, birth rate declines became evident, accelerating in the second half of the 1980s, and resulting in a slight decline in the 1981-1991 growth rate. From 1991 to 2001, fertility fell even more sharply.

In the period of rapid growth (1981-2001), the northern zone had the highest growth rate of 28.13%. The growth in the Southern zone, by comparison, had dropped to 13.7%. Overall, it had declined continuously over the past three decades, with the decline having accelerated between 1991 and 2001. The author goes on to present data from the Sample Registration System on the birth rate, the death rate and the rate of natural increase, from 1972 to 2000. He finds that while notable birth rate declines occurred across States, birth rates plateaued out at relatively high levels in the northern and north-western States. Natural increase was the highest at 2.1% per annum in Bihar, Madhya Pradesh, Rajasthan and Uttar Pradesh, while in Kerala and Tamil Nadu, it had fallen to 1.1% per annum.

One salient factor that is important for understanding these differentials is the IMR. The author draws the reader's attention also to the high infant mortality rate in India, particularly up to 1981. SRS data for 1971-1981 shows that it varied from 129 per thousand to 110 per thousand. Thereafter, the IMR fell steadily to reach 63 per thousand in 2002. This compares with IMRs of less than 10 in most developed countries and many developing countries. State wise IMRs display a wide variation, ranging from 91, 86, and 82 in Orissa, Madhya Pradesh and Uttar Pradesh respectively, to 12 per thousand in Kerala. Also noteworthy are the sharp rural-urban differences in the IMR, which are suggestive of lack of potable drinking water, sanitation and accessible medical facilities in rural areas. Thus, urbanization emerges as yet another underpinning of India's demographic trajectories.

Premi also profiles two other issues, to which we will return later—the issue of missing females and the issue of demographic ageing. To look into the matter of 'missing females' in the population, the author draws on the special census of India tabulation for the population aged 0-6 between 1991 and 2001. These data, which facilitate State wise comparison of the proportion of child population between these two census years, shows that the decline in the proportion of girls was quite substantial as compared to that of boys in Haryana, Punjab, Delhi and Uttaranchal. There can be four factors to account for the *worsening* of the Female Male Ratio, or the FMR, over time, the author argues: (i) relatively greater census undercounts of females (ii) emigration of females (iii) greater mortality among females and (iv) change in the Sex Ratio at Birth, or the SRB—the number of male births per 100 female births, that is, if more male children are born than female children, this also could make the FMR more adverse for females. The author rules out item (i), on the ground that post enumeration checks carried out by the Registrar General's office show it to be insignificant. Item (ii) also can be ruled out in the Indian context, he argues. As regards item (iii), recent data, from the mid 1980s, do not indicate excess female mortality. In fact, the trend seems to have been reversed. From the mid 1980s also, estimates of life expectancy at birth have been higher for females as compared to males (though in the case of some States like Bihar, Madhya Pradesh and Uttar Pradesh, males continue to have higher life expectancies). This leaves item (iv), namely, SRBs. SRBs, as per recent estimates are alarmingly high at 109.5 in 1981-90 and 111 in 1996-2000, as against a normal value of the SRB of 105. In Punjab and Haryana, the SRBs were as high as 126.3 and 125.5 in 1996-98. Premi thus shows that it is mainly the rise in the SRB that accounts for the increase of the Child FMRs between the 1981 and 1991 censuses.

Next, we turn to the author's analysis of demographic ageing. Due to fertility decline and also increases in longevity, the share of the elderly (60+) population in the country has been on the rise. The proportion of elderly, 5.6% in 1961, stands at 7.4% as of 2001. Notably, the proportion of female elderly had become higher than that of male elderly by that year. Notwithstanding this change in the age structure, India still has a predominantly young population, and hence, has a high potential for population growth. Premi conjectures that it will take another 60 to 70 years before the Indian population becomes a Stationary Population, i.e., a population with a zero growth rate.

Chapter 6, also by M.K. Premi, continues with the statistical profiling of India's demographic experience, focusing specifically on urbanisation and urban-rural differentials. Urbanisation, as we have noted, is a salient facet of India's demography. Rural-urban differentials in the IMR (Infant Mortality Rate) for instance, stem from better health facilities in urban areas. Schooling, as we have seen, an important determinant of fertility, is more widespread in urban areas, due to better facilities, as we see in Chapter 6. In this chapter, the author presents data to the effect that of the 1029 million persons enumerated by the 2001 census, 286 million, comprising 27.8% of the total population, were in urban areas. Even the increase in urban population in just a single decade preceding 2001 was larger than the population of any European country other than Germany and the Russian Federation, bigger than the population of any country in Africa except Nigeria and Egypt, and greater than the population of many countries in Asia and South America, the author tells us. The decadal growth rate of the urban population increased from 26.4% in 1951-1961 to 28.2% in 1961-1971, rising to a peak of 46.1% in 1971-1981. In 1981-1991, it declined to 37.5%, and in 1991-2001, to 31.5%. The percent urban rose from 18.0% in 1961, to 19.9%, 23.3%, 25.7% and 27.8% in 1971, 1981, 1991 and 2001 respectively.

Between 1991 and 2001, Tamil Nadu, Maharashtra and Gujarat were the most urbanised states. As of 2001, Tamil Nadu was the most urbanised State, with the proportion urban at 44%, followed by Maharashtra and Gujarat. A decade earlier, it was Maharashtra that had the highest urbanisation rate of 38.7%, followed by Gujarat and Tamil Nadu. The emergence of new towns in Tamil Nadu had dramatically increased its rate of urbanisation; with the declaration of 456 new towns on the eve of the 2001 census, Tamil Nadu's urbanisation rate jumped up by 9.7 points. Haryana and Punjab are other States that have seen spurts in their urbanisation rate. In Haryana, this resulted from a net addition of 12 towns and fast growth of cities like Faridibad and Gurgaon. In Punjab, the net addition of 37 new towns caused a sudden increase in its urbanisation rate. At the other end of the spectrum, the urban population in Kerala dropped from 26.4% in 1991 to 26.0% in 2001, as, on the eve of the 2001 census, 37 towns were declassified.

From 1981-91 to 1991-2001, when the share of the urban population declined from 37.5% to 31.5%, the Urban-Rural Growth Differential (URGD) dropped from 16.46 to 13.16. State level data show however, that States like Haryana, Tamil Nadu, Punjab and Karnataka showed increases in the URGD during this period. On the other hand, the URGD for States like Andhra Pradesh,

Bihar, Kerala, Rajasthan and West Bengal dipped below the levels for the 1981-91 decade. While the rate of urbanisation has been slowing down for the country as a whole, a parallel development that Premi highlights, is that the *rural-urban differentials in demographic indicators has also been on the wane.* Premi demonstrates this first, with data on the Crude Birth Rate or CBR. Since CBRs are affected by the age structure of populations (when one of the populations has a larger number of women in the reproductive ages, the CBR will be higher), the author carries out the same exercise for the TFR, or Total Fertility Rate, which is a measure of the number of children a woman has as she progresses through the childbearing years. The author finds that in regions where CBRs have declined, the rural-urban TFR differentials have mellowed. In some of the now low fertility States, the TFR differentials were relatively weak even as far back as 1972, subsequently becoming even smaller.

Tracing the trajectory of the rural-urban differential in the CBR, Premi finds that it declined from 7.7 points in 1971-73 to 6.6 points in 2002-04. Overall, the rural-urban differential in the CBRs has been in the range of 8-10 points in States like Assam, Bihar, Madhya Pradesh, Rajasthan and Uttar Pradesh. These are States where the overall CBR has remained above the national average. In States like Andhra Pradesh, Kerala, Maharashtra, Punjab, Tamil Nadu and Delhi, where the CBRs are relatively low, and there have been efforts to limit the rural CBR, the difference has been less than 4 points. In Kerala and Maharashtra, the rural-urban differential in the CBR has been less than unity.

The rural-urban TFR differential declined from 1.3 in 1971-74 to 1.1 in 2002-2003. The differentials for the currently low fertility states of Kerala, Tamil Nadu, Andhra Pradesh, was less than unity, even as far back as 1972. By 2002, the differential grew even smaller in these states, reflecting the further decline of rural TFRs. Punjab, Haryana, Karnataka and Orissa were other States where the differential was below unity in 2002-03.

The rural-urban differential in the Crude Death Rate (CDR) declined from 7.5 in 1971-73 to 2.5 in 2002-04. However, considerable State wise rural-urban differences continue to persist. In Kerala, J&K, West Bengal, Delhi, Haryana, Punjab, Rajasthan, Gujarat, and, and to a lesser extent, in Karnataka, Tamil Nadu and Maharashtra, the rural-urban differences in the CDR were below the national average by 2003, which is suggestive of improved health conditions in both rural and urban areas.

Rural-Urban differences in the IMR declined from 59 points in 1972 to 27 points in 2003. State wise rural-urban differences in the IMR however continue to be large and display no definite pattern in the past 30 years except that over the board declines have taken place. States where the rural-urban differentials were above the national average, as of 2003, are Andhra Pradesh, Assam,

Karnataka, Madhya Pradesh and Orissa. States where the rural-urban differentials in the IMR were below the national average, are Bihar, Haryana, Maharashtra, Tamil Nadu, Kerala and West Bengal. In Bihar, Haryana and Orissa, the rural IMR declined faster than the urban FMR between 1991 and 2003.

As of 2001, the rural-urban differentials in primary education were large in Himachal Pradesh, Jharkhand, Uttaranchal, Haryana, Orissa, Andhra Pradesh, and Tamil Nadu. They were low in Delhi, Kerala, Assam and Maharashtra. In the case of secondary plus education, the rural-urban difference was above the national average for J&K, Jharkhand, Orissa, Chattisgarh, Madhya Pradesh, Andhra Pradesh, West Bengal and Karnataka. It was low in Delhi, Kerala, and Tamil Nadu. Notably also, in Tamil Nadu, the government has made efforts to popularise secondary and higher education among both males and females, and the rural-urban differences in secondary plus education are on par for males and females. In most other states, the differentials are higher for females. In these States, urbanisation has had a strong effect in countering female exclusion in access to education, Prof. Premi points out.

As Chapter 5 shows, Kerala and Tamil Nadu have been at the forefront of the demographic transition. We focus specifically on these two states in the next chapter, Chapter 7, in which K.C. Zachariah and S. Irudaya Rajan write on the Demographic *Transition in Kerala and Tamil Nadu*. Kerala and Tamil Nadu are States that registered the lowest and second lowest population growth rates respectively among the States and Union Territories of India over the course of the 20th century (1901-2001). A more disaggregated picture shows however, firstly, that it was only after 1971 that Kerala's growth rate dipped below that of India, and secondly, that in the last decade (1991-2001), it was Tamil Nadu that registered the lowest growth rate.

The Crude Birth Rate, around 30 per thousand in Kerala in 1971-75, fell to around 18 in 1996-00. Corresponding figures for Tamil Nadu are 30.7 and 19.3. The TFR in Kerala fell from 3.4 in 1971-75 to 1.8 in 1996-00, as compared to 3.8 and 2.0 respectively in Tamil Nadu. The Crude Death Rate in Kerala, around 9 in 1971, as per SRS data, stayed at around 6 in the decade of the 1990s. In Tamil Nadu, the CDR, around 14 in 1971, fell steeply and hovered at around 8 in the 1991-2001 decade. The IMR differentials between the two States were far more dramatic. In Kerala, it dropped from around 60 per thousand live births in 1971 and dipped below 15 by around the mid 1990s. In Tamil Nadu, the IMR fell from about 110 in 1971 to around 50 in the mid 1990s, and further to around 45 in 2002. Notwithstanding Kerala's huge success in containing infant mortality, however, early age infant mortality in the State is worrisome. Further containment of infant mortality in Kerala, the authors show, will depend on how successfully early age infant mortality is averted.

Decomposing the IMR into its components, they highlight the fact that the contribution of post neonatal mortality (28 days to 365 days) is low compared to neonatal mortality, although both have been declining. Even within one month of life, mortality in the first week is a salient factor. Thus, as of 1997, out of 8 children that died within one month of life, 6 died in the first week.

Numerous factors, historical as well as policy-oriented, have gone into shaping Kerala's demographic trajectories, the authors point out. Among them is the high level of education in the state, the roots of which the authors trace back to British rule and the role of Christian missionaries who concentrated on education and health, rather than on proselytisation. The indigenous tradition of education by the native rulers meant that such initiatives were supported. As in the case of education, the British laid the grounds for the development of a health care system, to which also the native rulers were receptive, given their indigenous traditions of scientific medicine. Kerala's superior health conditions owes to numerous other factors as well, for instance, the even distribution hospitals across the state, easy access to medical facilities, due to the relatively small service area and good transportational facilities, and low cost of medical services as well as high demand for them on account of the high level of education, and a high degree of politicisation which makes for better delivery of public services. Improvements in standards of living for the poor, another factor at work, has come about from such developments such as minimum wages and working conditions, and land reforms ensuring house sites for the poor where vegetables and other food items can be grown as well. Other salient developments include the immunisation programme, and the World Bank population project which focussed on four backward districts of Wayanad, Malappuram, Idukki and Palakkad.

Notably, emigration from Kerala to the Gulf countries has had a significant impact on the status of women in Kerala, particularly Muslim women, who were forced to take up responsibilities related to education, children, banking, social obligations etc. With women at the helm, there has been a huge improvement in the education of girls. Modern ideas about having healthy and well-educated children and providing resources for them have played a role. The family planning programme has contributed to this, acting to change family size norms and create demand for contraception. Nonetheless, Child Woman Ratios (CWRs) computed by the authors to profile the timing and regional disparities in Kerala's fertility decline show that fertility was lower in 1956-66 than it was in 1946-56, which suggests that fertility declined in Kerala before 1965, when the family planning programme began. Trends in the CWR also suggest that fertility declined first in Southern Kerala, in the Travancore-Cochin region, and then in Malabar.

District-level birth rates in Kerala varied considerably, for instance, in 1988, the variation was from 14.8 in Alapuzha to 28.4 in Malappuram. In some districts in south Kerala, such as Alapuzha, Ernakulam, Kottayam and Pathanamthitta, the birth rates had dipped below replacement level, while in some northern districts like Malappuram and Kasargode, they were close to the all India average. Whereas in 1990, only five districts (Palakkad, Malappuram, Wayanad, Kannur and Kasargode) had TFRS above the replacement level, by the turn of the century, the situation had changed substantially. Thus, as per the 2001 census, Malappuram is the only district with a TFR higher than the replacement level. The lowest TFR of 1.5 were reported for districts like Alapuzha, Pathanamthitta and Ernakulam.

Though regional differences are getting eroded, and may disappear altogether in the coming decades, village level data smoothed by the kriging technique showed substantial inter-locality differentials in fertility persisting even into 1991. The lowest fertility area was along the coast from Trissur in the north to Kollam in the south, including regions around Kochi and Kottayam. The analysis showed also that fertility decline spread from a core area located between Alappuzha and Kochi. The Southern ghats were a barrier to fertility diffusion to the east, but the cultural barriers of South Malabar prevented diffusion into that region as well. These data demonstrate that fertility trajectories have been operating not only across time, but also across space, and suggest the operation of a 'demonstration effect' by which low fertility behaviour is imitated or copied.

This process, Guilmoto (2005) argues, is one by which '... interaction networks are shaped by proximity, both social and spatial', and 'diffusion' occurs across social groups as well as over contiguous areas'. NFHS-2 data, which show how the fertility of disadvantaged groups is comparable to that of the elites in low fertility States, bears witness to this phenomenon. The case of Andhra Pradesh, as shown by NFHS data for 1998-99, is noteworthy in this context. Rural-urban fertility differentials stand at 10% of the average fertility for the State, as compared to a figure of more than 25% for the country as a whole. Illiterates in A.P. have a fertility of only 4% higher than the AP average, as opposed to an all India figure of 22%. The fertility differences between the poorest and wealthiest groups is 13% for A.P. as compared to 45% for India. Data for 576 districts of India for 2001 showed moreover that the spatial patterning of fertility was far more pronounced than that of female education. It was found also that the spatial autocorrelation of fertility was more important than proximate variables like child survival, contraceptive prevalence or female age at marriage (Guilmoto 2005: 412-413, 415, 416, 418-420).

In Guilmoto and Rajan's 2001 study of the spatial diffusion of fertility, the authors use a measure of 'spatial autocorrelation' to capture the relationship between distance and the values of the Child Woman Index. They find that spatial correlation coefficients tend to grow stronger over time, increasing from moderate values in the 1950s to very high values by 1991, suggesting thereby that spatial aspects have become increasingly important as the fertility transition has occurred (Guilmoto and Rajan 2001: 728-730). The authors show also, using data from the census of India, that vertical diffusion across social groups was more pronounced in the early fertility-decline districts. They point to indications of this in data from the SRS and NFHS as well. Likewise, estimates based on NFHS and census data show that fertility decline among illiterates has been relatively more in Kerala, Punjab and Tamil Nadu, than elsewhere in India. This accounts for the acceleration of fertility decline among the early decliners (Guilmoto and Rajan 2001: 719, 724,725-728).

We now come to another factor in the fertility transition, namely the family planning programme. For about three decades since its inception, the family planning programme in India had been geared to 'couple protection'. Method-specific contraceptive targets were assigned so as to keep field staff under pressure, intensify contraceptive promotion, and facilitate programme evaluation. Due to the emphasis on meeting targets, quality of family planning services were neglected; 'poor counseling, lack of informed choice for clients, inadequate logistics support, and poor follow up services for family planning acceptors' were the major deficiencies (Khan & Townsend 1999: 44-45). By the last decade of the twentieth century, however, new policy winds began to blow, and a policy shift occurred with the emphasis on improving the quality of reproductive health services. Apprehensions that the policy reorientation could slow down fertility decline in India were belied by data from the NFHS of 1992-93 showing a huge unmet need for contraception which, it was thought, if catered to, could reduce fertility even without targeting pressures. Tamil Nadu's track record of focusing on maternal and child health, with no adverse impact on family planning, was also an encouraging sign. It was in this context that, in 1995, the Government of India decided to remove targets in one district in each of the six largest States (Murthy *et al.* 1999: 125-126). The objective was to focus on programme management designed to deliver quality reproductive health and family planning services. Though maternal and child health services improved in these districts, however, overall family planning performance initially suffered a setback. This has been explained in terms of disorientation at the field level, the need for training of staff and for the setting up of mechanisms to monitor quality of services. Be that as it may, a change in mindset had set in, along with a consensus on the desirability of a target free dispensation. Data for subsequent years showed that the family planning performance had begun to pick up, notwithstanding the continuation of the target free regime. Yet, there are indications that some States—Uttar Pradesh, Bihar and Madhya Pradesh, in that order, were particularly in need of strengthening their reproductive health programmes (Khan & Townsend 1999: 47-52, 54-60).

In Chapter 8, *The Decentralised Approach in the Indian Health and Family Planning Programme*, Nirmala Murthy tells us how, in 1996, the government declared the entire country target free, at the same time announcing its decision to provide a package of reproductive health services to ensure delivery of quality care. A decentralised approach was envisaged, of which one lynchpin was the CNAA, or the Community Needs Assessment Approach, by which the health workers were required to conduct household surveys to assess service requirements, which were then to be validated through discussions with anganwadi workers, women's health groups, panchayat members etc. Skeptics among policy makers believed that combining reproductive health care with FP would dilute the emphasis on FP services, and that this was not advisable, since the number one priority was population control. Programme managers, for their part, were not convinced that workers had the competence to develop work plans. They feared also that the workers would underestimate service needs so as to reduce their workload.

Subsequent to the CNAA guidelines, three approaches emerged. The first was the 'normative approach', by which health workers estimated requirements with respect to norms. For instance, the norm for prenatal care could be 100% of estimated pregnant women, while the norm for sterilisation could be (i) all women who delivered their third order child and (ii) half of those who delivered their second child. These norms ensured that areas with higher birth rates would have higher service requirements. Health workers were trained to use these norms, and at the same time, departmental staff were no longer to be used to recruit cases, so, health workers no longer had to compete with non-health staff to meet targets. Tamil Nadu, where this approach was implemented, was able to meet high levels of contraceptive acceptance and also increase maternal and child care services.

In the 'need-based approach', door-to-door surveys were carried out to identify couples who did not want more children, or wanted to space the next child. In Rajasthan, where this approach was carried out, a 150% increase in spacing methods was registered, along with a 25% decline in sterilisation. This, according to the workers, was because couples wanted to curtail childbearing but were scared of the sterilisation operation. Supervisors however did not accept this explanation. They felt workers were spending more time on surveys instead of motivating acceptors. To boost sterilisation acceptance, the State government announced that at least 70% of couples not wanting more children should be sought to be sterilised.

In the 'combination approach', workers estimated 'service requirements' using norms, and then carried out surveys to assess 'service needs' for health and FP services. Their workloads were set somewhere in this range. In practice, 'most workers used the 'service requirements' approach, so as not to clash with their bosses. They used surveys to increase contact with clients and for awareness-creation, for instance, by selective targeting of clients through inside knowledge of which clients preferred institutional deliveries and which did not, or which knew of use of ORS in case of diarrhoea, and which did not. This helped create awareness of the reproductive and childcare services that were being provided. It also gave workers a sense of ownership of the plans, instilling a professional commitment in them.

Of the 12 indicators used for programme monitoring, as many as five were related to mother care. Consequently, prenatal care and delivery by trained personnel had become the new programme priority, with health workers more interested in registering pregnant women for prenatal care than in recruiting family planning clients. NFHS1 and NFHS2 attested to this shift, by showing sizeable increases in delivery by trained personnel. Another fallout of this new policy shift was that health workers found their acceptability in the community had improved, since they were providing health services and were not merely out to implement family planning targets. Though their workloads had increased, they gained respectability. As regards quality of services, this too had increased, though there was a long way to go. On the criterion of client satisfaction, many women found that they got the contraceptive method of their choice.

The removal of targets initially was followed by a steep decline in contraceptive acceptance, especially in the number of sterilisation operations. In the more developed States, the decline was marginal (5% to 10%), and this was attributed to a decline in misreporting, with the pressure to meet targets no longer acting to inflate acceptance figures. In the underdeveloped States, the decline in sterilisations was substantial (more than 30%). District hospitals had cut down on the number of sterilisation camps, and doctors did not carry out as many sterilisation operations as before. Most cases however reported an increase in the adoption of spacing methods. At the same time, the birth rate continued to decline, from 27.5 in 1996 to 26.1 in 1999 and 25.0 in 2002, suggesting that programme effectiveness actually increased.

Sustainability of the decentralisation policy, Murthy asserts, depends on three factors: (i) implementation difficulties (ii) negative effects on the system and (iii) incentives for implementers. As regards implementation difficulties, workers felt that under CNAA, they were expected to meet targets for not just one, but eighteen services. They also suffered losses because they no longer got the special allowances for recruiting family planning cases. Supervisors, for their part, were unhappy because they could no longer decide on workers workloads, and so suffered an erosion of authority. Hence, they preferred the

State-specified norms. Since supervisors took no responsibility for implementing workers plans, this had a negative effect on the system. Programme implementers at the district level and below felt disappointed because they did not get any incentives in terms of devolution of powers, that would have enthused them to go along with the decentralised approach. Murthy argues that successful decentralisation involves bringing in the various stakeholders to the table. A good quality database is also a *sine qua non* for successful decentralisation, she argues.

It is useful here to briefly review how the quality of care approach has worked elsewhere. In the much written about ICDDR project in Matlab *thana*, Bangladesh, supply side deficiencies, such as accessibility of services and rapport with provider were found to be key determinants of contraceptive acceptance and use. Thus, demand was found to be a necessary but not sufficient condition; and supply side strategies like client oriented services, supervisory and peer support to staff, mechanisms to enforce provider accountability, and links with village leaders were critical to the supply side strategy (Phillips, Simmons, Koenig and Chakraborty 1988: 324-326). It has been found, more specifically, that the grassroots-level health worker can be a source of trust and credibility, reassure a client apprehensive of contraception and its side effects, act as a link to the delivery system so as to offset *purdah,* attenuate the cultural barriers between women and the outside world, and provide support to offset family counter pressures or the client's own ambivalence (Simmons, Baqee, Koenig and Phillips, 1988).

Reporting on data from Bangladesh, Koenig, Hossain & Whittaker (1997: 286) show that trust, rapport and confidence between client and the health outreach worker were critical factors in contraceptive adoption, and, especially, continued use of reversible contraceptives. The client-worker interface has been found to have a strong net effect on contraceptive use, even when measures of demand are controlled for (Phillips, Akbar, Rob and Mozumder, 1984; Phillips, Simmons, Koenig and Hossain 1986; cited in Simmons, Baqee, Koenig and Phillips 1988: 29). In another study, Koenig, Hossain and Whittaker show that after controlling for client characteristics, provider care in Bangladesh still increased the likelihood of contraception adoption (1997: 282-284). Likewise, in a study of 400 South Indian IUD acceptors, Prabhavathi and Sheshadri (1988) found that the likelihood of continued use depended on whether clients were given information on side effects, informed of alternative methods, and received follow up visits (Koenig, Hossain and Whittaker, 1997: 279).

In Chapter 8, we have tried to gauge such facets of family planning and quality of care from an analytical and statistical perspective. *In Chapter 9, Reproductive Health of Punjabi Women: Socio-Psychological Probings*—by

Komila Parthi, *we* look at anecdotal evidence. The chapter probes the reproductive health of 19 women in a sample drawn from Fatehgarh Sahib, a district that has the lowest FMR among all the districts of Punjab and of the country as well. From Fatehgarh Sahib district, the sample was drawn from a village and a town—Bhargrana and Sirhind respectively, which had the lowest FMRs. The intention was to draw a sample of women from a region where the prejudices against them were stark, and hence likely to show up in sharp profile. Women were sampled from three broad categories—(i) married women with no children (ii) married women with children and (iii) pre menstrual women. In all categories, women suffered intense reproductive health ailments, such as foul vaginal discharge, bad odour, lower abdominal pain, burning on urination, weakness, urinary infection, prolapse, and pain during intercourse. They also suffered psychological trauma, leading to stress and depression. All this on top of their household responsibilities was a heavy burden to bear. The case studies show that women's problems were not taken seriously, and that the women had reconciled themselves to their fate, which suggests that demand side factors need to be strengthened.

That women suffer in silence when faced with such problem is reflected in many of the case studies, for instance, in the case of Simran, a newly wed who had been suffering from abdominal pain brought on by menses, but had never taken any medication for her condition. When the affliction struck, she would cry out in pain and rest for a while, before continuing with her work. She also had heavy discharge, which left a stain on her clothes, but had taken no treatment for that condition either. There was a social context to her silence: a good daughter in law was not expected to be complaining of ill health in the first month of marriage itself. Another facet of the silence is that women themselves may not take their ailments seriously. Thus, Gurmeet, aged 23, reports that ever since she started menstruating, she has had a foul smelling discharge, coupled with weakness and discomfort, and backache. She took it all for granted and never sought any treatment. Another woman, Sunita Rani, a 20 year old who has not conceived after marriage, suffers severe reproductive health illness. Her heavy menstrual flow could be responsible for anemia, which, together with malnutrition, leads to low immunity. This could be the reason for her repeated illnesses. Her mother in law's response was to send her to her parents and to warn her not to come back until she was feeling better. For the family, it was her role as a mother that was all-important. Amarjeet, another 20 year old who has been married for nine months, had a swelling in her stomach and severe pain and breathlessness some three months after her marriage, in addition to the heavy vaginal discharge and abdominal pain since she started menstruating. Her parents took her to a doctor, who found no abnormality. In her husband's house, however, there was no one to take her to the doctor. The husband said he had no time to do it, and her mother in law believed that all her daughter in laws problems were due to her inability to conceive.

Women who already had children too were in a bad situation. Apart from being burdened with household work and caring for the family, and also having to manage their reproductive health problems, they were liable to suffer contraceptive-use related illnesses. Parampreet Kaur had been suffering from vaginal discharge and urinary infection ever since she started using the IUD as a contraceptive method. This inhibited her normal functioning at home. Bano, aged 35 also has had similar problems—she has had vaginal discharge along with discomfort and weakness, body ache and backache, since she began using the IUD. She too has never sought treatment. The reason, she says, is that it is difficult for her to leave the house, as there is always something to do a home. In another instance, Seetha, a 38 year old woman, had taken treatment from a doctor for her reproductive health ailments, but had not been completely cured. Going to the hospital means spending money—Rs. 20 on bus fare, and if a doctor is not available, the money goes to waste; moreover, if she takes regular treatment, there is insufficient money to meet her children's needs. In another case, 28 year old Jasbir, for whom pregnancy was a temporary escape from painful menstruation, had five pregnancies, of which three culminated in live births; one was stillborn, and one was aborted. Since her delivery the previous year—a home delivery carried out by a *dai*, she had vaginal discharge and back pain, severe abdominal pain, prolapse and weakness. She had taken no medical treatment due to poverty, lack of time, and lack of support from her family. Another woman, Swarn, a 38 year old mother, had had pre-menstrual tension, stomach ache and burning on urination since her first menstruation, but never sought any treatment, and leant to live with her ailments. After she got sterilised, she regularly had vaginal discharge, along with burning, pain on urination, bad odour, fever, lower abdominal pain, weakness and discomfort. The medication she took from a government hospital only given her temporary relief.

The women in the sample who were past menopause include 49 year old Satpal Kaur, who had not menstruated for the past year. She would feels giddy and depressed and have hot flushes and weakness throughout the day. Additionally, since the time she underwent sterilisation, she suffered from vaginal discharge coupled with bad odour, severe abdominal pain and fever. For Kaur, who works as a maid, work has become very burdensome. She got no relief despite having sought treatment. Lack of support from her husband and elder son at home makes matters worse. Amrinder Kaur too wasn't able to get any support from her husband for her reproductive health problems. Medication from a private practitioner has not helped her. Her husband says it is a natural process and she is overacting to it. She wonders why her husband does not permit her to go for detailed investigations. Another post-menopausal woman, 48 year old Tejpal Kaur, had severe depression and physical ailments like body ache, fatigue, weakness, palpitations and constipation since having spontaneously aborted. She never went to a doctor for treatment, since her husband thought that it was not essential and was of the view that all women suffer from such ailments.

Having profiled her case studies, Parthi recommends that the silence attached to women's health problems be removed, that the socialisation pattern be reformed so that young girls voice their problems, that health education be imparted to ensure that women seek timely treatment, and that a holistic approach be adopted in health care, one that also takes cognisance of the mental health problems that get intertwined with reproductive health concerns.

In Chapter 9, we have seen how women are powerless in seeking treatment for their reproductive health problems, partly because their health concerns are not prioritised by the husband or mother in law, partly because the women themselves seem to have internalised the values that underlie their powerlessness, and partly because they have learnt to live with the neglect of their health concerns, and endure in silence. Chapter 10—*The family: A neglected determinant of health in South Asia* by Carol Vlassoff and her colleagues add to the picture by providing evidence of how women's health concerns are neglected relative to men's. The authors underscore the crucial importance of family support in the treatment of disease, and particularly, in the case of stigmatising diseases like AIDS, and go on to focus specifically on family support in dealing with one stigmatising disease, namely, leprosy.

Their study is based on data from 1154 leprosy patients (496 males and 658 females) sampled from rural and urban sectors of four districts in Maharashtra. The authors show how women are neglected in terms of family support on a number of criteria. The gap between noticing a symptom and suspecting it to be leprosy, a criterion crucial to successful treatment (Gap 1) was approximately 14 months. While Gap 1 was smaller than the overall average in those cases where first reactions from family members were positive or where positive suggestions were made, it was much less in the case of males. In cases where the diagnosis was shared with the spouse too, Gap 1 was lower for males than for females. Gap 2—the gap between noticing the symptom and getting confirmation, another factor crucial for effective treatment, was lower in the case of both male and female respondents who shared the diagnosis with their spouse. However, in the case of the respondents who got positive suggestions from the family, Gap 2 was considerably lower for males than females.

The data show also that the delay in months between diagnosis and initiation of treatment was lower for males than for females for respondents who shared with their spouse or got a first positive response. The delay was lower for heads of households, perhaps because of their greater decision-making power. While this is true for both males as well as females, only 3.6% of the sampled women were household heads. As relatively few women in rural India are heads of households, they are likely to be disadvantaged in treatment seeming.

The delay in initiating treatment in the case of respondents who shared with their spouses was substantially less than the overall average for males, but far less so for females. While husbands may give emotional support, this evidently does not translate into actions like getting timely treatment for their wives or relieving them of their duties. We see also that, even in the case of respondents who shared with their spouse, vastly more males were regular in their treatments than females, suggesting that family support for females in ensuring that they got proper treatment was relatively poor. Overall, these data show that the family had a positive role in the treatment of disease, but males generally benefited more than females.

As we have seen, Chapters 9 and 10, which provide indications of the neglect of women's health concerns, feed into the rationale for a special focus on women's health in the country's health and family welfare programme. As Chapter 8 has shown, this could additionally facilitate the demographic transition by increasing levels of contraceptive use. Also noteworthy is the fact that chapters 9 and 10 do not just show how women's concerns are neglected, they indicate further this is grounded in their relative powerlessness in the household.

We now move on to a review of some other, related issues in the literature—of women's powerlessness, and its converse—their empowerment and autonomy. Women's autonomy is important in explaining demographic trajectories—not only in terms of a woman's control—or lack of control, over her reproductive health and childbearing, which can obstruct transitions to lower fertility or greater spacing of births, but also, in terms of the actions that she can take to protect her children's health and ensure their survival. A number of factors are at work. Caldwell (1986) argues that when women are not secluded and their morality is their own business and not that of society, they are free to go to health centres and wait in mixed queues, and it becomes possible to recruit young women to work outside the home as midwives or health workers. Within the household, a woman can take timely decisions on ensuring rest and treatment for sick children. In Kerala, the substantial autonomy for women was rooted in its matrilineal tradition, which was accompanied by 'a woman's right to decide with whom she consorted and for how long'; in Sri Lanka, the autonomy of women was attested by their sexual freedom before and after marriage, and in Costa Rica, where women played important decision-making roles in the family, chaperonage had been on the decline since the early 1940s (Caldwell 1986: 184-186).

Women's autonomy was a crucial factor in ensuring that Kerala was one of the four regions in the world that achieved good health at low cost. In Kerala, Sri Lanka, and Costa Rica—three of the four regions in the world where good health was achieved at low cost, both social and political will were at work, while in the fourth, China, it was political will alone that was the moving force (Halstead *et al.* 1985). In the case of China, education, health and improving the position of women were ideological aims, while in Sri Lanka, Kerala and Costa Rica, there were striking historical and social parallels—' ... a dedication to education, an open political system ... without a rigid class structure, a history of egalitarianism and radicalism and of national consensus arising from political contest with marked elements of populism' (Caldwell 1986: 182, 208).

As is well known, another key facet of women's agency is that associated with female education. The inverse relationship between female education and fertility, a familiar theme in demographic literature, has many facets. Educated women are likely to have a greater say in reproductive decisions as well as avenues of status and fulfillment other than childbearing. Not only is the opportunity cost of childbearing likely to be comparatively high for educated women, their greater aspirations for children makes them choose to have fewer offspring so that bigger investments per child is possible. Their better knowledge of contraceptive methods allows them to be more able to achieve planned family size, and reduce unplanned pregnancies. They are also likely have lower child mortality, which leads to lower fertility, since the risk of child death is reduced and the incentive to insure against child loss by having more children is weakened. Lower child mortality among educated women results from their being better informed of child nutrition, hygiene and health care, which is an important factor in a context of 'extraordinary beliefs' about the causes of disease and such traditional practices as cutting umbilical cords with unsterilised sickles. Educated mothers are also able to demand greater attention to children's health needs and to take advantage of public health services (Murthi, Guio and Dreze 1995: 748-749).

Another key theme in the literature on women's agency and its impact on childbearing and child survival is the relationship between female work force participation and child mortality. Women's work is believed to enhance women's agency in the society at large and in the family and childcare in particular. However, the double burden of work within and outside the home reduces the time available to them for childcare activities. Women's workforce participation also reduces dowry, which in turn reduces costs of rearing daughters. It also increases women's agency in the household and strengthens the mother's hand in resisting male pressure to discriminate in favour of boys. Women's work can impact on fertility also in that repeated childbearing keeps women out of the workforce and so has a cost (Murthi, Guio and Dreze 1995:749,754).

Multivariate analysis showed a negative and statistically significant relationship between female literacy and child mortality. The effects of female literacy however were stronger with respect to female child survival. Male literacy also reduces child mortality but reduces male child survival more (Murthi, Guio and Dreze 1995: 764). Women's agency variables like female literacy rate and female labour force participation have a statistically significant negative impact on female disadvantage in child survival, while variables pertaining to economic development and modernisation (poverty, male literacy, urbanisation and medical facilities), by reducing male mortality more than female mortality, increase female disadvantage in child survival (Murthi, Guio and Dreze 1995: 770).

These findings are not uncontested, however. In an India study by Bhattacharya (2006), it was found that out of the child mortality decline of 49.97 deaths per thousand between 1981 and 1991, 2.53 child deaths per thousand were accounted for increase in female literacy, while increased female labour force participation had no impact on child mortality. The two women's agency variables accounted for less than 6% of the child mortality decline. Modernisation and economic development variables, on the other hand, accounted for 40% of the decline; availability of safe drinking water had the greatest impact in reducing child mortality, accounting for a fall of 15.08 child deaths per thousand, with improved access to medical facilities accounting for 3.26 fewer child deaths per thousand and improved access to urban areas through *pucca* roads accounting for a decline of 1.36 child deaths. Thus Bhattacharya suggests that rather than women's agency, it was economic development and modernisation that had the greatest impact on both fertility and child mortality between 1981 and 1991 (Bhattacharya 2006: 278-279).

Bhattacharya finds also that both the women's agency variables had a negative and statistically significant effect on female disadvantage in child survival. Female literacy was found to reduce both male and female child mortality, but to reduce female child mortality more, and so attenuate female survival disadvantage. Female labour force participation was found to have *no* statistically significant effect on *male* child mortality, but significantly *reduced* female child mortality and so the gender disadvantage in child survival was lessened. The excess of female deaths over male deaths had declined by 4.9 per thousand between 1981 and 1991. Increase in female literacy accounted for a decline of 1.37, and increased female labour force participation, a decline of 1.24. Increased availability of safe drinking water led to a decline of 1.83. Overall, both economic development and women's agency variables were important in reducing female disadvantage in child survival. However, with continued economic development taking place, the two female agency variables will loose their relative importance (Bhattacharya 2006:279).

In a like vein, Mahuri (1995) suggests that maternal education as a factor reducing child mortality can be conditioned by the quality of available health interventions. In Matlab, Bangladesh, Mahuri (1995) found that for mothers with no schooling, child mortality in the intensive health interventions area (16.7 per thousand) was far lower than in the non-intensive area (25.7 per thousand), and particularly, in comparison to the control area, where the child mortality rate stood at 36.6 per thousand. In the case of mothers with some schooling, the differentials were far less—13.7, 17.1 and 17.7 respectively. While in the control area, the child mortality differential by whether mothers had schooling were quite large, the differential narrows down in the non-intensive area, and narrows down even more in the intensive intervention area (Mahuri 1995:820-821). Multivariate analysis showed that maternal schooling did not significantly affect the odds of child death in the intensive intervention area, but was associated with the odds of child death in the comparison area. It showed also that the intensity of interventions could decrease neither the female disadvantage in child death or the differentials in child death related to poor economic conditions or crowding (Mahuri 1995:824,826-828, 830).

We have seen how women's agency impacts on child mortality, and, more specifically, acts to reduce relative *female* child mortality. Chapters 11 and 12 focus on the issues of the whys of higher female mortality in the first place. Higher mortality among female, as compared to male children, which have led to a deficit of females in parts of South Asia, is rooted in the deprivation of the girl child in household allocations of life sustaining resources—food, nutrition and health care, and even the outright killing of girls or the aborting of female fetuses (Miller 1981). This, in a patriarchal social and cultural milieu such as that in India, derives in part from the expenses to be incurred for the upbringing of a daughter, who moves away to her husband's household and is 'lost' to her parents when she marries. Not only that, she is a drain on her parents' resources due to the flow of gifts (including dowry) from the bride's side to the groom's. A daughter does not have a claim on parental property, it is true, but she is customarily a recipient of presents from her parents' side for herself and her children, and, as per tradition, has claims on her brother's property; her children can expect to receive gifts from her brother, at least as long as she herself is alive. This also underscores the importance of a son as a source of help to parents in the discharge of responsibilities. A son is needed also to perform rituals, including death rituals, for his sister, and is expected to shield his sister and her husband in times of misfortune. Finally, sons bring *in* gifts and dowry, not to speak of a daughter in law to carry out household duties (Patel 2007: 142, 149-150, 161, 164, 163; Patel 2004).

Chapter 11, by John Hodinnott—*The intra-household distribution of food: an economic perspective*, provides a different sort of viewpoint on the discriminatory treatment of females. Citing evidence from the Philippines and Bangladesh, Hoddinott points out that nutritional adequacy at the household level correlates poorly with that at the level of the individual household member. The data he cites show that of the individuals comprising study households, a substantial proportion were subject to relatively low food intake even when aggregate levels of household nutrition were far higher, and further, that within households, food allocations favoured males over females. While disparities such as these have been explained in terms of the social and cultural manifestations of gender discrimination, Hoddinott argues that there are other dimensions involved as well.

In making his point, the author invokes the economic principles of *efficiency*, *equity* and *bargaining*. Of these, the first makes for a distribution of food such that the household's nutritional resources accrue preferentially to its economically more productive members. Citing data from Bangladesh, Hoddinott points out that men tend to do most of the agricultural work, including most of the work that is physically demanding. Thus, if they get a greater share of household food, it is likely to have the greatest impact on household income. Hoddinott draws on empirical data to indicate that this indeed forms a basis of food allocations deliberately tilted in favor of males. Maximisation of the household's productivity and income is the rationale here. One implication of this, the author points out, is that school meals programmes targeted at girls can be thwarted when households 'compensate' by reducing the quantities of food given to girls at home and reallocate the 'surplus' to the family's economically more productive. The principle of efficiency is not inexorable, however, for there are times when it is eclipsed by the principle of *equity*. Evidence from rural India suggests that the former is less likely to operate during seasons of plenty, at which time equity considerations are likely to come to the fore.

The third of Hoddinott's principles—*bargaining* draws upon game theory. The advantage to household members when they pool their resources, Hoddinott says, is jeopardised when any member implicitly threatens to go for an 'outside option', i.e., an economic opportunity that is available outside of a familial pooling arrangement. That forms a bargaining lever for laying claim to a greater share of a household's food resources. From this point of view, the subordinate position of females in the food entitlement hierarchy is a manifestation of women's lack of access to 'outside options'. By the same reckoning, policy interventions which increase women's access to 'outside options', for instance, changes in marriage laws giving a woman a share of her husband's estate on divorce, can be expected to bring about an improvement in the position of women within the household.

Chapter 11, essentially a non-technical introduction to issues of household food allocation, highlights the power structure in the household. While the author shows how this affects the distribution of food, we can extend the argument to include also access to health. This helps in explaining why women suffer from neglect of their health concerns—issues that we have seen in chapters 9 and 10. Secondly, Chapter 11 points out that household food allocations are not static—they are subject to changes in circumstances, such as better outside options for females. Moreover, as Hoddinott's principle of equity implies, in times of plenty, discriminations against females are likely to wane. In this context, since, when fertility declines, there would tend to be more resources to go around, we should expect the equity principle to operate. This has been argued by Dyson (1987), who take the view that fertility decline in India has reduced demographically determined risk in that it allowed a greater share of resources for females in smaller families, and made for an improvement of the survival chances of female children. Continued discrimination against girls in terms of how well fed and cared for they are did not translate into higher mortality rates for female children, but it acted to increase their frailty and susceptibility to morbidity.

Chapter 12, *Fertility Decline and the FMR in Rural India—State Wise Patterns and Trends, as Shown by Retrospective Data from the 1981, 1991 and 2001 Censuses*, by Rajiv Balakrishnan, throws some light on these issues. The chapter investigates two types of impact of fertility decline on the FMR. When fertility goes down and son-preference drives households to ensure they have the desired number of male offspring, the stage is set for the 'intensification effect', that is, an intensification of fatal daughter-discrimination. More specifically, higher birth order daughters are at grave risk, since, while a first daughter can entail manageable expenses, an additional daughter is more liable to represent an onerous drain on household resources, in terms of dowry, gifts etc. In India, the intensification effect appears to be a relatively recent phenomenon, beginning in the mid 1980s, when new technology made it possible for couples to follow the female foeticide route with ease and efficiency.

'Retrospective data'—the type of data drawn upon in this chapter—are data on children ever born (CEB) and children surviving (CS) as reported by mothers who were asked by census enumerators to provide details of their reproductive history. The data are about past events (births and deaths), and so they are called 'retrospective data'. The data were collected for mothers in various age groups, that is, 15-19, 20-24, 25-29 etc. When we consider data for 1991, then, mothers in the age group 55-59 would have entered their reproductive careers in 1956, and those aged 15-19 in 1991. So, these data allow us to trace patterns of offspring FMRs over time. We need to note that the retrospective data differ from the enumeration data in another fundamental way. The retrospective data are for different cohorts of mothers—the cohort of mothers who entered the reproductive ages in 1956, the cohort of mothers who entered the reproductive ages in 1961, and so on. So, they give a comparative picture of different such cohorts. The enumeration data, on the other hand, show data for the entire population at different points of time. Like all sources of data, the retrospective data have their limitations. Since these data are based on mothers' recollection of their own reproductive histories, they are susceptible to recall errors, and their accuracy may leave much to be desired. Through mathematical modeling, data of this kind have been used to estimate the overall child mortality rates when other more reliable sources of data are not available. In this paper, precise estimates are not the objective. The data are drawn upon to *roughly* gauge patterns and trends, and to look for underlying causes, rather than to attempt precise measurements. The data used are mostly for rural areas, though, while drawing on the 2001 retrospective data, urban areas and all areas have also been briefly considered.

The use of these retrospective data, as an alternative to population enumeration data, has two major justifications. Firstly, the age enumeration errors in the enumeration data pose a serious problem (Mari Bhat 2002a and Mari Bhat 2002b). In the case of retrospective data, we are not concerned with the mother's reporting of the age of the child—the data are on the mothers' recollection of all the children she has had. The second reason why enumeration data based juvenile FMRs are problematic is that excess female child mortality may not have fully manifested in the juvenile ages—the effect of excess female child mortality would be seen only after a sufficient ageing of a cohort of children has occurred. Composite variables like 'under five mortality' are prone to this sort of problem (Agnihotri 2000:29, 38, 95-96), and we can extend the argument to juvenile FMRs as well. Thus, though retrospective data has its limitations, so does the enumeration data of the census.

The retrospective data show that overall, *if one considers the entire period from 1956 to 1991*, fertility decline in India seems to have largely made the FMR more balanced, by having ensured that higher birth-order children, among whom girls are at heightened risk of fatal discrimination, are not born, i.e., it appears that the 'parity effect' had been the main moving force since the 1960s up to at least the mid nineteen eighties. Fertility decline, by preventing high birth order girls from being born, plausibly put the brakes on a worsening of the FMR, by acting to reduce female infanticide or fatal discrimination of girls. This effect was pronounced in Uttar Pradesh, Punjab, Gujarat, West Bengal, Orissa, Tamil Nadu, Andhra Pradesh, Haryana, Delhi, and Bihar. Also a tendency can be seen whereby the parity effect has been most potent in these parts of the country, where discrimination against daughters has traditionally been more acute.

It was investigated as to whether there could be factors other than parity acting to apply the brakes on the deterioration of the cohort FMRs. Female education was identified as one such salient factor, and the question was raised as to whether successive cohorts of women have more feminine FMRs merely because *more* of them are educated, rather than because they have lower fertility. The data do throw a little light on this. Firstly, they show that until 1986, offspring FMRs were more feminine for educated mothers than for illiterate mothers. At the same time, the parity effect operated for literate and for illiterate mothers both. Thus, the evidence of the parity effect having been salient and potent cannot be explained away in terms of increases in female literacy over time.

Notably, the nineteen seventies was a period of sharp fertility decline (Jha 2008: 86—Figure 4.1). By 1971, this seemed to have neutralised gender discriminatory practices, which, as Mari Bhat (2002b: 5252-5253) points out, had been rendered highly potent by the new access to life-saving factors. The net effect was arguably at the root of the child mortality declines for females relative to males since 1971 shown by SRS data (Mari Bhat 2002b: 5253). The feminisation of rural offspring FMRs between 1971 and 1986, shown by the 1991 retrospective data for rural areas, was especially steep for States like Uttar Pradesh, Delhi, and Rajasthan, as per the retrospective data. Juvenile FMRs compiled from census enumeration data corroborate this pattern of growing feminisation of the FMR between 1971 and 1981, particularly for Uttar Pradesh, Delhi and Rajasthan.

The intensification effect appears to be a relatively recent phenomenon, beginning in the mid 1980s, when new technology made it possible for couples wanting to eliminate undesired daughters to follow the female foeticide route with ease and efficiency. Between 1981 and 1991, the deterioration in the offspring FMRs that took place was substantial. The aggregate picture, taking all cohorts into account (the 1956 cohort up to the 1991 cohort), is that in States like Uttar Pradesh, Bihar, Rajasthan and Delhi, not only did the FMRs become very adverse for children ever born, they were even worse for children surviving, which suggests that not only pre-natal elimination of females pronounced in these regions, post natal elimination of females was pronounced also. It is a pattern that chimes in with the findings of Sudha and Rajan (2003). Between 1981 and 1991, when the revival of gender discrimination before birth occurred, this pattern can be seen notably for Bihar, Rajasthan and Gujarat. In the case of States like Punjab and Haryana, throughout a half century, we see a tendency for gender bias in birth to be the main operative factor, whereas in States like Uttar Pradesh, Bihar and Rajasthan, there is gender bias after birth also.

We see some corroboration for the parity effect having been overwhelming from a multivariate analysis using district level data separately for 1981,1991, and 2001, in which it was found that fertility (the Child-Woman Ratio) varied positively with the number of males per thousand females (Guilmoto 2005: 409). Thus, at the aggregate level, high fertility was associated with a high child FMR. This suggests that the intensification of daughter discrimination emerging after the mid nineteen eighties was not strong enough to offset the gains from the averting of high birth-order female births due to fertility decline. In other words, fertility decline in India has, on average, applied the brakes on the worsening of the FMR.

We need also to consider one other factor which operates in the *same* direction as the intensification effect, namely, the process of 'sanskritisation' or the emulation of upper caste lifestyles by the lower castes, which involves a withdrawal of women from the labour force as material conditions improve and it is no longer necessary for them to work. The 'effective co-operation' or partnership aspect of gender can, in this context, weaken (Dreze & Sen 1996: 155-159). This view that poverty reduction is likely to have been at the root of intensified female survival disadvantage is corroborated by cross sectional data for 296 districts, which show that higher levels of poverty go with more balanced FMRs, while, at the same time, female labour force participation makes the FMR more feminine (Dreze and Sen 1996: 157-163). In this context, we need also to consider Krishnaji's (1995) explanation for more balanced FMRs among working mothers, namely, that acute poverty makes it difficult for mothers to *fatally* discriminate in favour of their male children, since resources are at such a low level anyway that children of both sexes are at high risk (Krishnaji 1995). What these explanations imply is that the evidence we have considered of the 'intensification effect' operating since the mid nineteen eighties could in fact be due to declines in female work force participation. However, the retrospective data showed that in Bihar, Punjab, Uttar Pradesh and Gujarat, offspring FMRs have worsened for both working mothers as well as non-working mothers. Again, as in the case of literacy and the parity effect, we can't explain away the evidence of the intensification effect in terms of 'sanskritisation'.

Chapter 12 indicates also that the intensification effect had not occurred significantly in the South Indian States. This chimes in with a study by Sudha and Rajan (2003) to the effect that gender discrimination before birth was pronounced in those regions which historically had more acute levels of discrimination against females. Conversely, and also chiming in with the Sudha and Rajan (2003) study, the parity effect was found to be stronger in those parts of the country where discrimination against daughters was traditionally far worse. Though, between 1981 and 1991, northern states have seen a revival of gender discrimination before birth, which has caused a great deal of alarm, its magnitude appears to be small compared to what was traditionally the case; the data thus suggest that discrimination against females at birth, was far more acute a few decades earlier, *before* fertility decline set in. This plausibly was due to female infanticide, since technologies for identification of the female foetus were only a relatively recent development, occurring from the mid nineteen eighties. In Sates like Uttar Pradesh, Rajasthan and Bihar, a vast extent of infanticide seemed to have disappeared by 1981, plausibly due to the parity effect.

Notably, the retrospective data show that after 1986, up to 1991, in Punjab, Uttar Pradesh, Delhi and Bihar, the intensification effect occurred both among literate as well as educated mothers. Thus, whereas in earlier decades, women's education had acted to make the FMR more balanced, after the mid 1980s, there are indications that education no longer has been playing such a role. It is noteworthy that the finding to the effect that female education intensifies gender bias is echoed by a study based in rural Punjab by Das Gupta (1987), who found that educated mothers, who desired fewer children, were more resistant to having fewer sons. It is noteworthy also that this is contrary to the findings of other studies, which show that female literacy acts to reduce excess female child mortality (Bhattacharya 2006; Murthi *et al* 1995). Chapter 12 however has a very different in focus from the studies by Bhattacharya (2006) and Murthi et al (1995). Several points can be made here. Firstly, this chapter shows elimination of daughters before birth among educated women, whereas the studies by Bhattacharya (2006) and Murthi *et al* (1995) find a relationship between female education and mortality differentials by sex among *living* children. Secondly, Bhattacharya (2006) and Murthi *et al* (1995) deal with aggregate district level data for the country as a whole (for 1981 and 1991), and do not profile particular regions. Thirdly, we see in chapter 12, that the evidence of the intensification of daughter discrimination among educated mothers begins to be seen only after 1986, whereas Murthi et al (1995) deal with the situation in 1981. Fourthly, Bhattacharya (2006) and Murthi *et al* (1995) deal with 'all areas data', that is data for rural and urban areas combined, while here we are looking at data for rural areas only. As a final point, in both studies (Bhattacharya 2006; Murthi *et al* 1995), sex differentials in child mortality are studied using under 5 mortality data. This could potentially be a source of error—as Agnihotri (2000:29, 96) points out, when environmental conditions are harsh, male mortality tends to be high, and this can mask gender bias *in later years* when children have had a chance to fully age through the 0-5 age group. This is not a reason to reject the findings of Bhattacharya (2006) and Murthi *et al* (1995)—it only suggests that their findings be treated with caution.

Retrospective data for rural areas from the 2001 census corroborate the findings of the 1991 retrospective data for rural areas. They confirm that in the case of Punjab and Gujarat, offspring FMRs did grow more masculine between 1986 and 1991, plausibly due to the intensification effect. The 2001 retrospective data show this also for Delhi, Haryana and Himachal Pradesh. Notably, the 2001 rural areas retrospective data also confirm that the intensification effect had not occurred in the southern States up to 1991.

Chapter 11 had shown that the principles of efficiency, equity, bargaining contribute to changing intra-household food distribution scenarios, even as gender discriminatory practices remain unchanged. Chapter 12 complements this perspective by showing that socially determined risk too is a factor that can change to reduce intra household discrimination, and that this indeed has happened in India over the course of the demographic transition. It is noteworthy that the evidence in Chapter 12 of the salience and potency of the parity effect chimes in with Dyson's explanation of a decline in demographically determined risk. Dyson (1987) argues that fertility decline in India allowed a greater share of resources in smaller families, and hence made for an improvement of the survival chances of female children. Thus, according to Dyson, it was the fall in *demographically determined risk* that was behind falling female child mortality. In this context, though more children were surviving, continued discrimination against them in terms of how well fed and cared for they are did not translate into higher mortality rates for female children—it acted, rather, to increase their frailty and susceptibility to morbidity (Dyson 1987). That the decline of relative female child mortality was not linked to improvements in the health circumstances of girl children is suggested also in cause of death statistics for India for 1980, 1990 and 1998. The data show that mortality due to anaemia was higher among girls than among boys, which indicates higher levels of malnutrition among girl children (Sagar 2007: 181). The averting of high birth-order female births had critically reduced socially determined risk so that girl children became less burdensome to a point where fatal discrimination against them was less likely. If discriminatory practices still continued, they were not so deadly as before, in part because there were fewer high birth order girls in the household, and partly because, the decline in demographically determined risk (due to fertility decline) had given the girl child a reprieve. (It was not however found possible to separately quantify the effects of demographically determined risk and sociologically determined risk.)

We have profiled mortality and fertility trajectories, and probed the factors at work. We have also seen how fertility decline, via the parity effect, had applied the brakes to the worsening of the FMR until the mid eighties, after which it acted in the opposite direction by fueling the intensification effect and creating a tragic tailspin. We move on now to another major fallout of the demographic transition from high to low fertility and mortality, namely, changes in the age structure of the population. Due to mortality decline, the mean age of the population is liable to increase. This, along with a shrinking of the younger-age population when fertility declines, leads to the growth in the numbers of the elderly (those aged 60 and above) relative to the not old. While a fall in fertility always fosters ageing, a reduction in mortality can not only increase both the longevity of the elderly as well as the proportion surviving to older ages—it can also improve the survival chances of infants and young children, with the result that the age structure becomes 'juvenated'. As a consequence of countervailing juvenation and ageing effects over the course of demographic transitions from high to low levels of mortality and fertility, age structures can grow younger before they grow older, as was the case in the demographic history of the world's less developed regions between 1950 and 1985. The ageing that set in during this period was a precursor of things to come, data projected for 1985-2025 attests; the LDCs are on an ageing trajectory, as the more developed countries have been—but with a difference, for ageing in the demographic history of the LDCs has been projected to be much speedier than it was in the more developed world, on account of a faster fall in fertility (United Nations 1988).

Also salient is the fact that aging is taking place in the less developed countries of the world at levels of material development that are far lower than those prevalent in the developed countries when their populations began to age (U.N. Secretariat 1988). Consequently, a major concern fostered by demographic aging in the less developed regions of the world, where the economic situation does not permit resources to be set aside for old age on an adequate scale, is that the material needs of the enfeebled elderly will henceforth have to be shouldered by a smaller number of the more active young. It is here that the roots of the aging concerns of the LDCs lie, for these countries can ill afford the elaborate and expensive care arrangements that exist for the care of the elderly in the west. Also differing from ageing in the west, in the LDCs, it is the family that is the major source, not only of material resources for the care of the aged, but also, of assistance for what Habib (1988) calls ADL (Activities of Daily Living).

In Chapter 13, *Ageing in Kerala* by S. Irudaya Rajan and Sabu Aliyar, we are given an indication of the care burden on the young that ageing has imposed and will impose in the future, in an Indian State where longevity increases and mortality declines having proceeded far ahead of those of other States in the country. In Kerala, the proportion of elderly to the total population, at 10.5%, is the highest in the country. At the same time, the number of care-givers has declined due to the out-migratory flows of job seekers. Even when families are able to support the elderly, it has become more difficult for them to do so, because life expectancy is now far higher than it was in earlier times. One indication of an increasing burden of old-age care, the growth rate among the old-old (those aged 80+), was around 3% in 1991-2001, as against a population growth rate of 1% in the same period. In the coming decades, the growth rate of the old-old is expected to rise to about 4%. Another measure of old-age dependency, the index of ageing, defined as the proportion of the population aged 60+ to the population aged 0-14, is the highest in Kerala. It increased from 14 in 1961 to 15 in 1971 and 29 in 1991. By 2041, the index would be 228, five times higher than its value of 40 for 2001. By 2061, it is expected to touch 476. As per household survey compiled by the authors, in future, every household in Kerala would have to take care of one child and an aged mother or father or both.

Significantly, Chapter 13 also shows that family support for the elderly is extensive, going by that criterion of support, namely, co-residence. In Kerala as in the rest of India, a mere 2.5% of the elderly live alone. 62.5% live with a spouse, children and grandchildren, and 25.76 live without a spouse but with children or grandchildren. Another 7.65% live with their spouse. Thus, around 96% live with immediate family members. Another 1.36% live with relatives other than spouse, children or grandchildren, and 0.16% live with non-relatives.

Like Chapter 13, Chapters 14 and 15 too show extensive family care for the elderly in less developed settings. Chapter 14—*The family in south India: past, present and future*, by John C. Caldwell, P.H. Reddy and Pat Caldwell, is based on data for 9 villages in Southern Karnataka for different points of time—1979, 1983 and 1995. The authors explore several facets of the family, including the role of children in caring for elderly parents. That aspect of elderly care—co-residence with a child, develops naturally when a son marries and brings his wife home to live with him and his parents in what has become a 'Stem Family' (A 'Stem Family is one in which, 'in addition to the nuclear family, includes one or more parents / grandparents of the husband / wife). The stem family becomes a nuclear family when the older generation dies, and nuclear families in turn become stem families when the younger generation marries. Typically, parents stay with the eldest son, whose wife provides care for them. The other sons set up their own households when they get married. Fertility decline and the move towards single-son families, the authors prognosticate, will inevitably lead to a rise in the proportion of stem families. Meanwhile, mortality decline and a greater number of sons surviving to adulthood has meant that the proportion of nuclear families has grown. In the midst of all this change in family structure, what remains constant, the authors report, is the situation in which an older couple live with a married son. The high proportion of stem families in India, they argue, 'reflects the persistence of traditional filial obligations to parents'. Moreover, elderly respondents themselves overwhelmingly reported that they were treated by their children as expected or even better than expected. Also indicating the strength of elderly care, just 2% of males and 6% of females reported their living conditions as destitute.

In Chapter 15, *Family care for rural elderly in the midst of rapid social change: the case of Thailand*, John Knodel and Chanpen Saengtienchai draw on data from a variety of sources, including three surveys. Taking co-residence of the elderly with their children an indicator of family provisioned care for the elderly, the author's look at changes over time, in the decade of the nineteen eighties, which characterised by substantial out migration of young adults from the village to the city. Both census and survey data showed that at least four out of five Thai elderly who have living children lived with a child at both points of time that were compared. Moreover, urban and rural differences in levels of co-residence were small. While these data attest to extensive intergenerational residence, they underestimate the phenomenon, the authors believe. Censuses and surveys underestimate the true level of care, for even when the elderly do not reside in the same household, they may live in the same residential cluster as their children, whose proximity serves the same functional purpose as the more narrowly defined co residence. For instance, in rural areas, it is not uncommon for neighbouring adult children to bring their parents cooked food on a regular basis. Taking co-residence or daily contact as the criterion, it was found that 90% of the elderly with living children were ensconced in a family provisioned old age care arrangement.

According to SECAPT (Socio Economic Consequences of the Aging Population in Thailand), a survey carried out in 1986, national in coverage and extending to over 3000 elderly respondents, half of the non co-resident elderly lived by themselves, either alone or with their spouse. The remaining half live with a *laan* (grandchild, nephew or niece) or a child in law. The younger relative was economically active or an adult or both, or was a dependent cared for by the elderly. Comparing childless elderly to elderly with children, the former are less likely to be living in single households, and are more likely to live with siblings or laan.

In a 1994 survey carried out by the authors, only 3% of the 551 elderly that is, 15 elderly persons in the survey, lived alone. Of them 7 lived close to at least one married child, and in 3 cases, they lived next to relatives and thus were not isolated from the family network. In one instance, an elderly widow had a son staying in Bangkok, who provided support and visited occasionally. Another elderly widow too had a son who visited occasionally, but was a drunkard and was more of a burden according to informants. The remaining 3 elderly, who were truly deserted by their children, lived by begging or were dependent on neighbours. In these cases, the family support system had failed.

As in the case of elderly living alone, in the case of elderly living with their spouses, many did have access to extended family support. Thus, of the 13 households comprising elderly who lived with their spouses, 6 lived next in the close proximity of married children. Another household comprised of a government pensioner and his wife, who had moved into the area where they had family connections. In the case of the remaining 6 households, contact with children seemed to be occasional and support modest. However, it is possible that the elderly in these households were at a stage of life when they could manage, and that, when the need arose, help from children would be forthcoming. In fact, in a number of cases where the elderly seem to be living alone, a support system may be available to them in times of need.

Underscoring the family support arrangements for the elderly is the widespread sentiment, reinforced by culture, that children should care for elderly parents, out of a sense of obligation and gratitude. It is a sentiment that cuts across economic status, rural-urban residence, and age. In focus group discussions, both elderly and adults felt that though children may move out of the household after marriage or to seek jobs or higher education, at least one child should stay behind to care for parents. This sentiment is so strongly rooted that the elderly dependent on a child take it for granted that the child will not leave the village without making some arrangement for their care. Though out-migration of young adults takes place in many families, it is unlikely that one child would not stay back if the elderly parents are at a stage of life where they need care. Focus group participants, especially the elderly ones, did not view the migration of job-seeking young adults to the city with alarm.

Other Thailand based studies are noteworthy here, as they serve to complement the picture sketched out in Chapter 15. One study, which distinguishes between support from co-resident and non co-resident children, shows that material support from the latter, in the form of money, food and clothes—rose quite substantially with the number of living offspring (Knodel, Havavon and Siriboon 1992:84-86). Yet, a smaller number of children can make possible greater per-child educational investments and strengthen the earning capacities of the young, so that fewer offspring will not necessarily mean a reduction in the amount of material support for parents from children (Knodel, Havavon and Siriboon 1992: 90,95).

Chapters 14 and 15 have shown extensive levels of family care for the elderly in different Asian settings. This is corroborated with more recent national level data in Chapter 16—*Demographic Transition and Aging in India and China*—by Raja Gopal Dhar Chakrabarti. In both China and India, Chakrabarti reports, family supports for the elderly were extensive, as indicated by data on co-residence of the elderly with family caregivers. Only 7% of the elderly in China and 4% in India lived alone. NSS data for India show that in rural as well as urban areas, 70% of the elderly were economically dependent on others. Economic support was provided by children to 71.1% of rural elderly and 70.8% of urban elderly. Spouses and grandchildren too provided support. Under the category 'others', which include the government, 5.9% and 6.9% were supported in urban and rural areas respectively. In China, as many as two thirds of the elderly were dependent on children. Other family caregivers too were found to extensively support the Chinese elderly, as per survey data.

It needs to be noted however, that informal safety nets are not always reliable. In developing countries, the poor are especially vulnerable, because their children, on whom they depend, are also poor. It is noteworthy that this point has been made also in Chapter 15, where it is reported that while overall, the picture is one of extensive family support for Thai elderly, this does not mean that the elderly are adequately cared for, since poverty is so pervasive that resources are scarce for both the younger as well as the older generation. Chakrabarti too argues that family support systems are liable to come under increasing strain as the demographic transition increases the number of elderly and decreases the number of caregivers, thus increasing the per capita cost of elderly care. Increase in health care costs and lack of medical insurance compounds the problem, Chakraborti emphasises. In India, the effect of poverty can be gauged by the fact that the work participation rate among the elderly (93% of whom are 'main' and not 'marginal workers') is high—39%, as against 37.5% for the total work force population. Self-employment in agriculture on the family farm is a major sphere of elderly employment. 78% of the elderly work force is engaged in agricultural activities, and in the case of females, the figure is 84%. In urban areas, the elderly work in activities involving manual strength and physical hazard. Even more stark is the fact that in India, as many as 19% of the 80+ elderly work for a living. In China too the elderly working in rural areas was high, at 39.7%, but only 0.8% of them were working in urban areas.

India and China, which, between them, account for more than half of the developing countries' elderly and 64% of elderly in Asia, are ageing at a relatively low level of economic development, Chakrabarti points out. In both countries, provision for public support for the elderly is meagre, and culture and tradition emphasise filial piety and care of the elderly by their children. In India, the author tells us, only about 10% of the labour force is covered by old-age security schemes. As in the case of other poor countries, India has a large proportion of its labour force in the agricultural and in the informal sector, which are bypassed by these schemes. Though the government has schemes for the destitute elderly, the support levels are pathetic. States give pensions ranging from Rs. 55 to Rs.300. Even these meagre sums are accessible to only 10%-15% of the elderly in most states, while in Kerala, some 20% access some form of pension. Since 1995, the central government has started the National Old Age Pension Scheme, which pays Rs.75 per month to destitute persons aged 65 and above. According to one estimate, as of 2001, spending at both State level and central levels accounted for a mere 0.08% of GDP.

In China, most urban workers had been employed by State owned enterprises and were covered by social security benefits including old-age pensions. By the late 1980s, however, private businesses and factories had emerged upon the scene, and by the 1990s, only a quarter of the urban work force was protected by State provided benefits, with the remaining work force not covered by any form of social insurance. Moreover, under the medical reform in urban areas, free medical care was no longer available, and some form of cost sharing was introduced. In rural areas, the government and the collectives, once upon a time, provided the 'Five Guarantees'—food, clothing, medical care, housing and burial expenses to the childless and the infirm elderly. When collective farming was abolished under Deng Xioping's 'Four Modernisations', the family became the sole caregiver, recognised as such by both the Chinese constitution and the Chinese government. The government did seek to provide economic aid when, in 1991, the Ministry of Civil Affairs began a contributory pension scheme in rural areas, in which 3 Yuan had to be contributed per month. About 8.3 million people have participated in this scheme, which was to provide a pension of about 573.6 Yuan annually to half a million pensioners. The scheme however does not seem to have progressed beyond this point.

In both China and India, elderly staying in old age homes are miniscule. Still, China has far greater provision for elderly care in old age homes. In the whole of India, there are only 728 old age homes, of which only 547 'seem active'. 325 are free, 95 operate on a pay and stay basis, and 116 have free as well as pay and stay provisions. Throughout the country, there are only 278 old age homes to cater to the sick. 101 old age homes are exclusively for women. Kerala has the maximum number of old age homes found in any state—124. By comparison, China, at the end of 2001, had 8665 urban elderly welfare units, with 282,000 beds and 200067 occupants. It also had 26,550 rural elderly units, with 684,202 beds and 489,236 occupants. There were also 1343 homes for disabled veterans, with 45,448 beds and 31,404 occupants.

We have seen how ageing is taking place in the less developed world at a low level of material development, and we have seen how the burden of elderly care is heavy on the younger generation and will worsen in the years to come. We have also seen how family support for elderly is widespread, even if conditions of poverty mean that it falls short of what is needed. The role of informal systems of support, we have seen, is extremely meager. Theoretical issues in informal vs. formal care form the theme of the next chapter, that is, Chapter 17, on Old *age security: Families vs. Governments or Families and Governments* by Mussaddeq Chowdhury and Jeffrey Nugent. As an example of a formal system of elderly support, the authors cite the case of the social security system in the United States. The genesis of this arrangement was that of a private insurance scheme, by which individuals were to deposit a proportion of their incomes in an interest-bearing fund. On retirement, the insurer would receive benefits from the principal and interest. In 1939, the system was converted into a scheme of intergenerational transfer, whereby each generation of retirees is supported by the current generation of workers. In the LDCs formal schemes for the care of the elderly are unlikely to be sustainable, partly because the LDCs lack the administrative and tax resources, because of the lack of a market for insurance, and because the elderly in the LDCs do not have the kind of political clout as they do in the developed countries, which they use to advance their cause.

Among the issues Chowdhury and Nugent address is that of whether formal systems 'crowd out' (limit or constrain) informal arrangements. If the incentive for intergenerational transfer is altruistic, government schemes, by providing an alternative means of support for the aged, will 'crowd out' private transfers. However, the underlying motive can be 'inter temporal exchange'. This may arise from a recognition of the sacrifices made by one's parents, which forms the basis for reciprocity, or may stem from the desire to teach the young the norm of caring for aged parents. In either of these cases, public transfers will not undermine private ones. Then there is the phenomenon of 'crowding in', as opposed to 'crowding out'. 'Crowding in' can occur, for instance, when access to free or subsidised medical facilities by the elderly provide an impetus to complementary private transfers. The authors conclude from their discussions that formal schemes must be introduced only to the extent that they complement informal ones and that, simultaneously, existing informal systems need to be strengthened with incentives.

We have seen that a paucity of resources available to the household is a strong argument for the role of informal transfers as a 'crowding in' mechanism. The rationale for this stems also from factors pertaining to the household-sustaining roles that the elderly play in the household. The elderly are not merely dependents. In Thailand, Knodel, Saengtienchai and Sittitrai (1992) report, the typical pattern of co-residence of an elderly with a child means mutual assistance across the generations. We have already seen indications of this in Chapter 15, when instances were cited of the elderly caring for young dependents. In China and Australasia, studies show, the elderly are caregivers and productive members of the household (Davis-Friedman 1983; Quitugua

1982: 323; Treas 1979). It is a role that extends to the manufacture of handicrafts for household consumption, barter and sale; poultry raising; the cultivation of vegetable plots, the care of children; and shopping and house keeping tasks. Not only does this augment production and family income, it frees other household members, particularly women, for work outside the home (Treas and Logue 1986: 664). However, when the elderly 'grow increasingly frail, as their needs become consequently greater, as their assets are used up, and as their contributions diminish', they are liable to be accorded a low priority in the allocation of scarce resources—for the more economically productive expenditures on the younger generation might otherwise be comprised and care-givers burdened with greater opportunity costs, as evidences from South Asia testify (Treas and Logue 1986: 651-653).

The household entitlements of the elderly can have more intricate moorings, evidence also suggests. Levine (1987) argues, in her study of three Tibetan communities of northwest Nepal, that son preference and discrimination against daughters in the allocation of household resources needs to be seen in the light of an ethos according to which the household tends to value its members 'according to their current, past and future contributions'. In this context, formal supports to the elderly are likely to have a crucial bearing on their material welfare, freeing family heads of the need to make tragic decisions that impinge on the elderly. At the same time, it is important to note that the elderly are not a homogenous category. Health status, for instance, can be a facet of their heterogeneity. Thus, the 'frail elderly'—the 'neediest, oldest old' (Treas and Logue 1986: 660) require special care. It may also be necessary to assign a high priority to public health facilities for the older generation to strengthen the situation of the ailing elderly in the household (Treas and Logue 1986: 657). The disabled and ailing elderly, moreover, are quite different from the productive or potentially productive old, and policies for the former would need to be quite different from those for the latter. Other categories of salience are—elderly who have access to familial sources of ADL (Assistance in Daily Living) and those who have to depend more on other sources; elderly who belong to indigent households and those who are better off; and elderly who are especially vulnerable, such as son-less widows and the very old.

Care for the elderly can be hamstrung by a paucity of means, but it can also be hamstrung by a lack of skilled medical interventions and support, without which the elderly may be left to die a slow death. Professional care through home visits by trained personnel can be important in this context, even in an underdeveloped country setting. It is this facet that forms the focus of the next and last chapter -*The Hospice as an Agency for Elderly Care: Field Perspectives from the Indian State of Kerala*—by P. Thulasibai, a medical doctor providing professional care for the elderly through *Santhiheeram*, a hospice she established on the rural fringe of Thrissur city, Kerala. *Santhiheeram* is geared to cater to the ailing elderly in their homes through medical and nursing interventions, as well as emotional and psychological inputs. *Santhiheeram* seeks to tend to its charges '... with affection and love, so that their twilight days may by painless and peaceful'.

The hospice concept of home care, which is the inspiration of Santhiheeram, is, the author tells us, rooted in medieval times, 'symbolising a place where travellers, the sick, the wounded, or the dying can find rest and comfort'. In contemporary settings, the hospice provides comprehensive care for patients facing a life-threatening or terminal illness. Santhiheeram sends care givers to the homes of patients, to give food and medicine on time, clean and bathe them, make them do exercises, and so on. Family members are also instructed on how to take care of bed-ridden patients. Day and night care is given as per the request of family members, and doctor visits to patients in their homes are arranged as and when needed. In a number of cases, the author found that a widower or widow was staying alone, and home care by itself was not adequate. Thus, hospice care as a way of dealing with elderly care needs to be supplemented with institutionalisation, particularly in Kerala, where the absence of the younger generation in the household is a recurrent theme.

After elucidating these themes in hospice care, Dr. Thulasibai provides case study material of how things have worked on the ground. In one case, John, a 70-year-old man, came to her clinic with a bleeding maggot-infested ulcer under his toes. A part of his middle toe was gangrenous, and one of his toes was almost detached from his foot. The doctor went to his house, dressed the wound and gave medication. The floor of John's house was covered with cow-dung, which bred flies that infested the wound and produced the maggots. So, the household was advised not to use cow-dung any more. In one month, the wound healed completely, and John resumed his farm work, growing vegetables and selling areca nuts and coconuts in the market. Another case is that of Parvathy Amma, who was totally bedridden and whose son and daughter in law had taken leave from their jobs on loss of pay for six months to look after her. Santhiheeram volunteer Sathy was assigned the task of caring for the mother in the daytime, from morning to evening, till the son and daughter in law were back home. Through physiotherapy and regular exercises, the patient was able to walk about and attend to her personal tasks independently. Other case studies include that of 83-year-old Santhamma, and 84-year-old Janaki Amma, who were helped to recuperate from debilitating illness and to die in dignity.

We have now come to the end of our review of some of the contours, contexts, constraints and consequences of the demographic transition now occurring across Asia. It is a tale of great achievements in the fight against mortality and disease, and of sharp falls in fertility. We have seen also that vast regional variations in demographic indicators persist, and challenges in reducing fertility, mortality and infant mortality continue to be high in parts of India. In this context, there is a need to reform the health and family planning apparatus, so that it caters more and more to reproductive health and felt needs. At the same time, the demographic transition has thrown up new sorts of problems that demand to be tackled—the growing masculinity of the FMR as couples strive to have fewer children in a context of persisting son preference, and a burgeoning of problems associated with population ageing at a low level of resources. There is a need for a highlighting of these emerging concerns, and a will to surmount the obstacles in the way.

While underscoring the severity and grimness of the problems, however, this volume also holds out hope, for instance, the hope offered by the concept of the hospice, which, in a less developed country setting, where labour costs are low, can emerge as a viable low-cost approach to assist families in elderly care. It is important to work towards such solutions on a bigger scale.

At the same time, our mind-sets should be flexible enough to come to terms with the intricacies of the problems we face, rather than adopting a doctrinaire approach. Thus, there is a need for a constellation of counseling services to facilitate harmonious relationships between caregivers and elderly. With respect to health care, the challenge is not only to improve the levels of care, but to also ensure a thrust on women's health and welfare to counter factors militating against it, as well as to work towards a society where daughter discrimination has faded away. Efforts in that direction need to be tempered with wisdom, however, lest we fall into the trap of creating new apartheids in which the 'weaker sex' is favoured. That would go against the principle of a just society and non-discrimination on the grounds of gender. After all, shouldn't the goal be to move towards a better society, to create a superior socialisation pattern, to work for a future that is better than the past?

REFERENCES

Mary Arends-Kuenning. 2002. 'Reconsidering the Doorstep-Delivery System in the Bangladesh Family Planning Programme'. *Studies in Family Planning*. 33(1): 87-102.

Sajeda Amin and Alaka M. Basu. 2004. 'Popular Perceptions of Emerging Influences on Mortality and Longevity in Bangladesh and West Bengal'. Working paper 186. New York: Population Council.

Prabir C. Bhattacharya. 2006.'Economic development, gender inequality, and demographic outcomes: Evidence from India'. *Population and Development Review*. 32 (2): 263-291.

Commander, Simon. 1989. 'The mechanics of demographic and economic growth in Uttar Pradesh, 1800-1900', in Tim Dyson, ed. *India's Historical Demography: Studies in Famine, Disease, and Society*. London: Curzon Press.

David Arnold. 1989. 'Cholera mortality in British India, 1817-1947', in Tim Dyson, ed. *India's Historical Demography: Studies in Famine, Disease, and Society*. London: Curzon Press, pp. 261-284

Isabelle Attane. 2002. 'China's Family Planning Policy: An Overview of its Past and Future'. *Studies in Family Planning*. 33 (1): 103-113.

Mead Cain. 1978. 'The household life cycle and economic mobility in rural Bangladesh'. *Population and Development Review*. 4 (3): 421-438.

Mead Cain. 1981. 'Risk and insurance: Perspectives on fertility and agrarian change in India and Bangladesh'. *Population and Development Review.*

John C. Caldwell, P.H. Reddy and Pat Caldwell. 1982. 'The causes of demographic change in rural South India: A micro approach'. *Population and Development Review*. 8 (4): 689-727.

John C. Caldwell. 1986. 'Routes to Low Mortality in Poor Countries'. *Population & Development Review*. 12 (2): 171-220.

M. Das Gupta. 1995. 'Fertility decline in Punjab, India: Parallels with historical Europe'. *Population Studies*. 49 (3): 481-500.

Deborah Davis-Friedman. 1983. *Long lives: Chinese elderly and the communist revolution*. Cambridge. Mass: Harvard University Press.

Tim Dyson. 1987. 'Excess female mortality in India: Uncertain evidence on a narrowing differential', in K. Srinivasan and S. Mukherji Eds. *Dynamics of Population and Family Welfare*. Bombay: Himalaya.

Tim Dyson. 1989. 'The Historical Demography of Berar, 1881-1980', in Tim Dyson, ed. *India's Historical Demography: Studies in Famine, Disease and Society*. London: Curzon Press. pp. 150-196

Tim Dyson. 1991a. 'On the Demography of South Asian Famines—Part I'. *Population Studies*. 45:5-25.

Tim Dyson. 1991b. 'On the Demography of South Asian Famines—Part II'. *Population Studies*. 45:279-297.

Sumit Guha. 2001. *Health and Population in South Asia—From Earliest Times to the Present*. New Delhi: Permanent Black.

Tim Dyson and Monica Das Gupta. 2001 'Demographic Trends in Ludhiana District, Punjab, 1881-1981: An exploration of vital registration data in colonial India', in Ts'ui-jung Liu, James Lee, David Sven Reher, Osamu Saito and Weng Feng, eds. *Asian Population History.* New York: Oxford University Press, pp. in Tim Dyson, ed. *India's Historical Demography: Studies in Famine, Disease and Society.* London: Curzon Press. pp. 63-104

Christophe Z. Guilmoto. 2005. 'Fertility decline in India: Maps, Models and Hypotheses', in Christophe Z. Guilmoto and S. Irudaya Rajan eds. *Fertility Transition in South India*. New Delhi: Sage. pp. 385-435.

Christophe Z. Guilmoto and S. Irudaya Rajan. 2001. 'Spatial patterns of fertility transition in Indian districts'. *Population & Development Review*. 27 (2): 713-738.

Habib, Jack. 1988. Aging population structure and support for the elderly'. United Nations. Economic and Social Implications of Population Aging. New York: United Nations.

Anrudh K. Jain. 1982. 'The Impact of Development and Population Policies on Fertility in India'. *Population Studies.* 16 (4): 181-198.

R. Jeffery and P. Jeffery. 1983. 'Female Infanticide and Amniocentesis'. *Economic & Political Weekly*. April 16 issue.

M.E. Khan and John W. Townsend. 1999. 'Target Free Approach: Emerging Evidence', in Saroj Pachauri, ed. *Implementing a Reproductive Health Agenda in India: the Beginning.* New Delhi: Population Council, pp. 43-74.

Ira Klein. 1989. 'Population Growth and Mortality—Part I: The Climacteric of Death'. *Indian Economic and Social History Review*. 26(4): 87-403

Ira Klein. 1990. 'Population Growth and Mortality in British India, Part II: The Demographic Revolution'. *Indian Economic & Social History Review*. 27(1): 33-63.

Ira Klein. 1994. 'Imperialism, ecology and disease: Cholera in India, 1850-1950'. *Indian Economic & Social History Review*. 31(4): 491-517.

John Knodel, Napaporn Havavon and Siriwan Siriboon. 1992. 'The impact of fertility decline on familial support of the elderly: An illustration from Thailand'. *Population and Development Review*. 18 (1): 79-104.

John Knodel, Chanpen Saengtienchai and Werasit Sittitrai. 1992. 'The living arrangements of the elderly in Thailand: Views of the populace'. Comparative study of the Elderly in Asia, Research Report No. 92-20, Population Studies Centre, University of Michigan.

Michael A., Koenig, Mian Bazle Hossain and Maxine Whittaker. 1997. 'The Influence of Quality of Care upon Contraceptive Use in Rural Bangladesh'. *Studies in Family Planning*. 28 (4): 278-289.

Nancy E. Levine. 1987. 'Differential child care in three Tibetan communities'. *Population and Development Review*. 13 (2): 281-304.

Pradip K. Mahuri. 1995. 'Health Programs, Maternal Education and Differential Child Mortality in Matlab, Bangladesh'. *Population and Development Review*. 21 (4): 813-834.

Mahmood Mamdani. 1973. *The Myth of Population Control: Family, Caste and Class in and Indian Village*. New York: Monthly Review Press.

P.N. Mari Bhat. P.N. 2002. 'Returning a favour: Reciprocity between female education and fertility in India'. *World Development*. 30 (10): 1791-1803.

Kristy Mc. Nay. 1995. 'Fertility and Frailty: Demographic Change and Health Status of Indian Women'. *Economic and Political Weekly.* October 28, pp WS-81-WS86.

K. Mc. Nay, P. Arokiasamy, and R.H. Cassen. 2003. 'Why are educated women in India using contraception? A Multilevel Analysis'. Population Studies. 57 (1): 21-40.

Eva Mueller. 1972. 'Economic Motives for Family Limitation: a Study Conducted in Taiwan'. *Population Studies*. 26 (3): 383-417.

Nirmala Murthy. 1999. 'Decentralised Participative Planning and Monitoring', in Saroj Pachauri, ed. *Implementing a Reproductive Health Agenda in India: the Beginning.* New Delhi: Population Council, pp. 121-141

Mamta Murthi, Anne-Catherine Guio and Jean Dreze. 1995. 'Mortality, Fertility and Gender Bias in India: A District Level Analysis'. *Population & Development Review*. 21 (4): 745-782.

Nirmala Murthy, Lakshmi Ramachandar, Pertti Pelto and Akhila Vasan. 2002. 'Dismantling India's Contraceptive Target System: An Overview and Three Case Studies', in Nicole Haberland and Diana Measham eds. *Responding to Cairo: Case Studies of Changing*

Practice in Reproductive Health and Family Planning. New York: Population Council

Moni Nag and Neeraj Kak. 1984. 'Demographic Transition in a Punjab Village'. *Population and Development Review*. 10 (4): 61-78

NCAER. 1984. 'Demographic report, Rural Economic and Demographic Survey, 1981-82'.

Tulsi Patel. 1994. *Fertility Behaviour: Population and Society in a Rajasthan Village*. Delhi: Oxford University Press.

Tulsi Patel. 2007. 'The mindset behind eliminating the female foetus', in Tulsi Patel, Ed. *The Missing Girl Child*. New Delhi: Sage Publications, pp. 135-174

James F. Phillips; Akbar, Jalaluddin; Rob, Ubaidur; and Mozumder, Khorshed Alam. 1984. *Final Report on a Baseline Sociodemographic Survey in Munshigonj Subdivision*. Dhaka: ICDDR,B.

James F Phillips; Simmons, Ruth; Koenig, Michael A., and Hossain, M.B. 1986. 'Worker-Client Exchanges and the Dynamics of Contraceptive Use in Rural Bangladesh'. Paper presented at the annual meeting of the Population Association of America, San Francisco.

James F. Phillips; Simmons, Ruth; Koenig, Michael A., and Chakraborty, J. 1988. 'Determinants of Reproductive Change in a Traditional Society: Evidence from Matlab, Bangladesh'. *Studies in Family Planning*. 19 (6): 313-334.

K. Prabhavati and A. Sheshadri. 1988. 'Pattern of IUD Use: A Follow Up of Acceptors in Mysore'. *The Journal of Family Welfare*. 35 (1): 3-16.

Mark Rosenzweig 1988. 'Risk, implicit contracts and the family in rural areas of low income countries'. *The Economic Journal*. 98: 1148-1170.

Mark Rosenzweig and Oded Stark. 1989. 'Consumption smoothing, migration and marriage: Evidence from rural India'. *Journal of Political Economy*. 97 (4): 905-926.

Ruth Simmons; Majorie A. Koblinksy and James E. Phillips. 1986. 'Client Relations in South Asia: Programmatic and Societal Determinants'. *Studies in Family Planning*. 17 (6): 257-268.

Ruth Simmons; Baqee, Laila; Koenig, Michael A. and Phillips, James F. 1988. 'Beyond Supply: the Importance of the Female Family Planning Workers in Rural Bangladesh'. *Studies in Family Planning*. 19 (1): 29-38.

John W. Townsend; Khan, M.E.; and Gupta, R.B. 1999. 'The Quality of Care in the Sterilisation Camps of Uttar Pradesh', in Michael A. Koenig and M.E. Khan, Eds. *Improving Quality of Care in India's Family Welfare Programme—the Challenge Ahead*. New York: Population Council.

Judith Treas. 1979. 'Social organization and economic development in China: Latent consequences for the aged'. *The Gerontologist*. 19: 34-43.

Judith Treas and Barbara Logue. 1986. 'Economic development and the older population'. Population and Development Review. 12 (4): 645-674

David Quitugua. 1982. 'Care and support for the aging in Australasia'. *Unitas*. 55: 317-328.

Alpana D. Sagar. 2007. 'Between a Rock and a Hard Place', in Tulsi Patel, ed. *The Missing Girl Child*. New Delhi: Sage Publications, pp. 175-202

United Nations. 1988. *Economic and Social Implications of Population Aging*. New York: United Nations.

United Nations Secretariat, Population Division, Department of Economic and Social Affairs. 1988. 'Global trends and prospects of aging population structures', in United Nations. *Economic and Social Implications of Population Aging*. New York: United Nations.

Leela Visaria, Pravin Visaria and Anrudh Jain. 1994. 'Estimates of Contraceptive Prevalence based on Service Statistics and Surveys in Gujarat State, India', *Studies in Family Planning*. 25 (5): 293-303.

Leela Visaria and Pravin Visaria. 1999. 'Field-Level Reflections of Policy Change', in Saroj Pachauri, ed. *Implementing a Reproductive Health Agenda in India: the Beginning.* New Delhi: Population Council, pp. 75-118.

Leela Visaria. 2004. 'The continuing fertility transition', in Tim Dyson, Robert Cassen and Leela Visaria eds. *Twenty-first Century India: Population, Economy, Human Development and the Environment*. New Delhi: Oxford University Press.

Part II

THE HISTORICAL CANVAS

Chapter 2

Aspects of the Population History of South Asia in Southeast Asian Perspective

Tim Dyson

There are several reasons why the emerging field of Southeast Asian historical demography may be of interest to scholars concerned with the population history of South Asia. To begin with there are the profound and longstanding interconnections between the peoples of these two regions. These links almost certainly date back far into pre-history. The early historical influence of Indian civilisations in Southeast Asia is implicit in terms such as 'Greater India', 'Father India' and 'Indochina'—all of which have been used to refer to Southeast Asia in the past. Indeed, the title of the classic book by George Coedès on the history of Southeast Asia prior to the mid-fourteenth century—*The Indianized States of Southeast Asia*—reflects this ancient influence (Coedès 1968).

Furthermore, in more recent times, the forces of European colonialism and capitalism set up new economic and demographic interactions extending to such important subjects for population history as labour migrations and the spread of diseases. And, in still broader perspective, significant issues arise concerning the demographic consequences of the colonial era for populations in both regions.

The materials at hand to study South Asia's population history since about 1800 are probably better than those generally available for Southeast Asia. Indeed, the population history of the latter region appears to be relatively neglected by contemporary historical demographic research.[1] Therefore, as our understanding of South Asia's population history grows, so it may afford valuable lessons and perspective apropos the demographic evolution of Southeast Asia.

Touching on a variety of subjects, this paper roams over some of the above-mentioned concerns. Necessarily, it is selective. Those in search of overviews of the population history of these two regions must go elsewhere.[2] Instead, in somewhat free vein, a series of topics are discussed here which either involve some form of interaction between the populations of South and Southeast Asia, or which illustrate how some of the lessons emerging from study of the former region may help in interpreting the experience of the latter. Although the main focus will be on the populations of South and Southeast Asia, inevitably other parts of the continent are drawn in too. Moreover, at different points, the relevance of historical research for an understanding of recent experience merits some emphasis.

Early Links

It is appropriate to start by briefly outlining what is known about early Indian influences in Southeast Asia (excluding, here, most of Vietnam and the Philippines). The process of *Indianisation*, which Coedès described, occurred between the second and fourteenth centuries before the present (i.e. BP). It was largely a peaceful cultural transference, following trade, and few if any large-scale migrations were involved. Instead, comparatively small numbers of people—such as merchants, scholars and priests—gradually infused Indian systems of language, religion, art and administration throughout Southeast Asia. In its early stages, Indianisation involved *Hinduisation* and the establishment of 'court cultures' in the first 'Indian kingdoms' of the region. Later, the export of Buddhism saw cultural transfers at a more popular level, and pilgrimages between Southeast Asia and both India and Sri Lanka became quite common.

Two additional points should be made. First, there perhaps *already* existed basic socio-cultural similarities between the peoples of South and Southeast Asia, i.e., before the second century BP. In particular, the original 'Dravidian' inhabitants of South Asia may have shared important affinities with the peoples of Southeast Asia. The invasion of the so-called 'Aryan' tribes into South Asia—which is often thought to have occurred by way of Afghanistan around 3500 BP—eventually led to the predominance of Indo-European culture and languages throughout the northern two-thirds of the Indian subcontinent. But Dravidian culture and languages continued to prevail throughout most of southern and eastern India – as, indeed, is still generally the case today. Whatever their precise origins, any such initial socio-cultural similarities probably helped to facilitate the subsequent transfers of Indianisation.

Second, when Indianisation proper began, it mainly involved contact between the peoples of Southeast Asia and those living in southern and eastern (i.e. predominantly Dravidian) areas of South Asia. It is true that elements of northern Aryan Indian culture (e.g. Sanskrit) were central components of Indianisation. But it is important to appreciate that they affected Southeast Asia largely through the 'stepping stones' of the Dravidian civilisations of the Indian subcontinent's south and east.[3]

These fundamental socio-cultural commonalities between the peoples of southern and eastern India on the one hand, and those of Southeast Asia, on the other, may well have important demographic correspondences. In brief, the Indian peninsula is located where two of the world's major socio-cultural areas—namely those of West Asia and Southeast Asia—meet. The geographical line of divide between these areas roughly corresponds to the belt of the Vindhya and Satpura hill ranges in central India. Research suggests that in India there is a fairly sharp demographic line of divide corresponding to this basic socio-cultural division (Dyson and Moore 1983). Thus to the north and west of the line populations tend to experience relatively high rates of fertility and mortality, considerable excess female mortality, and exceptionally low female status. In contrast, populations in southern and eastern areas of the Indian subcontinent tend to have comparatively low levels of fertility and mortality, comparatively high levels of female autonomy, and there is relatively little excess female mortality. Despite considerable recent demographic change, this line of divide is still reasonably easy to detect—for example, in data from the 2001 Indian census (Dyson 2004). And there are reasons to believe that this fundamental socio-demographic contrast has existed for at least two thousand years (e.g. see Sopher 1980a, 1980b).

Two ways in which this north/south demographic division within India may shed light on the population history of Southeast Asia merit comment here. First, Southeast Asia's population history seems to have been characterised by comparatively low population densities. Several writers have speculated that part of the explanation for these low densities may have lain in relatively moderate levels of fertility (e.g. see Zelinsky 1950; Reid 1988: 160-62). In this context, it seems likely that populations in southern and eastern India also experienced comparatively modest levels of fertility—say not much above five live births per woman—prior to entering the fertility transition soon after the middle of the twentieth century.

Second, more recently, Southeast Asian countries have acquired a reputation for entering the demographic transition relatively early and/or traversing it relatively swiftly—and so too have Sri Lanka, and the States of southern and eastern India. In general, Southeast Asian countries have been comparatively successful in improving their levels of mortality—as have the states of southern and eastern India and Sri Lanka. Apropos fertility, Indonesia and Thailand are probably the best examples of early and fairly fast declines. Malaysia and Philippines entered the fertility transition in the 1960s (although their subsequent progress has admittedly been slowed *inter alia* by religious influences). More recently, countries like Myanmar (Burma) and Vietnam have experienced unexpectedly rapid fertility falls, albeit from later starting dates (United Nations 2001).

In this context, it is worth noting that the populations of southern and eastern India—and Sri Lanka—have also experienced relatively early and fast fertility falls. This relative homogeneity of experience has probably been heightened by the sharing of a comparatively similar socio-economic and political history—something which cannot be said of the countries of Southeast Asia (which also tend to be more socio-culturally diverse). Nevertheless, in accounting for an element of 'high level' correspondence between the relatively successful demographic experiences of Southeast Asian countries and populations living in the south and east of the India subcontinent, it might be wrong to entirely discount the ancient cultural interrelations preceding and during the period of 'Indianisation'. And it would probably be wrong too to dismiss other similarities—e.g. relating to the nature of kinship systems, the sharing of rice-based agriculture, and the relatively favourable position accorded to women in society (e.g. see Moore 1973; Whyte and Whyte 1978).

The Colonial Era

I now consider some of the main population interactions of colonial times. While several European countries (e.g. France, Holland, Spain) were involved in determining the development of nineteenth century Southeast Asia, I focus chiefly on the role of Britain—because it was the only country to have considerable influence upon populations in both South and Southeast Asia.

When the East India Company completed its domination of India up to the Sutlej river in 1818, it was soon followed by an eastern projection of the trade of India, based upon cotton, cotton cloth, and opium. As Cady (1964: 304) has written 'British hegemony in Southeast Asia was related ... to the larger geographical context extending from India to China. [The British Empire in Southeast Asia] was based on the enormous resources of the Indian subcontinent and finally functioned virtually on a free-trade basis'. In this context historical demographers have an obvious interest in the ensuing transfers of labour and disease.

Transfers of Labour from India

The main destinations for Indian labour within the two regions being considered were Burma, Peninsular Malaysia, Singapore and—within South Asia—Sri Lanka. Indeed, during most of the colonial era overseas labour migration out of India was chiefly to Burma, Malaysia and Sri Lanka. It is worth noting that Tamils (i.e. people from India's south-east) formed at least half of all migrants in these flows. Thus the 1931 census found that 48 per cent of Indian residents in Burma had been born in the Tamil Presidency of Madras (Visaria and Visaria 1982: 516). In 1970, of persons classed as 'Indians' in Peninsular Malaysia, 85 per cent were Tamil. In Singapore, in 1957, over sixty per cent of Indians were stated to be Tamil. And Tamils constituted virtually all of the Indian migrants who went to Sri Lanka (see Muthiah and Jones 1983). To the extent that non-Tamils were represented in these colonial labour migration flows from India, other southern cultural groups—predominantly Telegu and Malayee speakers—usually constituted most of the remainder.

Statistics on labour migration from India are available from the start of the indentured labour schemes in the early 1830s. Using this material, and addressing all destinations worldwide, Kingsley Davis estimated that between 1834 and 1870 about 9.8 million people left India and 7.8 million returned, giving a total net loss of about 2 million. Between 1870 and 1937 the corresponding figures were 20.4 and 16.1 million, giving a probable maximum net loss of 4.3 million over 67 years (see Davis 1951: 99).[4] The economic history of these migration flows—which mainly served to provide labour for agricultural plantation estates where 'locals' were often difficult to recruit—has been studied extensively (e.g. see Tinker 1974). Of course, in some of the destinations like Singapore and Malaysia (and Fiji) 'Indians' eventually became a significant fraction of the total population. But in the context of the aggregate demography of the Indian subcontinent—which probably had a population of between 236 and 255 million in 1871 (Dyson 2004)—the net losses were very small.

In this context, an area of interest concerns the comparative demographic experiences of different overseas Indian populations. Table 1 gives ethnic-specific death rates for Peninsular Malaysia since 1921. Most 'Indians' in Malaysia are of Tamil origin, and for the period in question a sizeable fraction were employed on agricultural estates. Addressing these Malaysian statistics Tan Poo Chang *et al.* (1987) note the comparatively high Indian death rate in 1921—which undoubtedly partly reflected very heavy mortality on the estates. But remedial health measures undertaken in the estates helped to reverse this position by 1940, although the mortality level of the Malay population remained largely unchanged. Following Independence in 1957 the health conditions prevailing in some estates actually deteriorated at times. And in the period between 1957 and the early 1980s the greatest fall in death rates was experienced by the Malays; 'the least decline, among the Indians, who generally remained in the estates' (Tan Poo Chang *et al.* 1987).

In this context the statistics for Indian Tamils in Sri Lanka—another predominantly agricultural estate population—suggest a striking similarity of experience to that in Malaysia. The statistics for 'Indian Tamils' in Table 1 should be interpreted with care—thus the 1921 death rate shown for this group is actually inclusive of Sri Lankan Tamils who constituted roughly half of the total 'Tamil' population of the island. Fortunately, however, Langford (1982) has shown that the death rates for both Tamil groups at that time were broadly comparable, and significantly higher than those of the dominant Sinhalese population. Consequently one can conclude from Table 1 that in *both* Sri Lanka and Malaysia estate death rates were initially comparatively high—presumably reflecting the appalling health conditions found on the estates. Then, during the 1920s and 1930s, this situation was reversed—as specific efforts to improve the health of estate workers led to relatively favourable death rates. Finally, in more recent times, after Independence, it is the majority ethnic populations whose death rates have declined the most (see Table 1).[5]

TABLE 1. Crude Death Rates for Peninsular Malaysia and Sri Lanka, by Ethnic Group, 1921-84

Year / Period	Peninsular Malaysia		Sri Lanka	
	Malays	Indians	Sri Lanka	Tamils
1921	25.4	37.2	31.2	35.4
1946-47	24.3	15.8	20.4	18.2
1950-53	18.7	13.6	11.0	12.1
1960-63	11.2	9.0	8.7	11.1
1970-71	7.6	8.5	7.7	13.3
1976-84	5.3	7.3	7.8	14.8

Notes: Malaysia gained independence in 1957, and Sri Lanka in 1948. For the periods shown the crude death rates for Malaysia relate to the specific years 1947, 1950, 1960, 1970 and 1984; and for Sri Lanka they relate to 1946, 1953, 1963, 1971 and 1976. The 1921 rate for Indian Tamils actually relates to the total Tamil population of Sri Lanka—and thus reflects Sri Lankan Tamils too. However, Langford (1984) has shown that death rates for both Tamil groups at that time were broadly comparable and significantly higher than those of the dominant Sinhalese population.

Sources: The rates for Peninsular Malaysia are taken from Tan Poo Chang *et al* (1987). For Sri Lanka the rates for 1946-71 have been taken from C.M. Langford (1982:13). For Sri Lanka the rates for 1921 come from the *Ceylon Administrative Report 1922*, Colombo, 1924, p. L25; those for 1976 are from the *Bulletin on Vital Statistics, 1977*, Department of Census and Statistics, Colombo, 1979.

Transfers of Labour into India

Another demographic consequence of nineteenth century colonialism and 'free-trade' was the increase in the size and diversity of the foreign community living *within* India. For selected language groups Table 2 gives the number of people reporting their 'mother tongue' according to the Indian censuses from

1881 to 1931. Again, care must be taken when interpreting these figures. In addition to migration, changes in the number of speakers of a particular language reflected factors such as natural increase, changes in the language classification system employed by the census (which rapidly became both more detailed and more complex) and changes in census coverage (relating especially to territorial jurisdiction, but also perhaps to enumeration level). It should also be borne in mind that these Indian censuses included much of Burma.

That said, the broad trends shown in Table 2 are fairly clear. For example, the 1881 census—which distinguished 162 different languages—commented that '[w]ith the exception of the few Chinamen employed in the tea gardens of Bengal and Punjab, the Chinese-speaking section of the population is confined to Burma, where there are 12,962 out of 14,466' (Registrar General, India 1883: 199). However, just ten years later the 1891 census showed that the number of speakers of Chinese had almost tripled. And the census report stated that the population of Chinese language speakers 'is scattered nearly all over India, since merchants, carpenters and caneworkers of this race are to be found in most large towns and cantonments' (Registrar General, India 1893:152). So employment-related migration—although often different in nature—was by no means all one-way.[6] There was migration into South Asia from elsewhere in Asia, both from the east and from the west.

Table 2 shows that there are fairly strong indications that the number of people reporting major Southeast Asian languages—such as Burmese or Shan—as their mother tongue increased markedly during the period 1881-1931, especially in Burma. In fact, in addition to 'Siamese' and 'Malay' the early Indian census volumes provide much detailed information regarding other East and Southeast Asian language groups (e.g. Indonesian, Mon-Khmer, Munda, Tibeto-Burman, Tai-Chinese and Man/Karen), the speakers of which were also primarily resident in Burma. In general these data suggest a considerable increase in the heterogeneity and size of these language groups, some of which at least was due to migration. Whatever the problems of interpretation, there can be little doubt that the size and diversity of both East and Southeast Asian populations resident in India (including Burma) increased significantly during colonial rule.

Transfers of Disease

It is clear from the preceding discussion that the possibility of disease transferences between the populations of South and Southeast Asia has existed for centuries. The point can be illustrated by the following statement, made around 860-873 AD by travellers visiting the Javanese kingdom of Mataram:

'In this country there are poisonous girls; when one has intercourse with them, he gets painful ulcers and dies ...' (quoted in Coedès 1968: 126).

TABLE 2. Number of Persons Reported in Selected Language Groups, India (and Burma), Censuses of 1881-1931

Language	Census Year					
	1881	**1891**	**1901**	**1911**	**1921**	**1931**
Arabic	21,188	53,351	42,881	42,102	42,729	54,788
Chinese	14,466	38,504	50,513	113,450	127,527	185,815
English	202,920	238,499	252,388	303,515	308,071	319,349
Italian	804	690	993	1,102	235	1,239
Japanese	2	93	363	1,130	977	4,304
Shan	59,723	174,871	753,262	898,832	843,810	944,887
Siamese	3	4	19,356	8,908	8,744	8,648
Malay	1,741	2,437	2,460	4,308	3,610	4,634
Burmese	2,248,479	5,560,481	7,474,896	7,893,504	8,423,256	8,853,538

Notes: As noted in the text, considerable caution is required when interpreting such figures. Changes in the number of speakers of a given language might reflect a host of factors as they differentially affected language groups. Of course, most Burmese and Shan speakers were resident in Burma. The Indian census volumes give much detailed data regarding other East and Southeast Asian language groups that were also primarily resident in Burma (e.g. Indonesian, Mon-Khmer, Munda, Tibeto-Burman, Tai-Chinese, and Man/Karen). In general such data suggest a very considerable increase in the heterogeneity and size of these language groups living in Burma during 1881-1931. Most of those who gave Siamese' or 'Malay' as their mother tongue also resided in Burma. The number of Siamese speakers given for the period 1881-1901 seems especially suspect. The statistics on speakers of English evince similar difficulties of interpretation, since much of the growth of this group over time reflects the increase of the 'Eurasian' population. However, the growth in the number of Japanese speakers is probably real, and certainly interesting.

Sources: Census of India, 1881, *Report on the Census of British India Taken on the 17th February, 1881*, Volume 1, HMSO, London, 1883; Census of India, 1891, *General Tables for British Provinces and Feudatory States*, Volume 1, Statistics, Eyre and Spottiswoode, London, 1892; Census of India, 1901, Volume 1-A, *India, Part II – Tables*, Office of the Superintendent of Government Printing, India, Calcutta, 1903; Census of India, 1911, Volume 1, *India, Part II – Tables*, Calcutta, 1913;Census of India, 1921, Volume 1, *India Part II – Tables*, Calcutta, 1923; Census of India, 1931, Volume 1, *India, Part II – Imperial Tables*, Manager of Publications, Delhi, 1933.

This explicit reference to some kind of venereal disease underscores the likelihood of early disease transfers. William H. McNeil implies that Indianisation probably involved the spread of new diseases into Southeast Asia. He speculates that the generally warmer and wetter climates of the region may—through enhanced levels of prevalence of micro-parasites—have restricted past rates of population growth, and thus contributed to the region's low historical population densities (see McNeil 1979: 109-11).[7] Disease transfers probably became more frequent during the colonial era because of the general increase in human mobility. Cholera, plague and influenza—each of which can be studied in some detail using historical data for India—merit particular mention, since they all featured prominently in the interactions between South and Southeast Asian populations.

(i) Cholera

The original 'home' of cholera is thought to lie in eastern India and Bangladesh. Prior to the nineteenth century, the disease sometimes spread to other parts of the Indian subcontinent, and perhaps Southeast Asia. But the first cholera *pandemic* began in 1817. And by 1822, the disease had spread to Southeast Asia, China and Japan. This pandemic may have been associated with a change in the cholera *vibrio*. However, in addition, it is almost certain that 'new, British-imposed patterns of trade and military movement ... (meant that) ... cholera overleaped its familiar bounds and burst into new and unfamiliar territories...' (McNeil 1979: 241). Transferences of cholera between these regions have continued into much more recent times. Thus the seventh cholera pandemic, starting in the early 1960s, involved a transference in precisely the opposite direction (i.e. from Southeast to South Asia). Possibly originating in the Celebes, the *el tor vibrio* spread rapidly through Indonesia and thence on to India (see Van Heyningen and Seal 1980: 29).

Cholera was a major concern of the British for virtually the whole of the colonial period in South Asia. Indeed, it can be argued that it received an inordinate amount of attention in official documents—partly because for the British it constituted a 'new' disease. Cholera was one of the main cause of death categories used by the vital registration system from the 1870s onwards (from the 1830s in the case of the major towns in India). Most of the annual Indian *Sanitary Reports* devote considerable space to the disease. There exists, then, a large body of data on cholera in India, much of which has not been analysed. However, it is apparent that cholera mortality fell considerably, and fairly steadily, during the twentieth century. A review by Arnold (1989) concludes that several factors were involved in the long-term decline of cholera in India. These included declines in the incidence of famine (especially after 1900), gradual improvements in water supplies and, perhaps, mass campaigns of inoculation. Arguably, however, the most important factor behind the decline in cholera was the establishment by the colonial authorities of a subcontinent-wide system of epidemiological surveillance which focussed on routes of transport, the situation in traditional areas of endemnicity, and the 'policing' of religious fairs. These developments need to be seen in the context of growing collaboration between the main European powers in the nineteenth century in order to restrict the spread of various diseases from Asia and Africa (McNeil 1979: 235-56).

(ii) Plague

The origins of the third plague pandemic are often located in China (around Pakhoi) in 1867. The pandemic eventually led to at least 13 million deaths worldwide. About 12.5 million of these were registered plague deaths in India. However this global figure of plague mortality is probably a severe understatement—since data for China are virtually non-existent. Bubonic plague reached the city of Bombay (now Mumbai) in 1896—probably by steamship from the then British controlled territory of Hong Kong. The disease became particularly entrenched in Bombay Presidency and rural Punjab. For some reason southern and eastern areas of South Asia were little affected—plague deaths in these regions being mostly restricted to the ports of Calcutta (Kolkata) and Madras (Chennai).

The socio-political dimensions of plague in India have received attention (e.g. see Catanach 1988), but scholars concerned with demographic and epidemiological issues have shown less interest in the subject. This is surprising because much of our modern understanding of the disease—such as the sometimes tight relationship between epidemics and epizootics—derives from work conducted in India between 1896 and 1920. And Waldemar Haffkine, a former associate of Louis Pasteur, first developed a successful anti-plague vaccine in Bombay. As Michelle McAlpin (1988) has rightly said 'India is a particularly fruitful area in which to understand some of the long unsolved problems of plague epidemics because the demographic data ... are quite good, because the research which led to understanding of the epidemiology of the disease was done in Bombay City and the Punjab, and because the British administration generated fairly full records of both the attempts to control the epidemic and ... (its) ... effects'. McAlpin's work examined the seasonality of the disease. A wider demographic treatment by Konings (1987) suggests that children and elderly people may have succumbed less than adults. Also, before 1912 slightly more men died of plague than women, whereas after that year the reverse applied. Konings suggests that in the pandemic's early stages men may have been more open to flea bites because their work patterns brought them into closer contact with rats, but by the pandemic's later stages men were more likely to be inoculated. Case mortality rates did not vary greatly by social class. But some groups—notably the Parsees—experienced lower death rates, perhaps because they were more likely to get inoculated. Addressing the issue of why plague was virtually eliminated by 1952, Konings concludes that many individual measures played a part.

Colonial Java was also particularly affected by this third plague pandemic—although to a lesser extent than was India. Terrence Hull (1987) has detailed how colonial competition between the British and Dutch administrations of these populations both hindered and helped efforts against the disease. For example, such rivalry delayed the acceptance among the Dutch in Java that the flea *X cheopis* was the main plague vector. Also in the context of Southeast Asia as a whole, which was not very badly affected, it may well be significant that southern and eastern areas of India largely escaped the ravages of this plague pandemic—perhaps reflecting the influence of similar environmental (e.g. climatic) considerations.

(iii) Influenza

The demography of the influenza pandemic of 1918-19 is another instance where analysis of events in South Asia can provide valuable indications for corresponding research in Southeast Asia. In only four months at the end of 1918 influenza caused more deaths in India than did plague during the entire period after 1896. The flu pandemic appeared in two main waves (a weaker third wave may have occurred in early 1919). The first main wave spread from Europe to Egypt—and then moved on sequentially to the seaports of Karachi, Bombay (Mumbai), Colombo, Rangoon, Singapore and Shanghai. In India the second wave—which was much more deadly—also began in Bombay Presidency, from where it spread rapidly inland in all directions. However, there are some signs that this second wave was also introduced independently to the eastern side of the Indian subcontinent by way of Rangoon— transport by sea thus moving faster than the overland route of transmission (Mills 1989).

The analysis of these events by Ian Mills (1989) is an outstanding study of this phenomenon for India. The study illustrates the wealth of material available for research in South Asian historical demography—in this case, both census and vital registration data, ecclesiastical returns, morbidity and mortality data relating to prison populations, plus information from various administrative reports. Here I mention some of the findings which may have special relevance for populations in Southeast Asia.

It appears from Mills' research that roughly half of the population of all regions of India suffered from influenza during the last months of 1918. However the case fatality rate (i.e. the chance of *dying* if one contracted the flu) showed a marked regional pattern. Case fatality—and therefore overall mortality—was relatively low in southern and eastern India, including Bengal, Assam, and both Upper and Lower Burma. Interestingly in this context, the influenza in Sri Lanka appears to have killed only about 1 per cent of the population—suggesting that the case fatality rate there was also comparatively low (see Langford and Storey 1992). In contrast, case fatality was extremely high in northern and western India (including much of contemporary Pakistan). Consequently these northern and western regions of South Asia experienced a truly tremendous quantum of death—indeed, it was not uncommon for more than one tenth of the entire population to die (e.g. see Dyson 1989b). In sum, influenza mortality was comparatively low in regions experiencing a narrow diurnal temperature range, while it was very high in areas where this range was high. A possible explanation is that it was pneumonic complications of the influenza which actually produced most deaths, and that such complications were more likely to occur where day and night-time temperatures differed a lot (Mills 1989).

If similar climatic considerations applied in Southeast Asia then we might speculate that influenza mortality may have been heaviest in part of northern Laos and Vietnam. However, as a whole Southeast Asia—being a predominantly tropical region which experiences comparatively limited diurnal temperature variation—should have escaped comparatively lightly—a conclusion for which the aforementioned data for Upper and Lower Burma analysed by Mills (1989: 227) and those for Sri Lanka analysed by Langford and Storey (1992) provide some support.

Vaccination and Smallpox

Having mentioned the exchange of certain diseases during the colonial era, it is perhaps appropriate to refer to one other development of the nineteenth century which eventually had more beneficial effects for the populations of the Indian subcontinent and Southeast Asia.

Edward Jenner discovered vaccination against smallpox in 1796, and he published his findings on the subject in 1798. It was appreciated rapidly that for really the first time in human history there existed a safe and effective measure against a common and extremely deadly disease.[8] Accordingly, in the last two years of the eighteenth century—and with active encouragement from Jenner himself—European ships began to try to transport cowpox lymph to various colonies, with what Ann Bowman Jannetta (2001: 293) has termed 'missionary zeal'. Involving huge distances, and long before any real refrigeration, this was an incredibly difficult task. But as pioneering research by Jayant Banthia on Indian data has shown, by February of 1802 a three-year old girl in Bombay City became the first person ever to be successfully vaccinated in South Asia. By the end of 1802 cowpox lymph had been successfully transported to Calcutta by way of the ports of Colombo and Madras (Banthia and Dyson 2000a). The Spanish were also particularly intent upon getting vaccination to their colonies in Latin America—and thence on to the Philippines. Knowledge of vaccination appears to have reached Canton in 1803 and viable lymph reached the city in 1805—from the west by way of the

British East India Company in Calcutta, and from the east via the Spanish Philippines (Shepherd 2001: 277; Jannetta 2001: 296). Dutch and French ships carried active lymph to their colonies in Southeast Asia from early in the nineteenth century. Thus the Dutch were vaccinating in Batavia (Jakarta) from 1804 and they also tried to get vaccination established in Japan from the 1820s—although with no success (Jannetta 2001: 297).

In this context research by Banthia on the various epidemiological, demographic and other rich data sets that are available for British India in the late eighteenth and nineteenth centuries conveys some idea of the massive devastation that smallpox wreaked. It is clear that at the start of the nineteenth century virtually everyone in India was afflicted by smallpox during childhood. And smallpox case fatality rates were extremely high—perhaps 25-30 per cent in unprotected populations—markedly above the rates which have been estimated for unprotected populations in eighteenth century Europe. Vaccination spread slowly in India during the first half of the nineteenth century, as generally seems to have been the case in Southeast Asia too. But from the 1870s onwards there were major gains in vaccination coverage, leading, in South Asia, to concurrent, major declines in the disease. Thus whereas at the beginning of the nineteenth century smallpox may well have accounted for more than 10 per cent of all deaths in India, by the end of the century, it had become a fairly minor cause of death (Banthia and Dyson 2000b).

Although during the last three decades of the nineteenth century India was struck by several massive famines—and there were other deleterious developments too, such as the spread of malaria following the construction of irrigation, road and rail works—it is important to bear in mind that the nineteenth century was probably a time of unprecedented population growth in South Asia. While it is hard to be precise, it is generally believed that the region's population grew comparatively fast during the seventeenth century—the age of the great Mughal rulers—perhaps at an average rate of between 0.2 and 0.3 per cent per year. In contrast, the region's average annual growth rate during the first seven decades of the nineteenth century was probably about 0.5 per cent, and perhaps even higher (Dyson 2004). And the average annual rate of population growth indicated for Madras Presidency by the census counts of 1822 and 1871 was 1.7 per cent (see Visaria and Visaria 1982: 467-69) although this may be something of an overestimate.

The most likely reason for this faster demographic growth in the nineteenth century was that the death rate in India declined slightly compared to previous periods. Smallpox being a prevalent and deadly disease, with probable significant secondary effects, it is likely that vaccination played a part in the decline in the death rate—although increased social stability (certainly compared to the volatile eighteenth century) probably played a role too.

Nevertheless, the conclusion from a comparatively rich data base that a modicum of mortality improvement accounts for South Asia's faster population growth during the nineteenth century may well have relevance for Southeast Asia—where some scholars are still inclined to maintain that fertility rise, rather than mortality fall, was the sole reason for that region's faster population growth during the nineteenth century (on this see Reid 2001: 45).

Malaria and Population Growth Trajectories

Malaria and its effects is another subject area where South Asian material—some of which embraced Burma—may serve as a useful reference standard for examining Southeast Asian experience.

Even today, much of the most valuable statistical data we have at the population level regarding, particularly, *epidemic* malaria, was collected by the colonial authorities in India. Special mention should be made of the work of Sir Rickard Christophers (1911). For example, with reference to the calamitous malaria epidemic in Punjab in northern India in 1908, Christophers showed that there was a fivefold increase in stillbirths in Amritsar, and he calculated that 30 per cent of all pregnancies were interrupted by the epidemic. These and other results are still cited in the epidemiological literature (e.g. see Bradley and Keymer 1984).

In Punjab malaria exhibited a highly seasonal pattern (a fact which facilitated its statistical identification). Sheila Zurbrigg (1994) has examined the period up to 1918, which contained several major epidemics, and the ensuing decades of malaria decline. Using annual time series of deaths from vital registration, and rainfall, price and other material, she reworked Christophers' original (1911) crude multivariate analysis to confirm that the incidence of food scarcity was probably an important determinant of epidemic severity. Christophers' findings in this regard have, she contends, effectively become 'sidelined' by modern researchers. Turning to the period of malaria decline after about 1918, it is important to appreciate that the reduction in malaria formed a significant component of total mortality decline, both in Punjab and indeed in South Asia as a whole. Zurbrigg argues that only a small fraction of the substantial gains made against epidemic malaria in Punjab before about 1940 can be attributed to remedial measures such as improved flood control and increased availability of medical services and quinine. Instead, much of the answer rests in reductions in hunger and improvements in nutrition.

Analysis of the demographic aspects of malaria—including its advance during the colonial era and its later decline—may prove a particularly strong common focal point for research into the historical demography of parts of South and Southeast Asia. In India the spread of malaria may have contributed to the very slow rates of population growth which occurred in some regions in the decades around 1900.

The census-based work of Arthur Geddes (1947/1970), which unfortunately is now almost forgotten, is especially important *vis a vis* the huge influence of malaria on South—and Southeast—Asia's past population growth. Using decennial census data for 600 administrative units for the period 1881-1931, Geddes analysed the indicated patterns of demographic growth, and he identified six main types of 'population change and variability'. Type 1, which he represented by Noakhali in present-day Bangladesh, he termed 'high natural increase'; in this type of trajectory the population grew fast and exponentially, and variation around the growth path was minimal. Type 2, illustrated by Jessore, which of course is close to contemporary West Bengal, was labelled 'stagnation'. In this type, population growth was minimal and its variability was slight; the main determinant of this pattern of population growth was the presence of *endemic* malaria. Two other of Geddes' six types of trajectory deserve special comment. Type 4, which he represented by Bhir, was termed 'recurrent crisis' by Geddes. In this, population growth over the long run was low or non-existent, but its *variability* was high. The experience represented by this type is one where comparatively fast short-run demographic growth is repeatedly interrupted—perhaps because of *epidemic* malaria, but famine and other diseases also played a major role in producing such 'recurrent crisis'. Type 6 Geddes named 'colonisation'; in this trajectory the population growth path was clearly heavily influenced by immigration. An example of 'colonization' was afforded by Montgomery, an area of Punjab, where major extensions of irrigation attracted many migrants. Lastly, it should be noted that Types 3 and 5 (represented by Geddes by the districts of Kadur and Bhir respectively) both involved a mixture of limited population increase and variability. The 'variable increase' regime (i.e. Type 5) represented the second fastest growth path (excluding the migration-influenced increase of 'colonisation').

The distribution of these six types of demographic growth in South Asia—and parts of Burma—was mapped by Geddes for 1881-1931. For this period, he showed that the very rapid growth trajectory of 'colonisation' characterised much of Punjab (reflecting the spread of irrigation). And with the establishment of tea estates it was also found in parts of Assam and central areas of Sri Lanka. 'Stagnation', reflecting a heavy load of endemic malaria, affected much of the northeastern Gangetic plain and West Bengal (although it was found too in other riverine and deltaic areas of the subcontinent). 'Recurrent crisis' prevailed throughout much of western and northwestern India—these were generally quite dry areas, with considerable potential for both famines and malaria epidemics.[9]

However, for present purposes, perhaps the most notable feature of the maps produced by Geddes was that the main areas of 'high natural increase' were located in what might be termed the 'littoral zone' surrounding the Bay of Bengal. By this, I mean much of Sri Lanka, large areas of southern and eastern India, most of what is now Bangladesh, and the majority of the coastal strip running down into Lower Burma. 'High natural increase' was the single most important population growth type throughout this entire region. It is significant that the next most frequent regime in this region was that of 'variable increase'—which also represented comparatively rapid demographic growth. And it is worth stressing that the available vital registration data suggest strongly that there was comparatively little annual variation in death rates for populations inhabiting this littoral zone. The results of the work of Geddes thus provides further support for an element of affinity between the demographic experiences of parts of the south and east of the Indian subcontinent on the one hand, and parts of Southeast Asia on the other. Conversely, the dominant impression of South Asia's population history as being one of 'recurrent crisis' has been coloured by events in northern and western areas of India. Almost certainly, however, such a characterisation was far less applicable to southern and eastern parts of India and South Asia.[10]

In summary, the nineteenth century saw fairly fast population growth in much of South Asia. In northern and western areas this growth was severely curtailed by famines (and later the 1918 influenza). But southern and eastern areas were comparatively unaffected. Indeed, their experience is broadly reminiscent of that of Java—where population growth rates appear to have been generally high from about 1815 onwards, being only *somewhat* reduced during 1891-1921 (see Carr-Saunders 1964: 282; Boomgaard 1989:1-2). Moreover, it seems likely that southern and eastern areas of South Asia experienced relatively modest levels of fertility in the nineteenth century—levels which, however, were quite sufficient to produce comparatively rapid population growth; this is another lesson which may have relevance for parts of Southeast Asia. The work of Geddes provides powerful evidence regarding the role of malaria, epidemic and endemic, as a key determinant of the demography of the Indian subcontinent in times past.

Administrative Interconnections

The administrative interconnections brought about by the colonial powers—especially during the nineteenth and early twentieth centuries—merit mention. In certain respects, I have already alluded to this (e.g. apropos British and Dutch competition over the aetiology and management of plague). However, colonial rivalry in matters pertaining to the health of 'subject' populations was considerable, and it affected all the major powers (e.g. see the contributions to Arnold 1988).

That said, a word is also in order concerning the establishment of systems of data collection—an important, but neglected field for research. In South Asia, the origins of both censuses and vital registration lie in the early nineteenth century. In Madras Presidency, for example, there were censuses in 1822, 1836-7, 1851-2, 1856-7, 1866-7 and 1871 (Visaria and Visaria 1982). Robert Keith Pringle—a former student of Thomas Robert Malthus at the East India Company's College at Haileybury near London—was a prime mover in this field. For example, he was involved in both the 1846 and 1851 enumerations of Bombay Presidency (notice the five year intercensal interval; a census planned for 1856 was cancelled due to administrative delays (N. den Tuinder, personal communication)). The first population totals pertaining to all areas under British rule were actually laid before Parliament in 1857 (Visaria and Visaria 1982). And there probably would have been a population count throughout British India around 1861 if it had not been for the so-called 'Mutiny' of 1857. In fact, most populations in South Asia were enumerated in various provincial censuses which took place during 1868-72. However, the first synchronous census of India occurred in 1881 and it marked the end of the provincial enumerations. By that time the establishment of civil registration for the general population (which dates from the 1860s) was also well underway.

Experience in India surely helped to condition the development of censuses, surveys and registration systems in other British colonies. Census years became synchronised (e.g. in India, Malaysia, Singapore and Hong Kong). Colonial administrators with Indian experience were moved on to work elsewhere. Burma, of course, was subject to the same basic census as was India itself. Evidence of the influence of the Census of India is easy to detect, however, in other early colonial enumerations such as the *Report on the Census of the Straits Settlements 1901* published in that year by the Government Printing Office in Singapore. Clearly, such influences would have worked strongest within a particular colonial regime (e.g. the British, French or Dutch). But the remarkably modern nature of the statistics produced for Thailand early in the twentieth century testifies to a much more pervasive western effect. A good example of this is afforded by the *Statistical Year Book of the Kingdom of Siam,* published, in English, in 1916.

The Rapid Mortality Gains of 1947-52

Coming lastly to more recent times, another feature of the demographic history of South Asia which probably has relevance for understanding of the population history of Southeast Asia concerns the very rapid mortality improvement which was experienced during 1947-52. Thus work by the present author (Dyson 1989b) on the good quality vital registration data available for the former central Indian province of Berar indicates that life expectation at birth rose from about 28 years in 1947 to around 37 years by 1952. This represents an annual gain in life expectation of about two years per year. And a very similar indication arises from the registration data for Sri Lanka (e.g. see Gray 1974; Langford 1996). Vital registration death rates for other locations in South Asia, although not generally of comparable quality, are also suggestive of an abrupt period of mortality improvement during 1947-52—although the falls in the death rate have sometimes been regarded as due to deterioration in the coverage of death registration (see Visaria and Visaria 1982).

In fact, however, there are good reasons to believe that such substantial and abrupt improvements in mortality in India and elsewhere in South Asia at around this time were largely real. Through its disruption of administration the Second World War not only contributed to calamitous events—such as the Bengal famine of 1943-44 which killed about 2.1 million people (see Dyson and Maharatna 1991)—but it also probably delayed some degree of mortality progress—already evident in much of the Indian subcontinent during the 1920s and 1930s—which would probably otherwise have occurred. With the end of the war, the rapid recovery of the global economy (which increased the demand for primary products like tea, coffee and timber) and the gaining of political independence, the countries of South Asia were able to make up for lost time.[11]

Almost certainly, these developments formed part of a much larger picture. And a broadly analogous analysis probably applies for much of Southeast (and East) Asia where, indeed, the effects of warfare were more direct. Certainly, death registration data for Malaysia, Philippines, Singapore and Taiwan strongly suggest that these locations too experienced major mortality gains at this short moment in time (see Dyson 1984: 62-63; Dyson and Murphy 1991).

Discussion and Conclusions

As was stated at the outset, this paper has had to be selective. There are other insights that the emerging field of South Asian—especially Indian—historical demography could well provide. For example, one example is that the age pattern of mortality has probably changed over time (see Bhat 1989, Dyson 1989c). Thus, whereas in recent decades, early-age (i.e. infant and child) mortality has been high relative to non-child (i.e. 'adult') mortality in India, this was probably not so much the case in the past. Consequently, demographic analyses which have assumed constant age patterns of mortality have tended to overestimate slightly past levels of mortality and fertility. Average levels of mortality in much of South Asia were probably not exceptionally high by historical standards. This point may apply for analyses for parts of Southeast Asia too. And, more generally, the conclusion that for various reasons (including the common practice of sexual abstinence and high levels of widowhood) pre-transitional fertility in South Asia was probably not very high finds clear resonance in research on Europe, China and Japan. The analysis of famines—and the reasons for their disappearance – may be another area where relevant lessons may apply. McAlpin (1983), for example, relates the major reduction in famine mortality in India after 1901 to the development of transport and the instigation of more effective systems of famine relief. Part of her argument is that the famines of the late nineteenth century reflected a period of increased vulnerability—when traditional ways of coping with food shortage had declined, but their modern counterparts were yet to be put in place. It is interesting to consider whether similar periods of increased vulnerability may have applied to other parts of Asia.

More directly, it is perhaps worth mentioning population data for 'hill tribe' peoples—often of Southeast Asian origin—who inhabit small states like Arunachal Pradesh, Meghalaya, Manipur and Nagaland adjoining Assam. Demographic analysis suggests strongly that such hill tribe populations generally experienced relatively modest levels of fertility and comparatively favourable levels of mortality in the past (Registrar General, India 1976). These are characteristics which Reid (1988:16), for example, has theorised may be relevant in connection with the past demography of upland peoples in much of Southeast Asia.

That said, the lessons will by no means be all one way. A promising avenue for research on early demographic dynamics in South Asia is afforded by the Christian parish records available for some coastal areas—perhaps especially those dating from the seventeenth century, set up by the Portuguese in Goa. So far, however, these have received little attention. There are few South Asian counterparts of the intense kind of study of parish records that has been undertaken in Philippines (e.g. see Smith and S-M Ng 1982). And, for still earlier periods, the chronicles of early European travellers to the Indian subcontinent may contain valuable qualitative insights relevant to population matters—much as Reid (1988) has shown can be derived for Southeast Asia.

A theme of this piece has been that, historically, there may well have been 'high level' correspondences between the demographies of Southeast Asia and those of southern and eastern parts of South Asia. And, within the time frame of demographically recorded history, there are clear signs of some commonality of demographic growth paths among populations inhabiting the coastal-zone around the Bay of Bengal. One can only hypothesise that this may have extended to much of littoral Southeast Asia.

Also, there little doubt that southern and eastern areas of South Asia and much of Southeast Asia experienced relatively fast population growth during the nineteenth century, compared to the century before. Perhaps this represents a comparable demographic response of different populations to the colonial era. The South Asian experience suggests that mortality decline was probably the main cause of this slightly faster population growth. Other possible parallels include the modest decline of malaria during the first part of the twentieth century, and the relatively rapid mortality improvement during 1947-52. It has also been argued that both southern and eastern South Asia and much of Southeast Asia may have shared social features that are conducive to comparatively fast demographic change.

The explanation for any such 'high level' correspondences lies beyond the scope of this paper. But possible prehistoric cultural circulations, the process of Indianisation and, later, the various socio-economic changes and interactions brought about by colonial rule, probably all played a part. The relatively mild climatic conditions shared by both southern and eastern areas of South Asia and much of Southeast Asia are probably also relevant. So too may be similarities relating to factors such as the distribution of wet-rice agriculture, water availability, systems of marriage and variations in female autonomy (which in Southeast Asia tends to be relatively high). Modern national boundaries are often poor guides to differences in such key aspects of life.

NOTES

1. A recent major edited volume, entitled *Asian Population History*, contains five chapters focussed on South Asia, nine dealing with East Asia, but only three focussed on Southeast Asia (one of which is general and the other two of which deal with Indonesia) (see Ts'ui-jung Liu *et al.* 2001).
2. For example on South Asia see Visaria and Visaria (1982), Dyson (1989a and 2004) and Guha (2001), and on Southeast Asia see Reid (2001)
3. This discussion of Indianisation is mostly based on the Introduction, Conclusion and Chapters 1-4 of Coedès (1968).
4. The figure is a maximum because of the relative paucity of statistics on return migration.
5. Although the Malaysian and Sri Lankan statistics presented in Table 1 are crude death rates, mortality measures standardised for age composition (e.g. infant mortality rates and age specific death rates) are sometimes available for these groups, and invariably they confirm the relative mortality trends shown (see Tan Poo Chang et al. 1987 and Langford 1984).
6. It is worth noting that during the nineteenth century it was the initial intention of the British to import Chinese labourers to work the newly established tea estates in Assam for much the same reasons that they imported Indian labour, for example, to Malaysia. However this idea was quickly dropped when the first Chinese 'coolie' imports from Singapore became disruptive after disembarking at Calcutta (Kolkata) (see Weiner 1978: 88-89).
7. However this view is not universally shared. Thus Reid (1988) considers that Southeast Asians were often quite healthy; he attributes past high death rates largely to the consequences of warfare. Reid too notes early references to transferences of venereal disease.
8. Inoculation, which was a traditional practice in parts of India (especially Bengal) and China, carried a small but significant chance of death. Of course, it took some time

before it was appreciated that the protection afforded by vaccination would wane and that therefore smallpox revaccination was required.

9. For a map of India's malaria regions which substantiates this point, itself taken from work by Christophers, see Learmonth (1970).
10. It is worth noting that with reference to the dry areas of Upper Burma Geddes (1949/1970) believed that the prevailing situation might be close to one of 'stagnation'.
11. The instigation of DDT spraying seems to be only a part of the explanation for this short period of exceptionally rapid mortality decline (see Langford 1996; Dyson 1989c).

REFERENCES

Arnold, D. (ed.) (1988) *Imperial Medicine and Indigenous Societies*, Manchester University Press, Manchester.

Arnold, D. (1989) 'Cholera Mortality in British India, 1817-1947', in T. Dyson (ed.) *India's Historical Demography*, Curzon Press, London, pp. 261-84.

Banthia, J. and Dyson, T. (2000a) 'Smallpox and the Impact of Vaccination upon the Parsees of Bombay', *The Indian Economic and Social History Review*, 37,1:27-51.

Banthia, J. and Dyson, T. (2000b) 'Smallpox in Nineteenth Century India', *Population and Development Review*, 25,4:649-80.

Bhat, M. (1989) 'Mortality and fertility in India, 1881-1961: A Reassessment' in T. Dyson (ed.) *India's Historical Demography*, Curzon Press, London, pp. 73-118.

Boomgaard, P. (1989) *Children of the Colonial State. Population Growth and Economic Development in Java, 1795-1880*, Free University Press, Amsterdam.

Bradley, D.J. and Keymer, A. (1984) 'Parasitic Diseases: Measurement and Mortality Impact', *Population and Development Review,* Supplement to Volume 10: 163-87.

Cady, J.F. (1964) *Southeast Asia, Its Historical Development*, McGraw-Hill, New York.

Carr-Saunders, A.M. (1964) *World Population, Past Growth and Present Trends*, Second Edition, Frank Cass, London.

Catanach (1988) 'Plague and the Tensions of Empire: India 1896-1918', in D. Arnold (ed.) *Imperial Medicine and Indigenous Societies*, Manchester University Press, Manchester.

Christophers, S.R. (1911) 'Malaria in Punjab', *Scientific Memoirs by Officers of the Medical and Sanitary Departments of the Government of India,* New Series No. 46. Superintendent of Government Printing, Calcutta.

Coedès, G. (1968) *The Indianized States of Southeast Asia*, edited by W.F. Wella and translated by S.B. Cowing, East-West Center Press, Honolulu.

Davis, K. (1951) *The Population History of India and Pakistan*, Princeton University Press, Princeton NJ.

Dyson, T. (1984) 'Future LDC Demographic Research: Some Thoughts on Data, Methods, Theory', in Départment de Démographie Université Catholique de Louvain, *La Demographie en Perspective, Chaire Quetelet*, Université Catholique de Louvain, Louvain-la-Neuve, pp. 45-75.

Dyson, T. (1989a) 'Indian Historical Demography: Developments and Prospects' in T. Dyson (ed.) *India's Historical Demography*, Curzon Press, London, pp. 1-15.

Dyson, T. (1989b) 'The Historical Demography of Berar, ' in T. Dyson (ed.) *India's Historical Demography*, Curzon Press, London, pp. 150-96.

Dyson, T. (1989c) 'The Population History of Berar Since 1881 and its Potential Wider Significance' *The Indian Economic and Social History Review* 26,2:167-201.

Dyson, T. (2004) 'India's Population—the Past' in T. Dyson, R. Cassen and L. Visaria (eds.) *Twenty-first Century India—Population, Economy, Human Development and the Environment*, Oxford University Press, Delhi, pp.15-31.

Dyson, T. and Moore, M. (1983) 'On Kinship Structure, Female Autonomy and Demographic Behaviour in India.' *Population and Development Review* 9,1:35-60.

Dyson, T. and Murphy, M. (1991) 'Macro-level Study of Socio-economic Development and Mortality: Adequacy of Indicators and Methods of Statistical Analysis', in J. Cleland and A. G. Hill (eds.) *The Health Transition: Methods and Measures*, Health Transition Centre, The Australian national University, Canberra, pp. 147-62.

Dyson, T. and Maharatna, A. (1991) 'Excess mortality during the Bengal famine: A re-evaluation' *The Indian Economic and Social History Review* 28,3:281-97.

Geddes, A. (1947/1970) 'The Social and Psychological Significance of Variability in Population Change', *Human Relations*, Volume 1, 1947; reprinted in Social Sciences Foundation Course Team (eds.) *Understanding Society*, Macmillan, London, 1947 pp. 620-36.

Gray, R.H. (1974) 'The Decline of Mortality in Ceylon and the Demographic Effects of Malaria Control', *Population Studies* 28,2: 205-29.

Guha, S. (2001) 'The Population History of South Asia from the Seventeenth to the Twentieth Centuries: An Exploration', in Ts'ui-jung Liu, J. Lee, D. S. Reher, O. Saito, and W. Feng (eds.) *Asian Population History*, Oxford University Press, Oxford, pp. 66-78.

Hull, T. (1987) 'Plague in Java', in N. G. Owen (ed.) *Death and Disease in Southeast Asia*, Oxford University Press, Singapore, pp. 210-34.

Jannetta, A.B. (2001) 'Public Health and the Diffusion of Vaccination in Japan', in Ts'ui-jung Liu, J. Lee, D. S. Reher, O. Saito, and W Feng (eds.) *Asian Population History*, Oxford University Press, Oxford, pp. 292-305.

Konings, E. (1987) 'From Rats and People: A Demographic Analysis of Bubonic Plague in Bombay Presidency, 1896-1952', MSc Dissertation, London School of Economics.

Langford, C.M. (1982) *The Fertility of Tamil Estate Workers in Sri Lanka*, World Fertility Scientific Report, No. 31, London.

Langford, C.M. (1984) 'Sex Differentials in Mortality in Sri Lanka: Changes Since the 1920s', *Journal of Biosocial Science* 16:399-410.

Langford, C.M. (1996) 'Reasons for the Decline in Mortality in Sri Lanka Immediately after the Second World War: A Re-examination of the Evidence', *Health Transition Review* 6,1:3-23.

Langford, C.M. and Storey, P. (1992) 'Influenza in Sri Lanka, 1918-1919: The Impact of a New Disease in a Pre-modern Third World Setting', *Health Transition Review*, Supplement to Volume 2, 97-123.

Learmonth, A.T.A. (1970) 'India's Population Geography in an Era of Change', in Social Sciences Foundation Course Team (eds.) *Understanding Society*, Macmillan, London, 1947 pp. 637-42.

McAlpin, M. (1983) *Subject to Famine: Food Crises and Economic Change in Western India, 1860-1920*, Princeton University Press, Princeton, NJ.

McAlpin, M. (1988) 'Bubonic Plague', in D. W. Attwood, M. Israel and N.K. Wagle (eds.) *City, Countryside and Society in Maharashtra*, University of Toronto Press, Toronto.

McNeill, W.H. (1979) *Plagues and Peoples*, Penguin Books, Harmondsworth, England.

Mills, I. (1989) 'Influenza in India During 1918-19', in T. Dyson (ed.) *India's Historical Demography*, Curzon Press, London, pp. 261-84.

Moore, M. (1973) 'Cross-cultural Surveys of peasant Family Structures: Some Comments', *American Anthropologist* 75,3: 911-15.

Muthiah A. and Jones, G.W. (1983) 'Fertility Trends Among Overseas Indian Populations', *Population Studies* 37,32: 253-72.

Registrar General, India (1883) *Report on the Census of British India taken on the 17th February 1881, Volume 1*, Her Majesty's Stationary Office, London.

Registrar General, India (1893) *General Report*, Her Majesty's Stationary Office, London.

Registrar General, India (1976) *Fertility Differentials in India, 1972,* Ministry of Home Affairs, New Delhi.

Reid, A. (1988) *Southeast Asia in the Age of Commerce: 1450-1680, Volume1*, Yale University Press.

Reid, A. (2001) 'South-East Asian Population History and the Colonial Impact', in Ts'ui-jung Liu, J. Lee, D.S. Reher, O. Saito, and W Feng (eds.) *Asian Population History*, Oxford University Press, Oxford, pp. 45-62.

Shepherd, J.R. (2001) 'Smallpox and the Pattern of Mortality in Late Nineteenth-Century Taiwan', in Ts'ui-jung Liu, J. Lee, D.S. Reher, O. Saito, and W Feng (eds.) *Asian Population History*, Oxford University Press, Oxford, pp. 270-91.

Smith, P.C. and S-M Ng (1982) 'The Components of Population Change in Nineteenth Century South-east Asia: Village Data from the Philippines', *Population Studies* 36,2: 237-55.

Sopher, D. (ed.) (1980a) *An Exploration of India*, Longman, London.

Sopher, D. (1980b) 'Indian Civilization and the Tropical Savanna Environments' in O.R. Harris (ed.) *Human Ecology in Savanna Environments*, Academic Press, London, pp. 185-207.

Tan Poo Chang, K.K. Kit, T.B. Ann, S. Nagaraj, T.N. Peng and S.N. Zulkifli (1987) 'Socio-economic Development and Mortality Patterns and Trends in Malaysia', *Asia-Pacific Population Journal* 2,1:3-20.

Tinker, H. (1974) *A New System of Slavery: The Export of Indian Labour Overseas, 1830-1920*, Oxford University Press, London.

Ts'ui-jung Liu, Lee, J. Reher, D.S. Saito, O. and Feng, W. (2001) *Asian Population History*, Oxford University Press, Oxford.

United Nations (2001) *World Population Prospects, The 2000 Revision, Volume 1,* United Nations, New York.

Van Heyingen, W.E. and J.R. Seal (1980) *Cholera, The American Experience, 1947-1980*, Westview Press, Boulder.

Visaria, L. and Visaria, P. (1982) 'Population (1757-1947)' in D. Kumar (ed.) *The Cambridge Economic History of India, Volume II, c. 1757-1970,* Orient Longmont, New Delhi, pp. 463-532.

Weiner, M. (1978) *Sons of the Soil: Migration and Ethnic Conflict in India,* Princeton University Press, Princeton, NJ.

Whyte, R. and Whyte, P. (1978) *Rural Asian Women*, Institute of South East Asian Studies, Singapore.

Zelinsky, W. (1950) 'The Indochinese Peninsula: A Demographic Anomaly.' *The Far Eastern Quarterly* 9,2: 115-45.

Zurbrigg, S. (1994) 'Re-thinking the 'Human Factor' in Malaria Mortality: The Case of Punjab, 1868-1940', *Parassitologia* 36: 121-35.

Chapter 3

Contextualising Long-run Demographic Change in Southern India

Ravindran Gopinath

This chapter, a broad survey of old Madras Presidency's demographic trajectories, highlights the character of pre-transitional mortality and fertility, and offers some explanations for the relatively early shift to lower levels of mortality and fertility in southern India.[1] The attempt is to first describe the long term movements in the Presidency's mortality and fertility curves, then disaggregate this large administrative unit into smaller, distinct constituent zones and go on to study individual districts.

The Data Base

The demographic data for this study are drawn from two sources: the Census of India and the Vital Registration System. Both go back to colonial times.

Census of India

The census of India, the most definitive and widely used source in demographic studies of the sub-continent, has a long history, and an ancestry that can be traced back to the19th century, when the maddening complexity of India was sought to be documented by the British authorities (Breckenridge and Van der Veer 1993). The Indian census was however not merely a neutral tool for information gathering; the classificatory logic of the census created conditions for the crystallisation and solidification of identities. In time, this led to new strategies of caste and status mobility and electoral mobilisation. (Cohn 1987).

The first census of British India in 1871/72, was not synchronous, but, since then, synchronous censuses have been conducted every ten years. All the post 1871-72 censuses were synchronous enumerations.[2] Even Britain itself could not boast of such an unbroken record, having had to skip the 1941 census.

Prior to the decennial British Indian censuses, in 1849, the Government of India had directed provincial governments to conduct quinquennial population enumerations on the lines of the ones carried out in the North West Provinces by revenue officials (G.O. No. 813, 27 March 1868 cited in Natarajan 1972). [3] Madras was the only Presidency to have implemented this directive in full, and was thus fortunate in having the longest history of population enumerations in this country.[4] Following this, Madras carried out four enumerations—in 1851-52, 1856-57, 1861-62 and 1866-67. The next, i.e., the fifth quinquennial census, was merged with the Imperial all India census of 1871-72. While the quinquennial and subsequent census enumerations suggest plausible and comparable rates of growth, the sudden increase in 1871 seems to have been caused by wider coverage. Historians' estimations of rates of population growth from the quinquennial data are thus of little use (Kumar 1992).

Two censuses of the colonial period require special mention. The 1931 census gained notoriety for its method of recording age and the smoothing of age distributions, which makes the published age figures incomparable with earlier and later census age distributions. This has enticed many a demographer to un-smooth the smoothed distribution, though none can claim complete success. Further, the Sarda Act, which made the marriage of under-fourteen year old girls punishable by law, also led to inaccuracies in the age returns of unmarried girls. The nationalist agitation was another factor—an unsettling circumstance, one that militated against this enumeration. The next census, i.e., the census of 1941, was held in wartime. The financial exigencies of the Second World War forced the government to drastically abbreviate the published report and tables of the 1941 census. The straitened circumstances also led to a change from household enumeration schedules to individual slips.

Caste data for the entire population was available for the last time in 1941. After independence, the recording of caste was discontinued, except for Scheduled Castes and Scheduled Tribes.[5]

Since 1951, post-enumeration checks were made regularly after each enumeration to check for accuracy. Another distinctive feature of the 1951 census was that it also published figures for 'divorced' men and women. (In the earlier censuses till 1941, this category was subsumed under 'widowed'). In the 1961 count, the category 'never married' was introduced. Similarly, nuptiality, featured in a publication from the 1941 census, based on a 2 per cent sample, often referred to as the Y-Sample, provided detailed age specific information on nuptial status and occupation and industry. In 1971, 'married' was replaced by 'currently married'. For 'currently married' women, age at marriage, children born in the last one year, number of children born and surviving, and age at birth of first child,[6] were recorded. Thus, we see a number of conceptual refinements with respect to marriage and fertility.

Vital Registration Data

The second basic source of demographic data tapped in this study is the *Report of the Sanitary Commissioner*—the annual series on births and deaths published by the government. (Its nomenclature subsequently changed to *Report of the Director of Public Health*). In the post independence years, these statistics at the district level were published in the annual series known as the *Vital Statistics of India*, which became available from 1958.

Report after report lamented the under-registration in these vital statistics. To make matters worse, the level of underreporting varied across time and by districts. The question, then, is that of whether we ought to discard this extremely rich though imperfect series. While the mainstream Indian demographer has judged registration data to be unusable, a long-term view of this data source suggests that between 1880s to the 1940s the data are of acceptable quality; after suitable corrections are made in the level of the reported statistics, they provide an invaluable source, not in making precise demographic projections, but in charting annual fertility and mortality movements.

For the more recent years, other problems present themselves. Thus, after Independence, the old Madras Presidency was divided into separate States on the basis of language. With the States reorganisation of 1956, the south-western, north eastern and northern districts of the erstwhile Presidency were amalgamated into the new states of Kerala, Karnataka and Andhra Pradesh. One consequence was that the demographic records of the newly formed States varied greatly in the attention paid to the collection of statistics.

For Madras City, vital registration data first became available in 1855. Registration was extended to the whole Presidency in 1865. The total number of deaths and births are available for Madras City and Madras Presidency from 1866 and 1870, respectively. Unhappy with the grossly deficient early returns, the Government had asked the Sanitary Commissioner, in December, 1868, to prepare standardised forms for the collection of vital statistics. In 1870, the recommendations of the Sanitary Commission were found to be imperfect by the Army Sanitary Commission, which suggested that the data collection should be in consonance with international designs. The Sanitary Commission opposed this on the plea that Indians were yet to be accustomed to registration. (As late as 1866, only in the Central Province of Berar were births registered). Given the absence of a tradition of registration in India, the local registrar charged with the duty of collecting these figures often thought of this exercise as 'the idle curiosity of an eccentric Sircar' (COI, 1911, XII,

I:20 in. Guilmoto 1988: 101).

Initially, the statistics that were generated were plagued by gross under enumeration. One reason for this was the *tahsildars'* failure to cite non-reporting villages. True, birth and death registration was compulsory in all the municipalities of Madras Presidency,[7] and the Sanitary Commissioner had repeatedly pleaded for the extension of the relevant Act to the whole of Madras. On comparing the vital statistics gathered from the areas within and outside the purview of the Act, however, it was found that villages and towns covered by the Act often produced much lower returns than areas where notification was not mandatory.[8] So, the problem lay not in the coverage of the Act, but rather, administrative failure. In 1921, the government instructed local bodies to use the services of their vaccinators in the off-season to correct birth and death returns by detecting errors and omissions in registration.[9] The incomplete compilation of results in the Collectors' offices too was seen as a major reason for incomplete statistics.[10] It was thought that the quality of statistics would improve if the work was transferred from the Revenue Department to the Health Department. A few years down the line, in 1926, it was claimed that '... in the last six years, the steady improvement which has been made is sufficient testimony to the efforts of the District Health Staffs, who have done great a deal in the detection of omissions and the setting right of irregularities in the village registers'.[11] This assertion is corroborated by an increase in the completeness of coverage of deaths using standard contemporary demographic estimation procedures.[12] Finally in 1932, as an experimental measure, the Director of Public Health took over the work of compilation from the Collectors.[13] Evidently, things then changed for the better: 'This transfer has not only effected an economy in the staff employed for the work, but also has been conducive to much greater efficiency. The Presidency figures became far more complete and accurate than they were ever before'.[14]

Both before and after Independence, a variety of official commissions had recommended the crucial need for the collection of vital statistics. These included the Royal Commission on Agriculture (1924), the Royal Commission on Labour (1928), the Central Advisory Board on Health (1939), Health Survey and Development Committee (1946), Vital Statistics Committee (1949) and the Committee on the Pattern of Statistical Units for Health Departments (1960). In view of the variations in the quality and coverage of vital registration, another committee—the Bhore Committee, underscored the need for a number of steps to improve the gathering of statistics on vital events (births and deaths) in India. To that end, it recommended the setting up of the Office of the Registrar General of India, which was done in 1951. In 1960, the work of collecting and compiling vital statistics was once again transferred from the Director of Health Services to the newly created Office of the Registrar General. In 1969, the

Registration of Births and Deaths Act was enacted to standardise and co-ordinate the registration of vital events across the country.

It is believed the Second World War impinged adversely on the collection of vital registration data. 'The machinery engaged in registration received the rudest shock during World War II when it went completely out of gear and the work was neglected in favour of all-out war efforts. The registration system has been on the downgrade ever since'.[15] In the case of Madras, however, neither the level of the uncorrected births and deaths nor the correction factors estimated in this study suggest such a marked deterioration during the War years. In the post-War period, though, the beginnings of a marked deterioration can clearly be discerned.

A study conducted by the Registrar General in 1966 to ascertain the level of under-registration in rural areas placed Tamil Nadu at second rank after Punjab in terms of the completeness of registration statistics [Registrar General, 1966 #4386]. This is supported by G.K.Mehrota's study, which places Tamil Nadu in the 'below 25%' category of under registration, Kerala and Mysore in the `25-49%' category, and Andhra Pradesh in the '50-74%' category.[16] Thus most of our study districts fall in the good or at least better data zone.

The registration of births and deaths worsened in the 1970s and then showed some improvement in 1981. In our study districts, the level of under-registration varied across districts, not necessarily in tandem with either State or national level trends. Despite this, the reconstruction of long-run vital rates, using clearly transparent methods, is useful to understand long-term processes of change.

Correction Procedures

Demographers have developed a number of techniques for estimating the completeness of death registration. To do this they compute death rates from sources other than death registration. They exploit the mathematics of the relationships between (i) age structure (% distribution of population in different age groups) (ii) age-specific mortality (mortality within an age group) and (iii) age-specific growth rate. Using data of this sort, for instance, from censuses, they calculate death rates, and then compare these with death rates calculated from registration data. The discrepancies give an indication of the extent of error in the registration records. An underlying assumption common to all such methods is that the population under study is closed to migration, which is not too restrictive a premise in the case of Madras Presidency, where migrants formed a very small proportion of the total population. In 1922, it was estimated that in the period 1911 to 1920, the number of emigrants was approximately 6.33 lakhs. This worked out to 60,000 per year or roughly 0.15 per cent of the total population, which is an extremely small number (Government of Madras 1923).

In this study we have chosen the Brass Growth Balance Method (Brass

1975) from the several so-called 'indirect methods' that have been developed to check the accuracy of demographic data.[17] The method allows age specific death rates to be calculated from age-wise census data. (To do this, we take cognisance of the extent to which age cohorts decrease in numbers as we go from younger to older age groups). When death rates so obtained are compared with figures from vital registration data, we get an indication of the extent of discrepancy. The advantage of this method is that it requires age specific vital registration death data only for the year of the census. To reduce chances of the vital registration mortality statistics for the census year being unrepresentative, we have taken a three year average of deaths by age, centred around the census year. (For data after 1941, however, we could not continue using the method).[18]

In this comparison of census and vital registration data, some modification of the census data had to be done as well. The age groups used in the census and the Report of the Sanitary Commissioner for Madras (hereafter RSCM] at the district level keep changing, and, to redistribute them in quinquennial groups, a process involving the use of 'age-splitting coefficients', developed by Carrier and Hobcraft (Carrier, Hobcraft and LSE 1971).

Data correction procedures were carried out also for fertility indicators computed from census-based age specific nuptiality tables, such as 'proportions married'. To that end, the demographic technique of 'standardisation' of age distributions was carried out, so as to facilitate comparability of the statistics.

Fertility Estimates for Colonial Madras

There is general consensus in virtually all the fertility estimates of India that Madras Presidency experienced lower mortality and fertility than the other provinces. Let us take a brief look at the evidence.

In a pioneering work on the Indian censuses, Kingsley Davis, using CWRs (Child Woman Ratios) to estimate regional fertility differentials,[19] found that, in 1931, Madras came lowest, with a CWR of 685, while Bombay and Bengal registered ratios of 766 and 754 respectively (Davis 1951: Table 19).[20] S.N. Agarwala, another noted demographer, suggests, citing vital registration returns, that for the period 1951-61, Madras State had the lowest birth rate in India; at 34.9 per thousand, the figure was below the all-India figure of 41.7. These figures are however, based on raw vital registration data with all its attendant deficiencies (Agarwala 1972: 117).

The distribution of births by birth order is another indicator of the level of fertility. More high-order births suggest high fertility while a high incidence of low order births point to lower fertility levels. Madras was one of top three states exhibiting the highest percentage of births (63) in the 1 to 3 order of births in the 1960s (Agarwala 1972: 123).

The next influential estimate of fertility, by S.B. Mukherjee (1976), was based on age distributions of the Indian population. His quasi-stable estimates of fertility for each of the five zones of India (Northern, Eastern, Central, Western, and Southern) gives the Southern region (which includes Madras, Coorg, Hyderabad and Travancore-Cochin) the lowest ranking in terms of birth rate, gross reproduction rate, and death rate for the period 1901 to 1961.

Estimates of zonal fertility rates from the census by Leela and Pravin Visaria also show the Southern zone to have the lowest fertility among all the zones (Visaria and Visaria 1984). The Visarias' estimates are much lower than Mukherjee's. Both sets of estimates however suggest a very stable and unchanging fertility level.

Alice Clark's estimates of the Gross Reproduction Rates (GRRs) for Madras, based on the 'variable r' method in combination with the new United Nations 'South Asia' model life tables, range between 2.64 and 3.29 for the period 1881-1931 (Clark 1989: 129). On inspecting the GRR trends of these three estimates and Hardy's estimate of the Crude Birth Rate, one fails to find any congruence in the direction of change, not to mention the levels of fertility. The important point of agreement, however, is that the South zone (or Madras) had the lowest fertility in India.

It is noteworthy also that the historically observed North-South differential in fertility has clear continuities with faster gains in fertility reduction in the south in more recent times. The regional patterning of fertility from 1951 to 1991 provides clear evidence of this and complements the observed colonial North-South demographic.[21]

Direct Estimates of Fertility

We now turn to direct estimates of fertility in Madras based on uncorrected vital statistics data. Figure 1 below plots the annual time series data for the CBR (Crude Birth Rate), decennial estimates of child-woman ratio, SMAM (the singulate mean age at marriage), and MarF15-49 (the proportion of women married between the ages of 15 and 49).

While the series is plagued by the problem of possibly changing levels of coverage, it does faithfully represent crisis years, as evidenced by the sharp drops in 1893, 1902 and 1918-19. Further, the movement in the raw CBR series agrees well with the CWR estimates (Figure 1).

The raw data suggests a more or less constant level of fertility in the pre-1921 period, followed by a secular increase till the end of the second half of the twentieth century. As expected, the earlier period, when crises occurred, is marked by greater fluctuations as compared to the post-1921 period. On the whole the level of fertility appears to be moderate.

FIGURE 1: Fertility and Nuptiality Trends in Madras, 1891-1947

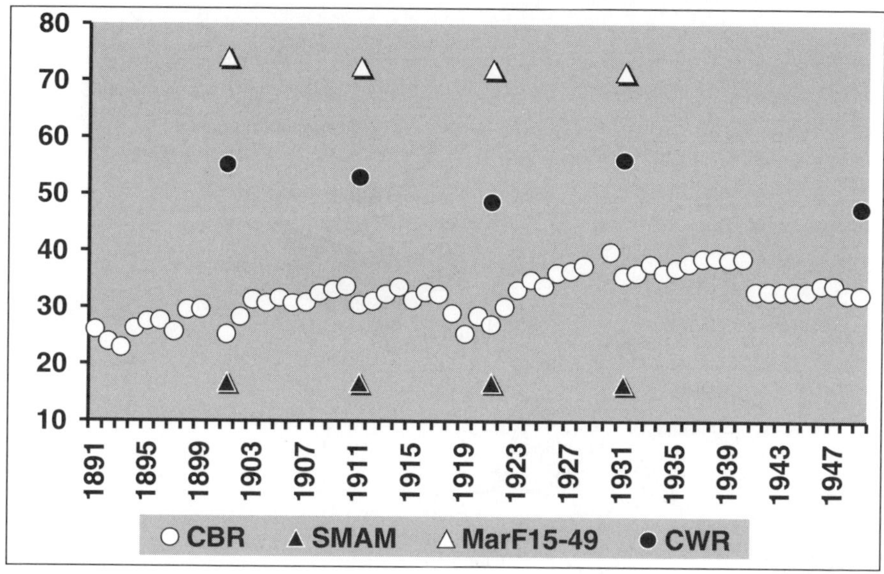

The Regions

As the English East India Company expanded northwards and then into the interior of the peninsula, annexing or partially tolerating vanquished local magnates and princes, colonial Madras Presidency came into being. Undivided Madras Presidency (Figure 2a), stretching from the 'dry' Deccan districts in the north (Bellary, Kurnool, Anantpur) to the 'wet' tropical Malabar Coast in the Southwest and the deltas in the east, was a creation of the colonial State. The early years of colonial rule saw a few changes in the territory of Madras Presidency. Malabar, which was initially part of Bombay, was transferred to Madras in 1800, and North Kanara was transferred to Bombay from Madras in 1862. Treaties with now ineffectual former rivals led to the continued existence of small French and Danish settlements and the larger Native states of Cochin, Travancore, Mysore and Hyderabad, on the peripheries of the newly created Madras Presidency.[22]

It would be futile to search for generalisations for an area as varied as Madras, with its many constituent regions and sub-regions. Regions are characterised by variations in resources which range from the most immutable such as rainfall, soil, vegetation and drainage to much more malleable ones such as education, communication, health and so on. Both are subject to the impacts of organised intervention, though to different degrees. State sponsored intervention, which continuously increased from the late nineteenth century, greatly grew in intensity and spread with the coming of independence.

FIGURE 2A: Rainfall Map, Madras Presidency (Selected Districts)

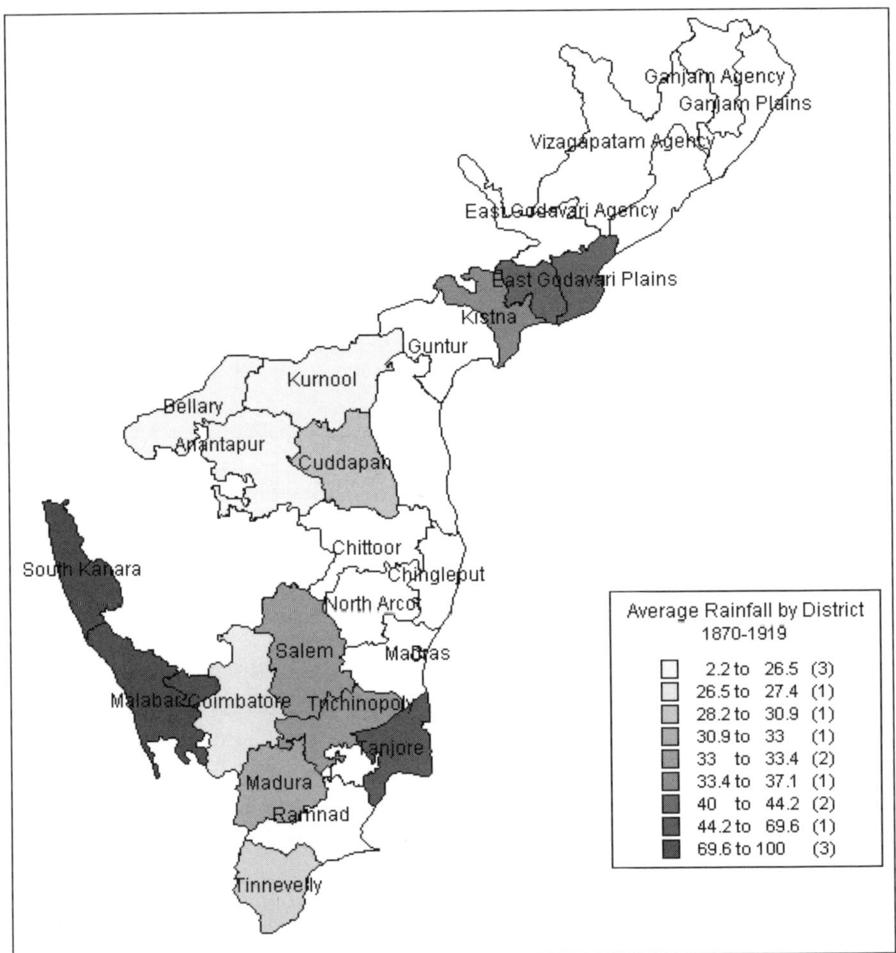

The census authorities divided the Presidency into five broad divisions: the Agency Division, the Deccan Division, East Coast Division, the Southern Division and the Western Division (See Figure 2b).

(i) The Agency Division, in the Northeast, was marked by low hills covered with dense jungle. It was populated largely by animistic tribes engaged in agriculture. With hardly any means of modern communication, it was very different from the other Divisions.

(ii) The Deccan Division, comprising of the districts of Cuddapah, Kurnool, Bellary and Anantapur in the Deccan, with scanty rainfall (less than 30 inches) was a 'dry' and rather infertile zone with a low

FIGURE 2B: Census Divisions, Madras Presidency

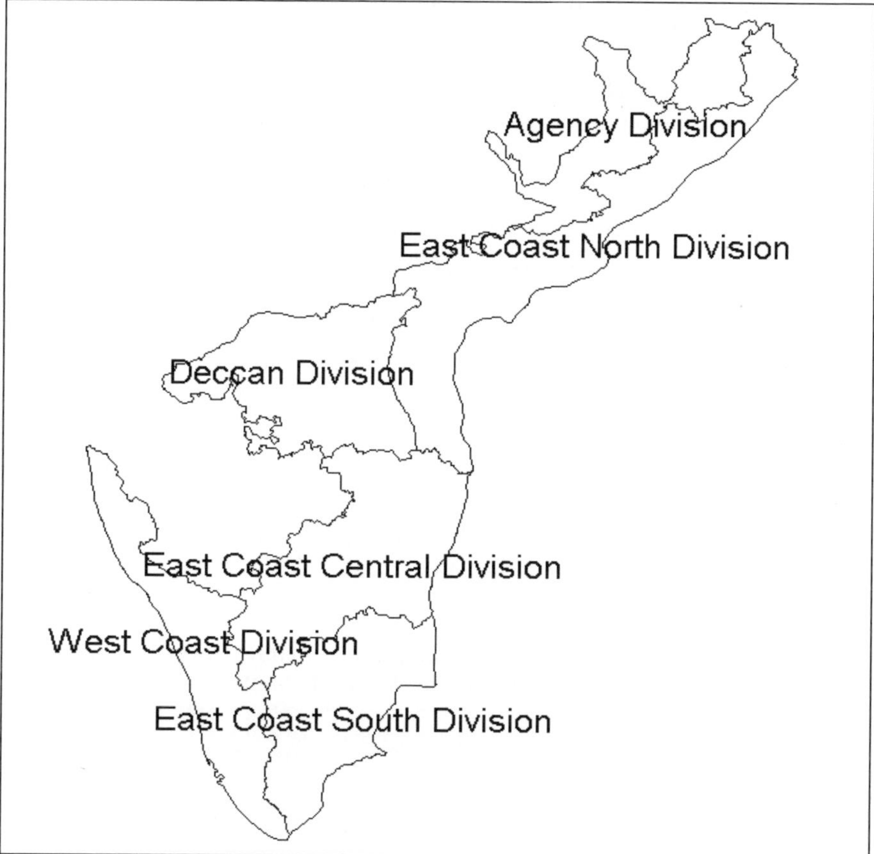

density and rate of growth of population. These districts had high mortality and moderate fertility.

(iii) The East Coast Division, which included the irrigated deltaic districts of East and West Godavari and Krishna, had the highest rate of population growth in the Presidency, with fairly high fertility and moderate mortality.

(iv) The large Southern Division with districts along the East Coast and Coimbatore, Madurai and Salem were agriculturally rich, with an annual rainfall of nearly 40 inches. Fertility increased progressively as one went southwards along the coast. The interior district of Coimbatore, Madurai and Salem stood between the high fertility East Coast and the low to moderate fertility levels of the West Coast.

(v) The West Coast districts of Malabar and South Canara (Dakshina

Kannada) was quite different from the rest of the Presidency with a very heavy rainfall, dense population, distinct social institutions and high level of literacy.

While the Western Division and the coastal districts of the East Coast were classed as 'non-famine districts', the Deccan districts and the interior districts of the Southern Division were 'famine districts'. Thus, the census divisions in many ways overlapped with the agro economic map of the Presidency.

Notably, a large number of writers have categorised and analysed social and historical change in Madras in terms of 'dry' and 'wet' ecotypes. To summarise, very broadly, the Deccan and interior Southern census Divisions corresponded with the 'dry' region. Parts of the interior areas of the East Coast districts of Krishna and Godavari also fell in this class. The Western and Eastern Divisions located along the Arabian and Bay of Bengal littoral comprised the 'wet' region. Several historians and geographers have emphasised the significance of these ecotypes in moulding the social, economic and cultural institutions and practices in each of these areas.

Figure 3 below clearly indicates that the 'dry' districts had lower inequality in landholding, and a much smaller amount of paddy cropping, as compared to the 'wet' districts.

FIGURE 3: Gini Coefficient of Landholding and % Paddy Grown, Wet and Dry Districts, Madras Presidency, 1920-21

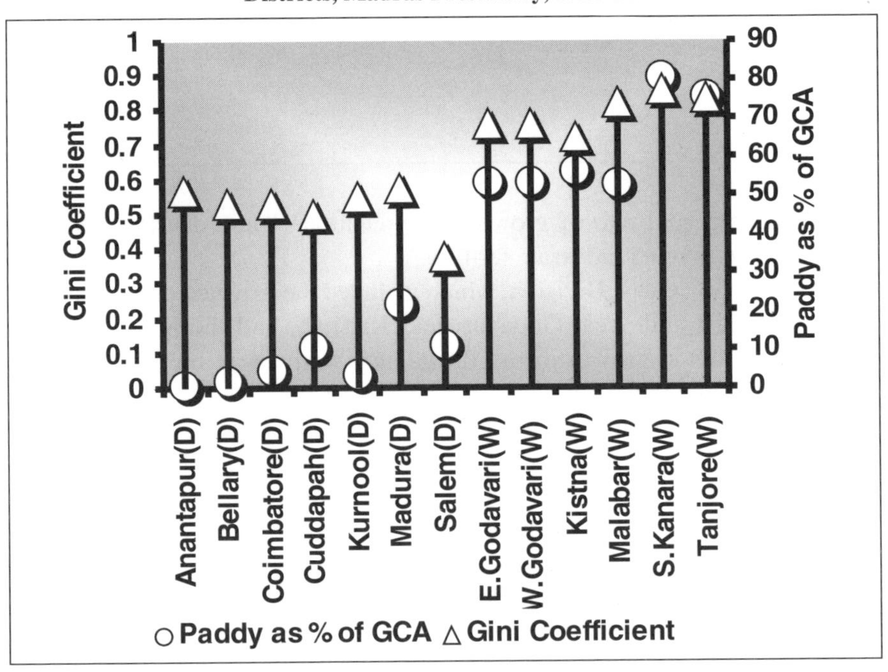

We now look at indices of risk in these two categories of 'wet' and 'dry' areas. Greater fluctuations in rainfall and food prices (captured by the coefficient of variation) are indicative of more uncertainty. Table 1 below provides these indices for prices in three 'wet' and three 'dry' districts.

TABLE 1: Coefficient of Variation of Prices of Staple Food Crops, Madras Presidency, 1870-1920

DRY	WET
51.16667	33.725

Table 2 below shows the percentage of remissions to total assessed revenue. The figures suggest that both the level and frequency of remissions, taken as a proxy for crop failures and risk, were much higher in the 'dry' districts than in the wet. Significantly the data point to the marked decrease in both the level and frequency of large remissions in the years after 1921. This has important implications in explaining the conundrum of Indian mortality decline.

Table 2: Remissions as a Percentage of Total Revenue Demand (Decennial Average), Selected Districts, Malabar Presidency, 1870-80 to 1940-50

Year	S. Kanara (Wet)	Malabar (Wet)	Salem (Dry)	Bellary (Dry)	Kurnool (Dry)
1870-80	5.4	0.6	12.3	8.0	10.2
1880-90	5.0	0.9	8.6	8.5	6.0
1890-90	2.4	0.2	3.8	10.8	10.5
1900-10	12.8	11.0	3.8	1.6	8.5
1910-20	1.3	0.7	2.6	1.3	2.6
1920-30	1.2	0.3	5.7	2.8	5.7
1930-40	1.1	2.1	4.2	-	-
1940-50	0.9	0.4	6.2	-	-

The greater intensity of cropping coupled with the preponderance of 'wet' paddy cultivation in the 'wet' districts as opposed to the 'dry' regions resulted in greater demand for agricultural labour. Not only was the proportion of agricultural labourers higher in the 'wet' areas, but so also was the index of female participation in the labour force. Labour intensive operations such as transplantation were entirely worked by female labourers.

Having thus demonstrated the difference between the 'dry' and the 'wet' regions in terms of cropping patterns, rainfall, inequality and the level of risk we move on study the economic structure and changes of the ten districts that have been included in this study in detail. The ten selected districts range from the very 'dry' to the very 'wet'. The driest of the 'dry' districts are the contiguous

Deccan districts of Bellary, Anantapur and Kurnool. The intermediate districts ('dry' but less arid than the Deccan region) are Salem, Madurai and Coimbatore. The 'wet' districts are all located on the coast- Malabar and South Canara on the south west coast and Krishna and Thanjavur on the Coromandel Coast (See Figure 2).

Table 3 shows that the 'dry' - 'wet' classification by district observed for the colonial period continued to largely hold good in the years after Independence. We find the average level of male literacy and the proportion of HYV crop acreage to the total cultivated area remained higher in the 'wet' districts compared to the 'dry' districts. However, the impact of rapid industrialisation, which began in the inter-War period, appears to have raised literacy in Coimbatore and adjoining Madura districts.

TABLE 3. Selected Economic Indices by District, 1956 to 1986

District	Mean WHYV/GCA	Literacy
Anantapur (D)	1.87	0.29
Bellary (D)	2.83	0.31
Kurnool (D)	4.18	0.31
Salem (D)	6.54	0.35
Coimbatore (D)	6.89	0.45
Madura (D)	11.51	0.46
S. Canara (W)	13.43	0.48
Krishna (W)	22.08	0.36
Thanjavur (W)	47.71	0.5

Note GCA: Gross Cropped Area; WHYV/GCA: Acreage under HYV rice as per cent of GCA, Literacy: Proportion of rural males classified as literate.

Data Source : BREAD (Bureau for Research and Economic Analysis of Development). http://ipl.econ.duke.edu/bread/index.htm. Select 'Data', Go to India Agriculture and Climate Data Set

Population Growth and Food Supply

There were no major famines during the first half of the twentieth century in Madras, except for limited famines in 1907-08 and 1918. However, this is not to say that these were years of great prosperity. Scarcities, associated price hikes, endemic diseases and epidemics continued to take their human toll. Further, the economic growth of these years benefited regions and classes very unequally. Despite the great deal of controversy that surrounds agricultural output statistics in British India, what the available data clearly suggests is that *food crop* output fell behind population increase in the 1920 to 1947 period (Blyn 1966: 331). The sluggish nature of agricultural growth of the last two decades of the colonial period with its associated low savings and investment rates continued into the early decades of the post-colonial period. Only from the late 1960s did the trend change direction for the better.

The weakening agricultural economy had been subjected to various external shocks - first, the Depression, and then, the War. The associated inflation of food prices and the attendant chronic hunger of the poor continued till the late 50s.[23] India became a major food importer in the years after Independence, with 1951 witnessing the first major food shortage. Consequently, to boost the country's food production, the First Five Year Plan emphasised land reforms, irrigation, fertiliser production and research and extension services. The Green Revolution saw the introduction of high yielding varieties of first, wheat and then rice, and crop yields shot up. From the end of the 1960s, food output stayed ahead of population increase. However, the 1970s witnessed a slackening of agricultural output growth. External shocks in the form of the oil price hike shook the economy. In this scenario, the State stepped in to introduce the Public Distribution System (PDS) so as to ensure equitable distribution.

We now turn to the performance of the ten of our individual study districts over a century, from 1881 to 1981. To that end, we take a look at prices. Price series form a good proxy index of food availability, and of well being.[24] A price increase inversely affects the economic well being of the population when the majority of the people are net buyers of food, which appears to have been the case in most of the districts. The inverse price-prosperity relationship was well recognised since the late nineteenth century and the Sanitary Commissioners regularly published food prices as a rough early warning signal for impending famines. As a number of other economists have argued in the past, the price variable provides a good index of analysing poverty (Sen 1985). The volatility of the price series rather than gradual changes provides a good measure of economic uncertainty. Both sharp price hikes and sudden falls meant increased economic uncertainty.

Economic uncertainty is suggested also by All India studies which show that the smallest cultivators, after selling a significant part of their output on the market became net buyers of food grains. Notably, the findings of the All-India Credit Survey and the National Sample Survey of 1954-55 suggest that for the period from the 1930s to the late 1950s, the average operated holding was inadequate for subsistence (India Cabinet Secretariat 1955). In another important study, of the distribution of marketed surplus of agricultural produce by size-level holding in India, Dharm Narain demonstrated that the smallest producers sold a disproportionately large part of their output, and often did not have enough to eat (Narain 1961: 36-37). A similar conclusion was reached by the All India Rural Credit Survey which estimated that about 35 per cent of the total production is sold by the cultivator (Reserve Bank of India 1955: 23). Some districts such as Malabar were chronically deficient in food and were net importers of the staple food grain for the entire period of this study.

To get back to our sample districts, in the first three decades after independence we see that the volatility of prices, which is captured by the coefficient of variation, was much greater for 'dry' crops as opposed to 'wet' crops.[25] Prices of both 'dry' and 'wet' crops registered a secular increase in the first three decades since 1956. All the districts displayed a marked spike in prices in 1974-75. The 'dry' districts of Anantapur, Kurnool and Bellary and to a much lesser extent, South Canara showed another earlier spike in 1965, which was much less extreme than the 1974 increase.

While cereal product prices moved up, the real wage series for this period shows interesting changes in direction and variation across districts. The real wage series has been computed by deflating the nominal male agricultural labour wages by the price of rice in the 'wet' districts and the average price of 'dry' cereals in the 'dry' districts. In keeping with all-India trends, we find a fairly sharp decline in real wages in the 'dry' districts till 1974 and a strong upward trend since then to 1986. The 'wet' districts on the whole show a much more stable trend. Krishna and South Canara register a marked upward drift in real wages post 1974. Thanjavur, on the other hand, is marked by a near stationary curve. Coimbatore, Madurai and Salem largely share the characteristics of the 'dry' and 'wet' districts depending on whether we use 'dry' crops or rice as the deflator. In short, what we see in the post-Independence decades is a definitely pervasive pattern of agricultural growth. Despite the general upward trend, however, the old inter-regional disparities stubbornly continued. This is seen in the fact that output per hectare was much lower in the 'dry' districts compared to the 'wet'. The late sixties mark the point from where a stronger upward trend becomes clear.

Regional Histories

The 'dry' and 'wet' agro-economic regions can be distinguished from each other in terms of climatic conditions, cropping patterns, concentration of land control, occupational structure and work force characteristics, and the degree of stability in economic and demographic indices. Related to these economic and ecological differences are social variations relating to caste, female autonomy, marriage practices and passage to modernity. We first broadly sketch out regional histories, and then sum up the salient features of these historical developments. In doing so, we contrast the dry regions with the wet regions.

The Dry Deccan

The 'dry' Deccan districts, located in modern Andhra Pradesh and Karnataka, apart from possessing a regional unity, constituted the 'Ceded Districts'. Bellary and Cuddapah districts were ceded to the East India Company by the Hyderabad Nizam for the maintenance in perpetuity of the Hyderabad

FIGURE 3: Real Wages by District, 1956-1988

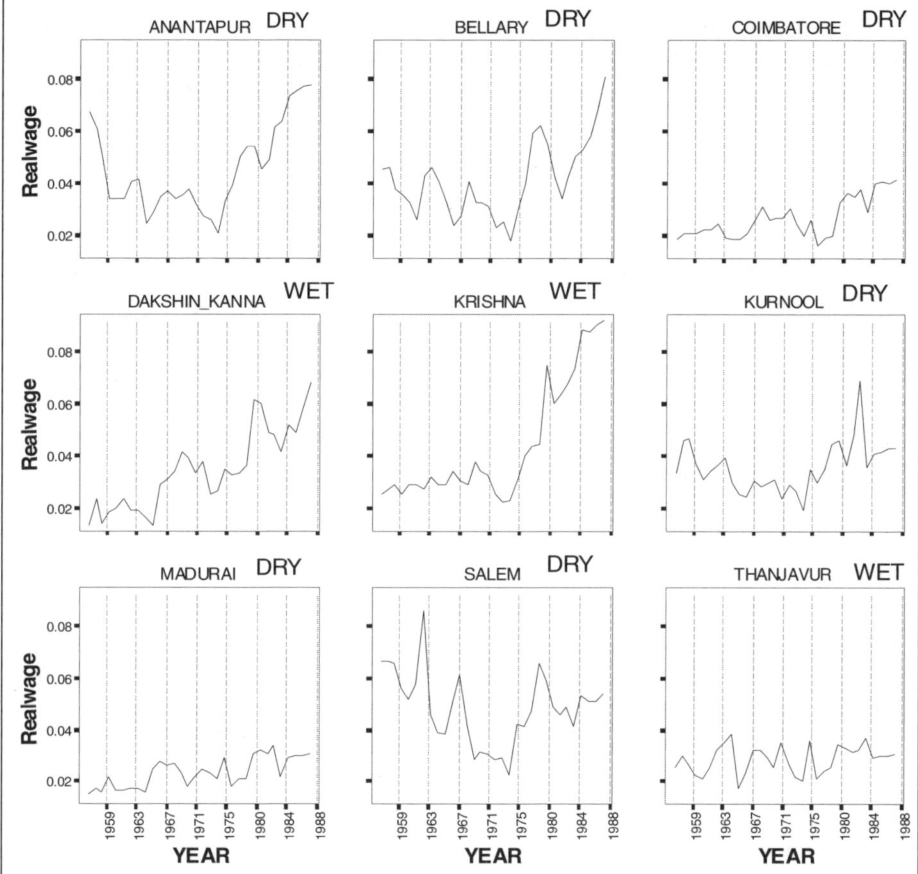

subsidiary force, while Kurnool was formally taken over in 1839. The early Ryotwari Settlement in the Ceded Districts resulted in a heavy land revenue burden. It was commented that most farmers in Bellary were 'if not annual bankrupts, at least annual applicants for remission' (Rajasekhar 1988: 11) According to Nilamani Mukherjee 'Poverty prevented the ryot from making the land productive and the high assessment deprived him of the fruits of his labour' (Mukherjee 1962:259).

The ceded districts (with the exception of Bellary, which was transferred to Mysore State) also form the majority of the Rayalaseema region of Andhra Pradesh.[26] Various observers have commented on the higher wage rates in the famine prone Rayalaseema districts compared to the more prosperous and labour abundant coastal districts of Andhra. Famine deaths (which were quite frequent) and out-migration of labour combined to deplete the numbers of labourers and increase the wage level (Rao 1981; Kumar 1965).

The changes in the cropping pattern in the 'dry' Ceded Districts that took place in the course of the early twentieth century in a bid to increase the means of subsistence was nothing less than a gamble with death. Pulses and other cereals declined and cotton increased (Rajasekhar and Rao 1991:13). In Bellary, the area devoted to cotton increased from 14 per cent in 1901 to 27 per cent in 1921 while the area under all food crops declined from 77 to 65 per cent (Rajasekhar 1988: 17). Both the area and average yield of the cotton crop declined from 7.4 per cent of the net cropped area in 1955-56 to 2.7 per cent in 1975-76, largely caused by the vagaries of the monsoon (Rajasekhar 1988: 35-36). From the late seventies and early eighties, however, the agrarian economy showed definite signs of growth in output as well as a decrease in inequality.

Observers such as Bruce Robert and Dharma Kumar have argued for a largely unchanging level of inequality in landholding across the colonial period. However, a detailed study of a single village in Rayalaseema disputes this in favour of an increase in skewedness. Our data at the district level also supports an increase in inequality.[27] Until the 20th century, the Brahmins and the Reddies were the chief landholding castes, with the intermediate castes of Yadavas and Valmikis working as smaller cultivators and agricultural labourers. In the course of the first half of the twentieth century, however, the Brahmins appear to have retreated from agriculture, faced with the problem of labour shortages, high wages and taxation - Brahmin dominance was diluted, with gains being made by non-Brahmins and Muslims, who also engaged in money lending (Sayana 1952:21).

In the period 1948 to 1956, large landholders in Rayalaseema region like their counterparts in coastal Andhra (albeit to a smaller extent) started alienating land, fearing impending land reforms by a the growing communist movement. In 1956, the Andhra Cultivating Tenants' Protection Act was passed, followed by the Andhra Pradesh Ceiling Act in 1961. In the post-land reforms period, the principal gainers were the Valmiki caste, who advanced at the expense of the non-Brahmin elite as well as the Harijans and the Muslims. Nonetheless, unlike in the earlier colonial period, the concentration in land distribution in the years from 1948 to 1982 is seen to have been largely constant (Rajasekhar 1988: 24).

Coastal Andhra (a 'Wet' Region)

The coastal belt of Andhra Pradesh was clearly more fortunate, both in terms of natural endowments as well as State sponsored investments. The development of the Krishna-Godavari canal systems and the fast pace of commercialisation distinguished this region from its less fortunate northern and eastern neighbours. The in-migration of landless labour from the north greatly speeded up the proletarianisation of the work force, while, unlike in other parts of the peninsula, nascent capitalism was being nurtured by a relatively independent peasantry rather than a small group of ritually and economically superior landlord elite (Rajasekhar and Rao 1991 : 5). The dominant peasants of this region such as the Kammas, Kapus, Khatriyas and Telagas also practised the *gosha* taboo, which prevented their women folk from participating in field labour.

In the years between the influenza epidemic of 1918 and 1925, grain prices sharply increased and the profits from rice cultivation grew. However, 1925 saw the beginnings of the downturn in commodity prices, which finally culminated in the Great Depression. Prices began to fall without a proportional decline in wages, squeezing small farmers out of land. In general, agricultural workers did better with their wages falling less rapidly than the price of their basic consumables (Sathyanathan 1935:31). With the fall of Burma to the Japanese, refugee capital flooded southern India and land and product prices spiralled till the imposition of controls in 1943.

Brahmins and Panchamas or Harijans appear to have been the most adversely affected caste groups. Reddies and Kammas - dominant peasants, emerged as the net gainers as the Depression lifted and gave way to the period of wartime inflation. We find an increasing influence of the Reddies and Kammas in the years since the Depression. The Reddies supported the Congress while the Kammas were largely aligned with the Communist Party of India. These groups played a major role in the abolition of zamindari through their participation in the kisan movement, finally acquiring some of the most fertile lands. It was only in late 1970s and the early 80s that there emerged an educated peasant middle class from the castes such as Kapu, Padmashali (weaver), Gouda (toddy tapper), Golla and Kurma (shepherds), as a result of State sponsored development policies (Srinivasulu 2002:21).

The Kaveri Delta (a Wet Region)

We now move further down the Coromandel coast to the Kaveri delta in Tamil Nadu. Tanjore, or Thanjavur as it is now called (Figure 2A), was located on the delta of the Kaveri and given to rice cultivation based on extensive irrigation from as early as the ninth century (Schendel 1991: 45). Caste and class neatly overlapped to distinguish the ritually superior *mirasidars,* largely Brahmins landlords, from the untouchable Adi-Dravida landless and poor farmers. Between the mirasidar and the agrestic serf (*adimai*) were intermediary cultivators. This group was divided into *ulkudi* and *porakudi* depending on whether they had hereditary rights or were mere tenants-at-will. The latter were distinguished from the agrestic serfs by their ownership of agricultural implements and their placement above the untouchables in the caste hierarchy. As in Malabar (which is discussed below) when the British introduced the *ryotwari* system here, the *mirasidar* was conveniently substituted for the actual cultivator or the *raiyat*. Western Tanjore sustained the classical exploitative relationship between *mirasidar* and agrestic serf, but in the less fertile east the relatively lower caste status of the *mirasidar* appears to have permitted inequities to be less pronounced than in the west. As in Malabar, the initially close support given to the *mirasidar* by the new State gradually got diluted by the end of the nineteenth century.

Rice and labour developed as the major exports of Tanjore in the middle of the nineteenth century. According to Kathleen Gough, labour out-migration depleted up to 20 per cent of the male workers, and a smaller number of female workers from the economy of the Kaveri delta (Gough 1981: 131). If this is indeed true, spousal separation would be significant in explaining the low fertility patterns observed in Tanjore.

By the turn of the century, as cheap Burmese rice inundated the south Indian market, the Tanjore *mirasidar* suffered. Retreating into rentier absenteeism and forging links with the urban job market were the preferred escape routes. To make matters worse, the Depression was devastating in its impact. The price collapse ruined the rice trade and the more or less simultaneous closing of labour markets spelt virtual doom for the agrestic labourer. Resistance soon developed, first in the east, where *mirasi* control weakened earlier. This was soon spearheaded, among others, by the Communist Party of India. As in Andhra, in the 1952 elections the CPI emerged as the second largest party in the region. Between Independence and the 1980s, though, the real wages of agricultural labour did not register a marked increase. However, Tanjore was fortunate in receiving crucial technology throughout its history. The Kaveri-Mettur irrigation scheme added a new delta in the eastern region. After 1965 under the Intensive Agricultural Development Programme (IADP) HYVs, artificial fertilisers and credit were introduced. HYVs soon became all pervasive. Though moderate in relation to the North of the country, this technological infusion appears to have borne results.[28]

Mirasidar control progressively declined and State intervention grew rapidly in the post-colonial period. Though there was no industrialisation, the tertiary sector did greatly develop.

Malabar (a Wet Region)

Crossing across the southern peninsula to Malabar district on the southwest coast, we find a region which bears an uncanny resemblance to Tanjore in terms of land relations and caste configurations.

Malabar's landholding structure, in contrast to the 'dry' districts of the Presidency, had been characterised by the continued dominance of large landholders. Small *pattas* under Rs10, medium *pattas* between Rs. 10 and Rs. 50 and large *pattas* of over Rs. 100 accounted for roughly 15, 21 and 24 percent of the cultivated area in 1904-05 (Schendel 1991). Nonetheless, despite the continued dominance of large holdings, from the 1920s, we find a trend towards easier access to land as suggested by the population to *patta* ratios. Small farm proliferation and some disengagement of large holders especially from 'wet' cultivation are evident in the course of the 20th century.

Population to Patta Ratio, Malabar, 1891-1951

Year	**1891**	**1904**	**1911**	**1921**	**1936**	**1941**	**1951**
Ratio	12.7	14.6	15.5	14.1	14.5	09.1	10.7

Source: Rent Rolls and Census.

The old British district of Malabar constitutes the northern and less developed half of the modern state of Kerala. By the Treaty of Seringapatam (1792), Malabar was ceded to the East India Company. The early colonial period saw Malabar being economically more closely integrated with the rest of the Madras Presidency. Malabar's recovery from the 1930s depression and the subsequent secular rise in agricultural product prices significantly contributed to a changed configuration of agrarian class power. Socially and economically powerful groups in the countryside greatly benefited from the new economic political situation at the cost of the weaker rent paying tenants and sub-tenants. This was facilitated by the juridical tenurial rights established by the British at the beginning of the century. The period saw a marked increase in litigation connected with land control and rent enhancements [Madras, #313@para 259].

While on the one hand, we find increasing inequality in the distribution of holdings and a significant increase in dwarf holdings, on the other, certain apparently small but significant tendencies appear to have been at work. As prices and productivity increased throughout the late nineteenth century up to the second decade of the twentieth century, all classes tried to maximise their share in the increased returns leading to a sharpening of conflict. In this context, the late nineteenth and early twentieth century witnessed recurrent violence by the Mapillas who were predominantly poor tenant farmers. British officials vigorously debated on the nature of the Mapilla 'outrages', attributing varying significance to agrarian discontent, poverty and fanaticism.

The first attempt at State intervention in agrarian relations in Malabar after their initial tenurial redefinitions was the Malabar Compensation for Tenants'

Improvement Act of 1887. This act was aimed to secure to tenants the full market value of the improvements made by them from the landlords at the time of eviction, and to check increasing evictions. The next phase of tenancy reform, especially in the post Mappilla Revolt period, was spearheaded by the Western educated and relatively well off *kanamdars*. The tenancy question became a major demand in all varieties of political activity after 1900. Finally, in December 1930, the Malabar Tenancy Act XIV came into force virtually conceding all the demands of the *kanamdars*. However, the Act did not benefit the poorer *verumpattom* tenants who were in most cases the actual cultivators of the soil. The interests of this section of the peasantry was taken up in the post-1930 period, under left wing leadership which went on to initiate wide ranging radical reforms in independent Kerala.

Small farm proliferation occurred not during the boom years of the late nineteenth and early twentieth century, but after agricultural prices started falling in the late 1920s as part of the onset of the great Depression. It was a time when the sharp increase in land revenue demand at the time of the Resettlement further lowered the already falling returns from agriculture. The Depression was marked by some disengagement of large holders from 'wet' cultivation, easier access to land, and militant organised peasant resistance to landlordism. Combined with this, the break-up of large Nayar *taravads* also contributed to the decline of landlordism, though not to a very significant extent in the Malabar region

Between 1911 and 1951, the composition of agrarian classes changed substantially. The number of 'Cultivating Landowners' sharply increased at the cost of 'Tenants' and 'Rent Receivers'. 'Agricultural Labour' showed a small increase. The phenomenon may be explained as a cumulative result of land reforms, the partitioning of Nayar *taravads*, increased tenant resistance to landlord rack-renting, and the move away from the agricultural sector into services by many of the erstwhile rent receivers. Thus we see clear evidence of a battle between different agrarian groups over the now increased returns from agriculture. The litigation, which mainly involved janmi-kanamdar problems, declined all over Malabar from 1933 onwards when the Depression began to take effect.

In the years after Independence, Kerala's economic history followed its earlier trajectory, though with one very crucial difference - a marked and unprecedented shift towards greater redistribution, with its correlate of increasing the exchange entitlements of the poor. The intensive and sustained progressive redistributive and social security policies followed by the State greatly improved the quality of life in the State. After the CPI came to power in the state in 1957, it passed the Agrarian Relations Act of 1960. However, the CPI government was dismissed by the Centre and a diluted version of its original act was finally implemented as the Kerala Land Reforms Act in 1970 by the Congress government. Notably, the concentration of operational holdings declined, with the Gini coefficient estimated to have gone down from 0.6316 in 1970-71 to 0.6077 in 1980-81 (Oommen 1994: 124). The abolition of landlordism was not however accompanied either by an increasing trend in output or productivity, but it did nonetheless provide to security to the poor, by investing them with ownership rights over their homesteads (Oommen 1994: 134). One significant spin off of progressive political milieu has been the greater participation and therefore empowerment of the people in relation to the political and developmental process. Notably, there are also other two sectors with respect to which Kerala has forged way ahead of the rest of the country, i.e., education and health.

Kongunad (a Dry Region)

The region of Kongunad included large parts of Coimbatore districts and smaller contiguous areas of Salem and Madurai (Baker 1984 - Map 2).[29] Kongunad or the 'dry' interior of the southern peninsula shows a marked difference in both agrarian structure and growth trajectory from the Tanjore in the east and Malabar to its west. In sharp opposition to the ritual caste based hierarchy of land control in the Kaveri delta, the upland plains of Kongunad were organised on a 'military style hierarchy which was buttressed not so much by ritual exclusiveness (although this was of course not absent) but by kinship rules and pyramidal systems of patronage and redistribution' (Baker 1984: 52-53). The dominant majority caste was that of the Vellalalas, known in Coimbatore as the Gounders. Their religious pantheon was peopled by local gods such as Murugan and more distantly, by the Vedic deities.

As it interacted with the valley, this region adapted and changed rapidly. Warfare and commerce were major growth industries in the early period. Though a 'dry' region with scanty rainfall, the presence of three tributaries of the Kaveri assured the presence of plentiful subsoil reserves of water. This was complemented by considerable fertile black and red soils. Further, its location in the middle of east-west routes, between the settled kingdoms to its northwest, west and east made it a buffer zone politically.

The significance of deep well irrigation, unlike the more corporate canal irrigation of the Kaveri delta, encouraged decentralised control. The entrepreneurial individual farmer rapidly expanded cultivation in the course of early colonial rule, leaving the less fertile tracts for cattle rearing. Early agriculture was dominated by the cultivation of 'dry' cereals (especially *cumbu*), and the export of the region's highly valued cattle by the Gounder owner-cultivators.

The farmers here found it easy to shift to commercial crops, namely cotton, in the years since the American Civil War. Cotton was soon joined by other lucrative crops such as tobacco and sugarcane. This continuous expansion of commercial agriculture continued, and by the 1950s, Coimbatore had the largest proportion of its total area (around 20 per cent) devoted to cash crops (Baker 1984: 207). The Depression had adverse effects here as elsewhere, but the scale of disruption was much less. Though iniquitous in the distribution of resources, 'the great majority of holdings was close to the optimal level of five to ten acres' (Baker 1984: 213).

One result of the Depression in Coimbatore was the migration of rural landed capital into the more profitable area of a small-scale industry geared to local consumer demand. As the towns grew in the 1940s with an increased out-migration from declining agriculture, the demand for these small industries went up. Thus in this region we see nascent industrial capital being generated from within the agrarian economy rather than being injected from elsewhere.

The Broad Patterns

To conclude this section, what we see, in many ways, is an essential continuity in the agrarian economy of south India from the Depression to post-colonial times. The most important change is the intensity of State intervention, which began in a very rudimentary way at the end of the nineteenth century and accelerated since the Depression to reach unprecedented levels in the post independence years. The very 'dry' Deccan, with neither a strong tradition of egalitarianism or significant popular movements that aimed at greater social and economic equity, gained the least. On the other hand, the growing political strength of the ritually subordinate dominant peasant groups in prosperous districts such as Krishna and Kaveri helped a much larger middle peasant groups to get empowered. The 'wet' districts of Tanjore and more specially, Malabar, continued with their earlier aggregate economic trends but the strength of the popular movements under the Left ensured the poor a greater role in government and development.

Demographic Trajectories

Though the regions studied above in terms of their historical trajectories neither overlap exactly nor cover all the census divisions, they do provide a dynamic social and historical context against which we can plot our demographic maps and curves with the hope of discovering some synergistic mechanisms.

The Deccan's Deadly Demography

As we have seen, the northern most set of districts in the old Madras

Presidency were located in the very dry Deccan plateau. We have selected three districts from this region - Bellary, Anantapur and Kurnool, now located in the modern Indian States of Karnataka and Andhra Pradesh.

Figures 4 and 5, which trace the birth and death rates for Bellary and Kurnool, show that fertility movements were closely related to mortality, especially in the years before the mortality transition.

FIGURE 4: Corrected CBRs & CDRs, Bellary, 1881-1981

FIGURE 5: Corrected CBR and CDR - Kurnool, 1881-1981

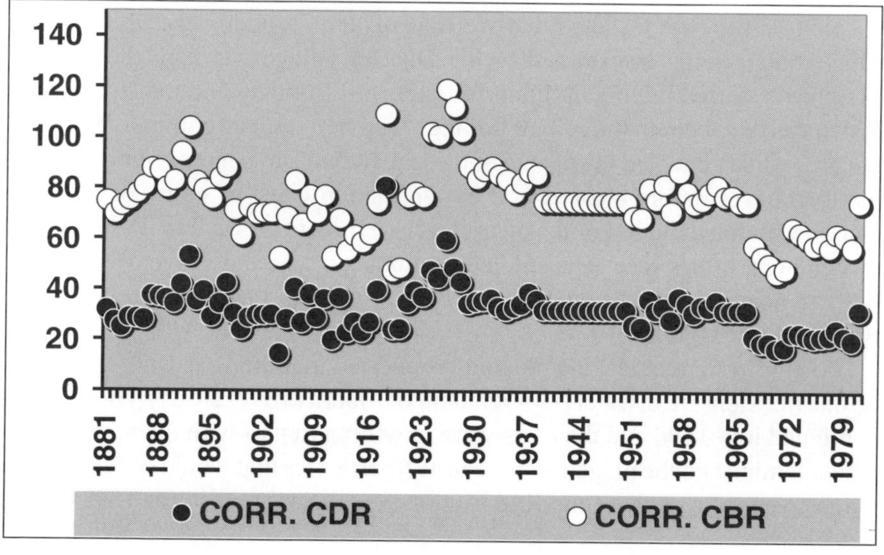

In this section we try to explain the historical events that moved the mortality and fertility curves up and down while sustaining very high mean levels in the Deccan districts.

The decade of the 1880s was one of recovery after the catastrophic famine of 1876-78. However, even this relatively benign phase was punctuated by sharp mortality hikes in the Deccan, in 1891-92 and then in 1896-97 (Figure 4 and Figure 5). Erratic monsoons and lethal epidemics that constantly preyed on a debilitated population explained the mortality fluctuations of the Deccan. Added to this was the role of the merchant, by now extending his area of operation in a context of increasing agrarian commercialisation; by purchasing grains from the region for transportation elsewhere, he contributed to local shortages and rising prices. When the fear of an impending famine became acute or when mortality peaked to excessive levels, fertility fell. Fertility decline was linked either to deferred marriages or the reduced fecundity that resulted from hunger.

The 1892 crisis also brought down fertility sharply. The Sanitary Commissioner commented that this fall cannot be ascribed merely to poor registration and 'must be regarded as a result of the distress, which prevailed in the Presidency during 1891 and 1892. It is an admitted fact that the fecundity of a population is directly dependent on, and largely influenced by, the general prosperity … and the high prices of articles of food and their insufficiency in quantity and inferiority in quality even when not carried to the extent of starvation and famine have a decided effect in lowering the birth rate' (Government of Madras. 1892: 16). The severity of the situation forced the government to open relief camps in the Deccan districts of Anantapur, Bellary and Kurnool.

1896 is the first instance that we find of famine prices elsewhere in the subcontinent being transmitted to the Deccan villages through the market. Merchants started buying up grain for export to Bombay and the North West Provinces that were in the grip of famine. 'The free railway communication of the present day enabled the agents of these merchants to penetrate into villages that had never before been visited by any one in quest of grain, beyond the *sowcars* [moneylenders] of the district' (Government of Madras. 1896: 17). In this context, prices rose. The southwest monsoon was above average in 1897 but the northeast monsoon was deficient, with the result that food prices remained at a high level.

To aggravate matters, astrologers prophesied that the year 1898-99 would be one of extensive disaster (Government of Madras 1897: 24-25). High prices continued into 1898 and the ryots were unwilling to part with their grain. The recent famine and the plague were seen as forerunners that would occur 'during the last year of a cycle of the Kali Yuga—the 'Vikari' (evil) year 1899-1900'

(Government of Madras. 1906: 2). The foreboding of evil times and the existing state of dearth led to a postponement of marriages and a pronounced fall in the birth rate in 1898. The Sanitary Commissioner commented: '…there is reason to presume that marriages have been deferred during the last three years, as far as possible, that is to say, as far as the caste custom directing the marriage of a female within a certain age will allow, because evil times have been prophesied' (Government of Madras. 1900: 2).

The next major mortality crisis was the influenza epidemic of 1918, which stands out as the deadliest killer of the twentieth century in southern India. The epidemic affected all the districts of the Madras Presidency, and the Deccan was no exception. However, the lethality of epidemic should be seen not only in terms of the virulence of the virus but also in the context of the worsening economic and epidemiological conditions of the War years.

In 1914, though prices remained stable and the season was favourable, mortality increased in Kurnool and Bellary because of cholera and fevers. Further, all three of our Deccan districts were hit by an increased incidence of epidemics. The unfavourable nature of the season in 1916 and the consequent rise in prices worsened with the failure of both monsoons in 1917. To add to Bellary's woes, the district was visited by a severe form of plague throughout the year. The rise in mortality was conspicuous in Bellary, Anantapur and Kurnool. Then in 1918 the flu struck the Deccan districts that were once again experiencing scanty rainfall. The birth rate, which had been falling in Bellary since 1916, continued on its downward course reaching its nadir in 1919, before embarking on a course of recovery.

In the period from 1881 to 1914 we see the natural rate of increase of Bellary's population exhibiting a secular decrease with the birth rate and the death rate trends converging in 1914. After 1914, excluding the excess mortality of 1918, the Deccan districts did not experience excess mortality. Mortality levels however remained high from the mid 1920s to the early 1940s with intermittent falls.

Located on the northern rim of the Madras Presidency, 'Bellary district [was] constantly exposed to infection from Hyderabad, Bombay and Mysore, but usually the disease becomes really serious only in the months of May and June. The Hampi festival contributed to the danger… of cholera. Probably the great increase in the incidence of cholera during the 1924 may be partly attributed to the drought and famine conditions….' (Government of Madras. 1924: 11). Subsequent mortality spikes in the graphs for the Deccan districts were caused by plague outbreaks and malarial epidemics.

The quotations from the Sanitary Commissioners' reports in the above narrative clearly demonstrate the unfailing regularity with which climate, market and disease combined to produce a dangerously volatile demographic regime, pushing up mortality while driving down fertility in the short-run. However, though the Deccan's demography was extremely unstable initially, after 1921, mortality fluctuations decreased markedly.

From the preceding discussion of the Deccan's frequent mortality spikes and its close connection with dearth and disease, the region's demography appears NOT to have been entirely governed by the Malthusian 'positive check'. Malthus, it will be recalled, had postulated that population tends to grow indefinitely till it is checked, by either the 'positive check' or the preventive check. The positive check refers to mortality increasing events whereas the preventive check pertains, in Malthusian terms, to fertility reduction through the postponement of marriage or increase in spinsterhood. Malthus saw these two checks as mutually exclusive but we find evidence of both working together in pre-mortality transition Deccan; the lethality and the associated high volatility of the pre-mortality transition regime seems to have held in check both nuptiality and fertility. Though less dramatic than sharp hikes in deaths, nuptiality played an important role in regulating the region's fertility. Thus we see that the Deccan registered relatively low proportions of married women compared with the other Census Divisions of the Presidency. (The low proportions married might be related to the relatively (relative to the country as a whole) not too early age at first marriage and the large proportions of widowed women. The only other Division that had lower proportions married was the West Madras Division (Figure 6), which was sociologically very different, with a dominant presence of matrilineal inheritance. The preventive check worked both through a relatively high age at marriage and a high incidence of widowhood, thereby

FIGURE 6: Married Females per 1000 Females, Madras Presidency, 1921-1951

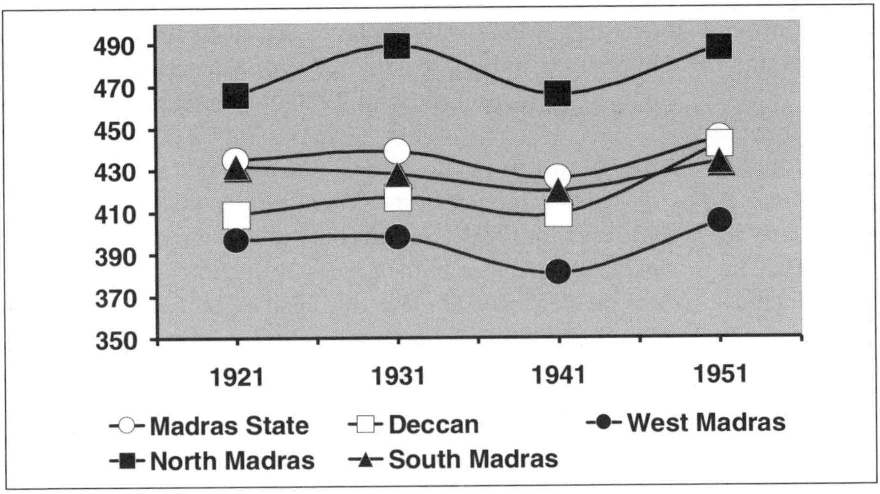

Source: Census of India (1951, Madras, Volume 1: 186-187).

reducing the female population at the risk of conception. Thus the Deccan districts provide an interesting instance where the simple Malthusian model moving from the positive to the preventive check needs to be qualified.

As Table 4 below shows, widowhood sharply declined from very high levels after 1931. In the initial period, both checks operated, preventive and positive, but later, when the positive check declined, the preventive check became more salient. The Coale index of marriage (I_m) showed an upward trend from 1881 to 1981, the fertility indices (I_f and I_g) registered a downward drift after 1941. After 1941, fertility declines occurred within marriage.

TABLE 4: Coale Fertility Indices, SMAM and Percentage Widowed, Bellary District, 1891-1981

Year	I_m	I_f	I_g	Widowed	SMAMm	SMAMf
1891	0.667	0.33	0.496	31.45	24.94	16.34
1901	0.767	0.449	0.585	21.37	23.02	16.03
1911	0.559	0.249	0.446	18.86	18.85	12.32
1921	0.734	0.411	0.56	24.68	24.00	16.17
1931	0.75	0.336	0.447	45.86	23.04	16.13
1941	0.767	0.505	0.658	20.29	23.43	16.73
1951	0.649	0.315	0.486	12.23	28.29	21.80
1961	0.846	0.383	0.453	12.17	24.41	16.52
1971	0.711	0.315	0.444	9.34	26.40	21.62
1981	0.846	0.429	0.508	7.38	24.83	18.12

Note: I_m, I_f and I_g refer to Coale's Indices of marriage, fertility and marital fertility respectively.

Widowed: Per cent of widowed women to total female population between ages 15 and 49.

Source: Based on Censuses of India.

The Demography of the Wet Zones

We now move to the next set of our study districts, which are representative of the 'wet' ecozone. These 'wet' districts, the polar opposite of the dry Deccan, were characterised by stable and regular rainfall, predominance of 'wet' paddy cultivation, and very steep social and economic class profiles. We take the old Malabar district of Madras Presidency (which now forms the northern part of Kerala state), Tanjore (now called Thanjavur) district, on the mouth of the Kaveri delta in Tamil Nadu, Kistna or Krishna as it is now called, on the Krishna delta in Andhra Pradesh, and the old South Kanara district of Madras, adjoining Malabar to its north on the western coast, presently constituting the Dakshin Kannada district of Karnataka State (Figure 2A). Malabar and Tanjore, located on the southwest and southeast coasts of the peninsula, despite the geographical distance between them, shared much more in terms of social, economic and demographic features, as compared to Malabar's immediate northern neighbour,

South Kanara.

Figures 7, 8 and 9 record the movement of the corrected crude birth and death rates in these three 'wet' districts. Compared to the Deccan districts, we find that the years of excess mortality were few and far between in the 'wet' zone. Mortality here appears to have had a lesser ability to dampen fertility.

FIGURE 7: Corrected CBR and CDR- Tanjore

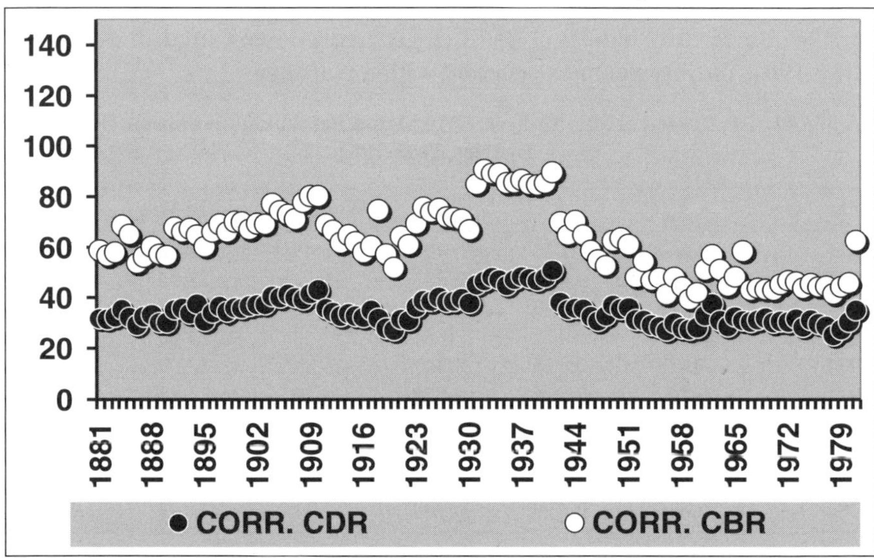

FIGURE 8: Corrected CDR, CBR and CWR, Malabar, 1881-1981

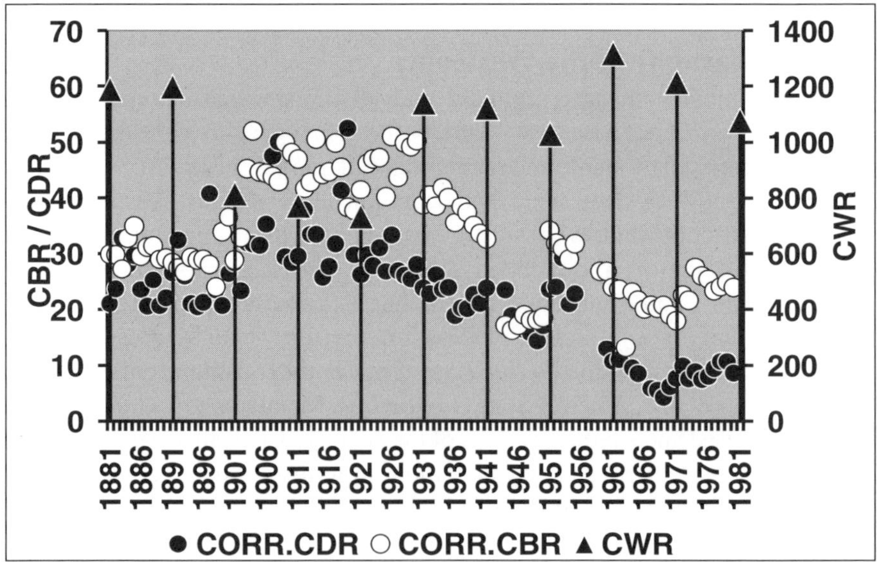

FIGURE 9: Krishna-Corrected CBR, CDR AND CWR

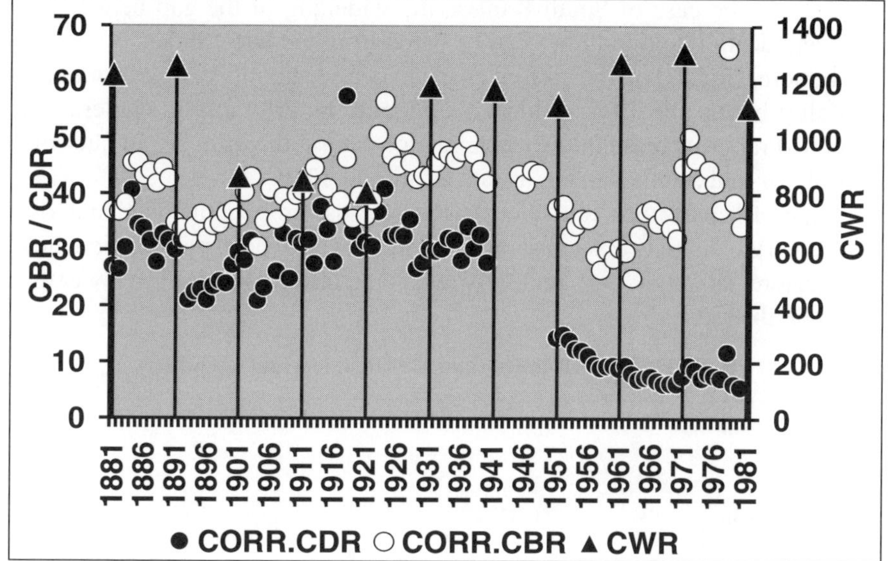

Cholera, smallpox, dysentery, diarrhoea and fever were the major killers in the 'wet' districts. The Sanitary Commissioner noted, 'the wetter the year the higher the fever mortality'. In South Kanara, mortality peaked in January, while in Malabar, it was July that claimed the most lives. In all other districts, December was the unhealthiest month (Government of Madras 1888: 16). Occasionally, as in 1924, floods also contributed to mortality hikes. Many of these years of mortality increases were accompanied by increased prices. This suggests the combination of economic distress and diseases in worsening the well being of the population. Likewise, the flu epidemic of 1918 and the cholera epidemic in Malabar and South Kanara in 1919 occurred at a time of increased post-War economic distress marked by unusually high prices.

Of the four 'wet' districts, Malabar had the maximum number of excess mortality years when the death rate exceeded the birth rate. The last year of excess mortality in Malabar was 1919. Unlike all the other districts of the Presidency, only Malabar and South Kanara registered higher mortality in 1919 than in the flu year of 1918. Fever was more widespread here in 1919 and this, coupled with increased deaths from dysentery and diarrhoea, pushed up mortality levels (Government of Madras 1919: 2).

Malabar's northern neighbour, South Kanara, displayed a much less lethal mortality regime. Unlike Malabar, South Kanara only experienced one year of excess mortality in 1890, in the period before 1919. Fevers and deaths from 'all other causes' had pushed up deaths in 1890 (Government of Madras 1890:2). In the case of South Kanara, the widening of the gap between the birth and death rate trend lines can be dated from the late 1890s.

Tanjore, situated on the eastern coast, experienced only one year of excess mortality before the 1918 influenza epidemic, in 1884 due to cholera. The sustained rapid increase in the crude rate of natural increase began later than in Malabar and South Kanara, as late as around 1918.

Figure 10 charts the Child-Woman Ratio across time for the 'wet' and 'dry' districts. Two districts that are somewhat outliers have been plotted separately. Coimbatore, although 'dry', regularly registered fertility levels even lower than the 'wet' districts.

FIGURE 10: CWR in Dry and Wet Districts and in Outliers

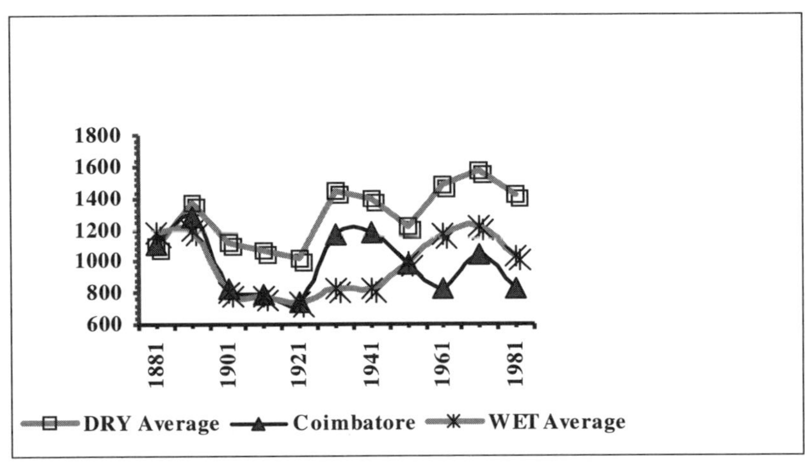

Except for the early years of the 1880s, when the Deccan was just recovering from the murderous famine of 1876-78, the 'dry' region consistently registered higher Child-Woman Ratios than the 'wet' regions. If one were to make adjustments for the higher infant and child mortality in the 'dry' regions, then these districts would return even higher CWRs than the 'wet' region. The 'dry-wet' differential in fertility showed a long-term increase, with the difference increasing very rapidly after 1951.

The above trends are for aggregated groups of 'wet' and 'dry' districts. Within each of these groups, individual districts, though conforming to the larger distinction, did exhibit variations that were related to district specific demographic and non-demographic determinants.

The single, major exception to this broad division on the basis of 'wet' and 'dry' eco-zones was Coimbatore district. Though 'dry' in terms of climate and agriculture, this district located between the southwest and southeast coasts.

We will return to explain the idiosyncratic demography of Coimbatore, when discussing the interior 'dry' districts.

Till the 1960s and 1970s, the demographic regime in southern India can safely be described as one characterised by 'natural fertility', with no significant level of illegitimate fertility. In such a scenario, fertility was a function of fecundity and the level of nuptiality, which in turn determined the proportion of the female population exposed to the risk of conception. We see also that figures for the proportion widowed are on the low side, in contrast to the corresponding figures for the dry zone.

The two maps below show the district-wise incidence of the widowed and the unmarried among women in the reproductive ages.

The incidence of unmarried women in the female population of reproductive age is primarily a function of the incidence of spinsterhood, widowhood and to a much smaller extent, age at first marriage. Excluding the Agency tracts in the extreme northeast of the Presidency, characterised by very uncertain demographic data collection, Malabar had the highest proportion of spinsters

FIGURE 11. Proportion of Unmarried Women Aged 15-49, Madras Presidency (Average of 1911 and 1931)

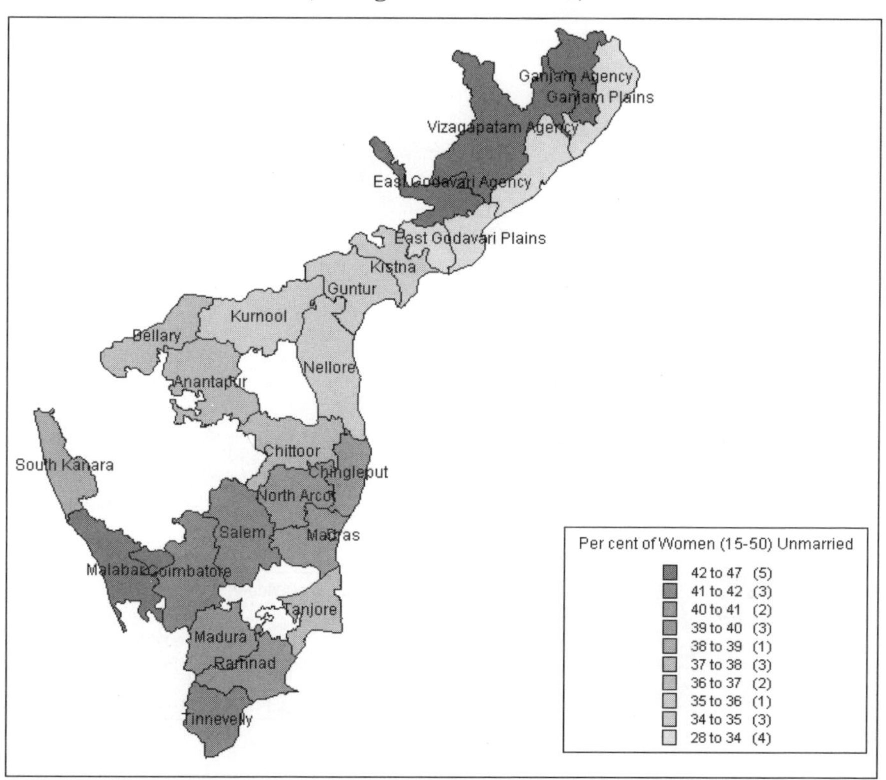

or never married women. One can discern a clearly marked corridor of districts with high proportions of unmarried women running northeast from Malabar to Madras. North and south of this corridor the proportions of unmarried women declined with the sole exception of Tinnevelly or Tirunelveli district at the extreme tip of the peninsula.[29]

The other related determinant of the proportion of married women is the incidence of widowhood in the population (see Figure 12). Widowhood in turn is the function of mortality and the strength of customs prohibiting remarriage. The high incidence of widowhood in the death prone Deccan is not surprising. Moderate mortality Malabar and South Kanara and Tanjore seem to have had a large proportion of widows as a result of the strength of the proscription of widow remarriage. Surprisingly, the famine prone interior districts of Madura and Salem registered very low levels of widowhood, possibly because of the weak hold of high Hinduism in the rural countryside.

FIGURE 12: Percentage of Widowed Women Aged 15-49, Madras Presidency, Average of 1911 and 1931

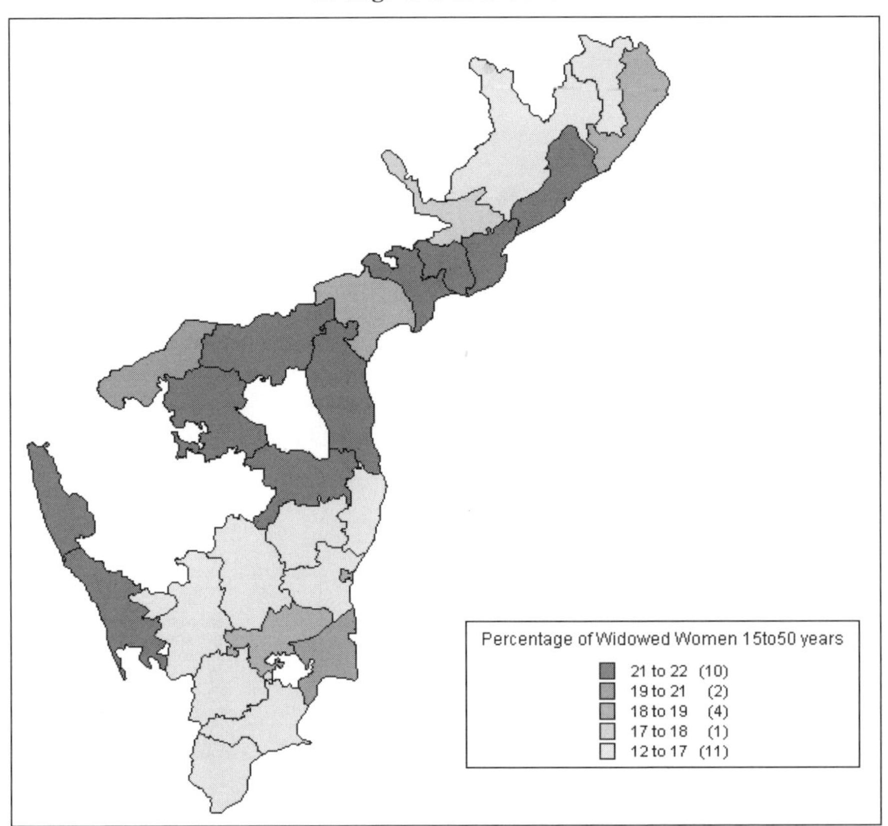

Thus we see the double incidence spinsterhood and widowhood had emerged as an important depressant of fertility.

The 'Dry' Interior

The 'dry' interior districts of the southern peninsula—Coimbatore, Madurai and Salem, form a third distinct demographic zone (Figure 2A). Located in the rain shadow of the Western Ghats, these districts were dependent on the vagaries of the monsoons. Though classified as 'famine districts', like the Deccan districts, these districts formed a demographic region exhibiting traits associated with both the 'dry' and 'wet' regions.

Figures 13, 14 and 15 show the corrected birth and death rates in each of these three districts. Years of excess mortality do not number more than three in any of these districts. Madura, Salem and Coimbatore experienced excess deaths only in three, one and two years respectively. All three districts showed an upward trend in births from 1881 to 1891, followed by a decline up to 1921, a rise until 1941, followed by a secular decline. This relatively benign demographic regime produced low marital fertility and total fertility, in accordance with the consensus in demographic analysis that high mortality regimes result in high fertility via the 'replacement' and 'hoarding' effects.

Demographers had in earlier discussions viewed pre-transitional populations as characterised by uncontrolled high fertility. Possibly influenced by this academic consensus, Louis Henry presented his concept of 'natural fertility'

FIGURE 13: Coimbatore CBR, CDR and CWR

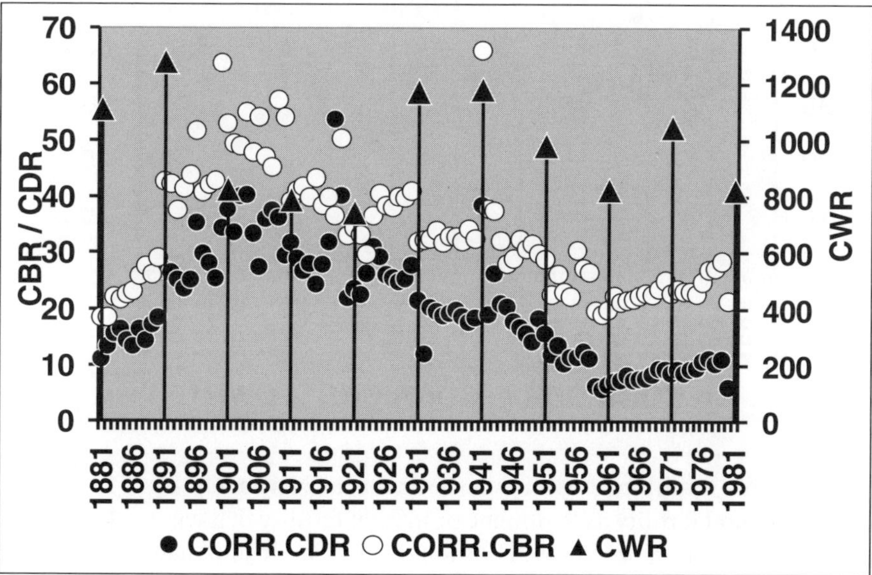

FIGURE 14: Madurai Corrected CBR, CDR and CWR

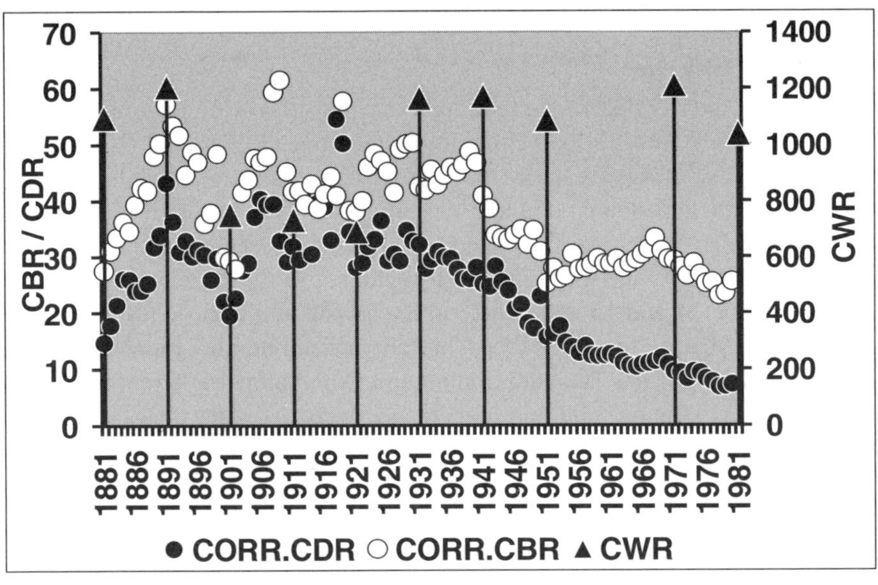

FIGURE 15: Salem CBR, CDR and CWR

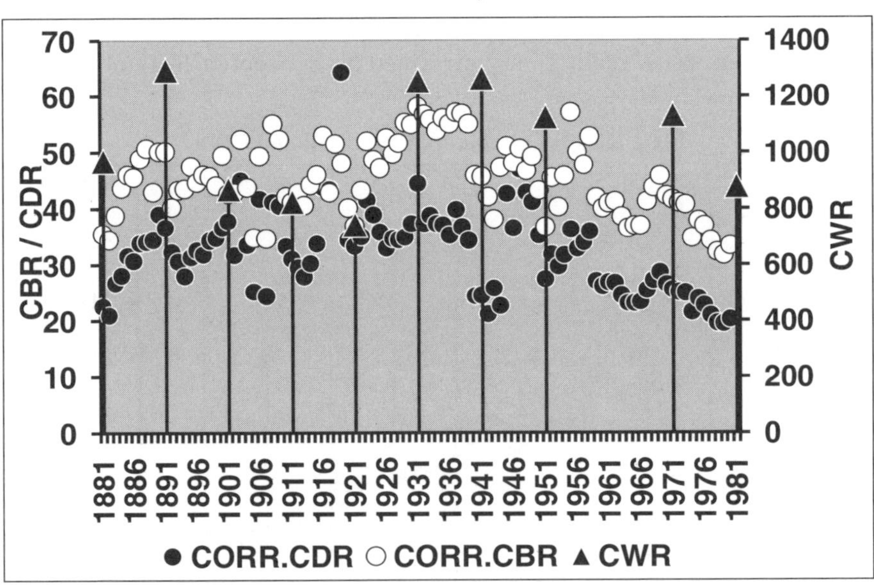

based on his family reconstitution of Crulai in Normandy in 1953. Henry defined natural fertility as legitimate or marital fertility that was unchecked by either contraception or induced abortion (Henry and Institut national d'etudes demographiques 1953). Subsequently, he further refined it to 'fertility in the absence of parity-dependent birth control or in the absence of behaviour to control births which is bound to the number of children already born and is modified when the number reaches the maximum which the couple does not want to exceed' (Henry 1961). There has been a large amount of work on the biological aspects of human fertility and the biological maximum is supposed to be fifteen live births per woman (Coale and Trussel 1974; Leridon 1977). However, even 'natural fertility' societies have experienced fertility levels much below this maximum. The conundrum is readily explained. The difference between total fertility and total fecundity in 'natural fertility' regimes can be explained largely by the 'exposure to risk' which is governed primarily by the length of sexual partnership, e.g. marriage, spousal separation, widowhood and lactational infecundability

Studies of natural fertility in India have estimated the natural fertility to be low in the pre-transitional period at six births per woman in the 1930s increasing to seven and nine in the 1970s and 1980s with improvements in healthcare (Iyer 2002: 171).[30]

Estimating the level of natural fertility in India for the historical period in terms of lactational infecundity, *post partum* amenohrrea, coital frequency, etc. is simply not possible in the absence of data. Assuming that that all births were legitimate and occurred within marriage, we use the Children per Married Women (CMWR) as a rough proxy index for natural fertility.

With an overwhelming majority of Indian men and women marrying and the relative insignificance of contraceptive use till the 1960s, Indian and southern Indian fertility can be assumed to fit Henry's natural fertility regime. Nuptiality then becomes the most significant proximate determinant of fertility. Nuptiality can be further broken down into age at first marriage and proportions married. Table 6 gives the estimates of average proportions single, married and widowed women in the reproductive ages across dry and wet districts and in the pre and post mortality decline periods. In both agro-economic regions the proportions single increased from the first period to the second period while the proportions married and widowed decreased.

The levels of nuptiality and the ratio of CWR to MCWR varied significantly across regions as seen in the Analysis of Variance (ANOVA) table below (Table 7). Widowhood however does not show significant variance across agro-economic zones, possibly due to differences in practices related to remarriage.

TABLE 6: Mean of Nuptiality Measures, Fertility Across Agro-Economic Zones and Time Periods

Nuptiality Variable	Agroeconomic Zone	Time Period	Mean
Per cent UF15-40	Dry	Pre-1931	7.80
	Dry	Post-1931	20.62
	Wet	Pre-1931	10.92
	Wet	Post-1931	31.04
Per cent MF15-40	Dry	Pre-1931	77.42
	Dry	Post-1931	76.91
	Wet	Pre-1931	75.29
	Wet	Post-1931	67.13
Per cent WF15-40	Dry	Pre-1931	14.78
	Dry	Post-1931	4.48
	Wet	Pre-1931	13.79
	Wet	Post-1931	3.55

Note: UF, MF, WF, denote Unmarried Females, Married Females and Widowed Females respectively The numbers following the variable refer to ages in years. Source: Census (various issues).

TABLE 7: One Way Anova: Nuptiality and Fertility Measures between "Dry" and "Wet" Agro-economic Zones

Nuptiality Variable	Agroeconomic Zone	Time Period	Mean
CWR0-9	Dry	Pre-1931	1298.67
	Dry	Post-1931	1304.30
	Wet	Pre-1931	1212.50
	Wet	Post-1931	1346.05
MCWR	Dry	Pre-1931	1671.03
	Dry	Post-1931	1637.77
	Wet	Pre-1931	1775.57
	Wet	Post-1931	1575.05
MCWR / CWR	Dry	Pre-1931	1.29
	Dry	Post-1931	1.27
	Wet	Pre-1931	1.51
	Wet	Post-1931	1.21

Nuptiality/Fertility Variable	Sum of Squares	F	Significance
Per cent UF15-40	383.688	5.703	0.020
Per cent MF15-40	208.695	9.116	0.004
Per cent WF15-40	26.11	0.659	0.420
CWR0-9	44644.57	1.423	0.238
MCWR	58166.81	1.592	0.212
MCWR_CWR	0.332	4.984	0.030

Note: See Table above for variable description. Source: Census (various issues)

Note: CWR, MCWR and MCWR_CWR denote Child Woman Ratio, CWR for Married Women, and MCWR/CWR, respectively. The numbers following the variable refer to age in years.

Source: Census (various issues).

TABLE 8: Correlation Matrix: Nuptiality Indicators, Region and Fertility, 1891-1981

Nuptiality/ Fertility	Correltion Statistics	Per cent UF15-40	Per cent MF15-40	Per cent WF15-40	CWR0-9	MCWR	MCWR _CWR	AGROECO
Per cent **UF15-40**	Pearson Correlation	1.000	-.354	-.623	-.002	-.052	-.056	.302
	Sig. (2-tailed)	.	.001	.000	.985	.658	.633	.020*
	N	84	84	84	84	76	76	59
Per cent MF15-40	Pearson Correlation	-.354	1.000	-.502	.300*	-.146	-.608	-.371
	Sig. (2-tailed)	.001	.	.000	.006	.207	.000	.004*
	N	84	84	84	84	76	76	59
Per cent WF15-40	Pearson Correlation	-.623	-.502	1.000	-.249	.155	.534	-.107
	Sig. (2-tailed)	.000	.000	.	.022*	.182	.000	.420
	N	84	84	84	84	76	76	59
CWR0-9	Pearson Correlation	-.002	.300	-.249	1.000	.083	-.621	-.156
	Sig. (2-tailed)	.985	.006	.022	.	.478	.000	.238
	N	84	84	84	84	76	76	59
MCWR	Pearson Correlation	-.052	-.146	.155	.083	1.000	.488	.168
	Sig. (2-tailed)	.658	.207	.182	.478	.	.000	.212
	N	76	76	76	76	76	76	57
MCWR_CWR	Pearson Correlation	-.056	-.608	.534	-.621	.488	1.000	.288
	Sig. (2-tailed)	.633	.000	.000	.000	.000	.	.030
	N	76	76	76	76	76	76	57
AGROECO	Pearson Correlation	.302	-.371	-.107	-.156	.168	.288	1.000
	Sig. (2-tailed)	.020	.004	.420	.238	.212	.030	.
	N	59	59	59	59	57	57	59

** Correlation is significant at the 0.01 level (2-tailed). Correlation is significant at the 0.05 level (2-tailed).
The variable agroeconomic takes the value of 0 and 1 for dry and wet districts respectively. MCWR_CWR =MCWR/CWR
Source: Census (relevant issues).

Overall fertility, represented by the Child Woman Ratio (CWR), was significantly correlated with the proportion of married women in the reproductive age groups (at the 95 per cent level) and inversely with the proportion of widowed women in the 15 to 40 year age group (at the 90 per cent level). The proportion single did not register any significant relationship with CWR. The average CWR is higher for the dry districts compared to that for the wet districts, but the Marital Child Woman Ratio (MCWR)[31] registered larger mean values in the wet districts than in the dry districts. Thus, while fewer women in the reproductive ages were married and thus exposed to the risk of conception, those who did marry exhibited higher fertility, Malabar being a case in point.

The proportions single and married varied significantly across dry and wet agro-economic regions. Wet districts showed greater positive association with single women and negative correlation with proportion married. Widowhood on the other hand did not exhibit any such significant variations across agro-economic regions.

While the Coale index of proportions married (I_m) was found to be higher in the higher fertility Deccan, deltaic coastal Andhra and South Canara districts, in contrast to moderate fertility Malabar and Tanjore, there is a statistically significant correlation between natural fertility and the index of proportion married (I_m) only in the districts with the highest natural fertility. Natural fertility sharply declines even in these regions in the years after 1970, accompanied in most cases with a sharp increase in the proportions married. In other words, there is no evidence of a simple monotonic relationship between natural fertility and proportions married. Only where natural fertility was very high, possible due to weak Malthusian positive and preventive checks do we find it directly being closely associated with marriages in the pre-transitional period.

Explaining Nuptiality Variations and Changes

For Madras Presidency as a whole, the SMAM for women showed virtually no trend and remained almost stationary (Table 8).[32] Given the approximate nature of age reporting, very small changes in the SMAM cannot be taken as conclusive evidence for change. Further, very small changes in the age at first marriage have no impact on the observed fertility levels. It takes bigger changes. Thus, it has been estimated that when the age at marriage increased from 15 to 19 years, the CBR, NRR and TFR decreased by only 10 per cent (D'Souza 1982). Madras had the highest proportion of single women amongst all the provinces in the country, and within Madras Presidency, Malabar and the West Madras Division registered the highest figures.

A comparison of the CWR and marital CWR (MCWR) yields interesting clues about fertility controlling mechanisms. MCWRs, with smaller denominators of married women only, would obviously be higher than CWRs. Table 8 below, which shows that between 1901 and 1931, the CWR accounted for 34%-61% of the MCWR. This unambiguously points to nuptiality as the major proximate determinant of moderate fertility in Madras. As mentioned earlier, the Malabar CWR was much lower than the all India average. However, the marital CWR ratios tend much closer to the all India average.

TABLE 8: Singulate Mean Age at Marriage, Child-woman Ratio and Proportion Married in the Madras Presidency, 1901-31

Year	SMAM	SMAM	Madras Presidency		Diff.	India		Proportion married (15-49)	
	Male	Female	CWR	MCWR		CWR	CMWR	Male	Female
1901	24.2	16.8	1128	1815	37.9			0.65220	0.740928
1911	23.4	16.8	1050	1395	24.7	1126	1438	0.78588	0.723266
1921	23.8	16.8	1019	1362	25.2			0.76965	0.719897
1931	22.6	16.6	1056	1419	25.6	1159	1483	0.79318	0.71640

Note: SMAM: Singulate mean age at marriage;
CWR: child-woman ratio (population aged 0-9/ Females aged 15-49*1000);
MCWR: CWR using married women as denominator (population aged 0-9/ Married Females aged 15-49*1000);
Diff.: Difference in percentage terms between CMWR and CWR.
Source: Census, Madras, 1901, 1911, 1921, 1931; Figures for India computed from Census, India, 1911, 1921

Widowhood in some districts exercised a countervailing influence on fertility by reducing the number of women at risk of conception. At the aggregated level of all our districts taken together the most significant variable raising fertility was the proportion of married women, and widowhood tended to significantly dampen fertility. We see also in table 9 that the proportions single, married and widowed varied in their influence on fertility across districts.

Notably, Malabar registered the smallest proportion of married women in the Presidency (Table 10). The small number of married women and the strong inverse relationship between widowhood and fertility combined to reduce Malabar's fertility to a very low level (Table 9).

In the 'dry' Deccan districts too, there is a positive association between fertility and the proportion married, but the relationship is not statistically significant. However, the relative smallness of the proportion married in the Deccan districts, especially till 1941, suggests the operation of the Malthusian preventive check in an un-Malthusian context of high mortality (Table 9 and Table 10). In other words, the preventive check and positive check appear to have worked in tandem.

TABLE 9: Relations of Nuptiality Variables with CWR by District, 1891-1981

District	Type	Proportion Unmarried	Proportion Married	Proportion Widowed
Anantapur, Bellary, Kurnool	Dry	x	.786	-.783
Madura	Dry	x	x	x
Salem	Dry	x	.853 (.007)	x
Coimbatore	Dry	x	.818 (.047)	x
Tanjore	Wet	x	.846 (.034)	x
Malabar[#]	Wet	x	.591 (.036)	-.584 (.038)
South Canara	Wet	x	x	x

[#]The correlation coefficient for Malabar is the nonparametric Spearman's rho whereas all others are Pearson's r.
Figures in parenthesis are p values. X denotes that the correlation coefficient was not significant.

Table 10 clearly indicates that the West Madras division had the lowest proportion of married women across censuses. This trend has continued right to the present with marriage incidence being the lowest in the modern state of Kerala. A variety of reasons, ranging from matrilineal inheritance among the dominant Nayar caste to restrictions on Nambudiri men's marriage to the easy dissolution of marriage, can be advanced to explain this phenomenon.

TABLE 10: Proportion married in the different Census divisions of Madras Presidency, 1921-51

Division	Number married per 1000							
	Males				Females			
	1921	1931	1941	1951	1921	1931	1941	1951
Madras State	422	428	405	428	435	439	426	445
Deccan	387	394	379	425	409	417	409	442
West Madras	386	386	362	375	397	398	381	405
North Madras	455	481	446	479	466	489	466	488
South Madras	419	418	399	415	432	428	420	434

Source: Census of India (1951, Madras, Volume 1: 186-187).

Marital fertility in Madras, though closer to all India levels, was still lower than the latter, as is clear on inspecting the CWR and CMWR (Children per 1000 married women) for Madras Presidency and India The relatively higher mean age at first marriage, suggested by the age wise nuptiality data, may have been a factor at work; this would, *ceteris paribus*, not merely postpone higher reproduction rate but slow the rate of population growth by increasing the length of a generation.

It must be added that the significance of lowered nuptiality as a depressant of fertility did vary across districts. Thus, we see in that the proportion of married women in the Deccan was lower than in the South Madras Division. Further, widowhood also contributed to keeping the fertility level much below biological limits. However, widowhood appears to be much less important than marriage as a determinant of fertility levels when examined using time point panel data for the all the districts of the Presidency together. This exercise shows that the correlation coefficient between CWR and the proportion of married women and between CWR and the proportion of widowed women were .300 and -0.249 respectively.

The agriculturally secure West Coast and the dearth-prone Deccan both had the lowest proportions married, while for North Madras and South Madras, the figures were much higher. Visakhapatnam and the Northeast had the highest proportion of married women.

While varying social customs provide the most ready explanation for variations in the incidence of marriage, it must be kept in mind that there are linkages between material changes and customs. Customs are not a historical constant. Changes in Madras were the result of the demands for transformation within different caste groups and State intervention from outside, as shown by (i) the two bills relating to *Nayar* and *Nambudiri* marriage reforms in Malabar (Bill 13 and Bill 14 of 1931, respectively) and (ii) the Child Marriage Restraint Act.

The Child Marriage Restraint Act, popularly known as the Sarda Act after Rai Sahib Haribilas Sarda who introduced it in the legislature, made the marriage of girls under the age of 14 punishable. The Act also prescribed eighteen as the minimum age at marriage for boys. However, no mention was made of the age of consent. The Sarda Act had a long history of discussion over the issue of child marriage in India. The age of consent was set at ten years for both married and unmarried girls in 1860. In 1891 the criminal code was amended to increase the age of consent to twelve years (Forbes 1996: 85). The interest shown in the issue by the League of Nations once again led to a renewal of debate and the Sarda Act was passed after a number of similar bills were defeated in the legislature.

Though the Act marked a major victory for middle class Indian women's organisations and definitely facilitated wider discussions on such issues, its effectiveness was never known, as the Government was hesitant to enforce it after receiving threats. Some Muslim leaders threatened to team up with the Congress if the Government was to implement the Act. According to a Government report the number of child marriages increased as people tried to celebrate these marriages before the Act came into effect (Forbes 1996: 89).

In 1921, for the Presidency as a whole, the percentage of married girls under the age of 15 to the total female population between ages 0 and 15 was 25.2 percent. The equivalent figure for males was 3.6 percent. In 1931 these figures came down appreciably to 1.9 percent for males and 10 per cent for females. By 1951 the male and female proportion married to the total population in that age group further declined to 0.06 percent and 2.5 percent respectively.[33]

Thus, the Census data do not corroborate the views of the Government or of the later commentators that the *Sarda Act* had little direct impact on the incidence of child marriage. Unfortunately, nuptiality data is not available annually. This compels us to depend solely on Census point estimates.

Historical literature, especially for Western Europe, is replete with examples of income affecting fertility by effecting changes in the age at first marriage. In the absence of time series data on marriages, examining short association between nuptiality and prices based on registration data is not possible in India. However, monthly registration of births in the annual registration data can be used as a very approximate indicator of marriage incidence, by dating the modal month of marriage nine to ten months before the modal month of births. When this is compared between periods of dearth and plenty one can get some rough indication of the nuptiality-economy interconnection.

In the post-independence period, the proportion married increases initially till the 1960s and in some districts till the 1970s followed by a decline. The Coale indices for dry and wet districts discussed in this paper suggest that this increase in nuptiality is accompanied by an opposite movement in natural fertility suggested by the Coale Index of marital fertility $I_{g.}$

One interesting pattern that can be seen in the monthly number of marriages is the distinctly seasonal nature of marriages, which peak after the main harvest. Despite marriages being virtually universal in the country as a whole, historical records do suggest the postponement of marriages during bad monsoon years. For instance, writing about the lowered birth rate in Madras in 1898, the Sanitary Commissioner wrote, 'there is reason to presume that marriages have been deferred during the last three years, as far a possible, that is to say, as far as the caste custom directing the marriage of a female within a certain age will allow, because evil times have been prophesied'.[34] This has to be seen in the context of a series of years of high prices, near famine conditions and plague epidemics in the dry districts of the Presidency since 1883. 'the late famine and the introduction of plague have been regarded as mere forerunners of much heavier disasters, which it has been prophesied will occur during the last year of the cycle of the Kali Yuga- the 'Vikari' (evil) year 1899-1900'.[35]

Though mediated through astrological prophesies of impending times of evil, the deferment of marriages in hard times definitely points to some form of the Malthusian preventive check at work, even in regions where the positive check worked with merciless efficiency.

Widowhood across regions and time periods appears as a statistically significant check on fertility. In the dry Tamil countryside, possibly the lowered significance of high Hinduism and the hold of localised religious cults, failed to keep a large proportion of widows from re-entering marriage and reducing the population exposed to the risk of conception. Malabar and Tanjore, on the other hand, with their extremely strong traditions of Brahmanical Hinduism appear to have ensured that widowhood was strictly enforced. South Canara is the only district that fails to conform to the above pattern. Despite a large proportion of single and widowed women, the nuptiality variable shows no association with fertility.

Across region and time, we find that in the dry districts, there is not much difference in the CWR and a very small decrease in the MCWR. On the other hand, in the wet districts, the CWR shows a small increase accompanied by a large decrease in the MCWR suggestive of a disruption of the natural fertility regime.

The Nonproximate Determinants—Mortality

Another important factor related to fertility decline is mortality, as the observed fertility level tends to decrease with sustained mortality decreases. Once again, we see that the level of mortality and the stability or lack of it (captured by the coefficient of variation of the crude death rate) in the pre-transitional demographic regime played a major role in determining the timing of the later fertility transition. Broadly speaking, famine-prone districts characterised by high and fluctuating mortality accomplished the fertility transition later than the agriculturally and economically more secure regions.

Mortality, in turn was determined largely by dearth and disease, and disease mortality was often magnified by economic distress. Mortality however, showed variations in long-term levels and volatility across both time and region.

This section attempts first, to explain the sustained secular trend of declining mortality, a conundrum that has resisted explanation for long. It is argued also that regions with long histories of adverse mortality conditions underwent later fertility transitions when compared to what was the case in districts where mortality was less pronounced.

Mortality was the result of lethal diseases, or the lack of adequate food, or, more usually, a combination of both. The fertility outcome of a sharp mortality increase could be twofold—it could increase fertility *via* the 'replacement' effect or it could depress fertility by lowering fecundity. Thus the mortality-fertility interconnection varied between regions with differing mortality regimes. Further, dearth varied in the quickness with which it impacted on mortality, depending on the agricultural calendar of the district and the presence or absence of insurance mechanisms.

While mortality and diseases can be captured by straightforward indices such as the Crude Death Rate or disease specific death rates, quantifying dearth is more complicated. In the absence of reliable time series data on income and output, the best proxy for income or dearth is the price of the staple food grain. Prices will go up when there is a scarcity in the local market and move down when there is plenty. The advantage with using price is that it is more reliable than the output series and it can be used for recording changes in chronically food deficit districts that were dependent on imported foodgrain, e.g. the district of Malabar. In such districts, near famine conditions arose when famine in another part of the country pushed up the cost of food.

However, an objection can be raised against the use of this proxy variable on the ground that if most of the farmers were self-sufficient subsistence producers, they would be immune to the vagaries of the market. In the case of southern India, this was not the case. Agricultural commercialisation had penetrated deep down the agrarian hierarchy. Some of the districts such as Tanjore and Malabar had close to a quarter of their agricultural workforce categorised as landless agricultural labour dependent on wages. In most districts, the highly skewed nature of landholding tended to make even the smaller self-cultivating middle and poor peasants dependent on the market for much of their annual supply of foodgrain. In such a context for the bulk of the agrarian population, price increases were inversely related to income. This attribute of food-crop prices appears to have been understood by the colonial administrators as far as back as the late nineteenth century, when, on the recommendations of the Famine Commission, 'warning' and 'scarcity' prices were prescribed as an early warning system to detect the onset of a possible famine. Nearly every annual report of the Sanitary Commissioner for Madras emphasised the crucial significance of high prices in pushing up the death rate.

Data and Methodology[36]

Demographic and economic time series are typically characterised by a significant trend component and the presence of autocorrelation in the error terms greatly reduces the optimal properties of Ordinary Least Squares when auto correlated series are used to derive relationships and estimates of determination.[37]

After satisfying that the estimated series are sufficiently stationary, the pre-whitened series are then used to estimate the fertility outcome of changes in mortality and the variations in mortality instability and mortality outcomes of changes in income. The response of the fertility variable to each of the lagged values of the mortality variable may be interpreted as the elasticity of fertility to mortality. The lag sum of elasticities has been calculated to capture both the immediate effects of mortality hikes and associated delayed effects of increased morbidity.

We have *a priori* knowledge that in India and in our study districts, mortality underwent a sharp reduction after 1921 with a concomitant rise in fertility. The exact years of onset of mortality decline and subsequent fertility transition varied from district to district. These discontinuities in the fertility-mortality relationship, suggested by visual inspections and non-parametric cross-correlations across time is highlighted by first specifying an OLS model and then testing it for parametric shifts using the Cumulative Sum of Squares method to graphically locate the dates of mortality and fertility transition across different districts.

As a first step we run various parametric tests of causal association between deaths and births. Our hypothesis that births responded with varying degrees of lag in different districts is first tested for the Malthusian short-term and then for normal mortality and fertility. Granger causality statistics have been estimated to establish the general direction of causation between deaths and births in the first two periods for representative study districts.[38]

CBR and CDR

This section draws on data for mortality and fertility, represented by detrended CBR and CDR series—taking into account data for all the study districts, spread across dry and wet agro-economic zones. These data are used to establish correlation and then causation between the two variables. The exercise has been carried out for representative districts from each of the agro-economic zones. We use the time series of crude birth and death rates to test two hypotheses: first, that the birth rate is the cumulative result of past mortality, and second that fertility is the result of the degree of uncertainty or volatility of the mortality regime.

The history of mortality and fertility trends in southern India in the colonial and post-colonial years can be broadly divided into three phases: the phase of high mortality up to 1921, falling mortality and rising fertility from 1921 to the 1960s and 1970s and finally a sustained fall in fertility and continued mortality decline. Phase I contains years till the onset of the mortality transition. Phase II is the interregnum between the mortality and fertility transitions and Phase III refers to the period after the onset of fertility decline. (In some of the representative districts the distinction between Phase II and Phase III is negligible).

As a preliminary test for the strength and direction of causation Granger causality tests were run between the de-trended CBR (CCBRRES) and CDR (CCDRRES) for each of the representative districts. When data from all the study districts for the period between 1881 and 1981 were used, Granger causation between the two variables was not evident.[39] However, when the data was split between dry and wet districts, [40] we find that that mortality lagged by four years significantly Granger caused fertility in the dry districts but this causal was not present in the wet districts.[41]

TABLE 11a: Granger Causality Tests, 1881-1921

District	Lag	N	Residual births do not Granger cause residual deaths		Residual deaths do not Granger cause residual births	
			F-Statistic	*p*	F-Statistic	*p*
Bellary	5	36	1.64721	0.18433	3.07618*	0.02676
Anantapur	2	35	1.36792	0.26870	2.91280	0.06840
Kurnool	5	36	1.55434	0.20935	5.41507*	0.00165
Malabar	5	36	0.94082	0.47197	1.12767	0.37155
Tanjore	5	36	2.54403*	0.05412	1.21916	0.32934
South Kanara	5	36	1.13901	0.36608	2.68293*	0.04493
Coimbatore	5	36	0.33278	0.88829	0.94525	0.46937
Krishna	5	36	1.33820	0.280851	1.09023	0.39013
Madura	5	36	1.19074	0.34198	5.41507*	0.00165
Salem	5	36	1.98087	0.11650	1.34178	0.27949

Note: Residual calculated by subtracting corrected death and birth series from smoothed death and birth series respectively;
P denotes significance probability

TABLE 11b: Granger Causality Tests, 1921-1940

District	N	Residual births do not Granger cause residual deaths		Residual deaths do not Granger cause residual births	
		F-Statistic	*p*	F-Statistic	*p*
Bellary					
Anantapur					
Kurnool				1.27171	0.35451
Malabar					
Tanjore					
South Kanara		0.36599	0.85961	2.13558	0.15227
Coimbatore					
Krishna					
Madura	20	1.94573	0.18178	0.76742	0.59586
Salem	20	1.85672	0.19786	3.35936	0.05480

Note: Residual calculated by subtracting corrected death and birth series from smoothed death and birth series respectively;
P denotes significance probability

Next, to examine the validity of the Malthusian positive check in the short run, the de-trended CBR series was regressed on current and lagged values of de-trended CDR and the price of the major cereal (PRRES). When data from both 'wet' and 'dry' districts were used together there is no statistically significant evidence of mortality or prices constraining fertility.[42]

To check whether our hypothesis of differential mortality-fertility linkages in 'dry' and 'wet' agro climatic regions is valid, the Chow break point test was applied to the data separating the dry and wet districts. The results given show the test to highly significant.

TABLE 12: Chow Breakpoint Test: 606

F-statistic	5.055001	Probability	0.000026
Log likelihood ratio	34.86779	Probability	0.000012

The explanatory variables used in the previous regression were then regressed on fertility separately for dry and wet districts. The regression results suggest that the inverse relationship between mortality and fertility was stronger in the 'dry' districts as compared with 'wet' districts.

TABLE 13: Regression of Residual CBR on lagged values of residuals of staple prices and CDR for both agro climatic zones

Dependent Variable: CCBRRES
Method: Least Squares
Sample(adjusted): 101 400

	DRY		WET	
Variable	**Coefficient**	**Prob.**	**Coefficient**	**Prob.**
CCDRRES	-0.087379	0.0592	0.238794	0.0024
CCDRRES(-1)	0.045726	0.3292	-0.063705	0.4291
CCDRRES(-2)	-0.040319	0.3517	-0.062941	0.4282
PRRES	0.006845	0.6870	0.685736	0.0002
PRRES(-1)	0.003965	0.8068	0.119649	0.4881
C	-0.114438	0.8293	-0.546678	0.3043
AR(1)			-0.100177	0.2906
n	77		151	

Having conclusively established that fertility determination differed in dry and wet districts, the time component is then introduced into the analysis to check whether the patterns of fertility determination showed temporal variations across these two agro climatic zones.

TABLE 14. Regression Results of Fertility on Lagged Values of Mortality and Prices for Dry Districts across Time (Dependent Variable: CCBRRES)

Variable	Period					
	1881-1924		1925-1950		1970-1980	
	Coefficient	Prob.	Coefficient	Prob.	Coefficient	Prob.
CCDRRES	0.208315	0.0455	0.419769	0.0092	0.091192	0.1486
CCDRRES(-1)	-0.022778	0.8195	-0.019422	0.9040	0.031645	0.6011
CCDRRES(-2)	-0.033555	0.7269	-0.166454	0.4163	0.037578	0.4863
C	0.149553	0.8430	1.308907	0.3526	0.016421	0.9737
PRRES	0.015226	0.5553	0.006751	0.8067	0.019934	0.4353
PRRES(-1)	-0.013189	0.7458	-0.026009	0.6484	-0.014033	0.7288
AR(1)	0.025269	0.7807	0.061695	0.6716	0.045292	0.5054
N	88		35		185	

TABLE 15. Regression results of Fertility on Lagged Values of Mortality and Prices for Wet Districts across Time (Dependent Variable: CCBRRES)

Variable	Period					
	1881-1924		1925-1950		1970-1980	
	Coefficient	Prob.	Coefficient	Prob.	Coefficient	Prob.
CCDRRES	0.030367	0.6892	0.007921	0.9594	0.566327	0.7500
CCDRRES(-1)	0.066655	0.3615	-0.016355	0.9117	-0.765831	0.9206
CCDRRES(-2)	0.067978	0.2820	-0.012264	0.9451	-1.245232	0.6786
C	-0.097694	0.8799	-0.944578	0.3211	-11.58232	0.8864
PRRES	0.620307	0.0136	0.078434	0.4576	0.157072	0.9648
PRRES(-1)	0.323975	0.2132	-0.029919	0.7549	2.160532	0.8633
AR(1)	0.063791	0.5338	-0.035240	0.7951	0.453635	0.8941
N	105		50		8	

The above sets of regressions clearly provide quantitative confirmation for our hypothesis that mortality-fertility-economy inter-linkages varied across both region and time.

Tables 14 and 15 show how the impact of the economic variable, represented by the price of the staple cereal and mortality impacted differently across region and time on fertility. The mortality variable was more powerful in explaining fertility changes in the 'dry' districts as opposed to the 'wet'. Further there is a progressive weakening of the impact of mortality in the explanation of fertility over succeeding time periods. Current mortality played an important role in determining fertility levels in the 'dry' districts whereas in the wet districts it did not have any statistical significance. [43] In the 'wet' districts lagged mortality played a more important, though statistically insignificant, effect on current levels of fertility.

Coming to the price variable we see that prices were more important in pushing up fertility in the wet districts, especially in the first period. In the dry districts prices did not show any causal relationship. However on dividing the entire study period into three different time periods we find that prices were (significantly) inversely related to fertility in both dry and wet districts in the second period, which it must be noted included the Depression.

To recapitulate, on taking the wet and dry districts together, without controlling for different agro-economic regimes and demographic variations no significant relationship was found between current and lagged values of prices and mortality on fertility. However on separating the dry and wet districts we found that the sum of lagged values for the coefficients for mortality was negative for the dry districts while those for the wet districts was positive. This suggests that in the dry districts taken as a whole mortality increases pushed down fertility, albeit weakly, while in the wet zone mortality hikes resulted in the pushing up of fertility, possibly for compensating increased deaths.[44] Similarly, prices showed no important relationship with fertility in the dry region. This is expected because of the much lower level of commercialisation of agriculture here.[45] In the wet regions, there was strong positive relationship of current prices with fertility in the pre-mortality decline period.

When the data aggregated by dry and wet zones was further divided by time periods we find that the weak inverse relationship between mortality and fertility was replaced by a positive significant relationship for un-lagged values of mortality and a very weak negative relationship for lagged values of mortality up to 1950. In the last period from 1970 to 1980 mortality showed no significant relationship with fertility. In this period, prices exhibited no relationship with fertility in both the wet as well as dry districts.

We had attempted to quantify the significance of emancipatory popular movements by including a variable for the electoral performance of the Left but this exhibited very high co linearity with the regional dummy and thus had to be omitted.

The last phase, which was inaugurated by the onset of the fertility transition, has however varied *across* the different regions of southern India. The fertility downturn can be noticed as early as the 1930s in Coimbatore and as late as the 1980s in Bellary. Mortality decline was a necessary though not sufficient condition for sustained fertility decline. Fertility decline followed the mortality transition with a lag. The length of this lag was however substantively determined by varied factors in different settings.

Let us consider districts which made an early transition. In Malabar, which lagged behind the national average in terms of conventional economic indices of growth, it was a greater democratisation which in turn increased the effectiveness of state welfare measures. These changes were helped by extant social practices accepted practices of relative gender equality, late marriage and non-marriage. In Krishna and Coimbatore on the other hand an agrarian order marked by lower levels of peasant inequity were impacted upon by rapid economic growth. On the other hand the dry Deccan did not have nature, history or the present in terms of emancipatory politics, economic prosperity or effective welfarist state intervention in its favour. Consequently this region lagged behind in making the transition to sustained fertility decline.

Conclusions

Inspired by works that have established firmly the critical role played by regions in the unfolding of southern India history, the other assumption made at the outset of this investigation was that regional and spatial variations have a crucial role in explaining varied trajectories of demographic change in India. Earlier works on Indian geography and demography have conclusively shown, despite some discordant views, the existence of a broad North-South divide for India as a whole.

We began with the premise that regional specificities and inter-regional differences, well established in studies of other areas of social change in peninsular India, may have produced distinctive demographic regimes and trajectories of change. To test this hypothesis, the districts of colonial Madras Presidency were divided into 'dry' and 'wet' on the basis of rainfall and cropping patterns along with a number of related social and economic correlates.

The 'wet' regions were devoted to labour intensive 'wet' paddy cultivation with associated structures of extreme caste discrimination and class inequities. Heightened caste-class inequalities were responsible for the precocious development of popular movements against caste oppression and landlord exploitation. The existence of large landlords and a high proportion of landless agricultural labourers ensured a greater development of agricultural commercialisation and consequently an increased sensitivity to the vagaries of agricultural price movements.

In contrast to these characteristics of the 'wet' districts, the 'dry' areas were given to considerable low value subsistence agriculture, and the relative weakness of high Hinduism and caste and class disparities. Commercial crops, in the form of cotton did make and appearance in the late nineteenth century, but with the retreat of magnate farmers from cotton in the face of falling cotton prices, this activity also became a small peasant enterprise. Lacking a politically articulate elite as well as a vociferous popular political movement, there were few adequately powerful agents in the 'dry' countryside who could demand greater attention for self-gain or more vicarious reasons from the State. In such a scenario of little developmental intervention, a failure of monsoons meant disaster in the form of famine.

The 'dry' districts, when aggregated, showed a persistently higher fertility and mortality than the wet districts. The divergence in observed fertility levels between the 'dry' and the 'wet' continued to increase in the post-Independence years. The explanation for this is essentially historical. The 'dry' regions as a whole exhibited a higher and more volatile mortality regime in relation to the 'wet'. As morality reduction was a necessary condition for any sustained fertility decline we find that the 'wet' region when aggregated achieved sustained reductions in fertility earlier.

More nuanced demographic trajectories were clearly discernable as well. While demographers since the time of Malthus have seen the positive check to precede the preventive check, the two being seen as features of different demographic regimes, the demographic behaviour of the famine and crisis mortality prone 'dry' Deccan districts of southern India was found to contradict the neat Malthusian spatial and temporal division between the operation of the positive and the preventive checks. Thus, the Deccan and even late nineteenth century Malabar, despite frequent mortality peaks, regulated nuptiality by ensuring that a large proportion of its population in the reproductive ages remained unmarried.

However, within the vast area of Madras Presidency, the nuptiality check was more powerful in some regions. The study identified a low nuptiality corridor extending northeast from Malabar district in the southwest to Chingleput district (where Madras city is located) on eastern coast. This finding is important, as it demands a qualification of the view that high fertility in India was related to the phenomenon of universal marriage.

After Independence, the new Indian State set about trying to compensate for the absolute absence of development under colonialism by intervening substantially in terms of agrarian and health policies in the countryside. The problem with developmental planning in India was that in the absences of any popular pressure in the country as a whole, the statist development schemes usually failed to reach the targeted recipients. In areas with significant levels of existing political mobilisation for social change and reform, State sponsored schemes aimed at improving health and demographic conditions fared better than in those areas with little political participation.

It is true that everyday life or death in the Indian countryside (and one may add the vicissitudes of the vibrant Indian stock market) continue to be substantially influenced by the whims of the Indian monsoon. Yet this is not to argue that every major change in India was dictated by the God Indra, who controlled the rains. To claim that one can explain the 'mortality transition' in India in terms of the beneficence of malevolence of the rain god appears to be an overstatement. Rains or rather the lack of it explained mortality only in those times when, and in areas where, the Sate had forsaken any substantive attempt at providing alternate irrigation or sources of livelihood. In the absence of any real welfarist state intervention, colonial Indian demographic processes were largely 'natural'. The deadly triad of monsoon failure, profit driven market forces and diseases continued to severely limit Indian life expectancy till the second decade of the twentieth century. Only when this lethal concatenation was broken did mortality begin to decline in India. Initially, as it has been pointed out correctly, it was the benign turn in the behaviour of Indra that stopped Indians dying in unusually large numbers.

While Indra's favours can explain the decline in the severity and frequency of famines on the subcontinent, it cannot explain satisfactorily the more complex processes of fertility change. This brings us back to our 'wet'—'dry' division. The proportion of married women to the total of fecund females in a population with little contraception and illegitimacy was the main proximate determinant of fertility in a 'natural fertility' regime such as that in southern India. This proportion was determined either by socially accepted mores of celibacy and rules of widowhood. The social availability of non-marriage as an option among the dominant castes, such as the Nairs of Malabar, appear to have garnered acceptability for such practices among a wider variety of subordinate castes. When relatively late marriage or significant levels of non-marriage was combined with strictly imposed rules against widow remarriage, fertility levels were reduced considerably from what they would have been without these checks. The fact that these practices were part of a dominant tradition helped greatly when subsequent 'modernisation' required age at marriage to be increased.

After 1921, there is a pervasive improvement in mortality across the Indian subcontinent. The exact timing of the sustained fall in mortality did vary, but it would not be incorrect to generalise that mortality had embarked on its downward course after the influenza pandemic of 1918 in India. The question then is: Why did the death rate fall in a context of a State which did little to actually make any substantial improvement in the lives of ordinary Indians? The colonial Government of India, after meeting its external obligations, remained faithfully wedded to the principle of a balanced budget and had very little funds to spare for public welfare. The per capita spending under the head Medicine and Health was ridiculously minuscule amounting to Rupees 0.07, 0.14 and 0.11 in 1900-01, 1920-21 and 1930-31 respectively. Only in 1946-47 do we find the per capita expenditure on health increasing to Rupees 44.69. It is pertinent to recall that the Sir Joseph Bhore's Report published in 1946 estimated that there were only 6000 beds available for about two and a half million patients in India. Thus no serious argument can be made about the colonial government's policies being significant in reducing mortality in India.

If we cannot credit the colonial State with any sustained and pervasive ameliorative initiative in reducing mortality, then we are forced to look for other explanations. Ira Klein, discounting the State's role in attenuating high levels of mortality in India, has argued for an epidemiological thesis to explain falling death rates in India. However, Sumit Guha (2001) has clearly shown the lack of empirical basis for Klein's (1990) thesis. Guha then goes on to argue that reductions in the volatility of Indian food output which in turn was determined by more timely and adequate rains explain India's falling mortality. Guha's argument is correct *per se*. While per capita food output decreased in the post-First World War period before 1947, so did the coefficient of variation in the food output series. What this implied was that although there was slightly less food to eat, the marked fluctuations (increasing output punctuated by famines) declined. This reduced mortality, especially crisis mortality. Agricultural output data and rainfall variation data do show a declining trend from the 1920s to the 1940s. Guha's contention that increased stability in food output despite stagnation and decline lowered mortality is well argued and plausible. However, it is more difficult to posit a direct simple correlation between the variations in the quantum of rainfall and output fluctuations. Even agriculture that is entirely monsoon dependent is affected not only by the variations in the quantum of rainfall, but also very significantly by the timing of the onset of monsoons and rainfall distribution across the monsoon months. This part of Guha's argument needs further substantiation before it can be accepted. At the moment the agricultural output driven mortality decline thesis, though partial, appears be the most plausible explanation for the conundrum of Indian mortality decline.

In this chapter, we have attempted to add to this thesis by arguing that, along with an increased stability in food availability, the two decades leading up to the Depression also witnessed a fall in the inequality of landholding distribution in some of the districts while in others the more marginal cultivators came into land. This ensured an increased access to scarce resources. Although not enough to ensure better farming practices it did however ensure a small amelioration in the vulnerability of the poorest cultivators to hunger and disease.

Thus the sharp current demographic divergence between the North and the South and within the different regions of southern India may be related in large measure to changes in politically economy which acted differentially on regions characterised by varying levels and patterns of nuptiality, fertility, mortality and agricultural production regimes.

NOTES

1. Notably, in Europe, demographers have for long looked to the past in trying to understand the triggers and timings of demographic transitions (Coale and Watkins 1986; Knodel and van de Walle 1979).
2. In recent years, though, political problems have forced the government to either abbreviate the scope of the census (1941) or omit certain areas (e.g. Assam in 1981 and Kashmir in 1991).
3. The census of the North West Provinces taken on the night of 31 December 1852 with a reference date of 1 January 1853 was the first census conducted on modern lines. This census was synchronously conducted with regular house to house numbering (Natarajan 1972).
4. Board of Revenue, "Circular to All Collectors, Dated 17 Feb. 1850, No. 298," (1850).
5. A provisional list of Backward Classes was also identified in the 1951 census.
6. Only married women were asked the last two questions.
7. [Madras, 1925 #4375@2]
8. Government of Madras, "Annual Report of the Sanitary Commissioner with the Government of Madras,1924," (Madras: 1925) in Adnan 1998:2.
9. Government Memorandum No. 812-1, P.H., dated 16 May 1921
10. [Madras, #4380@para 15]
11. [Madras, 1927 #4381@p.4]
12. These correction factors and the methods used in this study for correcting vital statistics data is discussed in the next section.
13. [Madras, 1936 #4383@p.3]
14. [Madras, 1936 #4383@p.3]
15. [Office of the Registrar General, 1971 #4385@p.18]
16. [Mehrotra, 1968 #4387]
17. The method is based on the assumption of a 'stable population', i.e., one with an unchanging age structure (% of population in different age groups) and a constant rate of population growth. In a population closed to migration, a stable population results from constant birth and death rates over a long period of time, and the entry rate into a population age group is equal to the rate of exit from the same population group. The Brass Method was amended by a number of scholars by eliminating the assumption of stability. However, possibly because of the later methods' sensitivity to errors of age misreporting, the estimated correction factors yielded by the Brass Growth Balance Method appear to be much more plausible. (The Bennet-Horiuchi and Hill estimation methods suggested extremely high levels of death registration at clear variance with the historical record).
18. This was so for more than one reason. First, annual registration of deaths at the level of the district became unavailable. Second, the sharp decrease in mortality relative to fertility in the post War period violates the assumption of stability.
19. The CWR has been computed as the ratio of children between ages 0-9 to the female population between ages 15 and 49.
20. While the low CWR agrees with other estimates of lower fertility in Madras vis-à-vis the other regions of India, however, it must be remembered that the CWR tends to be affected by the higher under-counts in the age 0-4 than in higher age groups
21. Fertility estimates for the period 1951-91 have been published in Guilmoto and Rajan (2001).

22. After Independence, with the creation of linguistically organised States, most of the Telugu speaking districts of coastal Andhra and the Deccan together with the Princely state of Hyderabad constituted the modern state of Andhra Pradesh. Some districts like Bellary, first went to Andhra and then finally came to rest with Karnataka
23. The findings of the All-India Credit Survey and the National Sample Survey of 1954-55 suggest that for the period from the 1930s to the late 1950s the average operated holding was inadequate for subsistence (India Cabinet Secretariat, 1955, 1958).
24. The commercialisation of agricultural throughout peninsular India was both pervasive and well developed. This situation continued into the post-Independence decades.
25. The values of the coefficient of variation, crop wise, are as follows. Bajra (52.06879), Jowar (52.9147), Maize (56.75747) and Rice (49.02679). However, in the years 1957-86 the Tamil districts registered higher coefficients compared to the Andhra and Karnataka districts.
26. Rayalaseema under British control, and Telengana under the rule of the Nizam, were backward in relation to the coastal region.
27. Our estimated Gini coefficient for Fasli 1330 and 1340 are 0.532612 and 0.558396
28. Schendel, *Three Deltas : Accumulation and Poverty in Rural Burma, Bengal and South India*.
29. The rest of the discussion on Coimbatore and Kongunad is based largely on this source.
29. The extremely poor quality of census and registration information gathering in Vishakapatnam Agency and East Godavari renders any analysis on the basis of these sources rather pointless.
30. Iyer rightly includes widowhood as a one of the depressants of natural fertility in India. However, Henry's two definitions and subsequent use of the term seems to exclude widowhood as a determinant of natural fertility; the latter being more related to the broad category of nuptiality.
31. The MCWR is defined here as the population aged 0-9 years / Number of married women aged 15 to 40 years multiplied by a radix of 1000. The 0-9 population rather than the 0-5 population has been used in estimating CWR and CMWR to reduce the errors of age misreporting in the early years and to even out the effects of high young age mortality.
32. Hajnal's index of Singulate Mean Age at Marriage (SMAM) has been used to estimate the mean age at first marriage.
33. Figures are from the census volumes for 1921, 1931 and 1951.
34. RSCM, 1898, p.26
35. RSCM, 1898, p.18.
36. This is a technical section. May be skipped by the general reader.
37. We first apply a smoothing function to separate the trend from the series and then estimate the deviations. A one-parameter double smoothing method, which is appropriate for series with a linear trend has been used. Being a one parameter model it is more parsimonious than a number of other smoothing procedures. This may be defined by the recursions:
    $S_t = \alpha y_t + (1-\alpha) S_{t-1}$
    $D_t = \alpha S_t + (1-\alpha) D_{t-1}$
    where S is the single smoothed series and D is the double smoothed series. Note that double smoothing is a single parameter smoothing method with damping factor $0<\alpha\leq 1$.
38. Granger causation estimates the extent to which current value of Y is explained by past

values of X. Granger causality can also run from X to Y and *vice-versa.* Granger causality is however different from cause in the more commonly used sense of the term.

39. Pairwise Granger Causality Tests
Sample: 1 908
Lags: 4

Null Hypothesis:	Obs	F-Statistic	Probability
CCDRRES does not Granger Cause CCBRRES	861	1.76221	0.13441
CCBRRES does not Granger Cause CCDRRES	0.45212	0.77089	

40. The variable AGROCLIM takes the value of 0 for 'dry' and 1 for 'wet' districts
41. Pairwise Granger Causality Tests
Sample: 1 908 IF AGROCLIM=0
Lags: 4

Null Hypothesis:	Obs	F-Statistic	Probability
CCDRRES does not Granger Cause CCBRRES	500	2.50164	0.04169
CCBRRES does not Granger Cause CCDRRES		0.52175	0.71980

Pairwise Granger Causality Tests
Sample: 1 908 IF AGROCLIM=1
Lags: 4

Null Hypothesis:	Obs	F-Statistic	Probability
CCDRRES does not Granger Cause CCBRRES	265	0.44481	0.77614
CCBRRES does not Granger Cause CCDRRES	0.36701	0.83202	

42. Dependent Variable: CCBRRES all
Sample(adjusted): 101 907 IF AGROCLIM<>NA
Included observations: 217
Excluded observations: 490 after adjusting endpoints
Convergence achieved after 3 iterations

Variable	Coefficient	Std. Error	t-Statistic	Prob.
CCDRRES	0.079628	0.049393	1.612121	0.1084
CCDRRES(-1)	-0.039589	0.048936	-0.808994	0.4194
CCDRRES(-2)	-0.002474	0.047774	-0.051779	0.9588
C	-0.158783	0.461906	-0.343756	0.7314
PRRES	0.032017	0.029726	1.077066	0.2827
PRRES(-1)	-0.018219	0.030996	-0.587777	0.5573
AR(1)	0.063105	0.070876	0.890359	0.3743

R-squared	0.025326	Mean dependent var	-0.062809
Adjusted R-squared	-0.002522	S.D. dependent var	6.104330
S.E. of regression	6.112024	Akaike info criterion	6.490119
Sum squared resid	7844.935	Schwarz criterion	6.599148
Log likelihood	-697.1779	F-statistic	0.909430
Durbin-Watson stat	1.822199	Prob(F-statistic)	0.488991

43. A p value of less than 0.5 may be used as a rough measure of statistical significance of a given coefficient.

44. As we have seen, fertility exhibits a direct relationship with rises in mortality as an attempt to counter increasing deaths. However, sustained very high mortality could dampen fertility via reduced fecundability.
45. In a population where a sizeable proportion of people depend on food bought from the market or where they are net buyers, an increase in staple prices would increase economic stress and reduce fertility *via* the Malthusian 'preventive check'. However, when the bulk of the population is not dependent on the market for food supplies or for selling their a significant part of their output, price will not have any significant impact on either mortality or fertility.

REFERENCES

Shapan Adnan. 'Fertility Decline under Absolute Poverty: Paradoxical Aspects of Demographic Change in Bangladesh'. *Economic and Political Weekly* 33 (1998): 1337-48.

Christopher John Baker. 1984. *An Indian Rural Economy 1880-1955 : The Tamilnad Countryside*. Oxford: Clarendon Press.

William Brass. 1975. *Methods for Estimating Fertility and Mortality from Limited and Defective Data*. Chapel Hill: Carolina Population Center.

Carol Appadurai Breckenridge and Peter Van der Veer. 1993. 'Orientalism and the Postcolonial Predicament : Perspectives on South Asia'. *South Asia Seminar Series*. Philadelphia: University of Pennsylvania Press).

Norman Carrier, John Hobcraft, and London School of Economics and Political Science. 1971. *Demographic Estimation for Developing Societies : A Manual of Techniques for the Detection and Reduction of Errors in Demographic Data*. London: Population Investigation Committee. London School of Economics.

Bernard S. Cohn. 1987. *An Anthropologist among Historians and Other Essays*. Delhi : Oxford: Oxford University Press.

Stan D'Souza. 1982. 'Nuptiality Patterns and Fertility Implications in South Asia', in Lado T. Ruzicka ed. Nuptiality and Fertility. Liege: Ordina Editions.

Kathleen Gough. 1981. *Rural Society in Southeast India*. Cambridge: Cambridge University Press.

Sumit Guha. 2001. Health and Population in South Asia. London : Hurst and Company.

Christophe Z. Guilmoto 1988.'The Sircar's Idle Curiosity: Critical Evaluation of Tamil Nadu's Demographic Sources, 1871-1981'. Madras Institute of Development Studies,

Christophe Z. Guilmoto and S. Irudaya Rajan. 2001. 'Spatial patterns of fertility transition in Indian districts'. *Population & Development Review*. 27 (2): 713-738.

L. Henry. 1961. 'Some Data on Natural Fertility'. *Eugenics Quarterly* 8 (2): 81-91.

Louis Henry and Institut national d'etudes demographiques (France). 1953. *Fécondité Des Mariages : Nouvelle Méthode De Mesure*. Edited by Démographiques Institut National d'Études, *Travaux Et Documents. Cahiers / France Institut National D'études Démographiques ; No.16*. [Paris]: Presses Universitaires de France.

Sriya Iyer. 2002. *Demography and Religion in India*. New Delhi: Oxford University Press.

Ira Klein. 1990. 'Population Growth and Mortality in British India, Part II: The Demographic Revolution'. *Indian Economic & Social History Review*. 27(1): 33-63.

John Knodel and van de Walle, Etienne. 1979. 'Lessons from the Past: Policy Implications of Historical Fertility Studies'. *Population and Development Review*. 5 (2): 217-245.

Dharma Kumar. 1992. *Land and Caste in South India : Agricultural Labour in the Madras*

Presidency During the Nineteenth Century. New Delhi: Manohar Publishers and Distributors.

Dharma Kumar. 1965. *Land and Caste in South India : Agricultural Labour in the Madras Presidency During the Nineteenth Century, Cambridge Studies in Economic History.* Cambridge: University Press, 1965.

H. Leridon. 1977. *Human Fertility: The Basic Concepts*. Chicago: Chicago University Press, 1977.

Government of Madras. 1888. 'Annual Report of the Sanitary Commissioner with the Government of Madras, 1888'. Madras: Government Press.

Government of Madras. 1892. 'Annual Report of the Sanitary Commissioner with the Government of Madras, 1892'. Madras: Government Press.

Government of Madras. 1890. 'Annual Report of the Sanitary Commissioner with the Government of Madras,1890'. Madras: Government Press.

Government of Madras. 1896. 'Annual Report of the Sanitary Commissioner with the Government of Madras, 1896'. Madras: Government Press.

Government of Madras. 1897. 'Annual Report of the Sanitary Commissioner with the Government of Madras, 1897'. Madras: Government Press.

Government of Madras. 1900. 'Annual Report of the Sanitary Commissioner with the Government of Madras, 1900'. Madras: Government Press.

Government of Madras. 1906. 'Annual Report of the Sanitary Commissioner with the Government of Madras,1906'. Madras: Government Press.

Government of Madras. 1919. 'Annual Report of the Sanitary Commissioner with the Government of Madras, 1919'. Madras: Government Press.

Government of Madras. 1923. 'Annual Report of the Sanitary Commissioner with the Government of Madras'. Madras: Government Press.

Government of Madras. 1924. 'Annual Report of the Sanitary Commissioner with the Government of Madras, 1924'. Madras Government Press.

Government of Madras. 1925. 'Annual Report of the Sanitary Commissioner with the Government of Madras,1924'. Madras : Government Press.

Government of Madras. 1929. 'Annual Report of the Sanitary Commissioner with the Government of Madras,1929'. Madras : Government Press.

Nilmani Mukherjee. 1962. *The Ryotwari System in Madras, 1792-1827*. Calcutta: Firma K. L. Mukhopadhya.

Dharm Narain. 1961. *Distribution of the Marketed Surplus of Agricultural Produce by Size-Level of Holding in India, 1950-51*. Institute of Economic Growth, *Occasional Paper No.2.*. London: Asia Publishing House.

D. Natarajan. 1972. *Indian Census through a Hundred Years. Census Centenary Monographs / Census of India 1971 ; No.2*. New Delhi.

M.A. Oommen. 1994. 'Land Reforms and Economic Change', in B.A. Prakash ed. *Kerala's Economy : Performance, Problems, Prospects*. Thousand Oaks, California: Sage Publications.

D. Rajasekhar and G.N. Rao. 1991. 'Commodity Production and the Changing Agrarian Scenario in Andhra: A Study in Interregional Variations, C.1910-C.1947', in Sumit Guha Sabyasachi Bhattacharya, Raman Mahadevan, Sakti Padhi, D.Rajasekhar and G.N.Rao eds. *The South Indian Economy: Agrarian Change, Industrial Structure and State Policy*. Delhi: Oxford University Press.

D. Rajasekhar. 1988. *Land Transfers and Family Partitioning : A Historical Study of an Andhra Village, Occasional Paper Series / Centre for Development Studies. No. 1.*

New Delhi: Oxford & IBH Pub. Co. and Centre for Development Studies Trivandrum.

G.N. Rao. 1981. 'Transition from a Subsistence to Commercialised Agriculture: Problems, Potentialities and Results: A Study of Krishna District in the 19th Century'. Paper presented at the seminar on *Commercialisation of Agriculture in India*, Centre for Development Studies, Thiruvananthapuram.

Reserve Bank of India. 1955. Committee of Direction of the All-India Rural Credit Survey. *All-India Rural Credit Survey : Report of the Committee of Direction*. Bombay: Reserve Bank of India.

Board of Revenue. 1850. 'Circular to All Collectors, Dated 17 Feb. 1850, No. 298'.

W.R.S. Sathyanathan. 1935. 'Report on Agricultural Indebtedness'. 71. Madras: Madras (India). Board of Revenue (Land Revenue and Settlement).

V.V. Sayana. 1952. *Land Sales, Land Values and Land Transfers*. Delhi: Chand

Willem Van Schendel. 1991. *Three Deltas : Accumulation and Poverty in Rural Burma, Bengal and South India, Indo-Dutch Studies on Development Alternatives ; 8*. New Delhi ; Newbury Park, CA: Sage Publication.

K. Srinivasulu. 2002. *Caste, Class and Social Articulation in Andhra Pradesh: Mapping Differential Regional Trajectories*. London: Overseas Development Institute.

India Cabinet Secretariat. 1955. 'The National Sample Survey. Eighth Round: July 1954-March 1955

India Cabinet Secretariat. 1958. No. 10. First Report on Land Holdings, Rural Sector'. Delhi: The Cabinet Secretariat, Government of India.

Willem Van Schendel. 1991. *Three Deltas : Accumulation and Poverty in Rural Burma, Bengal and South India*. Indo-Dutch Studies on Development Alternatives - *8*. New Delhi / Newbury Park, CA: Sage Publication.

Amartya Sen. 1985. 'Dharm Narain on Poverty: Concepts and Broader Issues' in John W. Mellor and Gunwant M. Desai *eds. Agricultural Change and Rural Poverty.* Baltimore and London: The Johns Hopkins University Press.

K. Srinivasulu. 2002. *Caste, Class and Social Articulation in Andhra Pradesh: Mapping Differential Regional Trajectories*.. London: Overseas Development Institute.

A.J. Coale and T.J. Trussel. 1974. 'Model Fertility Schedules: Variations in the Age Structure of Child Bearing in Human Populations'. *Population Index* 40 (2): 185-258.

D.A. Washbrook. 1976. *The Emergence of Provincial Politics: The Madras Presidency, 1870-1920*. Cambridge : Cambridge University Press.

Ansley J. Coale and Susan Cotts Watkins. 1986. *The Decline of Fertility in Europe : The Revised Proceedings of a Conference on the Princeton European Fertility Project.* Princeton, N.J.: Princeton University Press.

Part III

ETHNOGRAPHIC UNDERPINNINGS

Chapter 4

Fertility and Family Planning in Rural India: Anthropological and Ethnographic Perspectives

Tulsi Patel

Rapid fertility transitions have occurred in a majority of developing countries for over three decades now. Between the early 1960s to late 1980s, the Total Fertility Rate for the developing world declined by as much as an estimated 36 per cent—from 6.0 to 3.8 births per woman (U.N. 1995). Demographers have been grappling with this transformation in terms of looking for an argument that holds good theoretically as well as empirically, one that could account for why fertility declined even in the absence of the socio-economic transformations that demographic transition theory set store by. This search for an explanatory framework goes back even further, to the Ansley Coale led Princeton European Fertility Project, whose findings ran counter to the conventional demographic thesis of synchrony between socio-economic development and fertility decline. Regions of Europe geographically proximate with a common language and elements of a common culture, it was then argued, tended to experience fertility decline at more or less the same time. Thus, in this view, the classic predictors of the theory of demographic transition failed to account for the historic decline in fertility. Cultural institutions in different settings, it was argued, influenced the phenomenon independently of socio-economic conditions. Subsequently, culture became the 'grab bag' for explaining what economics was unable to do.

Other explanations for demographic transition include Caldwell's wealth flows theory (Caldwell 1982), The essence of the wealth flows theory is that the *direction* of the 'net intergenerational wealth flow', which, in traditional society, was from children to parents, gets reversed over the course of the demographic transition, and consequently, parents have fewer children, so that they can allocate more resources per child for child care, schooling, etc. Though of substantial value in incorporating anthropology into mainstream demography, the wealth flows theory is faulted on the ground that in it can be traced assumptions of evolutionary theory, long challenged in other social sciences.

Theories like Gary S. Becker's new home economics which influenced consumer choice theory (Becker 1960) draw on economics to explain fertility transition; higher fertility is inimical to investments in human capital, it is argued. Institutional theories (McNicoll 1994) too have a similar slant. For instance, in seeking to throw light on the underpinnings of high fertility, it is argued that a large family can have payoffs only in a situation of labour market competition, and may lead to more income for the family, as well as more security for its elders (McNicoll 1975: 4-5).

Another major strand in demographic theory is the importance of women's autonomy in explaining fertility decision-making. This view, that the status of women influences their fertility, was pursued in the 1980s (Mason). In this context, education was pointed out as the instrument for enhancing the status of women in order for fertility to decline. Subsequent empirical research has however shown diverse trends rather than a convincing theory.[1]

While demographic research is also influenced by micro-economic considerations and focuses on the individual and/or the couple, the sociological connections with institutions such as the family, kinship and also the macro structures, such as the State, market and socio-economic development remain to be teased out. Adoption of contraception for controlling fertility is now of prime concern to demography, with reliance on diffusion and modernisation theses along with the frequent use of the concept of culture. The dominance cultural theories are assuming over the economic reductionism of forty years in demography is however bordering on cultural reductionism. It places tremendous analytical weight on communication about contraception, neglecting the distinct possibility that when women get together they chat not only about bed time inconveniences, but also about their children's schooling, work, and other matters bearing on the socioeconomics of social life – issues that facilitate or obstruct contraceptive communication. This reproduces the functionalist myth that culture can be taken out of social, economic and political organisation. In fact, it is *in* those dimensions of life, shaping the form they assume. Instead of separating culture from context, contraception from socioeconomics, the real challenge is to construct whole demographies that illuminate the mutually constitutive relations and the implications of these relations for reproductive actors (Greenhalgh 1994: 9).[2]

Demography through Anthropological Fieldwork

In seeking to account for fertility decline in South India, Caldwell *et al* (1988) find that it runs counter to the 'classical' demographic transition theory: 'In contrast to what might have been anticipated from the classical version of that theory, fertility has declined significantly in the last 20 years in such poor agrarian countries as India, Indonesia and China, where most development indices are well below those which obtained at the onset of fertility decline in the countries experiencing the earlier fertility transition' (1988: 4). In describing the family planning programme at the local level, the authors say: 'The programme has never been one based merely on the provision of services, although since the emergency it has been closer to that model than ever before. There were always targets and these were used regularly to evaluate the caliber of program employees. The female health visitors and the more numerous auxiliary nurse midwives (now multipurpose health workers) visit each household at least every two months, not only with sales talk but with a message which includes moral imperatives. Given that they have official positions, are more educated, and are often higher in the caste hierarchy, it is frequently surprising that a mother of three or four children resists the suggestion of sterilisation during twenty separate visits in a three year period, especially when these are reinforced by statements from the doctor on visits to the health center. This is why families often suddenly agree to sterilisation in a spirit of newly discovered moral rectitude, sometimes implying that the daughter-in-law is benefiting the whole family by making a noble sacrifice, a concept very familiar to the Hindu tradition (Caldwell *et. al.* 1988: 74-75). Prolonged lactation and substantial periods of post-natal sexual abstinence provide satisfactorily long periods between births, and the demand for non-terminal methods arises from younger couples who fear they might conceive during the customary abstinence period. Terminal methods, however, are a major demand. ' An understanding of fertility transition necessitates an understanding of the sterilisation programme for most members of the community are offered nothing else. There has always been a degree of moral pressure, as is inevitable with a system of targets. The moral pressure is broader than the relationship between the health worker and the client' (Caldwell et al. 1988: 244).

The Political Economy Perspective

Mamdani (1972), in his monograph as a follow up study after ten years of contraceptive distribution and fertility control research in the Khanna region in Punjab through the 1960s, was trying to explore why fertility did not drop in ten years of apparent contraceptive acceptance by villagers. In the process, he dug deeper into the social meaning of fertility, high social value of more children, especially sons, for both the rich and the poor in the Khanna villages of Punjab. Using contraception when sons were needed on the farms was courting disaster. Household economics in the prospering Punjab state with emerging green revolution in the late 1960s and early 1970s continued to value high fertility which Mamdani brought up to show how economic actions are at once social. Just as a forest is known by its trees, a Jat (Punjabi peasant) is known by his sons. Sons for prosperity and sonlessness as doom, was common sense. Both household and macro level political economy favoured more sons, which lay behind the non-practice of contraception. That is why the villagers accepted contraceptives from the researchers without any intention of using them. Polite etiquette meant a non-refusal of contraceptives from the urban and educated researcher. In a like vein, in their study of the medical systems in Tamil Nadu, Djurfeldt and Lindberg (1976) report on an ethnography that speaks of the necessity and value of fertility, especially sons, in the context of fear of infant and child mortality. People were confronted with a dialogic relation with the government family planning employees who were chasing their own officially assigned targets and stressing on sterilisation more than other means of contraception.

Other studies—Jeffery *et al.* (1989) and Jeffery and Jeffery (1996), provide ethnographies to illustrate the effects of the macro-level political economy on the micro and family levels in dealing with childbirth and related practices. The authors report on women in Bijnor who come into close contact with the family planning programme through the agency of the Auxiliary Nurse and Midwife (ANM), a State employee who had access to various forms of birth control means such as pills, and copper-T (IUD). Sterilisation is the most favoured method by the Indian government. ANMs are given yearly quotas which they are encouraged to fill, and they often use very coercive tactics to 'motivate' people to get sterilised. People in the area were also distrustful of the ANMs for making health services at the government dispensary contingent upon their compliance with sterilisation. So, they checked with the researchers (the Jefferys) on the amount and quality of the pills ANMs gave them. Once an ANM asked a woman to pay for the second prescription for birth control pills when she went for a second prescription after having lost the first one. The ANM said that the only way to stop having children is to be sterilised. These instances show how women find little assistance in controlling their fertility; rather they are alienated from the government family planning programmes. One woman, Nijma, decided to opt for sterilisation without telling anyone in her family. She had been sick and was losing her sight. She did not have enough money to pay for medicines for herself or her ailing children and birth control pills made her sick. She had the operation one day when her in-laws were on a condolence visit to another town. She was compensated with Rs. 155. After the operation, the ANM who had promised to obtain treatment for her eye if she underwent the operation, never followed up on her promise.

In Jhakri, the Muslim village studied by the authors, sterilisation was rare. The records showed no vasectomy during the Emergency (1975-77). One woman in the village underwent sterilisation after an obstructed labour and dangerous cesarean section. Thus, while family planning officials try to achieve targets through various means, people work out what is in their best interest at different times in their lives. Jeffrey and Jeffrey tell also of how pressures to meet targets affect service providers, when they report false entries in the ANM's register, showing several women as having accepted IUDs when in reality the alleged acceptors claimed they never accepted the device. The registers also showed fewer births for the women than they actually had. The discrepancies can be traced to the pressure of the quota system through which the programme operated.

Anthropology and Demography

Influenced by the somewhat romantic picture of the anthropologist and ethnographer who lives in exotic, remote, distant villages, demography sees the role of anthropology in ethnographic descriptions obtained from the fieldwork method rather than in anthropological theory or concepts. This is partly because anthropology tends to focus on precisely the forces conventional demographic theory omitted in its method and analytical framework. In the Indian context, anthropologists and sociologists have produced ethnographic work either on fertility behaviour and family planning (Mamdani 1972, Jeffery et al. 1989, Patel 1994, Jeffery and Jeffery 1997, and Saavala 2001) or have described these in their work in closely related fields, such as health systems (Djurfeldt and Lindberg 1976), and everyday life of rural women (Jeffery and Jeffery 1996).

Over the last two decades, anthropology and demography have begun to speak to each other. There have been two developments enabling such a dialogue across these disciplines. First, demographic research has been in search of a theory which can explain the kind of changes taking place in the world in the wake of the onset of fertility transition in most countries. Second, demography has been opening up to the methodological intrusions by other disciplines into its own realm.[3] Demography has been rather accommodative and thus, anthropological demography has been institutionalised as a branch of demography rather than anthropology. The concern for population homeostasis—a kind of optimum balance between population and resources—i.e., a balance which includes the relationship between environmental resources and human populations, also brought anthropology and demography closer. Demographers like Caldwell and Caldwell (1987) have advocated the adoption of participant observation method for conducting micro studies in demography,[4] and Greenhalgh (1994) urges the creation, in fertility research, of 'whole demographies' that contextualise demographic behaviour not only in social and economic terms but in political and cultural terms as well.

Structuration and Practice Perspectives

Culturally sensitive exploration of pathways that operate in a society's fertility practice (whether high or low) enabled through ethnographic studies is gaining ground. Greenhalgh (1995) had recommended micro level village demographic ethnographies. Let us take two such studies in the Indian context. One, by Patel (1994), deploys Giddens (1984) structuration theory and the other, by Saavala (2001), uses Bourdieu's (1977) theory of practice.[5]

Patel finds, in her study of village Mogra, how values imbibed at an early age and put into practice in each couple's uniquely personal, and yet, socially accepted and expected ways of child bearing and rearing, paves the way for social acceptance in the normal course of life. Learning the rules of the game happens early in life. Their enactment, calibrated both through the 'rule book', on the one hand, and the individual/the couple, the family, wider influences and experiences, on the other, sets the stage for fertility trajectories. For Giddens, this practice constitutes 'structuration'.

Let us see how people express what they have learnt from the normative social practice. Sensitive data collection outside the pre-printed questionnaire give away a lot more about people and persons. Ethnography can tap their 'practical consciousness'. The importance of the social optimum number of offspring and sex composition is known, even to children and adolescents. We can visualise, from the ethnographic material presented below, how the norms situated outside an individual are activated in individual actions and behaviour, including statements in the course of conversation.

> Buddha, a 13-year-old Patel boy, was inquisitive about the number of children I, the ethnographer, had. He asked my 12-year-old daughter, as to how many her brothers and sisters were. On hearing that she had only one brother he responded with surprise, 'Oh no! you should have one more brother. Your parents must have at least one more son. One son is no son just as one eye is no eye (ek ank main ank nee, ne ek put mein put nee).' On another occasion, during the initial stage of fieldwork, when I lived all by myself, a Patel lady next door introduced me to her six-year-old son Hanuman, who was inquisitive about me. The boy looked around for sometime and whispered to his mother: 'But where are her children?'

As these instances suggest, even small children failed to understand the independence and individuality of an adult female. A woman without in-laws or children around, in their perception, is a deviant.

Young married girls generally bowed their heads and lowered their eyes as a sign of embarrassment and inhibition when asked about their reproductive activities.

> On asking whether they communicate with their spouses regarding sex and childbirth, Patel (1994) got the following responses that the adolescent typically give to the elderly. 'I don't know. How do I know? What is there to know (in this matter)? What can I say?' The less evasive responses included: 'We don't talk about this. You are embarrassing me. We will not do anything extraordinary. What happens to others will happen to us too.'

Parenthood, especially motherhood, is as critical as marriage in this village. The honor that is bestowed on woman when she attains motherhood, and the cementing of the marital tie that motherhood leads to, are too well known to require further elaboration. Here, we look through a sample of cases of how each person's individual fertility career has social norms in the background, as also, an ongoing social and personal assessment and learning from the experience for others.

> Rekha, a Charan mother, was verbally threatened by her husband when she did not bear a child seven years after marriage. Phatu, a Charan *patwari* (village accountant) in his thirties, has had no child even after more than 12 yeas of marriage. His wife is perpetually anxious about her future. Her husband's second marriage is her constant fear.

> Labu, a Bhambi, is one of the two currently married barren women. She is the first of two wives of her husband. As she did not bear a child despite several years of marriage, she went along with her husband's decision to have a second wife with a view to having children. The second wife, Kanwari was blind. Labu looked after her. Kanwari had three sons, who were brought up by Labu. Despite being blind, Kanwari has been cared for respectfully by her barren co-wife. She has greater authority in the family despite being the junior wife. The three parents live with one son each in three different houses adjacent to one another.

> During my fieldwork, Cuki had a son and Anadi was in an advanced stage of pregnancy. Cuki's childbirth silenced her husband's sisters and his brothers' wives. One a later visit to the field, I learnt that the birth of Anadi's daughter had made her quite confident in the family. Both Cuki and Anadi gained self-esteem as the stigma of barrenness was erased.

> Rajuji, a skinny old Patel in his late sixties, was generally reserved in interaction with fellow villagers as well as outsiders. Once I saw him holding his two-year-old daughter in one arm and carrying an empty pitcher in the other. He was walking towards the village pond to fetch water and also

herding his cattle for watering them. The sight of an old man fetching water is rare, although it is not uncommon for old men to be with small children, particularly their grandchildren. Rajuji was forced into work that was unusual for his age—carrying his own daughter, fetching water and herding cattle. He had to do it, as his wife was ailing and there was no one else in the household to relieve him. Rajuji had spent his entire life aspiring for a son. He married thrice. Two of his earlier wives died without a son. The second bore a girl who has been married off. The third wife had also borne a girl who was two years old (This was the one he was carrying). Rajuji's was the only Patel household without any gold and silver jewellery – the most sought after security plank after land. On being asked if he expected any girl or boy from his lineage (because they would also be his immediate neighbours) to fetch water, he responded with a bland expression: 'Who will come to help me? Even friends and relatives cease to exist when needed by a lonely person'. From the ethnographic work in the village it was very evident that people come forward with help only when they know that the help will be reciprocated. Social networks operate on the principle of implicit reciprocity.

Pemji, a shepherd in his forties, has only two surviving daughters out of seven daughters and two sons born. His elder brother, on the other hand, has three sons and two daughters. Due to his and his wife's illness, Pemji was heavily indebted. Consequently he wished to sell a part of his land to repay some of his debts. But his elder brother has been obstructing all his moves for nearly a decade. The land is in Pemji's deceased father's name. For any land deal, both brothers have to come together. Pemji cannot convince his brother who knows that the land will belong to him and his sons one day. If Pemji had a few sons or even one son, he would not have been indebted nor felt the need to dispose of the land. Even that was proving to be an impossible task.

Women's contribution to household subsistence does not automatically lead to their status enhancement. As Patel observes: 'Contribution to the family subsistence and improvement in status are mediated by a complex dialectics of patriarchal values and women's real life experiences' (1987: 126). Motherhood is crucial for a woman's status enhancement, especially when her offspring is a son. Afshar's (1985) and Kabeer's (1985) studies in Iran and Bangladesh respectively affirm this to be so. Having a son brings an all-encompassing confidence to the mother, visible in her demeanor and others' attitudes towards her.

Chandarki, a young Patel woman in her early twenties and mother of a son and daughter, once had a serious quarrel with her husband, while I and a few other people were present. He threatened to beat and drive her out of the house. At this, she retorted, addressing especially the by-standers: 'Don't think that I am a sonless woman. I will bring up my son in my natal home. When he grows up I will fearlessly come back to the village with all authority. I will approach all the village elders to listen to my son. Then I will live with my son on this man's (her husband's) property and constantly embarrass him. Only then will he realise that he had committed a blunder.'

Heerani, a Charan woman in her forties, was deserted by her husband after he married another. For several years she lived a miserable life. She had to do away with the Charan custom of *purdo* and work in the fields, and collect fuel and fetch water for herself and the children. She had two sons and as many daughters. She proclaimed with covert pride: 'He (the husband) will have to come back to me in the end. His name will be kept by my sons. When he is unable to stand on his own, his daughter will be in her conjugal home and his wife will be too weak to take care of him. How long can he then neglect me?'

Childbirth is power in ways more than one. It is in itself a women's domain. Almost all births in the village take place at home. Women are skilled in the job and do not depend on modern obstetricians. *Dai*s, local low caste birth practitioners and senior women are adept at handling childbirths with the knowledge of culturally prescribed nuances and notions of purity-pollution and theories of the birthing body and the environment.

Phooli, a Patel woman, came with her newly-born baby in her arms from the field a kilometer away. When I asked why she did not come home when the labour pains began, she said: 'The pain was bearable and irregular. So I thought the delivery was a few hours away. I continued to chop *bajri* stalks. Suddenly the pains shot up. I could hardly move to a smoother ground. As I squatted, the baby was born. I cut the umbilical cord with a sickle, buried it and the effluvia there itself, tore a piece of my *orno* (half-saree) and wrapped the baby in it, and set out for home with the baby. She is my fifth child, but the first I had all alone. I felt a strange courage in me to face it all by myself. God was kind enough to make it so smooth for me.'

The simple setting for childbirth and the matter-of-course attitude towards it go hand in hand. If the senior woman of the household feels less confident about handling the matter, she arranges for another experienced woman relative (neighbours are usually relatives) to stay with her overnight. Or, she is forewarned not to absent herself for long from home as she might be needed any time. Such an arrangement is usually made a few days in advance, especially if it is a woman's first child delivery. Even otherwise, the woman expert is kept regularly informed and can be called anytime; the prevailing norms do not allow her to refuse help, especially for child delivery. In fact, an opportunity to assist at childbirth, believed to bring *punna* (religious merit), is rarely foregone. Refusal evokes severe criticism and disrepute. I did not come across any case of refusal during fieldwork.

A modern doctor differs from the *dai* in many respects. There are indigenous ways of keeping a *dai* informed about the pregnant woman's condition. All precarious moments are discussed intensively with her. The modern doctor, on the other hand, keeps fixed hours of consultation, and fulfils a mandate that is restricted largely to professional expertise. The local birth expert conducts herself in an entirely different fashion. She sees the pregnant woman as a person belonging to a particularly household in the village. The *dai* also observes the patient in a wide context; the pregnant woman's health is seen in the context of her household, family, caste and economic condition. Unlike medical professionals in urban areas, the local birth attendant has no fixed schedule during which she is available for consultation. She may be approached at any time of the day—or night, if the situation demands. As the expert attendant's or the *dai*'s relationship with various households is informal, their availability for the purpose of consultancy or for attending on the patient depends primarily on personal terms.

It is usually possible to decipher from the child's name the particular stage of the parents' fertility trajectory. Certain names are proscribed or preferred for the first few children, while certain others are prescribed. Another set of names is usually meant only for children born after the couple's fertility expectations are met and the couple desires for no more. A few of the preferred names for the first few desired children are Asa or Asi (hope), Rana (king), Rani (queen), Sukhi (well-being), and names of deities such as Ram and Sita. Other names mean 'vegetation', 'courage', 'undefeated', 'immovable', 'magnanimous', 'wealth', 'jewels' and 'immortal'. As the first few children glorify the parents' status, their names are chosen accordingly. Parents who have lost infants in succession usually name the surviving one as 'natha' / 'nathi' (tethered), 'manga' / 'mangi' (borrowed), 'reta' / 'retai' (sand), 'uka' / 'ukli' (garbage heap) and 'koja' / 'koji' (ugly). All these names symbolise that the parents either had no rights over the infant or the infant was so ugly as to attract no one's fancy, thereby leaving it alone to grow up safely. Contrariwise, parents who did not desire any more children after say, two sons and two daughters, named their Johnny Come Lately children, especially daughters, 'madi' (one who gate crashed) or 'aai chuki' ('enough of coming'). I was told in personal communication that 'bhalya' (Punjabi for one who lost his / her way) used to be given to such an infant. I have come across a name '*Itishree*' given to a Bengali girl who I confirmed happened to be the fourth and last child of her parents. Itishree is a word made of two words, *iti*, meaning the end and *shree,* meaning Godess Lakshmi, often a name given to girls in India. By conjunction of the two words *iti* and *shree*, the word *'itishree'* becomes a beautiful name, in this case given to the last child of the couple. The child's position in the parents' fertility career itself rules out certain names and leaves open the possibility of certain others. The pool of preferred names may be divided into three categories – one, indicating desire for offspring, the other, anxiety about the offspring's survival, and third, suggesting the undesirability of the child.

We have already had a glimpse of the values that form the substratum of the first category, i.e., the desire for offspring. Now we move on to influences that work in the opposite direction, to curtail childbearing.

> Vena, a father of two sons and two daughters, initially agreed to his wife getting sterilised but revoked his consent immediately after his mother indicated her disapproval. He had agreed with his wife after she convinced him but chose to remain silent when his mother spoke against the decision.
>
> Bijoji, an old man owning a small patch of land, was perturbed when his only daughter gave birth to eight children in quick succession with two years' gap between each o them. He confided in me: 'It is no point having so many children without a stop. Three or four are enough. There are several means to put a stop these days. See how the whole house is littered.'
>
> Sugan, a young Charan woman in her late twenties and mother of three sons, always felt disgusted with her husband's indifference to her desire to get sterilised. He always diverted the issue and gave her false promises that her sterilisation would be arranged. As time passed, she feared another conception. During one of her occasional stays at her parental home, she got herself sterilised, much to the displeasure of her husband and mother-in-law. Sugan offered a vivid narrative of how she finally convinced her husband in spite of his strong reactions against her act: 'If we get a fourth son, how little land will each of the sons get! And if we had any daughter, how can we afford to marry her? The dowry expenses are rising day by day. Your salary is just sufficient to support the three boys and to educate them. Your opium addiction is no less expensive.' Sugan recalled that it took time before such an explanation finally pacified her husband's anger. She maintained that although the reaction of her husband and mother-in-law was hostile and painful (in the sense that she was not allowed to take proper rest after the operation), it did not last long. She summed up her gain: 'I am not reproducing like a goat.'

On the other hand, child loss—infant and child mortality, make for a strong and lasting case *against* sterilisation. Such an impact is not limited only to the woman or the couple on whom the misfortune of becoming childless was cast, but impacts the fertility course of their immediate kin and circle of relatives.

> Chidi, an old Harijan woman, strongly disapproved of the emerging trend towards fertility control. She was provoked when she overheard her daughter-in-law, a mother of four sons, being interviewed on the issue. She said: 'No one should get sterilised. There is no guarantee of life these days. Times are very adverse. There is a lot of sin spread all over the world. What can a woman do if all her children were to die after sterilisation? In Tanavara (a neighbouring village) a Sargari (woman of the Sargara caste) underwent tubectomy last year. She thought the three sons she had were enough for her. But as unfortunate as she is, two of her sons died of fever within two days of each other, and another died a month later. All the three healthy boys simply slipped out of her hands in less than a year of sterilsing. She couldn't do anything about it at all. She could only weep and wail. All this has driven her to mental illness and she talks incoherently. Her life is ruined. I will not permit my daughter-in-law to do such a thing. We will all share what we have. We will eat half instead of one *poori* (*poori khata adi khaon*) and be satisfied rather than ruin ourselves by trying all kinds of nonsense. It is a sin to sterilise and the sinner is punished sooner or later. Sterilisation leads to suffering'.

> Vaddi, aged 60, experienced the agony of mortality right from her childhood. In her childhood, a few of her siblings succumbed to mortality, and as a mother, she lost all four of her children. Such a trail of misfortune continued even in the case of her near relatives, particularly her husband's brother's family (all except one boy and a girl died). Given this background of personal tragedy, Vaddi turned hysterical whenever sterilisation was discussed. Vaddi's adopted son's (her husband's brother's orphaned son) wife, a mother of four daughters and two sons, recalled vividly: 'I wished to get sterilised after I had four children. Upon hearing this Maa-ji (mother-in-law) got so wild that I dared not mention it again. She called insulting names to those who had sterilised. To her they were blind and crazy. How can I even tell her that I want to get sterilised?'

Jhammu, a young woman in her twenties, was apprehensive about sterilisation. 'So many people have told me that sterilisation amounts to torturing all those beings who were destined to be born to a woman. Denying them entry in this world does not absolve the woman. She will have to bear all the remaining children in her next incarnation. There is no respite from this. One has to finish one's task before attaining *gati*.' A Hindu father's obligation to marry off his daughter at puberty to avoiding the sin of wasting potential births every menstrual cycle is linked with the fears Jhammu had.

'How shall we Feed them?': The Quest for Dignity

Let us now briefly review Saavala's (2001) careful and perceptive ethnography in Gopalpalli, a village of East Godavari district in Andhra Pradesh. The reasons behind the lack of food that many villagers have to face here is the grossly imbalanced land ownership – a majority of households do not have any land to cultivate, and consequently are dependent on wage labour. Irrigation in the area relies mainly on rainfall, unlike in the Godavari delta nearby. Only one paddy crop and a crop of pulses are cultivated annually in most fields. Consequently, labourers suffer from under-employment. The area has thus far averted both the direct benefits and curses of the 'Green Revolution'. Gopalapalli children have to be nourished and nurtured in conditions where food is objectively scarce for most families. In order to understand what the relation between economic conditions and fertility practices is, we have to look in ethnographic detail at the way Gopalapalli villagers speak about and act in relation to food and children.

The most common answer given by Gopalapalli villagers to the question of why a woman or a man opted for a small family, or why a small family in general would be better than having many children, came down to that of 'nourishing'. 'How could we fill all those bellies?' was a common rhetorical question. Similar answers were also given by rural Tamils in recent focus group discussions (Krishnamoorty et al. 1996). The question of having children is not formulated in terms of 'wanting' a small or a big family; in Telugu there is no direct equivalent to the English verb 'to want'. This is not a question of mere linguistics, but points to the basic way in which people conceptualise desirability – individual 'wants' are inseparable from the necessities for a good life that are, in turn, derived from their socially positioning.

When constantly hearing the expression 'difficult to feed, nourish children', one is tempted to adopt a straightforward economic explanation for fertility decline in the locality. The relationship between economic factors and fertility decline nevertheless turned out to be complicated and multifaceted. First, this trope was used not only by those who suffered from immediate food scarcity – it was a universally adopted way of denoting experienced difficulties of upbringing children. Second, it would be naïve to take such utterances as merely unproblematic reflections of objective reality. People do things by saying things and say things by doing things. Anthropology aims to reveal what lies behind ideas, expression and practices that appear unchallenged – not reducing but instead cultivating complexity, not simplifying conundrums but elaborating them. To gain full comprehension of the' difficulty of nourishing', probing was necessary – why did people use this expression when provoked, and what did they accomplish by saying so? Moreover, the expression 'to nourish' had to be contextualised to make sense. What is of more importance than searching for an abstract meaning of a metaphor or trope, is to look for the social consequences of phrases. Metaphors lead into social action; 'the tropes play on real life' (Hastrup 1995: 37).

The following was an angry outburst of a potter woman from Kummara caste of potters who was struck by economic deprivation. Savaala 2001 asked why she had got herself sterilised after giving birth twice. The author and others were sitting in front of their tiny mud house, facing her small, naked children playing in the alley and covered with muck and mire as it was the rainy season.

Pentamma (Kammara woman aged 24): 'We people cannot afford to have many children, we are just potters. How would we fill them, all those bellies? Our children are thin, they do not have proper clothes. Is it good to have ten such children around? No.... Those who have money have many children, it looks nice. But we cannot. That is why two is enough.'

Pentamma's answer was curt, even aggressive; it showed the contradiction between her aspirations and the reality. Her comment brings to the fore many facets related to having children. The question of poverty related directly to her caste identity; Pentamma used the idiom of *kulam* and poverty related to it in order to express the reasons for her accepting a sterilisation. As Kummaras are poor, they have to be pleased with few children, unlike those who are rich (rich equated here with the better-off peasant Kapus by whom the Kummaras are surrounded).

Pentamma pointed out the miserable living conditions of people of her caste, but simultaneously did not rule out the possibility of a better future if they just had fewer children. The second theme in her outpouring was the striving for dignity and improvement. Pentamma did not look forward to having many children because the fewer the children, the easier it was to feed and clothe them when they were small. She sought decency in her family, not to live surrounded by a flock of malnourished and ill children. In fact she coveted the appearance of the surrounding better-off Kapus by limiting the number of children. 'If we have many children, we look like poor people, if we have only few, we may appear respectable', was Pentamma's inference. The quest for dignity is pivotal for understanding the dialectics of hunger and hope for people who live in economic poverty.

In Hindu South Asia, food is a realm of sophisticated philosophical, religious, medical, and social meaning-giving (e.g. Appadurai 1984; Khare 1992a, 1992b). Already in the texts of the Upanishads from the first millennium BC, food is said to be the ultimate Reality, Brahman, and Cosmos. 'There is a non-dichotomous linkage between the Creator, body, and self through food' (Khare 1992a: 6). Thus food is essentially physical, but the physical cannot be separated from the social, spiritual, and mental well-being in Hindu philosophy, which informs the vernacular thinking.

There are two principal verbs used in Telugu for expressing nurturing, nourishing, bringing up a child, viz., *pencu* and *pooSincu.* They both contain the idea of nourishing others, giving cooked rice / food (*annam*). *PooSincu* also has a connotation of patronising, protecting, or bringing up an adopted child. In all relationships, affection is embedded in giving nourishment. The way to show affection towards a child is always in the material form of clothes and other consumer goods (cf. Osella and Osella 1996: 51; Trawick 1990: 215). When people talk about *annam*, they refer as well to all the other material things necessary for loving a child and making her / him into a whole person. Nurturing means giving a child cooked rice / food and other objects, services, and attention that embody their love and affection. Feeding others (i.e. giving away rice / food) is culturally more central than eating itself is. Already in the Laws of Manu it is said: 'He who prepares food for himself (alone), eats but sin' (Moreno 1992: 148). Feeding a child is the Dharmam—duty or virtue—of parents, but also the means for creating a sacrosanct social bond between them: '[T] he giver earns religious merit while the receiver accumulates a form of debt…. To be repaid sooner or later, in this life or the next' (Khare 1992b: 208).

Forcing an unwilling child to eat is regarded as benevolent care-taking. The typical way of feeding a child is that first the mother places a plate of cooked rice that she has mixed, with her hand, with a spoonful of curry (or just rice with some salt and oil, or tamarind water) in front of the child who sits on the floor, cross-legged. When the child gets impatient and rises up, the mother will follow her / him, pressing balls of *annam* she has worked out in her right hand into the child's mouth. Feeding another person with your own hand is full of affection – it is a bodily contact which no spoon or fork can convey.

By being fed by those who form the core of the regenerative powers of the household as deliverers of *annam* and deliverers of babies, a child attains personhood. Because there is a unity between self, body, *annam* and divinity, only through eating rice can one become a self—soul and body incorporated. If parents cannot feed a child rice, they are not able to give her / him full personhood, so to speak. Not being fed means corrosion of personhood through a looseness of social bonds. In South Asia personhood is fluid and social connections form the self which hardly exists as an 'inner, true self' separate from those relations' (e.g. Busby 1997a; Daniel 1984; Ewing 1990; Trawick 1990).

The connotation of mothers with *annam* is ubiquitous and indexical—a woman is supposed to take the main responsibility of feeding cooked rice to her spouse and children. Women's lives are coordinated by the necessities of preparing ingredients for food, cooking, and delivering meals to everyone and making them eat properly. It is a sign of success to a woman to see the family thriving and healthy, rather than thin and wasted. Affectionate love cannot be separated from bodily well-being: a loving wife's husband and children manifest her love in their plumpness and the glowing shine of their hair. The husband of a friend of mine is an emaciated, sickly man. Nagamani, my landlady, commented on his outlook and implied there to be something wrong with the wife as the husband was so gaunt. 'Does she not cook proper food for him?' she asked. By her remark she did not refer to the quantity or taste of the food cooked by my friend, but suspected some inauspicious or even harmful powers emanating from my friend and entering the husband's body through food given by her. In India, food is thought to easily absorb influences, words, and sins, especially from the person who gives the food (Khare 1992a). Affection is a bodily experience – it is digested and thus incorporated in the form of deified rice. By giving food prepared and cooked by herself, a woman passes her affection on to her dear ones in a corporeal way.

In the areas of paddy cultivation such as East Godavari District, civilization is conceptualised through rice-eating. Strangers and barbarians are by definition those who do not eat rice. 'Tribal' people, who live in the forest areas in the nearby hills to Gopalapalli panchayat, cultivate millets in their slash-and-burn fields (nowadays they have incorporated rice in their diet). One of their principal sources of energy during the hot season is *Khallu*, 'toddy' in Indian English, which is a self-fermenting drink tapped from palmyra trees. Also, some lower-caste Hindus and Malas produce and use toddy. For rice-eaters, those who eat millet as a staple diet and who drink toddy are associated with poverty, savagery, promiscuity and a general lack of humanity and civilization. Rice is valuable physically, socially and symbolically, for the politics of identity.

Eating is regarded as a habit; whatever kind of foodstuffs one eats and how much one eats becomes a habit, *alawaaTu*. There are many sayings that stress the permanence of habits acquired when one is small, and through practice; even hunger or eating bad food may become habits that do not wear off: 'You are what you eat and you eat what you are' (Khare 1992a:11). Children who grow up having to eat pork or beef, drink toddy, or with a staple diet other than rice, have incorporated these 'bad' habits into themselves. Gopalapalli people say that if you were brought up eating pork or beef – meat regarded as filthy or taboo – you will crave for it eternally, even if more highly prized meat such as mutton or chicken becomes available.

Saying that it is difficult to nourish children means that it is difficult to build up their personhood through prestigious food stuffs. Ability to nourish one's children means the ability to give them love and affection, to connect them socially, and also to connect them to divinity, auspiciousness, and civilization. A child who is deprived of a proper diet or rice is deprived of well-being in the widest sense of the word, not only of nutrients. The symbolic value of raising children in a desirably appropriate manner is expressed as 'filling the belly' and to be contextualised with sensitively careful ethnography to get to the deeper meanings of people's actions and decisions.

NOTES

1. The studies included in the volume edited by Basu and Jeffery (1996) is an illustration of this research close to home, i.e., in South Asia. It is noteworthy also that many of the status of women studies have omitted the context in which fertility is situated and dynamics of work in relation to women's status at the grass roots level; Patel's and Madhok's papers in Unnithan-Kumar (2004) are detailed reflections on this issue.
2. See Kertzer and Fricke, 1997 for an informed account of the relationship between demography and anthropology
3. 'Over the last decade or so a long line of demographers has bemoaned the disappointing state of the field. By these accounts demography is theoretically thin, substantively shrinking, and neglectful of global economic and political changes that are transforming its object of study' (Greenhalgh 1995: 11).
4. Caldwell et al (1988) conducted in South India a study following the method they advocated. Their appendix describing their methodological route and experience found few admirers in the demographic field, especially in the publishing industry two and a half decades ago.
5. Patel's (1994) study of a North Indian village was published in (1994) a year before Greenhalgh's call for use of Giddens' or Bourdieu's theories in demography.

REFERENCES

Appadurai, A. 1984. 'How moral is South Asia's Economy? A review article'. *Journal of Asian Studies*, vol.43, pp.481- 497.

Basu. A.M. and R. Jeffery (eds.) 1996. *Girls' Schooling, Autonomy and Feritlity Change in South Asia*. New Delhi: Sage.

Bourdieu, Pierre, 1977. *Outline of a Theory of Practice*. Cambridge: Cambridge University Press.

Busby, Judith, 1997a. 'Permeable and Partible Persons: A Comparative Analysis of Gender and Body in South India and Melanesia'. *Journal of the Royal, Anthropological Institute*, Vol.3, pp.261-278.

Caldwell, J.C., P.H. Reddy and P. Caldwell. 1988. *The Causes of Demographic Change.* Wisconsin: The University of Wisconsin Press.

Daniel, E. Valentine, 1984. *Fluid Signs: Being a Person the Tamil Way.* Berkeley: University of California Press.

Djurfeldt, G. and S. Lindberg. 1976. *Pills Against Poverty*. New Delhi: Oxford and IBH Publishing Company.

Ewing, Katherine P., 1990. 'The illusion of wholeness: Culture, Self, and the Experience of Inconsistency'. *Ethos*, Vol.18, pp.251-278.

George, A., 1984. *The Constitution of Society.* Cambridge: Polity Press.

Greenhalgh. S. 1995. *Situating Fertility: Anthropology and Demographic Inquiry*. Cambridge: Cambridge University Press.

Hastrup, Kirsten, 1995. *A Passage to Anthropology. Between Experience and Theory.* London: Routledge.

Jeffery, P., R. Jeffery and A. Lyon. 1988 *Labour Pains and Labour Power.* Delhi: Manohar.

Jeffery, P., R. Jeffery. 1996. *Don't Marry Me to a Ploughman! Women's Everyday Lives in Rural North India.* Boulder: Westview Press.

Jeffery, P., R. Jeffery. 1997. *Population, Gender and Politics.* Cambridge: Cambridge University Press.

Kabeer, N., 1985. Do Women Gain from High Fertility? In H. Afshar (ed.), *Women, Work and Ideology in the Third World.* London: Tavistock.

Khare, R.S., 1992a. 'Introduction'. In R.S. Khare (ed.), *The Eternal Food. Gastronomic Ideas and Experiences of Hindus and Buddhists.* Albany: State University of New York, pp.1-25.

...... 1992b. 'Annambrahman: Cultural models, meanings, and aesthetics of Hindu food'. In R.S. Khare (ed.), *The Eternal Food. Gastronomic Ideas and Experiences of Hindus and Buddhists.* Albany: State University of New York, pp.201-220.

Mamdani, M. 1972. *The Myth of Population Control.* New York: The Monthly Review Press.

Moreno, Manuel, 1992. 'Pancamirtam: God's Washings as Food'. In R.S. Khare (ed.), *The Eternal Food. Gastronomic Ideas and Experiences of Hindus and Buddhists.* Albany: State University of New York, pp. 147-178.

Osella, Filippo and Caroline Osella, 1996. 'Articulation of Physical and Social Bodies in Kerala'. *Contributions to Indian Sociology*, Vol.30, pp.37-68.

Patel, T. 1994. *Fertility Behaviour: Population and Society in a Rajasthan Village.* Delhi: Oxford University Press.

...... 2004. 'women in Fertility Studies and In Situ', in Unnithan-Kumar, M. ed. *Reproductive Agency, Medicine and the State.* New York, Oxford: Berghahn Books. pp.203-222.

Saavala, Minna. 1999. 'Understanding the Prevalence of Female Sterilization in South India'. *Studies in Family Planning,* vol.4, pp.288-301.

Saavala, Minna. 2001. *Fertility and Familial Power Relations: Procreation in south India.* London: Curzon.

Sadasivam, Bharati, 1986. 'Injectable Contraceptives in Mass Programme. Alarming Scope for Misuse'. *Economic and Political Weekly*, Oct. 25, pp. 1886-1887.

Trawick, Margaret, 1990. *Notes on Love in a Tamil Family.* Berkeley: University of California Press.

Part IV

INDIA'S DEMOGRAPHIC TRAJECTORIES

Chapter 5

India's Demographic Profile: Trends, Differentials and Contrasts

Mahendra K. Premi

India is the second most populous country in the world, next only to China. Its population touched one billion on May 11, 2000. On the census count of 1st March 2001, the population of India stood at 1.029 billion. As estimated by the United Nations, India accounted for a massive 1,025 million of the world's 6,134 million persons in mid 2001. At that point of time, of every 1,000 persons in the world, 167 were Indians, or, in other words, every sixth person was an Indian. India however, accounted for only 2.4 percent of the 135.2 million square kilometers of inhabited land area over which the world's population was distributed. It accounted for almost twice the population of Latin America and one and a quarter times the population of whole of Africa. Not only is India's population huge by world standards, it has been growing rapidly in recent decades. Thus, the 2001 population of India was almost three times the population of the country at the time of Independence. The country's increase of population during the 1990's has been greater than the total population of Western Europe comprising Austria, Belgium, France, Germany, Luxembourg, Netherlands, and Switzerland. Annually, India adds almost the total population of Australia or Sri Lanka.

Population Growth Pattern

The history of India's population growth since 1891 divides itself into four parts, the points of division being 1921, 1951 and 1981 respectively (Table 1). The year 1921 is called the year of the 'Great Divide', because it distinguished the earlier period of chequered population growth from a period of moderately increasing growth. The year 1951 marks the beginning of a period of rapid population growth. The third breakpoint is 1981, after which the high growth registers some definite signs of slowing down (Figure 1).

High mortality levels were responsible for the variable growth rates of population during the 30 years or more before 1921. A severe famine affected large areas of the country in 1896 and 1897. In Bombay Presidency especially, the effects of the famine were aggravated by a severe plague. As a result of the two scourges, the 1901 census recorded a population loss of about 2 percent in that province from the 1891 level of 18.8 million (Mitra 1978: 16).

TABLE 1: Population of India and its Growth, 1891-2001

Year	Total population (Millions)	Decadal growth		Average annual exponential growth rate (in percent)
		Absolute	Percent	
1891	235.9	—	—	—
1901	238.4	1.1	1.1	0.11
1911	252.1	5.7	5.7	0.56
1921	251.3	-0.8	-0.3	-.03
1931	279.0	27.7	11.0	1.04
1941	318.7	39.7	14.2	1.33
1951	361.1	42.4	13.3	1.25
1961	439.2	78.1	21.5	1.96
1971	548.2	109.0.	24.8	2.20
1981	683.3*	135.1	24.7	2.20
1991	843.4#	160.1	23.8	2.14
2001	1,028.6$	185.2	21.3	1.93

Notes: *In 1981, census was not conducted in Assam. Based on the 1971 and the 1991 censuses, the population of Assam as on March 1, 1981 has been interpolated to 18.04 million. As a consequence, the total population of India as of 1 March 1981 has been estimated as 683.3 million as against the earlier published figure of 685.2 million.

The 1991 Census could not be conducted in Jammu and Kashmir owing to disturbed conditions prevailing there. Hence, the population figures for India include the population of that state as have been worked out by 'interpolation.' That has resulted in the reduction of India's population for that year from 846.3 million to 843.4 million.

$ The population of India includes the estimated population of entire Kachchh district, Morvi, Maliya-Miyyana and Wakaner talukas of Rajkot district, Jodiya taluka of Jamnagar district of Gujarat State and entire Kinnaur district of Himachal Pradesh where population enumeration of Census of India 2001, could not be conducted due to natural calamities.

Sources: Census of India 2001; Premi (2003: 59).

Like the 1891-1901 decade, the 1901-11 decade witnessed several local famines and a severe one in 1907 in most parts of Uttar Pradesh. Plague was in evidence in the Bengal and Bombay Presidencies, and both plague and malaria were widespread in the Punjab and Uttar Pradesh where population growth was negligible. Yet, because the country as a whole suffered from famine less widely and for shorter durations, there was an appreciable rise in population size and growth rate compared with the previous decade.

During the 1911-20 decade, India suffered from an influenza epidemic that caused an estimated 7 percent of the total population to die. It was much more virulent in some provinces than in others (Mitra 1978: 22, 27).

Since 1921, the major causes of high mortality have been gradually brought under control and, between 1921 and 1951, the country witnessed a gradual rise in population growth rates (Figure 1). The decline in death rate became sharper after Independence in 1947, with the result that the population nearly doubled in 34 years - from an estimated 347.5 million in 1947 to 683.3 million in 1981. During the fifty-year period between 1951 and 2001, India's population increased by 668 million, which was country's total population in 1979.

It was not until the beginning of the 1970s that a decline in birth rate was observed. The birth rate decline seems to have been slightly faster during the second quinquennium of the 1980s than the decline in the death rate, resulting in a slight decline in the 1981-91 population growth rate. The decade of the 1990s has shown further decline in the birth rate and, consequently in the growth rate.

Population Distribution and Growth by Zones and States

The Indian census has divided the country into six zones—north, south, east, north-east, west and central (Box 1). (There were five zones till the 1991 census; the north-east zone has been created recently by bifurcating the east zone). States and union territories are grouped according to these zones in tables A1 and A2. Table A1 shows the distribution of India's population by

FIGURE 1: Average Annual Exponential Growth Rate, India, 1901-2001

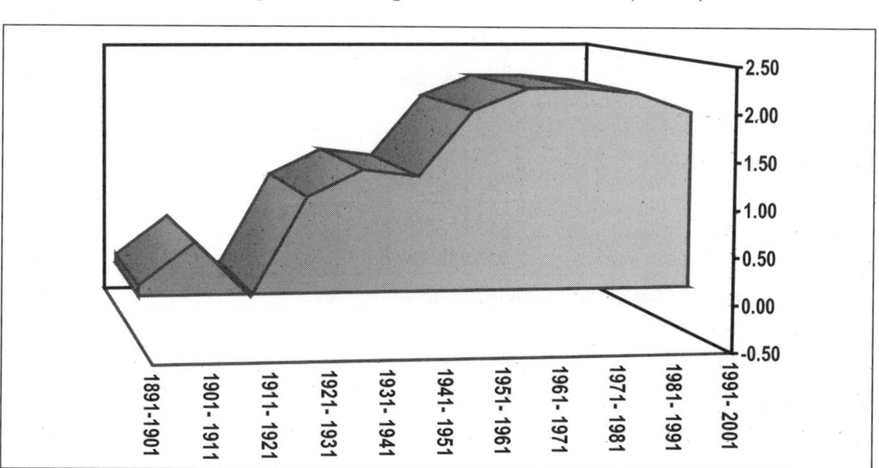

zones and by States and Union Territories over the past century, from 1901 to 2001.[1]

BOX 1 : Census Zones, India

Northern Zone	• Haryana • Himachal Pradesh • Jammu & Kashmir • Punjab • Rajasthan • Chandigarh (UT) • Delhi (UT)
Eastern Zone	• Bihar • Jharkhand • Orissa • Sikkim • West Bengal • A & N Islands (UT)
North Eastern Zone	• Arunachal Pradesh • Assam • Manipur • Meghalaya • Mizoram • Nagaland • Tripura
Central Zone	• Chhattisgarh • Madhya Pradesh • Uttar Pradesh • Uttaranchal
Western Zone	• Gujarat • Maharashtra • D & N Haveli (UT)
Southern Zone	• Andhra Pradesh • Goa • Karnataka • Kerala • Tamil Nadu • Lakshadweep (UT) • Pondicherry (UT)

Note : Goa was included in the Southern Zone up to 2001.

Appendix Table A2, and Figure 2, based on data in table A2, show the percentage share of area and population for each zone and each state and union territory.

FIGURE 2 : Zones of India by Population Share

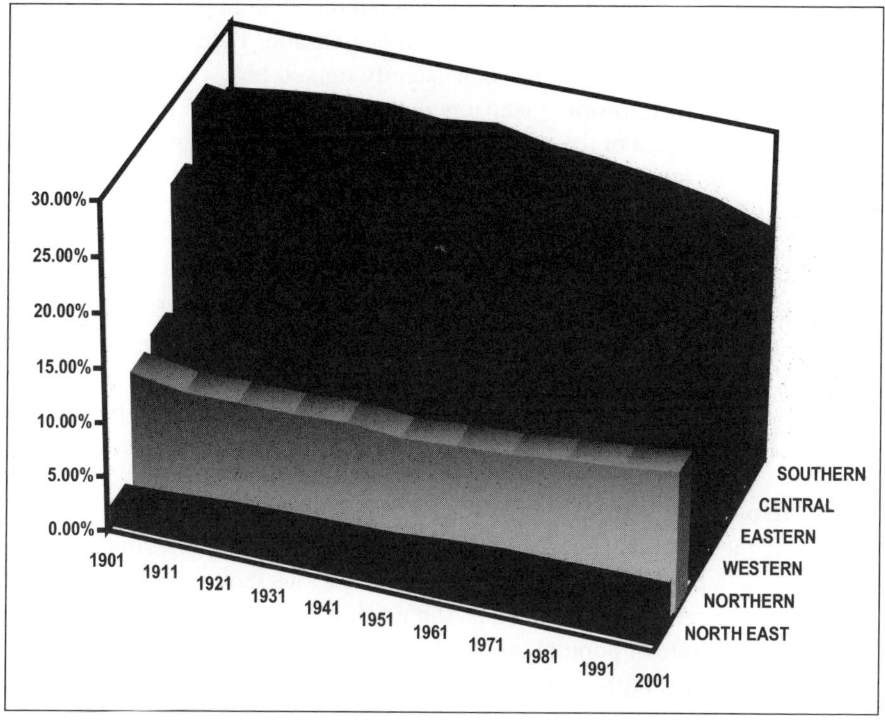

- The four states of the central zone – Chhatisgarh, Madhya Pradesh, Uttaranchal and Uttar Pradesh – put together, as of 2001, accounted for 22.4 percent of the land area and 24.9 percent of the total population – an increase of 0.63 percent in the share of the country's population in comparison to that in 1991 (Data in table A2, trend in Figure 2).
- While the share of the country's population enumerated in the Central zone declined from 27.5 percent in 1901 to 23.7 percent in 1971, the share of the population in the eastern zone increased during the 70 years up to 1971, except in 1951, when it declined slightly, owing to the exodus of Muslims to the newly created Pakistan (now Bangladesh). (Data in table A2, trend in Figure 2).
- The share of the southern zone in the country's population increased up to 1951, when it was 26.2 percent, but has been declining ever since. The decline during the 1990's has been quite sharp - from 23.4 percent in 1991 to 21.9 percent in 2001. (Data in Table A2, trend in Figure 2).

Madhya Pradesh in the Central Zone was geographically the largest Sate in the country before its bifurcation. Uttar Pradesh is largest in population.

Rajasthan in the north zone is the biggest State accounting for 10.4 percent of the total land area. Uttar Pradesh has remained the most populous state in the country over the entire period. At the other extreme, Lakshadweep with a population of 60,600 in 2001 has consistently ranked last.

The seven union territories taken together accounted for 16.5 million persons in 2001, or 1.6 percent of the country's population. Among them, the largest in population size is the almost entirely urban territory of Delhi, containing 13.8 million persons.

Population Growth, 1901-2001

The changing pattern of population distribution among the States is a consequence of differentials in decadal growth rates over time, which is partly due to differentials in the natural increase rate and partly due to in and out migration. Table A3 presents the decadal growth rates of India's population for each zone, state and union territory during successive time periods

Population Growth, 1901-21

- During the first two decades of the last century, the northern zone suffered a net loss in population of 1 per cent, due to various famines and epidemics.
- Among the remaining five zones, the north-eastern zone registered a very high growth rate of population of 40.6 per cent during 1901-21, mainly due to lesser depredation of famines and epidemics, and considerable immigration / in-migration. Assam, Manipur, Nagaland, and Tripura experienced very high population growth rates during 1901-21 (Table A3). The rapid population growth in Assam was mainly due to heavy in-migration to the tea gardens there.
- The southern zone also experienced fast growth rate of 11.02 percent during this period. Its growth rate was a result of almost uniform growth of population of its constituent units, except Kerala, where the population during the first two decades increased sharply by 22 per cent.

Population Growth, 1921-51

During the 30-year period between 1921 and 1951, the Indian population grew gradually from 251 million to 361 million, attaining an overall growth of 44 per cent. The northern, eastern, and southern zones had growth rates close to the national average. The central zone – Chhatisgarh, Madhya Pradesh, Uttar Pradesh and Uttaranchal - had a comparatively low growth of 35.6 percent, mostly due to higher incidence of mortality and substantial out-migration. The western zone, which experienced a growth rate of 56 per cent during this period, gained in population through in-migration besides natural increase. This was the period of initial industrial growth, particularly in and around Bombay and, to some extent, in Ahmedabad, Baroda, and Surat. Industry attracted migrants from almost all parts of the country.

Population Growth, 1951-81

During the thirty years from 1951 to 1981, India's population almost doubled, increasing from 361.1 million in 1951 to 683.3 million in 1981.

The northern zone experienced the highest growth rate of 111 per cent whereas the southern zone, which had higher than the national growth rates during 1901-21 and 1921-51, had the lowest growth during 1951-81.

At the zonal level, northern, north-eastern, and western zones had their population growth rates much above the national average (Table A3).

In these three decades, the death rate in India continuously declined without much decline in the birth rate, leading to higher natural growth rate. This effect was greater in the northern and western zones. Moreover, as a result of migration of Hindus and Muslims from East Pakistan (now Bangladesh), the growth of population in the north-eastern and eastern zone became quite high during this period. Significantly, the 1981 population census could not be held in Assam due to the large influx of Bangladeshi migrants.

Population Growth, 1981-2001

Examining the past two decades, one finds that during 1981-91 all the States and Union Territories experienced an increase in population, but at varying rates (Table A3) and except for a few cases, the addition in absolute numbers during 1981-91 was higher than between 1971 and 1981 (Table A1). The northern zone continued to lead the other zones, while the southern zone recorded the lowest growth rate (Table A3).

The decadal growth rate in the country as a whole declined from 23.9 per cent during 1981-91 to 21.53 in 1991-2001. The annual exponential growth rate declined below two percent (Table 1).

The northern zone had the highest decadal growth rate (28.13 per cent) during 1991-2001.

Other zones witnessed declines in growth rates of varying magnitudes.

It is noteworthy that the Southern Zone had a decadal growth rate of only 13.7 per cent, indicating a continuous decline over the past three decades, and a fast decline between 1991 and 2001 (Appendix Table 2).

Population Composition

Sex and age are the primary variables that are necessary for almost all classifications related to population characteristics. The sex and age structure of a population defines the limits of society's reproductive potential. This structure is also the basic demographic determinant of a nation's manpower supply and it influences requirements for various essential goods and services. The size of the school going population and school enrolment, the total working force and new entrants into the job market each year, and such events as new household formation are all a result of a particular sex and age structure of any given population.

The sex-age structure of a population at any time is the result of past trends in fertility, mortality, and migration. This, in turn, influences the current levels of birth and death rates and the rate of future population growth.

Sex Composition

In India, the overall sex ratio has throughout been unfavourable to females (Table 2). We see that in the period 1901-2001, the FMR became *increasingly* unfavourable to women. It is noteworthy, at the same time, that the 1981 and 2001 censuses recorded a slightly higher sex ratio as comparing to the corresponding figure in the previous census, which indicates feminisation of the FMR (Table 2). It was a serious matter, however, that after improvement in sex ratio in 1981, the 1991 census again recorded a FMR decline.

We also see that there have been periods when the decline in the sex ratio has been sharp, for example, between 1901 and 1911, between 1911 and 1921, and then between 1961 and 1971.

TABLE 2: Sex Ratio (Females per 1,000 Males) in India, 1901-2001

Census Year	Population (Millions)		FMR (Female-Male Ratio)
	Males	Females	
1901	120.8	117.4	972
1911	128.4	123.7	964
1921	128.5	122.8	955
1931	142.9	135.8	950
1941	163.7	154.7	945
1951	185.5	175.6	946
1961	226.3	212.9	941
1971	284.0	264.1	930
1981	353.4	330.0	934
1991	439.2	407.1	927
2001	531.3	495.7	933

Source: Premi (2003: 75).

There are four plausible reasons for India's low sex ratio: (a) greater undercount of females relative to males in the censuses, (b) greater emigration of females, (c) more adverse mortality conditions for females than for males, and (d) sex ratio at birth becoming more adverse to the female child than what it was in the past.

Estimates of the percentage of undercount by sex derived from the post enumeration checks of 1951, 1971, 1981 and 1991 censuses indicate that the differential between the male and female undercount has narrowed down (Table 3). Thus, under enumeration cannot be a reason for the worsening of the FMR.

Statistics on international migration for India are scarce. Moreover, the volume of inter-censal international migration in India, compared to the total population, has always been insignificant. Further, there is no evidence at all of female selective emigration or male selective immigration of a magnitude that can have even a minimal effect on sex ratio; accordingly, this factor is ignored.

The improvement in living conditions and availability of medical facilities throughout the country during the past half a century or more has led to greater survival of both males and females and should have led to narrowing down the gap if not reversing the prevailing trend. The difference between the female and male death rates reached its peak (-2.9 per thousand) in the 1951-61 decade, even though there was a steady reduction in mortality after 1921 of both males and females.

TABLE 3: Sex Differential in Under Enumeration per 1,000 Population, Post Enumeration Checks, 1951, 1971, 1981 and 1991 Censuses*

Year	Extent of under enumeration		Relative index of undercount (F/M)
	Male	Female	
1951	8.6	11.2	1.30
1971	15.3	18.3	1.20
1981	17.1	18.9	1.11
1991	17.3	17.9	1.03

Note: * = Data relating to extent of undercount by sex were not tabulated in the 1961 census.

Source: Premi (1991: 43); Census of India 1991 (1994: 9).

It is noteworthy that *recent* data do not show any evidence of increasing male and female mortality differential; on the contrary, there is evidence during the 1990s of the reversal of the past trend (Table 4). Hence, a female-male mortality differential cannot explain the declining sex ratio in recent years.[2]

Data relating to life expectancy at birth (Table 5) show that the difference between female-male life expectancy has been rising since 1981-85 (centred at 1983) becoming more favourable to females. This difference was of 1.7 years for the 1995-99 period (centred at 1997).

TABLE 4: Crude Death Rates* by Sex, India, 1983-2001

Period	Death rates by sex			Male-Female death rates
	Total	Male	Female	
1983-87	11.7	11.6	11.8	-0.2
1984-88	11.5	11.4	11.6	-0.2
1985-89	11.0	11.0	11.0	0.0
1986-90	10.6	10.6	10.6	0.0
1987-91	10.3	10.4	10.3	0.1
1988-92	10.2	10.2	10.1	0.1
1989-93	9.8	9.9	9.7	0.2
1995-97	9.0	9.2	8.7	0.5
1996-98	9.0	9.2	8.8	0.4
1997-99	8.9	9.1	8.6	0.5
1998-2000	8.7	9.0	8.4	0.6
1999-2001	8.5	8.9	8.1	0.8

Note: * = The crude death rates in the first seven rows are five-year moving averages, and those in the next four rows are three-year moving averages.

At the State level, Bihar, Madhya Pradesh and Uttar Pradesh continued to have higher male life expectancy than that of females. In contrast, all the four southern Indian states – Andhra Pradesh, Karnataka, Kerala and Tamil Nadu - had higher female life expectancy at birth than male by at least two years. Gujarat, Maharashtra and Punjab also registered significant improvement in female life expectancy over that of males in the last two decades (RGI 2003:5).

TABLE 5: Life Expectancy at Birth by Gender, India, 1970-75 to 1995-99

Year	Males	Females	Difference (F-M)
1970-75	50.5	49.0	-1.5
1976-80	52.5	52.1	-0.4
1981-85	55.4	55.7	+0.3
1986-90	57.7	58.1	+0.4
1987-91	58.1	58.6	+0.5
1988-92	58.6	59.0	+0.4
1989-93	59.0	59.7	+0.7
1990-94	59.4	60.4	+1.0
1991-95	59.7	60.9	+1.2
1992-96	60.1	61.4	+1.3
1993-97	60.4	61.8	+1.4
1994-98	60.6	62.2	+1.6
1995-99	60.8	62.5	+1.7

Source: RGI (2003: 3).

Finally, we consider changes in the Sex Ratio at Birth (SRB) as a cause of the deterioration in the FMR. In the absence of any hard data on the SRB in India, we have been assuming it as 105 male births for every 100 female births over the past four decades, if not more. Recent data on sex ratio at birth obtained from the Sample Registration System (SRS) during 1981-90, however, gave the SRB for India as 109.5, which has further increased to 111 during 1996-2000 (Table 7). This has been the result of large-scale female foeticide in certain parts of the country. Consequently, one is led to believe that it is mainly the rise in sex ratio at birth that has been responsible for a decline in overall sex ratio in certain states—especially the child sex ratio.

Child Sex Ratio

The 1991 census tabulated for the first time, sex ratios for the age group 0-6 and 7 and above. At the national level, the 'Child sex ratio (CSR)' (in the population aged 0-6 years) declined from 962 in 1981 to 945 in 1991. A decline of 17 points in the CSR in a decade is very substantial and a matter of serious concern.

The CSR declined by 38 points in Rajasthan, 33 points in Punjab, 28 points in Orissa, and 26 points in Madhya Pradesh between 1981 and 1991. In fact, all the major States and Delhi had declines in the CSR by various amounts between 1981 and 1991.

In the 2001 census, the child sex ratio declined further by 18 points - from 945 in 1991 to 927 in 2001. This decline is found in all the States and union territories except Kerala, Sikkim, Tripura and Mizoram (Table 6).

TABLE 6: Sex Ratio of Total Population and Child Population in 0-6 Years Age Group by States, 1991 and 2001

Sl. No.	India/States Union territories*	FMR					
		Total population			Child population (Population aged 0-6 years)		
		1991	2001	(4)-(3)	1991	2001	(7)-(6)
	INDIA	927	933	6	945	927	-18
1	Jammu & Kashmir	N.A.	900	N.A.	N.A.	937	N.A.
2	Himachal Pradesh	976	970	-6	951	897	-54
3	Punjab	882	874	-8	875	793	-82
4	Chandigarh*	790	773	-17	899	845	-54
5	Uttaranchal	936	964	28	948	906	-42
6	Haryana	865	861	-4	879	820	-59
7	Delhi*	827	821	-6	915	865	-50
8	Rajasthan	910	922	12	916	909	-7
9	Uttar Pradesh	876	898	22	927	916	-11

Sl. No.	India/States Union territories	1991	2001	(4)-(3)	1991	2001	(7)-(6)
10	Bihar	907	921	14	953	938	-15
11	Sikkim	878	875	-3	965	986	+21
12	Arunachal Pradesh	859	901	42	982	961	-21
13	Nagaland	886	909	23	993	975	-18
14	Manipur	958	978	20	974	961	-13
15	Mizoram	921	938	17	969	971	+2
16	Tripura	945	950	5	967	975	+8
17	Meghalaya	955	975	20	986	975	-11
18	Assam	923	932	9	975	964	-11
19	West Bengal	917	934	17	967	963	-4
20	Jharkhand	922	941	19	979	966	-13
21	Orissa	971	972	1	967	950	-17
22	Chhatisgarh	985	990	5	984	975	-9
23	Madhya Pradesh	912	920	8	941	929	-12
24	Gujarat	934	921	-13	928	878	-50
25	Daman & Diu*	969	709	-260	958	925	-33
26	Dadra & Nagar Haveli*	952	811	-141	1013	973	-40
27	Maharashtra	934	922	-12	946	917	-29
28	Andhra Pradesh	972	978	6	975	964	-11
29	Karnataka	960	964	4	960	949	-11
30	Goa	967	960	-7	964	933	-31
31	Lakshadweep*	943	947	4	941	974	+33
32	Kerala	1,036	1,058	22	958	963	+5
33	Tamil Nadu	974	986	12	948	939	-9
34	Pondicherry*	979	1,001	22	963	958	-5
35	A & N Islands*	818	846	28	973	965	-8

Source: Census of India 2001 (2001: 92, 94).

It is a very serious matter that the child sex ratio declined by 82 points to mere 793 in Punjab, by 59 points in Haryana, 54 points in Himachal Pradesh and Chandigarh, 50 points in Gujarat and Delhi, and 42 points in Uttaranchal. In contrast, the decline in CSR has been only of 12 points in Madhya Pradesh and of 7 points in Rajasthan (Table 6). Figure 3 shows how the deterioration in the CSR has varied across States.

Table 7, which presents the sex ratio at birth for India and major States for the 1996-2000 period, indicates that the SRB at the national level was around 111 male births for every 100 female births. It was 126.3 in Punjab and 125.5 in Haryana during 1998-2000. In contrast, SRB varied between 103 and 108 in the four southern states as also in Orissa and West Bengal. Consequently, one is led to believe that it is mainly the rise in sex ratio at birth in certain states that has been responsible for a decline in child sex ratio in those States at least.

FIGURE 3: Change in Child FMRS, States of India, 1991-2001

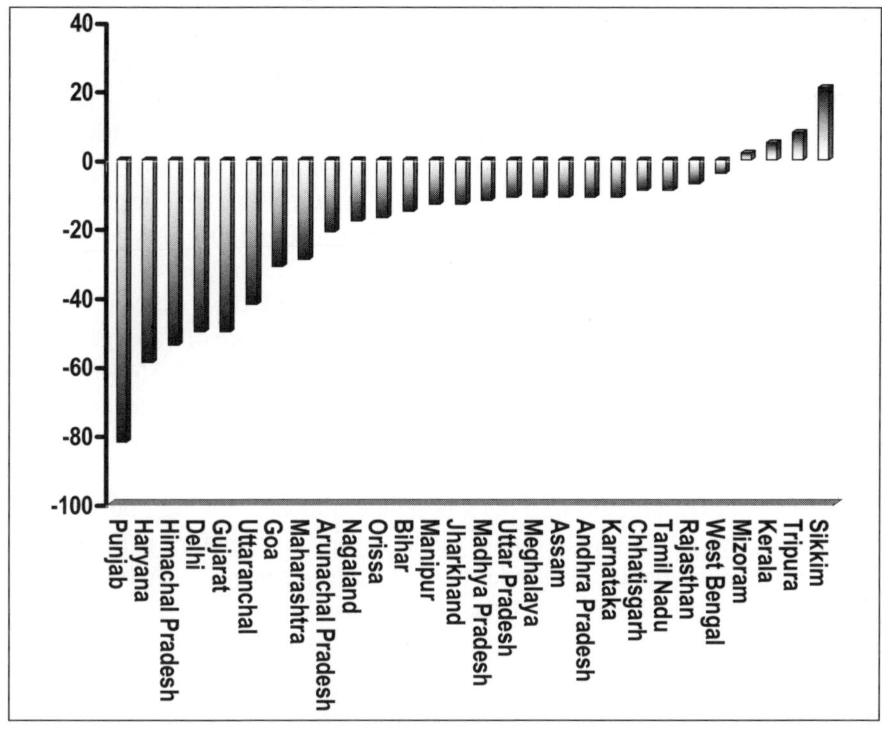

TABLE 7: SRS Based Estimates of Sex Ratio at Birth, major States, 1996-98 and 1998-2000

India / Major States	Sex Ratio at Birth	
	1996-98	1998-2000
INDIA	111.0	111.4
Andhra Pradesh	103.2	104.2
Assam	109.1	101.6
Bihar	111.5	111.6
Gujarat	113.9	117.5
Haryana	123.3	125.5
Karnataka	105.3	106.2
Kerala	107.1	107.5
Madhya Pradesh	109.9	110.3
Maharashtra	109.4	109.5
Orissa	107.6	107.8
Punjab	122.8	126.3
Rajasthan	114.8	114.0
Tamil Nadu	104.9	107.8
Uttar Pradesh	115.0	115.2
West Bengal	105.66	105.0

Age Composition

During the past forty years or so, India's population has grown steadily without being affected by any large-scale events like wars, pestilence, famine, or international migration. Consequently, its age structure has not got any distortions. It is noteworthy that India has a 'young' age structure with almost two-fifths of the total population in 1981 being of children below the age of 15 years, and only 6.2 per cent above the age of 60 years (Table 8). The proportion of children below the age of 15 years, however, declined to 37.3 per cent in 1991 census and to 35.3 percent in 2001 census. The proportion of persons aged 60 years and above, on the other hand, increased to 6.8 percent in 1991 and to 7.4 percent in 2001. The dependency ratio, a measure of the dependence of the very young and the old on the working age population,[3] 86 per cent in 1981, declined to 79 percent in 1991 and to 75 percent in 2001. Nevertheless, the 2001 rate is still much higher than the dependency ratio of many developed countries of the world. [4]

Because of its large base, India's population has a very high potential of future growth and may take 60-70 years, if not more, before it becomes a stationary population, i.e., a population with a zero growth rate. In framing the National Population Policy 2000, the Government of India has fixed the target date for population stabilisation (becoming stationary) as the year 2045. It is doubtful if the country's population would become stationary by then.

TABLE 8: Percent Distribution of India's Population by Broad Age Groups, 1961-2001

Census Years	Sex	Age groups				
		0-14	**15-44**	**45-59**	**15-59**	**60+**
1961	M	40.9	43.0	10.6	53.6	5.5
	F	41.2	43.3	9.7	53.0	5.8
1971	M	41.9	41.5	10.7	52.2	5.9
	F	41.9	42.4	9.7	52.1	6.0
1981	M	39.6	43.3	11.0	54.3	6.1
	F	39.8	43.5	10.4	53.9	6.3
1991	M	37.7	45.1	10.4	55.5	6.7
	F	37.8	45.1	10.4	55.5	6.7
2001	M	35.7	46.2	11.0	57.2	7.1
	F	35.2	46.2	10.8	57.0	7.9

Note: No census was conducted in Assam in 1981; hence India's population distribution for that year excludes Assam. Similarly, the 1991 age distribution excludes Jammu and Kashmir where no census was conducted in 1991.

The age structure of a country's population is normally presented in five-yearly age groups.[5] In this paper we compare the detailed age structure of India's population from 1981 to 2001 by sex[6] (Table 9).

TABLE 9: India's Age Structure by Sex, 1981,1991 and 2001

Age group	1981*			1991#			2001		
	P	M	F	P	M	F	P	M	F
0-4	12.55	12.28	12.85	12.28	12.11	12.46	10.74	10.73	10.74
5-9	14.08	14.03	14.13	13.35	13.28	13.42	12.47	12.54	12.40
10-14	12.92	13.16	12.65	11.84	12.01	11.65	12.14	12.33	11.93
15-19	9.64	9.89	9.37	9.48	9.76	9.17	9.74	10.14	9.32
20-24	8.62	8.43	8.82	8.93	8.67	9.21	8.73	8.70	8.75
25-29	7.62	7.49	7.77	8.30	7.99	8.64	8.11	7.81	8.43
30-34	6.37	6.28	6.47	7.00	6.92	7.10	7.22	7.02	7.44
35-39	5.84	5.79	5.90	6.28	6.37	6.19	6.86	6.77	6.96
40-44	5.14	5.24	5.03	5.10	5.28	4.91	5.42	5.61	5.21
45-49	4.39	4.47	4.31	4.33	4.38	4.28	4.61	4.67	4.54
50-54	3.82	4.02	3.61	3.73	3.91	3.54	3.56	3.73	3.37
55-59	2.47	2.47	2.46	2.58	2.53	2.62	2.69	2.55	2.83
60-64	2.73	2.73	2.73	2.73	2.75	2.70	2.68	2.55	2.81
65-69	1.43	1.39	1.47	1.54	1.50	1.59	1.93	1.78	2.08
70-74	2.33**	2.28**	2.38**	1.27	1.28	1.25	1.43	1.41	1.45
75-79				0.50	0.49	0.51	0.64	0.61	0.66
80+				0.77	0.77	0.76	0.78	0.74	0.83

Note: * = The data for 1981 exclude Assam where no census could be conducted that year.
= The data for 1991 exclude Jammu and Kashmir where no census could be conducted that year.
** = Data relate to persons aged 70 years and above.

Source: Census of India (1988:20); Census of India 1991, data released on CD; Census of India 2001, data released on CD.

The age pyramid of the 2001 census, presented as Figure 4, shows a decline in the proportion of both male and female children in 0-9 years age group, especially in 0-4 years age group, pointing towards fertility decline in the country.

Child Population Aged 0-14 Years

As indicated above, there is a perceptible decline in the proportion of children below the age of 15 years from 1971 onward (Table 8). The decline during the past 20 years has been largely due to a decline in birth rates, which will be considered in a later section of the paper.

Table 9 gives us sex and age-wise data in quinquennial age groups for the

FIGURE 4: Age Pyramid, India, 2001

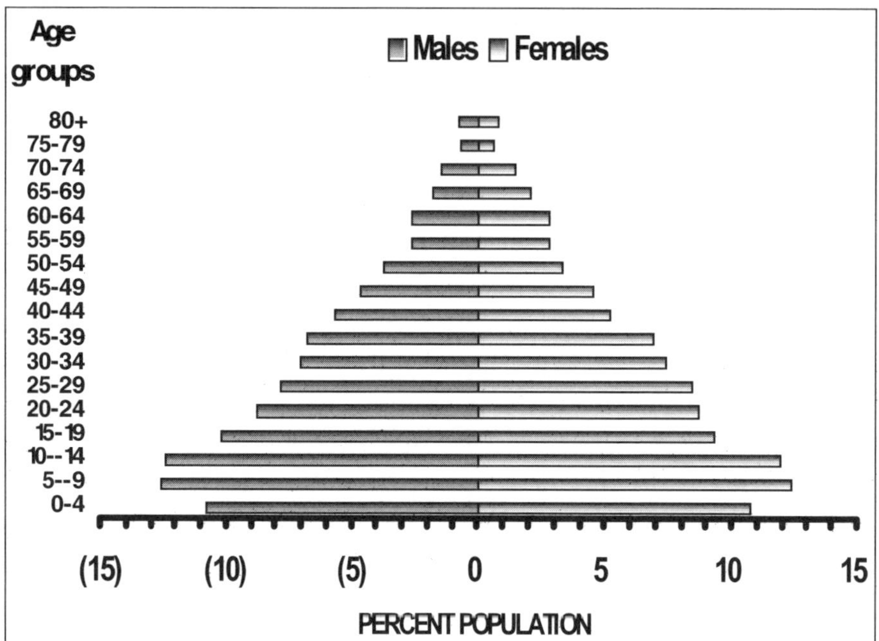

years 1981, 1991 and 2001. From the age data presented in this table, it is possible to examine changes from one age group to another. Taking the age group 0-4 years, one finds a small decline in the proportion of children between 1981 and 1991. The difference becomes pronounced between 1991 and 2001, indicating a faster decline in birth rate in the country. One notices a decline in the proportion of children in the 5-9 years age group as well.

Because of special tabulation of population aged 0-6 years, we consider here the variation in it by States for the years 1991 and 2001. Table 10 presents State wise and sex wise distribution of population in this age group. It is observed that the proportion of children aged 0-6 years has declined in all the States and Union Territories. A decline of a little over 2 percentage points in the proportion of children at the national level implies sharp fertility decline between 1991 and 2001.

Considering the major States, it is observed that the decline in the proportion of girls aged 0-6 years was quite substantial compared to that in respect of boys in Haryana, Punjab, Delhi and Uttaranchal. This points to an acute shortage of girls at birth in these regions. Maharashtra, Andhra Pradesh, Karnataka, Kerala and Tamil Nadu, on the other hand, experienced a decline in the proportion of both males and females during the 1990s by almost similar proportions, indicating an overall decline in birth rates.

TABLE 10: Percent of Population Aged 0-6 Years in Total Population by Sex and States, 1991 and 2001

State/UT	1991			2001			Difference (1991-2001)		
	P	M	F	P	M	F	P	M	F
INDIA	17.73	17.56	17.92	15.37	15.41	15.32	2.36	2.15	2.60
Jammu & Kashmir	NA	NA	NA	14.21	13.94	14.52	NA	NA	NA
Himachal Pradesh	16.03	16.23	15.83	12.66	13.15	12.16	3.37	3.08	3.67
Punjab	16.30	16.36	16.23	12.58	13.15	11.93	3.72	3.22	4.30
Chandigarh	14.92	14.06	16.00	12.13	11.66	12.75	2.79	2.41	3.25
Uttaranchal	18.33	18.22	18.46	15.56	16.04	15.06	2.77	2.18	3.40
Haryana	18.98	18.84	19.14	15.46	15.81	15.05	3.52	3.03	4.09
Delhi	17.06	16.28	18.01	13.96	13.63	14.37	3.10	2.66	3.64
Rajasthan	20.13	20.06	20.21	18.51	18.63	18.37	1.63	1.43	1.84
Uttar Pradesh	20.38	19.84	20.99	18.34	18.18	18.52	2.03	1.65	2.47
Bihar	20.70	20.21	21.24	19.59	19.41	19.78	1.11	0.80	1.45
Sikkim	18.37	17.56	19.29	14.28	13.48	15.19	4.09	4.07	4.10
Arunachal Pradesh	21.12	19.82	22.64	18.33	17.77	18.96	2.79	2.05	3.68
Nagaland	17.15	16.23	18.19	14.09	13.62	14.61	3.07	2.62	3.59
Manipur	16.69	16.55	16.83	13.09	13.21	12.97	3.60	3.34	3.86
Mizoram	18.60	18.15	19.09	15.88	15.62	16.17	2.71	2.53	2.92
Tripura	18.03	17.82	18.25	13.38	13.22	13.55	4.65	4.61	4.69
Meghalaya	22.18	21.84	22.54	19.84	19.83	19.84	2.35	2.01	2.70
Assam	19.73	19.20	20.29	16.33	16.07	16.62	3.40	3.14	3.68
West Bengal	16.98	16.56	17.45	13.88	13.67	14.10	3.11	2.89	3.35
Jharkhand	20.17	19.59	20.80	17.82	17.60	18.06	2.35	1.99	2.74
Orissa	16.89	16.93	16.85	14.11	14.27	13.95	2.78	2.66	2.90
Chhatisgarh	19.34	19.36	19.33	16.68	16.80	16.56	2.66	2.55	2.76
Madhya Pradesh	19.94	19.64	20.27	17.56	17.43	17.69	2.39	2.21	2.58
Gujarat	15.74	15.79	15.68	13.57	13.87	13.24	2.17	1.93	2.44
Daman & Diu	15.53	15.62	15.44	12.66	11.24	14.67	2.87	4.38	0.77
Dadra & Nagar Haveli	20.46	19.84	21.12	17.77	16.31	19.57	2.69	3.53	1.55
Maharashtra	17.11	17.00	17.23	13.63	13.67	13.59	3.48	3.33	3.64
Andhra Pradesh	16.49	16.46	16.51	12.77	12.87	12.68	3.71	3.60	3.83
Karnataka	16.63	16.63	16.63	12.94	13.04	12.85	3.68	3.59	3.78
Goa	11.74	11.75	11.72	10.58	10.73	10.42	1.16	1.03	1.30
Lakshadweep	18.30	18.32	18.28	14.62	14.42	14.83	3.68	3.90	3.45
Kerala	13.19	13.71	12.68	11.48	12.04	10.95	1.71	1.68	1.73
Tamil Nadu	13.33	13.51	13.15	10.98	11.24	10.71	2.36	2.27	2.45
Pondicherry	13.67	13.78	13.55	11.60	11.86	11.35	2.06	1.92	2.20
A. & N. Islands	16.51	15.22	18.09	12.54	11.78	13.44	3.97	3.44	4.66

Working-Age Population

Table 8 presents sex-wise data on working age population (15-44). This proportion has systematically increased from one census to another with the decline in the proportion of child population over the years. Though data in Table 9 do not show any increase in the proportion of young adults, their absolute size in 15-24 years age group has been constantly increasing leading to increased number of job seekers.

Among women, the proportion of women in the childbearing age group has systematically increased between 1971 and 2001 (Table 8) implying population momentum that can lead to more births even after decline in birth rates.

Elderly Population

Senior citizens (aged 60 years and above) numbered 76.6 million (37.8 million males and 38.8 million females) in 2001, registering an increase of 19.9 million persons compared to their number in 1991 (Census of India 2001).[7] This addition in a decade in the elderly population is greater than the total population of Australia or Sri Lanka. Further, in 2001, there were eight million senior citizens (3.9 million males and 4.1 million females) who had crossed the age of 80 years, and may be termed 'old old'.

The proportion of persons aged 60 years and above has been rising in India from one census to next. Table 11 indicates that their proportion in the total population increased from 5.6 percent in 1961 to 7.5 percent in 2001. Further, the proportion of older females in India's population has been higher than that of males. The absolute number of female senior citizens became higher than males for the first time in 2001 census pointing to their longer survival than that of males especially after the age of 50 years.

TABLE 11: Age Structure of Elderly Population, India, 1961-2001

Age Group & Sex	Census Year				
	1961	1971	1981	1991	2001
1	2	3	4	5	6
Persons					
60-64	2.56	2.62	2.73	2.73	2.68
65-69	1.11	1.28	1.43	1.54	1.93
70-74	1.96*	2.06*	2.33*	1.27	1.43
75-79				0.50	0.64
80+				0.77	0.78
Total	5.63	5.96	6.49	6.80	7.45

TABLE 11: (*Contd.*)

1	2	3	4	5	6
Males					
60-64	2.52	2.64	2.73	2.75	2.55
65-69	1.09	1.28	1.39	1.50	1.78
70-74	1.84*	2.02*	2.28*	1.28	1.41
75-79				0.49	0.61
80+				0.77	0.74
Total	5.45	5.94	6.40	6.79	7.10
Females					
60-64	2.60	2.61	2.73	2.70	2.81
65-69	1.12	1.27	1.47	1.59	2.08
70-74	2.09*	2.12*	2.38*	1.25	1.45
75-79				0.51	0.66
80+				0.76	0.83
Total	5.81	6.00	6.58	6.81	7.83

***Note*:** * = Figures relate to age group 70 and over.
***Source*:** Census pf India 1981 (1988: 20); Census of India 1991 (CD on Age Tables); Census of India 2001 (CD released in 2004).

Although the proportion of senior citizens in the country is small compared to most of the developed and many developing countries, their absolute size is greater than the total population of most countries in the world.

After examining the trends in population growth and its distribution, I shall now consider the change in fertility and mortality over time and how they determine the pattern of demographic transition in India.

Fertility and Mortality Patterns

In the civil registration system in India, which is more than a century old, registration of births and deaths is deficient in content, coverage and completeness. Some of the factors responsible for under-coverage of vital events are low levels of literacy, the overwhelming rural population, and the inadequacy of the registration machinery. In spite of the fact that the Government of India enacted the *Births and Deaths Registration Act* in 1969, which became applicable all over India from April 1, 1970, and which tried to unify the system of registration nationally and promoted uniformity and comparability, there has not been much improvement in the extent of registration of vital events at the national level.

In 1964-65, the Office of the Registrar General, India introduced a scheme of Sample Registration System on a pilot basis in a few selected states. It became operational during 1969-70 to cover both rural and urban areas all over the country. The Sample Registration System (SRS) provides yearly estimates of vital rates and other fertility and mortality measures at the national and state levels that are considered to be sufficiently reliable for most practical purposes.

Birth Rates, India and States

The national and State (major only) level estimates of birth rates covering the period 1972-2001 are presented in Table A 4. The estimates are 3-year moving averages, which are a little more stable than the annual estimates. The all India and State level data show clear declines in birth rates over the past two decades (Figure 5), which seems to be the result of certain socio-economic developments in the country and the massive family planning drive.

We see from Figure 5 that there has been appreciable birth rate declines in a number of States, for instance, in Haryana, Himachal Pradesh, Punjab, Delhi, Madhya Pradesh, Uttar Pradesh, Orissa, Gujarat, Maharashtra, Andhra Pradesh, Karnataka, Kerala and Tamil Nadu.

In the Southern States of Kerala, Tamil Nadu and Andhra Pradesh, and in States like Gujarat, Uttar Pradesh and Rajasthan, the major birth rate declines took place prior to the 1990's, after which the CBRs plateaued.

However, the plateaus in the case of the southern States were at far lower levels. Among the southern States, Kerala is the only one that achieved a birth rate of less than 20 per thousand from 1990 onward. By comparison, Bihar, Madhya Pradesh, Rajasthan and Uttar Pradesh are the four major states where the rural birth rate has remained well above 30 per thousand throughout the 1990s (Premi 2003: 185-90).

The three-year moving average in Tamil Nadu became less than 20 from 1993 onward. Further, Andhra Pradesh, and Karnataka in the southern zone Gujarat and Maharashtra in the western zone; West Bengal in the eastern zone; and Punjab in the northern zone had their birth rates in the 20-25, range especially during the second half of the 1990s (Table A 4). The other States had birth rates higher than the national average.

Death Rates, India and States

National and State level data from the SRS for the 1980s and the 1990s establish a clearly declining trend in death rates (Table A 4 and Figure 5), though the pace of decline seem to have slowed down. As in the case of birth rates, these rates are also three-year moving averages centred at mid-year. During the 1970s the national death rate declined from about 16 per 1,000 persons in 1972 to 12.5 in 1980. The death rate declined to 9.9 in 1990, and has become less than 9.0 in recent years.

The CDR has become less than 10 per 1,000 for the country and in a majority of bigger states for several years now. For most of the 1980s, Uttar Pradesh experienced the highest death rate (RGI: 1998). In contrast, among the major states only Kerala had its death rate below 7 per 1,000 throughout the 1980s and around 6 during the 1990s.

Karnataka, Kerala, Maharashtra, Punjab, Tamil Nadu and West Bengal among the major States had attained comparatively low death rate (below 10) in 1980's and 1990s while Bihar, Madhya Pradesh, Orissa, and Uttar Pradesh had death rates close to or above 10 per thousand.

Rate of Natural Increase

The difference between crude birth rate and the crude death rates in a closed population (not affected by in- and out-migration) indicates its natural increase rate. Table A 4 and Figure 5 indicate the changes in it over time for India and all its major states.

It is only in Kerala and Tamil Nadu that the growth had declined to 1.1 percent per annum. In these States, fertility has fallen below replacement level, as can be seen from Figure 5.

The other States that have experienced decline in growth rate during the latter half of the 1990s are Andhra Pradesh, Haryana, Himachal Pradesh, Karnataka, Maharashtra, Punjab, West Bengal and Delhi.

In contrast, the growth rate in Bihar, Madhya Pradesh, Rajasthan and Uttar Pradesh has continued to be more than 2 percent per annum and decline in it is rather slow. These four states would take fairly long time before their birth rates decline to replacement level of total fertility rate of 2.1.

Infant Mortality

Unlike most developed and many developing countries, where the infant mortality rate (IMR) is below 10 per 1,000 live births, India has suffered in the past and still continues to suffer from very high infant mortality rates. This is probably so because many infants suffer from birth abnormalities right after birth; and, after the first month of life, suffer from environmental hazards. Consequently, infant deaths increase sharply during epidemics.

Table 12 (based on SRS data) shows that IMR during the period 1970-2002 was consistently and substantially higher in rural areas than in urban areas. It indicates that IMR was as high as 129 in 1971. The IMR declined consistently during the 1980s becoming less than 100 in 1986 for the country and, by 1991, in rural areas as well.

Rural-urban differential in the IMR has been consistently high; the difference at the national level between the two in the 1970s was around 60 points which declined to around 40 points towards the end of the 1980s. The difference in the rural and urban IMR at the national level further reduced to around 30

FIGURE 5 : CBR, CDR and Rates of Natural Increase, India and States, 1972 to 2000

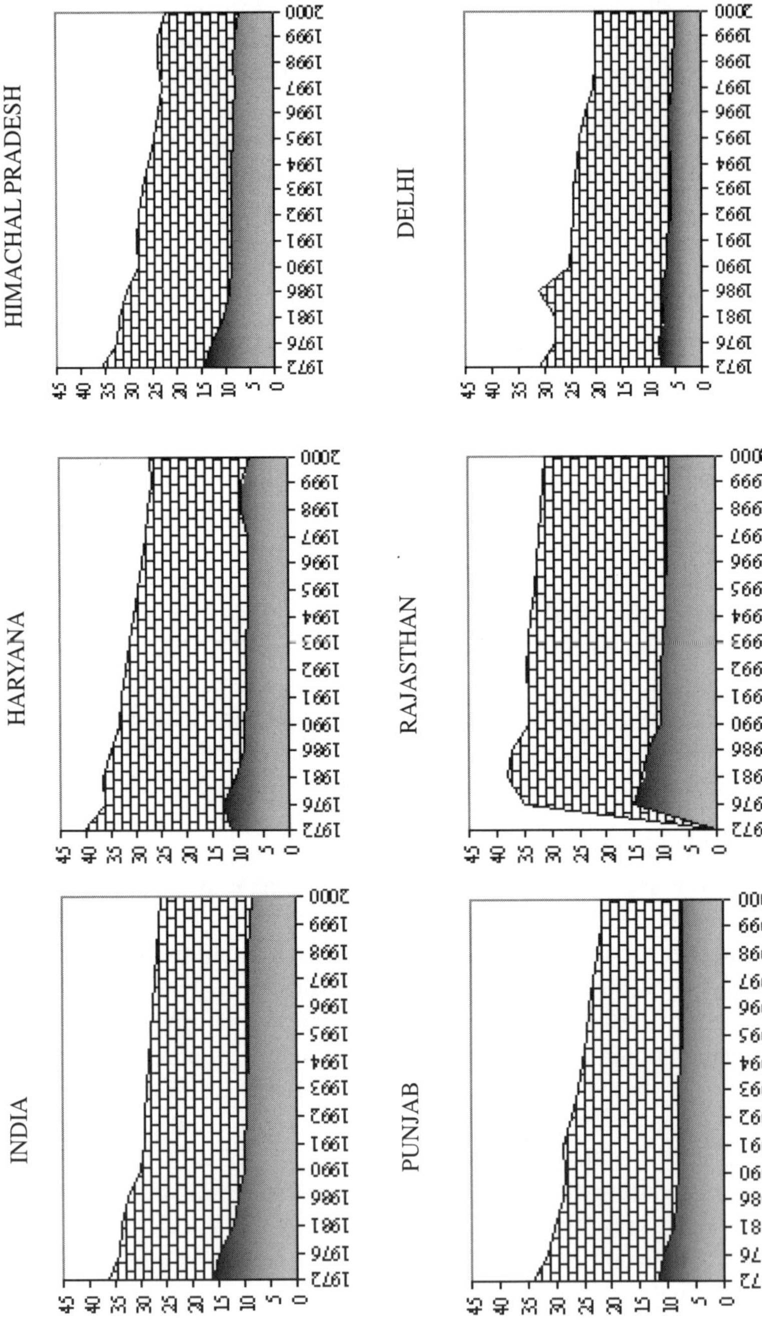

INDIA

HARYANA

HIMACHAL PRADESH

PUNJAB

RAJASTHAN

DELHI

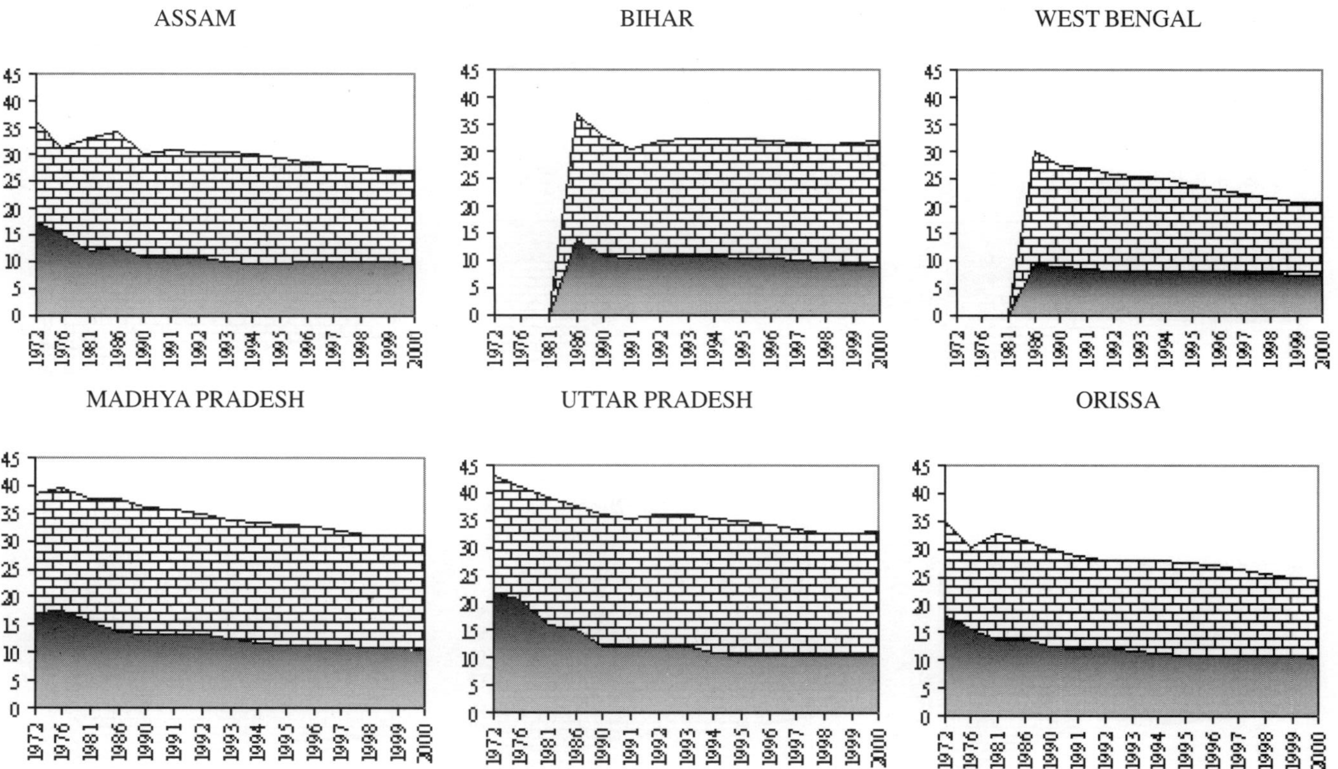
ASSAM
BIHAR
WEST BENGAL
MADHYA PRADESH
UTTAR PRADESH
ORISSA
45
40
35
30
25
20
15
10
5
0
1972
1976
1981
1986
1990
1991
1992
1993
1994
1995
1996
1997
1998
1999
2000

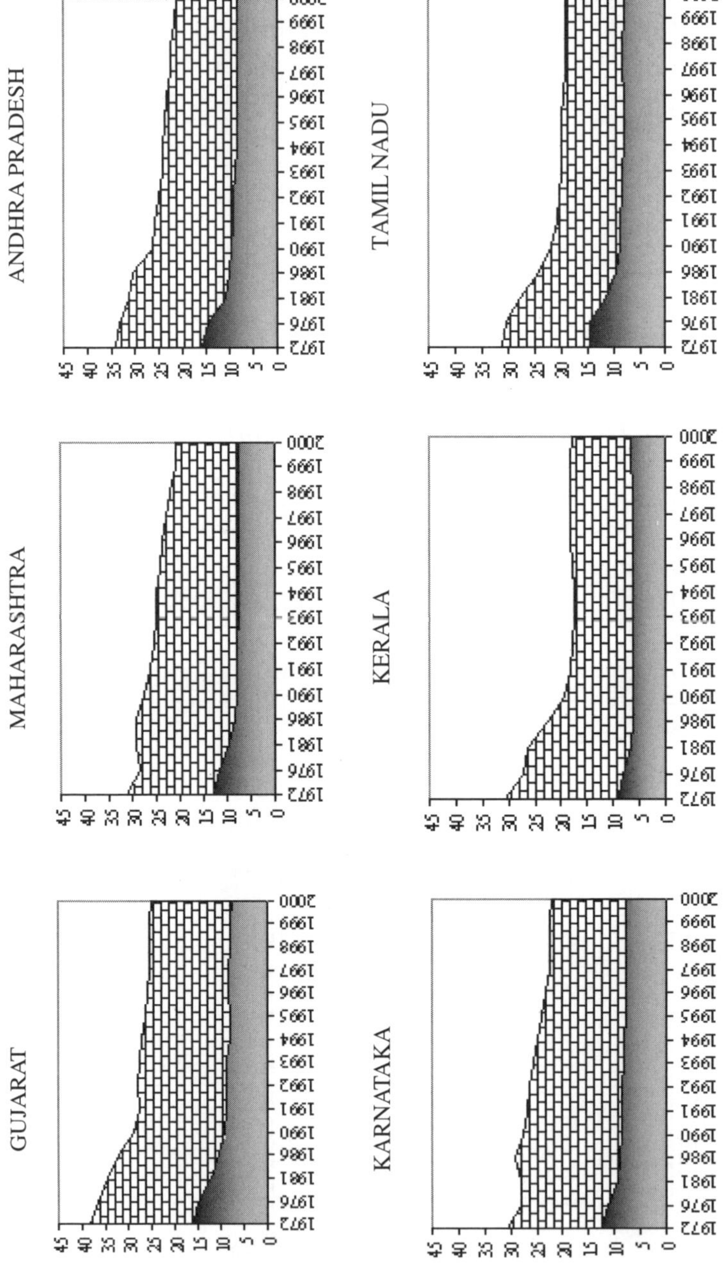

Note: the height of the brick wall from zero shows the CBR, the height of the black shaded area shows the CDR, and the height of the brick wall FROM the black shaded are shows the rate of natural increase.

during 1996-2002 (Table 12). A large difference between the rural and urban IMR is indicative of persistently poor living conditions and medical facilities in rural India, which need to be changed by unstinted efforts to provide potable drinking water, sanitation and accessible health facilities.

TABLE 12: Infant Mortality Rate in India, 1971-2002

Year	Total	Rural	Urban
1971	129	138	82
1976	129	139	80
1981	110	119	62
1986	96	105	62
1991	80	87	53
1996	72	77	46
1997	71	77	45
1998	72	77	45
1999	70	75	44
2000	68	74	43
2001	66	72	42
2002	63	69	40

Estimates of infant mortality rates by major States for the periods 1971-73, 1980-82, 1990-92, 1995-97, 1996-98, 1997-99 and thereafter continuously up to 2000-02 as obtained in the SRS are presented in Table 13. The rates are 3-year moving averages and are assumed to be centred at respective midpoints.

TABLE 13: Infant Mortality Rates for India and Major States, 1972, 1981, 1991, 1996, 1998, 2000 and 2001 (Three-year Moving Averages)

India/State	Years							
	1971-1973	1980-1982	1990-1992	1995-1997	1996-1998	1997-1999	1999-2001	2000-2002
India	134	110	80	72	74	72	68	66
Andhra Pradesh	109	86	71	65	65	65	66	64
Assam	137	104	78	76	76	76	75	73
Bihar	NA	110*	72	72	70	67	63	62
Gujarat	144	113	69	62	62	63	63	61
Haryana	90	99	71	68	68	68	67	65
Karnataka	93	68	73	56	55	56	58	57
Kerala	60	36	17	14	14	14	13	12
Madhya Pradesh	145	139	111	97	96	94	88	86
Maharashtra	107	75	59	50	48	48	47	46
Orissa	134	137	120	98	97	97	94	91
Punjab	112	82	57	52	52	53	52	51
Rajasthan	131	103	86	85	81	83	80	79
Tamil Nadu	114	89	58	53	53	53	51	48
Uttar Pradesh	182	152	98	85	85	85	83	82
West Bengal	NA	87*	66	56	54	53	51	50

While Kerala succeeded in achieving an IMR of 60 during 1971-73 and 36 in 1980-82 and just 12 in 2000-02, Uttar Pradesh had an IMR of 182 during 19971-73, 152 in 1980-82 and 82 in 2000-02, which was almost seven times the level in Kerala in the latest year. Madhya Pradesh and Orissa are the two other states with high IMR. It is noteworthy that none of the states in India could achieve an IMR of less than 50 even during the 1990s except Kerala and Maharashtra.

There was an overall decline in IMR during the 1990s. The State wise data, however, indicate little change, if at all, in the IMR during the latter half of the 1990s. Kerala recorded the lowest IMR at 12 during 2000-02 and is much below the anticipated level of less than 30 by 2010 in the National Population Policy, 2000. Karnataka, Maharashtra, Punjab, Tamil Nadu and West Bengal have made good progress in containing their IMRs.

Future Population Growth

Various national and international agencies and some individual researchers have been projecting population for India and its States from time to time. The latest available projections are those prepared by the Office of the Registrar General, India in 2002. These projections give the population of India and of major States up to 2026 (Table 11).

The age distribution of the 2001 population is estimated utilising data from the SRS. At the national level, the TFR (Total Fertility Rate) is assumed to decline from 2.9 per woman in 2001-05 to 2.0 in 2021-25, which will be below replacement level. Mortality assumption in terms of expectation of life at birth is 69.41 years in 2021-25 in respect of males and 74.34 years in respect of females. Keeping in view the insignificant size of net migration into India over recent years, this component has been ignored. Further, the sex ratio at birth has been assumed to remain constant at 106 male births for every 100 females births during the projection period.

Instead of having three alternative sets of projections with 'high', 'medium' and 'low' fertility assumptions, these projections were prepared only with 'medium' assumption of fertility decline. These projections assume a continuous decline in the population growth rate, which comes to 0.93 per cent per annum during 2021-26. The growth rate is still quite high if the country has to achieve stationary population by 2040 or 2050.

The data for the major states indicate that none is going to have stationary population by 2026. The annual growth rate during 2021-26 would, however, be less than five persons per 1,000 in Kerala and Tamil Nadu. These two states are expected to achieve stationary population by 2050 or even earlier.

In contrast, Madhya Pradesh, Uttar Pradesh and Chhatisgarh will continue to have annual growth rates above one per cent even beyond 2026 and would take a long time to arrive at population stabilisation. States like Andhra Pradesh, Karnataka, and Punjab might attain stationary population by 2050 or so.

TABLE 14: Population Projections ('000s), India and Major States, 2001-2026

India/State	Year					
	2001	**2006**	**2011**	**2016**	**2021**	**2026**
India	**1027015**	**1114201**	**1196555**	**1274936**	**1347021**	**1410840**
Andhra Pradesh	75729	80430	84674	88513	91985	94751
Assam	26638	29006	31271	33414	35369	37086
Bihar	82881	90832	98129	104869	110789	115752
Chhatisgarh	20796	22859	24789	26616	28300	29790
Gujarat	50597	54814	58691	62171	65230	67912
Haryana	21083	23039	24819	26431	27888	29188
Jharkhand	26908	29174	31197	33031	34631	35975
Karnataka	52734	56137	59189	61883	64267	66231
Kerala	31839	33569	35175	36533	37636	38523
Madhya Pradesh	60385	66801	72910	78773	84197	88940
Maharashtra	96752	104104	110941	117391	123411	128699
Orissa	36707	39053	41088	42922	44590	46022
Punjab	24289	25976	27456	28760	29867	30770
Rajasthan	56473	62431	67800	72772	76990	80727
Tamil Nadu	62111	65261	67972	70303	72270	73848
Uttaranchal	8480	9216	9906	10550	11118	11592
Uttar Pradesh	166053	183855	201350	218542	234478	248294
West Bengal	80221	85780	90886	95704	100101	103883
Delhi	13783	16065	18710	21789	25289	29210

We give below the shape of the age pyramid as it would appear in 2026 under assumed patterns regarding decline in fertility and mortality rates. This age pyramid takes the shape of an inverted top and changes in pattern of the two curves, one for 2001 and the other for 2026 can be clearly observed (Figure 6).

Demographic Transition

Coale and Hoover (1958) have related the Demographic Transition (DT) to economic development. According to them, agrarian peasant society is characterised by a high birth rate and a high death rate. The birth rate is high because of the need for more hands to work in agriculture. The death rates fluctuate in response to the variations in food production and the incidence of famines and epidemics. Death rates are high due to poor diet, primitive conditions of sanitation, and lack of preventive and curative medical facilities. When the agrarian economy starts undergoing changes, it becomes interdependent on production in other sectors of the economy and generates

FIGURE 6: Age Pyramids, India 2001 and 2026

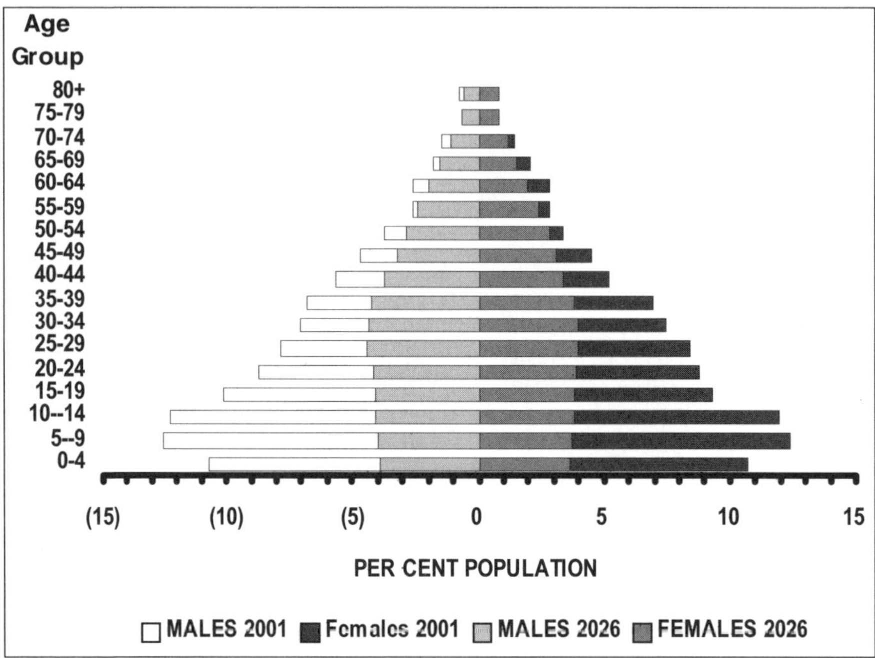

certain amount of food surplus; under that situation death rate starts declining. At a somewhat later stage birth rates also begin to fall slowly. The decline in birth rate usually occurs after a substantial time lag as compared to the decline in the death rate. With further improvement in agricultural production due to improved technology and mechanization, better medical facilities and control over communicable diseases, the death rate continues to decline and birth rate also follows suit almost at the same rate at which death rate declines. Under this regime, the population growth rate becomes more or less stationary for a while. With the growth in the economy, there is high degree of industrialisation and urbanisation, when a small family size becomes a norm not only for the urban high socio-economic groups, but also for the rural masses, the decline in birth rate becomes faster than the decline in death rate and the growth rate starts declining. With full development of the economy, from here on, reductions in death rate become very difficult, and birth rates and death rates become almost equal at a low level. Here death rates become almost stationary and birth rates fluctuate according to people's choice and government policies in regard to natality.

Demographic Transition in India

The first stage of demographic transition (DT) in India continued till about 1920 when both birth rates and death rates were very high.

The second stage of DT in the country began from the early 1920s and spread well up to 1971. During this period major causes of high mortality – famines and epidemics – were brought under control and, between 1921 and 1951, the country witnessed a gradual rise in population growth rates; the decline in death rate became sharper during the 1950s without any appreciable decline in birth rate resulting in higher population growth rates that continued during the 1960s (Figure 7).

Data for the past 20 years or so have registered a faster decline in birth rate than decline in death rate.

India seems to have entered the third stage of DT since 1971. The decline in death rate during the 1970s was almost the same as the decline in birth rate leading to a plateau in population growth rate during the 1960s and the 1970s.

According to the population projections prepared by the Office of the Registrar General, India in 1996 (RGI 1996), India is expected to enter the fourth stage of DT by about 2026. The Registrar General has also worked out the likely dates when the major states would achieve total fertility rate of 2.1 (equivalent to Net Reproduction Rate of one). Kerala and Tamil Nadu have already achieved that goal, and Andhra Pradesh, Karnataka, Maharashtra and

FIGURE 7 : Stages of Demographic Transition, India

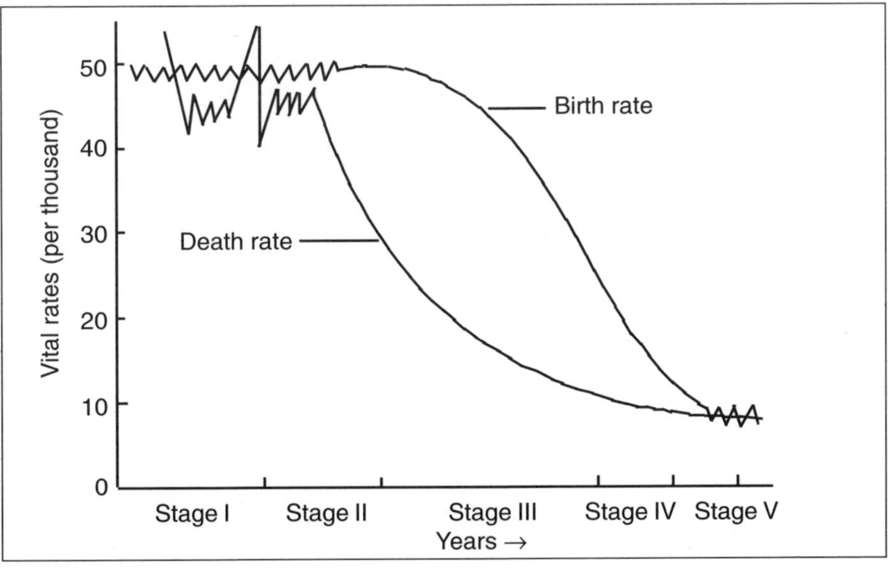

West Bengal are likely to achieve the same within the present decade. The problem states in this respect are Bihar, Madhya Pradesh, Rajasthan and Uttar Pradesh where the goal of TFR of 2.1 cannot be achieved before 2040. Although the TFR in the above states has also started declining, the pace of decline is very slow and there is hardly any downward movement in the natural increase rate (Table A 4 and Figure 5).

NOTES

1. Three new states—Chhattisgarh, Jharkhand and Uttaranchal - were created on the eve of the 2001 census. Chhattisgarh has been carved out from Madhya Pradesh, Jharkhand is the southern part of Bihar and Uttaranchal comprises the mountainous region of erstwhile Uttar Pradesh.
2. Mortality data by sex are not easily available for the earlier period. During 1901 and 1921, when the country suffered heavily due to various epidemics, female mortality was higher for various reasons. Due to prevailing social customs, women had to sit by the side of the dead body for hours together before its disposal, which many a time meant women getting infected with the disease. Further, women have always got lesser attention than males in illness, which should have resulted in higher female mortality, even after 1921.
3. Dependency ratio in India is defined as the ratio of population below the age of 15 years plus the population 60 years and above to the population aged 15-59 years.
4. In the developed countries (especially European and Japan) the child dependency ratio is low (around 25-30 percent) but the old age dependency ratio is higher (around one-third).
5. It is customary to use the age interval as 0-4, 5-9, 10-14, etc. to present age data. The age group 0-4 means all persons below the age of 5, 5-9 means all persons who have attained the age of 5 years but not exactly 10 years, etc.
6. Age data presented in Tables 8 and 9 are as reported by the respondents. There is a tendency among people to round off the age at digits ending in zero and five, and next on even numbers. Many married women in the age group 15-19 years who have already borne two or three children are often reported to be 20 years and over. Moreover, many small children in 0-4 years age group are completely missed.
7. 2004 CD on Age Data. Registrar General's Office, Government of India.

APPENDIX TABLE A.1 : Area and Population, Zones and States, India, 1921-2001 (Population figures in 000s)

Zone/State/ Union Territory	Area in Sq Kms (2001)	CENSUS YEAR										
		1901	1911	1921	1931	1941	1951	1961	1971	1981	1991	2001
1	2	3	4	5	6	7	8	9	10	11	12	13
NORTHERN ZONE	**716319**	**26949**	**26512**	**26675**	**29675**	**34888**	**38213**	**48034**	**61754**	**80913**	**103790**	**132985**
Haryana	44212	4623	4175	4256	4560	5273	5674	7591	10037	12922	16464	21145
Himachal Pradesh	55673	1920	1897	1928	2029	2263	2386	2812	3460	4281	5171	6078
Jammu & Kashmir	222236	2139	2292	2424	2670	2947	3254	3561	4617	5987	7804	10144
Punjab	50362	7545	6732	7153	8012	9600	9160	11135	13551	16789	20282	24359
Rajasthan	342239	10294	10984	10293	11748	13864	15971	20156	25766	34262	44006	56507
Chandigarh (UT)	114	22	18	18	20	23	24	120	257	452	642	901
Delhi (UT)	1483	406	414	488	636	918	1744	2659	4066	6220	9421	13851
EASTERN ZONE	**433681**	**54639**	**57806**	**56869**	**62874**	**72324**	**79897**	**99148**	**122935**	**151371**	**186800**	**227823**
Bihar	94180	21244	21567	21358	23438	26302	29084	36840	42125	52303	64531	82999
Jharkhand	70614	6068	6747	6768	7909	8868	9697	11606	14227	17612	21844	26946
Sikkim	7096	59	88	82	110	121	138	162	210	316	406	541
West Bengal	88752	16940	17999	17474	18897	23230	26300	34926	44312	54581	68078	80176
Orissa	155707	10303	11379	11159	12491	13768	14646	15549	21945	26370	31660	36805
A. & N. Islands (UT)	8249	25	26	27	29	34	31	64	115	189	281	356
NORTH EAST	**255083**	**4271**	**5059**	**6004**	**7172**	**8619**	**10261**	**14500**	**19582**	**24752**	**31548**	**38318**
Assam	78438	3290	3849	4637	5560	6695	8029	10837	14625	18041	22414	26656
Arunachal Pradesh*	83743	NA	NA	NA	NA	NA	NA	337	468	632	865	1098
Manipur	22327	284	346	384	446	512	578	780	1073	1421	1837	2167
Meghalaya	22429	340	394	422	481	556	606	769	1012	1336	1775	2319
Mizoram	21081	82	91	98	124	153	196	266	332	494	690	889
Nagaland	16579	102	149	159	179	190	213	369	516	775	1210	1990
Tripura	10486	173	230	304	382	513	639	1142	1556	2053	2757	3199

(Contd.)

APPENDIX TABLE A.1 (*Contd.*)

1	2	3	4	5	6	7	8	9	10	11	12	13
CENTRAL ZONE	**737857**	**65489**	**67596**	**65844**	**71136**	**80526**	**89292**	**106127**	**129995**	**163042**	**205293**	**255869**
Chhattisgarh	135039	4182	5192	5265	6029	6815	7458	9155	11637	14010	17615	20834
Madhya Pradesh	308087	12679	14249	13907	15327	17176	18615	23218	30016	38167	48566	60348
Uttar Pradesh	241005	46647	46012	44556	47479	53920	60274	70143	83848	105137	131999	166198
Uttaranchal	53331	1981	2143	2116	2301	2615	2946	3612	4493	5726	7113	8489
WESTERN ZONE	**504317**	**28543**	**31340**	**31087**	**35523**	**40618**	**48355**	**60282**	**77247**	**97053**	**120487**	**147928**
Gujarat	196024	9095	9804	10175	11490	13702	16263	20633	26698	34086	41310	50671
Maharashtra	307690	19392	21475	20850	23959	26833	32002	39554	50412	62783	78937	96879
D & N Haveli (UT)	491	24	29	31	38	40	41	58	74	104	138	220
Daman & Diu (UT)	112	32	32	31	36	43	49	37	63	79	102	158
SOUTHERN ZONE	**640186**	**58506**	**63781**	**64956**	**72596**	**81686**	**95070**	**111144**	**136647**	**166200**	**198473**	**225691**
Andhra Pradesh	275068	19066	21447	21420	24204	27289	31115	35983	43503	53550	66508	76210
Karnataka	191971	13055	13525	13378	14633	16255	19402	23587	29299	37136	44977	52851
Kerala	38863	6396	7148	7802	9507	11031	13549	16904	21347	25454	29099	31841
Tamil Nadu	130058	19253	20903	21629	23472	26267	30119	33687	41199	48408	55859	62406
Goa	3702	476	487	469	505	541	547	590	795	1008	1170	1348
Lakshadweep (UT)	32	14	14	14	16	18	21	24	32	40	52	61
Pondicherry (UT)	492	246	257	244	259	285	317	369	472	604	808	974
INDIA	**3287263**	**238396**	**252093**	**251321**	**278977**	**318667**	**361088**	**439235**	**548160**	**683329**	**846388**	**1028610**

Note: u = unavailable; UT = Union Territory. 1981 population total for Assam and 1991 population total for J & K are interpolated.
Source: Premi, Mahendra K. *India's Population: Heading Towards a Billion;* Census of India 2001, Series 1, India. *Final Population Totals.*

TABLE A2 : Percent Distribution of Area and Population , by Zones and States of India, 1901-2001

Zone/State/ Union Territory	Area in Sq Kms (2001)	CENSUS YEAR										
		1901	1911	1921	1931	1941	1951	1961	1971	1981	1991	2001
NORTHERN ZONE	**21.79**	**11.30**	**10.52**	**10.57**	**10.64**	**10.95**	**10.58**	**10.94**	**11.27**	**11.84**	**12.26**	**12.93**
Haryana	1.34	1.94	1.66	1.69	1.63	1.65	1.57	1.73	1.83	1.89	1.95	2.06
Himachal Pradesh	1.69	0.81	0.75	0.77	0.73	0.71	0.66	0.64	0.63	0.63	0.61	0.59
Jammu & Kashmir	6.76	0.90	0.91	0.96	0.96	0.92	0.90	0.81	0.84	0.88	0.92	0.99
Punjab	1.53	3.16	2.67	2.85	2.87	3.01	2.54	2.54	2.47	2.46	2.40	2.37
Rajasthan	10.41	4.32	4.36	4.10	4.21	4.35	4.42	4.59	4.70	5.01	5.20	5.49
Chandigarh (UT)	0.00	0.01	0.01	0.01	0.01	0.01	0.01	0.03	0.05	0.07	0.08	0.09
Delhi (UT)	0.05	0.17	0.16	0.19	0.23	0.29	0.48	0.61	0.74	0.91	1.11	1.35
EASTERN ZONE	**13.19**	**22.92**	**22.93**	**22.63**	**22.54**	**22.70**	**22.13**	**22.57**	**22.43**	**22.15**	**22.07**	**22.15**
Bihar	2.86	8.91	8.56	8.50	8.40	8.25	8.05	8.39	7.68	7.65	7.62	8.07
Jharkhand	2.15	2.55	2.68	2.69	2.84	2.78	2.69	2.64	2.60	2.58	2.58	2.62
Sikkim	0.22	0.02	0.03	0.03	0.04	0.04	0.04	0.04	0.04	0.05	0.05	0.05
West Bengal	2.70	7.11	7.14	6.95	6.77	7.29	7.28	7.95	8.08	7.99	8.04	7.79
Orissa	4.74	4.32	4.51	4.44	4.48	4.32	4.06	3.54	4.00	3.86	3.74	3.58
A. & N. Islands (UT)	0.25	0.01	0.01	0.01	0.01	0.01	0.01	0.01	0.02	0.03	0.03	0.03
NORTH EAST	**7.76**	**1.79**	**2.01**	**2.39**	**2.57**	**2.70**	**2.84**	**3.30**	**3.57**	**3.62**	**3.73**	**3.73**
Assam	2.39	1.38	1.53	1.85	1.99	2.10	2.22	2.47	2.67	2.64	2.65	2.59
Arunachal Pradesh*	2.55	0.00	0.00	0.00	0.00	0.00	0.00	0.08	0.09	0.09	0.10	0.11
Manipur	0.68	0.12	0.14	0.15	0.16	0.16	0.16	0.18	0.20	0.21	0.22	0.21
Meghalaya	0.68	0.14	0.16	0.17	0.17	0.17	0.17	0.18	0.18	0.20	0.21	0.23
Mizoram	0.64	0.03	0.04	0.04	0.04	0.05	0.05	0.06	0.06	0.07	0.08	0.09
Nagaland	0.50	0.04	0.06	0.06	0.06	0.06	0.06	0.08	0.09	0.11	0.14	0.19
Tripura	0.32	0.07	0.09	0.12	0.14	0.16	0.18	0.26	0.28	0.30	0.33	0.31

(*Contd.*)

TABLE A2 : (*Contd.*)

1	2	3	4	5	6	7	8	9	10	11	12	13
CENTRAL ZONE	**22.45**	**27.47**	**26.81**	**26.20**	**25.50**	**25.27**	**24.73**	**24.16**	**23.71**	**23.86**	**24.26**	**24.88**
Chhattisgarh	4.11	1.75	2.06	2.09	2.16	2.14	2.07	2.08	2.12	2.05	2.08	2.03
Madhya Pradesh	9.37	5.32	5.65	5.53	5.49	5.39	5.16	5.29	5.48	5.59	5.74	5.87
Uttar Pradesh	7.33	19.57	18.25	17.73	17.02	16.92	16.69	15.97	15.30	15.39	15.60	16.16
Uttaranchal	1.62	0.83	0.85	0.84	0.82	0.82	0.82	0.82	0.82	0.84	0.84	0.83
WESTERN ZONE	**15.34**	**11.97**	**12.43**	**12.37**	**12.73**	**12.75**	**13.39**	**13.72**	**14.09**	**14.20**	**14.24**	**14.38**
Gujarat	5.96	3.82	3.89	4.05	4.12	4.30	4.50	4.70	4.87	4.99	4.88	4.93
Maharashtra	9.36	8.13	8.52	8.30	8.59	8.42	8.86	9.01	9.20	9.19	9.33	9.42
Dadra & Nagar Haveli	0.01	0.01	0.01	0.01	0.01	0.01	0.01	0.01	0.01	0.02	0.02	0.02
Daman & Diu	0.00	0.01	0.01	0.01	0.01	0.01	0.01	0.01	0.01	0.01	0.01	0.02
SOUTHERN ZONE	**19.47**	**24.54**	**25.30**	**25.85**	**26.02**	**25.63**	**26.33**	**25.30**	**24.93**	**24.32**	**23.45**	**21.94**
Andhra Pradesh	8.37	8.00	8.51	8.52	8.68	8.56	8.62	8.19	7.94	7.84	7.86	7.41
Karnataka	5.84	5.48	5.37	5.32	5.25	5.10	5.37	5.37	5.34	5.43	5.31	5.14
Kerala	1.18	2.68	2.84	3.10	3.41	3.46	3.75	3.85	3.89	3.72	3.44	3.10
Tamil Nadu	3.96	8.08	8.29	8.61	8.41	8.24	8.34	7.67	7.52	7.08	6.60	6.07
Lakshadweep (UT)	0.00	0.01	0.01	0.01	0.01	0.01	0.01	0.01	0.01	0.01	0.01	0.01
Pondicherry (UT)	0.01	0.10	0.10	0.10	0.09	0.09	0.09	0.08	0.09	0.09	0.10	0.09
Goa	0.11	0.20	0.19	0.19	0.18	0.17	0.15	0.13	0.15	0.15	0.14	0.13
INDIA	**100.01**	**100.00**	**100.00**	**100.01**	**100.00**	**100.00**	**100.00**	**100.00**	**100.00**	**100.00**	**100.00**	**100.00**

Source: based on table A1.

TABLE A.3: Population Growth Rates of Various Zones, States and Union Territories, 1901-2001 (Figures in Percentage)

Zone/State/ Union Territory	1901-1921	1921-1951	1951-1981	1981-2001	1951-1961	1961-1971	1971-1981	1981-1991	1991-2001
1	2	3	4	5	6	7	8	9	10
NORTHERN ZONE	**-1.02**	**43.25**	**111.74**	**64.36**	**25.70**	**28.56**	**31.02**	**28.27**	**28.13**
Haryana	-7.94	33.32	127.74	63.64	33.79	32.22	28.74	27.41	28.43
Himachal Pradesh	0.42	23.76	79.42	41.98	17.85	23.04	23.73	20.79	17.54
Jammu & Kashmir	13.32	34.24	83.99	69.43	9.43	29.65	29.67	30.35	29.98
Punjab	-5.20	28.06	83.29	45.09	21.56	21.70	23.89	20.81	20.10
Rajasthan	-0.01	55.16	114.53	64.93	26.20	27.83	32.97	28.44	28.41
Chandigarh (UT)	-18.18	33.33	1783.33	99.34	400.00	114.17	75.88	42.04	40.34
Delhi (UT)	20.20	257.38	256.65	122.68	52.47	52.91	52.98	51.46	47.02
EASTERN ZONE	**4.08**	**40.49**	**89.46**	**50.51**	**24.09**	**23.99**	**23.13**	**23.41**	**21.96**
Bihar	0.54	36.17	79.83	58.69	26.67	14.35	24.16	23.38	28.62
Jharkhand	11.54	43.28	81.62	53.00	19.69	22.58	23.79	24.03	23.36
Sikkim	38.98	68.29	128.99	71.20	17.39	29.63	50.48	28.48	33.25
West Bengal	3.15	50.51	107.53	46.89	32.80	26.87	23.17	24.73	17.77
Orissa	8.31	31.25	80.05	39.57	6.17	41.13	20.16	20.06	16.25
A. & N. Islands (UT)	8.00	14.81	509.68	88.36	106.45	79.69	64.35	48.68	26.69
NORTH EAST	**40.58**	**70.90**	**141.22**	**54.81**	**41.31**	**35.05**	**26.40**	**27.46**	**21.46**
Assam	40.94	73.15	124.70	47.75	34.97	34.95	23.36	24.24	18.93
Arunachal Pradesh*	NA	NA	NA	73.73	NA	38.87	35.04	36.87	26.94
Manipur	35.21	50.52	145.85	52.50	34.95	37.56	32.43	29.28	17.96
Meghalaya	24.12	43.60	120.46	73.58	26.90	31.60	32.02	32.86	30.65
Mizoram	19.51	100.00	152.04	79.96	35.71	24.81	48.80	39.68	28.84
Nagaland	55.88	33.96	263.85	156.77	73.24	39.84	50.19	56.13	64.46
Tripura	75.72	110.20	221.28	55.82	78.72	36.25	31.94	34.29	16.03

(Contd.)

TABLE A.3 (*Contd.*)

1	2	3	4	5	6	7	8	9	10
CENTRAL ZONE	**0.54**	**35.61**	**82.59**	**56.93**	**18.85**	**22.49**	**25.42**	**25.91**	**24.64**
Chhattisgarh	25.90	41.65	87.85	48.71	22.75	27.11	20.39	25.73	18.27
Madhya Pradesh	9.69	33.85	105.03	58.12	24.73	29.28	27.16	27.25	24.26
Uttar Pradesh	-4.48	35.28	74.43	58.08	16.37	19.54	25.39	25.55	25.91
Uttaranchal	6.81	39.22	94.37	48.25	22.61	24.39	27.44	24.22	19.34
WESTERN ZONE	**8.91**	**55.55**	**100.71**	**52.42**	**24.67**	**28.14**	**25.64**	**24.15**	**22.78**
Gujarat	11.87	59.83	109.59	48.66	26.87	29.39	27.67	21.19	22.66
Maharashtra	7.52	53.49	96.19	54.31	23.60	27.45	24.54	25.73	22.73
D & N Haveli	29.17	32.26	153.66	111.54	41.46	27.59	40.54	32.69	59.42
Daman & Diu (UT)	-3.13	58.06	61.22	100.00	-24.49	70.27	25.40	29.11	54.90
SOUTHERN ZONE	**11.02**	**45.90**	**75.37**	**35.79**	**16.38**	**22.95**	**21.63**	**19.42**	**13.71**
Andhra Pradesh	12.35	45.26	72.10	42.32	15.65	20.90	23.09	24.20	14.59
Karnataka	2.47	42.79	94.41	42.32	21.57	24.22	26.75	21.11	17.51
Kerala	21.98	73.66	87.87	25.09	24.76	26.28	19.24	14.32	9.42
Tamil Nadu	12.34	39.25	60.72	28.92	11.85	22.30	17.50	15.38	11.72
Lakshadweep (UT)	0.00	50.00	90.48	52.50	14.29	33.33	25.00	30.00	17.31
Pondicherry (UT)	-0.81	29.92	90.54	61.26	16.40	27.91	27.97	33.77	20.54
Goa	-1.47	16.63	84.28	33.73	7.86	34.75	26.79	16.07	15.21
INDIA	**5.42**	**43.68**	**89.24**	**50.53**	**21.64**	**24.80**	**24.66**	**23.86**	**21.53**

Note: N.A. = Not Available.

Source: Premi, Mahendra K. *India's Population: Heading Towards A Billion* (1991); Census Of India 2001, Series 1, India. *Final Population Totals.*

TABLE A4: Crude Birth Rates, Crude Death Rates, and Natural Growth Rates (Three Year Moving Averages Centred at Mid Year), India and States, 1972-2000

India/State	Vital rate	1972	1976	1981	1986	1990	1991	1992	1993	1994	1995	1996	1997	1998	1999	2000
INDIA	CBR	**36.3**	**34.2**	**33.8**	**32.6**	**30**	**29.3**	**29.1**	**28.8**	**28.5**	**28.1**	**27.7**	**27.1**	**26.6**	**26.1**	**25.8**
	CDR	**15.9**	**15.2**	**12.3**	**11.3**	**9.9**	**9.9**	**9.7**	**9.5**	**9.2**	**9.1**	**9**	**9**	**9**	**8.7**	**8.5**
	NGR	**20.4**	**19**	**21.5**	**21.3**	**20.1**	**19.4**	**19.4**	**19.3**	**19.3**	**19**	**18.7**	**18.1**	**17.6**	**17.4**	**17.3**
Andhra Pradesh	CBR	34.1	33.6	31.3	30.6	26.1	26	24.9	24.2	24.1	23.6	23.2	22.6	22.6	21.7	21.3
	CDR	15.8	14.7	10.9	10	9.4	9.3	9.2	8.7	8.4	8.3	8.4	8.5	8.5	8.4	8.2
	NGR	18.3	18.9	20.4	20.6	16.7	16.7	15.7	15.5	15.7	15.3	14.8	14.1	14.1	13.3	13.1
Assam	CBR	36	31.1	33	34.4	30	30.9	30.4	30.4	29.9	29.3	28.4	27.9	27.7	27	26.9
	CDR	17.3	14.9	11.9	12.4	10.8	10.8	10.7	9.9	9.6	9.4	9.7	9.9	9.9	9.8	9.6
	NGR	18.7	16.2	21.1	22	19.2	20.1	19.7	20.5	20.3	19.9	18.7	18	17.8	17.2	17.3
Bihar	CBR	NA	NA	NA	36.9	32.6	30.5	31.7	32.3	32.2	32.2	32	31.6	31.1	31.5	31.9
	CDR	NA	NA	NA	13.9	10.8	10.4	10.5	10.6	10.5	10.4	10.2	9.9	9.4	9.1	8.8
	NGR	NA	NA	NA	23	21.8	20.1	21.2	21.7	21.7	21.8	21.8	21.7	21.7	22.4	23.1
Gujarat	CBR	38.6	36.8	34.8	32	28.6	27.5	27.9	27.7	27.3	26.4	26	25.6	25.5	25.4	25.2
	CDR	15.7	15.2	12	10.4	9	8.9	8.6	8.7	8.1	7.9	8.5	8.5	7.7	7.8	7.5
	NGR	22.9	21.6	22.8	21.6	19.6	18.6	19.3	19	19.2	18.5	17.5	17.1	17.8	17.6	17.7
Haryana	CBR	40.6	36.3	36.8	35.2	33.4	33.1	32	31.2	30.5	29.8	29	28.2	27.6	26.8	26.9
	CDR	11.2	12.9	10.6	8.9	8.8	8.4	8.3	8.2	8.1	8.1	8.1	8.1	9.1	9	7.5
	NGR	29.4	23.4	26.2	26.3	24.6	24.7	23.7	23	22.4	21.7	20.9	20.1	18.5	17.8	19.4
Himachal Pradesh	CBR	36	32.5	32	30.5	27.8	28.5	27.8	27	26	24.8	23.6	22.7	23.8	23.7	22.1
	CDR	14.6	12.8	10.3	9.2	8.7	8.7	8.8	8.7	8.6	8.4	8.3	7.9	8.2	7.9	7.2
	NGR	21.4	19.7	21.7	21.3	19.1	19.8	19	18.3	17.4	16.4	15.3	14.8	15.6	15.8	14.9
Jammu & Kashmir	CBR	32.3	31.9	31.2	32.7	N.A.	N.A.	N.A.	N.A.	N.A.	N.A.	N.A.	N.A.	N.A.	N.A.	19.6
	CDR	10.4	11.8	9	8.7	NA	NA	NA	NA	NA	NA	NA	NA	NA	NA	6.2
	NGR	21.9	20.1	22.2	24	NA	NA	NA	NA	NA	NA	NA	NA	NA	NA	13.4

(Contd.)

TABLE A4 *(Contd.)*

India/State	Vital rate	1972	1976	1981	1986	1990	1991	1992	1993	1994	1995	1996	1997	1998	1999	2000
Karnataka	CBR	30.7	27.8	27.9	29.2	27.6	26.8	26.2	25.5	24.8	24	23.3	22.6	22.3	22.3	22
	CDR	12.4	11.3	9.3	8.7	8.6	8.5	8.5	8.3	7.9	7.8	7.6	7.7	7.7	7.8	7.8
	NGR	18.3	16.5	18.6	20.5	19	18.3	17.7	17.2	16.9	16.2	15.7	14.9	14.6	14.5	14.2
Kerala	CBR	30.5	27.2	26.2	22.5	19.3	18.1	17.8	17.5	17.6	17.7	18	18.1	18.1	18	17.9
	CDR	8.9	7.9	6.7	6.2	6	6.1	6.1	6.1	6	6.1	6.1	6.3	6.3	6.4	6.4
	NGR	21.6	19.3	19.5	16.3	13.3	12	11.7	11.4	11.6	11.6	11.9	11.8	11.8	11.6	11.5
Madhya Pradesh	CBR	38.6	39.5	37.7	37.7	36.1	35.8	34.7	33.7	33.2	32.8	32.5	31.6	31.1	31.1	31.2
	CDR	17.1	17.6	15.6	13.7	13.1	13.1	13.1	12.3	11.7	11.3	11.1	11.1	10.9	10.7	10.2
	NGR	21.5	21.9	22.1	24	23	22.7	21.6	21.4	21.5	21.5	21.4	20.5	20.2	20.4	21
Maharashtra	CBR	31.1	28.4	29.1	29.3	27.4	26.2	25.6	25.2	24.9	24.3	23.7	23	22.2	21.1	20.9
	CDR	12.9	11.8	9.4	8.4	7.8	7.8	7.8	7.6	7.4	7.5	7.4	7.5	7.5	7.6	7.5
	NGR	18.2	16.6	19.7	20.9	19.6	18.4	17.8	17.6	17.5	16.8	16.3	15.5	14.7	13.5	13.4
Orissa	CBR	34.7	30.1	32.7	31.4	29.8	28.3	27.9	27.7	27.7	27.5	27.1	26.4	25.4	24.7	24.3
	CDR	17.9	15.3	13.5	13.4	12.4	12.1	12.2	11.7	11.3	10.8	10.8	10.9	10.9	10.7	10.5
	NGR	16.8	14.8	19.2	18	17.4	16.7	15.7	16	16.4	16.7	16.3	15.5	14.5	14	13.8
Punjab	CBR	34.1	31.5	30.2	28.6	28.2	28.5	27	26.1	25.2	24.3	23.9	23.2	22.4	21.8	21.5
	CDR	11.7	10.9	8.8	8.4	7.9	7.9	8	7.9	7.6	7.5	7.4	7.5	7.5	7.5	7.3
	NGR	22.4	20.6	21.4	20.2	20.3	20.7	19	18.2	17.6	16.8	16.5	15.7	14.9	14.3	14.2
Rajasthan	CBR	40.9	34.7	37.9	37.1	34	34.3	34.6	34.1	33.7	33.1	32.6	32	31.6	31.3	31.2
	CDR	NA	15.1	13.3	12.2	10.1	10.1	9.9	9.5	9.1	9.1	9	8.9	8.7	8.5	8.4
	NGR		19.6	24.6	24.9	23.9	24.2	24.7	24.6	24.6	24	23.6	23.1	22.9	22.8	22.8
Tamil Nadu	CBR	31.3	30.4	27.8	24.1	21.8	20.7	20.3	19.8	19.7	19.7	19.6	19.2	19.2	19.2	19.2
	CDR	14.5	14.4	11.4	9.6	8.7	8.6	8.5	8.2	8.1	8	8	8.2	8.2	8.1	7.9
	NGR	16.8	16	16.4	14.5	13.1	12.1	11.8	11.6	11.6	11.7	11.6	11	11	11.1	11.3

Uttar Pradesh	CBR	43.2	41.2	39.2	37.7	35.9	35.1	36	35.9	35.4	34.7	34.1	33.3	32.7	32.4	32.8
	CDR	21.7	20.7	16	15	12	12.1	11.9	11.8	10.9	10.5	10.3	10.4	10.4	10.4	10.3
	NGR	21.5	20.5	23.2	22.7	23.9	23	24.1	24.1	24.5	24.2	23.8	22.9	22.3	22	22.5
West Bengal	CBR	NA	NA	NA	29.9	27.4	26.7	25.8	25.2	24.8	23.9	22.9	22.2	21.5	20.9	20.6
	CDR	NA	NA	NA	9.1	8.5	8.4	8	8	7.9	8	7.8	7.7	7.4	7.2	7
	NGR	NA	NA	NA	20.8	18.9	18.3	17.8	17.2	16.9	15.9	15.1	14.5	14.1	13.7	13.6
Delhi	CBR	31.1	27.7	28	30.9	25.1	24.7	24.3	24.4	23.6	23.1	22	20.7	20.3	20	20.3
	CDR	7.8	8	7.1	7.6	6.4	6.4	5.6	5.9	5.8	6.1	6	5.5	5.2	5.1	5.1
	NGR	23.3	19.7	20.9	23.3	18.7	18.3	18.7	18.5	17.8	17	16	15.2	15.1	14.9	15.2

Notes: N.A. = Not available.

Figures for 1999 and 2000 are for those particular years and not the 3-year moving averages centred at the id-year. The data for J & K are not available for the years 1990 to 1999. Hence, the figures of India exclude Jammu and Kashmir for those years.

The aggregated estimates for India exclude Bihar and West Bengal for 1972, 1976 and 1981.

Sources: Registrar General, India (1998) and Sample Registration Bulletins for different years.

Chapter 6

Urbanisation and Rural-Urban Differentials in India

Mahendra K. Premi

Of the 1029 million people enumerated in the 2001 census of India, 286 million were in urban areas. Even the net addition to the urban population in 1991-2001, of the order of 68 million persons in a mere decade, is higher than the population of any country in Europe except the Russian Federation and Germany, or any country in Africa, except Nigeria and Egypt. It is also greater than the population of many countries in Asia and South America.

Urbanisation brings many changes—in the social fabric of cities and towns, and in terms of highly improved physical infrastructure. It entails opening of schools and colleges for the urban populace, leading to higher literacy and higher educational attainment compared to rural areas. Moreover, superior medical facilities at all three levels—primary, secondary and tertiary—are widespread and within easy reach. This results in lower mortality and higher life expectancy. Many a time, people come from nearby rural areas and from other towns and cities especially for specialised medical treatment. A number of people from rural areas come to cities and towns also to get better and higher education. Higher educational attainment in urban areas sustains the urge to provide good education to children, leading to smaller families and, hence, lower fertility. Finally, urbanisation means growth of jobs in secondary and tertiary sectors of industry, particularly in big cities and metropolises, implying better economic opportunities that attract migrants from far and wide. Thus, urbanisation leads to several types of rural urban differentials.

Considering the dynamics of population change, this paper brings out urban-rural growth differentials in the first instance. It then analyses the rural-urban variations in certain measures of fertility and mortality. Among the different fertility measures, we concentrate on the Crude Birth Rate and the Total Fertility Rate. Similarly, we examine rural-urban variations in the Crude Death Rate and the Infant Mortality Rate. As part of dynamics of population change, rural to urban migration is also analysed. The discussion on rural-urban differentials will not be complete until the variations in literacy and educational attainment on the one hand, and in economic activity on the other hand are discussed, and so, these aspects are also brought into the picture.

Trends in Urbanisation

India's urban population of 25.9 million in 1901—just 10.8 percent of the total population—has increased monotonically over time to 286.1 million in 2001, accounting for 27.8 per cent of the population of India. These changes over the past 100 years are a result of various historical, economic and demographic factors—the fall in the Crude Death Rate, especially since the beginning of the planning process in the country, more so in urban areas; decline in the incidence of famines and epidemics; rural to urban migration, industrial growth; and the country's partition into India and Pakistan in 1947.

It needs to be noted here that the urban population figures prior to 1961 and since 1961 are not strictly comparable as, on the eve of the 1961 census, the definition of urban settlements was substantially revised and made more restrictive,[1] which resulted in the declassification of 810 towns of the 1951 census. Consequently, we have concentrated on the urbanisation pattern that has emerged during the past 40 years.

The urban proportion of the total population in the country now stands at 27.8 per cent compared to 25.7 percent at the time of 1991 census count. The decadal urban growth rate has declined successively during the last two decades; it declined from 46.1 percent in 1971-81 to 37.5 percent in 1981-91 and to 31.5 percent in 1991-2001 (Table 1).[2] The increase in the proportion urban also slowed down over this period. Regarding the rural decadal growth rate, no pattern is observed over time; it increases in some decades and declines in others (Table 1 and Figure 1).

Urban Growth at the State Level, Emergence of New Towns and Declassification of Towns of the 1991 Census

As indicated above, India's urban growth rate declined from 37.5 percent during 1981-91 to 31.5 percent during 1991-2001. In this period, 1138 new towns emerged in the country—but 666 towns were either merged into bigger cities and towns, or were declassified, resulting in a net addition of 472 new towns (Table A2). As for the net addition to the country's urban population, it was of the order of 9.84 million persons.

TABLE 1: Urbanisation Rate and Decadal Growth Rates in Urban and Rural Population, India 1961-2001

Year	Population (in million)			Urbanisation rate	Decadal growth rate (per cent)	
	Total	Urban	Rural		Urban	Rural
1961	439.23	78.94	360.30	18.0	26.4	20.5
1971	548.16	109.11	439.05	19.9	28.2	21.9
1981	683.33	159.46	523.87	23.3	46.1	19.3
1991	846.39	217.55	628.84	25.7	37.5	20.0
2001	1028.61	286.12	742.49	27.8	31.5	18.0

Note 1: As the 1981 census was not conducted in Assam, the 1981 total and urban population figure for India include interpolated figures for that State.
2. The 1991 census was not held in Jammu and Kashmir. The 1991 total and urban population figures for India include the interpolated figures for that State.

Sources: Premi (1991: 41-52, 2003: 71); Census of India 1991 (1997: 170-71) Census of India 2001 (2001: 34); Census of India 2001, (2002, Primary Census Abstract on CD).

FIGURE 1: Decadal Population Growth Rates, India, Rural and Urban Areas, 1961, 1971, 1981, 1991 and 2001

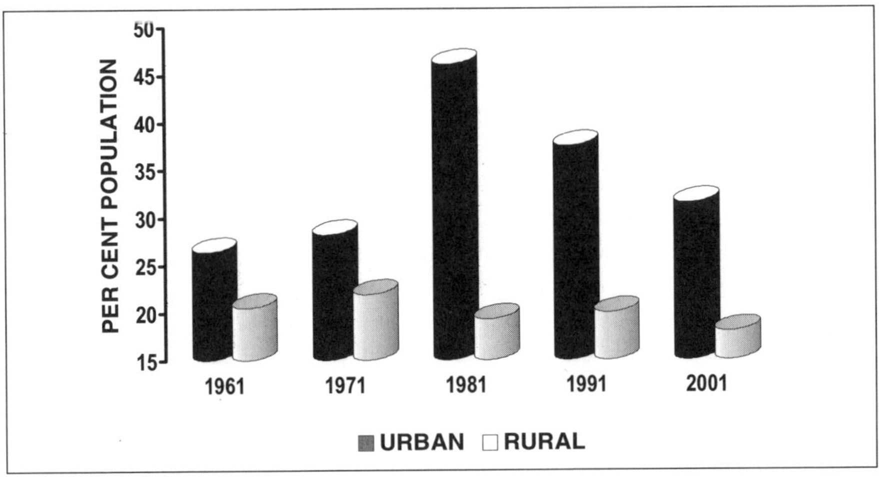

State level urban population data for the major States indicate that, as of 2001, Tamil Nadu was the most urbanised State, with its proportion urban at 44 percent (Table A1 and Figure 2). It is followed by Maharashtra, and Gujarat.

In 1991, Maharashtra, with an urbanisation rate of 38.7 percent was at the top, followed by Gujarat. Tamil Nadu could secure the third rank in that census with its urbanisation rate at 34.2 percent (Table A1 and Figure 2). Due to the declaration of 456 new towns on the eve of the 2001 census, there occurred a sudden jump of 9.7 percentage points in Tamil Nadu's urbanisation rate.

Besides Tamil Nadu, Haryana and Punjab have recorded substantial increases in their urban proportion during 1991-2001. Haryana, with proportion urban at 29 percent, and Punjab, with 34 percent urban in 2001 have gained by 4.4 percentage points each in this period. Haryana accounted for the observed urban growth pattern because of addition of 12 new towns (net of declassification), and very fast growth of some cities like Faridabad and Gurgaon, which are in the vicinity of Delhi. Punjab had a net addition of 37 new towns with a population of 4.19 lakh (Table A2), which caused a sudden increase in its urbanisation rate. Other major States showing an increase of more than 2 percentage points in their urbanisation rates are Maharashtra, Karnataka, and Gujarat (Table A1)

There are several major States—Andhra Pradesh, Bihar, Rajasthan, West Bengal, Madhya Pradesh and Uttar Pradesh—where the urban proportion between 1991 and 2001 has changed only marginally (Table A1 and Figure 2). It is noteworthy that the urban proportion has dropped in Kerala from 26.4 percent in 1991 to 26.0 percent in 2001. This is because the State suffered a net reduction of 37 towns compared to the 1991 census on the eve of the 2001 census count (Table A2).

FIGURE 2: Percent Urban, States of India, 1991 and 2001

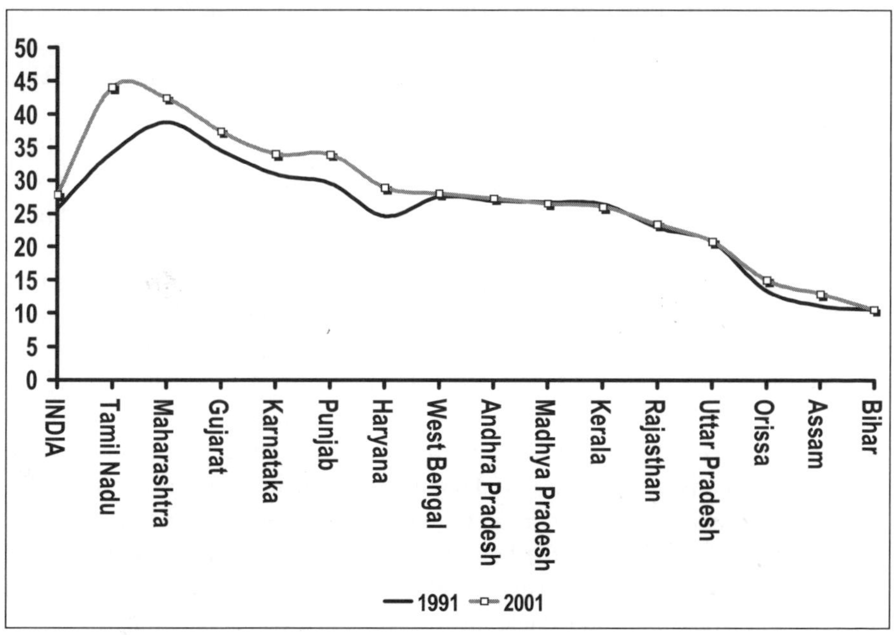

Urban-Rural Growth Differential (URGD)

At the national level, the URGD stood at 16.5 percent for the 1981-91 decade. It declined to 13.2 percent for the 1991-2001 decade (Table 2).

Table 2: Growth Rates of Total, Rural and Urban Populations and Urban-rural Growth Differential, India, 1981-91 and 1991-2001

Year	Growth rate	URGD		
		Total	Rural	Urban
1981-91	23.85	20.01	36.47	16.46
1991-01	21.35	17.97	31.13	13.16

Table A3 presents urban and rural decadal growth rates for 1980s and 1990s. Since rural and urban population distribution at the State level was not available for the newly constituted States of Chhattisgarh, Jharkhand and Uttaranchal for 1981, we have worked out the rural and urban growth rates for Bihar, Madhya Pradesh and Uttar Pradesh as they existed before bifurcation.

Amongst the major States, it was only Kerala where the rural growth rate was higher than urban growth rate during the 1990s, resulting in a negative URGD (Table A3 and Figure 3). As indicated above, the State suffered severely in respect of its overall urban growth due to declassification of many towns of the 1991 census on the eve of the 2001 census while not many new towns were added to its population. During the 1980s no major State had either negative or very low URGD. Chandigarh and Delhi as Union Territories and Sikkim, a small State, however, experienced substantial negative URGDs (Table A3).

In comparison to States like Tamil Nadu, Haryana and Punjab, where UGRDs increased over time, markedly so in the case of Tamil Nadu, in some of the States, i.e., Andhra Pradesh, Bihar, Kerala, Rajasthan and West Bengal, the UGRDs remained low and dipped to even lower levels (Figure 3). In Andhra Pradesh, a total of 79 towns (with a population of 14.46 lakh), were declassified on the eve of the 2001 census, while only 35 new towns emerged with a total population of 4.13 lakh. This depressed the urban growth rate very substantially during the 1990s (Table A1 and A2, and Figure 3). As indicated above, in Kerala, 36 towns with a population of 8.65 lakh persons were declassified and only 18 towns (with a population of 3.07 lakh) were added. This changed the balance between the urban and rural population growth rates during the 1990s. In old Bihar, in any case, the urban growth rate has been low in both 1981-91 and 1991-2001 decades. In the latter decade, 11 towns (with a population of 206,194 persons) were declassified and only 3 new towns (with a population of 31,604 persons) were added leading to decline in urban population of 174,590 persons. Hence, the URGD is low in Bihar. As in Bihar, in Rajasthan also, the difference in the population of declassified towns and new towns has been negative (29,590); hence, there has been a decline in urban growth in the 1990s compared to that in 1980s, and the URGD declined (Table A3 & Figure 3).

FIGURE 3: Urban-Rural Growth Differentials (UGRDs), States of India, 1981-1991 and 1991-2001

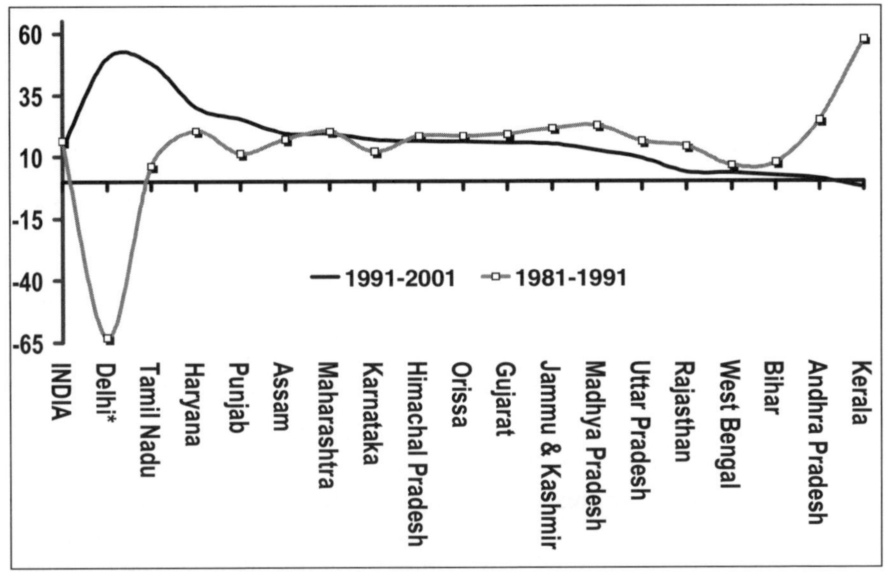

Dynamics of Population Change

The population of an area increases by births and decreases by deaths if the area is not affected by immigration and / or emigration. The difference between births and deaths over a specified time period is called 'natural increase'. Besides, if the area has also gained in population through larger immigration over emigration, there is increase due to migration. In contrast, some populations lose part of their natural increase (and, sometimes, even more than that) over a fixed period of time if the number of people going to other areas is greater than the number moving in.

We examine first changes in fertility, especially rural-urban differentials in the Crude Birth Rate over time, at the national level and for major States. CBRs are however affected by the age structure of the populations that we compare, for instance, when one of the populations has a larger number of women in the young reproductive ages, age specific fertility tends to be higher. So, we also compare the changes in Total Fertility Rate, a measure of the total number of children a woman has over her childbearing years, which is not affected by changes in age structure.

Birth Rates in India

At the national level, the Crude Birth Rate (CBR) varied from a high of 36.3 per thousand persons in 1972 to 24.8 in 2003, a decline of around ten points in three decades. When we examine rural and urban CBRs, we find that the difference between the two has fluctuated between 6 to 8 points. With a faster decline in rural CBRs in recent years, the difference has somewhat narrowed down (Table 3).

TABLE 3: Crude Birth Rates (Three-Year Moving Averages Centered at Mid-Year), and Rural Urban Differentials, India, 1972-2003

Residence type & differential	Period							
	1971-1973	1980-1982	1990-1992	1995-1997	1999-2001	2000-2002	2001-2003	2002-2004
Rural	37.7	35.4	31.2	29.4	27.5	27.1	26.7	26.4
Urban	30.0	27.6	24.0	27.9	20.7	20.3	20.0	19.8
Combined	36.3	33.8	29.6	27.7	25.8	25.9	23.3	24.8
Rural-urban differential	7.7	7.6	7.2	7.5	6.8	6.8	6.7	6.6

State-wise CBRs for the major States (including Delhi) by rural / urban residence, from 1971 to 2003, obtained from various publications of the Sample Registration System, are presented in Appendix Table A4. Since there are large variations in year-to-year estimates of States' CBRs, the estimates are three-year moving averages in order to minimise those fluctuations. The table also gives rural-urban differentials.

The CBR continued to remain above 30 per 1,000 in Bihar, Madhya Pradesh, Rajasthan and Uttar Pradesh, while the current rates have declined to mere 16.3 per 1,000 persons in Kerala and 18 in Tamil Nadu (Table A4 and Figure 4A). In 2003, birth rates were between 20 and 21 in Andhra Pradesh, Himachal Pradesh, Maharashtra and West Bengal (Table A4 and Figure 4A). There has been a decline in the CBR of 10 points or more in many States over a period of 30 years, as in the case of country as a whole (Table A4 and Figure 4A).

The CBRs in urban areas are considerably lower than in rural areas, expectedly so, because, as explained earlier, people in urban areas are particular to have small families enabling them to give good education to their children. Moreover, due to better health facilities and lower infant mortality rates, parents are more confident about child survival and this checks the tendency to have a larger number of children as a strategy of compensating for anticipated child loss.

At the national level the difference between the rural and urban CBRs has remained almost the same (between 6 to 8 points) in recent years (Table A4 and Figure 4B). At the State level, the rural-urban differential in CBRs in some States like Assam, Bihar, Madhya Pradesh, Rajasthan and Uttar Pradesh has been around 8-10 points. These are the States where the overall CBR has remained much above the national average. There are other States like Andhra Pradesh, Kerala, Maharashtra, Punjab, Tamil Nadu and Delhi where this difference has been less than four points. These States have recorded quite low overall CBRs. Also, in these Sates, there have been constant efforts to limit the rural CBR (Table A4 and Figure 4A).

It is noteworthy that the rural-urban differential has largely narrowed down in the recent past. The rural-urban difference in the CBR has been as low as less than one in Kerala and Maharashtra in recent years (Table A4 and Figure 4B).

Total Fertility Rate

The number of 'Children Ever Borne' by a woman as she passes through her childbearing span and completes her fertility history is known as the *Completed Fertility Rate*. It is a measure that requires data for at least 35 years for a set of women entering the age of 15 years in a particular year. To overcome this problem of data requirement, we try to estimate the Completed Fertility Rate by an indirect procedure, in which we assume that Age-Specific Fertility Rates for women of different ages at *a point of time* represents the fertility trajectory of a cohort of women entering the child bearing ages. If Age Specific Fertility Rates (ASFRs) are computed for a particular year (or a set of three or five years) for each five-yearly age group, we get seven different figures for seven age groups between 15 to 50 years. Using sets of seven ASFRs would make both spatial and temporal comparison difficult, and hence, we summarise these figures into one, to arrive at the *Total Fertility Rate* or the TFR. The TFR sums up, in a single number, the fertility of all women who, at a given point in time, have passed through ages between 15 to 50 years during that year. It is a 'pure' measure of fertility, as it is not affected by variations in age structure. This measure is very helpful in comparing fertility performance of different populations or social groups at a point of time as well as temporally.

TFRs for India by rural-urban residence over a period of thirty years are shown in table 4. The TFR declined from a high of 5.1 children per woman in 1972 to 3.7 children in 1991, a decline of 1.4 points in almost 20 years. Then it declined to 3.0 children per woman in 2002. Rural urban differentials in TFR have varied between 1.4 and 1.1 children (Table 4).

Table A5 shows the TFRs of the major States from 1971-73 to 2001-03. The figures are three-year moving averages centered at midpoint. Among the major States for which we have complete data sets for the past 30 years, TFR was high and continued to be so in Madhya Pradesh, Rajasthan and Uttar

TABLE 4A : Crude Birth Rates, States of India, 1972-2003

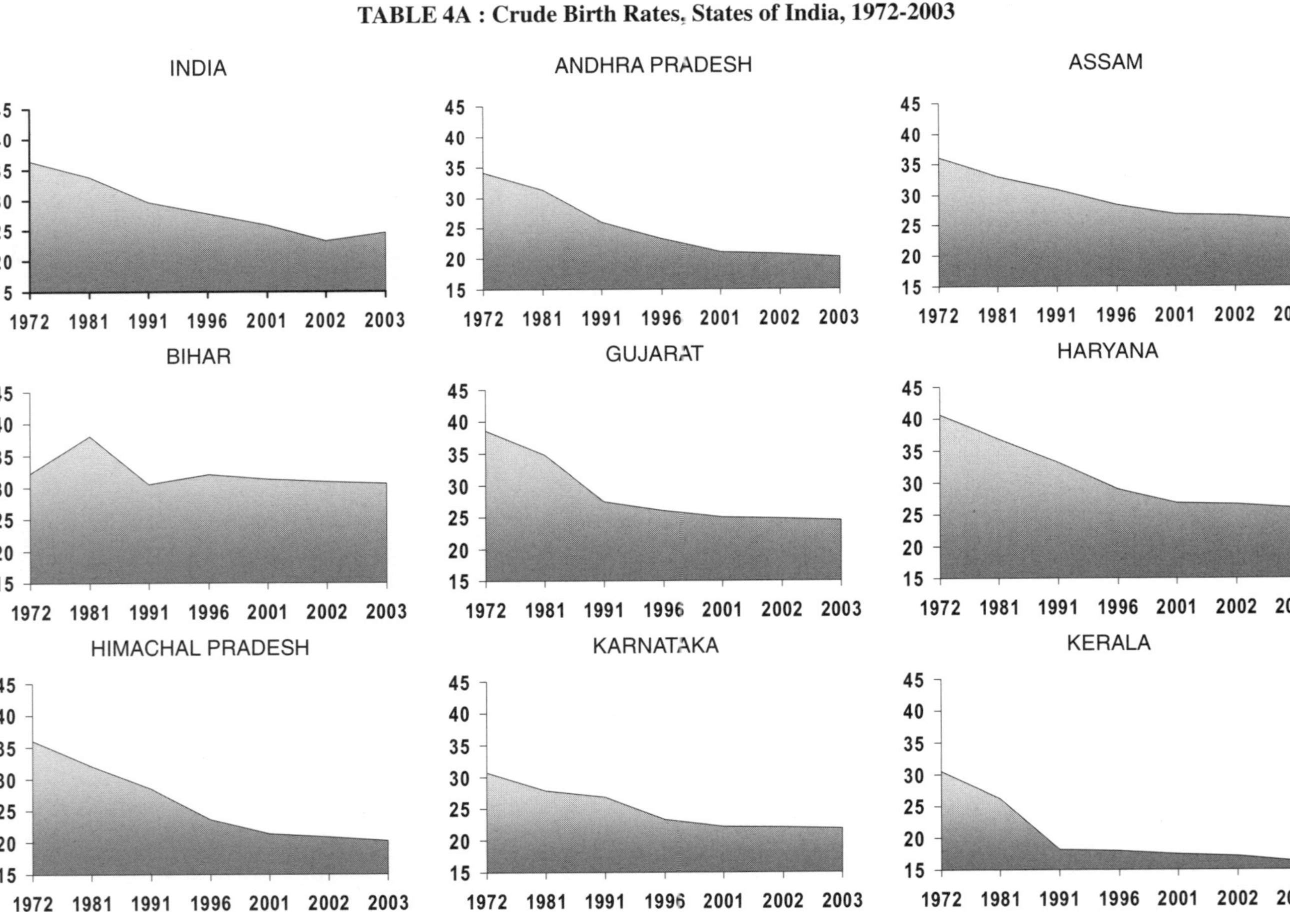

TABLE 4A : (*Contd.*)

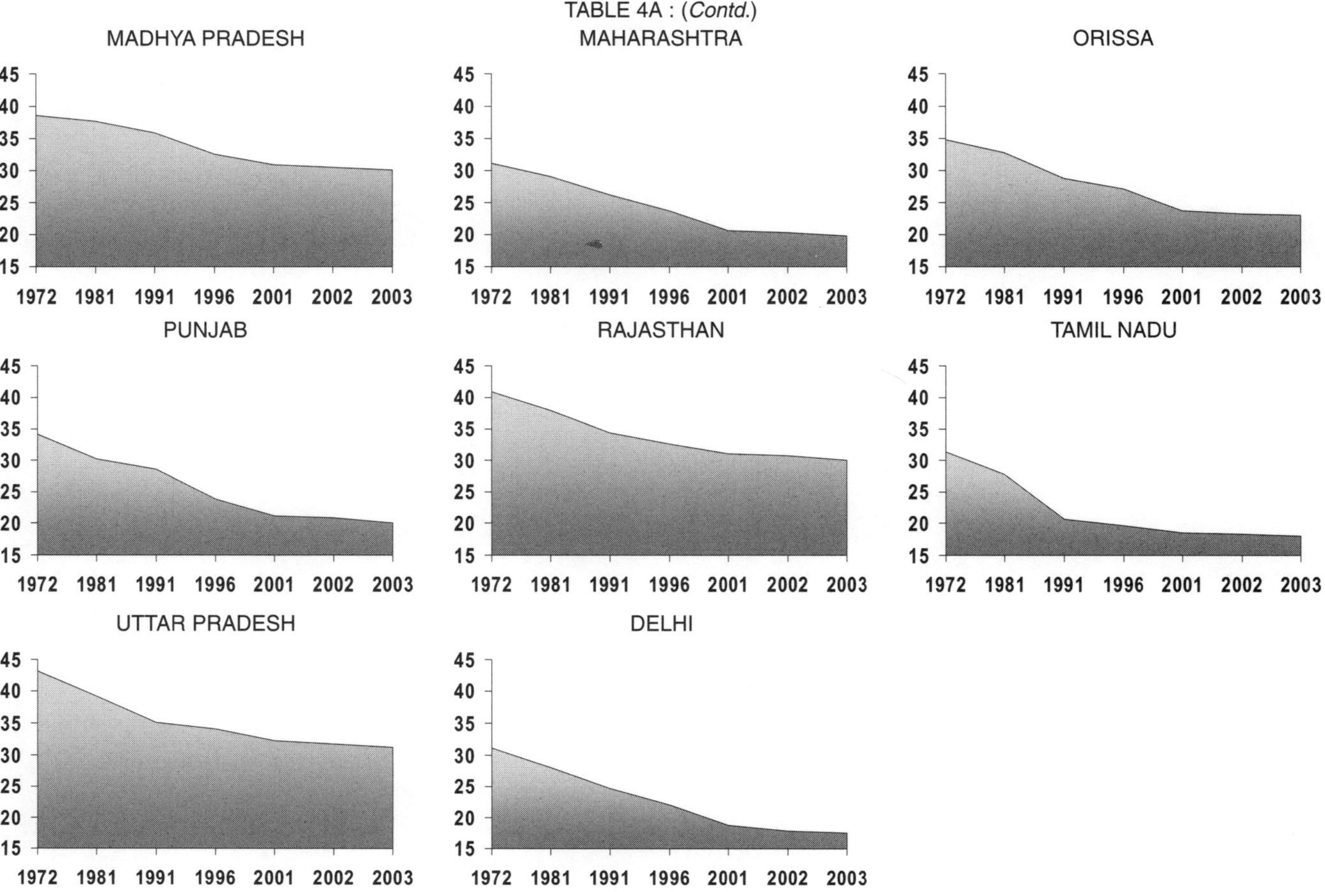

TABLE 4B : Rural-Urban Differentials in the Crude Birth Rates, States of India, 1972-2003

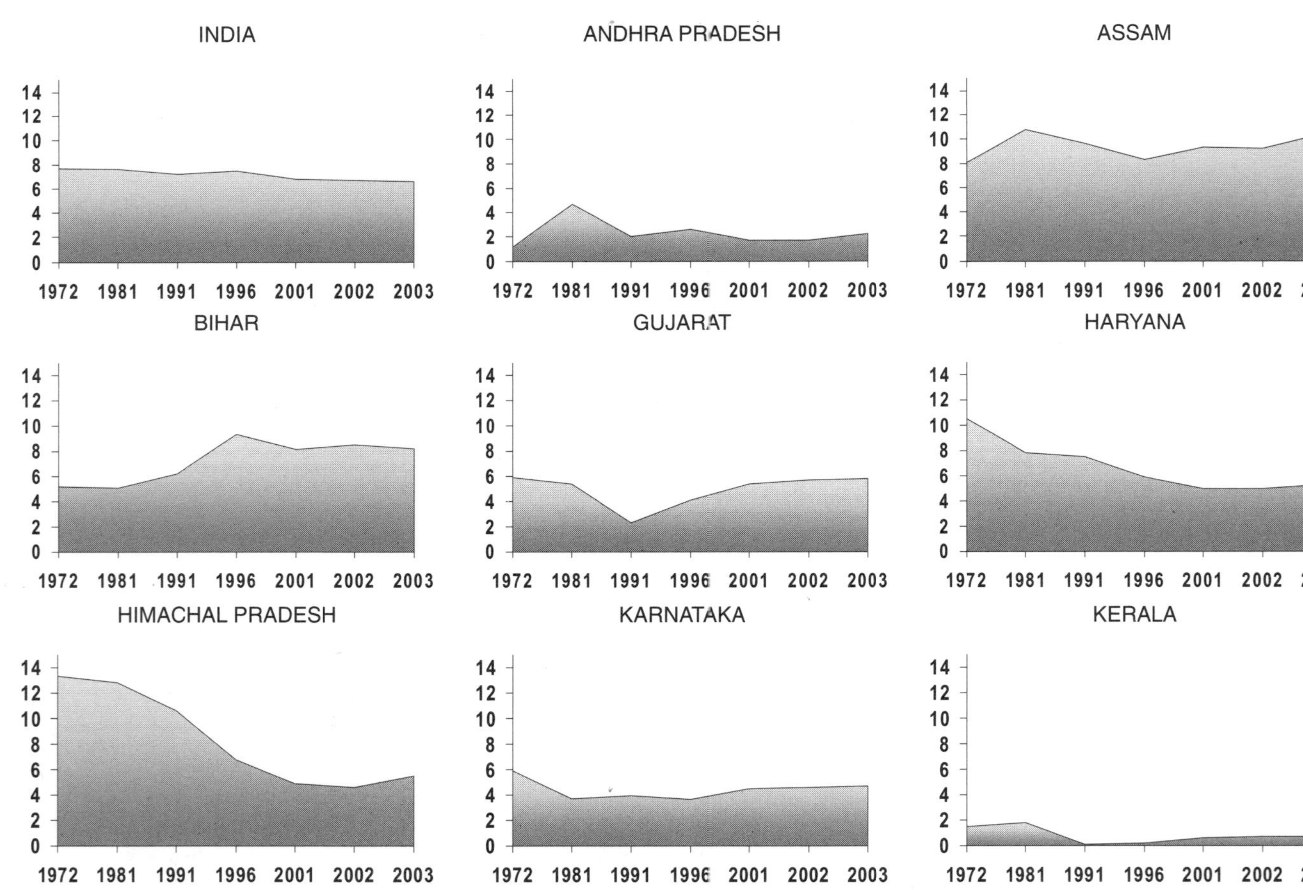

TABLE 4B : (*Contd.*)

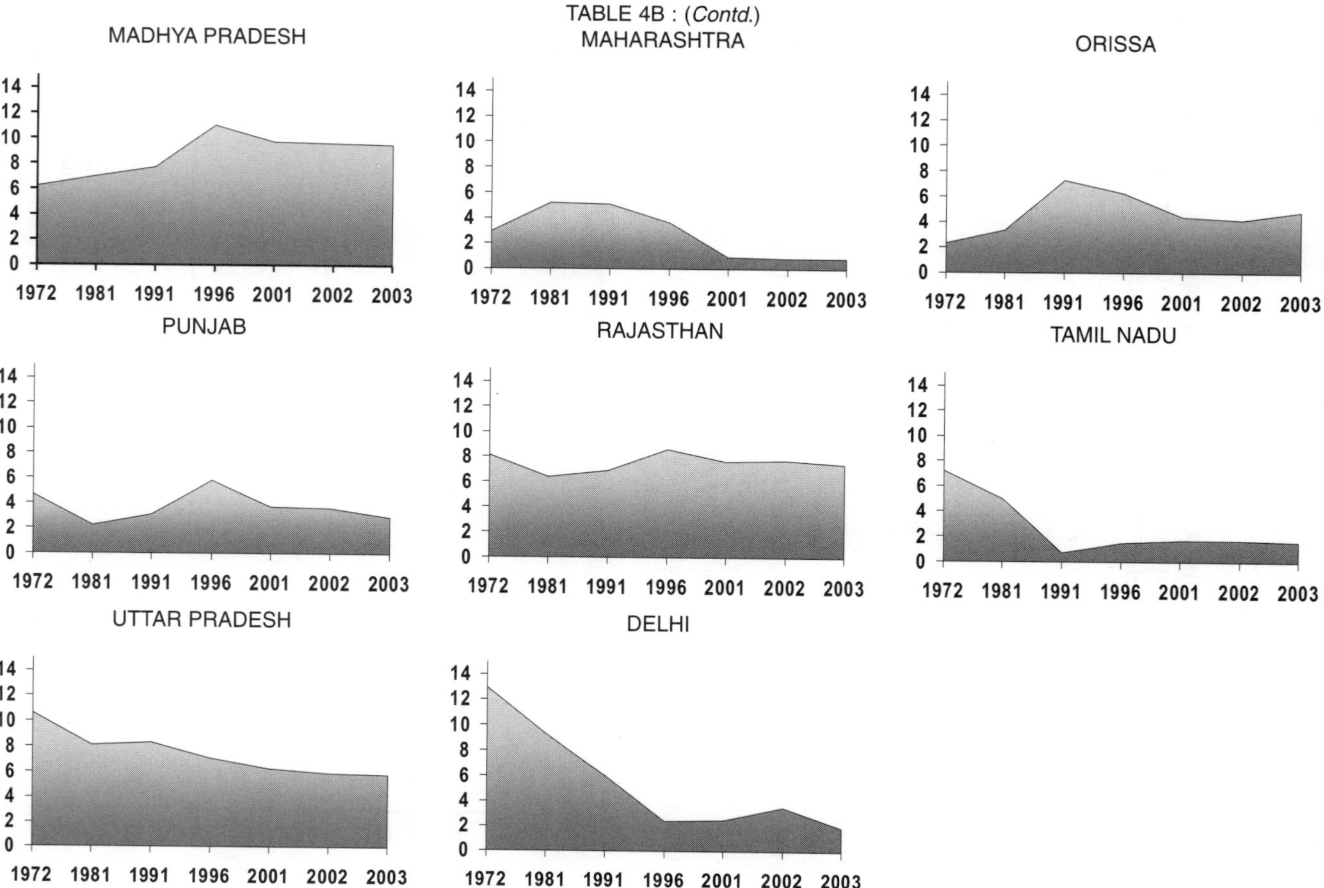

Pradesh over three decades (Table A5 and Figure 5). Even in 2002, the TFR was as high as 4.3 in Bihar, 3.8 in Madhya Pradesh, 3.9 in Rajasthan and 4.4 in Uttar Pradesh (Table A5).

TABLE 4: Total Fertility Rates for Rural, Urban and Combined Areas (Three-Year Moving Averages Centered at Mid-Year) and Rural Urban Differentials, India, 1972-2002

Residence type	1971-1973	1980-1982	1990-1992	1995-1997	1999-2001	2000-2002	2001-2003
Rural	5.3	4.8	4.0	3.7	3.5	3.4	3.3
Urban	4.0	3.4	2.7	2.5	2.3	2.3	2.2
Combined	5.1	4.5	3.7	3.4	3.2	3.1	3.0
Rural-urban differential	1.3	1.4	1.3	1.2	1.2	1.1	1.1

Among the low fertility States, Kerala and Tamil Nadu had TFRs of as high as 4.0 and 3.8 in 1972. Andhra Pradesh, another low fertility State, had a TFR of 4.5 in that year (Table A5). In Kerala, the TFR declined to 1.8 (below the replacement level) in 1991 itself and continued to remain so thereafter. In Tamil Nadu, TFR did not fall as rapidly; it declined to 2.2 in 1991 and to 2.0 in 2002 (Table A5). The other States with low fertility over the past 30 years have been Andhra Pradesh, Karnataka, Maharashtra and Orissa (Figure 5).

FIGURE 5: TFRs, States of India, 1972, 1991 and 2002

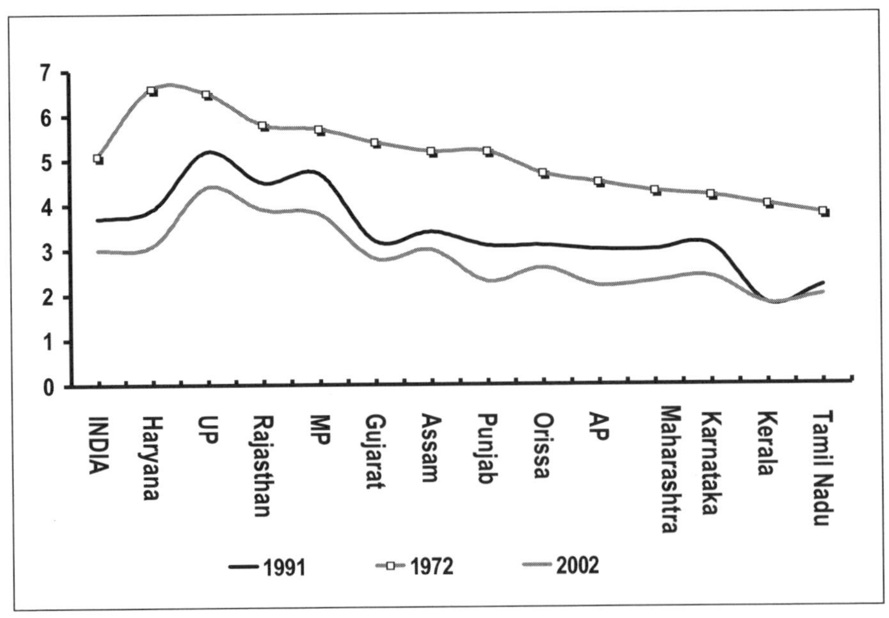

As of 2002, rural-urban differentials in TFRs varied from 0.1 in Kerala to 1.7 in Madhya Pradesh to 1.3 in Uttar Pradesh (Table A5). Among the currently low fertility States (Kerala, Tamil Nadu, Andhra Pradesh), rural-urban differential was less than one, even way back in 1972 (Table A5 and Figure 6a). By 2002, in the low fertility States, the rural-urban differentials had grown even smaller, indicating that the rural TFR had substantially declined (Figures 6a and 6b).

FIGURE 6a: R-U Differentials in TFRs, States of India, 1972

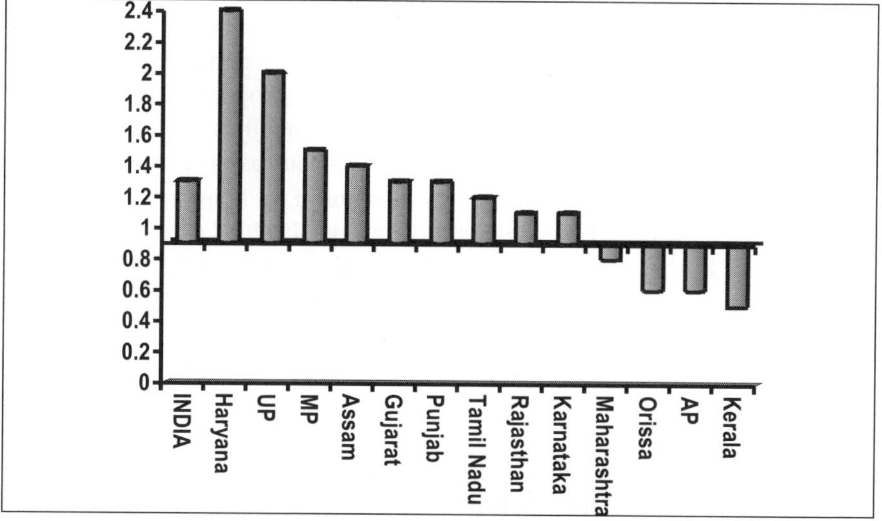

FIGURE 6b: R-U Differentials in TFRs, States of India, 2002

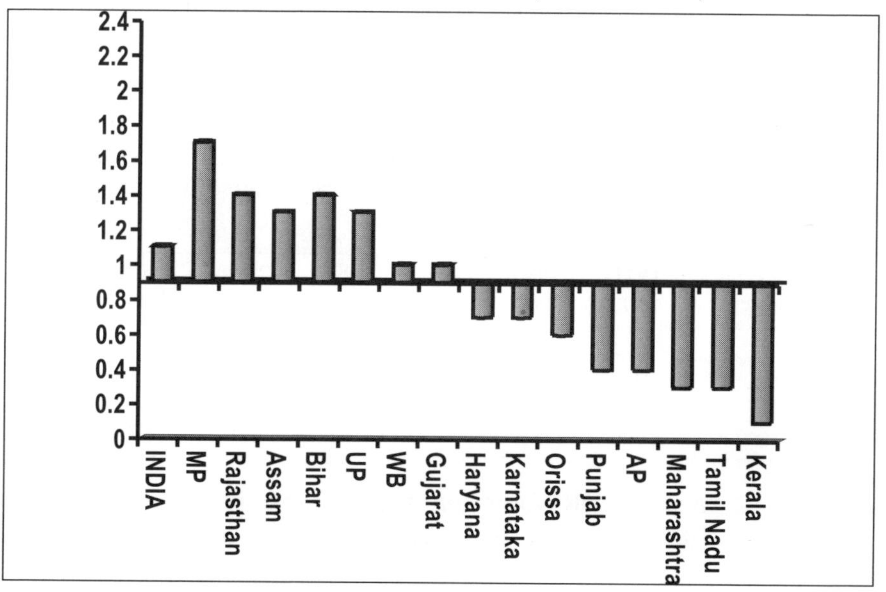

Mortality Differentials

With regard to mortality differentials in urban and rural populations, we examine here the Crude Death Rate and the Infant Mortality Rate. Like the Crude Birth Rate, the Crude Death Rate is also affected by differences in age structure of the populations under comparison; hence, they do not tell much about mortality. The CBR and CDR are, however, used for computing rates of natural increase (CBR minus CDR) for different populations to provide temporal and spatial comparisons.

The *Infant Mortality Rate* (IMR) is regarded as a very good indicator of health and social well-being since low IMR implies good health facilities, especially to the newly born child, implying a higher proportion of institutional deliveries or those attended by doctors and/or trained midwives. This also implies higher literacy and educational level of both parents, better nutrition of the mother and the child and higher social status of the household. In contrast, regions with high IMR have comparatively poor health facilities and a low proportion of births take place in health institutions and more often deliveries occur at home attended by traditional *dais*. In many cases when the child is of low birth weight, it has low survival chances.

We shall now examine separately the urban-rural differentials in CDRs and IMRs.

Crude Death Rate

At the national level, the CDR has varied from a high of 15.9 per thousand persons in 1972 to 7.9 in 2003, a decline of eight points in three decades. Examining the rural and urban CDRs over time, it is found that the difference between the two, a high of 7.5 points in 1972, declined monotonically to 2.5 points in 2003. With a faster decline in rural CDRs in recent years, the difference has substantially narrowed down (Table 5).

TABLE 5: Crude Death Rates for Rural, Urban and Combined Areas (Three-Year Moving Averages Centered at Mid-Year) with Rural Urban Differentials, India, 1972-2003

Residence type & differential	1971-1973	1980-1982	1990-1992	1995-1997	2000-2002	2001-2003	2002-2004
Rural	17.4	13.5	10.7	9.7	9.0	8.8	8.5
Urban	9.9	7.7	7.0	6.5	6.2	6.1	6.0
Combined	15.9	12.3	9.9	9.0	8.3	8.2	7.9
R-U differential	7.5	5.8	3.7	3.2	2.8	2.7	2.5

Table A6 presents CDRs for major States to bring out the pattern as it has evolved from 1971-73 to 2002-04. One clear indication is that there has been a sharp decline in the CDR across the board over time. However, there is continued evidence of inter State disparities, and of rural-urban differentials (Figure 7).

FIGURE 7: CDRs, States of India, 2003

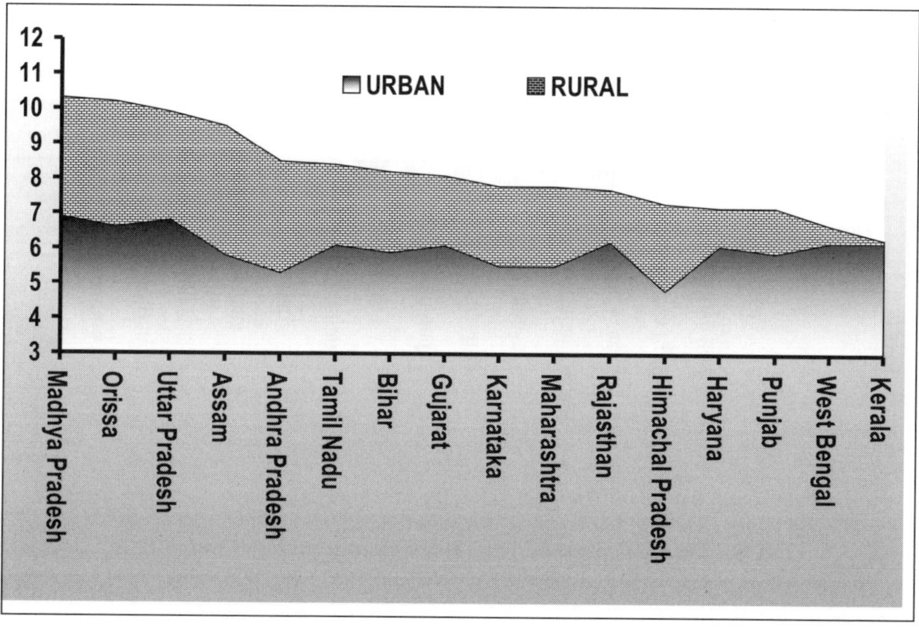

While there has been a constant decline in the rural-urban differential in the CDR over the past three decades, there are States like Andhra Pradesh, Assam, Madhya Pradesh, Uttar Pradesh and Orissa where the rural-urban differential continued to be more than three points in 2003 compared to 2.5 points at the national level (Figure 8a). Uttar Pradesh, while having experienced a considerable proportionate decline in the CDR between 1972 and 2003, also showed a high differential at 3.1 points in 2003 (Table A6 and Figures 8a and 8b). In Tamil Nadu, Himachal Pradesh and Rajasthan, the decline in the CDR differential has been phenomenal. Moreover, in Rajasthan, the CDR differential had dipped substantially below the national average in 2003 (Table A6, Figures 8a and 8b).

The difference in rural and urban CDRs in Punjab, Haryana, Rajasthan, Gujarat, Kerala, Punjab, J & K, West Bengal and Delhi fell below the national average by 2003. This was also so to a lesser extent in Karnataka, Tamil Nadu and Maharashtra. The rural-urban CDR differential became less than one point in Kerala, West Bengal and Delhi from at least 2001 onwards (Table A6). This is indicative of improved health conditions in both rural and urban areas. It also suggests that, of recent, the rural population in some States at least has been getting good medical facilities.

FIGURE 8a: CDR, Rural-Urban Differentials, States of India, 2003

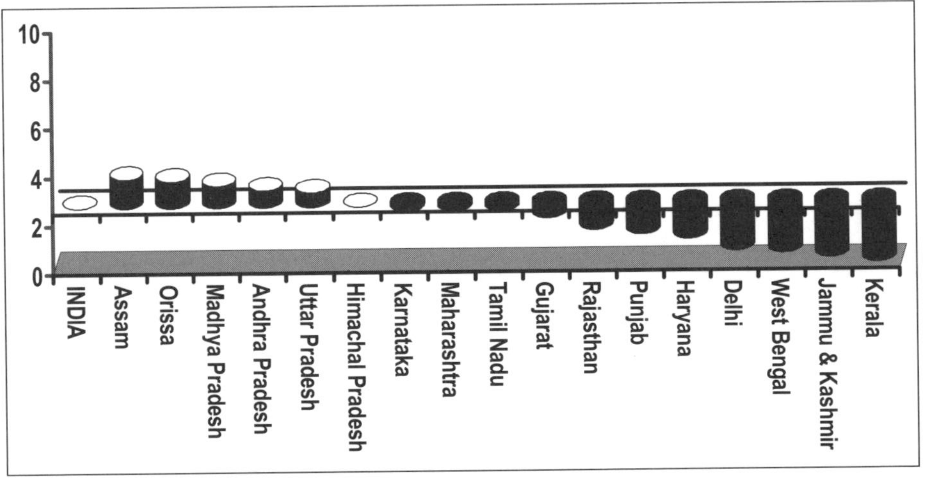

FIGURE 8b: CDR, Rural-Urban Differentials, States of India, 1972

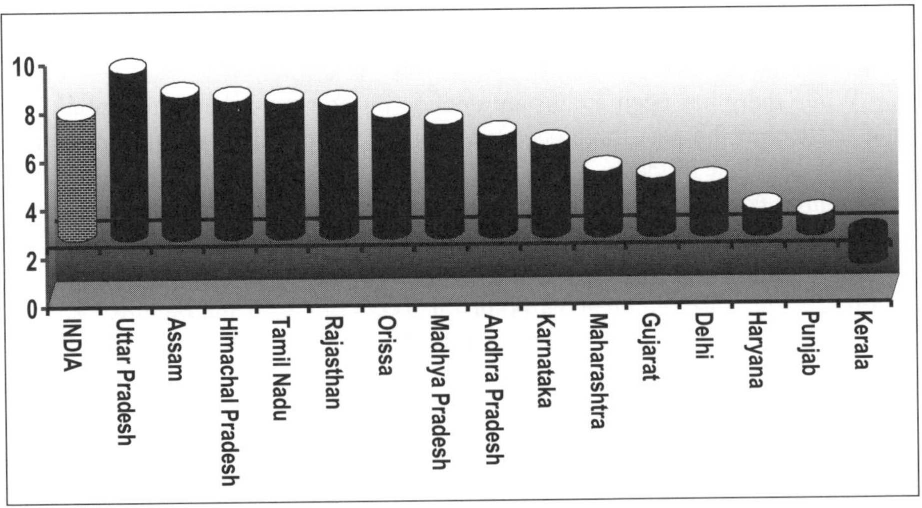

Infant Mortality Rate

As indicated above, IMR indicates the existing health conditions, especially of infants. Table A7 presents data on IMR at the national level and for major

States as three-year moving averages centered at midpoint from 1971-73 to 2002-04. It also gives rural urban differentials in the IMR.

At the national level, IMR declined substantially during the past three decades, from a high of 134 per 1,000 live births in 1972 to a low of 60.3 in 2003. The rural-urban differential also declined from 59 points in 1972 to 27 points in 2003 (Table A7). There are, however, large variations in rural urban differentials in the IMR at the State level, and no single pattern emerges over the past thirty years except that rural-urban differentials in the IMR have declined across the board.

In rural areas, the decline in the IMR between 1991 and 2003 was marginal in Andhra Pradesh and Assam while in urban areas, Andhra Pradesh showed a substantial IMR decline (Table A7 and Figure 9). In Bihar the urban IMR in 2003 was higher than what it was in 1991 (Table A7 and Figure 9). Madhya Pradesh, Orissa and Uttar Pradesh continued to have relatively high IMRs (above the national average) in 1991 as also in 2003 (Figure 9).

FIGURE 9: IMR, States of India, 1991 and 2003

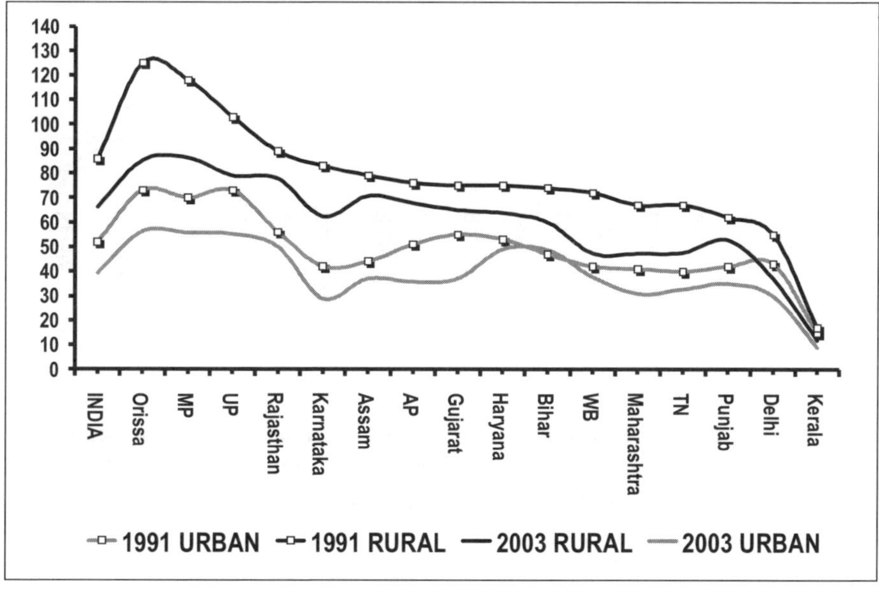

States can be classified into two categories. In the first, the rural-urban differential continued to remain high, mostly ABOVE the national average. As of 2003, these States were: Andhra Pradesh, Assam, Karnataka, Madhya Pradesh and Orissa (Table A7 and Figure 10). The R/U differential in Uttar Pradesh remained high till the middle of the 1980s, mainly due to the persisting high urban IMR in the State, but then declined sharply in the following years

(Table A7). In the second category are States where, in 2003, the R/U differential in IMR was low in comparison to the national average. These include the States of Bihar, Haryana, Maharashtra, Punjab, Tamil Nadu, Kerala and West Bengal (Figure 10).

In Bihar and Haryana, the rural IMR declined faster than the urban IMR (Table A7). This is strikingly so also in the case of Orissa (Table A7 / Figure 9). Other States registered a decline in IMR in both rural and urban areas. The R/U differential in IMR in Kerala, as low as 15 points in 1972, declined even further, to just 2 to 3 points in recent years (Table A7 and Figure 10).

FIGURE 10: IMR, Rural-Urban Gap, States of India, 1991 and 2003

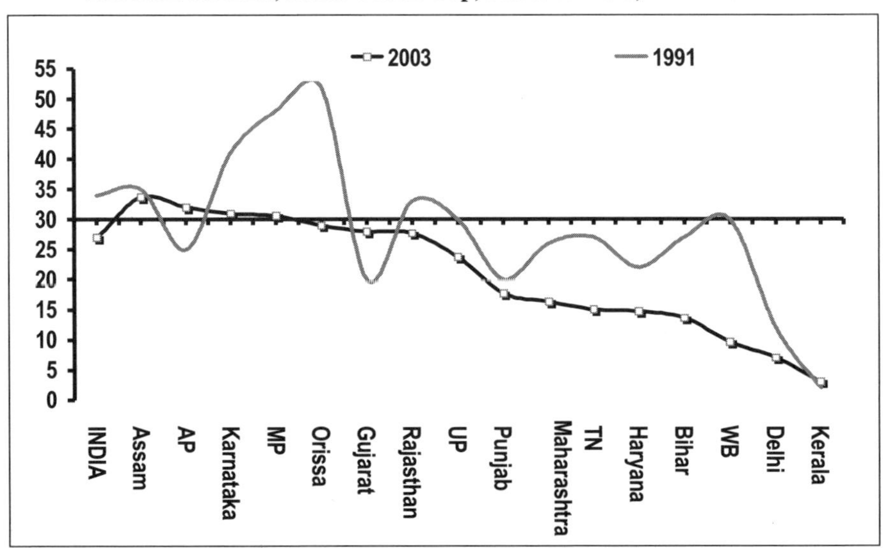

Migration in India

It was observed earlier that besides natural increase, the urban population also increases by net rural-to-urban migration. Examining the pattern of 'lifetime migration' (which is based on birthplace data—'born elsewhere other than the place of birth'), it is noteworthy that between 1961 and 1991, there had been a substantial decline in the proportion of migrants to the total population—from 33 percent in 1961 to 27.4 percent in 1991. In 2001, this proportion, however, increased to 29.9 percent.

There were 307 million lifetime migrants in a population of 1028.6 million, as of the 2001 census of India. 273 million moved within the country on the birthplace criterion, while 34.2 million were *immigrants*. A majority of these immigrants were from Pakistan. They had migrated to India at the time of partition of British India into India and Pakistan in 1947. The total immigrants in the country on the 'place of last residence' basis numbered just 5.16 million. The number of inter-censal immigrants during 1991-2001 was only 0.74 million persons, largely from Bangladesh, Nepal, Pakistan and Sri Lanka. It seems that the census could not count properly all the immigrants into the country, probably because a large number of illegal migrants from Bangladesh reported themselves as Indians.

Of the total lifetime internal migrants, 51.7 million moved from rural to urban areas while 13 million moved from urban areas to rural areas, leading to an addition of 34.7 million persons to the urban population through net migration. Further, 2.55 million persons *immigrated* into urban areas, so that the total addition to the urban population due to migration stood at 37.25 million persons.

Table A8 presents data on net rural-to-urban inter-censal migration, total inter-censal migration and net rural-to-urban migration as proportion of total inter-censal migration, 1991-2001.

Net inter-censal rural-to-urban migration as percentage of all inter-censal migration in the country stood at 15.2 per cent for all persons, 24 .8 percent for males and 10.4 percent for females. There has been greater urban-to-rural migration than rural-to-urban migration in Sikkim, and in the union territories of Daman and Diu and Lakshadweep, resulting in negative net rural-to-urban migration.

There are large inter-State differences in net inter-censal rural-to-urban migration as proportion of total inter-censal migration. Delhi stands out in this respect, with its net inter-censal rural-to-urban migration at 58% of total inter censal migration (Table A8 Figure 11). Net rural-to-urban migrants in Delhi comprised as much as 9.3 percent of the total population. Like Delhi, Chandigarh also has a large proportion of net rural-to-urban migrants (Figure 11).

Net rural-to-urban migration as percentage of inter-censal migration in 1991-2001 was higher than the national average in Punjab, Haryana, Jharkhand, Gujarat and Maharashtra. It was higher only for males in Bihar, Orissa and Uttar Pradesh (Table A8 and Figure 11). All the above States except Uttar Pradesh, Bihar, Jharkhand and Orissa have a robust economic base and attract migrants. Net rural-to-urban migration, especially of males, in the four southern States of Andhra Pradesh, Karnataka, Kerala and Tamil Nadu has been fairly low for various reasons.

Female net rural-to-urban inter-censal migration has been higher than the national average of 10.4 percent in Gujarat (18.5 percent), Maharashtra (15.2 percent), Haryana (13.6 percent), Punjab (11.7 percent) and Karnataka (11.2 percent). As the reasons differ from State to State for higher female rural-to-urban migration, detailed analysis of the extant data would be useful.

FIGURE 11: Net Inter-Censal Rural-Urban Migration as a Proportion of Total Inter-Censal Migration, States of India, 1991-2001

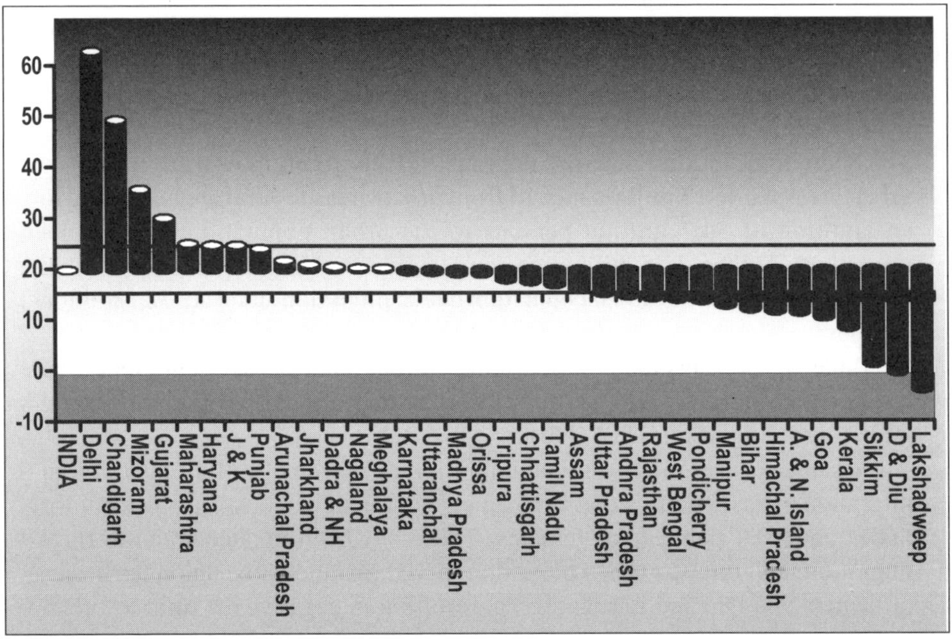

Literacy and Educational Attainment

Literacy level and educational attainment are regarded as two very important indicators of social and economic development. The United Nations, in its World Development Report, uses the Adult Literacy Rate and attainment of middle or higher level of education along with the Infant Mortality Rate, Life Expectancy at Birth and Per Capita Income as development indicators (Srinivasan and Shariff 1997).

From the demographic viewpoint, the literacy rate (LR) and level of educational attainment are regarded as key variables affecting fertility, mortality (especially infant mortality) and migration. It has been recognised the world over that fertility levels are highest among illiterate women and fall with increases in educational attainment. Similarly, the CDR declines with the level of education. The death rate is significantly lower among persons who have attained high school or better education. It is mothers' education that has a negative correlation with the Infant Mortality Rate. This becomes clear when the respective data are tabulated by rural and urban residence. At higher educational levels, especially in urban areas, mothers are capable of taking right decisions in case of child's illness. They are also more particular about nutrition requirements of the young children.

Education also plays an important role in migration decision-making. People with a certain level of education have rising expectations and try to search for white-collar jobs in both rural and urban areas.

Literacy in the Indian Census

In the Indian census, a person is recorded as literate if he or she is able to read and write a simple message with understanding in any language. In the 1991 census, all children below the age of 7 years were considered illiterate. Also, to compute refined (or net) literacy rate, the base population has been designated as 'population aged 7 years and above'. Based on this definition, the 1991 census reported that 52 percent of India's population was literate. The male literacy rate was 64 percent and female literacy rate was 39 percent. The net literacy rates in 2001 indicate a very significant increase in respect of both males and females. Presently, almost two-thirds of India's population is literate; the male LR has risen to three-fourths, while the female literacy rate, at 54.2 percent, means that more than half the females have become literate for the first time. In urban areas, the male literacy rate in 2001 crossed 80 percent, while that for females became almost three-fourths (Table 6).

The literacy rate in the country in the population aged 7+ years improved from 43.7 percent in 1981 to 52.2 percent in 1991, and then to 65.1 percent during the next decade. There are large urban-rural differentials in literacy rates. Between 1981 and 1991, the literacy rate increased substantially in both rural and urban areas but, in 1991, the urban LR of 73.0 percent was quite above the rural LR of 44.5 percent, implying urban-rural differential of 28.5 percentage points. The rural LR, however, increased from 44.5 percent in 1991 to 58.7 percent in 2001 (Table 6); this improvement was more in absolute terms as also proportionately than that in urban LR. The urban-rural differential in literacy rate in 2001 declined to 21.2 percentage points.

TABLE 6: Literacy Rates in India by Sex and Rural Urban Residence, 1981-2001

Year	Total			Rural			Urban		
	M	F	T	M	F	T	M	F	T
1981	56.5	29.8	43.7	49.7	21.8	36.1	76.8	56.4	67.3
1991	64.1	39.3	52.2	57.8	30.4	44.5	81.0	63.9	73.0
2001	76.2	52.0	65.1	70.7	46.1	58.7	86.3	72.9	79.9

Note: The 1981 figures exclude Assam where the census could not be held. The 1991 figures exclude Jammu and Kashmir for the same reason.

Source: Census of India 2001, Series 1, India, *Provisional Population Totals*, Paper 1 of 2001; Census of India 2001 (2002, CD of Primary Census Abstract).

Difference in Urban Rural Literacy Rates in Major States

As indicated above, at the national level, the difference between urban and rural literacy rates in 1991 was 28.4 percent. It declined to 21.2 percent in 2001. The urban-rural difference in the literacy rate declined in all the major States between 1991 and 2001, by various amounts (Figure 12). The difference was low in comparison to the national average, in Kerala, Assam, Bihar, Chhattisgarh, Himachal Pradesh, Karnataka, Rajasthan, Uttaranchal, West Bengal and Delhi but for altogether different reasons. In some States like Kerala, Karnataka, Uttaranchal, West Bengal and Delhi, both urban and rural literacy rates were high. This implied low urban minus rural literacy rates (Table A9). In contrast, the difference between urban and rural literacy rates continued to remain high in Andhra Pradesh, Jharkhand and Madhya Pradesh (Figure 12).

FIGURE 12: Rural-Urban Literacy Differentials, Total Population, States of India, 1991 and 2001

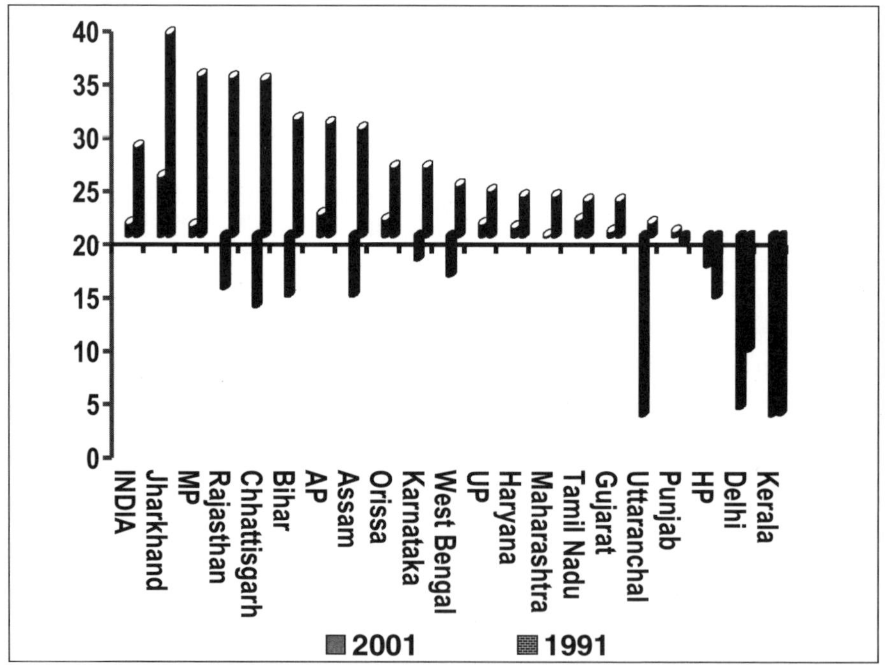

Educational Level Attained and Rural Urban Differential

At the national level three-tenths of the people (27.5 percent of males and 32.3 percent of females) were literate (but had not attained any formal educational level). 26.2 percent had completed only primary level in 2001. Thus, 56 percent of India's literate population had completed hardly primary education (Table A10). The situation in some States was quite bad; for example, among the major States, more than three-fifths of the people had no formal education or only primary pass in Chhattisgarh, Madhya Pradesh, Orissa, Rajasthan and West Bengal. The situation has been worse in respect of females in almost all the States. At the other end of the scale, the proportion of people in the above two categories was just 37 percent in Delhi and 44 percent in Kerala in 2001. Other States where this proportion is below 50 percent are Jammu and Kashmir, Himachal Pradesh, Punjab and Uttaranchal.

Of the total literate persons in India, 28 percent completed at least high / secondary school education. This proportion was one-fifth in rural areas and two-fifths in urban areas. The proportion of literate persons having completed secondary and higher education was 47 percent in Delhi, 37 percent in Punjab, 34 percent in Himachal Pradesh, 33 percent in Jammu and Kashmir, Haryana, Karnataka and Maharashtra, and 32 percent in Kerala. Delhi is the national capital and facilities for higher education have expanded fast in this metropolis compared to others. Punjab has also expanded its higher education facilities in both rural and urban areas. Similarly, higher education facilities have expanded in Haryana, Himachal Pradesh, Jammu and Kashmir, Karnataka and Maharashtra. Kerala has the highest literacy rate but, it seems, facilities for higher education have not expanded there proportionately.

We have examined rural urban differentials in educational attainment of literate persons who had not completed any educational level, studied up to primary, those who completed at least secondary education and those who had done their graduation or higher levels of education. These differentials are presented separately for males and females (Table A11).

The rural-urban difference in India among those who were literates but without any educational qualification was 16.9 percent for females and 12.8 percent for males. The differences narrowed down among those males and females who had completed the primary or middle level of education. As one would expect, the proportion of those having completed secondary and higher education is much higher in urban areas than in rural areas. Among 'graduates and above' the difference for males was 9.9 percent. It was 9.2 percent among females (Table A11).

Conversely, in the case of those who have no formal education, both males and females, there is a higher proportion in rural areas as compared to urban areas in all the major States. This difference is quite large in respect of the educationally backward States like Chhattisgarh, Madhya Pradesh, Rajasthan, Assam, and Orissa. In contrast, rural-urban differentials were considerably low in States like Delhi, Kerala, Tamil Nadu, Punjab and Himachal Pradesh. These are the States where the proportion of literate without educational level has been low.

The rural-urban difference in primary education has been large (for both males and females) in Himachal Pradesh, Jharkhand, Uttaranchal, Haryana,

Orissa, Andhra Pradesh and Tamil Nadu. The difference has been low in Delhi, Kerala, Assam and Maharashtra.

Considering the number of persons having completed at least secondary education, States where the rural-urban difference is quite large compared to the national average (for both males and females) are: Jammu and Kashmir, Jharkhand, Orissa (marginally, in the case of females), Chhattisgarh, Madhya Pradesh, Andhra Pradesh, West Bengal, and Karnataka (Table A 11 and Figure 13). The rural urban difference is low in Delhi, Kerala and Tamil Nadu. In Delhi and Kerala, it is difficult to draw a line between rural and urban sectors. In Tamil Nadu, efforts have been made consistently to popularise secondary and higher education both among males and females. Thus, the rural-urban educational differentials in higher education are on par for males as well as females in the State (Table A11). We see also that in most of the other States, rural-urban differentials are higher for females (Figure 13). Evidently, in these States, urbanisation has had a relatively strong effect in nullifying female exclusion, and this manifests in the observed rural-urban contrasts.

The pattern of rural urban differential among graduates (the numbers in the category 'graduate and above' are a part of the secondary and above category) is almost similar to the one observed for those completing at least secondary education (Table A11).

FIGURE 13: Urban-Rural Literacy Differentials for those with Secondary Education and Above, States of India, 2001

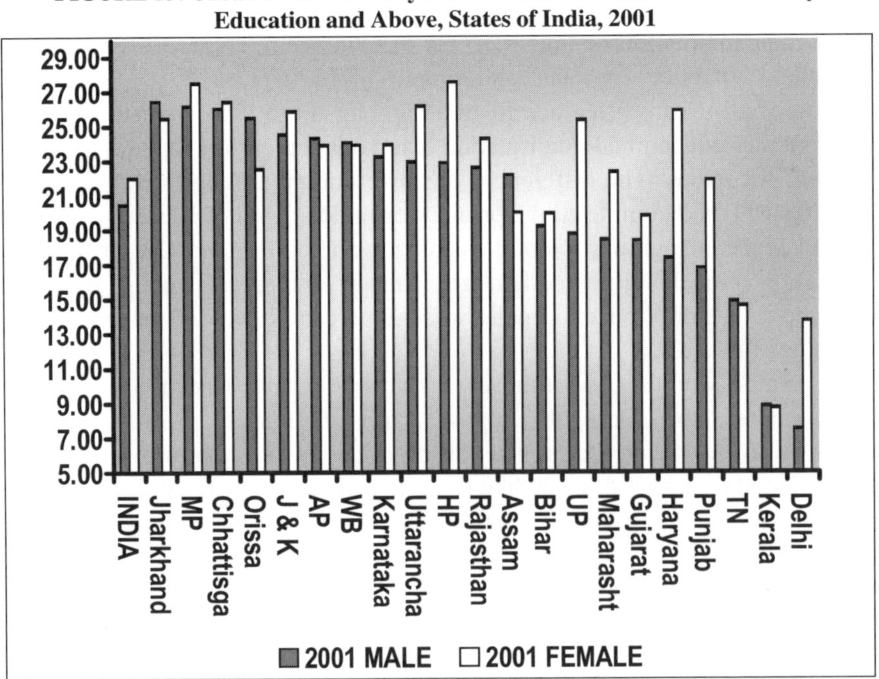

Economic Characteristics

One of the major aspects of human societies from very early times in the context of survival and subsistence has been the organisation of labour. Some people work for the production of subsistence and wealth. They are classified as workers, in contrast to non-workers who are not engaged in the production of goods and services. Further, workers are classified according to the sector of economy they are engaged in, the nature of work they perform, employment status (whether they are employers, employees, or independent workers), and their earnings. All these aspects of any population specify its economic characteristics.

The age of entry into the work force, the age of retirement, and the distribution of workers into primary, secondary, and tertiary sectors of the economy largely depends on the level of industrialisation a country has achieved.

Table 7 gives the work participation rates for India, for 1991 and 2001, by rural-urban residence and sex. The WPR improved between 1991 and 2001, largely because of an increase in the female WPR. It can also be observed that while the difference between male rural and urban WPRs is small as it should be, the R/U difference is large in female WPRs since the urban female WPR is considerably lower than the rural female WPR.

TABLE 7: Work Participation Rates by Residence and Sex, India, 1991 and 2001

Residence Category	1991			2001		
	Persons	Males	Females	Persons	Males	Females
Total	37.5	51.6	22.3	39.3	51.9	25.7
Rural	40.1	52.6	26.8	42.0	52.4	31.0
Urban	30.2	48.9	9.2	32.2	50.8	11.5
R-U	9.9	3.7	17.6	9.8	1.6	19.5

State-wise Work Participation Rates and Rural Urban Differentials

While the male WPR has remained almost the same between 1991 and 2001, the female WPR increased substantially over the past one decade due to special efforts made by the Census Organisation to net female economic activity as close to reality as was possible with a large army of enumerators on the one hand and peoples perceptions on the other hand.

There are considerable State wise variations in the WPR by sex and rural urban residence (Table A 12). As every able-bodied male above a certain age must work to eke out a living, male WPR has remained uniformly high over time, with little State-to-State and rural-urban variations. Among the major States, male WPR improved by more than two percentage points between 1991 and 2001 in Himachal Pradesh, West Bengal, Karnataka, and Kerala. States with lower than 50 percent male work participation rates (for example, Bihar, Jharkhand, Uttar Pradesh and Uttaranchal) sound an alarm of possible high unemployment. It is disturbing to note that male WPR has declined in Orissa by one percent and Uttar Pradesh by 2.4 percent during the 1990s. This needs further probing by making detailed analysis.

Female WPR increased substantially in Haryana, Himachal Pradesh, Punjab, Rajasthan, Bihar, Orissa, West Bengal, and Uttar Pradesh. It, however, declined in Assam, Maharashtra and Kerala (Table A 12) for different reasons, in spite of very liberal definition of economic activity with special emphasis on female work.

The rural-urban differential in the overall WPR came to almost 10 percentage points, mostly because of very low female WPR in urban areas. Female WPR in urban areas was below 7 percent in Uttar Pradesh, Bihar and Jharkhand. Urban female WPR was 15 percent and above only in Himachal Pradesh, Karnataka and Tamil Nadu.

Conclusions

Of the 1029 million people in India, 286 million were living in urban settlements as of 1st March 2001. The net addition to the urban population has been of 68 million persons during 1991-2001. This addition in a decade is higher than the population of any country in Europe except the Russian Federation and Germany, or any country in Africa except Egypt and Nigeria. The proportion urban in the country now stands at 27.8 percent compared to 25.7 percent at the time of 1991 census count.

The decadal urban growth has declined successively between 1981 and 2001. All available data of urban population from the 2001 census and their analyses indicate that the slowing down of urban growth is largely due to a decline in natural increase and a limited increase of new towns.

State level urban population data indicate that, among the major States, Tamil Nadu is most urbanised (44 percent), followed by Maharashtra and Gujarat. Tamil Nadu, Haryana and Punjab have recorded substantial increase in their urban population's decadal growth rates during 1991-2001 in comparison to their 1981-91 growth rates. In contrast, there are several major States—Andhra Pradesh, Bihar, Rajasthan and West Bengal—where the urban proportion has changed only marginally.

Ninety-three towns and urban agglomerations in the country got upgraded to class I category during the 1990s. The 393 UAs and cities in 2001 account for two-thirds of the urban population and 19 percent of country's total population.

The number of metropolitan cities in the country increased from 12 in 1981 to 23 in 1991, and to 35 in 2001; the number increasing almost three times in two decades. Of the 286 million urban dwellers in the country, 37.8 percent were living in 35 metropolises. There are six mega cities—Mumbai, Kolkata, Delhi, Chennai, Bangalore and Hyderabad—that account for 60 million persons and cover 21 percent of the total urban population. These data clearly depict the nature of concentration of India's population in fewer places and smaller areas.

The Urban Rural Growth Differential declined somewhat during the 1990s compared to the 1980s at the national level and in most major States. The URGD, however, increased in Assam, Haryana, Karnataka, Punjab and Tamil Nadu during the period under consideration. The reasons for the phenomenon are specific for each State.

We examined in this paper rural-urban differentials in fertility, mortality and migration. With a faster decline in the rural as compared to the urban CBR, there has been a decline in rural-urban differential in many States. There are, however, some States where the rural-urban differential increased in recent years. Regarding the Crude Death Rate, the rural-urban differential is generally small, since over time, the decline in the rural death rate was faster than its urban counterpart.

There are large variations in 'net rural-to-urban migration' as proportion of total inter-censal migration. It was as high as 58 percent in Delhi and 45 percent in Chandigarh to a low of 3.6 percent in Kerala and 7 percent in Bihar and Himachal Pradesh. While Delhi and Chandigarh have been attracting migrants from various parts of the country, Kerala, Bihar and Himachal Pradesh have been sending their people outside the respective States.

Future Prospects

India's latest population projections prepared in 2005 provisionally put the country's population in 2026 at 140.5 crores out of which 53.9 crores are likely to live in urban areas, giving rise to an urbanisation rate of 38.2 percent. This proportion is lower than what was expected in 2016 in the projections made in 1996 (RGI 1996).

Looking at the large cities that did not qualify as a metropolis in 2001, we find the possibility of some 13-15 cities becoming metropolises by 2011 due to natural growth of population and some migration. Also, almost 70-80 Class II and Class III towns are likely to become class I cities in 2011. Taking this into account, we expect that the proportion of urban population living in Class I cities would be around 70 percent, if not more.

Future urbanisation would mean a shift in demographic composition in the nation's urban population, its labour force structure, and in the natural and social environment. Further, the envisaged increase in the number of cities would require provision of additional infrastructure in terms of housing, roads, water supply and sanitation (including sewerage disposal systems that do not pollute the rivers and other water bodies), schools, hospitals, office buildings, shopping complexes, etc.

The data on natural increase in urban population during 2001-2003 gives an annual growth rate of 1.39 percent, which is lower than 1.57 percent observed during 1991-2000 decade. Hence, one may expect some decline in the proportion of natural increase in urban growth during 2001-2011.

With liberalisation and globalisation of the Indian economy since the beginning of the 1990s, it was expected that foreign investment would bring large number of industries into the country leading to the creation of jobs in the secondary and tertiary sectors and faster urbanisation. Contrary to this expectation, urban growth has slowed down. It is possible that as a consequence of pressures from the World Trade Organisation to open the Indian economy further for foreign investment in industry, the urbanisation rate and the proportion urban in the country will increase during 2001-2011 with substantial rural-to-urban migration.

The Government of India has, however, planned a very big programme of rural development including creation of rural infrastructure. Under this programme, it is proposed to provide at least 100 days of employment to one adult in every poor family in 200 worst affected districts in the first instance. A sum of Rs. 175 thousand crores was earmarked in 2004 for the next five years for rural employment generation programmes. The success of this programme is likely to somewhat contain rural to urban migration. If this happens, the urbanisation rate in the country will further slow down. Under that situation, the component of net rural-to-urban migration in total urban growth would decline leading to slow urbanisation during 2001-2011 as well.

NOTES

1. Tests for eligibility for places to be treated as towns in 1951 and 1961 censuses were:
   1951: All areas having a municipal corporation, municipal area, town area committee, all civil lines not included in municipal limits, and cantonments. Further, tests prescribed for distinguishing towns from villages in different States were based on ideas common to all States, but they were not identical nor had they been applied with meticulous uniformity. In the case of princely States, the definition of town was applied a little indiscriminately.
   1961: All areas having a municipal corporation, municipal area, town committee, notified area committee, and cantonments board. All other selected places with (a) density of not less than 1,000 persons per sq. mile (b) a population of 5,000 (c) three-fourths of

the working population should be working outside agriculture (d) or any other place, which according to the Superintendent of the State, possesses pronounced urban characteristics and amenities (Census of India 1991, 1997: 165).

2. The high urban growth rate in 1971-81 was basically due to *reclassification* of a large number of settlements as urban; these settlements had been *declassified* on the eve of the 1961 census while applying the revised concept of 'urban'.

REFERENCES

Census of India 1961 (1964). Volume 1, India, Part II-A (i), *General Population Tables*. Delhi: Manager of Publications.

Census of India 1991 (1996). *Population Projection for India and States, 1996-2016*. New Delhi: Registrar General, India.

Census of India 1991 (1998). Series 1, India, Part II-A (i), *General Population Tables*. Delhi: Controller of Publications.

Census of India 2001 (2001). Series 1, India, *Provisional Population Totals*, Paper 1 of 2001. Delhi: Controller of Publications.

Census of India 2001 (2001). Series 32, Kerala, Provisional Population Totals.

Census of India 2001 (2002). Compact Disc release on Cities, Towns and Urban Agglomerations. April.

Census of India 2001 (2004). Compact Disc release on Primary Census Abstract (ORGCCI) Office of the Registrar General and Census Commissioner, India.

Press Release on Rural and Urban Population, 20 July 2001.

Premi, Mahendra K. (1991). India's urban scene and its future implications. *Demography India*, Volume 20, No, 1, January-June.

Premi, Mahendra K. (2003). *Social Demography: A Systematic Exposition*. New Delhi: Jawahar Publishers and Distributors.

Srinivasan K. and Abusaleh Shariff (1997). *India. Towards Population and Development Goals*. United Nations Population Fund for United Nations System in India. Delhi: Oxford University Press.

TABLE A1: Urban Population, Urbanisation Rate and Decadal Growth Rates, India, States and Union Territories, 2001

States/Union Territory	Population (in 000)		Urbanisation rate (Percent)		Decadal growth rate (Percent) 1991-2001	
	Total	Urban	1991	2001	Total	Urban
INDIA	**1028837**	**286120**	**25.7**	**27.8**	**21.6**	**31.5**
Andhra Pradesh	76210	20809	26.9	27.3	14.6	16.3
Arunachal Pradesh	1098	228	12.8	20.8	27.0	106.1
Assam	26656	3439	11.1	12.9	18.9	38.2
Bihar	82999	8682	10.5	10.5	28.6	29.4
Chhattisgarh	20834	4186	20.1	20.1	18.3	36.6
Goa	1348	671	41.0	49.8	15.2	39.9
Gujarat	50671	18930	34.5	37.4	22.7	32.9
Haryana	21145	6115	24.6	28.9	28.4	50.8
Himachal Pradesh	6078	596	8.7	9.8	17.5	32.7
Jammu and Kashmir	10144	2517	24.9	24.8	30.0	41.4
Jharkhand	26946	5994	22.2	22.2	23.4	29.1
Karnataka	52851	17962	30.9	34.0	17.5	29.2
Kerala	31841	8267	26.4	26.0	9.4	7.6
Madhya Pradesh	60348	15967	26.7	26.5	24.3	30.1
Maharashtra	96879	41101	38.7	42.4	22.7	34.6
Manipur	2389	570	27.5	23.9	30.0	12.7
Meghalaya	2319	454	18.6	19.6	30.7	37.6
Mizoram	889	441	46.1	49.6	28.9	38.7
Nagaland	1989	353	17.2	17.7	64.4	69.5
Orissa	36805	5517	13.4	15.0	16.3	30.3
Punjab	24359	8263	29.5	33.9	20.1	37.9
Rajasthan	56507	13214	22.9	23.4	28.4	31.3
Sikkim	541	60	9.1	11.1	33.1	62.1
Tamil Nadu	62406	27484	34.2	44.0	11.7	44.1
Tripura	3199	546	15.3	17.1	16.0	29.5
Uttar Pradesh	166198	34540	20.8	20.8	25.9	33.0
Uttaranchal	8489	2179	25.6	25.7	19.3	33.3
West Bengal	80176	22427	27.5	28.0	17.8	19.9
Union Territories						
A. & N. Islands	356	116	26.7	32.6	26.8	54.8
Chandigarh	901	809	89.7	89.8	40.3	40.5
Dadra & Nagar Haveli	220	50	8.5	22.9	58.9	326.4
Daman and Diu	158	57	46.8	36.2	55.5	19.9
Delhi	13851	12906	89.9	93.2	47.0	52.3
Lakshadweep	61	27	56.3	44.5	18.0	-7.3
Pondicherry	974	649	64.0	66.6	20.6	25.5

Note: Jammu and Kashmir's total and urban population for 1991 has been obtained by exponentially interpolating the 1981 and 2001 populations.

Source: Census of India 2001, Data released in Compact Disc.

TABLE A2: The Number and Population of New Towns, and the Number of Merged / Declassified Towns, 2001

India / State	New Towns	Merged/ Declassified Towns	Population of Declassified Towns	Net Addition of Towns	New Towns' Population
India	**1138**	**666**	**4,988,158**	**472**	**14,828,319**
Andhra Pradesh	35	89	1,446,269	-54	412,881
Arunachal Pradesh	7	0	0	7	57,095
Assam	37	5	28,084	32	269,798
Bihar	3	11	206,194	-8	31,604
Chhattisgarh	19	17	16,121	2	219,006
Goa	17	4	18,698	13	134,117
Gujarat	43	65	649,852	-22	622,604
Haryana	15	3	21,378	12	203,221
Himachal Pradesh	2	3	4,728	-1	27,832
Jammu and Kashmir	1	0	0	1	5,105
Jharkhand	33	14	111,544	19	243,000
Karnataka	45	81	203,315	-36	1,161,889
Kerala	18	55	865,254	-37*	307,047
Madhya Pradesh	40	15	59,909	25	368,813
Maharashtra	79	37	222,654	42	1,082,900
Manipur	4	2	36,833	2	21,800
Meghalaya	4	0	0	4	53,696
Mizoram	0	0	0	0	0
Nagaland	0	0	0	0	0
Orissa	18	4	17,123	14	155,500
Punjab	41	4	18,505	37	418,808
Rajasthan	17	17	186,147	0	156, 559
Sikkim	1	0	0	1	14,670
Tamil Nadu	456	93	280,881	363	5,742,147
Tripura	7	2	26,114	5	65,620
Uttar Pradesh	45	11	74,888	34	471,134
Uttaranchal	9	6	36,687	3	74,727
West Bengal	105	112	424,133	-7	1,080,331
Union Territories					
A. & N. Islands	2	0	0	2	16,221
Chandigarh	0	0	0	0	0
Dadra & Nagar Haveli	1	0	0	1	28,566
Daman & Diu	0	0	0	0	0
Delhi	35	5	7,656	30	1,381, 628
Lakshadweep	0	1	5,670	-1	0
Pondicherry	0	5	19,523	-5	0

***Note*:** Of the 55 merged or declassified towns in Kerala, population figures of only 36 declassified towns are available (Census of India 2001, Series 32, Kerala, Appendix to Table 5).

TABLE A3: State-wise Growth Rates of Total, Rural and Urban Populations and URGD, 1981-91 and 1991-2001

State/ Union Territory	Total Growth Rate		Rural Growth Rate		Urban Growth Rate		URGD	
	1981-1991	1991-2001	1981-1991	1991-2001	1981-1991	1991-2001	1981-1991	1991-2001
India	**23.85**	**21.35**	**20.01**	**17.97**	**36.47**	**31.13**	**16.46**	**13.16**
Northern zone	28.17	27.94	23.62	22.32	40.01	40.83	16.39	18.51
Haryana	27.41	28.06	22.92	20.63	43.41	50.78	20.52	30.15
Himachal Pradesh	20.79	17.52	19.39	16.09	37.80	32.52	18.34	16.32
Jammu & Kashmir	28.93	29.04	24.39	25.58	45.95	40.73	21.56	15.15
Punjab	20.81	19.76	17.69	12.28	28.94	37.59	11.25	25.31
Rajasthan	28.44	28.33	25.46	27.49	39.61	31.17	14.15	3.68
Chandigarh*	42.16	40.34	130.06	39.18	36.17	40.45	-93.89	1.28
Delhi*	51.46	46.31	109.96	1.50	46.88	51.32	-63.08	49.84
Eastern zone	23.40	21.85	21.92	21.26	30.45	24.46	8.53	3.20
Bihar	23.54	27.11	22.59	26.79	30.21	29.18	7.62	2.39
Orissa	20.06	15.94	17.91	13.80	36.17	29.78	18.26	15.98
Sikkim	28.48	32.98	39.25	30.05	-27.45	62.16	-66.70	32.11
West Bengal	24.73	17.84	23.01	16.94	29.49	20.19	6.48	3.25
A & N Islands	48.68	26.94	47.88	16.60	51.02	55.30	3.14	38.70
North-Eastern zone	27.46	22.02	24.35	19.72	50.77	36.25	26.42	16.53
Arunachal Pradesh	36.87	26.21	27.70	15.19	167.04	101.29	139.34	86.11
Assam	24.24	18.85	22.55	16.68	39.58	36.21	17.03	19.53
Manipur	29.28	30.02	27.36	36.55	34.67	12.81	7.31	-23.75
Meghalaya	32.86	29.92	32.00	28.24	36.76	37.27	4.76	9.03
Mizoram	39.68	29.13	-0.04	20.97	161.01	38.68	161.05	17.71
Nagaland	56.13	64.38	52.98	63.37	73.18	69.44	20.20	6.08
Tripura	34.29	15.74	27.81	13.38	86.73	28.78	58.92	15.40
Central zone	25.91	24.56	22.47	22.42	40.87	32.64	18.4	10.22
Madhya Pradesh	26.84	22.66	22.24	19.79	44.90	32.20	22.66	12.41
Uttar Pradesh	25.48	25.48	22.58	23.62	38.73	32.88	16.15	9.26
Western zone	24.15	22.61	17.42	15.95	37.44	33.84	20.02	17.89
Gujarat	21.19	22.48	15.24	17.12	34.37	32.66	19.13	15.54
Maharashtra	25.73	22.57	18.65	15.16	38.87	34.31	20.22	19.15
Dadra & Nagar Haveli	33.57	59.20	30.99	34.12	69.58	330.33	38.5	296.21
Daman & Diu	28.62	54.59	8.18	86.41	63.81	20.56	55.63	-65.84
Southern zone	19.42	13.26	14.22	7.65	33.59	26.35	19.37	18.7
Andhra Pradesh	24.20	13.86	18.41	13.58	43.23	14.63	24.82	1.05
Goa	16.07	14.87	0.73	-2.17	48.61	39.38	47.88	41.55
Karnataka	21.11	17.25	17.66	12.05	29.62	28.85	11.96	16.80
Kerala	14.32	9.42	3.56	10.05	60.97	7.64	57.41	-2.41
Tamil Nadu	15.39	11.19	13.33	-5.20	19.59	42.79	6.27	47.99
Lakshadweep	28.47	17.19	4.50	48.93	56.28	-7.44	51.78	-56.37
Pondicherry	33.64	20.54	0.82	11.97	63.61	25.39	62.79	13.42

TABLE A4: CBRs, Three-Year Moving Averages Centered at Mid-Year, India and States with Rural Urban Differentials, 1972-2003

State or Union Territory and Area		1972	1981	1991	1996	2001	2002	2003
India	**Rural**	**37.7**	**35.4**	**31.2**	**29.4**	**27.1**	**26.7**	**26.3**
	Urban	**30.0**	**27.6**	**24.0**	***21.9***	**20.3**	**20.0**	**19.7**
	Combined	**36.3**	**33.8**	**29.6**	**27.7**	**25.9**	**23.3**	**24.6**
	R-U	**7.7**	**7.6**	**7.2**	**7.5**	**6.8**	**6.7**	**6.6**
Andhra Pradesh	Rural	34.3	32.2	26.4	23.8	21.4	21.1	**20.7**
	Urban	33.1	27.5	24.4	21.2	19.7	19.4	**18.2**
	Combined	34.1	31.3	26.0	23.2	21.0	20.7	**20.2**
	R-U	**1.2**	**4.7**	**2.0**	**2.6**	**1.7**	**1.7**	**2.2**
Assam	Rural	36.8	33.9	31.7	29.4	27.8	27.5	27.2
	Urban	28.7	23.2	21.3	21.1	18.5	18.3	16.9
	Combined	36.0	33.0	30.9	28.4	26.8	26.6	26.0
	R-U	**8.1**	**10.7**	**9.6**	**8.3**	**9.3**	**9.2**	**10.3**
Bihar	Rural	32.7	38.6	31.2	33.0	32.3	31.9	31.5
	Urban	27.5	33.5	25.0	23.7	24.2	23.4	23.3
	Combined	32.3	38.1	30.5	32.0	31.3	30.9	30.6
	R-U	**5.2**	**5.1**	**6.2**	**9.3**	**8.1**	**8.5**	**8.2**
Gujarat	Rural	40.1	36.3	28.2	27.3	26.7	26.6	26.5
	Urban	34.2	30.9	25.9	23.2	21.3	20.9	20.7
	Combined	38.6	34.8	27.5	26.0	25.0	24.8	24.5
	R-U	**5.9**	**5.4**	**2.3**	**4.1**	**5.4**	**5.7**	**5.8**
Haryana	Rural	42.5	38.2	34.7	30.3	27.8	27.6	27.3
	Urban	32.0	30.4	27.2	24.4	22.8	22.6	22.0
	Combined	40.6	36.8	33.1	29.0	26.8	26.6	26.0
	R-U	**10.5**	**7.8**	**7.5**	**5.9**	**5.0**	**5.0**	**5.3**
Himachal Pradesh	Rural	36.8	32.8	29.2	24.1	21.7	21.2	20.6
	Urban	23.5	20.0	18.6	17.3	16.8	16.6	15.1
	Combined	36.0	32.0	28.5	23.6	21.3	20.8	20.2
	R-U	**13.3**	**12.8**	**10.6**	**6.8**	**4.9**	**4.6**	**5.5**
Jammu & Kashmir	Rural	34.9	33.5	N.A	N.A	20.5	20.1	19.8
	Urban	22.6	21.9	N.A	N.A	16.3	18.8	15.1
	Combined	32.3	31.2	N.A.	N.A.	19.7	19.7	18.8
	R-U	**12.3**	**11.6**	**N.A.**	**N.A.**	**4.2**	**1.3**	**4.7**
Karnataka	Rural	32.3	29.0	27.8	24.4	23.5	23.4	23.1
	Urban	26.4	25.3	23.9	20.8	19.0	18.8	18.4
	Combined	30.7	27.9	26.8	23.3	22.1	22.0	21.8
	R-U	**5.9**	**3.7**	**3.9**	**3.6**	**4.5**	**4.6**	**4.7**
Kerala	Rural	30.7	26.5	18.2	18.0	17.5	17.1	16.4
	Urban	29.2	24.7	18.1	17.8	16.9	16.4	15.7
	Combined	30.5	26.2	18.1	18.0	17.4	17.1	16.3
	R-U	**1.5**	**1.8**	**0.1**	**0.2**	**0.6**	**0.7**	**0.7**

State or Union Territory and Area		1972	1981	1991	1996	2001	2002	2003
Madhya Pradesh	Rural	39.6	38.9	37.3	34.3	32.8	32.4	32.1
	Urban	33.4	31.9	29.6	23.3	23.1	22.8	22.6
	Combined	38.6	37.7	35.8	32.5	30.9	30.5	30.1
	R-U	**6.2**	**7.0**	**7.7**	**11.0**	**9.7**	**9.6**	**9.5**
Maharashtra	Rural	32.0	30.8	28.0	25.1	21.0	20.6	20.2
	Urban	29.1	25.6	22.9	21.5	20.1	19.8	19.0
	Combined	31.1	29.1	26.2	23.7	20.6	20.3	19.8
	R-U	**2.9**	**5.2**	**5.1**	**3.6**	**0.9**	**0.8**	**0.8**
Orissa	Rural	34.8	33.0	29.6	27.8	24.2	23.7	23.6
	Urban	32.5	29.7	22.3	21.5	19.8	19.6	18.8
	Combined	34.7	32.7	28.8	27.1	23.7	23.2	23.0
	R-U	**2.3**	**3.3**	**7.3**	**6.3**	**4.4**	**4.1**	**4.8**
Punjab	Rural	35.1	30.7	28.2	25.4	22.1	21.8	20.8
	Urban	30.4	28.5	25.1	19.6	18.4	18.2	17.9
	Combined	34.1	30.2	28.6	23.9	21.2	20.9	20.0
	R-U	**4.7**	**2.2**	**3.1**	**5.8**	**3.7**	**3.6**	**2.9**
Rajasthan	Rural	42.4	39.1	35.7	34.2	32.3	32.0	31.4
	Urban	34.3	32.7	28.8	25.6	24.7	24.3	24.0
	Combined	40.9	37.9	34.3	32.6	31.0	30.7	30.0
	R-U	**8.1**	**6.4**	**6.9**	**8.6**	**7.6**	**7.7**	**7.4**
Tamil Nadu	Rural	33.4	29.4	21.3	20.1	19.5	19.2	18.6
	Urban	26.2	24.4	20.6	18.6	17.8	17.5	17.0
	Combined	31.3	27.8	20.7	19.6	18.5	18.3	18.0
	R-U	**7.2**	**5.0**	**0.7**	**1.5**	**1.7**	**1.7**	**1.6**
Uttar Pradesh	Rural	44.6	40.4	36.7	35.3	33.3	32.7	32.3
	Urban	34.0	32.3	28.3	28.2	27.0	26.8	26.5
	Combined	43.2	39.2	35.1	34.1	32.2	31.7	31.2
	R-U	**10.6**	**8.1**	**8.3**	**7.1**	**6.3**	**5.9**	**5.8**
West Bengal	Rural	N.A.	36.4	30.0	25.4	22.8	22.6	22.3
	Urban	25.4	20.0	18.1	16.2	14.0	14.0	13.7
	Combined	N.A.	32.4	26.7	22.9	20.6	20.5	20.0
	R-U	**N.A.**	**16.4**	**11.9**	**9.2**	**8.8**	**8.6**	**8.6**
Delhi	Rural	42.7	36.3	30.2	24.6	21.0	20.9	19.3
	Urban	29.8	27.0	24.2	22.2	18.5	17.4	17.4
	Combined	31.1	28.0	24.7	22.0	18.8	17.8	17.6
	R-U	**12.9**	**9.3**	**6.0**	**2.4**	**2.5**	**3.5**	**1.9**

Notes: N.A. = not available.

Data for Bihar, Madhya Pradesh and Uttar Pradesh from 1972 to 1996 relate to States as they existed before bifurcation. From 2000 onwards CBRs are for the States as they presently constitute.

TABLE A5: Total Fertility Rates for Rural, Urban and Combined Areas (Three-Year Moving Averages Centered at Mid-Year), India and Major States and Rural Urban Differentials, 1972-2003

India and Major States		1972	1981	1991	1996	2000	2001	2002
India	**Rural**	**5.3**	**4.8**	**4.0**	**3.7**	**3.5**	**3.4**	**3.3**
	Urban	**4.0**	**3.4**	**2.7**	*2.5*	**2.3**	**2.3**	**2.2**
	Combined	**5.1**	**4.5**	**3.7**	**3.4**	**3.2**	**3.1**	**3.0**
	R-U	**1.3**	**1.4**	**1.3**	**1.2**	**1.2**	**1.1**	**1.1**
Andhra Pradesh	Rural	4.6	4.1	3.1	2.7	2.5	2.4	2.3
	Urban	4.0	3.0	2.5	2.2	2.0	2.0	1.9
	Combined	4.5	3.9	3.0	2.6	2.3	2.3	2.2
	R-U	**0.6**	**1.1**	**0.6**	**0.5**	0.4	**0.4**	0.4
Assam	Rural	5.3	4.2	3.6	3.5	3.3	3.2	3.1
	Urban	3.9	2.6	2.1	2.1	1.8	1.8	1.8
	Combined	5.2	4.1	3.4	3.3	3.1	3.0	3.0
	R-U	**1.4**	**1.6**	**1.5**	**1.4**	1.4	**1.4**	1.3
Bihar	Rural	N.A.	N.A.	4.7	4.6	4.7	4.6	4.5
	Urban	N.A.	N.A.	3.4	3.2	3.3	3.2	3.1
	Combined	N.A.	N.A.	4.6	4.5	4.5	4.4	4.3
	R-U	N.A.	N.A.	**1.3**	**1.4**	1.4	**1.4**	1.4
Gujarat	Rural	5.7	4.7	3.4	3.3	3.2	3.2	3.2
	Urban	4.4	3.6	2.9	2.6	2.3	2.2	2.2
	Combined	5.4	4.4	3.2	3.1	2.9	2.9	2.8
	R-U	**1.3**	**1.1**	**0.5**	**0.7**	0.9	**1.0**	1.0
Haryana	Rural	7.0	5.3	4.2	3.8	3.3	3.3	3.2
	Urban	4.6	3.7	2.9	2.8	2.6	2.5	2.5
	Combined	6.6	5.0	3.9	3.5	3.2	3.1	3.1
	R-U	**2.4**	**1.6**	**1.3**	**1.0**	0.8	**0.8**	0.7
Karnataka	Rural	4.5	3.8	3.3	2.8	2.6	2.6	2.6
	Urban	3.4	2.9	2.5	2.2	2.0	1.9	1.9
	Combined	4.2	3.6	3.1	2.6	2.4	2.4	2.4
	R-U	**1.1**	**0.9**	**0.8**	**0.6**	0.7	**0.7**	0.7
Kerala	Rural	4.1	3.0	1.8	1.8	1.8	1.8.	1.8
	Urban	3.6	2.5	1.8	1.8	1.8	1.7	1.7
	Combined	4.0	2.9	1.8	1.8	1.8	1.8	1.8
	R-U	**0.5**	**0.5**	**0.0**	**0.0**	0.1	**0.1**	0.1
Madhya Pradesh	Rural	6.0	5.5	4.9	4.4	4.4	4.3	4.2
	Urban	4.5	4.0	3.3	2.6	2.6	2.5	2.5
	Combined	5.7	5.2	4.7	4.1	3.9	3.9	3.8
	R-U	**1.5**	**1.5**	**1.6**	**1.8**	1.8	**1.8**	1.7
Maharashtra	Rural	4.6	4.0	3.4	3.2	2.6	2.6	2.5
	Urban	3.8	3.1	2.5	2.4	2.2	2.2	2.2

India and Major States		1972	1981	1991	1996	2000	2001	2002
	Combined	4.3	3.7	3.0	2.8	2.5	2.4	2.3
	R-U	**0.8**	**0.9**	**0.9**	**0.8**	0.4	**0.4**	0.3
Orissa	Rural	4.8	4.3	3.4	3.3	2.8	2.8	2.7
	Urban	4.2	3.7	2.4	2.3	2.1	2.1	2.0
	Combined	4.7	4.3	3.1	3.1	2.7	2.7	2.6
	R-U	**0.6**	**0.6**	**1.0**	**1.0**	0.7	**0.7**	0.6
Punjab	Rural	5.5	4.1	3.3	3.0	2.6	2.5	2.4
	Urban	4.2	3.4	2.8	2.3	2.1	2.0	2.0
	Combined	5.2	4.0	3.1	2.8	2.4	2.4	2.3
	R-U	**1.3**	**0.7**	**0.5**	**0.7**	0.5	**0.5**	0.4
Rajasthan	Rural	5.9	5.8	4.8	4.4	4.4	4.3	4.1
	Urban	4.8	4.4	3.5	3.0	2.9	2.8	2.7
	Combined	5.8	5.5	4.5	4.2	4.1	4.0	3.9
	R-U	**1.1**	**1.4**	**1.3**	**1.4**	1.5	**1.5**	1.4
Tamil Nadu	Rural	4.3	3.7	2.4	2.2	2.1	2.1	2.1
	Urban	3.1	2.8	2.0	1.8	1.8	1.8	1.8
	Combined	3.8	3.4	2.2	2.1	2.0	2.0	2.0
	R-U	**1.2**	**0.9**	**0.4**	**0.4**	0.3	**0.3**	0.3
Uttar Pradesh	Rural	6.8	6.1	5.5	5.1	4.9	4.8	4.7
	Urban	4.8	4.2	3.8	3.8	3.5	3.4	3.4
	Combined	6.5	5.8	5.2	4.9	4.6	4.6	4.4
	R-U	**2.0**	**1.9**	**1.7**	**1.3**	1.4	**1.4**	1.3
West Bengal	Rural	N.A.	N.A.	3.6	3.0	2.7	2.6	2.6
	Urban	N.A.	N.A.	2.0	1.8	1.6	1.6	1.6
	Combined	N.A.	N.A.	3.2	2.7	2.4	2.4	2.3
	R-U	N.A.	N.A.	**1.6**	**1.2**	1.1	**1.0**	1.0

***Notes*:** N.A. = not available.

Data for Bihar, Madhya Pradesh and Uttar Pradesh from 1972 to 1996 relate to States as they were before bifurcation. From 2000 onward Total Fertility Rates are for the States as they presently constitute.

TABLE A6: CDRs, Three-Year Moving Averages Centered at Mid-Year, India and Major States, 1972-2003

India/State	T / R / U	1971-1973	1980-1982	1990-1992	1995-1997	2000-2002	2001-2003	2002-2004
India	**Rural**	**17.4**	**13.5**	**10.7**	9.7	9.0	**8.8**	**8.5**
	Urban	**9.9**	**7.7**	**7.0**	**6.5**	**6.2**	**6.1**	**6.0**
	Combined	**15.9**	**12.3**	**9.9**	**9.0**	**8.3**	**8.2**	**7.9**
	R-U	**7.5**	**5.8**	**3.7**	**3.2**	**2.8**	**2.7**	**2.5**
Andhra Pradesh	Rural	17.0	12.1	10.1	9.2	9.0	8.9	8.5
	Urban	10.3	6.6	6.5	5.9	5.6	5.5	5.3
	Combined	15.8	10.9	9.3	8.4	8.2	8.1	7.7
	R-U	**6.7**	**5.5**	**3.6**	**3.3**	**3.4**	**3.4**	**3.2**
Assam	Rural	18.1	12.3	11.1	10.2	9.8	9.7	9.5
	Urban	9.7	7.8	7.3	6.1	6.2	6.2	5.8
	Combined	17.3	11.9	10.8	9.7	9.5	9.3	9.0
	R-U	**8.4**	**4.5**	**3.8**	**4.1**	**3.6**	**3.5**	**3.7**
Bihar	Rural	NA	NA	10.9	10.6	8.6	8.3	8.2
	Urban	NA	NA	6.5	6.9	6.5	6.1	5.9
	Combined	NA	NA	10.4	10.2	8.3	8.0	8.0
	R-U	NA	NA	**4.4**	**3.7**	**2.1**	**2.2**	**2.3**
Gujarat	Rural	17.0	12.8	9.3	9.1	8.5	8.5	8.1
	Urban	12.1	9.7	7.8	6.4	5.9	6.1	6.1
	Combined	15.7	12.0	8.9	8.5	7.7	7.7	7.4
	R-U	**4.9**	**3.1**	**1.5**	**2.7**	**2.6**	**2.4**	**2.0**
Haryana	Rural	11.9	11.4	8.9	8.4	7.6	7.4	7.2
	Urban	8.3	6.8	6.9	6.9	6.7	6.7	6.1
	Combined	11.3	10.6	8.4	8.1	7.4	7.3	6.9
	R-U	**3.6**	**4.6**	**2.0**	**1.5**	**0.9**	**0.7**	**1.1**
Himachal Pradesh	Rural	15.1	10.7	9.0	8.5	7.4	7.4	7.3
	Urban	6.9	5.2	5.6	6.0	5.3	5.1	4.8
	Combined	14.6	10.3	???	8.3	7.3	7.2	7.1
	R-U	**8.2**	**5.5**	**3.4**	**2.5**	**2.1**	**2.3**	**2.5**
Jammu & Kashmir	Rural	NA	9.7	NA	NA	6.0	5.9	5.8
	Urban	NA	6.0	NA	NA	5.9	5.7	5.4
	Combined	NA	9.0	NA	NA	6.0	5.8	5.7
	R-U	NA	**3.7**	NA	NA	**0.1**	**0.2**	**0.3**
Karnataka	Rural	14.2	10.4	9.3	8.5	8.2	8.0	7.8
	Urban	7.9	6.4	6.3	5.5	5.9	5.9	5.5
	Combined	12.4	9.3	8.5	7.6	7.5	7.3	7.1
	R-U	**6.3**	**4.0**	**3.0**	**3.0**	**2.3**	**2.1**	**2.3**
Kerala	Rural	9.1	6.8	6.1	6.2	6.6	6.5	6.3
	Urban	7.8	6.3	5.9	6.0	6.2	6.2	6.2
	Combined	8.9	6.7	6.1	6.1	6.5	6.4	6.3
	R-U	**1.3**	**0.5**	**0.2**	**0.2**	**0.4**	**0.3**	**0.1**

India/State	T / R / U	1971-1973	1980-1982	1990-1992	1995-1997	2000-2002	2001-2003	2002-2004
Madhya Pradesh	Rural	18.1	16.9	14.2	11.8	10.8	10.6	10.3
	Urban	10.9	9.2	8.4	7.7	7.3	7.2	6.9
	Combined	17.1	15.6	13.1	11.1	10.0	9.9	9.6
	R-U	**7.2**	**7.7**	**5.8**	**4.1**	**3.5**	**3.4**	**3.4**
Maharashtra	Rural	14.5	10.5	9.0	8.7	8.5	8.3	7.8
	Urban	9.3	7.1	5.7	5.4	5.7	5.7	5.5
	Combined	12.9	9.4	7.8	7.4	7.4	7.3	6.9
	R-U	**5.2**	**3.4**	**3.3**	**3.3**	**2.8**	**2.6**	**2.3**
Orissa	Rural	18.5	14.0	12.6	11.2	10.7	10.4	10.2
	Urban	11.0	7.9	7.0	7.5	6.7	6.5	6.6
	Combined	17.9	13.5	12.1	10.8	10.2	10.0	9.7
	R-U	**7.5**	**6.1**	**5.6**	**3.7**	**4.0**	**3.9**	**3.6**
Punjab	Rural	12.4	9.5	8.6	7.8	7.5	7.3	7.2
	Urban	9.1	6.7	6.0	6.1	6.1	6.2	5.9
	Combined	11.7	8.8	7.9	7.4	7.1	7.0	6.8
	R-U	**3.3**	**2.8**	**2.6**	**1.7**	**1.4**	**1.1**	**1.3**
Rajasthan	Rural	17.6	14.5	10.6	9.5	8.4	8.1	7.7
	Urban	9.6	8.0	7.6	7.1	6.4	6.3	6.2
	Combined	16.2	13.3	10.1	9.0	8.0	7.8	7.4
	R-U	**8.0**	**6.5**	**3.0**	**2.4**	**2.0**	**1.8**	**1.5**
Tamil Nadu	Rural	16.9	13.1	9.4	8.7	8.6	8.5	8.4
	Urban	8.8	7.9	6.9	6.6	6.1	5.8	6.1
	Combined	14.5	11.4	8.6	8.0	7.8	7.7	7.6
	R-U	**8.1**	**5.2**	**2.5**	**2.1**	**2.5**	**2.7**	**2.3**
Uttar Pradesh	Rural	22.9	17.1	12.9	10.7	10.5	10.3	9.9
	Urban	13.5	9.9	8.7	8.2	7.7	7.4	6.8
	Combined	21.7	16.0	12.1	10.3	10.0	9.8	9.3
	R-U	**9.4**	**7.2**	**4.2**	**2.5**	**2.8**	**2.9**	**3.1**
West Bengal	Rural	NA	NA	9.0	8.0	7.1	7.0	6.7
	Urban	NA	NA	6.8	7.2	6.5	6.3	6.2
	Combined	NA	NA	8.4	7.8	6.9	6.8	6.5
	R-U	NA	NA	**2.2**	**0.8**	**0.6**	**0.7**	**0.5**
Delhi	Rural	12.0	8.8	8.0	5.6	5.4	5.6	5.5
	Urban	7.3	6.9	6.2	6.0	5.1	5.0	4.9
	Combined	7.8	7.1	6.4	6.0	5.1	5.1	4.9
	R-U	**4.7**	**1.9**	**1.8**	**-0.4**	**0.3**	**0.6**	**0.6**

Notes: N.A. = not available.

Figures for Jammu and Kashmir in the third column are the 3-year average of 1972-74.

Data for Bihar, Madhya Pradesh and Uttar Pradesh from 1972 to 1996 relate to States as they were before bifurcation. From 2000 onward, Crude Death Rates are for the States as they presently constitute.

TABLE A7: Infant Mortality Rates, India and Major States, 1972-2003

India/State	T / R / U	1971-1973	1980-1982	1990-1992	1995-1997	2000-2002	2001-2003	2002-2004
India	**Rural**	**144**	**119**	**86**	**78**	**71.7**	**69.0**	**66.3**
	Urban	**85**	**64**	**52**	***46***	**42.0**	**40.0**	**39.3**
	Combined	**134**	**110**	**80**	**72**	**65.7**	**63.0**	**60.3**
	R-U	**59**	**55**	**34**	**32**	**29.7**	**29.0**	**27.0**
Andhra Pradesh	Rural	119	94	76	72	73.0	70.7	67.7
	Urban	64	47	51	39	37.0	36.0	35.7
	Combined	109	86	71	65	64.3	62.3	60.0
	R-U	**55**	**47**	**25**	**33**	**36.0**	**34.7**	**32.0**
Assam	Rural	141	105	79	79	76.0	73.3	70.7
	Urban	84	71	44	44	35.7	35.7	37.0
	Combined	137	104	78	76	73.0	70.3	67.7
	R-U	**57**	**34**	**35**	**35**	**40.3**	**37.6**	**33.7**
Bihar	Rural	NA	NA	74	73	62.7	62.3	62.3
	Urban	NA	NA	47	55	51.7	50.3	48.7
	Combined	NA	NA	72	72	61.7	61.0	60.7
	R-U	NA	NA	**27**	**18**	**11.0**	**12.0**	**13.6**
Gujarat	Rural	157	121	75	68	68.3	67.0	65.0
	Urban	106	91	55	46	41.3	38.3	37.0
	Combined	144	113	69	62	60.7	59.0	56.7
	R-U	**51**	**30**	**20**	**22**	**27.0**	**28.7**	**28.0**
Haryana	Rural	93	106	75	70	67.0	64.3	63.7
	Urban	69	56	53	61	54.3	51.7	49.0
	Combined	90	99	71	68	65.0	62.3	60.7
	R-U	**24**	**50**	**22**	**9**	**12.7**	**12.6**	**14.7**
Himachal Pradesh	Rural	NA	NA	NA	NA	57.0	53.3	52.3
	Urban	NA	NA	NA	NA	32.3	28.7	25.7
	Combined	NA	NA	NA	NA	55.3	51.7	50.7
	R-U	NA	NA	NA	NA	24.7	24.6	26.6
Karnataka	Rural	101	76	83	65	67.3	65.0	60.0
	Urban	63	46	42	31	25.0	25.0	29.0
	Combined	93	68	73	56	56.7	55.0	52.0
	R-U	**38**	**30**	**41**	**34**	**42.3**	**40.0**	**31.0**
Kerala	Rural	61	38	17	13	12.3	11.7	12.0
	Urban	46	28	15	15	10.3	9.0	9.0
	Combined	58	36	17	14	11.7	10.7	11.0
	R-U	**15**	**10**	**2**	**-2**	**2.0**	**2.7**	**3.0**
Madhya Pradesh	Rural	154	150	118	102	91.7	89.0	86.3
	Urban	96	80	70	60	54.3	54.7	55.7

India/State	T / R / U	1971-1973	1980-1982	1990-1992	1995-1997	2000-2002	2001-2003	2002-2004
	Combined	145	139	111	97	86.3	84.3	82.0
	R-U	**58**	**70**	**48**	**42**	**37.4**	**34.3**	**30.6**
Maharashtra	Rural	117	84	67	60	54.7	51.7	47.3
	Urban	84	52	41	32	31.7	31.3	31.0
	Combined	107	75	59	50	46.0	44.0	41.0
	R-U	**33**	**32**	**26**	**28**	**23.0**	**20.4**	**16.3**
Orissa	Rural	139	143	125	102	94.3	90.0	85.3
	Urban	78	65	73	65	61.0	57.3	56.3
	Combined	134	137	120	98	91.3	87.0	82.3
	R-U	**61**	**78**	**52**	**37**	**33.3**	**32.7**	**29.0**
Punjab	Rural	120	89	62	56	55.3	54.3	52.7
	Urban	79	54	42	39	36.7	35.3	35.0
	Combined	112	82	57	52	51.7	50.7	48.3
	R-U	**41**	**35**	**20**	**17**	**18.6**	**19.0**	**17.7**
Rajasthan	Rural	140	113	89	89	82.7	81.0	77.7
	Urban	82	65	56	60	56.7	55.0	50.0
	Combined	131	105	84	84	79.0	77.7	73.3
	R-U	**38**	**48**	**33**	**29**	**26.0**	**30.0**	**27.7**
Tamil Nadu	Rural	127	101	67	60	54.0	51.0	47.7
	Urban	76	57	40	41	35.0	32.7	32.7
	Combined	114	89	58	53	48.0	45.3	42.7
	R-U	**51**	**44**	**27**	**19**	**19.0**	**18.3**	**15.0**
Uttar Pradesh	Rural	189	160	103	88	85.3	82.7	79.0
	Urban	124	98	73	66	61.7	58.3	55.3
	Combined	182	152	98	86	82.0	79.7	76.0
	R-U	**65**	**62**	**30**	**22**	**23.6**	**24.4**	**23.7**
West Bengal	Rural	NA	NA	72	59	53.3	51.3	47.3
	Urban	NA	NA	42	44	36.7	35.7	37.7
	Combined	NA	NA	66	56	50.3	48.7	45.0
	R-U	NA	NA	**30**	**15**	**16.6**	**15.6**	**9.6**
Delhi	Rural	NA	NA	**55.0**	**38.7**	**32.3**	**32.3**	**37.0**
	Urban	NA	NA	**43.0**	**38.0**	**30.7**	**29.3**	**30.0**
	Combined	NA	NA	**44.0**	**38.2**	**31.0**	**29.7**	**30.7**
	R-U	NA	NA	**12.0**	**0.7**	**1.6**	**3.0**	**7.0**

Notes: N.A. = not available.

Data for Bihar, Madhya Pradesh and Uttar Pradesh from 1972 to 1996 relate to States as they were before bifurcation. From 2000 onward infant mortality rates are for the States as they presently constitute.

TABLE A8: Net Intercensal Rural-to-Urban Migration, India and States, 2001

Place of Enumeration	Net rural-to-urban migration (in '000)			Total Intercensal migration (in '000)			Net R-U migration as % of intercensal migration		
	P	M	F	P	M	F	P	M	F
India	**14328.7**	**7726.5**	**6602.2**	**94604.9**	**31222.5**	**63382.4**	**15.15**	**24.75**	**10.42**
Andhra Pradesh	734.0	420.7	313.3	7428.5	2696.1	4732.4	9.88	15.61	6.62
Arunachal Pradesh	31.7	16.1	15.6	186.9	101.3	85.6	16.97	15.93	18.20
Assam	180.6	103.6	77.0	1613.6	534.8	1078.8	11.19	19.38	7.14
Bihar	363.7	168.3	195.3	4995.0	589.0	4406.0	7.28	28.58	4.43
Chhattisgarh	285.5	135.1	150.4	2245.4	702.3	1543.1	12.71	19.23	9.75
Goa	16.8	9.2	7.6	295.0	137.7	157.3	5.70	6.65	4.86
Gujarat	1642.2	916.9	725.3	6475.9	2549.1	3926.7	25.36	35.97	18.47
Haryana	536.5	295.6	240.8	2684.4	916.6	1767.8	19.98	32.25	13.62
Himachal Pradesh	53.1	29.5	23.6	770.3	283.0	487.3	6.89	10.41	4.85
Jammu & Kashmir	88.5	49.7	38.8	443.5	165.0	278.5	19.95	30.14	13.92
Jharkhand	329.8	155.6	174.2	2033.3	467.4	1565.9	16.22	33.28	11.13
Karnataka	830.7	443.0	387.7	5642.7	2175.6	3467.2	14.72	20.36	11.18
Kerala	116.8	6.9	109.8	3205.0	1176.8	2028.2	3.64	0.59	5.41
Madhya Pradesh	855.5	417.1	438.4	5969.2	1725.6	4243.6	14.33	24.17	10.33
Maharashtra	3126.3	1814.2	1312.2	15408.3	6802.4	8605.9	20.29	26.67	15.25
Manipur	5.2	1.6	3.6	65.1	20.8	44.3	8.04	7.89	8.11
Meghalaya	10.8	5.2	5.5	69.6	38.2	31.3	15.47	13.71	17.63
Mizoram	32.0	16.6	15.4	103.3	55.6	47.7	31.00	29.94	32.23
Nagaland	12.6	7.4	5.2	81.3	46.9	34.3	15.50	15.66	15.29
Orissa	453.7	241.6	212.1	3181.1	906.4	2274.7	14.26	26.66	9.32
Punjab	474.4	281.5	192.8	2459.4	815.6	1643.8	19.29	34.52	11.73
Rajasthan	500.2	245.5	254.6	5267.4	1350.2	3917.1	9.50	18.18	6.50
Sikkim	-2.4	-1.5	-0.9	69.3	34.0	35.2	-3.41	-4.40	-2.45
Tamil Nadu	457.1	217.6	239.6	3774.8	1490.6	2284.2	12.11	14.60	10.49
Tripura	29.7	14.2	15.6	227.0	80.9	146.0	13.10	17.51	10.65
Uttar Pradesh	992.4	502.4	490.0	9556.6	1697.9	7858.7	10.38	29.59	6.24
Uttaranchal	146.0	79.1	66.8	1001.6	381.8	619.8	14.57	20.72	10.79
West Bengal	600.1	290.6	309.5	6513.3	1702.2	4811.1	9.21	17.07	6.43
Union Territory									
A. & N. Island	4.8	3.1	1.8	72.6	38.6	34.0	6.66	7.99	5.16
Chandigarh	105.1	60.9	44.2	235.3	129.8	105.5	44.64	46.87	41.90
Dadra & Nagar Haveli	7.8	5.0	2.8	49.5	33.5	16.0	15.74	14.89	17.52
Daman & Diu	-2.5	-2.2	-0.3	49.9	36.8	13.1	-5.06	-5.99	-2.44
Delhi	1294.6	770.6	523.9	2226.8	1244.9	981.9	58.14	61.90	53.36
Lakshadweep	-1.2	-0.8	-0.5	14.5	9.1	5.4	-8.40	-8.27	-8.63
Pondicherry	16.9	6.5	10.4	189.6	85.8	103.8	8.90	7.59	9.99

TABLE A 9: Difference Between Urban and Rural Literacy Rates, India and Major States, 2001 and 1991

India / States	T/R/U	2001			1991		
		Persons	Males	Females	Persons	Males	Females
India	**Total**	**64.8**	**75.3**	**53.7**	**52.2**	**64.1**	**39.3**
	Rural	**58.7**	**70.7**	**46.1**	**44.7**	**57.9**	**30.6**
	Urban	**79.9**	**86.3**	**72.9**	**73.1**	**81.1**	**64.1**
	U-R	**21.2**	**15.6**	**26.7**	**28.4**	**23.2**	**33.5**
Andhra Pradesh	Total	60.5	70.3	50.4	44.1	55.1	32.7
	Rural	49.8	61.7	36.7	35.7	47.3	23.9
	Urban	71.9	80.0	62.0	66.3	75.9	56.4
	U-R	22.1	18.4	25.2	30.6	28.6	32.5
Assam	Total	63.3	71.3	54.6	52.9	61.9	43.0
	Rural	64.7	71.0	57.7	49.3	58.7	39.2
	Urban	79.1	83.0	74.5	79.4	84.4	73.3
	U-R	14.4	12.0	16.8	30.1	25.7	34.1
Bihar	Total	47.0	59.7	33.1	37.5	51.4	22.0
	Rural	64.7	71.0	57.7	34.2	48.4	18.4
	Urban	79.1	83.0	74.5	65.2	75.4	52.9
	U-R	14.4	12.0	16.8	31.0	27.0	34.5
Chhattisgarh	Total	64.7	77.4	51.9	42.9	58.1	27.5
	Rural	68.1	81.8	54.7	36.7	52.4	21.0
	Urban	81.4	87.1	74.8	71.4	82.7	58.9
	U-R	13.4	5.3	20.1	34.7	30.2	37.9
Gujarat	Total	69.1	79.7	57.8	61.3	73.1	48.6
	Rural	61.3	74.1	47.8	53.1	66.8	38.6
	Urban	81.8	88.3	74.5	76.5	84.6	67.7
	U-R	20.5	14.2	26.7	23.4	17.8	29.1
Haryana	Total	67.9	78.5	55.7	55.8	69.1	40.5
	Rural	55.3	72.2	37.3	49.9	64.8	32.5
	Urban	76.2	86.5	64.7	73.7	82.0	64.1
	U-R	20.9	14.3	27.3	23.8	17.2	31.6
Himachal Pradesh	Total	76.5	85.3	67.4	63.9	75.4	52.1
	Rural	52.5	66.6	36.9	69.9	73.9	49.8
	Urban	69.8	76.8	61.7	84.2	89.0	78.3
	U-R	17.2	10.2	24.8	14.3	15.1	28.5
Jharkhand	Total	53.6	67.3	38.9	41.4	55.8	25.5
	Rural	59.7	68.2	50.7	32.7	48.1	16.4
	Urban	85.3	89.7	80.2	71.7	80.9	60.3
	U-R	25.6	21.5	29.5	39.0	32.9	44.0
Karnataka	Total	66.6	76.1	56.9	56.0	67.3	44.3
	Rural	63.4	73.1	53.2	47.7	60.3	34.8
	Urban	81.2	86.1	75.7	74.2	82.0	65.7
	U-R	17.8	13.0	22.6	26.5	21.7	30.9

India / States	T/R/U	2001			1991		
		Persons	**Males**	**Females**	**Persons**	**Males**	**Females**
Kerala	Total	90.9	94.2	87.7	89.8	93.6	86.2
	Rural	90.0	93.6	86.7	88.9	92.9	85.1
	Urban	93.2	95.9	90.6	92.2	95.6	89.1
	U-R	3.2	2.3	3.9	3.3	2.7	4.0
Madhya Pradesh	Total	63.7	76.1	50.3	44.7	58.5	29.4
	Rural	59.8	72.9	46.7	35.5	50.5	19.2
	Urban	80.8	87.9	72.9	70.7	81.0	58.9
	U-R	21.0	15.0	26.2	35.1	30.5	39.8
Maharashtra	Total	76.9	86.0	67.0	64.9	76.7	52.3
	Rural	60.5	74.1	47.0	55.5	69.8	41.0
	Urban	80.6	89.4	71.1	79.3	86.6	70.9
	U-R	20.1	15.3	24.1	23.8	16.8	29.9
Orissa	Total	63.1	75.3	50.5	49.1	63.1	34.7
	Rural	57.8	71.7	42.8	45.5	60.0	30.8
	Urban	79.4	87.4	70.5	72.0	81.2	61.2
	U-R	21.6	15.7	27.7	26.5	21.2	30.4
Punjab	Total	69.7	75.2	63.4	58.5	65.7	50.4
	Rural	61.3	74.1	47.8	52.8	60.7	43.9
	Urban	81.8	88.3	74.5	72.1	77.3	66.1
	U-R	20.5	14.2	26.7	19.3	16.6	22.2
Rajasthan	Total	60.4	75.7	43.9	38.6	55.0	20.4
	Rural	70.4	81.9	58.4	30.4	47.6	11.6
	Urban	85.5	91.0	79.1	65.3	78.5	50.2
	U-R	15.1	9.1	20.7	34.9	30.9	38.6
Tamil Nadu	Total	73.5	82.4	64.4	62.7	73.7	51.3
	Rural	54.5	65.4	43.5	54.6	67.2	41.8
	Urban	76.1	83.2	68.7	78.0	86.1	69.6
	U-R	21.6	17.8	25.2	23.4	18.9	27.8
Uttar Pradesh	Total	56.3	68.8	42.2	40.7	54.8	24.4
	Rural	59.3	70.4	48.0	35.8	51.2	18.1
	Urban	80.6	86.7	74.1	60.2	69.3	49.4
	U-R	21.2	16.2	26.1	24.3	18.1	31.3
Uttaranchal	Total	71.6	83.3	59.6	57.7	72.8	41.6
	Rural	90.0	93.6	86.7	52.7	70.1	35.1
	Urban	93.2	95.9	90.6	74.0	80.8	65.5
	U-R	3.2	2.3	3.9	21.3	10.7	30.4
West Bengal	Total	68.6	77.0	59.6	57.7	67.8	46.6
	Rural	66.2	77.1	55.3	50.5	62.1	38.1
	Urban	82.5	89.0	76.0	75.3	81.2	68.3
	U-R	16.3	11.8	20.7	24.8	19.1	30.2
Delhi	Total	81.7	87.3	74.7	75.3	82.0	67.0
	Rural	78.1	86.6	67.4	66.9	78.5	52.2
	Urban	81.9	87.4	75.2	76.2	82.4	68.5
	U-R	3.9	0.8	7.8	9.3	3.9	16.3

TABLE A 10: Educational Level Attained by Persons of all Ages by Sex and Residence, 2001

India/States	Literates without edu. level		Primary		Middle		Secondary but < graduate		Graduate and above	
	M	F	M	F	M	F	M	F	M	F
INDIA	**27.51**	**32.29**	**24.82**	**28.20**	**16.62**	**15.30**	**23.46**	**18.80**	**7.59**	**5.41**
Andhra Pradesh	26.00	31.59	28.96	33.81	10.33	10.09	26.04	19.70	8.67	4.81
Assam	30.81	32.42	22.25	23.47	17.60	19.47	23.55	21.13	5.79	3.52
Bihar	28.47	35.80	24.85	30.61	14.59	13.17	23.67	16.87	8.42	3.55
Chhattisgarh	36.97	44.97	25.37	27.66	14.61	12.97	16.96	10.63	6.09	3.77
Delhi	15.94	18.27	19.19	22.04	16.30	15.20	30.40	26.17	18.17	18.32
Gujarat	26.65	30.25	25.55	29.34	15.89	13.26	25.22	21.45	6.69	5.70
Haryana	21.87	26.51	24.79	29.74	17.05	16.12	29.40	21.51	6.90	6.12
Himachal Pradesh	20.70	22.99	24.70	31.03	17.20	16.95	31.07	24.69	6.34	4.33
Jammu & Kashmir	20.66	27.24	20.19	23.69	23.21	20.81	28.46	22.36	7.47	5.89
Jharkhand	27.00	33.93	25.16	28.16	16.74	15.17	23.15	17.87	7.95	4.87
Karnataka	25.62	28.90	26.08	30.24	12.68	12.33	27.00	23.01	8.62	5.52
Kerala	19.96	20.98	24.30	23.22	24.21	23.14	26.04	26.82	5.49	5.84
Madhya Pradesh	33.59	42.53	26.50	26.95	16.02	13.27	17.12	12.22	6.77	5.03
Maharashtra	25.26	29.65	23.03	28.80	15.37	14.27	27.80	20.88	8.54	6.39
Orissa	30.08	32.84	27.36	32.10	14.87	13.93	20.46	17.07	7.23	4.07
Punjab	19.73	20.41	23.66	28.31	17.54	16.11	32.67	28.42	6.41	6.75
Rajasthan	33.87	47.93	25.44	25.45	17.53	12.08	17.14	10.55	6.02	3.99
Tamil Nadu	25.45	27.51	27.91	29.84	16.63	17.92	23.91	20.19	6.10	4.54
Uttar Pradesh	27.10	34.55	23.25	27.32	20.08	16.82	22.23	16.17	7.34	5.15
Uttaranchal	22.85	27.66	23.14	27.63	20.39	17.38	24.09	19.07	9.53	8.27
West Bengal	34.47	39.50	23.09	25.88	17.38	16.61	17.07	12.97	7.99	5.03
RURAL AREAS										
INDIA	**30.39**	**26.68**	**26.95**	**30.47**	**17.04**	**14.96**	**19.96**	**13.91**	**4.26**	**1.91**
Andhra Pradesh	34.19	29.60	31.96	36.41	10.68	9.43	22.04	13.78	4.70	1.83
Arunachal Pradesh	31.82	26.44	26.10	29.30	16.67	15.24	17.70	11.80	4.95	2.32
Assam	32.41	30.26	23.10	24.19	17.73	19.62	21.62	18.93	3.77	1.86
Bihar	28.90	26.53	26.06	32.16	14.84	12.88	22.73	14.44	6.46	1.99
Chhattisgarh	28.12	22.51	26.75	28.60	14.52	11.89	13.29	6.10	3.34	1.04
Delhi	30.32	26.36	21.47	27.48	18.91	18.30	31.60	23.18	10.10	8.51
Gujarat	30.78	27.49	28.08	31.85	15.49	12.50	20.97	15.84	3.03	1.83
Haryana	34.07	30.15	27.47	34.22	17.63	16.36	27.14	16.33	3.54	1.65
Himachal Pradesh	38.66	35.89	25.94	32.62	17.63	17.29	30.03	23.26	4.64	2.65

India/States	M	F	M	F	M	F	M	F	M	F
Jammu & Kashmir	38.28	32.03	23.05	26.88	25.31	21.96	23.76	16.99	4.26	2.06
Jharkhand	32.79	27.86	28.43	31.04	17.30	14.32	18.73	11.12	4.08	1.40
Karnataka	34.63	31.49	28.95	33.49	13.43	12.36	21.97	16.29	4.46	1.69
Kerala	29.00	29.70	25.09	23.89	24.64	23.78	24.97	25.75	4.24	4.58
Madhya Pradesh	26.39	22.56	28.75	28.02	15.72	10.96	12.78	5.86	2.79	0.96
Maharashtra	33.14	27.34	25.34	32.07	15.37	14.00	23.08	14.62	4.66	1.71
Manipur	31.26	30.41	20.63	24.35	24.99	22.78	26.11	23.23	9.07	6.22
Meghalaya	28.69	26.21	22.36	24.14	11.77	11.10	12.76	9.50	1.98	1.36
Mizoram	17.85	16.20	28.66	27.79	14.67	13.78	8.74	5.52	2.49	0.79
Nagaland	32.56	31.47	27.70	31.22	20.56	20.31	23.78	19.15	4.70	2.71
Orissa	30.90	27.90	28.86	33.53	15.08	13.90	18.04	14.15	4.87	2.22
Punjab	37.12	34.64	26.55	33.01	18.46	16.77	29.88	24.35	2.78	2.20
Rajasthan	26.02	20.36	27.43	25.81	17.54	9.52	13.64	5.22	3.16	0.82
Sikkim	26.35	28.40	25.96	29.09	14.28	15.24	16.76	13.70	3.89	2.35
Tamil Nadu	28.29	24.60	32.17	33.80	17.17	18.26	19.85	15.39	3.06	1.79
Tripura	18.27	14.38	31.82	33.85	18.95	17.70	10.61	6.92	3.56	1.50
Uttar Pradesh	27.98	25.78	24.56	29.68	20.99	16.75	20.38	11.79	4.64	1.63
Uttaranchal	31.37	26.88	25.53	30.63	22.16	18.34	21.01	15.59	5.83	3.72
West Bengal	25.23	21.89	25.09	27.87	16.88	15.18	12.97	7.89	4.07	1.47
URBAN AREAS										
INDIA	**19.02**	**21.88**	**20.61**	**24.55**	**15.80**	**15.83**	**30.39**	**26.68**	**14.18**	**11.06**
Andhra Pradesh	16.58	19.93	22.86	29.48	9.63	11.19	34.19	29.60	16.75	9.81
Assam	17.16	20.01	18.38	20.46	17.02	18.85	32.41	30.26	15.04	10.42
Bihar	20.38	24.97	18.13	24.45	13.20	14.30	28.90	26.53	19.38	9.75
Chhattisgarh	21.37	25.57	21.19	25.18	14.90	15.81	28.12	22.51	14.42	10.93
Delhi	15.80	18.00	19.02	21.70	16.11	15.00	30.32	26.36	18.74	18.94
Gujarat	19.09	21.92	22.24	26.65	16.41	14.08	30.78	27.49	11.48	9.86
Haryana	16.99	18.28	19.25	22.26	15.84	15.71	34.07	30.15	13.85	13.60
Himachal Pradesh	12.88	13.72	15.61	18.62	14.07	14.31	38.66	35.89	18.78	17.45
Jharkhand	17.28	21.81	18.06	23.89	15.52	16.44	32.79	27.86	16.35	10.00
Karnataka	17.16	19.73	21.72	26.14	11.55	12.30	34.63	31.49	14.94	10.34
Kerala	16.95	18.24	22.10	21.41	23.03	21.42	29.00	29.70	8.92	9.23
Madhya Pradesh	19.98	23.58	21.71	25.20	16.67	17.02	26.39	22.56	15.25	11.65
Maharashtra	18.16	21.46	20.43	25.43	15.36	14.55	33.14	27.34	12.92	11.22
Orissa	16.85	20.39	20.87	26.78	13.98	14.02	30.90	27.90	17.40	10.91
Punjab	15.57	15.42	19.03	21.14	16.07	15.11	37.12	34.64	12.20	13.69
Rajasthan	22.82	28.21	20.38	24.78	17.50	16.80	26.02	20.36	13.27	9.85
Tamil Nadu	22.97	24.51	23.31	26.20	16.05	17.60	28.29	24.60	9.38	7.08
Uttar Pradesh	19.90	22.25	19.18	22.14	17.28	16.97	27.98	25.78	15.67	12.87
Uttaranchal	16.65	18.54	17.47	20.89	16.21	15.22	31.37	26.88	18.29	18.47
West Bengal	21.50	25.32	19.13	22.39	18.37	19.12	25.23	21.89	15.77	11.29

TABLE A11: Difference (Rural—Urban) in Educational Level Attained by Persons of All Ages

India/States	Literates without edu. level		Primary		Middle		Secondary and Above		Graduate and Above	
	M	F	M	F	M	F	M	F	M	F
INDIA	**12.77**	**16.86**	**6.34**	**5.92**	**1.23**	**-0.87**	**-20.35**	**-21.91**	**-9.92**	**-9.15**
Andhra Pradesh	14.04	18.63	9.10	6.93	1.05	-1.75	-24.19	-23.80	-12.04	-7.98
Assam	16.63	15.39	4.72	3.73	0.71	0.77	-22.06	-19.89	-11.28	-8.56
Bihar	9.54	13.54	7.92	7.72	1.64	-1.41	-19.10	-19.84	-12.93	-7.76
Chhattisgarh	20.74	26.80	5.56	3.42	-0.39	-3.92	-25.91	-26.30	-11.08	-9.89
Delhi	2.12	4.53	2.44	5.78	2.80	3.29	-7.36	-13.61	-8.64	-10.43
Gujarat	13.34	16.07	5.84	5.20	-0.92	-1.58	-18.26	-19.68	-8.45	-8.03
Haryana	7.23	13.17	8.22	11.96	1.79	0.64	-17.24	-25.77	-10.30	-11.95
Himachal Pradesh	8.88	10.46	10.33	14.00	3.56	2.98	-22.77	-27.44	-14.14	-14.80
Jammu & Kashmir	9.15	13.64	8.82	8.92	6.46	3.19	-24.43	-25.76	-9.92	-10.72
Jharkhand	14.19	20.31	10.36	7.15	1.78	-2.12	-26.33	-25.34	-12.27	-8.60
Karnataka	14.02	16.44	7.23	7.35	1.87	0.06	-23.13	-23.84	-10.47	-8.65
Kerala	4.10	3.75	3.00	2.48	1.62	2.37	-8.71	-8.60	-4.68	-4.64
Madhya Pradesh	19.98	30.61	7.04	2.83	-0.96	-6.05	-26.06	-27.39	-12.46	-10.69
Maharashtra	13.40	16.13	4.90	6.64	0.01	-0.55	-18.31	-22.23	-8.25	-9.51
Orissa	16.31	15.80	8.00	6.75	1.09	-0.12	-25.39	-22.43	-12.54	-8.68
Punjab	6.76	8.26	7.53	11.86	2.39	1.66	-16.67	-21.78	-9.43	-11.49
Rajasthan	15.40	30.42	7.05	1.03	0.04	-7.28	-22.49	-24.17	-10.11	-9.03
Tamil Nadu	4.78	6.26	8.86	7.59	1.11	0.65	-14.76	-14.50	-6.32	-5.29
Uttar Pradesh	9.53	17.91	5.38	7.54	3.71	-0.22	-18.63	-25.23	-11.03	-11.24
Uttaranchal	8.82	13.19	8.06	9.74	5.95	3.12	-22.83	-26.05	-12.47	-14.75
West Bengal	19.50	22.27	5.96	5.48	-1.50	-3.94	-23.96	-23.81	-11.70	-9.82

TABLE A12: Work Participation Rates by Residence and Sex, India and Major States, 1991 and 2001

India / States	T/R/U	1991			2001		
		Persons	Males	Females	Persons	Males	Females
INDIA	Total	**37.5**	**51.6**	**22.3**	**39.3**	**51.9**	**25.7**
	Rural	**40.1**	**52.6**	**26.8**	**42**	**52.4**	**31**
	Urban	**30.2**	**48.9**	**9.2**	**32.2**	**50.8**	**11.5**
	R-U	**9.9**	**3.7**	**17.6**	**9.8**	**1.6**	**19.5**
Andhra Pradesh	Total	45.1	55.5	34.3	45.8	56.4	34.9
	Rural	50.3	57.9	42.5	50.9	58.5	43.2
	Urban	30.8	48.9	11.9	32.2	51.1	12.6
	R-U	**19.5**	**9.0**	**30.6**	**18.7**	**7.4**	**30.6**
Assam	Total	36.1	49.4	21.6	35.9	49.9	20.8
	Rural	36.7	49.3	25.3	36.4	49.8	22.3
	Urban	30.9	50.2	7.5	32	51	10.3
	R-U	**5.8**	**-0.9**	**17.8**	**4.4**	**-1.2**	**12**
Bihar	Total	32.2	47.9	14.9	33.9	47.7	18.8
	Rural	33.2	48.9	16.3	34.8	48.4	20.2
	Urban	25.1	41.9	5.1	25.6	41.9	6.9
	R-U	**8.1**	**7.0**	**11.2**	**9.2**	**6.5**	**13.3**
Chhattisgarh	Total	NA	NA	NA	46.5	53	40
	Rural	NA	NA	NA	50.4	54.3	46.6
	Urban	NA	NA	NA	31.1	48	13
	R-U	**NA**	**NA**	**NA**	**19.3**	**6.3**	**33.6**
Gujarat	Total	40.2	53.6	26.0	42.1	55	28
	Rural	45.5	54.9	35.6	47.6	55.6	39
	Urban	30.2	51.1	7.2	33.1	54.1	9.1
	R-U	**15.3**	**3.8**	**28.4**	**14.5**	**1.5**	**29.9**
Haryana	Total	31.0	48.5	10.8	39.8	50.5	27.3
	Rural	31.9	48.5	12.6	43.1	50.9	34.2
	Urban	28.3	48.5	5.1	31.5	49.5	10.3
	R-U	**3.6**	**0.0**	**7.5**	**11.6**	**1.4**	**23.9**
Himachal Pradesh	Total	42.8	50.6	34.8	49.3	54.7	43.7
	Rural	43.6	50.5	36.6	50.6	54.7	46.5
	Urban	35.0	52.4	14.1	36.9	54.4	15
	R-U	8.6	-1.9	22.5	13.7	0.3	31.5
Jammu & Kashmir	Total	N.A.	N.A.	N.A.	36.6	49.8	22
	Rural	N.A.	N.A.	N.A.	37.9	49.1	25.8
	Urban	N.A.	N.A.	N.A.	32.7	51.8	9.5
	R-U	**NA**	**NA**	**NA**	**5.2**	**-2.7**	**16.3**

India / States	T/R/U	1991			2001		
		Persons	Males	Females	Persons	Males	Females
Jharkhand	Total	N.A.	N.A.	N.A.	37.6	48.2	26.4
	Rural	N.A.	N.A.	N.A.	41.1	49.9	31.9
	Urban	N.A.	N.A.	N.A.	25.7	42.6	6.3
	R-U	**NA**	**NA**	**NA**	**15.4**	**7.3**	**25.6**
Karnataka	Total	42.0	54.1	29.4	44.6	56.9	31.9
	Rural	46.5	56.0	36.6	49.2	58.3	39.9
	Urban	32.0	49.8	12.9	35.7	54.1	16.1
	R-U	**14.5**	**6.2**	**23.7**	**13.5**	**4.2**	**23.8**
Kerala	Total	31.4	47.6	15.8	32.3	50.4	15.3
	Rural	32.1	47.9	16.9	32.6	50.2	15.9
	Urban	29.6	46.8	13.0	31.6	50.8	13.5
	R-U	**2.5**	**1.1**	**3.9**	**1.0**	**-0.6**	**2.4**
Madhya Pradesh	Total	42.8	52.3	32.7	42.7	51.6	33.1
	Rural	46.8	54.0	39.3	47.1	53.1	40.7
	Urban	29.6	46.8	19.2	30.6	47.6	11.7
	R-U	**17.2**	**7.2**	**20.1**	**16.5**	**5.5**	**29.0**
Maharashtra	Total	43.0	52.2	33.1	43.5	53.5	32.6
	Rural	49.7	53.2	46.1	50.4	54.2	46.5
	Urban	32.3	50.6	11.4	34	52.6	12.7
	R-U	**17.4**	**2.6**	**34.7**	**16.4**	**1.6**	**33.8**
Orissa	Total	37.5	53.8	20.8	38.9	52.8	24.6
	Rural	38.7	54.7	22.6	40.3	53.4	27.1
	Urban	29.7	48.4	8.1	30.7	49.4	9.8
	R-U	**9.0**	**6.3**	**14.5**	**9.6**	**4.0**	**17.3**
Punjab	Total	30.9	54.2	4.4	37.6	54.1	18.7
	Rural	31.2	55.0	4.4	39.7	54.5	23.2
	Urban	30.1	52.3	4.5	33.4	53.4	9.7
	R-U	**1.1**	**2.7**	**-0.1**	**6.3**	**1.1**	**13.5**
Rajasthan	Total	38.9	49.3	27.4	42.1	50.1	33.5
	Rural	42.0	50.1	33.2	45.9	50.8	40.7
	Urban	28.2	46.6	7.2	29.6	47.6	9.2
	R-U	**13.8**	**3.5**	**26.0**	**16.3**	**3.2**	**31.5**
Tamil Nadu	Total	43.3	56.4	29.9	44.8	58.1	31.3
	Rural	48.5	58.3	38.5	50.4	59.4	41.3
	Urban	33.3	52.8	13.1	37.6	56.4	18.4
	R-U	**15.2**	**5.5**	**25.4**	**12.8**	**3.0**	**22.9**
Uttar Pradesh	Total	32.2	49.7	12.3	32.6	47.3	16.3
	Rural	33.5	52.5	14.2	34.1	47.8	18.9

India / States	T/R/U	1991			2001		
		Persons	Males	Females	Persons	Males	Females
	Urban	27.1	46.4	4.8	26.9	45.1	6.2
	R-U	**6.4**	**6.1**	**9.4**	**7.2**	**2.7**	**12.7**
Uttaranchal	Total	NA	NA	NA	36.9	46.4	27.1
	Rural	NA	NA	NA	39.6	46.0	33.3
	Urban	NA	NA	NA	29.1	47.6	7.3
	R-U	**NA**	**NA**	**NA**	**10.5**	**-1.6**	**26.0**
West Bengal	Total	32.2	51.4	11.2	36.8	54.2	18.1
	Rural	35.2	52.1	13.1	37.9	54.3	20.7
	Urban	29.6	49.6	6.2	33.8	54.1	11.1
	R-U	**5.6**	**2.5**	**6.9**	**4.1**	**0.2**	**9.6**
Delhi	Total	31.6	51.7	7.4	32.8	52.2	9.1
	Rural	29.1	48.2	5.5	32	49.7	10.1
	Urban	31.9	52.1	37.5	51.6	22.3	39.3
	R-U	**-2.8**	**-3.9**	**-32**	**-19.6**	**27.4**	**-29.2**

Chapter 7

Demographic Transition in Kerala and Tamil Nadu

K.C. Zachariah and *S. Irudaya Rajan*

Formed on 1 November 1956 as a result of the reorganisation of India's states on a linguistic basis, Kerala, situated on the southwest edge of the peninsula, takes its name from the word *keram*, which means 'coconut' in Malayalam. The State accounts for 1.3 per cent of India's land area and supports 3.1 per cent of the country's population. Kerala's population, as enumerated by the census of 2001 in around 7 million households, was around 32 million. The average household size in the State was 4.7 persons. As of 2001, Kerala had 14 districts, 63 taluks, 159 census towns, 999 *panchayats* and 1,364 villages. It also had 3.1 million people belonging to the Scheduled Castes and 0.4 million to the Scheduled Tribes. (These groups constitute 9.8 per cent and 1.1 per cent of the total population respectively).

Kerala has the highest literacy rate in India. Even at the time of its formation, nearly half the Keralite population was literate. For the population aged 7 and above, the literacy in the 2001 census was 90.92 per cent, as against 89.81 in 1991. The male literacy rate was 94.20 per cent in 2001 in comparison to 93.62 per cent in 1991. The female literacy rate was 87.86 per cent in 2001 as against 86.17 in 1991. The difference between male and female literacy, almost 20 points in 1961, declined to six points in 2001. On the other hand, the male and female literacy rates for India were 75.85 and 54.16 respectively in 2001. The gender gap was 22 per cent for India as against just 6 per cent for Kerala.

The work participation rates for males and females in Kerala are lower than for the country as a whole. The 2001 census ranked Kerala as the nineteenth (out of 35 States and Union Territories) with regard to female work participation rate. This is the same position Kerala held in earlier decades. In 1991, the male and female work participation rates were 47.8 and 15.9 respectively. The current rates, as per the 2001 census, are 50.4 and 15.3.

The per capita income (per capital net national product at factor cost), estimated at Rs. 10,754 for 2001-02 (at 1993-94 prices) as against 10,306 in 2000-01, registered an increase of 4 per cent during the previous year. The net state domestic product at constant (1993-94) prices was estimated at Rs 36,079 crores in 2001-02 as against Rs 34,450 crores in 2000-01. At current prices, the State income was an estimated Rs 69602 crores in 2001-02 as against 63094 crores in 2000-01, registering a growth rate of 10.3 per cent.[1]

A glaring manifestation of the unemployment problem in Kerala is the large number of out-migrants from the State. Firm figures are not available, but according to our own earlier estimate, there were about 618,000 migrants in 1991 (Zachariah *et al.* 1994). The most accurate estimate of the number of emigrants in Kerala in the second half of 1998 was 1.36 million, according to a study conducted at the Centre for Development Studies (CDS), Kerala, (Zachariah, Mathew and Irudaya Rajan 2003). A just completed study at the CDS puts the emigrants at 1.84 million persons, roughly 27 emigrants per 100 households. Emigrants send home remittances, and one estimate of its flow has been estimated at 18,465 Crores (Zachariah and Irudaya Rajan 2004). The rate of net migration from Kerala stood at -0.16 percent during decade 1961-71, -0.22 percent during 1971-81, -0.31 percent during 1981-91 and -0.27 percent in the last decade 1991-2001 (Mari Bhat and S Irudaya Rajan, 1990; Irudaya Rajan and Aliyar 2005).

Population Size and Growth

Until 1971, Kerala's growth rate was always higher than India's. It was only in the 1971-81 decade that Kerala's growth rate fell below the all India rate. Overall, over the last century, Kerala's population doubled five times (6 million in 1901 to 32 million in 2001) whereas India's population grew slightly more than three times (238 million in 1901 to 1027 million in 2001). Between 1991 and 2001, Kerala registered the lowest growth rate among the 35 States and Union Territories in India followed by Tamil Nadu. While Tamil Nadu's growth during the last century was almost similar to India's (19 millions in 1901 to 62 millions in 2001), its growth rate during the last decade works out to be 1.06 per cent, the lowest after the formation of the state of Kerala (Table 1 and Figure 1).

Kerala is one of the most densely populated regions in India. Among the major states, Kerala had the highest density until 1981. In 1991, West Bengal occupied the prime position, but the difference between Kerala and West Bengal was only 17 persons per square kilometre in 1991. It increased to 85 per square kilometre in 2001. However, Kerala's density of 819 persons per square

TABLE 1: Population Size and Growth in Kerala, Tamil Nadu and India, 1901-2001

Year	Kerala		Tamil Nadu		India	
	Population	Growth Rate	Population	Growth Rate	Population	Growth Rate
1901	6396262	—	19252630	—	238396327	—
1911	7147673	1.11	20902616	0.82	252093390	0.56
1921	7802127	0.88	21628518	0.34	251321213	-0.03
1931	9507050	1.98	23472099	0.82	278977238	1.04
1941	11031541	1.49	26267507	1.13	318660580	1.33
1951	13549118	2.06	30119047	1.37	361088090	1.25
1961	16903715	2.21	33686953	1.12	439234771	1.96
1971	21347375	2.33	41199168	2.01	548159652	2.22
1981	25453680	1.76	48408077	1.61	683329097	2.20
1991	29098518	1.34	55858946	1.43	846387888	2.14
2001	31838619	0.91	62405679	1.06	1027015247	1.93

Note: Compiled from various Censuses.

FIGURE 1: Population Growth Rates, Kerala, Tamil Nadu and India, 1901-2001

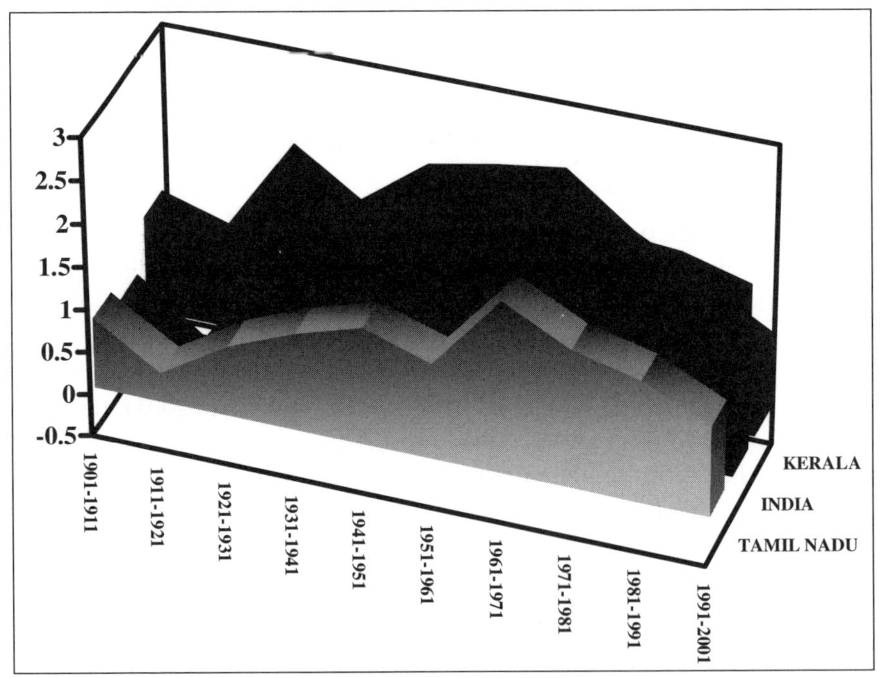

Data source: Table 1.

kilometre as per the 2001 census was nearly thrice than the all India average, much higher than that of Tamil Nadu (478 persons per square kilometre). Even at the beginning of this century, Kerala's population density was higher than the all India figure (Table 2). Over a period of the last 100 years, the population pressure on land was much higher in Kerala as compared to Tamil Nadu and India, which tends to be ignored when we discuss Kerala's demographic transition.

TABLE 2: Sex Ratio and Population Density, Tamil Nadu and Kerala, 1901-2001

Year	Sex ratio			Population density		
	Kerala	Tamil Nadu	India	Kerala	Tamil Nadu	India
1901	1004	1044	972	165	148	77
1911	1008	1042	964	184	161	82
1921	1011	1029	955	201	166	81
1931	1022	1027	950	245	180	90
1941	1027	1012	945	284	202	103
1951	1028	1007	946	349	232	117
1961	1022	992	941	435	259	142
1971	1016	978	930	549	317	177
1981	1032	977	934	655	372	216
1991	1036	974	927	749	429	267
2001	1058	986	933	819	478	324

Note: Compiled from various Censuses.

Kerala's sex ratio is unique among the Indian States in as much as it is the only one with an excess of females and the only one where this excess has grown consistently during the past century (Table 2 and Figure 2). At the beginning of 20th century, both Kerala and Tamil Nadu registered excess females in its population but the excess of females was much higher for Tamil Nadu than Kerala. Tamil Nadu's sex ratio was about 1044 females per 1000 males as against 1004 for Kerala, i.e., an excess of 40 females in Tamil Nadu. Over the years, Kerala improved its position of 4 excess females per 1000 males in 1901 to 58 in 2001. Tamil Nadu, on the hand, went from 44 excess females per 1000 males in 1901 to a deficit of 14 females in 2001.

Of the 14 districts of Kerala, half registered growth rates higher than the State average. The lowest growth rate was observed in Pathanamthitta whereas the highest growth rate was registered in Malappuram. Overall, the northern districts of Kerala follow a higher growth pattern and southern districts follow the lower population growth rate (see Table 3a). On the other hand, among the 30 districts of Tamil Nadu, only ten districts have registered their growth rate more than 1.0 percent (See Table 3b). The lowest growth rates are in the southern parts of Tamil Nadu. The lowest growth rate of 0.4 percent was observed in

FIGURE 2: Sex Ratio (Females per 1000 Males) for Kerala, Tamil Nadu and India, 1901-2001

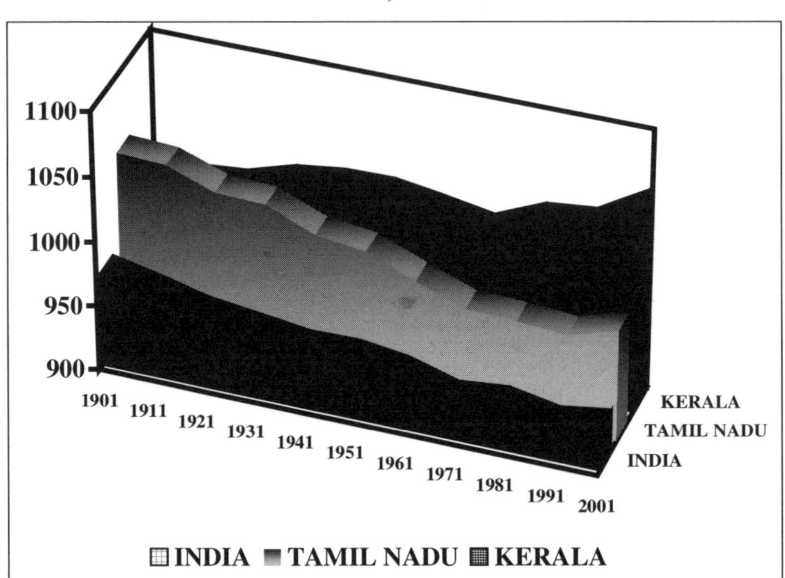

Kanniyakumari, Theni and Sivaganga districts.

Population density in Kerala was lower than the State average in six out of 14 districts. The highest density was found in Alappuzha and the lowest in Idukki. Density played a major role in the accessibility of social facilities, such as schools and hospitals and indirectly contributed to the early process of demographic transition. In Tamil Nadu, the highest population density of 24231 persons per square kilometre was in Chennai district. The next highest, in Kanniyakumari (992 persons per square kilometres) is almost double the State average (Table 3b).

In the Idukki and Wayanad districts of Kerala, sex ratios were favourable to males in 1991 and in 2001; only one district in Kerala (Idukki) has more males than females. The highest sex ratio of 1085 females per 1000 males was found in Thrissur. Pathanamthitta district took the first position in the 2001 census, with 1094 females per 1000 males. In Tamil Nadu, the situation is quite different. Though the State reported 986 females per 1000 males, half of the districts in Tamil Nadu registered excess females in their total population. The highest FMR of 1049 females per 1000 males was found in Toothukudi district. The situation however is much worse when one considers child sex ratios. Four districts (Dharmapuri, Salem, Namakkal and Theni) reported their child sex ratios below 900 indicating the practice of female infanticide in Tamil Nadu (for more details, see Vella 2005).

TABLE 3A: District Profile of Kerala as of the 2001 Census

Districts	Population	Growth Rate 1991-01	Sex Ratio		Population Density	% Urban	Literacy (%)		WPR (%)	
			(Total)	(0-6)			M	F	M	F
Kasaragod	1203342	1.16	1047	984	604	19.42	90.84	79.8	49.3	20.8
Kannur	2412365	0.69	1090	956	813	50.46	96.38	89.57	50.0	15.2
Wayanad	786627	1.57	1000	954	369	3.76	90.28	80.80	55.7	22.8
Kozhikode	2878498	0.94	1058	966	1228	38.25	96.30	88.86	48.8	8.1
Malappuram	3629640	1.59	1063	979	1022	9.81	91.46	85.96	42.8	6.6
Palakkad	2617072	0.94	1068	963	584	13.62	89.73	79.31	52.2	21.1
Thrissur	2975440	0.83	1092	953	981	28.21	95.47	89.94	50.8	15.1
Ernakulam	3098378	0.87	1017	948	1050	47.65	95.95	90.96	55.4	17.1
Idukki	1128605	0.67	999	970	252	5.07	92.11	85.04	58.4	28.1
Kottayam	1952901	0.65	1025	957	884	15.35	97.41	94.45	52.4	13.9
Alappuzha	2105349	0.51	1079	962	1489	29.36	96.42	91.14	49.7	20.2
Pathanamthitta	1231577	0.36	1094	968	467	10.03	96.62	93.71	47.6	13.2
Kollam	2584118	0.71	1070	961	1038	18.03	94.63	88.60	48.5	16.7
Thiruvananthapuram	3234707	0.93	1058	955	1476	33.78	92.68	86.26	51.5	14.4
Kerala	31838619	0.9	1058	963	819	25.97	94.20	87.86	50.4	15.3

Note: Sex ratio is defined as number of females per 1000 males. WPR: Work Participation Rate. All information is compiled from the Census of India 2001 reports.

TABLE 3B: District Profile of Tamil Nadu as of the 2001 Census

Districts	Population	Annual Growth Rate 1991-01	Sex Ratio		Population Density	% Urban	Literacy (%)		WPR (%)	
			(Total)	(0-6)			M	F	M	F
Thiruvallur	2738866	2.0	970	957	800	54.5	85.3	68.4	55.0	19.8
Chennai	4216268	0.9	951	972	24231	100.0	90.0	80.4	54.1	13.5
Kancheepuram	2869920	1.7	972	961	647	53.5	84.7	68.8	55.2	24.0
Vellore	3482970	1.4	997	943	573	37.9	82.0	62.8	54.7	27.4
Dharmapuri	2833252	1.5	938	869	294	15.8	71.6	50.6	57.9	40.5
Tiruvannamalai	2181853	0.7	996	948	352	18.4	79.2	55.6	57.8	39.6
Villupuram	2943917	0.7	983	961	406	14.5	75.1	52.4	57.5	40.0
Salem	2992754	1.5	929	851	573	46.4	74.4	55.2	60.3	35.2
Namakkal	1495661	1.2	967	889	436	36.8	77.6	57.0	64.4	48.2
Erode	2574067	1.0	971	939	314	46.2	75.3	55.1	66.5	44.3
Nilgiris	764826	0.7	1015	979	300	59.5	88.5	71.6	54.9	35.4
Coimbatore	4224107	1.9	959	963	566	66.0	84.6	69.1	63.2	28.7
Dindigul	1918960	0.9	986	930	317	35.0	79.8	58.9	60.4	40.7
Karur	933791	0.9	1010	930	311	33.2	79.6	56.8	63.1	43.2
Tiruchchirapalli	2388831	0.8	1000	955	542	46.7	86.5	69.3	56.9	31.1
Perambalur	486971	0.8	1007	937	278	14.5	77.9	54.4	58.0	49.7
Ariyalur	694058	0.9	1007	949	358	11.4	77.2	51.2	58.0	41.5
Cuddalore	2280530	0.7	985	957	626	33.0	81.6	60.3	55.3	29.6
Nagapattinam	1487055	0.8	1014	963	548	22.2	84.9	68.0	55.5	23.6
Thiruvarur	1165213	0.6	1013	970	538	20.2	85.4	67.9	57.1	27.1
Thanjavur	2205375	0.7	1020	959	649	33.9	84.5	66.7	56.4	24.9
Pudukkottai	1452269	0.9	1015	955	312	16.9	82.5	60.0	57.6	35.5

Sivaganga	1150753	0.4	1035	952	275	28.2	83.1	61.7	55.8	33.5
Madurai	2562279	0.7	978	926	733	55.9	86.2	69.3	56.5	27.6
Theni	1094724	0.4	979	891	357	54.1	81.9	61.2	57.6	37.3
Virudhunagar	1751548	1.1	1011	958	409	44.4	84.0	63.6	59.5	41.3
Ramanathapuram	1183321	0.6	1033	964	287	25.3	83.0	63.4	55.0	33.1
Toothukudi	1565743	0.7	1049	953	339	42.3	88.3	75.1	56.3	30.7
Tirunelveli	2801194	1.1	1042	957	411	46.5	85.2	67.4	55.3	39.1
Kanniyakumari	1669763	0.4	1013	968	992	65.1	90.4	84.8	53.0	12.7
Tamil Nadu	62405679	1.1	986	942	478	43.9	82.3	64.5	57.6	31.5

With respect to the literacy rate, Kottayam district ranks first, both with respect to male as well as female literacy. The lowest rates are found in Palakkad district. In Tamil Nadu, the highest female literacy was observed in Kanniyakumari district.

As regards male and female work participation rates, Idukki leads as number one, whereas the Malappuram is lagging behind all the districts. Namakkal and Peramballur have registered the highest female participation rates.

Mortality and Life Expectancy

Although a civil registration system has been in existence in Kerala for long, its performance was highly unsatisfactory until recently. As a result, not much confidence can be placed on either the level or trend in vital rates implied by this source. Recent data published by the civil registration system in Kerala is of importance, however, as it can provide below-district level estimates of fertility and mortality. It is unfortunate that a systematic attempt has not been made either by demographers or by the government to produce below-district level data on fertility and mortality on a regular basis using the civil registration system. Hence, we have to depend upon the Sample Registration System (SRS) as it offers data of more acceptable quality.

According to the SRS, the crude death rate (CDR) in Kerala hovered around six during the last 10 years (Figure 3) and the infant mortality rate

FIGURE 3: Crude Death Rates for Kerala, Tamil Nadu and India, 1971-2002

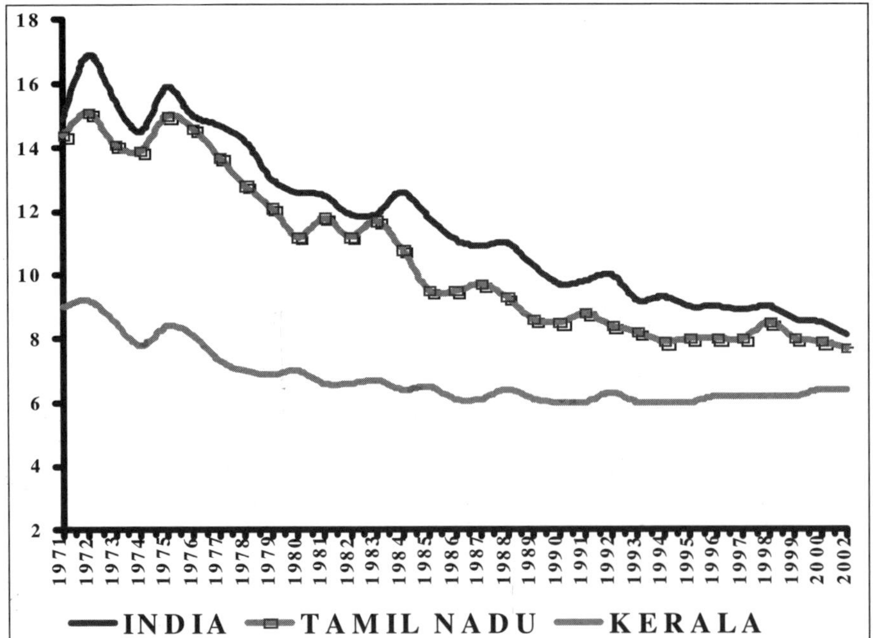

(IMR) has marginally declined from 16 per thousand live births in 1991 to 10 per thousand in 2002 (Figure 4). The life expectancy at birth in Kerala is 68 years for males and 74 years for females, with a gender gap of six years.

Over the last 30 years, the IMR has shown a lot of fluctuation (Figure 5). We see also that the contribution of neo-natal mortality (mortality in the first 28 days of life) is quite high (Figure 5). The contribution of post neo-natal mortality (28 to 365 days) is low compared to neo-natal morality (0-28 days), even though both have been declining over time (Figure 5). Again, if we decompose the one-month mortality into two components such as 0-7 days and 7-28 days, it reveals an interesting scenario of the health situation in Kerala. For instance, in 1997, out of the 7.5 children that died in one month, six died in the first week of life (Table 4 and Figure 6). The pattern holds also for peri-

FIGURE 4: Infant Mortality Rates for Kerala, Tamil Nadu and India, 1971-2002

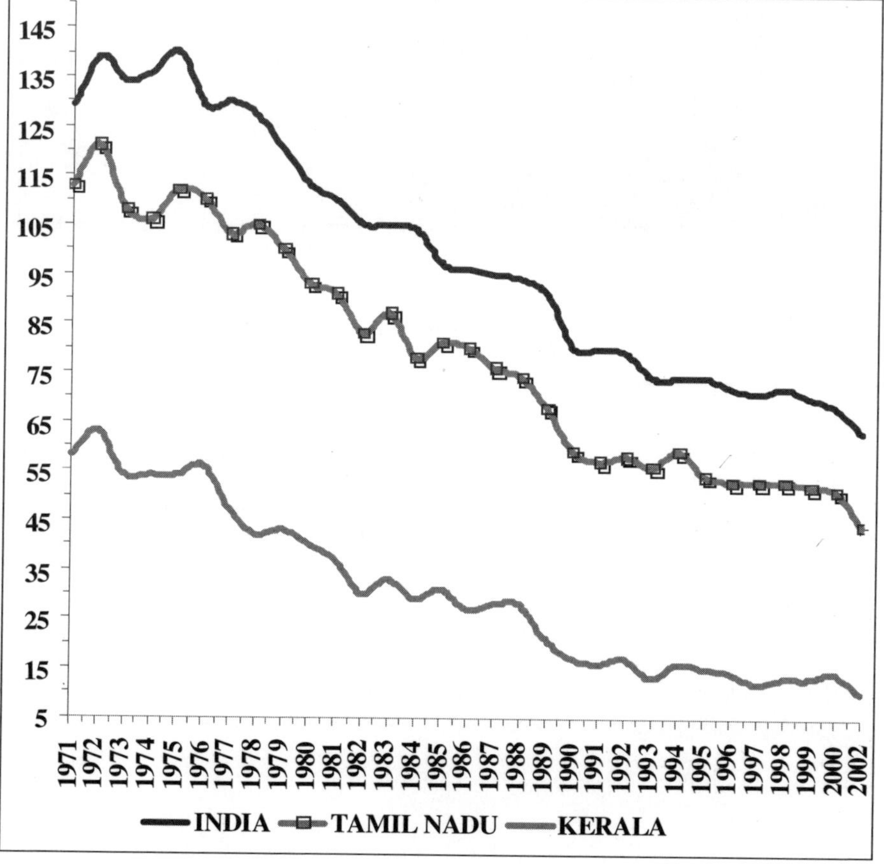

natal morality (still birth plus one week mortality rate) and mortality due to stillbirth (Figure 7).[2]

FIGURE 5: Infant Mortality Rate (IMR) and its Components (NMR & PNMR), Kerala, 1971-2000

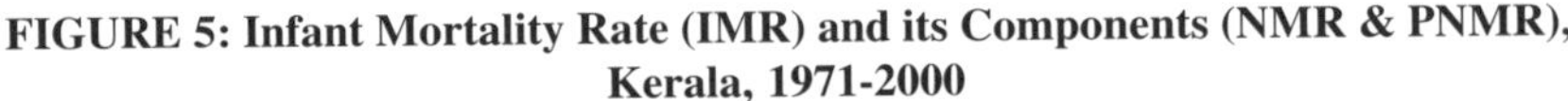

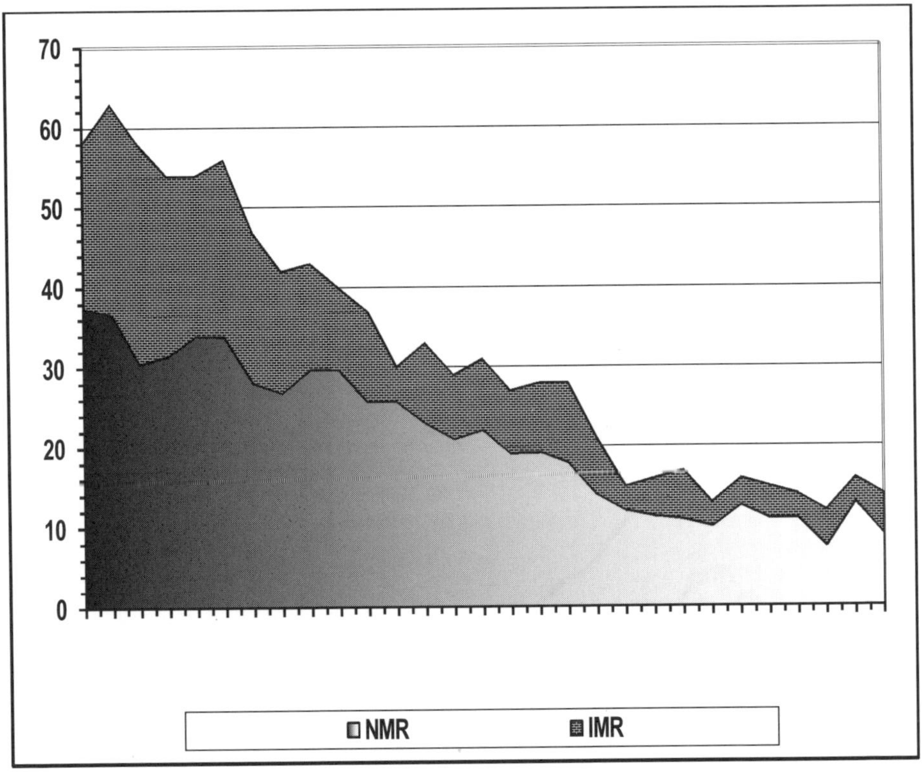

Note:

- NMR - Neonatal Mortality Rate (deaths per 1000 live births in the first 28 days of life). The height of the shaded portion from zero shows the NMR.
- IMR - Infant Mortality Rate (deaths per 1000 live births in the first year of life). The height of the brick wall from zero shows the IMR. Note that in the above diagram, the whole of the brick wall is not visible. Only that portion of the brick wall that is above the shaded portion is visible.
- PNMR - the Post Neo Natal Mortality Rate, i.e., the number of infant deaths of more than 28 days and less than a year per 1000 live births. The difference between the shaded portion and the height of the brick wall from zero shows the PNNMR. Thus, the PNNMR is shown by the visible portion of the brick wall.

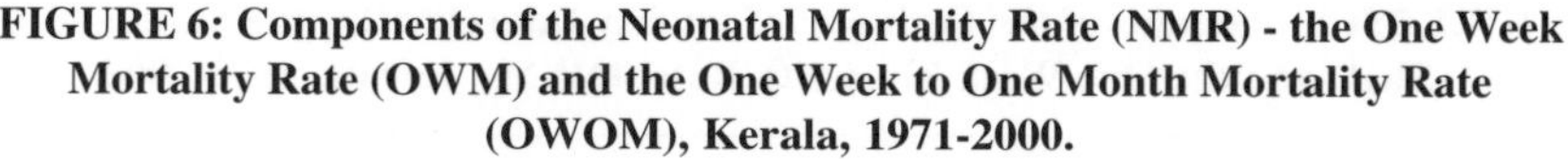

FIGURE 6: Components of the Neonatal Mortality Rate (NMR) - the One Week Mortality Rate (OWM) and the One Week to One Month Mortality Rate (OWOM), Kerala, 1971-2000.

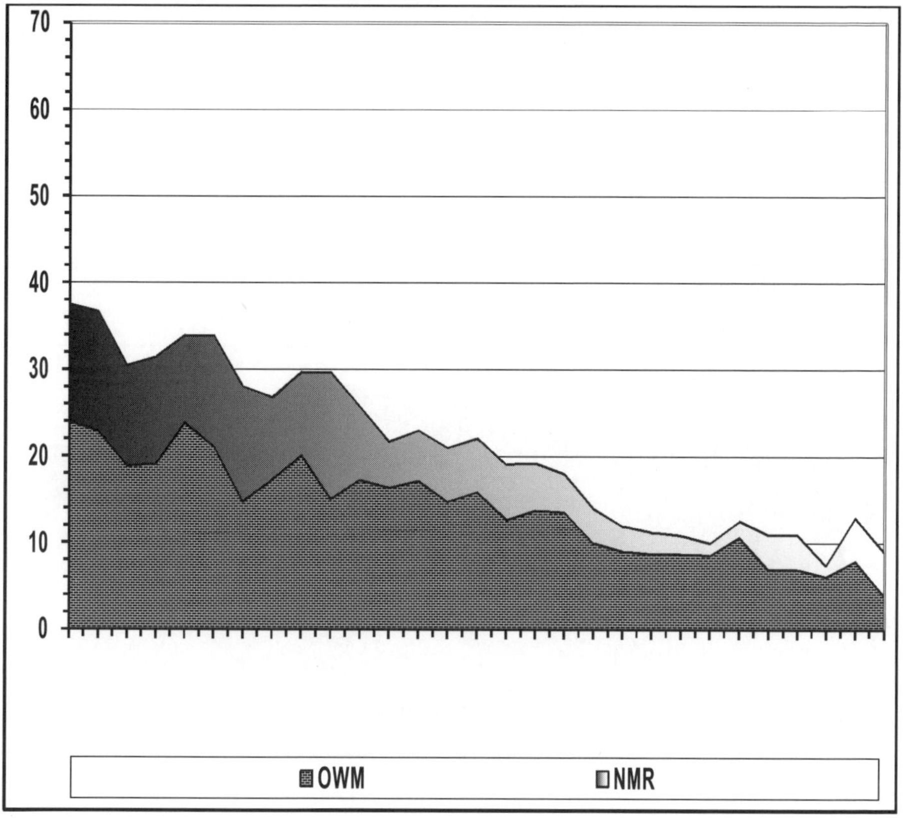

Note:

- OWM - One Week Mortality (0-7 days mortality) is the number of infant deaths in the first week of life per 1000 live births. The height of the brick wall from zero shows the OWM.
- NMR - Neonatal Mortality Rate (deaths per 1000 live births in the first 28 days of life). The height of the shaded portion from zero shows the NMR. Note that in the above diagram, the whole of the shaded portion is not visible. Only that portion of the shaded portion that is above the brick wall is visible.
- OWOM - The One Week to One Month Mortality Rate (7 to 28 days mortality) is the number of infant deaths of more than one week and less than 28 days per 1000 live births. The difference between (a) the shaded portion from zero and (b) the height of the brick wall from zero shows OWFW. Thus OWFW is shown by the visible portion of the shaded portion.

FIGURE 7: Components of the Perinatal Mortality Rate (PMR) - the Stillbirth Rate (SBR) and the One Week Mortality Rate (OWM), Kerala, 1971-2000

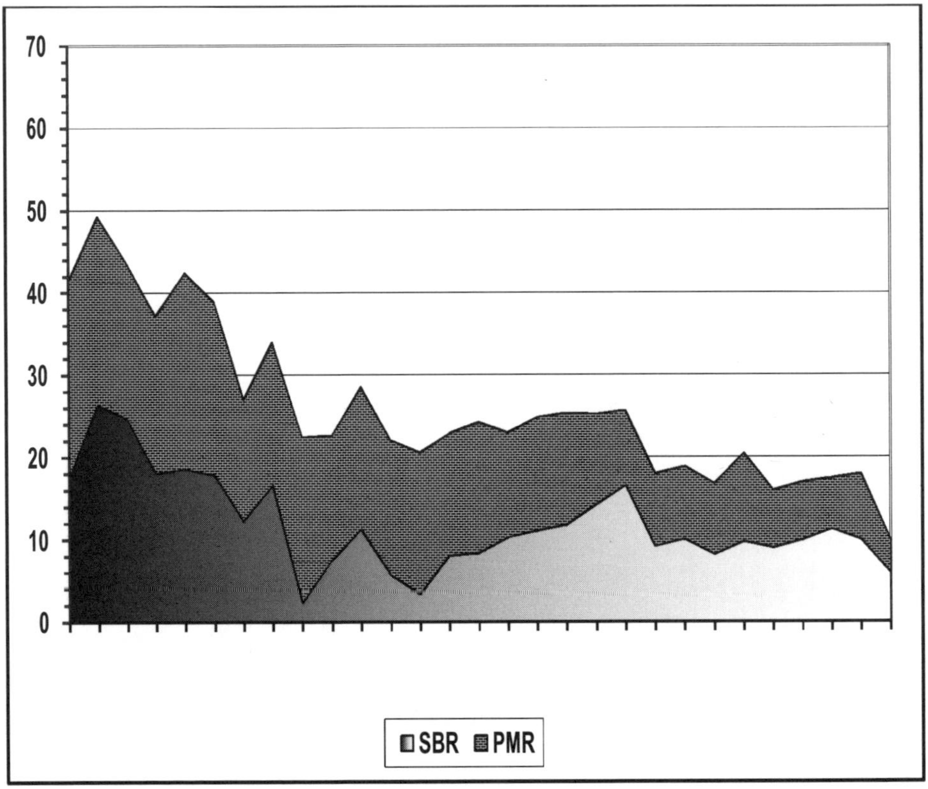

Note:

- SBR - the Stillbirth Rate, is the number of stillbirths per thousand live births. The height of the shaded portion from zero shows the SBR.
- PMR - The Perinatal Mortality Rate, is the number of stillbirths plus infant deaths in the first week life (0-7 days) per thousand live births. The height of the brick wall from zero shows PMR.
- OWM - The One Week Mortality Rate, is the number of deaths in the first week of life per thousand live births. OWM is shown by the visible portion of the brick wall.

Fertility

Reliable data on fertility trends in Kerala have been available only since the introduction of the Sample Registration System (SRS). However, estimates made by several authors using census data are available for different periods. The census-based estimates shown here are taken from Bhat (1987). Table 5

TABLE 4: Different Components of Infant Mortality Rates, 1971-2000

Year	PMR	SBR	OWM	OWOM	NMR	PNMR	IMR
1971	41.5	17.5	24.0	13.5	37.5	20.5	58
1972	49.3	26.4	22.9	13.8	36.7	26.3	63
1973	43.6	24.7	18.9	11.6	30.5	26.5	58
1974	37.2	18.1	19.1	12.4	31.5	22.5	54
1975	42.5	18.6	23.9	10.1	34.0	20.0	54
1976	39.0	17.9	21.1	12.8	33.9	22.1	56
1977	27.1	12.3	14.8	13.3	28.1	18.9	47
1978	34.0	16.7	17.3	9.5	26.8	15.2	42
1979	22.5	2.4	20.1	9.7	29.8	12.9	43
1980	22.7	7.6	15.1	14.6	29.7	10.5	40
1981	28.6	11.3	17.3	8.4	25.7	11.7	37
1982	22.1	5.7	16.4	5.3	25.7	8.7	30
1983	20.6	3.4	17.2	5.8	23.0	10.0	33
1984	22.9	8.1	14.8	6.2	21.0	7.7	29
1985	24.3	8.4	15.9	6.2	22.1	9.2	31
1986	23.0	10.3	12.7	6.4	19.1	8.3	27
1987	24.9	11.1	13.8	5.5	19.3	8.6	28
1988	25.4	11.8	13.6	4.4	18.0	9.7	28
1989	25.3	14.3	10.0	4.0	14.0	7.0	21
1990	25.7	16.6	9.1	2.9	12.0	3.3	15
1991	18.0	9.2	8.8	2.5	11.3	5.1	16
1992	18.9	10.1	8.8	2.1	10.9	5.8	17
1993	16.8	8.2	8.6	1.4	10.0	3.3	13
1994	20.5	9.8	10.7	1.9	12.6	3.2	16
1995	16.0	9.0	7.0	4.0	11.0	4.0	15
1996	17.0	10.0	7.0	4.0	11.0	3.0	14
1997	17.5	11.3	6.2	1.3	7.5	4.5	12
1999	18.0	10.0	8.0	5.0	13.0	3.0	16
2000	10.0	6.0	4.0	5.0	9.0	5.0	14
2002	n.a	n.a	n.a	n.a	n.a	n.a	10

Notes:

- PMR refers to perinatal mortality and is defined as the number of stillbirths and infant deaths of less than seven days during the year divided by number of liver births and stillbirths during the year multiplied by 1000.
- SBR refers to Still Birth Rate and defined as number of stillbirths during the year divided by number of live births and stillbirths during the year multiplied by 1000.
- OWM refers to One Week Mortality (0-7 days mortality) and defined as number of infant deaths of less than one week during the year divided by number of live births during the year multiplied by 1000.
- OWOM refers to One Week to One Month Mortality (7-28 days mortality) and defined as number of infant deaths of more than one week and less than a month during the year divided by number of live births during the year multiplied by 1000.
- NMR refers to Neo-natal Mortality Rate (0-28 days mortality) and defined as number of infant deaths of less than a month during the year divided by number of live births during the year multiplied by 1000.
- PNMR refers to Post Neo-natal Mortality Rate (28 days to 1 year) and defined as number of infant deaths of more than a month and less than a year during the year divided by number of live births during the year multiplied by 1000.

presents estimates of some fertility measures for Kerala and India from 1951-81.[3]

TABLE 5: Estimates of CBR and TFR, Kerala and India

Decade	Crude birth rate		Total fertility rate	
	Kerala	India	Kerala	India
1951-61	43.9	47.1	5.6	6.3
1961-71	37.1	43.0	5.0	6.0
1971-81	28.1	37.2	3.4	5.2

Source: Mari Bhat, 1987.

The figures in Table 5 and Table 6 show that the CBR (the Crude Birth Rate) in Kerala came down from 44 per 1,000 in 1951-61 to 18 per 1,000 in 2000. The TFR, which reflects the total number of live births a woman will eventually have if she bears children under current fertility rates, declined in Kerala from 5.6 in 1951-61 to 2.6 births in 1981-85 and 1.8 in 1996-2000.

Even in 1951-61, Kerala had lower fertility than the all-India average, the difference being about three per 1,000 in the CBR and 0.7 births per woman in the TFR.[4] Our estimates suggest that there was indeed some decline in fertility in Kerala between 1951-61 and 1961-71, and rapidly falling fertility after 1961-71. As fertility declined faster in Kerala, the gap between the two has increased, and now it is as much as 8.6 per 1,000 in the CBR and 1.4 births per woman in the TFR. While the small difference in the 1951-61 fertility levels between Kerala and India was almost certainly due to the higher age at marriage among Kerala women, the large differences in fertility levels that we see at present arose mainly from the greater use of contraception in the State.

However, average estimates for the decade presented in Table 5 do not give enough information on the date of the onset of the rapid decline in fertility. The child-woman ratios computable from the census age distributions could be more helpful. Table 7 shows these ratios calculated from the last five censuses for Kerala as whole, and for its southern and northern parts.

Two kinds of ratios are presented, one obtained by dividing the population of ages 0-4 by women in the age interval 15-49 (CWR1), and the other by dividing the population of 5-9 by women in the age interval 20-54 (CWR2). The former ratio provides information on the level of fertility in the last five years preceding the census. The latter ratio gives the same information for the 5-9 years preceding the census. Let us explain this by an example, taking 1991 as the reference year. CWR1 is a measure of the children born between 0 and 4 years prior to 1991, i.e., in 1986-1991, to mothers aged 15-49 years. Thus:

TABLE 6: SRS Estimates of CBR and TFR, Kerala, Tamil Nadu and India

Year	Crude birth rate			Total fertility rate		
	Rural	Urban	Total	Rural	Urban	Total
KERALA						
1971-75	30.0	28.4	29.3	3.8	3.2	3.4
1976-80	26.6	25.0	26.3	3.2	2.7	3.1
1981-85	24.6	24.3	24.6	2.7	2.4	2.6
1986-90	20.7	21.4	20.9	2.1	2.0	2.1
1991-95	17.8	17.9	17.8	1.8	1.7	1.7
1996-00	17.7	18.0	17.9	1.8	1.8	1.8
TAMIL NADU						
1971-75	32.9	25.8	30.7	4.2	3.0	3.8
1976-80	30.4	26.5	29.2	3.9	3.2	3.6
1981-85	28.3	25.1	27.3	3.5	2.8	3.2
1986-90	23.4	22.3	23.0	2.7	2.2	2.5
1991-95	20.5	19.4	20.1	2.3	2.0	2.2
1996-00	20.0	18.2	19.3	2.1	1.8	2.0
INDIA						
1971-75	37.2	29.3	35.6	5.3	3.8	4.8
1976-80	34.7	28.1	33.4	4.8	3.4	4.5
1981-85	35.2	28.1	33.6	4.8	3.4	4.5
1986-90	33.0	26.1	31.4	4.3	3.0	4.0
1991-95	30.5	23.4	28.9	3.9	2.7	3.5
1996-00	28.2	21.1	26.5	3.5	2.3	3.2

Note: Compiled from various issues of Sample Registration System.

- The children in the age group 5-9 in 1991 would have been in the ages of 0-4 in 1986
- The women in the age group 20-54 in 1991 would have been in the age group 15-49 in 1986.

Thus, CWR1 and CWR2 give us the ratio of children aged 0-4 to mothers in the reproductive ages (15-49) at different points of time, i.e., 1986 and 1991. It should be noted that CWR2 is also influenced by the changes in mortality, though to a lesser degree.

Table 7 and Figure 8 show that both CWRs had increased between 1951 and 1961. There could have been two factors at work. One, a fall in infant and child mortality, and the other, a rise in fertility; a temporary increase in fertility just before its secular fall has been observed in number of populations (Dyson and Murphy 1985).

Between 1961 and 1971, we see a reduction in both the child-woman ratios in Kerala, which suggests that the level of fertility in 1956-1966 was lower than that of 1946-56. These finding supports the conclusion reached by P.R.G. Nair (1974) based on the trend in school enrolment rates to the effect that the fertility had begun to fall in Kerala even before the intensification of the family planning programme in 1965.

The trends in CWRs also indicate that fertility decline in 1961-1971 was far steeper in the Travancore-Cochin region as compared to the Malabar region. This suggests that fertility decline had begun earlier in Travancore-Cochin. It is quite possible that fertility had begun to fall in Travancore-Cochin even before 1961 because the increase in the child-woman ratios observed during 1951-61 was relatively small. However, to be certain, better information of the trend in infant and child mortality during this period is required.

Interestingly, there is a striking similarity in the pattern of change in the CWRs of the Malabar region and that of the nine districts adjacent to Kerala (Bhat and Rajan 1990).[5] Both sets of ratios have shown impressive declines. In the 1981-1991 census decade, however, the percentage decline was much higher for CWR2 than CWR1, indicating accelerated fertility decline between 1976-1986, especially the southern part of the State. The same phenomenon was observed in northern Kerala around 1986-91.

TABLE 7: Changes in Child-Woman Ratios in Kerala, 1951-91

Census Year	Kerala		Southern Kerala*		Northern Kerala*	
	CWR	% Change	CWR	% Change	CWR	% Change
Child-Women Ratio, 0-4						
1951	559		590		501	
1961	638	14	647	10	622	24
1971	550	-14	526	-19	591	-5
1981	406	-26	360	-32	482	-18
1991	290	-40	330	-19	252	-30
Child-Women Ratio, 5-9						
1951	544		576		481	
1961	698	28	722	25	657	37
1971	666	-5	656	-9	682	4
1981	524	-21	475	-28	605	-11
1991	403	-23	270	-43	339	-44

Notes: *Comprising of Thiruvananthapuram, Kollam, Alappuzha, Pathanamthitta, Kottayam, Idukki, Ernakulam, and Thrissur Districts in 1981 and Pathanamthitta in 1991 (roughly, the old Travancore-Cochin)

**Comprising of Kannur, Wayanad, Kozhikode, Malappuram, and Palakkad districts in 1981 (roughly the old Malabar).

FIGURE 8: Per cent Changes in CWR, Kerala and Regions, 1951-61 to 1981-1991

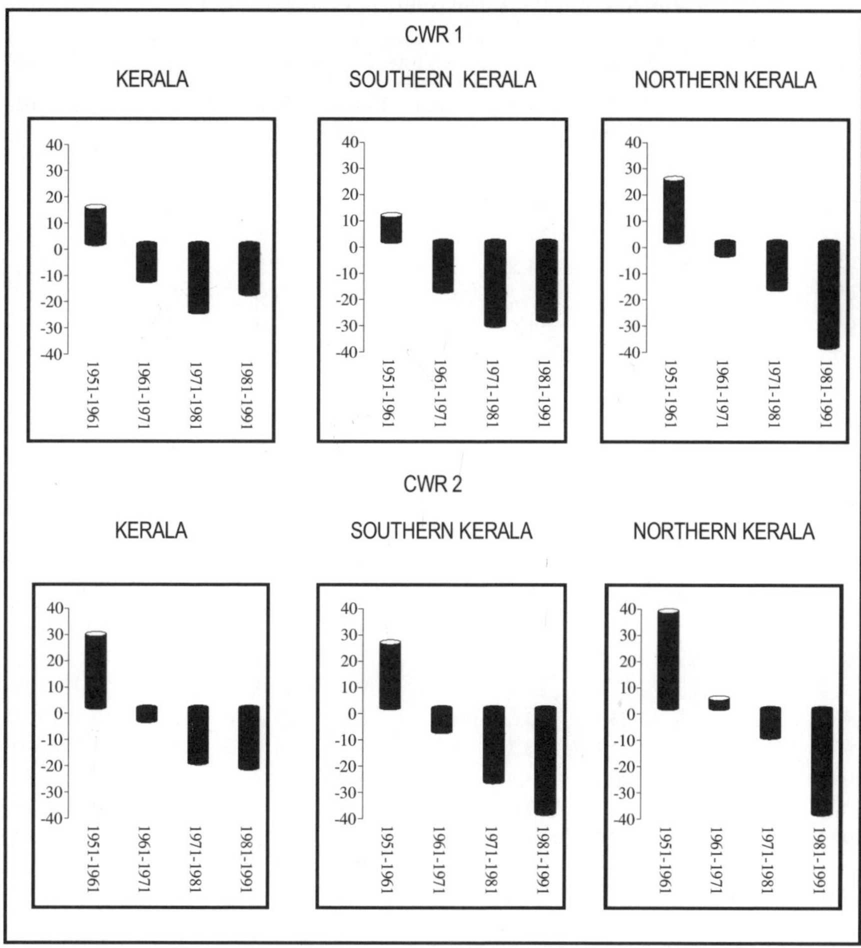

Fertility indicators derived from the Sample Registration System are provided in Table 8. A few conclusions may be drawn from these figures. According to the SRS, the CBR in Kerala declined from 31.1 in 1971 to 25.6 in 1981 (5.5 points) and to 16.6 in 1993 (9.0 points). The current CBR for Kerala is 16.9 as per the latest SRS bulletin, a slight increase compared to 1993 figures. (Figure 9 shows the comparative picture for Kerala, Tamil Nadu and India).

The TFR also registered the similar decline through out the period under study. For instance, the TFR was 4.1 children per woman in 1971, 3.1 children in 1980 and 2.1 children in 1990 and 1.7 in 2000.

TABLE 8: Crude Birth Rates, Crude Death Rates and Infant Mortality Rates, SRS Estimates, Kerala, Tamil Nadu and India, 1971-2002

Year	Crude birth rate			Crude death rate			Infant mortality rate		
	Kerala	Tamil Nadu	India	Kerala	Tamil Nadu	India	Kerala	Tamil Nadu	India
1971	31.1	31.4	36.9	9.0	14.4	14.9	58	113	129
1972	31.2	32.4	36.6	9.2	15.1	16.9	63	121	139
1973	29.2	30.0	34.6	8.5	14.1	15.5	54	108	134
1974	26.8	29.2	34.5	7.8	13.9	14.5	54	106	136
1975	28.0	30.7	35.2	8.4	15.0	15.9	54	112	140
1976	27.8	30.7	34.4	8.1	14.6	15.0	56	110	129
1977	25.8	29.8	33.0	7.3	13.7	14.7	47	103	130
1978	25.2	28.8	33.3	7.0	12.8	14.2	42	105	127
1979	25.8	28.9	33.7	6.9	12.1	13.0	43	100	120
1980	26.7	27.9	33.7	7.0	11.2	12.6	40	93	113
1981	25.6	28.0	33.9	6.6	11.8	12.5	37	91	110
1982	26.2	27.7	33.8	6.6	11.2	11.9	30	83	105
1983	24.9	27.9	33.7	6.7	11.7	11.9	33	87	105
1984	22.9	28.0	33.9	6.4	10.8	12.6	29	78	104
1985	23.3	24.7	32.9	6.5	9.5	11.8	31	81	97
1986	22.5	23.8	32.6	6.1	9.5	11.1	27	80	96
1987	21.7	23.6	32.2	6.1	9.7	10.9	28	76	95
1988	20.3	22.7	31.5	6.4	9.3	11.0	28	74	94
1989	20.3	23.1	30.6	6.1	8.6	10.3	21	68	91
1990	19.6	21.6	30.2	6.0	8.5	9.7	17	59	80
1991	18.3	20.8	29.3	6.0	8.8	9.8	16	57	80
1992	17.7	20.7	29.0	6.3	8.4	10.0	17	58	79
1993	17.4	19.5	28.5	6.0	8.2	9.2	13	56	74
1994	17.4	19.0	28.7	6.0	7.9	9.3	16	59	74
1995	18.0	20.3	28.3	6.0	8.0	9.0	15	54	74
1996	18.0	19.5	27.5	6.2	8.0	9.0	14	53	72
1997	17.9	19.0	27.2	6.2	8.0	8.9	12	53	71
1998	17.9	19.2	26.5	6.2	8.5	9.0	13	53	72
1999	17.9	19.3	26.0	6.2	8.0	8.6	13	52	70
2000	17.9	19.2	25.8	6.4	7.9	8.5	14	51	68
2002	16.9	18.5	25.0	6.4	7.7	8.1	10	44	63

Source: Compiled from Sample Registration System.

Note: CBR refers to number of live births during the year divided by the population in the same year multiplied by 1000; CDR refers to number of deaths during the year divided by the population in the same year multiplied by 1000. IMR refers to Infant Mortality Rate and defined as number of infant deaths during the year divided by number of live births during the year multiplied by 1000.

FIGURE 9: Crude Birth Rates for Kerala, Tamil Nadu and India, 1971-2002

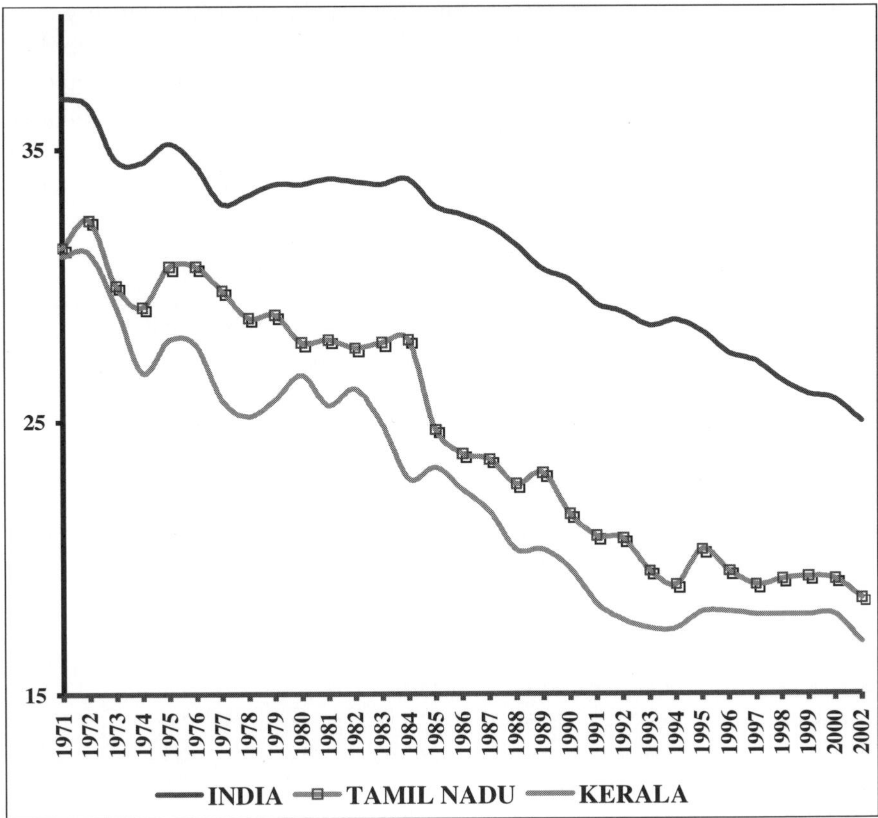

Kerala achieved replacement level of fertility at the beginning of the 1990s. At this stage, many demographers in India and abroad thought that further decline would be unlikely. Against their predictions, Kerala's TFR declined further to 1.7 by the year 1993 and has remained around the figure for the last 5 years.[6]

District Level Differentials

The birth rate varied considerably from region to region and from district to district. According to unofficial tabulations of the SRS data, in 1988, the birth rate varied from 14.8 in Alappuzha to 28.4 in Malappuram. While the birth rates in some districts in south Kerala such as Alappuzha, Ernakulam, Kottayam, Pathanamthitta seemed to have definitely dipped below the replacement level in the 1990s, the birth rate in some of the northern districts such as Malappuram, Kasaragod was reported in 1984-90 to be near the all-

India average. Such large inter-district variation in the birth rate in Kerala was confirmed by a more recent analysis by Bhat who has estimated fertility rates for all districts of Kerala using 1981 and 1991 censuses (Bhat, 1996). According to these estimates, the TFR varied from 1.6 in Ernakulam to 3.4 in Malappuram during 1984-90. In the beginning of 1990, only five districts (Palakkad, Malappuram, Wayanad, Kannur and Kasaragod) in Kerala have registered TFRs above the replacement level. The remaining districts had fertility below replacement level (details, see Table 9)

TABLE 9: Crude Birth Rate by Districts of Kerala, 1971-2001

District	Crude birth rate			Total fertility rate		
	74-80	84-90	94-00	74-80	84-90	94-00
Trivandrum	22.8	19.6	16.4	2.3	1.8	1.6
Kollam	23.3	18.5	16.2	2.7	1.8	1.6
Alappuzha	21.0	16.7	15.2	2.3	1.6	1.5
Pathanamthitta	n.a	17.2	14.5	—	1.7	1.5
Kottayam	20.1	16.6	15.6	2.4	1.7	1.6
Idukki	26.7	19.8	17.0	2.9	1.8	1.6
Ernakulam	21.4	16.9	15.7	2.4	1.6	1.5
Thrissur	22.2	18.7	16.1	2.5	1.9	1.6
Palakkad	22.5	18.8	17.3	3.4	2.4	1.8
Malappuram	33.6	29.5	22.4	4.3	3.4	2.4
Kozhikode	26.3	20.5	17.4	3.0	2.0	1.7
Wayanad	31.4	23.4	19.5	3.8	2.3	2.0
Kannur	28.8	20.5	16.6	3.5	2.1	1.7
Kasaragod	n.a	24.4	18.9	2.5	—	1.9
Kerala	25.0	20.3	17.1	2.9	2.0	1.7

Sources: Mari Bhat, 1996; Guilmoto and Irudaya Rajan, 2002.

As per the latest estimates based on the 2001 census, Malappuram is the only district in Kerala where the TFR is above replacement level (Guilmoto and Irudaya Rajan, 2002). The lowest TFR of 1.5 is reported for many districts including Alappuzha, Pathanamthitta and Ernakulam. More detailed spatial study on the fertility in Indian districts indicates that Alappuzha in Kerala was the forerunner of fertility decline even during the 1960s (Guilmoto and Irudaya Rajan, 2001).

If we assess the district level fertility estimates for Tamil Nadu, the trend indicates a fast decline in fertility in all districts. As per the latest estimates (1994-2000), Dharmapuri was the only district where the TFR was around 2.6 children. The TFR for Chennai was the lowest among all districts of Kerala and Tamil Nadu (Table 10)

TABLE 10: District Level Fertility Estimates for Tamil Nadu

District/State	Crude birth rate			Total fertility rate		
	1974-80	1984-90	1994-2000	1974-80	1984-90	1994-2000
Tamil Nadu	28.2	21.9	17.2	3.5	2.3	1.8
Chennai	24.7	19.4	13.5	2.7	1.8	1.3
Chengalpattu	31.0	24.4		3.8	2.5	-
Thiruvallur	-	-	18.4	-	-	1.9
Kancheepuram	-	-	17.7	-	-	1.9
North Arcot	32.9	24.6	-	4.3	2.6	-
Vellore	-	-	18.6	-	-	1.9
Tiruvannamalai	-	25.7	17.7	-	2.8	2.1
South Arcot	32.6	25.6	-	4.1	2.8	-
Cuddalore	-	-	18.7	-	-	2.1
Villupuram	-	-	18.9	-	-	2.1
Dharmapuri	32.1	26.3	20.9	4.2	3.0	2.6
Salem	24.1	19.5	17.4	2.8	2.0	1.9
Namakkal	-	-	15.3	-	-	1.7
Coimbatore	23.1	17.6	16.4	2.7	1.7	1.7
Erode	22.4	16.9	14.7	2.6	1.6	1.6
Nilgiris	27.2	19.2	16.3	3.0	1.6	1.6
Madurai	28.4	22.1	16.9	3.5	2.2	1.8
Theni	-	-	16.7	-	-	1.8
Dindigul	-	20.4	17.0	-	2.1	1.8
Tiruchchirapalli	26.2	21.1	16.6	3.2	2.2	1.8
Ariyalur	-	-	19.2	-	-	2.1
Karur	-	-	16.3	-	-	1.8
Perambalur	-	-	18.2	-	-	2.0
Thanjavur	26.5	21.4	17.1	3.3	2.3	1.8
Nagapattinam	-	-	17.9	-	-	1.9
Thiruvarur	-	-	17.3	-	-	1.8
Pudukkottai	30.1	22.2	19.0	3.9	2.3	2.0
Ramanathapuram	30.9	24.5	18.6	4.0	2.6	2.1
Virudhunagar	-	23.2	18.0	-	2.4	1.9
Sivaganga	-	21.4	16.8	-	2.3	1.9
Tirunelveli	29.9	22.5	17.8	3.9	2.4	1.9
Toothukudi	-	22.1	17.2	-	2.4	1.8
Kanniyakumari	26.6	19.7	15.4	3.4	2.1	1.6

Sources: 1974-80 and 1984-90: Bhat, P.N.M. (1996), 1994 -2000: Guilmoto and Rajan (2002).

Note: A dash indicates that the district had not been formed at the time of the census (1981 or 1991) or had been reorganised by the 2001 census.

Modeling Fertility at Village Level in Kerala, 1991 Census

Rural data from the 1991 census have been used to understand both determinants and differentials of fertility at the lower levels. As was done in our earlier studies, original village data have smoothed using the kriging technique. The result shows that fertility variations across rural Kerala were still sizeable in 1991, as recorded fertility levels in some localities could be twice as high as in other localities. The lowest fertility area is found along the coast from Thrissur in the North to Kollam in the south and includes the regions around Kochi and Kottayam (Map 1). Interestingly enough, Thiruvananthapuram is not part of this zone, which historically corresponds to the State of Cochin as well as the north of the Travancore State. Fertility is, however, significantly higher in the highlands to the east of the Coast. The influence of Coimbatore area in Tamil Nadu, whose fertility level is as low as in Alappuzha district, is visible in the border district of Palakkad.

The highest local fertility is recorded in the Malappuram district, most notably in the lowlands around Malappuram city. Malappuram is actually the only district in Kerala where child-woman ratios tend to decrease in hilly areas. The singularity of this district in terms of high fertility is mainly related to the proportion of Muslims, which account for no less than two-thirds of the district total. The analysis shows the clear demarcation between South and North Malabar, which used to be part of a single district of the Madras presidency during the colonial period.

This analysis also shows that fertility decline in Kerala has proceeded from a core area located between Alappuzha and Kochi. The Southern Ghats represented a visible barrier to the diffusion of fertility decline to the East, though the cultural barrier in South Malabar proved to be formidable. There, fertility rates resemble those observed in the Deccan Plateau, though recent estimates from the 2001 census show these regional differentials in Kerala to fade gradually. In the coming decade, district fertility levels in Kerala may become almost indistinguishable.

Fertility is expressed in terms of child woman ratio (CWR) in this analysis. As Kerala villages are relatively large, 1380 villages are used for regression analysis.

Using linear regression, the estimated coefficients are as follows:

Child Women Ratio = 538.2621-3.618+4.712MNW-0.747MW-
1.326FAL+0.2785PSch-
2.037SC-0.942ST-0.665D,

Where, FL = Female Literacy
MNW = Male non Workers
FMW = Female marginal workers

Map 1: Child-Women Ration

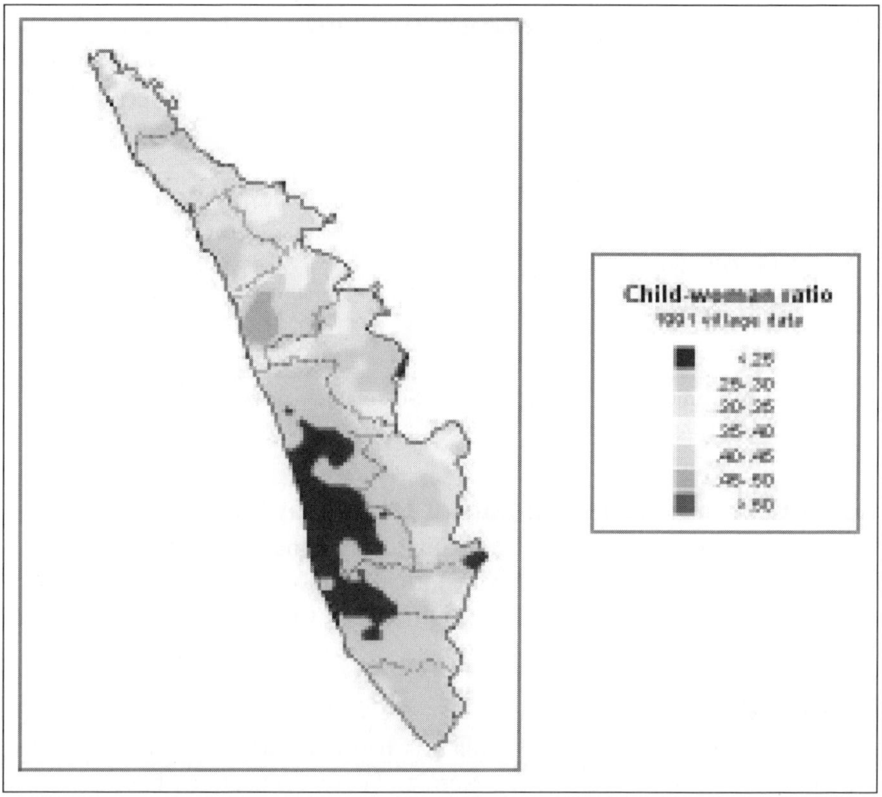

FAL= Female agricultural Labours
PSch = Primary School
SC = Scheduled Caste
ST = Scheduled Tribe
D = Density.

The results confirm the earliest fertility studies carried out in Kerala. However, a few observations can be made: variables such as female agricultural labor, female marginal workers, Scheduled Caste, Scheduled Tribes, settlement pattern and female literacy were found to be negatively significant whereas male non-workers is found be positively significant. Of the eight regression coefficients (the constant associated with each explanatory variable), all coefficients except the one corresponding to primary school found to be significantly different from zero.

TABLE 11: Results of Regression Analysis at Village Level Data, 1991

Child women ratio	Regression coefficient	T	P>lTl
% female literate	-3.61759	-17.592	0.000
% male non workers	4.711763	6.582	0.000
Population density	-.6647932	-2.788	0.005
% female marginal workers	-.7470145	-7.667	0.000
% female agricultural labourers	-1.325806	-11.968	0.000
Primary school	.2785184	1.038	0.300
% Scheduled Caste population	-2.037485	-8.708	0.000
% Scheduled Tribe population	-.9420171	-3.489	0.000
Constant	538.2621	13.933	0.000
N=1380			
R^2 = 0.3707			

Note: Child Woman Ratio = (population aged 0-6/Total female population age 7+)*1000
Primary school in the villages Dichotomous (Yes –1, No = 0)

Socio-Economic Determinants of Demographic Transition

In 1980, it was argued that the fertility decline that took place in Kerala in recent years was caused as much by historical developments as by recent policy interventions. This is true not only with respect to fertility decline, but also with respect to mortality decline.

Historical Aspects

From the very beginning, Kerala has had extensive contacts with other cultures, both within and outside Kerala. These connections have played a significant role in the socio-economic development of the state. From the other side of the Ghats came the caste and land tenure system; from West Asia came Christianity, Islam and Judaism; fro Europe also came Christianity as well as the modern administrative system, the plantation industry, modern education, public health and so on.

The Aryans, arriving two or three centuries before the Christian era, introduced the caste system, a dominant socio-economic and political force even today. The system had been so rigid in Kerala that people of lower caste could not come closer than a prescribed minimum distance when approaching those of higher castes.

Foreign influences have left some permanent marks on the population of Kerala. The State has a fairly balanced religious and caste composition that includes Nairs, Ezhavas, Christians and Muslims. As a result, no one group can profit at the expense of the other. Rather than forming permanent alliances, the various groups shift their alliances to suit their self-interests. The characteristic instability of the elected government and the give-and-take policies of each administration can be traced to a large extent to the balanced religious and caste composition of the population.

Historically, what distinguished Kerala most from the rest of India were the high density of population in the State and its achievements in the field of health, education and land reforms.

Kerala is one of the most densely populated states in India. Population density in Kerala was more than twice that of all-India even in 1901 and despite significant out-migration and fall in fertility, Kerala's population grew more rapidly than India's and by 1991, the density of the population grew to three times the India average. The high population density and the peculiar settlement pattern in the state make land reforms and other socio-economic reforms more relevant for fertility decline in Kerala than in other States in the country).

The modern formal educational system in the state owes its origin to the British rule in India and to the Christian missionaries who, finding a sizeable Christian population in the State, concentrated their efforts on education and health instead of proselytising. Fortunately, the indigenous tradition favoured education and the local rulers were supportive; by the end of the 19th century every village in the states of Travancore and Cochin had a primary school.

The influence of Europeans on health was similar to that on education. They provided the initial impetus for the development of a health care system, whereupon the indigenous tradition of scientific medicine and the wholehearted support of the local rulers carried the development forward.

It is against this historical background that recent socio-economic development and policy interventions are best viewed.

Health

The physical environment in most parts of Kerala is healthy and has always been so, except for Malaria tracts in the hills (Malaria has now been eradicated). Kerala also has a long tradition of medical and health treatment (the Ayurvedic system). The rulers have always taken an interest in health matters and have committed sufficient funds to both curative and preventive medicine. In addition, foreign missionaries established private hospitals with trained health personnel.

Health conditions in Kerala have always better than those in other parts of India, and recent developments have accentuated the disparity. The extent of this difference is indicated by the IMR, which in 1990 was about 17 in Kerala and 80 in India. The chance of an infant dying during the first 12 months of life elsewhere in India today is more than four times than the corresponding chance in Kerala. The continued improvement in the health conditions of the people is tied to their educational attainment and to the health policies which have brought medical facilities within their reach and their means.

The hospitals in Kerala are evenly distributed throughout the State. The easy access to medical facilities (due to relatively small service area and good transport facilities), the relatively low cost of medical services and the high demand for them (due to more educated population) are all important reasons for the comparatively better health conditions in Kerala than in other States of India.

Kerala is not so better off with respect to reported morbidity. The reported morbidity rates in Kerala are several times higher compared to those in other states of India. One reason for the higher rate in Kerala could be the high humidity conditions and the long rainy season. However, an important factor is also the much higher awareness and demand for medical treatment among the population of Kerala.

Education

The contrast between Kerala and India is equally striking with respect to educational attainment. In 1991, more than 90 percent of the people in Kerala were literate compared to 52 percent in India. Among females, the rates were 87 per cent in Kerala and 39 percent in India. The improvements in literacy levels in the decade 1981-91 was greater in Kerala than in India (21 percentage points compared to 16).

The development of education in the State owes much to the importance given to it in the Kerala culture and to the effort of the European missionaries. Historically, education was provided by using temples as centers, with non-formal education imparted to both men and women through religious stories and devotional songs. More recently, the rulers of both Travancore and Cochin gave considerable impetus to education by having the State pay the entire cost of primary education. These official efforts were supplemented by private efforts which began with the foreign missionaries' establishment of church-managed schools and colleges.

Formal channels of education i.e., the schools and colleges managed by the government, by private persons or organisations and recognised by appropriate government agencies are only part of the picture. There are a number of other educational institutions as well, including tutorial colleges and 'parallel' colleges. The parallel colleges in Kerala are a unique institution. While the tutorial colleges take students who fail in public examination, the parallel colleges take students who fail to gain admission to a recognized institution. Such students can study in parallel colleges and take the same examinations as those from recognised institutions. Thus through the system of parallel colleges, a higher level of education, especially in liberal arts, is made accessible to people from all walks of life.

Formal schools and colleges are more easily accessible to people of Kerala.

Although the average population served by a school is greater, Kerala spends a much higher proportion of its revenue for education than does India taken as a whole. Further, the State spends proportionately more money on primary education than on higher education as compared to the whole of India.

Two aspects of these educational developments are particularly relevant to the demographic transition. First, education is so widespread that there are practically no illiterate women or men in the prime reproductive ages. Second, the supply of educated personnel has been far in excess of demand, so that the problems of the educated unemployed are becoming progressively worse.

Political Awareness

Every aspect of life in Kerala is politicised. Newspaper reading and political discussions are a principal pastime of the average person. Protest marches, general strikes, bandhs, hunger strikes and other public demonstrations are as much a daily occurrence in Kerala as the monsoon in July. For some people participation in processions and protest meetings is a full-time job.

Such politicisation has many disruptive consequences, but it is not without beneficial effects. It has had the effect of making public services much more readily available for the poor in Kerala. Political awareness and the politicization of all issues, even those affecting only a small minority of the population, may be responsible for better delivery of government services than would otherwise be the case. What the people are eligible for, they obtain – by application, appeal or agitation.

Land Reform and other Distributive Policies

Undoubtedly, the most significant development in the recent political economy of the State is the shift in political power from the rich to the poor. Along with this shift, and as a consequence of it, there has been considerable transfer of wealth and income to the lower strata of the society. These changes have been brought about through land reforms, job reservation, enforcement of minimum wages, pension benefits for agricultural laborers and other deprived classes, reservation in educational institutions and on public bodies for the economically and socially backward.

Land reform was the principal means used to bring about a major distribution of wealth. The first post-independence legislative measure was adopted in 1957. It sought to assure permanent tenure to all tenants, to give tenants the right to purchase their land and to impose a ceiling on the total acreage a primary family unit could own. The proposal aroused considerable opposition, and as a result of the agitation, which followed, the government was dismissed. The Land Reform Act was finally passed in 1963, although its actual implementation was delayed by several more years. By 1969, tenancy was altogether eliminated, and rental income from land was virtually abolished throughout Kerala. The 1968 amendments to the Land Reform Act lowered the ceiling on landholding to ten acres, removed some of the exemptions from the ceiling and gave the 'hutment dwellers' the right to purchase about one-tenth of an acre of land per household at a nominal price.

The impact of these land reforms on the distribution of wealth has not been fully evaluated. It is likely to be greater on the Malabar area than in the former Travancore-Cochin area. Eviction from the huts had in fact been banned in much of Kerala some years before the Land Reform Act (in as early as 1949 in Travancore).

The Land Reform Act created a large middle class of owner-cultivators. These people should have gained by the reforms, as they were no longer required to pay rents to their landlords. But agrarian reforms simultaneously raised the wages and other benefits of farm workers. Since Kerala's middle-class farmers are accustomed to using hired labour for all their agricultural work, the higher wages increased the cost of cultivation considerably. At the same time, the prices of many agricultural products are controlled by the government. It is therefore doubtful whether land reforms have actually increased the income of the middle-class farming families.

Agricultural laborers constitute nearly one-fourth of the total workers in Kerala. They have benefited from the land reforms in two aspects. Most of them used to live in houses located on land owned by other people; they now have a permanent right to their house sites and to a piece of land immediately adjacent (ten cents in rural areas but much less in towns). They can, therefore, live in their houses without fear of eviction and begin to cultivate fruit trees and vegetables on their household plot. These workers have also benefited from the Minimum Wages Act and other agrarian reforms that fix wages and working conditions for all agricultural operations. The gains from higher daily wages have been partly offset, however, by losses due to the reduction in the number of days a wage earner can find work and in employment opportunities for other family members, especially grown-up children.

One long-term effect of these reforms will be the problems of finding house sites for the children when they grow up. No land owner will be prepared to lend his land to these children for fear that he will never get it back. These children will have to migrate out and find a place elsewhere to put up a house of their own.

The 1980s

Universal Immunisation Program

One of the very significant achievements of Kerala in the field of health is the great progress it made in immunising children and pregnant women in the 1980s. This was done under the umbrella of what is commonly known as the universal immunisation program (UIP) which is an international project supported by the World Health Organization (WHO). Although immunisation was a part of the MCH programs from the early 1970s, the UIP was launched only in 1985. The program was introduced in a phased manner beginning with just 30 districts in India. By 1989, all the districts in Kerala were brought under this program.

Under the UIP program, every child in the country was to be given three doses each of DPT and OPV, one dose of BCG, one does of measles vaccine, before the first birth day of the child. Pregnant women were to be given two doses of tetanus toxoid early in their pregnancy. The program was so successful that in just one year (1989), the all India IMR declined from 91 to 80 and Kerala's IMR declined by 11 points between 1988-90.

Universal (Total) Literacy Campaign

Total literacy campaign (TLC) in Kerala's education progress is like the UIP in Kerala's health progress. This campaign was aimed at eradicating illiteracy from the entire State. It began in Ernakulum district in 1989 and spread to Kottayam town and later to the entire State. It was supposed to have made every one between ages 5 to 60 literate. The initial program was completed in 1990 and a follow-up program initiated catering to special groups such as the Scheduled Castes and Tribes.

The TLC was a popular movement carried out by volunteers, directed by popular committees representing political parties, trade unions, student organisations, *mahila samajams*, etc. In addition to the popular committees, literacy brigades were constituted. The campaign was sponsored though the Kerala Sastra Sahitya Parishad in association with the Kerala Association for Non-Formal Education and Development. It was given the caption 'Operation Flood Light' under the general name 'Lead Kindly Light'. One noteworthy feature of the program was the *kala jathas* in which several artists gave performances at various places in the State. Street performances were also organised in thousands of places.

The State claimed 100 percent literacy (among five-60 years olds) by the end of 1990, but the change in the literacy rate in the State as a whole was relatively small as the level of literacy was already very high—a change of about 2 percentage points. But the program was able to achieve much more in changing people attitudes regarding the need to be literate.

World Bank Population Project (IPP-III), Kerala

The India population project III was started in Kerala in April 1984 and concluded in March 1990. It covered the four backward districts of Wayanad, Malappuram, Idukki and Palakkad. The main objectives of the project were to reduce fertility and mortality rates by improving the MCH services in the project districts, and improving coverage and quality of health and family welfare services through better facilities, training and management. The inputs included physical facilities such as buildings, equipments, and other supplies, vehicles, additional staff, training facilities and support for Information, Education and Communication (IEC) and the Management Information and Evaluation System (MIES).

The final evaluation of the project indicated that a significant decline in birth rate took place during the project period in Wayanad and Idukki districts with only moderate declines in Palakkad and Malappuram. Most of the married women availed of ante-natal care, and about 60 percent of children were fully immunised. A majority of the births took place in hospitals and were attended either by a doctor or a nurse.

Gulf Migration

The 1980s saw Kerala becoming as much part of the countries of the Gulf as it is part of India. The State has become integrated with these countries, economically and socially. Practically every household in Kerala is affected directly or indirectly by the emigration of the workers to the Gulf. A significant proportion of the households are directly affected in the sense that one or more of their members have emigrated to the Gulf and contribute to the household expenditure. Others are affected indirectly thorough socio-economic changes in the State, and changes which can be traced to the emigration. The latter include female education, prices, housing, employment, wages, transportation and status of women.

Around 1975, the estimated migrants in the Gulf from India was about 154,000, a majority of whom were from Kerala. A study conducted by the Department of Economics and Statistics, Government of Kerala in 1987 placed the total out-migrants from Kerala at 680,000, of whom 301,000 were Gulf emigrants (Government of Kerala, Department of Economics and Statistics, 1994). In our earlier study, we have estimated that nearly 10 percent of households from Ernakulum, Palakkad and Malappuram districts had at least one emigrant who had been living in Gulf countries at least six months, the largest being in Malappuram with 15 percent (Zachariah *et. al.*1994). A rough estimate of the number of emigrants from Kerala in 1991 based our Kerala Fertility Survey data is about 600,000. Another estimate made during the same period by the Bureau of Economics and Statistics indicated that the estimated number of emigrants in Gulf and other foreign countries numbered around 669,000. This trend continued even today with 1.84 million in 2004, from

1.36 million in 1999 (Zachariah, Mathew and Irudaya Rajan, 2003; Zachariah and Irudaya Rajan, 2004).

Emigration had a very significant impact on the status of women in Kerala, especially Muslim women. Since the man of the house was away in a Gulf country, women were forced to take the responsibilities usually borne by the man – responsibilities related to education of children, banking, investments and similar financial responsibilities, social obligations, etc. One important aspect of this change is the tremendous improvement in the education of girls who benefited more than boys, as some of the boys themselves had emigrated. A large proportion of the emigration was from the Muslim communities in the backward coastal areas. Emigration opened up these communities to modern ideas about female education, maternal and child health and family planning (more details on this aspect, see Zachariah and Irudaya Rajan 2001). Increase in the income of the households thorough remittances and transfer of goods has enabled many of the households to improve their housing conditions, consume nutritious food, acquire modern consumer items, and educate their children and to utilise doctors and hospital facilities for health problems. In these and several other ways, emigration played significant role in the demographic transition in Kerala in the 1980s.

Other Determinants of the Demographic Transition

Fertility and mortality experienced a very significant decline during the 1980s. The extent of the decline was larger than predicated in the beginning of the decade. What were the factors associated with this accelerated decline? The immediate or proximate causes for the decline in fertility were the increase in age at marriage and the increased use of family planning, especially sterilisation.

Family planning was also a proximate determinant of mortality decline. However, the most important proximate determinant of mortality decline was the UIP, especially antenatal care. This program not only provided immunisation to mother and children but more importantly, it brought the population closer to the health system and this indirectly increased the utilisation of health facilities for delivering babies, for treating the sick and for family planning. The IPP-III, which covered four backward districts including Palakkad and Malappuram, is also a factor which has to be reckoned with.

Whatever the immediate means by which fertility and mortality rates were reduced, the basic underlying factors were a series of socio-economic changes which made it an economic necessity for the parents to improve the quality of their children – quality in terms of health, nutrition and education. The socio-economic changes were described in detail in the study done by Zachariah (1984). The additional factors in the 1980s were the accelerated emigration to the countries in the Gulf which continued throughout the period, the UIP which was introduced in 1985, the World Bank project which was executed during 1985-90, and the Sakshartha program (the universal literacy program) which begun in Ernakulum in 1980.

In the World Bank study (1984), prime importance was given to education for generating a series of changes, which brought about and quickened the demographic transition. The introduction of formal education as a criterion of public services brought about a basic change in society after centuries of fundamental stability. Society became, so to say, unhinged, with the ushering in of a movement away from inherited and towards achieved status, from interdependence of caste to competition, from traditional authority to modern bureaucracy.

In the changed economic perspective, children of high quality become not merely desirable, but they became essential for upward social mobility and even for sheer economic survival both for the well-to-do and for the poor. Formerly, the rich could fall back on the family's land or connections to make a decent living and maintain their status in the society. This was no longer possible. Lacking adequate education (and good health) a person could not make a living on the basis of caste or religion or from land alone. For the poor and those of lower caste, education offered the only hope of getting out of the circle of illiteracy, poor health and poverty. With recent political changes, and with all the social and economic reforms favouring them, the poor saw a chance to improve their lives. Education and good health were key prerequisites.

Education and health care are getting more and more expensive each day. Even without any changes in the cost per child, the total cost to a family to educate and to provide good health to children would have increased because of the decline in infant and child mortality and the consequent increase in the number of surviving children.

On the positive side, though the short term economic benefits of children have shrunk as the tight employment situation has reduced their chances of obtaining paid work outside the home, there is reason to believe that the long-term benefits of children might have increased. But these benefits come only if the necessary initial investment is made in a child's education. With the increase in both the cost per child and the number of surviving children, most families in Kerala simply do not have the resources to make the initial investment too often. They have, therefore reduced their family size, opting for a well-endowed small family over an ill-endowed large one.

It is, however, doubtful whether the recent sharp decline in marital fertility and infant mortality, which has embraced all socio-economic groups, was caused solely by these long-term changes in attitude concerning the need for quality children. More likely, it was precipitated by more recent policy interventions (land reforms, agrarian reforms, the UIP, the TLC, and the (universal) family planning program) and accelerated migration to Gulf.

The land reforms and other re-distributive policies which were introduced in the State in the late 1960s continued to accelerate the need for healthier and well-educated children; the increased emigration opened up some of the hitherto closed populations to modern ideas about family size, education and health and provided the needed income to realise them; the UIP, the World Bank project and the family planning program helped to translate the manifest or latent desire for fewer and healthier children into actual fertility and mortality reductions; and the universal literacy program helped not only in creating additional demand, but also in the better utilisation of the government's policies and programs in health and family planning.

Not all families are directly involved in emigration in the sense that one of their members is an emigrant, but almost all families in Kerala now directly or indirectly affected by it in terms of increased income and exposure to modern ideas about education, nutrition, health, family planning and family size. Emigration not only helped to created additional demand for health services, education and family planning, but also provided additional income to achieve these objectives.

The official family planning program is not merely a means for providing contraceptive services; it has also been an independent causal factor in changing family size norms, and in creating and strengthening the demand for family planning. In Kerala, it went one step further. As a result of the economic incentives offered to officials and acceptors, the program was able to create demand even where it did not exist previously. Thus the program provided services where demand existed, strengthened demand where it was weak, and created demand especially among the poor where no demand existed previously.

The role of the UIP in creating demand for antenatal care and child immunisation is even larger than that of family planning. The program by its very effective communication strategy played a major role in creating demand for higher nutritional levels among pregnant women and their children and a host of other health-related practices.

The interaction between fertility and mortality decline which were strengthened in this decade is a major additional factor. The universal literacy program worked in the background to strengthen this interaction. The MCH program had an impact not only on mortality but also on fertility. It brought the people to closer to health system which also delivered family planning. Similarly, the accelerated fertility decline resulted in fewer unwanted births, and births at older ages, thus reducing the infant mortality.

A good deal of credit should go the official policies in education, family planning and health, not only in provided the needed services but also in creating additional demand for these and related services. The socio-economic changes created the necessary milieu in which family planning and MCH programs were not only desirable but also necessary and essential. The family planning and MCH programs created additional demand for themselves, and also provided the means by which fertility and mortality could be reduced.

NOTES

1. The calculation of State income does not include remittances arising out of migration. If remittances have to be included in the State income, it would have been more than 20% percent than the present state domestic product (State Planning Board 2003).
2. The current peri-natal mortality rate is 18 for Kerala whereas the still birth rate is 11. Both are extremely high in Kerala, given the level of IMR (Irudaya Rajan and Mohanachandran 1999).
3. The inter-censal estimates of fertility shown in the table are somewhat higher than the official estimates. This is because any census-based estimate of the CBR is derived either explicitly or implicitly assuming a level of infant and child mortality. The official estimates of infant and child mortality are biased downward, so are the birth rate estimates. It may also be noted that the estimates of fertility measures from the SRS for 1971-81 are somewhat lower than the census-based estimates.
4. We do not have reliable estimates of fertility levels for periods before 1951 but it is unlikely that the levels were much higher than that of 1951-61
5. The nine districts belong to Tamil Nadu and Karnataka. They are: Kannyakumari, Tirunelveli, Madurai, Ramanathapuram, Coimbatore and Nilgiri districts of Tamil Nadu and Mysore, Kodagu and Dakshina Kannada districts of Karnataka.
6. According to the SRS, the crude birth rate declined by just 1 point during the last 10 years and almost no change in the total fertility rate (TFR).

REFERENCES

Bhat, P.N. Mari. 1987. Mortality in India: Levels, Trends and Patterns.Ph.D Dissertation. University of Pennsylvania, USA.

Bhat, P.N. Mari, and S Irudaya Rajan. 1990. Demographic Transition in Kerala Revisited. *Economic and Political Weekly.* Vol. 25, No. 35-36, pp. 1957-80.

Bhat, P.N. Mari, 1996. Contours of Fertility Decline in India: A District Level Study Based on the 1991 Census. Chapter 4, pp. 96-177 in K Srinivasan, eds. *Population Policy and Reproductive Health.* Hindustan Publishing Corporation, New Delhi.

Guilmoto, C.Z. and S. Irudaya Rajan. 2001. Spatial Patterns of Fertility Transition in Indian Districts. *Population and Development Review*, Vol. 27, No.4.

Guilmoto, C.Z. and S. Irudaya Rajan. 2002. District Level Estimates of Fertility from India's 2001 Census. *Economic and Political Weekly*, Volume XXXVII, No.7, pp.665-672.

Guilmoto, C.Z. and Irudaya Rajan (eds) 2005 Fertility Transition in South India. Sage Publications, New Delhi.

International Institute for Population Sciences. 2000. *National Family Health Survey (NFHS-2), 1998-99.* Mumbai.

Irudaya Rajan, S. and U.S. Mishra. 1996. Fertility Transition in Kerala: Implications for Educational Planning. *Productivity*, Vol. 37, No. 3, October-December, pp. 386-96.

Irudaya Rajan, S. and U.S. Mishra. 1997a. Kerala: Restructuring Welfare Programs -

Emerging Trends. *Economic and Political Weekly*, Vol. 32, No. 6, pp. 261-63.

Irudaya Rajan, S. and U.S. Mishra. 1997b. Population Ageing: Causes and Consequences. Chapter 12, pp. 222-236 in K.C. Zachariah and S. Irudaya Rajan. eds. 1997. *Kerala's Demographic Transition: Determinants and Consequences*. Sage Publications, New Delhi.

Irudaya Rajan, S. and K.C. Zachariah. 1998. Long Term Implications of Low Fertility in Kerala, India. *Asia Pacific Population Journal*, Vol. 13, No.3, pp. 41-65.

Irudaya Rajan and P Mohanachandran. 1999. Estimating Infant Mortality in Kerala. *Economic and Political Weekly*, Vol. 34, No. 12, pp.713-717.

Irudaya Rajan, S. 2005. Emerging Demographic Change in South India. pp. 23-52 as Introduction in Guilmoto, C.Z. and Irudaya Rajan. eds. 2005 Fertility Transition in South India. Sage Publications, New Delhi.

Irudaya Rajan, S and Sabu Aliyar. 2005. Fertility Change in Kerala. Chapter 5, pp. 167-190 in Guilmoto, C.Z. and Irudaya Rajan (eds) 2005 Fertility Transition in South India. Sage Publications, New Delhi.

Krishnamoorthy, S., P.M. Kulkarni and N. Audinaryana. 2005. Causes of Fertility Transition in Tamil Nadu. Chapter 7, pp. 227-247 in 281 in Guilmoto, C.Z. and Irudaya Rajan, eds. 2005 Fertility Transition in South India. Sage Publications, New Delhi.

Rajna, P.N., P.M. Kulkarni and N. Thenmozhi. 2005. Fertility in Tamil Nadu: Level and Recent Trends. Chapter 6, pp. 191-226. 281 in Guilmoto, C.Z. and Irudaya Rajan, eds. 2005 Fertility Transition in South India. Sage Publications, New Delhi

State Planning Board, Government of Kerala. 2003. *Economic Review 2002*, Thiruvananthapuram.

Vella Stephane. 2005. Low Fertility and Female Discrimination in South India: The Puzzle of Salem District in Tamil Nadu. Chapter 8, pp. 248-281 in Guilmoto, C.Z. and Irudaya Rajan (eds) 2005 Fertility Transition in South India. Sage Publications, New Delhi.

Zachariah, K.C. 1984. The Anomaly of the Fertility Decline in India's Kerala State: A Field Investigation. Staff Working Paper No. 700, World Bank, Washington D.C.

Zachariah, K.C., S. Irudaya Rajan, P.S. Sarma, K. Navaneetham, P.S. Gopinathan Nair and U S Mishra, 1994. Reprinted in 1999. *Demographic Transition in Kerala in the 1980s*. Centre for Development Studies Monograph Series, Thiruvananthapuram.

Zachariah, K.C. and S. Irudaya Rajan. eds. 1997. *Kerala's Demographic Transition: Determinants and Consequences*. Sage Publications, New Delhi.

Zachariah, K.C. and S. Irudaya Rajan. 2001. Gender Dimensions of Migration in Kerala: Macro and Micro Evidences. Asia Pacific Population Journal, Volume 16, No.3, pp. 47-70.

Zachariah, K.C., E.T. Mathew and S. Irudaya Rajan. 2003. *Dynamics of Migration in Kerala: Dimensions, Differentials and Consequences*. Orient Longman Private Limited. Hyderabad.

Zachariah, K.C. and S. Irudaya Rajan. 2004. Gulf Revisited. Centre for Development Studies, Working Paper No. 363, September. Thiruvananthapuram (www.cds.edu).

Part V

FAMILY PLANNING AND REPRODUCTIVE HEALTH

Chapter 8

The Decentralised Approach in the Indian Health and Family Planning Programme

Nirmala Murthy

Decentralisation involves transferring authority and responsibility to lower levels of government. It can take a number of forms: political decentralisation, in which citizens or their representatives get power to decide policies and programmes at local levels; functional decentralisation, in which central government transfers some of its functions such as planning and personnel, to local level governments, while retaining control over budget and policy making functions; or fiscal decentralisation, in which local level governments participate in budgetary and financial decision-making (Gilson *et al.* 1994).

India practices all three forms of decentralisation, to varying degrees, at different administrative levels. For example, the enactment of the 73rd–74th Amendment to the Constitution allows devolution of powers to plan, implement and monitor development programmes, including those of health and family welfare, to local governments. Not all elements of this policy however have been implemented uniformly in all the States. Functional decentralisation is practiced mainly at the State level and to some extent, at the district level, when district level managers are willing to take responsibility. For example, under functional decentralisation, local administrators can decide whether to compress the duration of a training course or lower the qualifications or offer incentives to recruits to fill staff posts in backward regions under their jurisdiction. Fiscal decentralisation is practiced very selectively and usually at levels where own sources of revenue are available. Local governments that depend almost entirely on grants from the State or central government, on the other hand, have little scope to practice financial decentralisation. They get funds tied to various schemes and programmes, along with guidelines on how to spend them.

In India, the first major decentralisation initiative began in mid 1960's, with Community Development Planning based on the Balwant Rai Committee report. In 1987, Karnataka State undertook political decentralisation of all development programmes to the district level, to *Panchayati Raj* Institutions. The State government however could not sustain that undertaking because of its inability to correspondingly devolve the financial and personnel functions to local governments (Satishchandran TR, 1993). Later in 1993, with the 73rd–74th amendment to the constitution, GOI facilitated this type of decentralisation by allowing transfer of development budget to the local self-government bodies. In the context of population, India's National Population Policy (2002) shows the GOI's commitment to decentralisation. In the NPP, decentralisation planning and implementation is one of the 12 operational strategies to address deficiencies in the family welfare programme, by giving planning and implementation responsibilities to local *panchayats*. Some State policies have gone even further, by giving *panchayat*s a role in resource mobilisation and performance based allocation.

Decentralised Approach: Advantages and Risks

A decentralised approach is needed in situations where there is high variability in delivery and utilisation of services, as is the case in different regions of the country, due to different demand and supply constraints. Different regions also have different opportunities. For example, the more developed States have better health facilities and more educated clientele than the under-developed States. The decentralised approach has many advantages in such situations. It facilitates the best use of locally available resources to overcome the local constraints (Box 1).

Decentralisation also has a few risks especially in the context of sensitive services like reproductive health and family planning. Local government authorities might not, for example, adhere to the national policy guidelines such as not offering cash incentives to contraceptives acceptors. Local authorities being usually more susceptible to cultural barriers, might not provide abortion services or contraceptives to adolescents. The decentralised approach can also lead to increase in inequity if resource-rich regions provide more and better quality services than resource-poor regions (Box 1).

Indian Family Planning Programme: Need for Decentralisation

India has created a vast rural public health infrastructure consisting of 137 thousand sub-health centers, 23 thousand primary health centers, about 3 thousand rural hospitals and over 500 district hospitals to deliver health and family planning services. This impressive infrastructure however has failed to provide adequate quantity and quality of services especially to the rural poor (Verma *et al.* 1994). Health centers are not well equipped or staffed. Sterilisation operations are still conducted in makeshift camps in villages that lack basic amenities and cleanliness. People have to wait long for surgeons to arrive from district hospitals and sometimes return home if the camp is canceled. Surveys show 30-40 percent acceptors suffering from contraceptive side effects and going to private doctors for treatment. Researchers blame this situation on the centralised system of setting contraceptive targets. Under this system, the 'health staff is rewarded if they fulfill the targets and punished if they do not. Everybody focuses on recruiting contraceptive acceptors and pays little attention to pre-existing infections, to counseling women and to addressing the issue of side effects because the programme strategy has become persuasion, incentive and pressure' (Murthy & Barua 1998).

BOX 1: Advantages and Risks of Decentralised Approach

Advantages	(i)	Increased local accountability for health outcomes.
	(ii)	Higher responsiveness to local health needs.
	(iii)	Efficient management of resources.
	(iv)	Use of local information in planning.
	(v)	Better inter-agency coordination.
Risks	(i)	Disregard for national policy guidelines.
	(ii)	Cultural barriers detrimental to the programme.
	(iii)	Increased inequity.

As a result, the Indian family planning programme became a sterilisation programme in which operations were conducted in unhygienic conditions and by 'speed' doctors performing 300-500 operations in a single day (Banarage 1998). Health staff did not feel they were under obligation to provide *quality* services; after all, they were providing *free* services and, and, besides, women were getting monetary incentives for undergoing sterilisation operations (Ramasundaram 1994). Field experiments, on the other hand, have shown that 'target and incentive' was not the correct strategy to increase contraceptive use. Contraceptive use actually increases when the programme provides a broad range of mother and child-care services of acceptable quality (Measham & Heaver, 1996; Ramasundaram 1995).

Soon after the Cairo conference in April 1995, which reflected the new wisdom, the GOI declared two districts in each State to be 'target-free'. This was to be an experiment to find out how well the FP programme would function without contraceptive targets. In April 1996, before the experiment could be evaluated, the GOI declared the entire country to be 'target-free'.

The GOI also decided to provide a package of reproductive health services through the family planning programme and to adopt a decentralised planning approach to help deliver quality reproductive health and family planning services. The need for decentralisation was justified because health and family planning indicators showed wide variations between States and among districts within each State (Table 1).

TABLE 1: District Variations in Selected RCH Indicators from RCH-RHS (2002-03), IIPS, Deonar Mumbai

State	CPR (Any Method)	Modern method	Full Imm.	Safe Delivery	CBR
Andhra Pradesh	53.7-71.9	53.4-71.4	28.1-83.6	49.3-96.7	14.6-17.9
Assam	12.2-70.2	12.1-44.1	0.7-47.3	8.5-56.1	11.8-22.8
Bihar	22.9-36.8	18.9-33.9	9.5-41.3	15.4-49.2	19.7-32.8
Chhattisgarh	34.9-57.3	31.4-56.9	48.9-68	25.9-66.4	14.6-24.8
Delhi	60-66	50.3-60.6	40-71.2	64.5-77.9	14.6-24.1
Gujarat	41.2-69.8	37.8-60.8	31-73.2	50.3-86.4	16.0-25.5
Haryana	41.6-69.9	36.4-65.3	36.7-90.8	34.4-78.3	18.6-30.5
Jharakhand	22.7-50.7	19.3-45.8	7.7-51	21-55.6	15.5-25.8
Karnataka	41.7-73.7	40.3-73.5	48.1 95.2	41.2-95.7	14.3-24.4
Kerala	52.6-84.5	37.6-61.9	54.5-92.3	91.2-100	15.7-22.6
Madhya Pradesh	27.3-67.2	27.2-65.9	10.5-60.5	13.9-88.9	16.1-27.9
Maharasthra	55.2-73.6	53.4-73.4	36.2-96	52.6-94.2	11.9-21.3
Orissa	43.6-61.9	34.9-47.4	36.7-74	18.1-61.7	18.2-19.3
Punjab	64.7-70.6	49.8-59.1	49.6-90.7	80.4-95.3	16.6-20.7
Rajasthan	24.5-57.4	23.4-54.1	12.3-36.6	28.6-57.4	21.1-32.6
Tamil Nadu	43.9-71.3	42.3-65.2	84.7-98.4	77.7-98.9	15.1-22.3
Uttar Pradesh	21.3-55.1	14.3-51.1	14.3-51.6	9.8-50.7	19.7-36.5
West Bengal	68.3-82.4	47.5-62.7	27.9-64	49.8-88.5	11.6-23.6
Overall	12.2-84.5	12.1-73.5	0.7-98.4	8.5-100	11.6-36.5

The GOI's decision to replace the target system with decentralised planning received an enthusiastic initial response from many quarters for a variety of reasons. Policy makers responded positively because decentralisation was a national policy. Health Workers welcomed it because no targets meant less work for them. District administrators were happy because with decentralisation they expected devolution of financial and administrative powers to their level.

Implementing Decentralisation Through CNAA

The CNAA, or Community Needs Assessment Approach (CNAA), required that health workers set their own targets. Outlining how this was to be done, CNAA guidelines to health workers stated: 'Work out the (service) requirement by conducting a household survey. Validate the estimate of requirement through discussion with anganwadi workers, members of Mahila Swasthya Sangha (women's health group), panchayat members etc. Relate this estimate with the birth rate of the area and with the achievements in the previous year to ensure that the estimated needs are realistic. Then develop a plan that meets the needs and is realistic' (GOI, 1998)

Many policy makers were not convinced that CNAA would help curtail population growth. The National Family Health Surveys had shown that there was already 20 percent unmet need for contraception and meeting that 'need' would bring about the required fertility decline. Combining FP with a package of RH services would, it was felt, dilute the programme emphasis on FP services. The proponents of this view believed that India's number one priority was population control and the new approach was not likely to help achieve it.

Apart from this, there was discontent from different quarters.

- Programme managers were not convinced that workers were capable of developing their work plans. They feared that workers would underestimate service needs in their areas to reduce their workload. They were also not likely to work without the target pressure, it was felt.
- Health workers were happy about the targets being removed but were not happy about having to involve community members in the planning exercise. 'They (community members) don't know what is good for them. Then how can they help us to plan'? workers asked.

The GOI promised to review the CNAA after one year, 'when details would be worked out, mistakes would be corrected, and confusion would be sorted out' (Reddy *et. al.* 2000). The CNAA guidelines were deliberately kept broad so that different States would develop different approaches as per their needs. As expected, some States undertook surveys to assess community's health needs; some used service norms to calculate service needs; some used past performance as indicative of service needs. Broadly, three main approaches emerged:

(i) The normative approach
(ii) The need-based approach
(iii) The combination approach

The Normative Approach

In this approach, States developed norms for various health and family planning services, using which health workers estimated service requirements in their areas. For example, the norm for prenatal care could be 100 percent of estimated pregnant women; the norm for sterilisation operation could be all women who delivered their third or higher order child and half of those who delivered their second child. These norms automatically ensured that districts with higher birth rates would plan to meet higher requirement for health and family planning services than districts with lower birth rates.

Health workers were trained to use these norms. This usually resulted in somewhat higher contraceptive targets but workers hardly complained, because they thought the targets were rationally decided. The policy of decentralised planning had also envisaged not involving other departmental staff for recruiting FP cases, as was practiced under the previous system. As a result, health workers did not have to compete with non-health staff for recruiting cases nor did they have to bribe women to accept contraceptives.

Tamil Nadu, where this approach was implemented most effectively, was able to maintain a high level of contraceptive acceptance and at the same time, increase maternal and child care services (Ramasundaram 1995).

Need-Based Approach

In this approach, couples are given contraceptive choice. Workers carry out house-to-house surveys to enlist couples that do not want more children or want to space the next child, but are not using contraception. Health workers liked this approach because it made their family planning work systematic. They knew which method to promote with whom. But they also found that converting people's 'needs' into actual use was still hard work. For their bosses, it meant that workers were not doing a sincere job of assessing needs.

This approach was mainly tried in Rajasthan where, at the end of one year, the State recorded a 150 percent increase in use of spacing methods but a 25 percent decline in sterilisation acceptance. Workers explained this decline as due to low demand for sterilisation. 'Couples who did not want more children also did not want to undergo sterilisation operation because they are afraid of the operation', they said. Supervisors did not accept this explanation. 'Workers were spending more time doing the survey and less on motivating couples', they said. Therefore, to boost sterilisation acceptance, the State government asked health workers to aim at sterilising at least 70 percent of couples who did not want more children. After establishing that norm, sterilisation performance did increase but remained below the levels achieved during the target era (Table 2).

Combination Approach

This approach was the closest to the GOI's planning guidelines. It included the use of norms and of the need assessment surveys. First, workers estimate service 'requirements' using State norms. Then they carry out surveys to assess 'needs' for health and FP services and set their workloads somewhere within or close to the range (Table 3). In practice, most workers accepted the 'requirements' as their workloads because their bosses had decided the norms and therefore they were safe if they accepted them. They used surveys for increasing contacts with community and to identify services that needed awareness-creation (Murthy and Nagaraj 1998). For example, workers knew who among their clients preferred institutional deliveries and who did not; who did not want more children, and who did not know/use ORS during diarrhea. These surveys also helped create awareness in the community about the reproductive and child health services being provided. Workers felt ownership of the plans they had developed and showed higher commitment to fulfilling them

TABLE 2: RCH Performance Before and after Initiating Decentralisation Through CNAA in Three States

Indicator	Year	State			India
		Karnataka	Rajasthan	Tamil Nadu	
% children fully immunised	1993	52.2	21.1	64.9	35.4
	1999	67.6	30.1	90.1	42.0
% Couples using modern contraceptive methods	1993	46.4	27.1	45.5	36.2
	1999	56.5	38.1	50.3	42.8
% Share of Spacing Methods	1993	10.2	10.4	12.7	
	1999	8.0	15.2	8.5	
% Delivery by trained professional	1993	50.9	21.8	71.2	34.2
	1999	64.7	32.2	80.9	42.5
Birth Rate (SRS estimate)	1993	25.9	33.2	23.5	28.7
	1999	22.7	32.1	19.0	26.5

Source: National family Health Survey, 1993, 1998.

Impact of Decentralisation through CNAA

Considering the size of the country and the socio-economical differences between States, the GOI had expected the States to follow different approaches to community needs assessment with different impact. There was also no denying that this approach had demystified the system of target setting. Yet the policy was expected to produce some positive impacts such as:

(i) Priority for reproductive health services,
(ii) Improving quality of services,
(iii) Increasing client satisfaction with services,
(iv) Improving effectiveness of family planning programme, and
(v) Enhancing community participation in service planning.

Though no formal policy impact assessment was carried out, case studies carried out by several non-governmental organisations showed significant achievements in some areas and not at all in others.

TABLE 3: Sub-center Action Plan: An Example from Karnataka

Service	Service Norm	Service Need	Performance	
			Past	Planned
• ANC Registration	138	136	162	140
• Early ANC Registration (before 16 weeks)	82	121	72	85
• High risk pregnant women referred	20	44	19	20
• Therapeutic Iron supplement to pregnant women	69	122	85	70
• TT injection to Pregnant Women	138	136	140	140
• Three prenatal visits by pregnant women	138	125	110	135
• Institutional delivery	46	95	23	45
• Deliveries by midwifery trained persons	130	123	75	125
• Weighing of newborn	130	121	76	120
• Referral of high risk newborn	12	40	2	10
• Children protected against six vaccine preventable diseases	130	124	125	130
• Children given Vitamin-A Prophylactic	130	125	84	130
• Spacing Method	69	56	91	70
• Sterilisation	62	75	38	60

Priority for Reproductive Health Services

Most case studies indicated that prenatal care and delivery by trained persons had become the new programme priority. Health workers were showing more interest in registering pregnant women for prenatal care than in recruiting family planning cases. That was because out of 12 indicators used for programme monitoring, five were related to mother care (early registration of pregnancy, minimum three prenatal check-ups, TT and IFA, deliveries by midwifery trained persons, and treatment of RTI). All major States recorded sizable increases in delivery by trained persons (from 34 percent in 1993 to 42 percent) as shown in NFHS 1, 1993 and NFHS 2, in 1998).

Because they were providing more health services and not just pursuing family planning targets, workers reported their image in the community had improved. A worker from Tamil Nadu for example reported 'Now that the target pressure is off we are able to inquire about health problems of women and of children. People do not call us family planning workers. They also consult us about other ailments' (Visaria and Visaria, 1999).

Workers in Rajasthan reported becoming more productive because 'earlier we used to wander around looking for family planning cases; now we work more systematically'. Though they were carrying more workload, providing 15-18 services, their work gave them more respectability, they felt (Population Council 1997). In spite of the increased workload they were happy because supervisors did not 'scold' them for not meeting targets.

Quality of Contraceptive Services

With no pressure to fulfill targets, health staff were expected to screen women for contraindications, treat them for pre-existing infections, and help them make informed choice of contraception. Contraceptive side effects was one of the indicators used for monitoring that effect. A study in Karnataka found nearly 50 percent decline in the reported side effects after the targets were removed, may be because women received the methods they desired and were not forced to accept any method to fulfill method-specific targets (Johnson *et al.* 2000).

However, by and large, the programme's quality of contraceptive service had a demographic impact. Still, States reported improved quality in terms of increased contraceptive use among young couples, and not in terms of women screened for contraindications or counseled for informed choice. RCH household surveys however found that only 30 percent women were informed about contraceptive side effects and only 25 percent had received after-care, indicating the extent of work needed to improve the quality of contraceptive services (IIPS 1999).

Client Satisfaction with Services

Women, by and large, reported no change in the way health workers provided services because of decentralisation (Chatterji 1999). Several case studies also reported that community leaders did not know about the FP programme being decentralised though they had heard about targets being removed. But one change many women noticed was that they got the contraceptive methods of their choice. A woman in Rajasthan village said: 'In my time, the ANM forced me go for operation. But now I see she gives oral pills to women if they don't want an operation'. Also, health staff had become conscious about satisfying clients. Some reported referring cases to private doctors if government health centers did not have equipment and supplies. By doing so, they thought women were getting better quality service because private doctors thoroughly examine patients and prescribed more drugs than government doctors (Bhatia and Cleland 1999).

Effectiveness of Family Planning Programme

The initial impact of decentralisation in target setting was a sudden decline in contraceptive acceptance, especially in sterilisation operations all over the country. But that decline was not uniform. In the developed States, the decline was marginal i.e. 5 to 10 percent. In underdeveloped States, it was substantial, more than 30 percent. Health officers attributed the 'less than 10 percent decline' to reduction in misreporting. 'Now that the targets are removed, workers do not have to exaggerate their performance', they said. But they attributed the more than 30 percent decline to the removal of the targets. Many officers reported that workers were interpreting 'no targets' to mean 'no work'. A case study in Uttar Pradesh reported that it was so not only in the case of the field level workers, but also with service providers at higher levels. District hospitals had drastically reduced the number of sterilisation camps they held because there was no target pressure on them. Workers complained that doctors did not conduct as many operations as they did before because they had no targets; only workers had them.

Most States reacted to the initial decline in contraceptive acceptance in different ways. Some went back to setting the targets; some announced incentives for acceptors; most adopted norm-based planning, keeping the façade of decentralised planning. May be as a result, the contraceptive acceptance improved in subsequent years (Table 4 and chart 1). The no-target policy however, was not a disaster for the family planning. The programme statistics in most States reported increased use of spacing methods, especially among younger couples. The birth rate continued to decline from 27.5 in 1996 to 26.1 in 1999, to 25.0 in 2002 in spite of the declines in sterilisation rates during that period (Table 4 and chart 1), suggesting that programme effectiveness might have actually increased.

TABLE 4: Contraceptive Acceptance by Method and Birth Rates, 1993-2000, India

Year	Sterilisation$	IUD$	Oral Pill$	Birth rate@
1993-94	4497000	6017000	4302000	28.7
1994-95	4580000	6702000	4873000	28.7
1995-96	4422000	6858000	5091000	28.3
1996-97	3870000	5681000	5250000	27.5
1997-98	4239000	6173000	6395000	27.2
1998-99	4207000	6083000	6944000	26.5
1999-00	4595000	6200000	7748000	26.1
2000-01	4735000	6046000	7640000	25.8
2001-02	4827000	6262000	8691000	25.4
2002-03	4793000*	6121000*	9237000*	25
2003-04	4875000*	6079000*	8751000*	NA

$. http://mohfw.nic.in/dofw%20website/achievements/achieve-main.htm on 9.8.2005.
@. http://cbhidghs.nic.in/HII2004/2.02.htm on 9.8.2005.
* Figures are provisional.
NA. Not available.

CHART 1: Contraceptive Acceptance and Birth Rates, India, 1993/94–2003/04

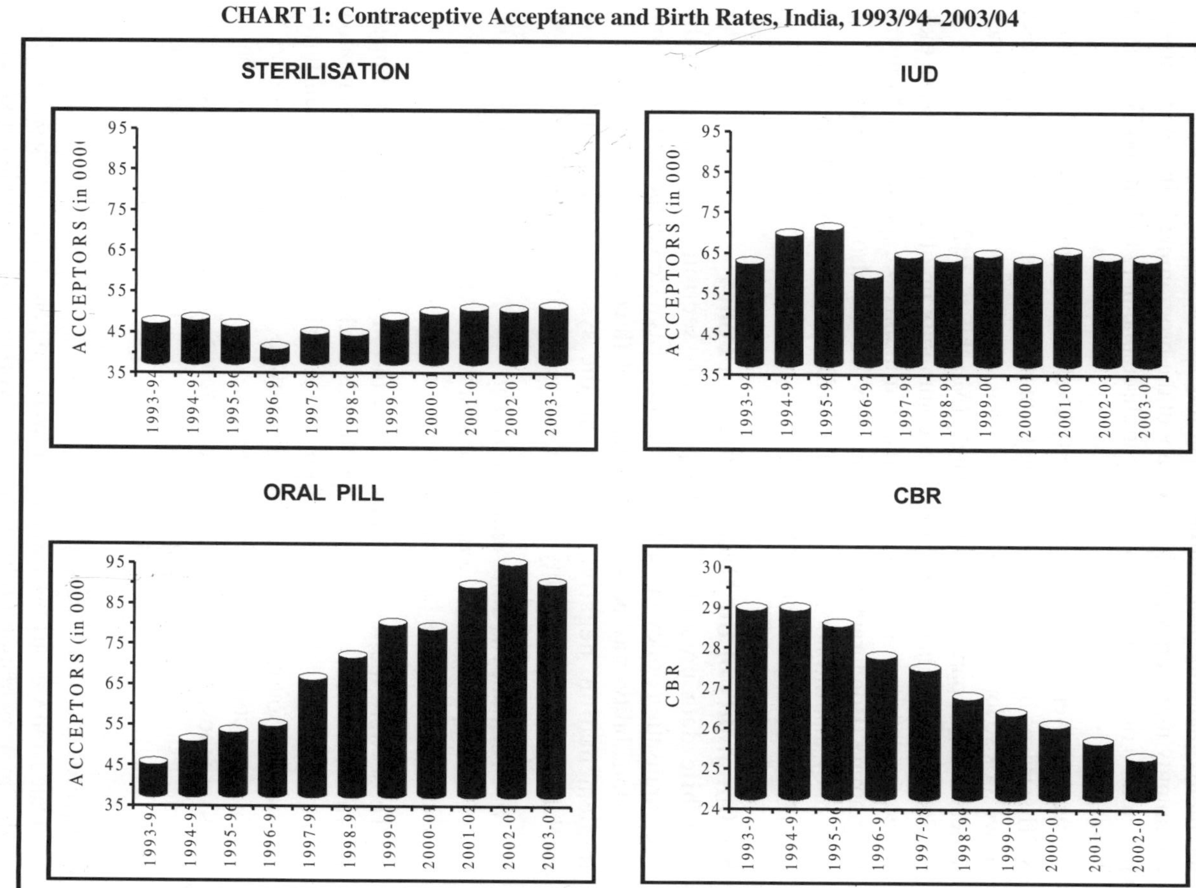

Community Participation

The policy had the least success in promoting community participation in the family planning programme. According to one study, only 20 percent of community members vaguely knew about the programme being made target-free and no one had heard about decentralised planning (Khan and Townsend 1998).

Workers were organising community level meetings to inform people about RCH services but were not involving them in planning the services because, 'If we took so long to understand how to calculate the needs how could women understand and participate in planning?' (Murthy *et. al.* 2001).

State officers also did not insist on community involvement because they were afraid that it might increase the community's expectations from the programme (Bondurant 1997). Community leaders also had little interest in the policy that did not involve transfer of funds or control of health staff to them (Kalway and Rawat 1999).

Sustainability of the Decentralisation Policy

While data presented in the previous section suggested that the decentralisation policy in the FP programme was a step in the right direction, its sustainability may be gauged in terms of three criteria, namely, ease of implementation, negative impacts on the system, and incentives for implementers. Sustainability of any policy is low if:

(i) The policy is *difficult to implement,*
(ii) The policy has *negative* effects on the system, and
(iii) Implementers have no *incentives* to implement the policy.

Those were the lessons learned from the Philippines local government reform effort, which was the most ambitious health decentralisation initiative ever undertaken in Asia. In this reform, the central government had transferred additional resources and administrative powers to the local governments to implement public health services. However, some of the local authorities began to misuse those powers particularly in personnel selection and in financing of technical support. The result was decrease in service quality and decline in service delivery (World Bank 1994).

Implementation Difficulties

Data from various field studies showed two potentially serious difficulties in the implementation of this policy: (1) Workers thought their workload had increased and (2) supervisors complained that their authority had been undermined.

'Under the CNAA, we are expected to meet targets of not 1 but 18 services', workers complained. In most States they also suffered financial losses because they were not getting the special allowances they used to get for recruiting family planning cases.

Decentralised planning also meant that supervisors could not decide workloads of workers under them; workers decided their own workloads. Supervisors therefore felt a loss of authority. 'Earlier we told them what to do, now they tell us what they would do. In that case how can we control them?' supervisors asked (Salunke & Narvekar 1997). Supervisors therefore preferred State-specified norms because the norms did not give the workers the flexibility to decide their workloads (Murthy and Nagaraj 1997).

Negative Effects on the System

For many years, the States had looked upon family planning as the Center's programme and merely complained about irrational targets the Center was imposing on them. But when the GOI stopped setting the targets, the States stepped into that role. One negative effect of this development on the system was that States developed their own planning guidelines that were sometimes contrary to the GOI's guidelines. Some continued with the targets as before; some even introduced incentives for family planning acceptors. As a result, the planning process became less transparent. Workers reported that they still had targets though they called them by different names like 'self-determined targets', 'expected level of achievements (ELA)', and 'service needs'.

Another negative effect on the system was the weakening of teamwork among health staff. Supervisors took no responsibility for implementing workers' plans. Workers complained, 'Earlier when we had targets, the entire health team felt responsible for them. But now our plans are our responsibility. We get no cooperation from our doctors'. Doctors organised fewer service camps and carried out fewer operations than before. If the policy had required doctors to plan, instead of workers, perhaps the entire health team would have been involved in implementing plans and teamwork would have been better.

Lack of Incentives for Implementers

The removal of targets was a good enough incentive for the health staff to want to implement the policy. But programme administrators at the district level and below were disappointed with it because the policy offered them no incentives in the form of devolution of powers to go along with the decentralisation concept.

Incentive for health workers in implementing this policy was the promise of their improved status in the system. They could decide their workloads and were not pulled up by supervisors for not meeting the targets. State level administrators also had the incentive that they could control the programme by developing work norms that reflected States' priorities. Most high performing States also received financial envelopes i.e., unallocated funds to implement their priorities. These envelopes, though not very large, were a beginning of decentralisation at the State level in priority setting in the family planning programme.

On the other hand, supervisory staff at the district level and below or the community leaders had no incentive in implementing the decentralisation policy. Supervisors had no role in deciding the targets and lost the power over workers in terms of supervising their achievements. Community leaders were disappointed that *panchayats* received no fund to implement this policy (Kalway and Rawat 1999). They were expected to participate in consultation meetings with health workers to discuss the local health needs and to develop local plans accordingly. That participation did not materialise as envisaged. 'Why would they want to participate?' asked one doctor. 'In pulse polio, we pay them to participate. In RCH, there is no money even for a cup of tea if they come for meetings'.

Thus these case studies showed that decentralisation through CNAA had meager chance of being effective or sustained. Therefore search for other approaches to decentralisation also began simultaneously.

Other Approaches

Decentralisation is usually a political decision. However, the decentralisation through the CNA approach attempted in the Indian FP programme was an administrative decision. It involved no structural or procedural changes in the programme, only a tactical change of allowing workers to estimate their own workloads using the centrally determined guidelines. This decision was a part of GOI's commitment, announced during the ICPD, to making its family planning services user friendly and sensitive to clients' needs.

However the CNA approach tried out to fulfill this commitment lacked two essential elements of decentralisation: (1) local situation analysis and (2) involvement of local community. It also lacked substantive involvement of three other administrative levels in the system i.e. district, block and PHC that have the implementation responsibility. CNAA was also criticised for being narrowly focused on estimating the number of potential beneficiaries of various health and family planning services and not on addressing local problems and constraints in implementing the health and family planning programmes (Murthy and Vasan 1999). Decentralisation planning was needed to address issues such as reducing variability in the access, utilisation and quality of existing health care facilities and exploring options for augmenting service delivery to meet local needs. Since such issues are handled mostly at the district level and sometimes at the block level, decentralisation was needed first at those levels and not at the health worker level. Other approaches being tried to introduce decentralisation at these levels include:

a. District Health Societies

GOI agreed to start autonomous health and family welfare societies at State and district levels to manage donor funded health programmes, especially in States that were facing severe budgetary deficits. These societies helped introduce functional decentralisation in the health programmes at the district level. There are now close to 200 such societies managing project funds and health activities at the district level. They are expected to undertake district level health assessments, set local priorities, and find solutions to local problems.

This model has become a vehicle for decentralised planning and implementation at the district level. Experience so far shows that it is a powerful tool for decentralisation in the hands of dynamic district collectors who take interest in the programme. However, in situations where collectors have short tenures and an overload of responsibilities, these societies function only as a fund-flow mechanism (Narayana 1993; Murthy N. 2002).

b. Sector Investment Programme

Sector Investment Programme (SIP) assisted by the European Commission (EC) is another approach to decentralisation being tried in 11 States. This programme addresses systemic issues such as gaps in infrastructure, sub-optimal use of health staff, and inefficient financial management etc. through the district Health and Family Welfare (H&FW) agencies set up as autonomous societies. SIP releases funds to district H&FW Agencies based on pre-determined performance benchmarks so that they can have smooth fund flow to implement the district plans. A review of SIP experience however, showed that lack of funds is not the only bottleneck for implementing a decentralisation approach. Lack of clear guidelines from the States / Center also affects the decentralisation process. Without such guidelines the district level staff hesitates to take decisions especially those regarding local purchases and financial transactions (Dayalchand & Murthy 2002).

c. District Cluster Strategy

In this strategy, the aim is to build partnerships between government and non-government health functionaries at community level to deliver health services in remote and under served areas. These functionaries form 'Health and Nutrition Teams' to undertake micro planning that contain actions needed to overcome constraints encountered in delivering services in the remote and under-served areas (Example: Box 1). Engagement with this strategy has heightened interest and enhanced commitment of health functionaries towards delivering the health services. The strategy helps to ensure (1) adequacy of consumable items (2) geographical reach of services (3) improved service utilisation and quality.

BOX 1: Action, Constraints and Solutions for Improving PNC Services (an example)

Expected actions	Constraints	Solutions
AWW to take newborn weight in their areas	(i) Lack of weighing scales at AWW	(i) Supply of weighing scales from CDMO
	(ii) Cultural barrier against weighing newborns	(ii) Organise behavior change communication through TBAs
	(iii) Postnatal visits low because workers do not understand the need	(iii) Joint training of HW, AWW & TBA to be organised by CDMO & CDPO

d. State Innovations in Family Planning Services (SIFPSA)

Under SIFPSA, an autonomous agency is created at the State level to promote development of District Action Plans based on adequate and reliable district level data, by involving stakeholders and by devolving appropriate authority to the district level. Autonomous district agencies (DIFPSA) are established to implement these plans. These agencies have authority over their budgets. District Magistrates chair these agencies and have health officers, NGO representatives, local industrialists and prominent citizens as their members.

e. Strengthening District Health Management

This is another approach to strengthen decentralisation at the district level. In this, the aim is to make efficient use of available resources. Using a quality of care framework, certain priority areas are identified for improvement, such as maintenance of facility or equipment, mobility of health staff and medicine to peripheral health centers etc. State and district level committees are set up that involve a broad range of stakeholders, to ensure that funds flow to peripheral institutions. For example: PHC and CHC medical officers are authorised to carry out petty repairs of buildings; health staff is given fixed travel allowance to improve their mobility; a drug management system is developed to ensure adequate and timely drug supply to health centers. However, effectiveness of this approach is conditional on reforms in government policies and procedures. For example, a CHC medical officer would have little incentive to undertake repair works at his CHC if he is required to get a completion certificate of works from engineers of rural works department before getting paid. Many such procedures need modifications for encouraging local initiatives and decentralised management.

f. Marginal Budgeting for Bottlenecks (MBB)

This tool attempts to identify major bottlenecks in the health system, estimates the cost of removing them and improvements expected as a result. In this tool certain health services are defined as 'tracer' interventions that have high impact at relatively low cost on the health outcomes. For example, in maternal and neonatal care 'safe delivery using the 5 cleans' is defined as a tracer intervention.

Using this tool, district planning teams select major bottleneck, identify actions needed to remove them, decide who will implement those 'actions', and who will pay for them. For example, if a team identifies accessibility to immunisation service as the bottleneck, then the associated 'actions' could be micro planning of regular outreach sessions, fixed day clinic sessions and catch-up sessions in remote areas. After these actions are implemented the tool is used again to identify the next bottleneck and new 'actions'. MBB thus is a dynamic process decentralised planning but requires a large quantity of data.

Emerging Challenges

The preceding description of various efforts at decentralisation shows a lot of interest and vigorous search for effective decentralisation approaches to planning and implementation of the health and family planning programme. Many tools and methodologies are being developed. Some of them are very data and analysis dependent; some involve many stakeholders; some involve devolution of planning and financial authority to local levels.

Reviews of many of these approaches show that the necessary conditions for their success are: availability of local database, better communication between different levels of administration and capacity building of programme managers at different levels (Dayalchand & Murthy, 2002; Anirudh Krishna, 2003).

Creating reliable databases for use in local planning is a challenge. For example, during a planning exercise in one district participants commented, 'Our infrastructure looks better on paper than on the ground'. They refused to believe the official data presented to them. One officer said, 'Our data shows 95% ANM positions are filled. But that is misleading. Do you know that because supervisory posts are vacant and Government does not want to fill those posts that many ANM are holding additional charge as supervisors? They are not working as ANMs. In reality, there is a severe shortage of ANMs'. In another district, participants said, 'Your data shows we have many hospitals but you must see their condition. Most are very old buildings, ready to collapse. Our staff cannot use those buildings; they provide services under a tree'.

It is not unusual to find that local administrators dispute official data and even do not trust the survey data. Under those conditions, allowing local authorities to suggest modifications or engaging them in situation analysis strengthens the decentralisation process.

Successful decentralisation processes provide opportunities for different stakeholders to participate because each stakeholder groups view health problems and solutions differently. Administrators usually think the problem is clients' lack of awareness. Service providers see the problem as clients not accepting their advice. Community members blame under-utilisation on the cost or lack of access to services'. It is therefore important to ensure that the three groups are adequately represented in the decentralised planning process and the consultations should be structured such that each group participates fully in it. Participative methods like voting – brainstorming, round robin and consensus building help to get diverse views of stakeholders' on the table.

How One Team Selected a Problem for Decentralised Action Planning

In this workshop, the three stakeholder groups (administrators, service providers, community representatives) discussed various problems in their district such as women being not aware, staff demanding money, poor work environment, political interference, unsafe areas, long distances etc. for low utilisation of maternal care services by poor women. The list contained nearly 14 problems. Thereafter they individually selected one or two problems as the 'most important problem' to be addressed through decentralised planning. The workshop facilitator compiled the results.

When facilitator informed the three groups that they had selected 'services not affordable' as the most important problem, the administrators' group vehemently disagreed. They first suspected compilation errors but found none. They again discussed those problems and again voted on them. This time, the administrator's group had selected 'women not aware of services' while other two groups had selected 'non affordability' as the most important problem.

When the three groups presented their respective selection in the plenary, the administrator's group refused to accept 'non-affordability' as the problem. Government services are free, they argued. Members from the other two groups tried to describe the ground realities of the 'free' government services that make even poor women seek private services, which they cannot afford. Finally after much debate all agreed to accept community members' view that poor women indeed find the maternal services not affordable because of time, distance, payment they have to make at government clinics etc.

Experience has also shown that these processes need external facilitation to ensure that pressures of hierarchy and barrier of language do not affect participation by different stakeholder groups. External facilitators could help the teams to not get bogged down by many programme constraints and feel helpless. Typically, local planners tend to get bogged down by problems such as women being illiterate and poor; traditional society, joint families, corruption, bad personnel policies etc about which they can do little. They look up to the government for help and all solutions. They rarely think of mobilising local resources (cash or kind) as feasible. They feel safe if there is a government order permitting them to take any action. In such situations, techniques such as appreciative inquiry can help local planners to recognise the positive aspects of their situations and utilise opportunities that exist (Amanda Trosten-Bloom 1999). Best Practice literature can also aid in finding solutions to problem.

GOI/State governments should provide the most critical help of removing bottlenecks in the process of decentralisation.

Another prerequisite for decentralised planning and management is good quality local data. Though local planners usually have a fairly good idea of local situation and problems, some form of quantification does help to resolve conflicts and build consensus among planners. Decentralisation would get a huge boost if periodic surveys are undertaken to generate district level data and planners are trained in using the data.

Most of those efforts discussed above, with the exception of CNAA, have been tried on a small scale and in a project mode. The emerging challenge therefore is how to scale them up and sustain them. Meeting that challenge may require:

(i) Developing a cadre of facilitators who know national health programmes and strategies, understand management practices and have critical thinking capacity.

(ii) Establishing sound accountability through proper monitoring and supervision of locally developed plans. Involving communities in the monitoring would strengthen the local government's accountability.

(iii) Involving non-health but related sectors such as education, women and child welfare, rural development etc. in the decentralisation process through greater inter-sectoral collaboration.

(iv) Initially expecting decentralisation only in tasks that are delegated to the district level such as service provision, supervision, coordination, in-service training etc. Later decentralisation might be extended to areas such as deciding programme policies, budgets, resource mobilisation, allocations etc. That would ensure that the process is well established and can be sustainable.

REFERENCES

Banarage A. 1998. *Women, Population and Global Crisis*. Zed Books: London.

Bhatia J.C. and John Cleland. 1999. 'Health seeking behavior of women and cost incurred: an analysis of prospective data', in Saroj Pachauri ed. *Implementing a Reproductive Health Agenda in India: the Beginning*. Population Council, New Delhi, 207-232.

Bose, Ashish. 1996. 'In search of a New Strategy for Family Planning in India', in Ashish Bose and P.B. Desai eds. *Population and Planning in India*. Delhi: BR Publishing Corp.

Bondurant Tony. 1997. 'The introduction of the target free approach in West Bengal: a case study'. Paper presented at the national workshop on the performance of family welfare programme under target free approach, Lucknow Uttar Pradesh, November 24-25.

Chatterji, S. and Pappu K. 'Health Watch Case Study: West Bengal', in *Community Needs based Reproductive and Child Health in India – Progress and Constraints*, Health Watch Trust, Jaipur, India.

GOI. 1986. National Health Policy. New Delhi: Ministry of Health and Family Welfare.

GOI. 1998. *Manual on Community Needs Assessment Approach*. New Delhi: Department of Family Welfare, Ministry of Health and FW.

Health Watch. 1999. 'Voices from the Ground: A review of Post-ICPD family welfare programme implementation'. SAHAYOG, Premkuti, Pokharhali, U. P. India.

IIPS. 1999. 'Findings from District Reproductive & Child Health Surveys'. Deonar Mumbai, monograph.

Jain Anirudh. 1997. 'Consistency between contraceptive use and fertility in India'. *Demography India*. Vol. 26, Number 1.

M. Johnson Samuel, M. Lingaraju, P. Prabhuswamy, 2000. 'Has abolition of targets improved the quality of family planning and health services? – A Survey in Karnataka'. *Journal of Health Management*. New Delhi: Sage Publications. 2 (1): 99-112.

Jejeebhoy S. 1997. 'Addressing women's reproductive health needs: Priorities for the family welfare programme'. *Economic & Political Weekly*. March 1-8.

Kalway K. and Rawat M. 1999. 'Family Welfare Programme in MP after ICPD: a case study', in *Community Needs based Reproductive and Child Health in India – Progress and Constraints*, Health Watch Trust, Jaipur, India.

Khan M.E., Townsend, J.W. 1998. 'Has the Indian family welfare programme lost momentum under the TFA? Emerging evidence'. Paper presented at the workshop on the TFA approach. World Bank, New Delhi, April 2-3.

Lubhaya Ram. 1997. 'Target Free Approach for Family Welfare: a review of experiences in Rajasthan'. The Futures Group International, 4/2 Shanti Niketan, New Delhi.

Measham A.R. and Heaver R.A. 1996. *India's Family Welfare Programme: Moving to a Reproductive and Child Health Approach*. Washington D.C.: The World Bank.

Mukhopadhyay S. and Sivaramayya J. 1999. 'Forging New Partnerships: Towards empowerment'. in Saroj Pachauri ed. *Implementing a Reproductive Health Agenda in India: The Beginning*. New Delhi: Population Council. Pp. 335-353.

Murthy, N. 'Decentralised Health Planning: Lessons from Two Districts in India'. *Journal of Health and Population in Developing Countries*. 1(2), 1-10.

Murthy, N. 1999. 'The Quality of Family Welfare Services in Rural Maharashtra: insights from a client survey', in Koenig and Khan eds. *Improving Quality of Care in India's Family Welfare Programme*. New York: Population Council. 33-48.

Murthy, N. Barua, A. 1998. 'Integrating reproductive health in health programmes in India', in Maithreyi Krishnaraj *et al.* eds. *Gender, Population and Development*. New Delhi: Oxford University Press. 293-309

Murthy N., Nagaraj, G.V. 1998. 'Implementing decentralised planning in family welfare programme: an experience from Dharwad district'. Working Paper, Foundation for Research in Health System, Ahmedabad.

Murthy N., Vasan A. 1999. 'Improving District Family Welfare Services: A decentralised planning model'. *The Journal of Health Management*. New Delhi: Sage Publications. 1 (1): 35-53.

Nirmala Murthy, Lakshmi Ramachandar, Pertti Pelto, and Akhila Vasan. " Dismantling India's old Contraceptive Target System: an overview and three case studies (a chapter in a casebook by the Population Council, reference to be completed).

IIPS. 1995. *National Family Health Survey (MCH and Family Planning), India 1992-93*.

Operations Evaluation Department (OED). 1998. *Lessons form Experience in HNP*. Report Number 18642, World Bank.

Pachauri, Saroj. 1998. 'Defining a reproductive health package for India: A proposed framework', in Maithreyi Krishnaraj *et al*. eds. *Gender, Population and Development*. 310-339. New Delhi: Oxford University Press.

Population Council. 1997. 'Implementing target free approach in Family welfare Programme'. Case studies prepared for the National Workshop on Target free Approach, November 24-25, Lucknow.

Ramachandran, Vimala. 1996. 'NGOs in the time of Globalisation'. *Seminar*. No. 447, November.

Ramasundaram, S. 1994. 'Quality of Care in Health and Family Welfare Programme'. Paper presented at the Seminar on Quality of Care, Gujarat Institute of Development Research, April 28-29, 1994, Ahmedabad, India.

Ramasundaram, S. 1995. 'End of the target era'. *Voices*. 3(2). Bangalore, India.

Reddy, M. Ramakrishna, Rayappa, P. Hanumamtha, Raju, K.N.M. 2000. 'Target Free Approach in family Planning—a critique'. *Demography India*. 29 (2): 255-276

Ross, J.A. 1997. *'The Policy Project, Targets for family planning in India: an analysis of policy change, consequences and alternative choices'*. New Delhi: The Futures Group

Salunke Subhash and Sharad Narveka. 1997. *Target Free Approach for Family Planning: a review of experience in Maharashtra.* The Policy Project, The Futures Group International, New Delhi 1997

The Futures Group International. 2001. *'Review of Implementation of Community Needs Assessment: Approach for family welfare in India'*. Policy Project II, New Delhi, India

The World Bank. 1994. 'Philippines Devolution and health Services: managing risks and opportunities'. Country department 1, population and human resources operation division, east Asia and pacific Region office

The World Bank. 1995. *India's Family Welfare Programme: Toward a reproductive and child health approach*. Population and Human Resources Operations Division, South Asia Country Department II

The World Bank. 1997. *India: Reproductive and Child Health Project.* Project appraisal document, 32-36, Population and Human Resources Operations Division, South Asia Region.

UNFPA. 1998. 'Participatory planning and quality of care for Population & Development: UNFPA's experience in India'. unpublished

Verma, Ravi K., Roy T.K., Saxena P.C. 1994. 'Quality of Family Welfare Services in Selected Indian States'. (monograph). International Institute of Population Sciences, Mumbai.

Visaria L. and Visaria P., 1999. 'Field level reflections of policy change', in Saroj Pachauri (ed). *Implementing a Reproductive Health Agenda in India: The Beginning*. Population Council, New Delhi, 77-109.

Chapter 9

Reproductive Health of Punjabi Women: Socio-Psychological Probings

Komila Parthi

Reproductive health—the ability to reproduce and to regulate fertility; to undergo pregnancy and child birth safely; be free of obstetric and gynecological disorders, and have the capacity for enjoyment of sexual relations free from the fear of pregnancy or of contracting disease—is a rubric under which are included urinary tract infections, sexually transmitted diseases, vaginal discharge, prolapse, uterine and cervical cancers, and pelvic inflammatory disease.[1] These contribute towards high morbidity rates and impact on occupational roles, apart from having a bearing on stress levels, and hence, impacting on relationships of women with their spouses and children. The cultural silence attached to reproductive health problems adds to the stress and trauma women face.

Community-based studies on self-reported gynecological morbidities and reproductive tract infections (Koenig *et al.* 1996; Bang *et al.* 1989) have identified iatrogenic factors such as sterilisations (Char and Vaidya 2000; Bhatia *et al.* 1997; Oomman 1996; Bhatia and Cleland 1995; Bang *et al.* 1989); and childbearing and surgical procedures such as sterilisation and induced abortion (Ravindran *et al.* 1999). Personal hygiene also has been implicated in reproductive tract infections. Thus, in China, rural women who did not bathe frequently were at increased risk of having bacterial vaginosis (Kaufman *et al.* 1996). According to another study (Oomman 1996), women using sand as filler in cloth rags during menstruation and rarely having an opportunity to wash and change these rags reported susceptibility to infection.

Impact of Reproductive Health Problems on Women

Apart from reproductive health problems, women in their childbearing years typically experience anxiety and mood disorders (Kessler *et al.* 1993). Jaswal's (2001) study of low-income women in Mumbai shows that 50.6 percent of the women reported at least one gynecological morbidity, and further, that 27.5 percent of these women also reported common mental disorders. Similarly, Chandra (2001) found that depression was prevalent amongst women reporting pelvic pain, menstrual irregularities and gynecological cancers.

Each phase of the childbearing years—puberty, menstruation, pregnancy, and menopause, is associated with its own peculiar traumas.

During puberty, the sex steroid hormones play a vital role in causing vulnerability to anxiety and depression. In the pre-menstrual phase, some women may report recurrent depressive and anxiety symptoms, while amongst others, chronic depression may occur (Rubinow & Roy-Byrne 1984). O'Brian (1994) reports that premenstrual syndrome has often not received the attention it deserves, largely as most women suffer only minor psychological symptoms with the ovarian endocrine cycle. Mild physiological symptoms occur in as many as 95 percent of women of reproductive age, only 5% being completely symptom free. Five percent of the women report that their lives are completely disrupted during the second half of their cycle. Symptoms may be so severe that they lead to suicide, para suicide, and acts of violence against others.

During pregnancy, panic disorder symptoms are released amongst some women (Klien *et al.* 1995). Obsessive-compulsive disorders can also get exacerbated (Altshuler *et al.* 1998). In case a woman suffering from a psychiatric ailment plans to conceive or is pregnant, it is a worrisome thought for the clinician. If she is on psychotropic medication, it diffuses readily across the placenta; hence adequate clinical antenatal care is imperative. In the post-partum period, there is an increased risk for new onset or recurrence of mood disorders (Altshuler *et al.*, 1998; Dean *et al.*, 1989). Also, studies from India and Pakistan demonstrate a greater risk for post-natal depression in mothers who have a girl child, especially if the mother already has living girl children (Patel *et al* 2002; Rahman et al forthcoming; Chandran *et al* 2002).

Menopause, yet another traumatic phase of a woman's life, is a time of physiological and psychological changes. Daly *et al.* (1994) point out that the quality of life may be severely compromised in women with menopausal symptoms; conversely, perceived improvements in quality of life in users of hormone replacement therapy seem to be substantial. At the same time, research studies reveal several cross-cultural variations in the perception of menopause, with western women reporting a higher incidence of depression (Pearce *et al.*1995).

Psychological Trauma in the Reproductive Years

Menstruation, though a natural cyclical event, impinges on a woman's privacy. It constrains her capacity to work and is also referred to as a 'curse'. Moreover, the childbearing years of a woman's life are fraught with trauma—of both pregnancy and infertility.

It is true that reproduction causes acute physical discomfort, mental tension and sometimes even personal embarrassment, but it is the socio-cultural setting which defines pregnancy as a happy or sad event. In patriarchal societies, a newly married woman is subjected to pressure to produce an heir (a male child) and, in doing so, carve out a niche for herself in the family. In case a male child is born, the next message is: *eek akh nal thooda zindagi chaaldi hai duuji aakh vi taan chaheedi hai (*one can't live one's life with just one eye one needs two eyes, so one more son is desirable). In case it is a girl, the reaction is: Why did she have to come? In case it is twins, the boy is named *Jagtaar Singh* (ruler of the universe) while the girl is named *Ayee-Gayee* (go as you have come). Repeated pregnancies leave a woman with little choice but to fall prey to the pregnancy-ultrasound-abortion-pregnancy cycle till the two-eyes target is met, even if, in the long run, it subjects her to infections and suffering. Apart from the mental suffering that she undergoes, economic pressures in terms of expenditure at the time of delivery, whether in terms of the *dai*'s, hospital expenses, and ceremonies, are also highly demanding. Loss of wages during the natal and postnatal period may be involved as well.

As we have seen, pregnancy is a source of trauma for a woman—but so is the fear of infertility. Thus, a woman is caught between the devil and the deep blue sea; being able to reproduce and *not* being able to reproduce—both situations are as grim. While menopause brings with it the period of *aaram* (relief), it is a harbinger of miseries as well. As one respondent puts it: *Har maheene di khicchaal muk gayee hai par hoon hoor beemariyaan vadd gayeeyan ne. Dhuii dukhdee rehndee hai, goode taan jawaab de chuuke ne. Ghar de pucchde naheen han, bachee aapne vich rehnde ne, nooan suundeyaan nahee haan, saara din kale bbethe rehni haan;* 'It's a relief that menstruation is over, but it has caused so many other physical ailments like backache and inflexible knees. My husband has lost interest in me. The children don't bother, and the daughters-in-law don't listen to me. No one takes me to the doctor. I sit all by myself the whole day'.

At any stage of a woman's lifespan, she has to be silent about her reproductive health problems, or bear the brunt of being 'labeled', i.e., she has to suffer the social stigma of having been 'loose' and hence, infected.

All this calls for one to delve into women's mindsets. The association between diseases related to female's sexuality and reproduction, and women's role behaviour and position in society will also need to be factored in, before a holistic picture begins to emerge.

Objectives

The main objectives of the paper are to profile women suffering from reproductive health problems, explore the nature and causes of their afflictions, and report on the mental health problems that are rooted in their reproductive health ailments.

Methodology

A case study method was reckoned as the most appropriate. A group of 19 currently married women in the age group of 15-50 years was taken up for a detailed study. Though each woman was distinct in her own right, their common concerns have been woven together. For the purpose of the present study, the district with the lowest sex ratio in Punjab (and the districts of the rest of India as well), that is, Fatehgarh Sahib, was identified. From Fatehgarh Sahib, a village and town with the lowest FMRs—village Bhagrana and town Sirhind, were selected. The intention was to capture the village and town for the study wherein the incidence of sex selective abortion was of the highest order in all probability. Further, within the village and the town, households for the case study were adopted with help of the local *dai* who was conversant with the reproductive status of every women.

Women were sampled from three broad categories: (i) married women with *no* children yet (ii) women with children and (iii) pre-menopausal women. Five women each were selected from categories (i) and (iii). From the second category, the longest in the entire reproductive span, nine women were sampled.

Both qualitative and quantitative techniques were used for the collection of data. Two self-constructed questionnaires were designed, the first to collect data on the socio-economic and demographic characteristics of the women and the second to capture their reproductive health problems. In addition, two standardised questionnaires to measure women's stress (Perceived Stress Scale, Cohen, Kamarack and Mermelstein, 1983) and depression levels (Beck Depression Inventory, Beck et al., 1961) were administered. Observations, opinions and beliefs voiced by the respondents about their problems were also noted down. Each case was scrutinised meticulously, and events that triggered trauma were, in particular, recorded.

Findings from Quantitative Data

An analysis of the nineteen case studies reveals that women in all the three categories experienced reproductive health problems such as vaginal discharge. Amongst the newly married women with no children, it was associated with stains on clothes, burning on urination, foul smell, pain on intercourse, and abdominal pain. Women with children had most of these problems and also reported the problem of prolapse or 'something coming out', which causes extreme discomfort. They also suffered from weakness, discomfort, and backache. In the case of pre-menopausal women, an overall fall in the incidence of problems was evident (Table 1).

As far as problems associated with the menstrual cycle is concerned, aches and pains, followed by heavy and irregular flow, were the most often reported problem by newly married women with no children, as well as by women in the childbearing age who had borne children. In both the groups, an equal proportion of women reported pre-menstrual tension and nausea. Amongst the pre-menopausal women, irregularity and aches and pains during menstruation were reported as the major problem. Further, the cessation of menses brought in its wake general weakness and giddiness, as well as hot flushes, palpitations and insomnia (Table 1).

An analysis of stress and depression levels reveals that these prevail amongst all the three categories of women, notably in the case of women with children. This could be attributed to their multiple obligations. At times, these women also participate in the economic struggle by taking up some job, manual or other.

TABLE 1: Women by Reproductive Status and Reproductive and Mental Health Problems, Fatehgarh Sahib, Punjab, 2005

Category of problem	Problem	Category of women		
		Newly married with no children	Of childbearing age with children	Pre-menopausal
Menstruation	Irregular menstruation	1	3	2
	Scanty menstruation	1	0	1
	Body aches/pain	4	4	1
	Heavy Flow	2	3	-
	PMT	1	1	-
	Nausea	1	1	3
	Hot Flushes	-	-	2
	Weakness	-	-	1
	Dizzy/Fatigue	-	-	2
	Palpitations	-	-	1
	Constipation	-	-	1
	Insomnia	-	-	1
Reproductive health	Vaginal Discharge	5	9	5
	Stains on Clothes	2	0	-
	Burning on Urination	1	3	-

Contd.

	Foul Smell	2	5	3
	Abdominal Pain	2	3	4
	Pain on intercourse	1	0	-
	Urinary Infection	0	2	-
	Weakness	1	5	3
	Discomfort	0	4	2
	Backache	0	2	-
	Prolapse	0	2	1
	Fever	-	-	1
Mental health	Stress	3	7	3
	Mild Stress (vis a vis daily hassles)	2	2	1
	Depression	3	3	2
	Mild depression	0	2	1

Note : Sample Size
- For Newly Married Women With No Children (5)
- For Women of Childbearing Age With Children (9)
- For Pre-Menopausal Women (5)

Findings from the Case Studies

The case studies delineate women who are currently suffering from a reproductive health problem and its impact on their psychological state of mind. These are placed in the socio-economic status of each respondent, so as to synthesise text and context. Names of respondents have been disguised for reasons of confidentiality

Category 1: Newly Married, Childless Women

In Punjab, in accordance with patriarchal and patrilocal tradition, a woman moves to her husband's patrilineal residence after marriage. By this stage, she has already been trained in the management of household chores, and has acquired the social skills of developing long lasting relationships at home. This is a time of transition when she willingly accepts new roles such as those of 'wife', daughter-in-law and 'mother', a time when she is faced with the challenges of adjusting to the new family and bearing it an heir. Any delays in conception are viewed with the suspicion that the daughter in law is infertile, which prods her to trips to medical institutions. At this juncture, as the transition from girlhood to womanhood takes place, a girl is faced with mixed feelings of both pleasure and pressure.

Case 1

Simran, aged 24 years, belongs to a Hindu Backward Caste. She has been married to the village barber for a month and a half. She is a matriculate, and is aware of the fact that she's better educated than a number of girls her age in the village. She is rustic, unsophisticated and demanding in temperament. Her family comprises her husband, mother-in-law, a younger brother-in-law and an unmarried sister-in-law. She complains about her sister-in-law throwing frequent temper tantrums, for which she requests some kind of advice or treatment. Attired in her best finery even at home, she displays an attitude of belligerence, at least in the absence of her mother-in-law, who is away in town.

Simran, who began menstruating at age 16 and has had regular menses ever since, complains of abdominal pain brought on by menstruation. She has never taken any medication for her abdominal pain; she cries out in pain and rests for a while before getting back to work. She also has excessive white discharge, which leaves stains on her clothes, and has never undergone any treatment for that problem either; she seems to have accepted it as a fact of life, and taken it for granted. '*Eh taan vihaaha ton pehlan vi vagda si, us veele tan koi nahin pucheya*; 'it flowed even before marriage, no one asked about it at that time', she says. Suddenly she appears upset and says: '*bahut jalan vi hondi hai, jis din vihaaha hoiya si pet vich dard vi bahut hoi si, par ki kehndi, soocheya ki sayaad ees tarahan hi honda hai*'; 'I had burning also, and, on cohabiting the first time after marriage, experienced pain in the stomach, but assumed that probably that's how it is, and never spoke about it to anyone'. She now has so many questions to ask: What is her problem? Does it need treatment? Where should she go for treatment? Is it serious? Will it in some way affect her fertility? Should she tell her husband? How will her husband react if he comes to know?

The psychological tests administered to her do not confirm her as being high on stress or depression. Still, there are grounds for concern, as the responses studied individually reveal that she is sad, cries more than she did earlier, and is unable to take decisions without first consulting her mother-in-law or husband. These are all indicative of a suppressed undercurrent which, if not monitored, may take a serious turn.

A good daughter-in-law is not expected to be complaining of ill health within the first month of marriage. If she does so, it will adversely affect her standing in the household. So Simran had refrained from talking about her illness. Now, as she discusses her problems with the interviewer, her ignorance about her health condition surfaces. She becomes anxious as the discussion progresses. Adjusting to a new environment is itself stressful, she says. Further, her ill health, which she never took cognisance of so far, now awakens innumerable apprehensions in her. She needs someone qualified who she can speak her mind to and confide in. It is imperative that she have a counselor in the close vicinity who can suggest ways by which she can overcome her physical and mental turmoil.

Case 2

Gurmeet, 23 years, educated up to class 12, belongs to a Jat Sikh family. She has been married for three years now to an affluent farmer and *chakki* owner (wheat miller). Attired simply, she is warm, modest and soft-spoken. Her family comprises of her father-in-law, mother-in-law, and husband.

Her reproductive history reveals that her menstruation started at 17 years of age, and has been regular ever since. It however has been accompanied by severe backache. Also, during menstruation, she suffers from white, foul smelling discharge coupled with stains, discomfort and weakness. She says that vaginal discharge occurred even before marriage but she took for granted that it was normal and never sought any treatment. *Saangdi si taahiyaan kissi nu dasseya vi nahee*; 'I was too embarrassed and never told anyone about it'. In three years of marriage, she has not been able to conceive. She has been under treatment from private doctors, civil hospitals and even from indigenous healers (*babajis* and *hakims*).

Her white discharge and backache take a backseat as she discusses her infertility problem, which is emotionally more painful for her. Since her husband is an only son, '*Bujurgan di akhree aas han asi*'; 'We're the elder's last hope'. She does softly add, though: '*Mainu lagda hai ki nuks ehna vich hai*'; 'I have a feeling that the deficiency lies with my husband and not with me'.

As expected, her perceived stress score is high. She also complains of body aches, high anxiety, fatigue, poor appetite, and frequent vomiting. She is moving fast towards depression. Her husband being the only son, her role of a dutiful daughter-in-law becomes even more critical: she has to produce an heir for the family. Her mother-in-law is extremely worried and pleads with me to suggest some treatment or to recommend an infertility center of repute. To end her turmoil, she is ready to mobilise all her economic resources.

The family as a whole is under severe stress because of the 'infertile' status accorded to their daughter-in-law. The young lady succumbs to the pressures at home and undergoes various treatments, while in her heart she is convinced that it is 'their son' who needs to be examined. She has silently undergone the trauma for the last two years now, waiting for the kindness of the almighty, hoping that some day...

This state of affairs will not end until she gathers enough courage to tell her in-laws that it is their son who should be subjected to tests and investigations also, rather than she alone. To maintain her balance, she needs the support of a therapist who can convince the family that both husband and wife need to be put under treatment.

Case 3

Bimla, 24 years, belongs to a Hindu Scheduled Caste, and is educated up to the primary level. She has been married for two years, and lives in a nuclear family with just her husband. She is dressed shabbily, and is crude in her approach.

Though menstruating normally since 14 years of age, she complains of scanty periods ever since. She speaks with tears in her eyes, and responds with an uncontrollable surge of emotion at the mere mention of '*aapki sehat kaisi hai*?'; How is your health?. '*Ki daseeye sehat kaisi hai, shaadi ton baad baccha thera si, bus do maheene vich gir gaya, private doctor kol puree safayee layee vi gayee si. Us samay di bus bimar payee haan. Safeed pani painda hai pet vich bahut dard rehnda hai, boo vi bahut aaoundi hai. Sas, saure' naal nahin haan, te vaada koi naheen hoonda si kuch daasan hoon jaada ma-pe de ghar rehnee haan. Doctor noo deekhaya kahnde kuch nahee hai, dawai-buuti koi aasar naheen kardi. Ultrasound vi kara ke vekh lita hai. Koi aaram nahin hai. Gharwala kehnda hai hameshha maree rehndi hai, hun baccha nahien thareya than chaad daanga*'; 'What shall I tell you about my health? Soon after my marriage, I conceived, but within two months, I had a spontaneous abortion, for which I had to visit a private doctor. Ever since then, I have had white discharge accompanied by severe lower abdominal pain. The doctor recommended an ultrasound, but no abnormality was found. My husband has threatened to abandon me if I do not conceive'.

Bimla's perceived stress scores are high, which are indicative of her distressed state of mind. She also has a high score on depression. She reports body aches and pains, anxiety, insomnia, fatigue, heart palpitations and poor appetite.

Her husband's constant threats to leave her makes her anxious. Brawls are a regular feature between the two of them, and, under such conditions, conception becomes impossible. Her tense state of mind anyway inhibits normal relations. She prefers to stay at her parent's house to avoid regular clashes with her husband.

She has conceived once, and doctors have confirmed after ultra sounds conducted on her that there are no indications of physiological malformation. So, family counseling and support are called for. Inter-spousal support rather than merely parental support would prove a more effective strategy. Family counseling focused on enhancing inter-spousal harmony and effective communication is needed.

Case 4

Sunita Rani, 20 years, a Sikh, belongs to the Backward Caste, is educated up to the primary level, and has been married for three months now. Her family comprises of her husband, mother-in-law, brother-in-law, and sister-in-law. Neatly dressed, she talks in a moderated tone. Her eyes are eloquent. They speak more than her words.

Rani has been menstruating normally since 13 years of age, but with pre-menstrual tension, heavy flow, painful periods, severe backache and nausea. She claims that the severity of all these symptoms increased subsequent to her marriage. She stays unwell throughout the month—one week on account of menstruation, and in the remaining three weeks, she suffers from fever, poor digestion and vomiting. She undergoes severe vaginal discharge, the reason for which is unknown to her. She also complains of weakness. Heavy menstrual flow could be responsible for anemia, which, coupled with malnourishment, leads to low immunity levels. This may account for her repeated illnesses. Rani has not been able to conceive till date, which upsets her mother-in-law the most. *Eek vaar bacha ho jayee taan sab kuch theek ho jayeega boolde tan haan nahin bacha kithon therega'*; 'Once Rani delivers a baby, all her problems will vanish. She needs to cohabit with her husband, but then, we don't know if she will conceive'.

The mother-in-law unscrupulously packs off Rani to her '*maika*' (parents house) every few days and warns her to not come back until she is feeling better. Rani feels embarrassed and helpless. Her eyes say that she seeks help, lest she be packed off for good. Her stress and depression are under control primarily because of a supportive sister-in-law, but she too feels : 'How long can this be sustained?' The mother-in-law is an overpowering lady and openly says '*Keeni der tak ek bimaar noo sambde rahange asi';* 'How long will we keep supporting a sick daughter-in-law?'. Unfortunately, the family's emphasis was more on her getting into the mothering role, than on her ill health. She has never been treated so far.

Rani reports that her first sexual experience traumatised her completely. Ever since, she has kept unwell. Her poor appetite may be a genuine disorder or, at times, a form of silent protest. Her 'illness' may be just a pretext to keep herself away from her husband. Her physiological and psychological state of mind is somewhere deeply impacted upon, and that requires intervention.

Research studies confirm that women reporting premenstrual symptoms are prone to less of sexual desire, less sexual activity, less frequent orgasms and less satisfaction with orgasm during the late luteal period as compared to the other phases of menstruation (Clayton *et al.* 1999). Rani's case is distinct also because she falls in the high-risk group. She is predisposed to the risk of premenstrual syndrome by factors which include her age group of 20-30 years (Freeman *et a*l. 1995a); her menses lasting more than six days (Deuster *et al.* 1999); and life stressors involving major life events, relationships with significant others, work, and social support (Severino & Moline 1989). Management of such cases can be to follow a non-pharmacological approach, i.e., to focus more on diet and exercise, combat nutritional deficiencies by adding supplements, and by psychotherapy. Rani needs to be counseled on how to identify stress events that trigger menstrual exacerbation.

Case 5

Amarjeet, aged 20 years, is a Hindu, belongs to a Scheduled Caste, is educated up to middle school, and has been married for nine months. Her family comprises her husband and her mother-in-law. Her husband has a photographer's shop in the nearby town and her mother-in-law works as a sweeper in the local government school. They live in their own *pucca* house.

Amarjeet is good looking, well groomed, eager to share information, and possesses an overall positive outlook. She had been menstruating regularly since 14 years of age, until her marriage. Subsequently, her menses were irregular, and marked by a heavy unmanageable flow, coupled with stomach ache and backache. She suffers from vaginal discharge with bad odour, and has severe abdominal pain not attributable to menstruation. She has not conceived so far. Three months after her marriage, she had a swelling in her stomach along with severe pain and breathlessness. She complained to her husband but no one in her marital household took cognizance of her ill health. Her parents took her to a private doctor, who conducted an ultrasound. No abnormality was however detected. Even after medication, she still complains of severe pain—but her husband does not take her to the doctor, nor is she allowed to visit her parents anymore. Now there is no one to take her to the doctor. She says '*mera gharwala mainu kehnda hai mere kol time koi nahin hai aapne aap chalee ja, kiveen javaan kithe javaan mainu taan kuch pata hi naheen hai, je taan main Maulijagran vich hondi te aap hi chalee jandee par ithe tan mainu kuch pata hi nahin hai*'; 'My husband claims that he has no time (to take me to the doctor), and that I can go by myself. In my parents village (M*aulijagran)* (near Chandigarh), I could have managed my way, but here I know nothing of the way the land lies'. Even her mother-in-law is not bothered; she assumes all her daughter in law's problems are due to her inability to conceive.

Amarjeet reports high perceived stress and depression scores, which are an indication of a distressed mind. Her physical complaints include head, stomach and body ache, anxiety, insomnia, fatigue, heart palpitations and a poor appetite. She had so many expectations out of marriage but none of them were fulfilled. This makes her disinterested in every thing around her; '*Har cheez layee taan tok dende ne ki kuch karan da dil hi nahin karda, pehle main ine sone taaran de phuul te chiriya bana ke veechdi si. Main bacheyan nu sikha kaar paise vi kama sakdi haan , par karan den taan na. Main ithe kissi cheez di koi kadar na payee. Meri taan zindigi barbad ho gayee hai*'; 'My husband obstructs anything I want to do. Before I got married, I used to make lovely flowers and birds out of golden wire and sell them. My husband does not let me do anything now. I can take classes for children and earn money but he won't let me do it. Nothing that I do has ever been appreciated in this house. My life seems to have collapsed completely ever since I got married'. She says it's not just her health that is ignored at home; anything she asks for is turned down immediately.

She accepts that she had developed a bad temper; on a few occasions, she even hit her husband. At times, she would throw a tantrum primarily to seek his attention. Broken hearted and frustrated with life, she has given up and says: 'It is futile to retaliate. It is better to accept the fate destined for you'. She says she makes a conscious effort to mellow down and not complain.

Category 2: Mothers in the Childbearing Years

In the existing socio-cultural milieu, the childbearing years are viewed as a high stress prone period for women. It is a phase of adjusting within a new family, coupled with the pressure of bearing a male child to carry on the lineage. Epidemiological data point to this period as a time of increased women's vulnerability to mood disorders (Weissman & Olfson 1995). In particular, the post partum period is a traumatic time; in the first three months, a significant proportion of women have to be admitted to hospital (Kendall *et al.* 1987). One study puts the figure at as high as 12.5 per cent for the entire postpartum period (Duffy 1983). It is noteworthy also that when women undergo pregnancies, deliveries, abortions and adopt contraception, susceptibility to 'exogamous infections', i.e., infections attributable to external agents, is the highest. The stresses and strains of the childbearing years also can lead to a deterioration of mental health; thus there is a strong relationship between the childbearing years and mental illness.

Case 6

Raakhi, aged 28 years, is a Muslim and belongs to a Backward Caste. She is shabbily dressed. She has been married for nine years now. Her family comprises her husband and two sons. Her third child, a son, died three hours after birth, from unknown causes. The child turned blue soon after birth and died. Raakhi has a sharp, probing mind, and displays no hesitation in responding to any of the questions put to her by the interviewer. Indeed, she even has queries of her own, on her health problems, such as: Why do they occur? What should the line of treatment be?

Raakhi has been menstruating regularly since 15 years of age. She complains that when she menstruates, she has a stomach ache. Moreover, she has been suffering from severe body and backache ever since she became an acceptor of laparoscopy as a method of contraception. Her vaginal discharge, which she attributes to *garmi* (heat) and unhygienic living conditions, is foul-smelling. She experiences burning on urination, and has lower abdominal pain. She sought treatment at the nearby sub-centre and was prescribed some medication, which she took religiously. On the approach of the summer months of May-June, her trauma recurs. The exact cause is unknown. Medications provide only temporary relief.

Raakhi reports high scores on perceived stress and depression. Evidently, this was not due to her health condition alone. On probing, she discloses that she has been accused by her sister-in-law of being 'loose', who believed she was having illicit relations with her brother-in-law. She complains of body and backache, anxiety, fatigue, chest pain and constipation. Poor health, coupled with disturbed familial relations, seriously impacts her psychological state of mind. She tends to ruminate about her physical health. She also expresses guilt because she spoke extra nicely to her brother-in-law on a few occasions, and may have been mistaken then. Overall, her life is plagued by poor inter-spousal communication, with distrust creeping in, which diminishes her quality of life.

Case 7

Gulshan Kaur, aged 34 years, is a Backward Caste Hindu. She is illiterate. Married for fifteen years, she is lean, dark, and looks anemic. Her family comprises of her husband, one daughter and a son. She manages to earn a thousand rupees a month working as a maid—washing utensils and clothes in other people's homes. She lives in a semi-*pucca* house with limited amenities. She is shabbily dressed and very talkative, but is in a rush to end the conversation, as she has to go back to work. She had come home at lunchtime to give food to her children, and to wash clothes (as water is supplied for limited hours at this time of the day).

Gulshan Kaur traces her medical history right from her childhood and wants to know if there would be any consequences of her earlier problems now. She has been menstruating regularly since age 14. Menstruation for her has always been painful. It hampers her daily routine at least in the initial two days. She has had no abortions and is an 'acceptor' of tubectomy as a contraceptive method. She got herself sterilised at the Government Hospital and has been suffering from severe vaginal discharge, urinary infections and backache ever since. *Gilla jihaa lagda hai, te badboo vi aaundi hai, eene sharam aaundi hai kissi noo ki dasseeye, ghar-ghar jaana hoonda hai te ees haalat vich*; 'There is a feeling of wetness and a foul smell emits, which is embarrassing, particularly since I have to visit houses for work. Also, it is something that one can't tell anybody about'.

Her perceived stress scores revealed that she is under tremendous strain due to her dual charge of managing the house as well as of her job as a maid in other people's houses. She is unable to control the important things in her life, feels nervous and stressed out, and often finds herself thinking of the things she has to accomplish. Her high stress levels make her feel sad. She feels discouraged about the future, and she does not enjoy things the way she used to. She feels overpowered by the difficulties in her life and has no clue as to how she can overcome them.

Overall, she is hospitable with a warm and forthcoming disposition. She suffers physical as well as psychological problems, yet she tries to maintain a balance, primarily for the sake of her children. The entire burden is on her, as her husband is a happy go lucky man. His irresponsibility frightens and irritates her. She has apprehensions about his moral behavior too.

Poor women working as maids constantly reel under the turbulence of income generating work and attending to their household responsibilities. They need specialised support systems.

Case 8

Parampreet Kaur, aged 24 years, a Sikh, is an undergraduate. She lives in a joint family comprising her husband, herself, her two children (one son and one daughter), father in law and mother-in-law, and her brother-in law's family. She belongs to an agricultural family with a land holding of 10 acres, which is just enough to manage the household expenses, given that the household demands and expenses have been increasing at a very fast pace.

Kaur has been regularly menstruating since the age of 16 years. She is using the Intrauterine Device (IUD) but reports that ever since she began using it, she has suffered from vaginal discharge and urinary infection, accompanied by weakness and discomfort. She says '*Boj painda hai, eisa lagda hai jiven kucch bahaar aa reha hai*'; 'I have a feeling of heaviness, and I feel that something is coming out of me'. Her condition inhibits her normal functioning at home, particularly activities such as washing clothes, utensils, taking care of the livestock and most of all, her sexual activity. She shyly puts forth her problem and inquires about the line of treatment for it.

She reports severe anxiety. Her psychological assessment reveals that she has mild levels of perceived stress primarily due to her physical condition. Her daily work gets hampered and this adds to her turmoil. She remains upset, is nervous and stressed, and feels that things are not going her way. The whole day passes in taking care of the needs of the family. In addition to the family, there lies the responsibility of the livestock and the labourers working in the fields, who also need to be provided with food, water and tea. She caters to the enormous burden of household responsibilities the whole day, which leaves her fatigued, with no energy to take care of herself.

She has no outlet for her pent up tensions, no mechanism for letting off stream, which contributes to her pent up emotions getting transformed into stress and anxiety. She needs someone to open up to. She needs to let go. A qualified person who could guide her towards enhancing her coping skills would be a blessing for her.

Case 9

Bano, aged 35 years, a decently dressed, illiterate *dalit* Muslim, speaks about her health and familial problems with no inhibitions. She is the second wife of a man whose earlier wife had died. There is a considerable age difference between the two. They have a married son from the first wife living with them. The other members in the family include her two sons aged eleven and eight. Her husband and the elder (step) son work as *kumhars,* making pots in the village and selling them in the town. Their earnings barely suffice to make ends meet for the family. She is concerned about her newly wedded daughter-in-law who has not conceived in 3 months of marriage.

Bano has been regularly menstruating since the age of 12 years. She uses the Intrauterine Device (IUD) but reports that ever since its use, she has been suffering from vaginal discharge, along with weakness and discomfort. '*Shareer dukhda raheenda hai, sir te dhui than jiven hann hi nahee'*, she also reports; 'I have a bad body ache and worst of all is my headache and backache'. She wants to continue with the IUD and not opt for any other contraceptive device, which she feels are cumbersome. She is ready to tolerate the discomfort of vaginal discharge. She is completely open about her discomfort and has no apprehensions about discussing them. She, however, has never sought any treatment; '*Ghaul kar jayeeda hai gharon nikalna hi muskil hai, soochdi hi rehni haan, jadoon bahut dukhi ho jaani haan tan aaram kar leeni haan. Aurat di zindagi taan hai hi isi tahran di, ki kareeye'*; 'I am keen to undergo treatment, but I find it difficult to leave the house. There is always something to do at home. A woman's life is like that. What can one do?'

She constantly keeps repeating that she has been feeling very unwell for about three-four months; *'teen char maheene ton bahut zayada tabeeyat kharaab rehndi hai'*. A feeling of insecurity has crept in ever since her stepson got married about three months ago. An identity crisis and a feeling that she is no longer the boss of the house makes her force the daughter-in-law to stay at her parents place most of the time. She even tells her son that he should find some work in the town and live there with his wife. Family counseling is what is urgently required for a family like this, whereby they all can live together in harmony.

Case 10

Seeta, 38 years of age, is a Hindu Brahmin, married for sixteen years. She has been educated up to high school. Her family comprises of her husband, herself, her mother-in-law, three daughters and one son. No one in the household has any employment. They live by the rent they get from a shop that they let out. Her husband, an alcoholic, is mentally disturbed and incapable of seeking work.

Seeta has been menstruating regularly since 15 years of age. When she menstruates, she gets a lower backache. She has undergone one abortion; the foetus was female and she already had three daughters. Her subsequent ultrasound confirmed the next foetus to be a male, so her son was born. The couple have accepted the condom as their contraceptive choice ever since. Seeta complains that after intercourse, she suffers from vaginal discharge along with bad odour and burning on urination. She attributes her vaginal discharge to condom usage. Further, she claims that '*garmi*' (heat) leads to her problem, which she also apprehends to be due to wrong eating habits/ hot food ('*garam cheez khane se hota hai*').

After suffering for about a month, she sought treatment from a private medical practitioner, but the medication he prescribed provided only palliative relief. Now, she either continuously takes medication or refrains from sexual activity. She prefers to follow the latter course but remains keen on a permanent cure. No tests were advised so she does not really know what her problem is and why it recurs. In addition to her reproductive health problems, she suffers from tuberculosis, for which she is undergoing treatment from the government hospital. She is getting treated there for epilepsy also. She alternates between allopathic to homeopathic medicine, and consults *babaji*s (indigenous medical practitioners) also.

Her high perceived stress and mildly high depression are attributable not just to her reproductive health problems but also to the socio-cultural set up. '*Saare ghar ka bhaar mere par hai, kya kya karron, kaise sambhaloon saab kuch, sarkari haspatal jaane ka matlab hai 20/- rupees ka bus kiraya aur aage aagar* doctor *chutti pe hai to paisa barbad. Private doctor* paise *bahut lete hain aur paisa itna thooda hoota hai ki es maheene dawai kha li to bachhon ki jaroorat kaise poori hogi, barabar treatment naheen le pati isliye koi bhi bimari jaar se naheen nikalti*'; 'The pressure of the entire household is on me. I cannot afford regular treatment. That is why my problem does not get completely cured. Going to the government hospital means I need to spend 20/- rupees on bus fare. In case the doctor is not available, all that money is wasted. Private doctors are very expensive. If I take regular treatment, then there is insufficient money to meet my children's needs'.

Poor economic status of the family, husband's irresponsible behavior, increasing demands of the children, health care expenditure for her mother-in-law and herself, are all overpowering. Seeta's problems underscore her health needs, each one of which necessitates early redressal. Her problems being multifarious, she needs adequate medical, psychiatric and social support.

Case 11

Amarjeet, aged 38 years, a Sikh belonging to a Backward Caste (*lohar*), married for nineteen years, lives in a joint family comprising of her husband, her mother-in-law, herself, one daughter, and two sons. She is educated up to class ten, and is a housewife. She lives in a *pucca* house with all the basic amenities. Till a month ago, her brother-in-law was also living in the same household along with his family. This used to be one reason for unrest at home. He now has a separate dwelling close by. Dressed neatly, hospitable, she is warm and forthcoming.

Her reproductive history can be traced from her regular menstruation since the age of 15 years. Within one year of marriage, she conceived her first child—a female baby. Her second daughter passed away soon after birth; it was a home delivery, so the cause of death is unknown. Her subsequent pregnancy resulted in an abortion; the pre-natal diagnostic test had confirmed it to be a female foetus. Two successive deliveries resulted in live births, both male children.

Earlier, menstruation was accompanied by just mild backache, but in the last two years, Amarjeet has suffered from premenstrual tension, backache, painful periods along with big clots coming out, weakness, burning on urination and nausea. She also complains of frequent white discharge, coupled with bad odour. She has taken treatment from a female private practitioner for her problems. No tests were conducted on her and she was advised to take medicines that have not helped her very much.

Amarjeet's perceived stress and depression scores are high. She claims she was earlier a relaxed person, but, with increasing age, factors such as physical health problems, emerging reproductive health problems, husband's ill health, children's increasing demands, and constant bickering with her mother-in-law, have lead to an upset state of mind. She complains of her inability to make decisions, and also, that she does not look as attractive as she used to.

Her problems can be adequately addressed only if she is closely monitored and provided psychotherapy.

Case 12

Jasbir, aged 28 years, belongs to a Sikh Backward Caste (*julaha*) family. An illiterate housewife married for nine years, she lives in a joint family comprising of her husband, herself, her father-in-law, one son, two daughters, and two unmarried brothers-in-law. They live in a semi-*pucca* house with limited facilities. Dressed shabbily and excessively overworked, she just wanted a quick discussion and solutions to her problems.

Her menstruation started at the age of 13 years, and she complains of having always had heavy and painful periods. She views pregnancy as a temporary getaway from her painful menstruation. She has had five pregnancies, of which three culminated in live births. One was stillborn, and one foetus was aborted, primarily, she claims, because she had completed her family; she did not undergo any pre-natal diagnostic tests. *Roti khaan de taan paise han nahin test kithoon karande pheereye*; 'There is limited money to eat food. Where is the money to undergo tests?', she asks. She says that ever since her delivery last year—a home delivery conducted by the local *dai*—she has been suffering from vaginal discharge coupled with back pain, severe abdominal pain, prolapse and weakness. She adds that she has taken no medical treatment for any of her problems, on account of constraints such as poverty, lack of time, and lack of support from her family.

She reports high perceived stress and mild depression. Her ill health, coupled with the daily chores and responsibilities, tire her out completely and she finds it difficult to cope. She has no choice but to silently nurse all her woes, as no one at home empathises with her. She says all the men folk in the household are trying so hard to earn a living that expecting them to take some time off to take her to a doctor is asking for too much. *Patta nahin kaad taakan aidaan hi chaalega. Ki eihi zindagi hai?;* 'I don't know for how long things will remain like this, maybe forever. Is this life, I wonder?'

Working hard the whole day long and having lost hope of brighter days, she deserves a break. She needs a sympathetic ear, for one thing. In addition, she needs an income-generating alternative, which can give her back her lost self-confidence and self esteem.

Case 13

Swarn, aged 37 years, belongs to a Hindu Backward Caste (*Darjee)* family. She is an illiterate housewife. Married for twenty-one years, she lives in a nuclear family comprising, apart from herself, her husband, three sons and two daughters. Dressed decently, she discusses her health concerns openly, while remaining discreet about her familial problems. She appears worried about her husband's health, her son's future, and the poor economic condition of the family. Her worries about her daughter's marriage however ends on a positive note, with the daughter being 'happily married'. On this subject, Swarn maintains a discreet silence, and says that she (the daughter) is with them (the parents) and is in her ninth month of pregnancy. The younger daughter still has to be married.

Swarn had been menstruating regularly since 14 years of age, and reports premenstrual tension, stomach ache and burning on urination ever since. No treatment was ever sought for these problems. She considers them 'normal' and has been suffering from these problems for so many years that she has learnt to live with them. *'Eeh saariyan beemariyan maheene de naal hi hoondiyan haan hoon ehne saal toh hoo reeha hai, apne aap theek vi ho jaandi hai, ki eelaz layeeye'*; 'All these diseases are related to menstruation, and once menopause occurs, the problems too will vanish. So, any treatment seems to be of little avail.

Having achieved desired family size, Swarn underwent one abortion before getting sterilised. After sterilisation, vaginal discharge became a regular feature, along with burning and pain on urination, bad odour, fever, lower abdominal pain, weakness and discomfort. She is extremely upset by all this. She has been on medication from government and private hospitals, but they give her only temporary relief. She is looking for a permanent cure for her ailment. She finds it embarrassing to be suffering from a problem which cannot be openly discussed with anyone. *Patta nahin mainu kyun ehojee gandi bimmarri ho gayee hai te doctor vi koi sahi ilaj nahin* karde; 'I don't know why I have to suffer from a dirty disease for which even the doctors have no permanent cure'.

Her high perceived stress and depression scores are indicative of the turmoil she undergoes due to her ailments. Often she feels nervous and 'stressed'. She finds that difficulties are piling up so high that she cannot overcome them. Daily life hassles have started to upset her and she finds no solution to them. She feels incapable of taking decisions and has developed a poor appetite along with a declining interest in sex. Her physical problems seemed to have made her so upset as to have affected familial harmony as well. Reporting her various physical health and other problems provides an outlet to her inner turmoil. She expostulates: *'Hoon aaye ho taan kuch kaar ke vi jaoo. Sirf kagaz bhar ke te naa jaoo'*; 'Now that you have come to us, don't just fill up the papers, do something for us'.

Overall she feels upset and distressed and seeks advice and a way out. She needs a detailed medical investigation before she can be put on medication, as her problems appear chronic. However, in the mean time, psychotherapy and coping skills are advisable.

Case 14

Anita, a house wife aged 27 years, belongs to a Hindu Backward Caste (*Ramdasi)* family. She is educated up to the middle level. Married for nine years, she lives in a nuclear family comprising herself, her husband, two daughters and one son. She and her family cohabit with the families of two of her brothers-in-law in a one-room semi-built house served by a single toilet. Her minimal communication with her sisters-in-law is limited to petty issues of fighting over who left the toilet dirty or about the mis-behaviour of other's children. Dressed decently, she is shy and a difficult respondent. She requires a lot of confidence-building before she begins to talk about herself and her problems. She is apprehensive about so many details being noted, and that her time is being wasted with no substantial gain. She repeatedly asks: '*Kya aap sarkari hospital se aaye ho, hamare liye kya karooge aap*'; Have you come from the civil hospital? What will you do for us?

Her menstruation started at the age of 13 years and she has been suffering from premenstrual tension ever since. She has had no abortions and is a condom user. She claims that condom use results in vaginal discharge along with bad odour, weakness and discomfort. She has been taking medicines from the private and government dispensaries but that did not give her any relief. She seeks help and advice on where she could get more effective treatment. '*Doctor kehte hain ki condom nahin use karoo operation karraoo ya phir copper-T istemaal karoo. Copper-T lagvaee thi usse hi to beemaree laagee thi, operation naheen karra saktee kyunki bacche choote hain aur ghar mein koi dhyaan rakhne ko naheen hai*'; 'The doctor advised me to get sterilised or use an IUD, but it was because of an IUD that my vaginal discharge started in the first place. I can't get myself sterilised because my children are young and there is no one to take care of the house during the recouping period'.

She reports high scores on perceived stress, which indicates that she has a problem handling her daily activities. She feels nervous and stressed out, is unable to control the critical things in her life, is not in a position to manage even minor irritants, and often finds herself thinking of the things she would like to have in life. She has high rising aspirations for her children and herself, and is frustrated because she has not been able to achieve her aspirations. To top it all, she says, she has to suffer from a 'dirty disease' such as vaginal discharge, which one cannot even talk about.

An introverted temperament makes her closed to any kind of advice. This evidently is at the root of her unwillingness to discuss her problems. She responds to any suggestion that she visit a particular doctor with disbelief and mistrust. She needs someone who can invoke the spirit of trust so that she can be relieved of her physical ailments and psychological fears.

Category 3: Premenopausal Women

Premenopause or peri-menopause is a period when women have irregular menses. During this stage, oestogen levels decrease, and menstrual periods become irregular and then cease. Post-menopause, defined retrospectively after 12 months without menstruation, is reached at an average age of 50.4 years

(World Health Organization 1981). Menopause, as described by Cole and Rothman (1990), was considered a 'sign' rather than a symptom indicative of a disease. The signs, which occur during peri-menopause, and disappear once hormone levels stabilise, are divided into 3 categories (Dennerstein *et al.* 1993): vasomotor (e.g. hot flushes, night sweats); psychosomatic (e.g. headaches, palpitations, dizziness); and psychological (e.g. tiredness, forgetfulness, irritability, nervousness, loss of concentration). It is the period when the hormonal levels undergo the greatest change, putting women at a greater risk of mood disturbances. It is a period of change—physiological, psychological, and social, when women are faced with innumerable types of turmoil, which together act to make them disturbed.

Case 15

Satpal Kaur, Hindu, 49 years old, belongs to a Scheduled Caste, is illiterate, works as a maid in three houses, and earns about a thousand rupees a month. The family has its own house with three spacious rooms, and a big courtyard. The house is well kept in spite of Kaur's health and familial problems. Kaur was married at the age of 18 years to a blind man; '*kismat ke khel hain beta, kya karen';* 'its destiny, what can be done about it?' she expostulate stoically. She has four children—two daughters and two sons. Her second born child, a daughter, died after two days of her birth. '*Jadoo toona kar ta si, suuk ke maar gayee beecharee';* 'Someone cast a spell on her and she died'. Her two living daughters are both happily married. Her elder son sells vegetables, but is an alcoholic; whatever little he earns is blown up in liquor. He is now divorced, and his wife has shifted to her parents home. The younger son, unmarried, works in a factory and contributes a meager amount towards household expenditure.

Satpal Kaur has been regularly menstruating since the age of 15 years. She says she did not experience any discomfort on account of menstruation. However, she has been experiencing problems related to the cessation of her menstruation for the last one year now; she feels giddy, is depressed, and experiences hot flushes and weakness throughout the day. In addition, ever since having undergone sterilisation, she has been suffering from vaginal discharge coupled with bad odour, severe abdominal pain and fever. Work has become a burden for her, whether it is her household work, like cooking, cleaning and washing or moving about from house to house to earn a livelihood. She has sought treatment from public and private institutions but has not got much relief. So she has given up taking any more treatment. '*Jadoon takaan chalega, eh beemari vi raheegi eh jayega te beemari vi theek ho jayeegi'*; 'The disease is due to menstruation—once it ceases, the disease will also end'.

Satpal Kaur's psychological assessment confirms high perceived stress and depression. Her mental state is primarily due to the change in her physiology. In addition are the circumstances at home—lack of support from her husband and elder son. She feels they are more of a burden on her than a support. She says that earlier, it was just her husband who was an alcoholic. Now her son's alcoholism has ruined the family completely. She paints an overall picture of misery and sees no way out; '*maut ton hi mukti milegi*'; 'only death will bring deliverance', she says.

Economic independence for her has been out of compulsion, for she was married to a blind man, who couldn't earn the daily bread for his household. The burden of the entire household has been on her all these years. Now, at 49 years of age, she has the additional burden of an alcoholic divorced son, who has added to her miseries. Her pathetic circumstances make her say that only death will free her. She needs a break from the daily grind, which has kept her enslaved all these years. She needs sensitive family counseling. Furthermore the son can be referred to a de-addiction center, which will help him overcome his problem and be able to shoulder his responsibilities more effectively.

Case 16

Sukhjeet Kaur, aged 48 years, a Sikh from a Backward Caste (*Lohar*), lives in a joint family comprising her husband, herself, her four children (including two daughters and two sons), her father-in-law and mother-in-law, and her brother-in law's family. An undergraduate, she belongs to an affluent business family, which has no spending constraints on health care.

Sukhjeet has been menstruating regularly since the age of 15 years. She complains that, whenever menstruation occurs, she gets headache and nausea. In the past one year, her menstruation has been irregular. The duration has increased and the discharge is also more profuse. She has been advised hysterectomy by the doctor. She reports feeling giddy, has hot flushes and suffers from insomnia and mental depression. In addition, ever since she underwent sterilisation, she has been suffering from vaginal discharge, along with severe abdominal pain, weakness, discomfort, and a feeling that something is coming out. She lives in a joint family where the household chores are multifarious, and the workload weighs on her immensely. This contributes heavily towards elevating her stress levels.

In the last one month, she has not been able to deal with life's hassles. She is unable to control the way she spends her time and has not ever felt on top of things. She has an intense feeling that things just don't seem to go the way she wants them to, it is this that leads to her feeling of hopelessness and depression. She puts off making decisions and gets so upset at times that she wants to kill herself but she pushes away the thought because of the children. '*Aurat di koi zindagi nahin hai, saara din lage rahee da hai phir vi koi nahin puchhda haar kissi nu time te saab kuuch deeta jaanda hai phir vi koi khush nahin hoonda. Bachee vi haar samay naraaz raheende ne, koi eh naheen puchda, ma tusi theek ho. Doctor kol le chaaleye'*; 'A woman has no life, the whole day I slog at home try and maintain timings for food and other needs of everyone at home, yet no one is happy, even the children are annoyed over something or the other. No one asks me 'Mother, how are you feeling? Shall we take you to the doctor?'' All this upsets her and she doesn't know whom to seek help from. *'Kale aye haan kale tur jawange, koi naal nahin aaya koi naal nahee jayeega, appne pharz nibha ke bina kissi nu kuch kahee tur javange'*; 'We have come alone and shall go back alone, nobody will accompany us, so it is better to accept this fact and stop expecting anything'.

Torn between household responsibilities and her own needs, she has compromised her health, both physical as well as psychological, for the sake of the family. At this juncture of her life, she has an intense fear that one day, her children will leave her in their own self-interest, while she will be left to suffer and fight her loneliness. What an irony—after having spent a lifetime taking care of all the needs of her family, she has no assurance of security in her old age.

Case 17

Amrinder Kaur, aged 49 years, a Sikh from a Backward Caste (*Lohar*), belongs to an affluent business and agrarian family. She is an undergraduate. She lives in a joint family comprising her husband, herself, her two sons, father-in-law and mother-in-law, and her brother-in law's family. Kaur has been irregularly menstruating since the age of 16 years. She reports stomachache, heavy periods and lower backache. It is a real testing time for her. She can't even talk about it to anyone at home. '*Eh gaalan kis naal kareeye, ghar de kehnde ne* ki *aam ji gaal hai, haar aurat nu hoonda hai tusi jyada hi mahsoos karde ho'*; 'When I bring it up with my husband, he just comments that it is a natural process all women go through, and that I overreact to it'. Adding to her state of misery is the problem of vaginal discharge and its presence in the urine, bad odour, severe lower abdominal pain, weakness, and frequent fever. She has been on medication from a private practitioner but to no avail. She remains perturbed and upset primarily due to the fact that these are not really *'beemari'* (a disease) yet it has so much suffering attached to it. One can't even talk about it. Even the doctor says *'kucch nahin hai, phikar ki koi baat nahin hai';* 'It is nothing serious, don't worry about it'.

On the psychological assessment, she reports perceived stress due to her poor coping skills with respect to daily life hassles. This gets further aggravated due to her reproductive health problems. *Kya baat karen apni beemari ki, ehsi to koi beemari nahin hai par phir bhi pareshan hain*; 'What can I say about my disease? There is no such disease, according to the doctors, but still, I suffer'. She is left with no option but to suffer in silence.

She perceives shrinking support and declining concern from her husband, which unnerves her the most. In addition, she has a feeling of insecurity creeping in as to what her problem is and why her husband does not permit her to go ahead with a detailed investigation. To help her cope with her mental trauma, she needs immense confidence-building, which is possible only by paving a way towards her holistic health care by an experienced therapist.

Case 18

Tejpal Kaur, aged 48 years, belongs to a Sikh Backward Caste (*Ramdasi*) family. She got married at the age of 23 years. She lives in a nuclear family comprising, apart from herself, her husband, who is working with the Punjab Roadways, and her children—a son and a daughter, both students. She is educated up to middle level and is a housewife. She is meticulous, soft spoken and forthcoming. She is conscious about personal hygiene and the cleanliness of the house. Her worries include her husband's indifferent health and the future of the children.

She has been menstruating regularly since the age of 12 years. For the last couple of months, she has been experiencing scanty periods, and that upsets her. '*Ho sakda hai hun jaan da vela hai tan karke ghat gaye hain';* 'Maybe its time for the cessation of the menstruation and so it's scanty'.

She reports having lost twin male children after normal births; she had high blood pressure, which resulted in the death of the children. She also reports having undergone a spontaneous abortion in the second month, which caused her immense depression. Ever since then, she had numerous physical ailments, which include body ache, fatigue, weakness, palpitations and constipation. In addition, there is her vaginal discharge. She has been suffering from it for a long time now. She cannot remember distinctly how long. She attributes it just to eating wrong / 'hot' food. She has never gone to a doctor for treatment as her husband thinks it is not essential and that all women suffer from such ailments. 'A*am ji gal hai doctor kol jaan di ki loor hai, saariyan auratan noo ho jaanda hai*'; 'It is a problem which all women suffer from, so no advice from a doctor is needed'. She feels that if she could get a diagnosis to her problem, a lot of her suffering could be averted, but she wants it sitting at home, as she cannot go for treatment without her husband's permission.

She does not report being high on perceived stress, but is unable to control the important things in her life. She experiences nervousness and is stressed out. She also finds herself thinking about her husband's health (he suffers from severe skin allergies) and her children's secure future. She does acknowledge that she feels sad, puts off taking decisions, needs extra effort to get started, gets tired easily, and is less interested in sex now.

She tries to cope with these problems but does not get very far. An earnest effort by a therapist can effectively change her mindset and nurture the ability to cope with the mundane household worries and stay away from stresses of life. This can be made possible if a psychologist is made to play an active role in public health units.

Case 19

Preet Kaur, aged 50 years, a Sikh, belongs to a Backward Caste (*Kumhaar).* She lives in a nuclear family comprising herself, her husband, and her four children—two sons and two daughters. The family lives in a two room semi-pucca house. Kaur is illiterate. Her husband works as a labourer and earns just enough to meet the household's daily needs. She is decently dressed but disinterested in carrying forward the conversation. Somewhere in her a feeling persists: '*Tussi saade layee ki karooge?*; 'What will you do for us?'

She has been menstruating since the age of 15 years. In the past two months, her menstruation has been irregular. This has resulted in multifarious physical health problems, including dizziness. In addition, she reports that she has been having frequent vaginal discharge along with bad odour, severe abdominal pain, weakness, and discomfort. She attributes the vaginal discharge to eating 'hot' and wrong food. In the summer months, she reports, her condition worsens. She has been under medication from a private practitioner, which provides only a temporary relief. *Ghar vich hoor ehne kharche hain ki appne ute kina paisa kharch karde raheeye. Is ton changa hai ki chup chap bardasht karro te kissi nu kucch na kahoo. Eh tan bimari hi eisee kharaab hai jis da koi eelaj nahin hai*; 'There are so many expenses that one can't cope. How does one spend so much on a disease which has no cure? It is torture, but one has to learn to live with it'. She suffers from fatigue, aches and pains, insomnia, and anxiety. All this inhibits her normal functioning. Her married daughter is in the family way, and that too has added to her stress level.

Her psychological assessment reveals that she is under high-perceived stress and mild depression. She remains nervous and finds it tough to cope effectively with the important changes occurring in her life. She reports feeling sad, pessimistic about the future, does not enjoy things the way she used to earlier, gets annoyed or irritated more easily, and cries more often than she used to. Overall, she feels upset with life and her living conditions. No matter how much effort she puts into rectifying things, she says, they still go wrong and she is helpless. '*Sarkar nu kahoo kuch kare na te sadee sehat da kheyal rakh di hai te na hi naukri dendi hai ki asi koi kaam kar ke char paise kamma layeeye*; 'You must intimate to the government that we need to be provided with better health care facilities, and also with employment, so that we can earn some money and make a decent living'.

A lot of effort goes into making her cooperate in the interview. Probing into her health and familial problems is a tough task as she is reticent to a high degree. Her behaviour is understandable as she is undergoing so much of trauma in life that she has lost her self-confidence and has no faith in others. She has become sad, dejected and negativistic in her approach. She feels there is no way out. Living in poverty and coping with the mundane activities of the household have altogether depressed her. She admits that she has inadequate support from her family; otherwise, she would have helped her husband and made a better living for the family. Being a woman is a handicap. You live like a dependant throughout your life.

Concluding Remarks

Punjab, one of the most developed States of India, remains a traditional society in several ways. The joint family persists here to a large extent. A young newly married girl, for the initial year or so after marriage, is provided with adequate social support to adjust to the new family circumstances, with a hope that she will produce an heir. An implicit message is that she has to learn to cope with a tough situation till such time that she has produced a child, preferably a male one. To attain that goal, she may have to undergo innumerable pregnancies, abortions, and ultrasound tests. During this period, numerous reproductive health problems that she suffers from, including vaginal discharge, pain / burning on urination, foul smell, and abdominal pain, take a back seat. The fact that these reproductive health problems can lead to infertility is evidently not appreciated. In fact, a high incidence of infertility amongst young couples is itself emerging as an area of concern. This calls for in depth research studies.

Women in the second category—those in the child bearing age who have had children—too often neglect their health needs. Their gynecological morbidities such as vaginal discharge, discomfort during menstruation or intercourse and the related backache or abdominal pain, are martyred at the altar of their own self-effacing. Their reasons for not taking treatment include poor economic condition, which makes it difficult to incur expenses on medical care. Added to this is the primary obligation of looking after children and elders, as also the demands of domestic chores, all of which leave little time to visit the doctor. Mixed feelings about reproductive health issues prevail. On the one hand, they are not taken seriously, as it is considered normal for women to be suffering from reproductive health problems. On the other hand, the symptoms may be taken as a signal of a dangerous disease. Reasons for not seeking treatment are put forth until such time as it does not inhibit a woman from carrying out the household chores.

Women in the third category—those in the pre-menopausal stage, are now on the other side of the divide, with changed social roles and expectations. Menopause is accepted as a natural phase, which brings with it reproductive health problems such as vaginal discharge, burning on urination, and foul smell. Treatment is not sought because it is felt that as it is now time for the cessation of the menses, things will automatically get sorted out. Further, these women have a declining interest in sex, which leads to an indifference to reproductive health. The incentive to seek treatment also gets diluted. Moreover women's attitude towards holistic health needs the sanctions of their husbands before they can actually reach out for treatment. This also may not be forthcoming in desired degree at this stage of life.

Women's health problems, both physiological and psychological, need to be sensitively addressed and redressed particularly since a woman is socialised from childhood to maintain silence about her problems. In all the three stages—of puberty, childbearing and menopause, it clearly emerges that reproductive health problems have a genesis in the socio-cultural setting women are placed in and the expectations from them at a particular stage. Each stage has its own traumatic psychological impact, leading to stress and depression, and not being without long-term implications. Women reel through their lives in misery, assuming its what they are destined for. Will this trial by fire never end?

Recommendations

- The 'silence' syndrome attached to reproductive health problems to be removed. This will reduce the associated mental health problems of women.
- A reform in the socialisation pattern for young girls would contribute towards their being more open about voicing their problems. To ensure that they seek timely treatment, adequate health education too needs to be imparted.
- A holistic health care package to women at the primary, secondary and tertiary care levels is necessary. It must comprise of an assessment of their mental health in addition to diagnosis of physical health. This will require the inclusion of mental health care specialists as regular members of any health team.
- Vital issues concerning the health of working women, infertile couples, and menopausal women need to be identified and focused upon. It is important that this vulnerable, silent half of society is focused upon as a research priority. This will help in identifying interventions through effective policy-making.

NOTE

1. Moreover, studies confirm that sexually transmitted diseases increase the risk of acquiring and transmitting HIV infection by three to five times (Cohen 1998; Wasserheit

1992) and bacterial vaginosis may be a cofactor for HIV transmission, especially among younger women (Sewankambo *et al.*, 1997). (The susceptibility to sexually transmitted diseases is higher among the younger women, as they have fewer antibodies to fight pathogens and greater cervical ectopy) (World Health Organisation 1997).

REFERENCES

Altshuler, L.L., Hendrick, V., & Cohen, L.S. 1998. Course of Mood and Anxiety Disorders during Pregnancy and the Postpartum Period. *Journal of Clinical Psychiatry*, 59 Suppl. 2, 29-33.

Bang, R.A., Bang, A.T., Baitule, M., Choudhary, Y., Sarmukaddams and Tale, O. T. 1989. 'High Prevalence of Gynecological Diseases in Rural Indian Women'. *The Lancet*, 14, January, pp-85-88.

Beck, A., Ward, C.H., Mendelson, M., Mock, J. and Erbaugh, J. 1961. 'An inventory for measuring depression'. *Archives of General Psychiatry*, 4, 561-571.

Bhatia, J.C. and Cleland, J. 1995. 'Self-Reported Symptoms of Gynecological Morbidity and their Treatment in South India.' *Studies in Family Planning*. 26(4) : 203-16.

Bhatia, J.C., Cleland, J., Bhagavan, L., & Rao, N.S.N. 1997. 'Levels and Determinants of Gynaecological Morbidity in a District of South India'. *Studies in Family Planning*. vol. 28, no. 2, pp. 95-103.

Chandra, Prabha, S. 2001. 'The Interfaced between Psychiatry and Women's Reproductive Health', in Davar, Bhargavi, V. Ed., *Mental Health from a Gender Perspective*. New Delhi : Sage Publications India

Chandran, M.P. Tharyan, J. Muliyil, S. & Abraham, S. 2002. 'Post-partum Depression in a Cohort of Women from a Rural Area of Tamil Nadu, India: Incidence and Risk Factors'. *British Journal of Psychiatry*, 181, pp. 499-504.

Char, A. and Vaidya, S. 2000. 'Gynaecological Morbidity among Women Seeking Sterilization Services in Rural Maharashtra'. Paper presented at the workshop on *Reproductive Health in India: New Evidence and Issues*, Pune, February-March.

Cole, E., & Rothman, E. 1990. Commentary on 'Sexuality and the Midlife Woman'. *Psychology of Women Quarterly.* 14, 509-512.

Cohen, S., Kamarck, T. and Mermelstein, R. 1983. 'A Global Measure of Perceived Stress'. *Journal of Health and Social Behaviour*, 24, pp.385-396.

Daly, E, Gray, A, Barlow, D, McPherson, Roche, M and Vessey, M. 1994. Measuring the Impact of Menopausal Symptoms on Quality of Life. *Selections from British Medical Journal*, Vol. 9. 1050-54.

Dean,C., Williams, R.J., and Brockington, I.F. 1989. 'Is Puerperal Psychosis the Same as Bipolar Manic-Depressive Disorder? A family study'. *Psychological Medicine*. 19, 637-647.

Dennerstein, L., Smith, A., Morse, C., Burger, H., Hopper, J., and Ryan, M. 1993. 'Menopausal Symptoms in Australian Women'. *Medical Journal of Australia*. 159, pp. 232-236.

Dennerstein, L., Brown, J.B., Golts, G., Morse, C.A., Farley, T.M.M. & Pinol, A. 1993. 'Menstrual Cycle Hormonal Profiles of Women with and Without Pre-Menstrual Syndrome'. *Journal of Psychosomatic Obsteterics & Gynaecology,* 14, 259-268.

Duffy, C.L. 1983. 'Postpartum Depression: Identifying Women at Risk'. *Genesis*, 11, 21.

Jaswal, Surinder, K.P. 2001. 'Gynaecological Morbidity and Common Mental Disorders in Low Income Urban Women in Mumbai', in Davar, Bhargavi, V. Ed., *Mental Health from a Gender Perspective*. New Delhi: Sage Publications India.

Kaufman, J., Lan Liquin, W. Tongyin, and A. Faulkner. 1996. 'A Survey of RTI Prevalence, Risk Factors and Field-Based Diagnosis Method among 2020 Rural Chinese Women in Yunan Province'. Unpublished paper.

Kessler, R.C., McGonagle, K.A., Swartz, M., *et al.* 1993. 'Sex and Depression in the National Co-Morbidity Survey: I. Lifetime Prevalence, Chronicity and Recurrence'. *Journal of Affective Disorders*, 29, 85-96.

Kendell, R.E., Chalmers, J.C., & Platz, C. 1987. 'Epidemiology of Puerperal Psychosis'. *British Journal of Psychiatry*. 150: 662-673.

Klein, D.F., Skrobala, A.M., & Garfinkel, R.S. 1995. 'Preliminary Look at the Effects of Pregnancy on the Course of Panic Disorder'. *Anxiety*.1: 227-232.

Koenig, M., Jejeebhoy, S., Singh Sagari and S. Sridhar. 1996. 'Undertaking Community Based Research on the Prevalence of Gynaecological Morbidity: Lessons from India'. Unpublished document.

Mellner, Christin 2004. Women's Subjective and Objective Health Overtime: the Role of Psychosocial Conditions and Physiological Stress Responses. Doctoral thesis, Department of Psychology, Stockholm University, Stockholm.

Oomman. N. 1996. 'Poverty and pathology: Comparing rural Rajasthani women's ethnomedical models with biomedical models of reproductive morbidity: Implications for women's health in India'. Dissertation submitted to the School of Hygiene and Public Health, Johns Hopkins University, Baltimore.

Patel, V., Rodrigues, M. and Souza, N De. 2002. Gender, Poverty and Post-Natal Depression: A Cohort Study from Goa, India'. *American Journal of Psychology.* 159, pp. 43-47.

Pearce, J., Hawton, K., and Blake, F. 1995. 'Psychological and Sexual Symptoms Associated with the Menopause and the Effects of Hormone Replacement Therapy'. *British Journal of Psychiatry*. 167, 163-173.

P M S O'Brien. 1994. 'Selections from BMJ'. Vol 10, March 1994, pp. 54-56.

Rahman, A., Iqbal, Z., & Harrington, R. (Forthcoming). 'Life Events, Social Support and Depression in Childbirth: Perspectives from a Rural Community in the Developing World'. *Psychological Medicine.*

Ravindran, T.K.S., Savitri, R. and Bhavani, A. 1999. 'Women's Experiences of Utero-Vaginal Prolapse: A Qualitative Study from Tamil Nadu, India.' in M. Berer and T.K.S. Ravindran eds., 'Safe Motherhood Initiatives. Critical Issues'. pp. 165-72. London: Blackwell Sciences Limited for Reproductive Health Matters.

Ravindran, T.K.S., Savitri, R. and Bhavani, A. 1999. 'Women's Experiences of Utero-Vaginal Prolapse: A Qualitative Study from Tamil Nadu, India.' in M. Berer and T.K.S.Ravindran eds., 'Safe Motherhood Initiatives. Critical Issues'. pp. 165-72. London: Blackwell Sciences Limited for Reproductive Health Matters.

Rubinow, D.R., and Roy-Byrne, P.P. 1984. 'Premenstrual Syndromes: Overviews from a Methodological Perspective'. *American Journal of Psychiatry*. 141,163-172.

Sewankambo, N. *et al.* 1997. 'HIV-1 Infection Associated With Abnormal Vaginal Flora Morphology and Bacterial Vaginosis'. *Lancet*. 350(9083), pp. 546-550.

Wasserheit, J.N. and Holmes, K.K. 1992. 'Reproductive tract infections: challenges for international health policy, programs and research in A. Germain et al. *Reproductive Tract Infections.* N. York: Plenum Press.

Wasserheit, J. 1992. 'Epidemiological Synergy: Interrelationships between Human Immunodeficiency Virus Infection and Other Sexually Transmitted Diseases'. Sexually Transmitted Diseases. 19 (2): 61-77.

Cohen M.1998. 'Sexually Transmitted Diseases Enhance HIV Transmission: No Longer a Hypothesis'. *Lancet*. 351 (Suppl.3): 5-7.

Weissman, M.M., and Olfson, M., 1995. 'Depression in Women: Implications for Health Care Research'. *Science*. 269, 799-801.

World Health Organisation. 1981. *Research on Menopause*. Geneva: World Health Organisation.

World Health Organisation 1990. 'Measuring Reproductive Morbidity, Report of a Technical Working Group'. Geneva: World Health Organisation.

World Health Organisation 1997. 'Young People and Sexually Transmitted Diseases'. *Fact Sheet*. Geneva: WHO, No. 186.

Part VI

GENDER AND THE FEMALE-MALE RATIO

Chapter 10

The Family: A Neglected Determinant of Health in South Asia

Carol Vlassoff, Shobha Rao, Varsha Garole, Neelima Karandikar, Mandana Azar and *Asanwari Kanade*

In South Asia the family influences almost every aspect of life. Nonetheless, its potential role in determining the health behaviour of individuals has been neglected in the health and social science literature. Interestingly, far more attention has been devoted to family support in the West where public institutions provide far greater social, health, and financial security than in the developing world. The evidence presented here clearly demonstrates the importance of family support in determining the course of disease, and in coping and treatment

Social support is a coping mechanism that acts as a buffer once a health problem or condition has been defined as serious (Shuval 1981). In many societies, kinship networks play an important role. Indeed a supportive traditional kinship system in times of need, especially during illness, is important in many societies (Olukayode 1981). In illnesses that are accompanied by social stigma, significant others, such as kin, may play an even more vital role.

Role of the Family in Health and Illness: Evidence from the Literature

In the West, considerable research has demonstrated the importance of support from the family and society in determining health outcomes. Health professionals and social scientists have increasingly come to appreciate the irrefutable evidence to the effect that social support has profound effects, not only on the emotional and psychological well being of patients, but also on compliance and adherence to treatment regimens.

Social support has been defined by Lin *et al.* as 'support accessible to an individual through social ties to other individuals, groups and larger community' (Lin *et al.* 1979). It refers to the 'interpersonal exchanges that provide information, emotional reassurance, material assistance, and a sense of self-esteem' (Revenson and Gibofsky 1994: 5). Many studies give broad definitions of social support such as the above. However, on closer examination, family members and friends stand out as the major source of support.

A study of Chinese-Americans living in Washington D.C. shows a clear relationship between social support, stressful life events and illness. Although the link between stressful life events and illness has been well established in previous research, this study is unique in that it also examines the role of social support. Interestingly, social support was found not only to correlate negatively with illness symptoms but was a better predictor of symptoms than stressful life events. The authors' findings strongly suggest that social support has as much, if not more, of an effect on illness than stressful life events. The implications are that although stressful life events are usually 'unmanipulatable' (Lin *et al.* 1979: 116); social support can be manipulated or improved upon by services and health care interventions.

Several studies have examined the impact of family/social support on various chronic diseases such as hypertension, cancer, diabetes, and rheumatoid arthritis. Research on social support networks of elderly patients in New Mexico concludes that social support helps to buffer stress effects linked to diagnoses of cancer. It also provides assistance in decision making, adherence to medication regimens and transportation, hence improving compliance with treatment (Goodwin et al. 1991). In a previous study by the same author, married cancer patients were diagnosed earlier, took more appropriate treatment, and survived longer than unmarried patients (Goodwin *et al.* 1987).

Becker and Maiman (1980), in a paper on strategies for enhancing patient compliance, review a number of studies demonstrating the influential role of family support in problems of obesity, coronary heart disease, arthritis and hypertension. In hypertension, intervention consisting of family support in combination with *exit interviews*—individualised instructional sessions with a health educator, of 15-20 minutes duration, following examination and prescription of regimen by physicians, to reinforce and clarify the physicians instructions—were found to be the most effective strategy for enhancing compliance with the prescribed medication (Green *et al.* 1975). A more global view suggests that people's 'perceived sense of support' may lead to a more 'generalised sense of control', perhaps explaining the mechanism by which social support acts to enhance health status (Fishman 1995:175). The impact of social support is however not unqualifiedly beneficial. Thus, while Revenson and Gibofsky (1995) recognise the invaluable contribution of family / spousal support in enhancing the impact of medical interventions in rheumatic disease, they also warn against certain unhelpful types of support such as minimising illness severity, offering pessimistic comments, pitying the patient, and being overprotective (Revenson and Gibofsky 1995: 6).

Two other studies, on family support and diabetes, indicate the importance of family and social support and the separate roles they play. La Greca *et al* (1994) finds that the support of family and friends was of different kinds for adolescents—families gave more material help such as assisting with injections and supervising diets. Interestingly, girls received more emotional diabetes specific support from friends than boys. This study highlights the importance of looking at gender differences when investigating family and social support. In another study, Garay-Sevilla *et al.* (1995) examined compliance with diet and medication in 200 diabetic patients in Mexico. Their observations were consistent with previous research in that adherence to medication and diet strongly correlated with social support. This study is one of only a few which dissect social support into various parts such as family structure and function, roles of family members and control of behaviour and independently studies their effect on compliance. Control of behaviour was the only parameter of social support found to influence compliance in diabetics.

Evidence suggests also that status within the household affects access to information about disease, preventive measures and treatment. For example, there is growing evidence that the mother's freedom to make decisions has considerable influence on the health of her children (Dyson and Moore 1983). In Jordan, Doan and Bisharat (1990) reported that women's autonomy in the household had a strong influence on the nutritional status of their children. In households where the mother-in-law was present and the young wife had little decision making power, children's weight for age was significantly lower than in families where the mother was head or co-head of the household. In Mali, household status was an important determinant of treatment seeking for malaria. The household heads, most of whom were male, had ultimate decision making power with respect to choice of treatment and payment for treatment (Traore and Coulibaly 1992).

Despite the growing evidence that family support and family roles have a great impact on health and illness outcomes, few studies have explored the reasons for this association. This is even more true in the case of stigmatizing diseases, although with the advent of HIV/AIDS new insights are beginning to emerge. The literature on the role of social and family support to those infected with HIV/ AIDS has been concerned more with the consequences on the patient's quality of life than on the course or outcomes of disease (Nunes et al., 1995; WHO, 1992). Research indicates that fear of rejection is a major concern of patients suffering from HIV/AIDS (Lie and Biswalo, 1994; Turner *et al,* 1993), and that AIDS patients may experience even more stress from the fear of loss of social support than from fear of the physical consequences of the disease (Hart *et al,* 1992). These findings highlight the special role of social and family support in helping patients to deal with stigmatising diseases, an area that has received less attention in the literature than non-stigmatising diseases.

Role of the Family in Health Behaviour in South Asia

It is well accepted that in South Asia the family is critical in determining the behaviour of its members. Major decisions customarily are taken in consultation with family members in these communities, and family opinions cannot be ignored easily. 'Family life and close friendships play a central role in Indian life. The centrality of social relationships in Indian life stands in contrast to the peculiarly western preoccupation with work and professional advancement' (Lepore.*et al.* 1991).

South Asian demographers have paid considerably more attention than health scientists to the role of the family, especially in relation to fertility and family planning. For example, in a study of a tribal community in South India (Gurumurthy 1985), it was found that interference of the members of kinship groups emerged as the second most powerful variable, explaining 14 per cent of the variation in fertility. Likewise, Koenig and Foo (1992), in a review of reproductive behaviour, patriarchy and women's status in rural North India, indicate that in 95 per cent of cases, husbands and mothers-in-law had granted permission to wives before they underwent sterilisation. Mothers-in-law tend to stop childbearing with the entry of daughters-in-law into their household to avoid the disgrace on becoming pregnant at a late stage of life (Opler, 1964; Yadav and Singh, 1986; Jeffreys *et al,* 1989).

Despite the evidence of the important role of the family in decision making and behaviour in family planning, there are surprisingly few detailed analyses of decision making dynamics and the influence of the patriarchal system on fertility outcomes (Koenig and Foo 1992). Even more importantly, the role of the family in determining family planning and ultimately, population growth outcomes, has not been enunciated in family planning policies.

The role of the South Asian family has received relatively more attention in psychiatric disorders than in other health problems. The research indicates that strong familial support contributes to better treatment outcomes. In a study of schizophrenia in Chandigarh, India, Leff *et al.* (1990) suggest that tolerance and acceptance among family members led to a better response to treatment. The authors note, however, that the contribution of family support in rural societies requires a more detailed analysis.

In a stigmatised disease such as leprosy, the role of the family may be even more important in determining the course and outcome of the disease. A negative attitude in the family could ruin the life of a patient whereas a positive attitude from the time of detection could lead the patient to a complete cure. Unfortunately, the existing research tends to portray a negative impression of the leprosy patient's family. For example, Mull *et al.* (1989) cites several cases of family rejection of leprosy patients, including the withdrawal of love from one's own mother, as well as problems of finding marriage partners for patients and their family members. Similarly, Ramu *et al,* (1975) report that in South India, leprosy affliction resulted in the break-up of joint families. Kaur *et al.* (1994) observe that in North India, stigma due to leprosy may result in strained relationships between family members, and that discrimination and fear of spreading infections were more common in joint families. The instability of leprosy patients in this regard is also highlighted in a study in Maharashtra, India (Vlassoff *et al.*).

Research evidence for the role of positive family attitudes in leprosy, as well as in other diseases, is scanty. In stigmatised diseases a supportive environment would seem essential in ensuring positive health behaviour and appropriate interventions on the part of the patient. Leprosy, therefore provides a good example of the role of family in health seeking behaviour and health outcomes, with far reaching implications for health and disease control policies. We therefore have chosen a recent study in Maharashtra, India, to illustrate the role of family support in detecting, treating and coping with leprosy.

Evidence from a Study of Leprosy in India

The study reported on here was conducted between 1993 and 1996. It involves both qualitative and quantitative data, as described below.

Data and Methods

The study was carried out in four districts of Maharashtra State, in which four urban and four rural or tribal sectors were selected. For each sector, complete lists of current patients and those released from treatment (but still under surveillance) were obtained. A random sample, stratified on the basis of age and sex, was then selected. The sample was also stratified by type of living arrangement. In Maharashtra about 10 per cent of patients are staying in leprosy colonies and about 5 per cent in special homes or institutions. Similar proportions of such patients were maintained in the study sample.

A total of 1154 patients (496 males and 658 females) were interviewed, using a semistractured questionnaire, to investigate various aspects of the experience of leprosy, including its detection, approaches to and compliance with treatment; the impact of the disease on social, family and personal life, and the role of the family in mediating this impact. Most patients on treatment were contacted at clinics whereas those from homes and colonies were interviewed in their homes.

This analysis focuses on the influence of the family on the course of disease and in coping and treatment seeking. "Family" is defined as the entire group (of two or more people) who are related to each other by blood, marriage, or adoption. In this analysis we do not treat family support as a single entity but rather consider various aspects that represent our concept of family support. These include (1) position of the patient in the family as household head (2) sharing the diagnosis with spouse (3) a supportive reaction of the family after detection and (4) positive suggestions of the family for treatment.

Although in most analysis "type of family" (joint / nuclear) is considered as a key independent variable, we have not used it as an indicator of familial support for several reasons. First, family type may change at the time of detection and during the course of disease as patients may divorce, remarry, stay separately, or cohabit with other patients. In this study we did in fact find an increase in the percentage of nuclear families after detection of leprosy (Rao *et al.* 1996). Further, patients may be married both at the time of interview and at detection of the disease but not necessarily to the some person. In an earlier study, this was found to be the case. Similarly, many patients, particularly women, who had been living alone for many years, said that they were married because they did not wish to admit that their spouse had abandoned them.

Also, family type is highly influenced by the life cycle stage of its members. In rural South Asia, a young married couple usually lives with in-laws, but when the couple has children, or when other sons marry, the older son may move out with his family (Vlassoff and Vlassoff 1983). Hence the type of family changes from joint to nuclear for the same individual is a natural course and is not necessarily related to other factors such as disease. In our analysis, therefore, family type is difficult to associate causally to disease variable.

Results

The distributions of the indicators used for family support are summarised in Table 1. A high proportion of male, as compared to very few female, patients were heads of household. Similar proportions of males and females shared their first diagnosis of leprosy with their spouse, although the proportion of females was somewhat higher. Considerably more females said that the family's first reaction after learning of the diagnosis was positive and more women said that the family had made positive suggestions. However, as will be seen, women's reported perceptions of positive behaviour on the part of the family were less influential than men's in determining the course of disease, coping, and treatment seeking behaviour.

TABLE 1. Respondent by Sex, Household Headship and Family Support Indicators

Sex	Position in family		Shared diagnosis with		First reaction of family		Suggestions by family	
	Head	Other	Spouse	Others	Positive	Negative/ Natural	Posi- tive	Negative/ Natural
Males (%)	64.0	36.0	30.3	69.7	54.5	45.5	75.9	24.1
(N)	306	172	115	265	211	176	356	113
Females (%)	3.6	96.4	38.4	71.6	61.3	38.7	83.2	26.8
(N)	23	613	187	300	381	241	500	101
Total (%)	29.5	70.5	34.8	65.2	58.7	41.3	80.0	20.0
Total Resondents	329	785	302	565	592	417	856	213

Role of the Family in Determining the Course of the Disease

As with most other diseases, in the case of leprosy, early detection is critical in determining treatment and the possibility of a cure. In leprosy, the initial symptoms, patches and redness of the skin, are not painful and may be ignored easily. It is interesting to see, then, in which situations early noticing and discussion of symptoms with family members take place and how these affect the further course of treatment.

The 'course of the disease' shown in Table 2 is measured by (1) gap (in months) between noticing a symptom (primarily the appearance of a skin change) and suspecting it as a symptom of leprosy; (2) gap (in months) between suspecting the initial symptom to be leprosy and obtaining medical confirmation (3) delay (in months) in initiating medical treatment after diagnosis and (4) irregularity in compliance with treatment, as reported by patients. Irregularity is measured by the proportion of patients reporting that they were irregular in treatment, rather than in time, because assessments of time, on and off treatment, over the long duration required by the treatment schedule, was poorly recalled by the patients.

The initial gap (Gap 1) between noticing a symptom and suspecting it to be leprosy was, on average, approximately 14 months. For heads of households this gap was much smaller (11.7 months) and especially for female (8.2 months) (Table 2). In cases where the first reaction on the part of the family member was positive, and where positive suggestions were made, this gap was also smaller than for the overall sample. However, when broken down by sex, the gap was much less in the case of males. Sharing the diagnosis with the spouse also appeared to reduce the gap much more for males than females. If anything, for females, sharing seems to have had a negative impact. The data show also that the gap between obtaining the diagnosis and the initiation of medical treatment was far smaller for heads of household than for those in other positions.

TABLE 2: Response to Disease by Household Headship and Family Support Indicators

Type of response	Overall average	Position as head			Sharing with spouse*			First reaction positive			Positive suggestions		
		T	M	F	T	M	F	T	M	F	T	M	F
Gap 1 (in months)	13.9	11.7	12.0	8.2	14.1	11.4	15.9	13.3	10.5	14.9	13.4	12.9	13.7
N	(917)	(264)	(244)	(20)	(221)	(86)	(135)	(484)	(180)	(304)	(697)	(289)	(408)
Gap 2 (in months)	13.2	7.6	7.2	12.8	9.2	9.3	9.1	12.3	9.4	14.7	13.3	11.9	14.6
N	(202)	(54)	(50)	(4)	(48)	(17)	(31)	(117)	(52)	(65)	(152)	(71)	(81)
Delay (in months)	16.8	5.2	5.6	0.0	9.6	4.0	12.9	15.9	10.3	19.0	18.7	20.7	16.3
N	(43)	(32)	(10)	(22)	(10)	(2)	(8)	(21)	(12)	(9)	(28)	(15)	(13)
Irregularity (%)	12.3	8.3	8.8	0.0	16.4	10.0	21.0	12.5	10.8	13.5	10.6	8.7	11.9
N	(1085)	(316)	(297)	(19)	(239)	(101)	(138)	(560)	(204)	(356)	(721)	(300)	(421)

*N for "sharing with spouse" for male and female does not add to total who shared with someone because this N refers only to a subset of those who shared with others.

Note:

'Gap 1' refers to gap in months between noticing a symptom (primarily the appearance of a skin change) and suspecting it as a symptom of leprosy.

'Gap 2' refer to gap in months between suspecting the initial symptom to be leprosy and obtaining medical confirmation.

'Delay' refer to delay (in months) in initiating medical treatment after diagnosis. 'Irregularity' refer to irregularity in compliance with treatment, as reported by the patient

The second gap (Gap 2)—that between noticing the symptom and obtaining medical confirmation—may be even more important than the first in determining the possibility of early and effective treatment. Here family support obviously played a significant role, especially for males. Sharing the diagnosis with the spouse seemed to reduce the gap for both men and women, but in the case of other family support indicators (i.e. position as head, positive reactions and suggestions from the family) Gap 2 was considerably lower for males than for females. Thus, family support seemed to favour males in reducing the gap in treatment.

The delay in initiating treatment was, on average, small. However, among those who delayed initiation, head of households had smaller delays than those in other positions. Presumably, the greater decision-making power of household heads allows them to act quickly and effectively. While this was true for both males and females, only 3.6 per cent of females were heads of household. In reality, as few women in rural India are heads of household, they will be less likely to be detected and treated as early as men. The delay in initiating actual treatment for those who shared with their spouse was substantially less. Interestingly, however, this was not true in the case of females, maybe because although husbands would give emotional support, it does not necessarily lead to immediate and positive action such as taking their wives for treatment or reliving them from work by way of substitution. This is substantiated by the higher percentage of irregularity in treatment of female patients in spite of sharing with their spouse.

A positive reaction after first sharing of the diagnosis resulted, for males, in smaller gaps in the entire interval between appearance of the symptoms and initiation of the treatment. Again, such a trend is not true for female patients. A possible explanation may be that women tend to say that they received a positive reaction in order not to speak badly of their family. Similar observations hold true in the case of irregularity in treatment. For the most part, irregularity in treatment seeking was less for those who received support from their families than for those who did not. Overall these results confirm the role of positive support from the family in determining the course of disease, although males generally benefited more than females.

Role of Family in Coping

When affected by leprosy, the social costs for a family may be very high. It has been noted that the costs of accepting the diagnosis of leprosy 'is simply too great in terms of overall family well being' (Mull *et al.* 1989). Therefore, successful coping will require considerable acceptance and understanding on the part of the family, failing which the leprosy afflicted may seek to hide the disease for as long as possible, thereby delaying effective treatment.

'Coping' is considered in terms of (1) how the patient handles the disease, that is, whether or not he or she hides the disease from others by withdrawing from social participation, or by taking treatment secretly, etc. and (2) the extent of self-stigma developed on the basis of selected questions regarding how the disease affects marriage prospects, divorce or separation, perceptions of causation of the affliction, hopes for cure of the disease, attitude towards maintaining contacts with family and society, etc. (Scores were computed, with possible values ranging from 0 to 3).

The majority, 81.6 per cent of the patients, appeared to be coping well with the disease (Table 3). This is probably due to the influence of effective treatment with multi-drug therapy (MDT). However, 18.4 per cent still hid their symptoms as a way of coping; fear of rejection by the family was stated as the main reason for hiding. Overall, hiding of the disease was less among heads of the household, but this was the case only among males.

Otherwise, too, males seemed to benefit more from family support than females in terms of not hiding the disease. Interestingly, sharing with spouse increased concealment of the disease among both males and females. Depending on the situation, helping a patient to hide the disease may be positive, if it motivates the patient to obtain early and effective treatment before the disease advances and becomes debilitating. On the other hand, hiding may be indicative of denial and hence a negative reaction. Since sharing with the spouse effectively reduced the delay in treatment for both males and females in our sample, it seems that shared concealment by the spouse had a positive rather than negative effect. A positive reaction on the part the family led to less hiding of the disease among males, but not among females. This again casts doubt on the perceptions of females about positive familial reactions. Although not shown in the table, responses obtained to the question on hiding revealed that, for 41.3 per cent of the patients (45.4 per cent of males; 38.7 per cent of females), negative reactions of family members led to hiding the disease.

The first recognition or diagnosis of leprosy is often extremely disturbing to the individual, as are its later symptoms, if allowed to progress. The social stigma attached to the disease, resulting from a long tradition of superstition and misconception about its cause and transmission, sharpens this negative image. Self stigma of the leprosy patient could be very severe in families where support is low, hindering the overall effectiveness of the treatment. Individuals with higher self stigma scores are therefore likely to cope less successfully with the disease. We found that the average self-stigma scores in tribal communities are lowest (.60) in comparison to the rural (.75) and urban (.89) scores. This observation is consistent with earlier reports that stigma among tribal communities is low (Gokhale *et al* 1993).

Average self-stigma is significantly lower for heads of household than for

TABLE 3: Illness Response by Household Headship and Family Support Indicators

Type of coping	Overall average	Position as head			Sharing with spouse*			First reaction positive			Positive suggestions		
		T	M	F	T	M	F	T	M	F	T	M	F
Response													
Hiding (%)	18.4	15.7	15.2	22.7	24.5	23.0	25.5	18.2	12.9	21.2	18 3	16.4	19.6
N	(1132)	(325)	(303)	(22)	(297)	(113)	(184)	(582)	(209)	(373)	(948)	(396)	(552)
Self-stigma score*	.79	.70	.70	.69	78	.77	.78	.84	.90	.80	.78	.79	.78
N	(1149)	(328)	(306)	(22)	(304)	(116)	(188)	(563)	(210)	(353)	(948)	(396)	(552)

* Details of derivation of self stigma scores are in the appendix.

the overall average (Table 3). Interestingly (although not shown in the Table), self-stigma was considerably high for males in other positions (.91) than for females in other positions (.80). This again reveals the gender difference in dealing with the disease. Males perhaps finding it more difficult to accept than females because it may mean a loss of social status. Neither sharing with spouse nor a positive first reaction from family significantly affected self stigma scores. However, first reactions of the family, if negative, did seem to affect self-stigma. Patients who received negative reactions from their families on first sharing had higher self stigma in case of both males (1.56) and females (1.29). This indicates the importance of the family's role in influencing a patient's ability to cope with disease.

Role of the family in determining treatment

It is well known that people often opt for various sources of treatment, including home remedies, offerings and prayers, and traditional and religious healers before seeking medical help. Treatment seeking patterns vary considerably from family to family, depending on factors such as family customs, religion, convenience and costs. It is for these reasons that the family's role in determining the timing and choice of treatment assumes importance.

In our analysis, both traditional and modern methods of treatment are considered. These include (1) religious treatment (offerings, fasting, pilgrimages, etc.) (2) traditional practices (traditional healers, applications of oils, drinking decoctions, etc.) and (3) medical treatment (MDT). The family's role in positive treatment seeking may be confounded by the prevalent cultural practice of seeking help from religious and traditional sources. Reasons for consulting traditional, as well as modern sources, deep-rooted and widespread in South Asia, include lack of funds, easy accessibility and the positive, welcoming reception of the patient. Heads of households and those who shared their problem with their spouse were less likely than others to have sought religious or traditional treatment before diagnosis (Table 4). Moreover, sharing the diagnosis with a spouse reduced the tendency to consult non-medical sources. Positive reactions on the part of the family appeared to have little effect on choice of treatment before diagnosis, although females who said they received positive feedback from the family were more likely to have consulted religious help. Generally, household position and family support led to greater reliance on medical treatment, although this was true mainly for men. Even after diagnosis, and despite taking MDT, many patients, especially females, continued to rely on religious and traditional sources.

Discussion

We have considered four major family support indicators in the context of

TABLE 4: Choice of Treatment by Household Headship and Family Support Indicators

Type of coping	Overall average	Position as head			Sharing with spouse			First reaction positive			Positive suggestions		
		T	M	F	T	M	F	T	M	F	T	M	F
Before Diagnosis													
None	10.3	10.8	10.6	13.6	7.7	6.2	8.6	7.7	9.2	6.9	8.1	8.5	7.9
Religious	14.5	11.1	11.2	9.1	10.7	8.0	12.4	15.6	13.5	16.7	16.6	152	17.0
Traditional	4.2	2.4	2.6	0.0	3.4	1.8	4.3	4.1	2.9	4.8	3.2	2.5	3.7
N	(1134)	(325)	(303)	(22)	(298)	(113)	(185)	(584)	(207)	(377)	(864)	(355)	(509)
After Diagnosis													
Religious	27.3	22.5	21.9	31.6	24.1	13.0	30.9	30.1	25.1	329	28.1	31.6	25.6
Traditional	13.7	10.1	10.5	5.0	11.5	7.8	13 7	11.9	9.5	13.3	12.9	12 3	13 3
Medical	85.4	90.3	91.5	73.9	85.1	92.2	80.7	86.3	89.1	84.8	86.7	87.9	85,8
N	(1135)	(329)	(306)	(23)	(302)	(115)	(187)	(592)	(211)	(381)	(856)	(356)	(500)

leprosy, but these indicators could vary as could the diseases to which they are applied. Position as household head generally helped patients to go early for diagnosis, follow appropriate treatment and cope better with the disease. Greater decision making power associated with headship seems to promote positive health behaviour. As women are rarely heads of household in rural India, the observation implies that empowering women with decision-making through other avenues, such as income generation or literacy, could improve their health status.

Sharing the diagnosis with the spouse appeared beneficial, especially for males, as it reduced the delay in initiating medical help and increased regularity in treatment. It also led to hiding of the disease as a coping mechanism, which, in turn, led to earlier treatment. This suggests that counselling the spouse regarding positive action and the availability of MDT would be a powerful intervention.

Immediate positive reaction of the family after diagnosis and positive suggestions for treatment also led to more appropriate treatment seeking and coping. In general, however, males benefitted from family support much more than females. This could be due to the fact that women's avowal of positive reactions on the part of their families may be more indicative of their unwillingness to criticise family members than of the real situation.

It is important to emphasise that family support, despite its usually positive role in health behaviour, can also be problematic in certain situations. For example, both men and women who reported that they received positive reactions from their families were also more likely to consult religious as well as medical sources. While this is not necessarily negative, such alternative advice may confound the recovery process. For example, in an earlier study, patients who visited 'jaundice specialists' were advised to stop MDT treatment, impeding their cure (Vlassoff *et al.*). Similarly, expenditures on costly offerings or pilgrimages may unnecessarily add to the costs of treatment. These considerations must be kept in mind when advocating the importance of family support to patients. Advice to religious leaders and traditional practitioners about the need for appropriate treatment and referral of patients also should be considered.

While it seems obvious that more attention to family roles and gender relations within the family could improve the effectiveness of health programmes in South Asia, more research is needed on how illness and disease are perceived and cared for by families. Priority should be given to research on the roles of family members in activities that promote or hinder health, as well as in care giving. Families are already an important health resources for their members and it is likely that they can become more effective if provided with relevant and timely information. Women are universally respected as the key health providers in the family, yet their role as potential partners is largely ignored by the formal health care sector (Vlassoff and Bonilla 1994). We have also seen that women and men differ greatly in terms of the family support they receive, in their interpretations of this support, and in the use they make of it. Gender sensitivity is therefore important in understanding the influence of family dynamics in health and in designing interventions to improve the positive influence of family support on health outcomes.

REFERENCES

Doan R.M. and L. Bisharat (1990) Female autonomy and child nutritional status: the extended-family residential unit in Amman, Jordan. *Social Science and Medicine* 38(7)783-789.

Dyson, T. and M. Moore (1983) Kinship structure, female autonomy, and demographic behaviour in India. *Population and Development Review* 9, 35.

Fishman, T. (1955) The 90-second intervention: a patient compliance mediated technique to improve and control hypertension. *Public Health Report* 110(2): 173-177.

Garay-Sevilla, M.E., L.E. Nava, J.M. Malacara, R. Huerta, J. Diaz de Leon, A. Mena and M.E. Fajardo (1995) Adherence to treatment and social support in patients with non-insulin dependent diabetes mellitus. *Journal of Diabetes and its Complications* 9:81-86.

Gokhale, S.D. (1993) Rehabilitation in leprosy: a socio-cultural cause-effect study. Unpublished project report. WHO/TDR.

Goodwin, J.S., W.C. Hunt, C.R. Key and J.M. Samet (1987) The effect of marital status on stage, treatment, and survival of cancer patients. *Journal of the American Medical Association* 258(21): 3125-3130.

Goodwin, J.S., W.C. Hunt and J.M. Samet (1991) A population-based study of functional status and social support networks of elderly patients newly diagnosed with cancer. *Archives of Internal Medicine* 151;366-370.

Green, L.W., D.M. Levine and S. Deeds. 1975. Clinical Trials of Health Education for Hypertensive Outpatient: Design and Baseline Data. *Preventive Medicine.* 4;417-425.

Guarnaccia, RJ., Parra, P., Deschamps, A., Milstein, G. and Argiles, N. (1992) Si Dios quiere: Hispanic families' experiences of caring for a seriously mentally ill family member. *Culture, Medicine and Psychiatry* 16:187-215.

Gurumurthy, G. (1985) Kinship interactions and fertility among Yanadis—a tribal community in South India. *Demography India 14(2):* 197-203.

Hart, G.K. Mann and M. Stewart (1992) Les consequences du SIDA dans la vie des hemophiles et de leur soignants familiaux au Quebec: stress, au stress et soutien social. *Sante, Ment. Que.* 17(1):97-110.

Jeffrey, P., R. Jeffrey and A. Lyon (1989) *Labour Pains and Labour Power: Women and Childbearing in India.* New Delhi: Manohar.

Kaur, H. and V. Ramesh (1994) Social problems of women leprosy patients—a study conducted at 2 urban leprosy centres in Delhi. *Leprosy Review* 65,361-375.

Koenig, M.A. and G.H.C. Foo (1992) Patriarchy, women's status and reproductive behaviour in rural North India. *Demography India* 145-166.

La Greca, A.M., W.F. Auslander, P. Greco, D. Spetter, E.B. Fisher, Jr. and J.V. Santiago (1994) I get by with a little help from my family arid friends: adolescents' support for diabetes care. *Journal ofPediatric Psychology* 20(4):449-476.

Leff, J., Wig, N.N., Bedi, H., Menon, D.K., Kuipers, L., Korten, A, Ernberg, G., Day, R., Sartorius, N. and Jablensky, A. (1990) Relatives' expressed emotion and the course of schizophrenia in Chandigarh. A two-year follow-up of a first-contact sample. *British Journal of Psychiatry* 156, 351-356.

Lepore, S.L., M.N. Palsane and G.W. Evans (1991) Daily hassles and chronic trains: a hierarchy of stressors? *Social Science and Medicine* 33(9): 1029-1036.

Lie, G.T. and P.M. Biswalo (1994) Perceptions of the appropriate HTV/AIDS counsellor in Arusha and Kilimanjaro regions of Tanzania: implications for hospital counselling. *AIDS-Care* 6(2):139-151.

Lin N., Simeone, R.S., Ensel, W.M. and Kuo, W., Social support, stressful life events, and illness: a model and an empirical test. *Journal of Health and Social Behaviour*

Mull, J.D., C. Shear Wood, L.P. Gans and D.S. Mull (1989) Culture and 'compliance' among leprosy patients in Pakistan. *Social Science and Medicine* 29(7):799-811L

Naik, S.S., P.S. Hambarde, and A.N. Desai (1991) Problems and needs of women leprosy patients in Bombay and Goa—a preliminary report. *Indian Journal of Leprosy* 63(2):213-222.

Nunes, J.A., S.J. Raymond, P.K. Nicholas, J.D. Leuner and A. Webster (1995) Social support, quality of life, immune function, and health in persons living with HIV. *Journal of Holistic Nursing 13(2):* 174-198.

Olukayade, R. (1981) A study of the role of socio-cultural factors in the treatment of mental illness in Nigeria. *Social Science and Medicine* 15A:49-54.

Opler, M E. (1964) Cultural context and population control programs in village India. pp.201-221 in E.W. Count and G.T. Bowles (eds.), *Fact and Theory in Social Science*. Syracuse: Syracuse University Press.

Ramu, G., M.P. Dwiwedi and C.G.S. Iyer (1975) Social reaction to leprosy in a rural population in Chingleput District (Tamil Nadu) *Leprosy in India* 43(3):56-169.

Rao *et al.* (1996). Women and Leprosy. Ongoing Research Project funded by the Special Reference on Research and Training in Tropical Disease, World Health Organisation, Geneva.

Revenson, T. and A. Giebofsky (1995) Marriage, social support, and adjustment to rheumatic disease. *Bulletin on the Rheumatic Diseases* 44(3):5-7.

Shuval, J.T. (1981) The contribution of psychological and social phenomena to an understanding of the etiology of disease and illness. *Social Science and Medicine* 15A:337-342.

Traore, S., S. Coulibaly and M.C. Sidibc (1993) Comportements et couts lies au paludisme chez Ies femmes de campements de pecheurs dans la zone de Selingue au Mali. *SER Project Reports* No. 12. WHO, Geneva.

Turner, H.A., R.B. Hays and T.J. Coates (1993) Determinants of social support among gay men: the context of AIDS. *Journal of Health and Social Behaviour* 34(1):3 7-53.

Vlassoff, C. and E. Bonilla (1994) Gender differences in tropical diseases: what do we know? *Journal of BiosocialScience* 26(l):37-53.

Vlassoff, C.S. Khot and S, Rao (Forthcoming) Double jeopardy: women and leprosy in India. In M.E. Khan (ed.) *Work, Health and Contraception from Women's Perspective.* Centre for Operations Research and Training, Baroda.

Vlassoff, C. and M. Vlassoff (1983) Family type and fertility in rural India: a critical analysis. *Journal of Biosocial Science* 15:407-419.

World Health Organization (1992) *Living with AIDS in the Community.* WHO, Geneva (WHO?IDS/HCS/92.1).

Yadav, R.C. and B.N. Singh (1986) Presence of daughters-in-law in the household: a good contraceptive. *Demography India* 15(2):249-252.

APPENDIX

Note on Self-Stigma Scores

Self-stigma scores were developed to assess the level of self-stigmatisation of leprosy patients. Leprosy patients were interviewed using a structured questionnaire. Nine relevant questions were selected from this questionnaire to develop a self stigma scale. These questions concerned reasons for not marrying, decision to divorce, perceived cause of leprosy, withdrawal from day to day activities, reasons for not keeping in contact with family, hiding of the disease, etc. Each of these questions had multiple possible responses. A three point scale was developed to assess self stigmatisation as low, medium or high (values at 1, 2, 3 respectively). If the response indicated no self stigma a score of 0 was applied. Not all questions were answered by all patients and hence not all questions had scores, but the score was averaged over all questions for which the respondent answered. Below are examples of how scores were derived:

Question	Response	Score
Who decided to divorce?	Self	3
	Spouse	1
	Other	0
Cause of hiding disease	Lacked courage, fear of bring abandoned	3
	Fear of contaminating others, fear of stigma	2
	Waiting for symptoms to disappear, no need to share	1
	Did not hide the disease	0

Chapter 11

The Intra Household Distribution of Food: An Economic Perspective

John Hoddinott

Food is vital for survival, yet many people in the developing world do not have access to sufficient quantities to permit them to live active and healthy lives. In general, this is not a problem of insufficient production. In most countries, sufficient food is produced to feed the population, or resources exist to import food where production is below requirements (Kanbur 1990). Hunger arises because of individuals lack the resources necessary to obtain access to food, something Sen (1981) refers to as a failure of entitlements. At an aggregate level, there are many studies of the reasons for this, and a plethora of estimates of the extent of hunger.

This essay examines access to food but at a highly disaggregated level. We seek to unpack the rules governing intra household food entitlement using methods derived from neoclassical economics. The focus is on explaining these allocations in terms of three broadly defined economic principles: (i) efficiency, which comes into play when labour productivity linked nutritional demands forms a basis for the claim to food; (ii) equity; and (iii) bargaining, wherein the distribution of resources is affected by the ability of members to threaten credibly to leave the household.

All this is pot to say, of course, that economic considerations are the sole factor governing the allocation of food amongst members. Food and its distribution contain social and culture commutations and the absence of their consideration here should not be interpreted as a claim that they are unimportant. My argument is more modest, that is, economic considerations are important as well. We begin with a brief review of some important measurement issues and an examination of data from the Philippines and Bangladesh. These data, while not representative of south Asia as a whole, provide a useful means of motivating our discussion.

Measurement Issues

Any discussion of food allocations within families would be incomplete without a brief discussion of measurement issues. Note that families and households are separate concepts. Families are perhaps easier to measure as they typically refer to related kin who may or may not be living together. Households are comprised of people who "live together" in some sense, for example by eating from a common pot and/or answerable to a common head. A family can be a household, but a household can consist of non-family members.

The most direct measure of food allocation is that of nutrient intake, obtained by measuring portions served to each individual. This approach involves tradeoffs between precision, cost and invasiveness. That is, greater precision in measurement entails greater intrusion into the privacy of households being studied. It also requires that more time and effort be expended in making these measurements. Typically, attempts to reduce such difficulties increases the likelihood of inaccurate measurement. Harriss (1990) describes these potential inaccuracies as errors of omission and commission. The former include: failing to measure snacks, condiments, sauces and spices, food consumed outside the household, and the exclusion of extraordinary events such as feasts and fasts. Errors of commission include those derived from the standardisation of the containers used to measure quantities—that is, errors induced by the use of containers by the study that differ from those used by the household. Errors of commission also arise where the nutrient content of food actually consumed by the household differs from laboratory analysis of the nutrient content of that food. The timing of measurements can matter substantially as well. A 24 hour observation period can produce misleading information if it is subject to some exceptional event such as the illness of a particular household member. Also, seasonal data are necessary where intake and activity levels vary over the year. A further problem is that of reflexivity—the possibility that individuals will change their behaviour when being observed.

Faced with these difficulties, one might be tempted to measure food allocations in terms of some nutritional outcome instead of intake. Such measures include a child's height given her age and her weight given her height. Indicators such as these, however, capture a number of features other than nutritional status, including genetic background, maternal characteristics and morbidity.

Intra Household Disparities in Food Allocations: Evidence from Two Micro Samples

In this section, two studies are cited as examples where researchers have been particularly sensitive to problems of measurement. One is drawn from a study of households in the rural Philippines by Senauer and Garcia (1993). The data were obtained via a 24 hour food weighing method at both the household and individual levels. Foods were weighed prior to cooking in the morning and leftovers were measured after dinner. For the individual level data, interviewers were present at the meal table and weighed food served to each person and any leftovers (snacks and foods eaten between meals) were also accounted for. Some of the findings of that study are as follows: amongst households where caloric-acquisition was greater than 70% of standard caloric requirements, roughly 25% of the individuals residing in such households received less than 65% of the calories they required. Again, amongst households where caloric acquisition was greater than 85% of standard caloric requirements, roughly 40% of the individuals residing in such households received less than 85% of the calories they required. Most of the correlation coefficients between individual and household level caloric, protein, iron and retinol adequacy are far from equal to unity.

Data from another study of households, in rural Bangladesh, by Pitt, Rosenzweig and Hassan (1990), shows a marked gender bias with males over 12 and under 6 receiving a statistically significant higher level of caloric intakes.

These data tell us three things. First, many people in these samples are receiving fewer calories per day than those recommended by the World Health Organisation (WHO) and other organisations. Second, it suggests that food is distributed unequally amongst household members. In the majority of households in these two studies, there is enough food for everyone to meet basic dietary needs; but because of the inequitable allocation of food, this does not happen. (There are also households where individuals obtain amounts in excess of their requirements even though there is not enough food for everyone to meet their needs). Third, the distribution of food within families is not random; rather it can be the case that certain groups such as women may appear to receive less than their fair share.

Findings such as these are important. First, they may be important indicators or explanators of welfare; perhaps it is the case that discrimination with respect to access to one commodity is replicated in other aspects of family life. It has been argued that differentially poor access to both food and health care is responsible for excessively high female mortality in parts of south Asia and North Africa. The consequences of this are dramatic. It has been estimated that the cumulative loss of life that this has generated over the last century amounts to something like 60-100 million females (Sen 1990). Second, many policy interventions designed to reduce hunger are targeted at households perceived as being in need. The evidence presented suggests that such schemes are liable to two types of omission: (1) there is no guarantee that food will reach those most in need within such vulnerable households; (2) calorie deficit individuals in households not receiving assistance will be excluded from such schemes.

Economic Explanations of the Intra Family Allocation of Food

We now turn to three possible economic explanations for patterns of food allocation such as those described. By economic explanations, we mean those based on the notion that food preferences—what food is purchased, who consumes how much and so on—are assumed to be fixed. This is not to say that food consumption is fixed. This can vary with factors such as prices and incomes. Rather, it assumes that "tastes" do not change, at least over the period of time being studied. If we did not make this assumption, it would not be possible to disentangle changes in food consumption that are a function of tastes from those due to changes in income and prices. Another important assumption is that individuals seek to maximise their levels of wellbeing or utility. This is dependent, in part, on food acquisition, either directly, in the sense that wellbeing increasing with acquisition, or indirectly, in that higher levels of acquisition make individuals more productive and hence better able to obtain those commodities that they do desire. Maximisation is subject to a number of constraints, among them a budget constraint ("you cannot purchase more food than your income allows"); a time constraint ("there are only so many hours in a day"); and, in some circumstances, a biological constraint (how the body transforms food into energy). Put very crudely, economic explanations can be summarised as "maximisation subject to constraints with preferences fixed."

Efficiency

The notion of efficiency used here is the idea that parents or family decision makers allocate food within the family according to the incentives or returns they face. Consider the following example. Suppose that an individual's productivity (measured, for example, by how much he or she can produce working on their farm or as the wage he/she receives working for some one else) is a function of his/her "knowledge" (measured say by level of education), physical health and "effort"—how hard they work. Health is, in turn, a function of nutrient intake, innate healthiness, other health inputs and work effort (hard work leads to a deterioration in health). Now suppose the household obtains an extra 100 calories. How should these be allocated?

Some members' health will respond more readily to the increase in nutrient intake than others. So, all other things being equal, these calories should go to the person whose health increases the most by the increased intake. Second, productivity rises with better physical health. So again, all other things being equal, these marginal calories should go to the individual who will obtain the greatest increase in productivity. Pitt, Rosenzweig and Hassan (1990) argue that in rural Bangladesh, men tend to undertake the bulk of agricultural work, including most of that which is especially physically demanding. As a consequence, an increase in calories they obtain is likely to have the greatest impact on agricultural productivity and hence on household income.

This tells us two things. First, we should be cautious about making inferences directly from the data earlier cited. The data on physical labour for the Bangladeshi sample previously discussed indicates also that there are marked differences in activity levels amongst men and women 12 and older. There is also much greater variability with women predominating in moderate activities and men either doing very light or very heavy work. This pattern is consistent with the fact that men have greater caloric consumption and this exhibits greater variability, suggesting that food allocations might be based, at least in part, on productivity considerations.

Second, they suggest that policy interventions designed to improve the food intake of particular household members may fail. Suppose there is concern regarding the wellbeing of young girls in a particular area; specifically there is a perception that they do not get enough food to eat. A possible policy response is the implementation of a school meals programme in schools where girls are recorded as being particularly malnourished. However, the success of this intervention cannot be ascertained in the absence of information on the pattern of food allocation among household members. Households seeking to maximise productivity might respond by reducing the amount of food girls receive at home and increasing the amount of food consumed by other household members. Consequently, the programme may not achieve the goals that have been set for it.

Equity

We have assumed that food allocation is based on efficiency considerations; but it seems unreasonable to assume that these are the sole consideration. It may be the case that the family, or family decision makers, prefer certain members to others. This could be expressed in terms of a bias towards males, towards the able bodied at the expense of dependents, on lower order children to the detriment of higher order children. Perhaps on a more positive note, it could also be the case that the household takes steps to compensate particular individuals who, say, have particularly poor endowments. For example, sickly children receive more food than their healthier siblings.

In the context of developing countries, it is useful to note that constraints on food acquisition may be particularly important in determining how equitably food is allocated. A study in rural south India considered food allocation in both the surplus (post-harvest) and lean (preharvest) seasons (Behrman 1988). During the surplus season, when food is relatively plentiful, households exhibit what is described as inequality aversion with respect to food allocation amongst children. That is, food is allocated relatively equally. But during the lean season, when food is less plentiful, efficiency considerations predominate with older children, particularly males receiving relatively more and younger children and females receiving less.

Finally, it is worth noting that the notion of an 'equitable' food allocations can be problematic. Suppose a fixed quantity of food is to be distributed amongst two children in an 'equitable' fashion. Curry and Tiefenthaler (1993) suggest that this could include an equal split (the quantity of food is divided 50/50); a proportional split—if each child has different food needs, each gets an equal percentage of their optimal food requirement but not necessarily the same amount of food; or equal losses of food—each child has some optimal food intake, but receives an amount less than the optimum which is the same for both children. Note that depending on their innate healthiness, basal metabolic rate and so on, the health outcome for these children may also differ. Notions of what constitutes an equitable distribution have not received extensive coverage in the economics of intra household allocation and remain an important topic for future study.

Bargaining

Frequent reference has been made to the "household" and the "family" as the unit of analysis. It is implicitly assumed that everyone, or at least all decision makers, agree on the observed allocation of food, even when certain groups lose out on a systematic basis. In some, indeed perhaps all family situations, this seems strange. Family members do not always cooperate with each other—they may bicker, bargain and occasionally walk out on each other. This feature of family life is not captured in our discussion thus far. The feminist economist Nancy Folbre (1986) sums it up nicely when she states:

> The suggestion that women and female children voluntarily relinquish leisure, education and food would be somewhat more persuasive if they were in a position to demand their fair share. It is the juxtaposition of women's lack of economic power with the unequal allocation of household resources that lends bargaining power much of its persuasive appeal.

A bargaining approach to household behaviour, including the distribution of food and other resources, is an area of ongoing study and debate. A great deal of work on the subject, both theoretical and empirical is in progress, and has been summarised in Haddad, Hoddinott and Alderman (1994). There is no consensus on findings in this area, nor is there any one unique model; indeed there is some disagreement over the value of this whole approach. Here, we give a flavour of this growing literature.

One approach has been to borrow from non-cooperative game theory. It is assumed here that individuals cannot enter into binding and enforceable agreements with other household members. Instead, each person takes the other person's actions as given, and subject to such a constraint (and others) makes decisions that maximise his/her own welfare. A second approach borrows from cooperative game theory. Here, individuals can enter into binding contracts with each other. In one variant of this theoretical approach, individuals are seen to form a family/household because they are better off by pooling their resources than if they were to remain single. What becomes critical here is the distribution of gains from household formation. It is possible to show that this depends on individuals' outside options—that is, the wellbeing they can obtain if they leave the household. In turn, this suggests that policy interventions that increase, say women's position in society, for example, changes in marriage laws that guarantee a woman a certain share of the household estate should she be divorced by her husband, will improve her position within the household.

Can these models be applied to food acquisition and allocation within the household? A number of studies use income or education as proxies for women's and men's bargaining power within the household. Work undertaken by Hoddinott and Haddad (1995) found that in the Cote d'lvoire, increasing women's share of household cash income lead to an increase in the share of the family budget devoted to food, with corresponding decreases in outlays on commodities often consumed by men, such as alcohol and cigarettes. A Brazilian study by Thomas (1990) found that additional non labour income (that is, income such as dividends, rents and pensions that are derived from sources other than wage or own business labour) in the hands of women increases food expenditures five times as much as a comparable increase in men's non labour income. This effect is even larger if calories instead of expenditures is used as the dependent variable.

There are no studies that directly match control of income to food allocation. Some studies that try to pick this up indirectly by looking at the relationship between women's income or education and the health of male and female children. Somewhat puzzlingly, these pick up mixed effects. Thomas (1994) presents evidence from Brazil, Ghana and the United States that suggests that women "prefer" girls and men "prefer" boys. In his study, maternal education and non labor income has a larger impact on the height of a daughter relative to a son, and vice versa in the case of men. But this is not a universal finding. Haddad and Hoddinott (1994) find that the height of boys younger than 5 years increases when mothers' share of household cash income rises. Haddad and Hoddinott rationalise their finding by noting that at birth, and in the early years of life, girls are biologically more robust than boys. As a result, a mother favouring an equitable health outcome (the fourth concept of equity listed above) will, at the margin, allocate more resources to boys rather than girls.

I believe that ultimately a bargaining approach will lead to new insights regarding the intra family allocation of food. But having noted the results of these studies, it is important to inject some caution into this discussion. First, measuring bargaining power in an unambiguous way has proven to be rather difficult. For example, suppose we observe that food purchases rise with women's income. This could be interpreted as an increase in women's bargaining power, that leads them to increase household consumption of goods they see as being especially valuable. But equally, increases in income may be associated with increased time spent working in the wage labour market. As a result, women may substitute more expensive prepared foods for cheaper foodstuffs which take longer to prepare at home and this is why food purchases rise.

Second, these models suggest that any measure that increases the relative position of women or men will affect the distribution of food or other resources within the household. Consider a scheme whereby a woman receives a monthly payment from the state for each child in the household. Under the cooperative model described here, this might improve the intra household distribution of resources in ways favoured by women. But suppose that household formation is preceded by some form of binding agreement (such as a prenuptial contract) which includes the promise of transfers from husband to wife. Once the new child allowance scheme is in place, one might expect subsequent generations of husbands to reduce their transfers, offsetting the effect of the payment of child allowances.

Conclusions

This paper has provided a non-technical introduction to the allocation of food amongst family members. Three explanations are developed based around the notions of equity, efficiency and bargaining. There are two points worth emphasising. First, although social and cultural factors are undoubtedly important, in the context of low income households resident in developing countries, it is likely that economic considerations are important factors in the allocation of food amongst family members. Second, it is probably a mistake to assume that families will respond passively to policy interventions. Understanding how families allocate food amongst members leads to an understanding of the probable success and limitations of such interventions.

REFERENCES

Bardhan, P. 1973. 'On the Incidence of Poverty in Rural India in the Sixties' *Economic and Political Weekly.* Vol 8.

Behrman, J. 1988. 'Intra Household Allocation of Nutrients in Rural India'. *Oxford Economic Papers.* Vol. 40, pp. 32-54.

Behrman, J. 1992. 'Intra Household Distribution and the Family'. Mimeo, University of Pennsylvania.

Behrman, J. and A. Deolalikar. 1988. 'Health and Nutrition', in H. Chenery and T.N. Srinivasan, *eds.Handbook of Development Economics* vol I. Amsterdam: North Holland.

Curry, A. and J. Tiefenthaler. 1993. 'Fairness Concepts and the Intra Household Allocation of Resources'. Mimeo. Colgate University, USA.

Dandekar, V. and N. Rath. 1971. 'Poverty in India' *Economic and Political Weekly,* vol 6.

Dasgupta, P. 1993. *An Inquiry into Wellbeing and Destitution.* Cambridge: Cambridge University Press.

Folbre, N. 1986. 'Hearts and Spades: Paradigms of Household Economies'. *World Development.* Vol. 14. pp. 245-255.

Haddad, L. and J. Hoddinott. 1994. 'Women's Income and Boy-Girl Nutrition Outcomes in the Cote d'lvoire'. *World Development.* Vol. 22, pp. 543-553.

Haddad, L., J. Hoddinott and H. Alderman. 1994. 'Intra Household Resource Allocation: An Overview'. Policy Research Working Paper 1255. The World Bank, Washington D.C.

Harriss, B. 1990. 'The Intra Family Distribution of Hunger in South Asia', in J. Dreze and A. Sen, eds. *The Political Economy of Hunger,* vol I. Oxford: Clarendon Press.

Hoddinott, J. and L. Haddad. 1995. 'Does Female Income Share Influence Household Expenditure Patterns?' *Oxford Bulletin of Economics and Statistics.* Vol. 57. pp. 77-96.

Kanbur, S.M.R. 1991. 'Global Food Balances and Individual Hunger'in J. Dreze and A. Sen *eds.The Political Economy of Hunger.* Vol I. Oxford: Clarendon Press.

Pitt, M., M. Rosenzweig and Md. Hassan. 1990. 'Productivity, Health and Inequality in the Intra Household Distribution of Food in Low Income Vountries'. *American Economic Review.* Vol. 31. pp. 1139-1156.

Reutlinger, S. and H. Alderman. 1980. 'The Prevalence of Calorie Deficient Diets in Developing Countries'. *World Development.* Vol. 8.

Sen, A. 1981. *Poverty and Famines.* Oxford: Oxford University Press.

Senauer, B. and M. Garcia. 1993. 'An Intra Household Analysis of a Philippine Food Subsidy Program'. Mimeo. International Food Policy Research Institute, Washington DC.

Strauss, J. and D. Thomas. 1994. 'Human Resources: Empirical Modelling of Household and Family Decisions'. Mimeo. RAND.

Sukhatme. 1981. 'On the Measurement of Poverty' *Economic and Political Weekly.* Vol. 16.

Thomas, D. 1990. 'Intra Household Resource Allocation: An Inferential Approach'. *Journal of Human Resources.* Vol. 25. pp. 635-664.

Thomas, D. 1994. 'Like Father Like Son, or, Like Mother, Like Daughter: Parental Education and Child Health'. *Journal of Human Resources.* Vol. 29. pp. 950-988.

United Nations. 1987. *First Report on the World Nutrition Situation.* Rome: FAO.

Chapter 12

Fertility Decline and the FMR in Rural India—State-wise Patterns and Trends, as shown by Retrospective Data from the 1981, 1991 and 2001 Censuses*

Rajiv Balakrishnan

In parts of Asia, mortality has traditionally been higher for boys than among girls, due to the deprivation of the girl child in household allocations of life sustaining resources—food, nutrition and health care. This, coupled with the outright killing of girls or the aborting of female fetuses has led to a deficit of females in the region (Miller 1981). At the root of the phenomenon lie the cultural props to son-preference. In a patriarchal social and cultural milieu, a daughter moves away to her husband's household and is 'lost' to her parents when she marries. So, the expenses that have to be incurred for her upbringing are a drain on household resources. Not only that, a daughter imposes a burden on her parents on account of the flow of gifts (including dowry) from the bride's side to the groom's. A daughter does not have a claim on parental property, it is true, but she is customarily a recipient of presents from her parents' side for herself and her children, and, as per tradition, has claims on her brother's property—her children can expect to receive gifts from her brother, at least as long as she herself is alive. This also underscores the importance of a son as a source of help to parents in the discharge of responsibilities. A son is

* Based on paper presented by the author at a Ford Foundation sponsored seminar organised by the Council for Social Development, on *Demographic Transition in South Asia: Contours, Contexts, Constraints & Consequences*, New Delhi, 28 Feb–01 Mar, 2005.

needed also to perform rituals, including death rituals, for his sister, and is expected to shield his sister and her husband in times of misfortune. Finally, sons bring *in* gifts and dowry, not to speak of a daughter in law to carry out household duties (Patel 2007: 142, 149-150, 161, 164, 163; Patel 2004).

To look a little closer at the elements in this picture, let us, as a point of departure, briefly sketch out some of the key elements of the social milieu of dowry, and its effects on female survival. Clark (1983), in her study of the Leva Kanbi Patidars of Central Gujarat in the 19th century, shows that it was predicated on the superiority of the bride-receiving family. The author draws on data for four villages of Kaira district—Nadidad, Anand, Borsad and Petlad, which together constituted the prestigious *Charotar* tract and accounted for the greatest demographic concentration of the Patidar elite (Clark 1983:1) These Patidar aristocrats, known as the *kulia* (of good family), derived their high status not only from their lineage, but also from the fact that their ancestral villages belonged to the *Charotar* (Clark 1983: 3, 16). Other families sought to buy their way into this prestige circle by offering a daughter in marriage, along with the inducement of dowry. In turn, the *kulia* made enormous and growing dowry demands. Rising marriage expenses too contributed to the financial burden on the wife-givers (Clark 1983: 3, 8, 14). Daughters, in this context, were liable to impose a serious financial burden on the *akulia* (the non-*kulia*) and infanticide came to be seen as a remedy when the attraction of prestigious marriages seemed out of reach. The *kulia* families, for their part, seem to have practiced female infanticide so as to avert the transfer of their wealth through marriage payments (Clark 1983: 14-15, 17). Colonial administrators, initially distressed by their prognosis that increasing marriage expenses were liable to siphon off the growing prosperity of the region and hence limit the revenue base, sought to promote marriage circles, or *ekada*, based on the principle of the *exchange* of brides, as a counter to hypergamy (Clark 1983: 3-4, 8-9). Despite the reform effort, however, *kulia* marriages continued to persist, as did its complement—female infanticide. Eventually, however, since the Levi Patidars were seen as efficient land-managers, the colonial administration implicitly connived in the practice of female infanticide and the fatal neglect of girl children (Clark 1983: 12, 18). Notably, the hypergamy of the Patidars had a different basis from that of the Jadejas, originally from Sind, who, through conquest, established principalities in Kathiawad, Gujarat, and were, in the Raj, limited to '… the archaic profession of warrior rule …'. Since they occupied the highest caste niche in the region, they could not, under the principle of hypergamy, be givers of daughters. So they practiced 'wholesale infanticide' (Clark 1983: 15). Significantly, the Jadejas, who lost the patronage of the colonial government to the resource maximising Kanbis, were more sternly dealt with under the colonial government's initiatives to stamp out infanticide, and with considerable success (Clark 1983: 2, 18).

Dowry and the burdensomeness of daughters are one side of the coin. The other is that a son, who typically co-resides with his parents after his marriage, and is a source of economic and social security to his natal household, brings in a daughter in law to help with household work. This can make all the difference between a prosperous household and a pitiful one. Not surprisingly, therefore, the arrival of a son is celebrated, while that of a daughter is mourned (Patel 2004; 2007: 143, 150). Nonetheless, a daughter too has a place in the traditional scheme of things. The 'sacrifice', or giving away, of a virgin to a suitable recipient brings religious merit or *punya* for the donors (the parents), as does the subsequent flow of gifts from them on ritual and life cycle occasions. It brings social prestige as well, through the forging of hypergamous ties, and the building of both symbolic and social capital. Hence, a daughter, who is treated like delicate china, is lovingly raised to be a caring, responsible and efficient wife. By the same token, however, if she suffers a serious illness that is likely to leave her physically or mentally compromised, her chances of a favourable marriage are likely to be poor, and it is liable to be felt that it is better for her to die (Patel 2007: 142, 144-145, 156-157, 164).

Women themselves have internalised the value system in which son preference is rooted, notes Visaria (2007:72-74). Based on her discussion in the field with women in Gujarat and Haryana, the author says that patriarchal values gave her respondents a sense of security. After all, while the daughter leaves the household when she marries, the son stays with the mother and is expected to take care of her. Bose (2007) too touches on the theme of women having internalised patriarchal values when he reports on his intensive field work to investigate DEMARU (Daughter Eliminating Male Aspiring Rage for Ultrasound) in three districts in the country where child FMRs, as per 2001 census data, were the most masculine—Fatehgarh Sahib in Punjab, Kurukshetra in Haryana and Kangra in Himachal Pradesh. He points out that women know that when they have a male son, their status will go up in the family, community and the village. There will be gifts, celebrations, and congratulatory visits—all of which will be conspicuous by their absence if the child is a girl (Bose 2007: 81-82). The author's fieldwork showed also that people were widely aware that increasing dowry and rising marriage costs meant that daughters have become greater financial liabilities (Bose 2007: 86-87).

The pressure to have sons intensifies typically if the first-born is a girl child. Women's status derives as mothers of sons, and even though there is a perception that daughters take better care of their parents and are emotionally closer to their mothers, more sons are desired than daughters. With women now a days wanting fewer children, they like to ensure that at least one if not two of them are sons. The pressure comes to be cruelly felt when a woman has had one or two daughters and is pregnant with a third one. Not surprisingly, therefore, the FMR for *last births* is far more masculine than the FMR for all live births or first or second live births (Visaria 2007: 67, 72-76). Other notable studies too show that higher parity girl children are at greater risk of female survival disadvantage (Das Gupta 1987; Khan *et al.* 1989).

Sketching out the ethnographic underpinnings, Patel (2007) points out that when parents have more than one daughter and the burdens of dowry and gift giving hence increase, the responsibilities of rearing a daughter tend to transmute into daughter dislike. This leads us to the all-important distinction between the first daughter and subsequent ones. The birth of a second daughter is met with 'solemn gloom', while, conversely, the failure to beget a son is a source of deep despair. The first child that is born to a family is received with much joy, regardless of whether it is a boy or a girl, for childbirth validates the mother's fecundity and is proof that she is free of the dreaded curse of barrenness. A second or additional daughter is however perceived as an onerous burden. Daughter dislike, arising in this context, leads to gender discriminatory practices, like incurring less medical, educational or nutritional expenses on a female, as compared to a male child. Or, the apprehension of what a daughter may have to go through, if her in-laws are not satisfied—bride burning, or divorce and the accompanying stigma, shapes the mindset of the burdensome daughter. This fosters receptivity to technologies like ultra sound, which can reveal the sex of the to-be-born child, thus allowing the female foetus to be aborted. It is felt that it is better to spend a relatively small amount on averting a female birth than to incur heavy financial losses later in life if a daughter is born (Patel 2004: Patel 2007: 142-145, 147, 151, 153-156, 164).

FMRs from the Census Enumerations

Let us now briefly look at the data on FMRs from the census of India. From 972 females per thousand males in 1900, the FMR declined steadily to 930 in 1971. The 1981 census showed a brief reversal of the trend, with the FMR having risen to 934, but by 1991, it fell sharply to 927. In the next decade, there was some improvement, with the 2001 census recording a FMR of 933 (Jha and Ojha 2008:214). Thus, overall, the FMR has been growing *increasingly* masculine. There is a conundrum here, for if daughter discrimination is indeed so deep rooted in the Indian context, as our review of its socio-cultural underpinnings indicates, then why, in 1900, was the FMR relatively so feminine? The conundrum becomes even more compelling when we consider that between the 1901 and 1941 censuses, the *child FMR* (FMR for children in the ages 0-4) *was above 1000 females per thousand males*, touching a high of 1040 in the 1921 census. Between 1951 and 1961, child FMRs remained at

992. Thereafter, in 1971 and 1981, it hovered around 980. Subsequently, a precipitous decline occurred, with the 1991 census recording a child FMR as masculine as 954 (Bhat 2002a: 5107—Table 2). One could thus logically ask whether daughter discrimination is a relatively recent phenomenon. We try now to probe a little deeper.

First, however, it is necessary to put the census data on which the FMRs are based under a microscope. To do so, we start by taking a close look at two seminal papers by Mari Bhat (2002a and 2002b). The author compiles census data to show that the FMR for the 0-4 age group remained at around 1040 females per 1000 males for the first 30 years of the 20th century, which suggests that mortality was *higher* among male children. If that was indeed the case, and it was not a result of reporting errors, then when the cohort of children aged 0-4 years survives into the age group 5-9, then in the 5-9 age group also, we should see an excess of girls. *What we see, however, is that the FMRs for the age group 5-9 in the above mentioned 30-year period hovered around 960, and thus were highly 'masculine'.* The FMRs for the next higher age group, 10-14, were even more masculine, ranging between 830 and 950. How can we explain these data? Mari Bhat argues that age misreporting accounts for the discrepancies, as the ages of young male children tend to be overstated. Consequently, (i) fewer male children are enumerated than their actual numbers in the very young ages (0—4) and (ii) because ages of young male children are overstated, more male children are *reported* at the older ages than what is actually the case.

Is there an underlying cause for such a pattern of overstatement of the age of boys? Mari Bhat (2002a: 5107) explains: 'As boys are generally better fed than girls in cultures with strong son preference, in censuses and surveys, their ages get exaggerated more than girls when enumerators or parents are forced to assess age on the basis of a child's physiological features' (Bhat 2002a: 5107). The exaggeration of the ages of male children is affirmed also by the fact that the fertility rate estimated from the number of children in the 0-4 age group have been found to be too low, while fertility rates derived from population data for the higher age groups, i.e., 5-9 and 10-14, have been found too high (Bhat 2002a: 5107). Over time, however, the accuracy of age reporting is believed to have gone up, since literacy and better ability to correctly report age, and the requirement of a birth registration certificate to enroll in school could be expected to have led to a greater awareness of age. Consequently, we should expect *declines* in the 0-4 FMRs over time, making them more masculine, and correspondingly, a feminisation of FMRs at higher ages. Census data do in fact show such a pattern. From 1037 in 1931, the 0-4 FMR for India fell sharply to 992 in 1951, and then further to 953 in 1991. The 10-14 FMRs, on the other hand, which were ranged from 825 to 829 between 1901 and

1921, rose to 899 in 1991 (Bhat 2002a: 5107).

There are indications of the improvement of age reporting over time also in the *single ages* population data from the census of India for 1961, 1971, 1981 and 1991. These data, which allow us to calculate age specific FMRs, make it possible to assess abnormal fluctuations. Since single age FMRs change only gradually from one single age to the next; the *degree* of fluctuations in the FMR between one age and the next allows one to gauge *extent* of age misreporting. The mean of these deviations, known as the *Sex Ratio Index*, provides an indication of the quality of age reporting. Higher values of the index suggest poor quality data. The values of the Index for India, for census data from the 1961, 1971, 1981 and 1991 censuses—5.2, 4.9, 4.1 and 3.8 respectively, point to a clear improvement in the quality of the age data over time. It is interesting to note also that Sex Ratio Index calculated from NFHS (National Family Health Survey) data for 1992-93 (3.9) is very close to the index for 1991 computed from census data. This, notwithstanding the intensive training to NFHS investigators engaged in collecting age data, which should have led us to expect the NFHS data to be more accurate (Bhat 2002a: 5108).

Another way in which the single age population data have been used to gauge the effects of age misreporting is through the computation of FMRs for *cumulated age segments*, i.e., for population in the age segments 0-1, 0-2, 0-3, 0-4, and so on. When these FMRs are plotted as a line, they show a characteristic pattern of a peak at the age segment 0-3, at which point the FMR is highly feminine, followed by an increase in masculinity (Bhat 2002a: 5108). Let us dwell on this a little. Firstly, that the decline is spurious (due to misreporting of age) and not *actually* age-related is evidenced by the fact that it cannot be explained by sex differences in mortality. Thus, a graph of expected sex differentials in mortality, based on SRS (Sample Registration System) data[1] shows that *unlike* the line plotted with census data for 1991, our SRS based graph of *expected FMRs* for cumulated age segments shows a *gradual* and *not* a sharp decline, *with no telltale peak at age 3.* The sharp variation in the unadjusted census data are, it can be inferred, due to the overstating of the ages of boys, due to which, a percentage of boys in every age segment gets recorded in a higher segment. Correcting for this source of error will obviously mean that a certain number in the higher age segment should be transferred to the lower segment. On the assumption that the numbers should be such as to bring the adjusted values in line with the values computed as above by using SRS data on mortality differences by sex and age, we ask the question: at a given age above 3 years, what percentage of *enumerated* male children should be taken to be in a lower age segment? If we take this percentage at age 3 to be 3 percent and at higher ages to be 8 percent, and make adjustment for these age transfers, then our adjusted line comes very close to the line that we have generated for expected FMRs (Bhat 2002a: 5108-5109).

With age distortions getting corrected over time, the fall in age 0-3 FMRs between 1961 and 1991 have been phenomenal, ranging, in most states, from 20 to 40 points. For the North Eastern States, where the 0-3 FMRs were pronouncedly feminine to begin with, the declines were in the range of 40 to 70 points (Bhat 2002a: 5106, 5109). If these declines were real and *not* related to errors in age reporting, then the FMRs in a higher age group, let us say, 04-14, should also have correspondingly become more masculine, because, when the 0-3 age group of 1961 grows older, then it should bring about a decline in the FMR of the age group 04-14. Looking at the all India 04-14 FMR, we see that it remained stationery throughout the period from 1961-1991. If, on the other hand, the fall in the FMR at age 3 was *entirely* due to improvement in age reporting, then, when the exaggeration of the age of boys is less than earlier, fewer boys would have been reported in the higher age group. Consequently, the 04-14 FMR should have *become more feminine* over time. This too did not happen (Bhat 2002a: 5109—figure 4). Thus, the fall in the 0-3 FMRs was 'partly real and partly spurious'. There are however regional variations to be taken note of. In the case of the North West ('Greater Punjab', including Haryana and Himachal Pradesh), the dramatic increase of masculinity of the 0-3 FMR between 1981 and 1991 was followed by a corresponding masculinity in the 04-14 age group between 1991 and 2001, suggesting that the survival of children in the 0-3 age group was reflected in the higher age group, and hence, that what we are looking at are genuine intensifications of FMR masculinity (Mari Bhat 2002a: 5109-5110). A similar argument could be made for States like Tamil Nadu and Bihar, and to a lesser extent Andhra Pradesh, where 0-3 FMRs had grown more masculine by significant amounts between 1981 and 1991. To a degree, due to age misreporting, these could be spurious trends, but the direction of the change is worth taking note of in these cases. A caveat is in order here—we are only *roughly* allowing for a time lag for the 0-3 FMR to affect the higher age group (1961-1991). Thus, in the 1981-1991 decade, the changes in the 0-3 FMR that are closer to 1991 are liable to reflect in the 04-14 age group only *after* 1991. Keeping this caveat in mind, we note that the 04-14 FMR does show indication of change in the expected direction in the case of States like Tamil Nadu and Bihar. As far as the remaining States are concerned, the 0-3 FMRs need to be taken with a pinch of salt, Mari Bhat's data suggest. At one extreme of the spectrum are States which had abnormally high 0-3 FMRs in 1961, like Assam and West Bengal, and in these cases, the evidence suggests that the decline was spurious (Bhat 2002a: 5106—Table 1).

As is well known, the declines in the all India FMR at ages 0-6, from 945 in 1991 to 927 in 2001, sent alarm bells ringing in the country. However, we need to consider firstly, that age misreporting also affects 0-6 FMRs, and makes them seem unduly feminine. Thus, the all India 0-6 FMR of 945 for 1991 is far higher than the expected value of 935. Secondly, due to improvements in age reporting, the masculinity of the 0-6 FMR could be expected to have increased by 2001. Consequently, it is likely that a considerable part of the 0-6 FMR decline of 18 points indicated by census data between 1991 and 2001 was due to improvements in age reporting (Bhat 2002a: 5109). As we note later in this paper, this is one rationale for looking at an alternate data source for studying child FMRs. Having said that, it needs to be noted that, for the purposes of this paper, accuracy is not a goal *per se*. We are concerned here more with broad patterns and trends. Arguably, the data do represent these, as is suggested by comparing the census enumeration data with the 'retrospective data' (to be discussed presently) that are drawn upon for this paper.

We have looked at the conundrum of why child FMRs are feminine to begin with and we have said that it was due to age mis-statements. But we also noted that the FMR for the population as a whole too was feminine in the early 20th century. Between 1901 and 1951, the decline in the FMR could only have been due to the growing masculinity of the FMR at higher ages (15+), since at age 0-14—an age group for which reporting errors are small (Mari Bhat 2002a: 5106—Figure 1) the FMR was *becoming more and more feminine*. Up to 1951, the greatest change in the FMR was in the 55+ age group (Bhat 2002a: 5107—Table 2). We can attribute this to three mortality-related factors that were salient in the pre-Independence period, namely, the elimination of war and banditry, the control of famines, and the containment of epidemics (Davis 1951). War and banditry in pre-British rule had the effect of pushing up male mortality in particular, and its effects appear to have persisted down to the beginning of the 20th century, due to which the FMRs of that time were tilted in favour of females. The effects of British rule in containing war and banditry, in terms of improved male survival, had begun to be felt in the 1800s, but … 'the scar of the earlier turmoil may have still been felt at the beginning of the 20th century in the form of high FMR of the elderly population'. That scar, however, 'would have disappeared fast in the first half of the past century' (Mari Bhat 2002b: 5247). Far more pertinent, according to Mari Bhat (2002b: 5248-5250), is famine mortality, which, historical data show, decimates males more than females. Thus, in India's 'famine decade' of 1801-1901, when famines ravaged various parts of the country, survival rates declined more for males than for females, *particularly in the older age groups* (25-50). This was due to a number of factors, among them, (i) a higher storage of body fat in females, (ii) the tradition by fasting by women and the custom by which they eat after men and children, which 'condition Hindu women to low calorie intake while men, not accustomed to hunger, succumb to starvation early' and (iii) wandering of men in search of food, which makes them feeble and sick, and vulnerable to mortality. 'Indeed', according to Mari Bhat, 'reduction in the sex differentials in mortality after the institution of the famine code has been chiefly attributed to the absence of wanderings in later droughts and famines, as men became aware [of] where they would get relief' (Mari Bhat 2002b: 5250). After a famine, male mortality begins to improve, and FMRs become more masculine, as the Indian data attest. This occurs mostly in the older age groups, particularly 35-54 and 55+ (Mari Bhat 2002b: 5249).

What about the role of epidemics? Could the epidemics that occurred in the beginning of the 20th century have had sex selective mortality impacts? The three likely suspects are plague, influenza, and cholera. Women, who spent more time at home than men, were more susceptible to that carrier of plague mortality—the rat flea. Along with influenza, it plausibly accounts for why the FMR grew more masculine in the first two decades of the 20th century. As for cholera, several pandemics in the 19th century, perhaps due to the improvement of transport and communications, followed from river and railway traffic, fairs and festivals, and movement of troops, pilgrims, and labourers. Males were 'the first victims of the disease', though cholera decimated women and children too when it was accompanied by droughts and famines.[2] Given the mode of transmission and the particular susceptibility of males, '... when cholera mortality began to decline in the 1920s, adult men were standing to gain more than women' (Mari Bhat 2002b: 5251).

After 1951, the 0-14 FMR and the 15+ FMR *both show increasing masculinity* (Bhat 2002a: p. 5107—Table 2, p. 5111- Figure 6, p. 5112). Cohort analysis further shows that in the 1901 to 1951 period, FMR declines were large and statistically significant for the age groups 40-49, 50-59 and 60+, while for the age group 20-29, the decline was smaller but also significant. In the period 1951-1991, on the other hand, FMRs in the age groups above 30 showed a tendency to *become more feminine*, with the trend reversal statistically significant in the age groups 40-49 and 50-59. By contrast, a statistically significant decline occurred in the FMR for the 0-9 age group. The subsequent age group, 10-19, also showed a statistically significant decline, which suggests that the childhood FMR decline in 1951-1991 was real and not spurious (Mari Bhat 2002a: 5108, 5112).

Post Independence, a number of developments have acted to reduce mortality—government programmes in immunisation and disease control, the proliferation of Primary Health Centres and Sub Centres, increase of hospitals and hospital beds, and growth in the number of registered doctors. At the same time, transportation and communication between rural and urban areas provided rural inhabitants access to urban facilities. This in turn led to new possibilities of discrimination. 'As access to health care began to improve, mortality rates became more and more subject to household decisions. If sex preference earlier revealed itself only through intra household allocation of food and personal care, since the 1950s, the sex bias in the provision of health care would have also begun to have an effect on the sex ratio'. We however have no data to throw light on these developments in the first two decades of Independence (Mari Bhat 2002b: 5252-5253). We know that mortality began to decline in India after 1921, but it was only after World War II—roughly at around the time of Independence, that accelerated mortality decline set in. (While life expectancy rose by a mere 8 years from 1900 to the 1940s, it rose further by as much as 30 years over the second half the 20th century). We can thus argue that changes in the adult FMR prior to 1940 were due to the moderate declines in mortality in the earlier half century, while the steep mortality decline in the later half impacts on child FMR declines (Mari Bhat 2002b: 5247).

A subsequent development that occurred is that female mortality began to decline relative to male mortality. The Sample Registration System, set up in the late 1960s, shows a change in the sex-wise pattern of mortality from a 1.5 year excess life expectancy for males as compared to females in 1970-75 to a 1.5 year excess life expectancy for females as compared to males in 1991-95. Mortality reductions in the 0-4 and 5-9 age groups (especially in former), the 15-39 age group, and the 65+ age group favoured females, while in the remaining age categories, the differences were marginal (Mari Bhat 2002b: 5252-5253).

SRS data on the sex difference in the average annual change in child death rates between 1971 and 1998 show that in the States of Andhra Pradesh and West Bengal, there were no differences in the rates of change. In Tamil Nadu, concomitant with a rising incidence of female infanticide, mortality improvements were better for boys than for girls. In the remaining Sates, mortality declined faster for females as compared to males, with the steepest declines in the States of Uttar Pradesh, Haryana, Madhya Pradesh Punjab and Rajasthan. In these regions, as per census data, the largest masculinisation of the juvenile FMR had taken place. SRS data show also that it was in rural areas, which witnessed the sharpest deterioration in juvenile FMRs, where the relative female mortality falls were the greatest (Mari Bhat 2002b: 5253-5254). Thus, if we are to accept the SRS data as genuine and the census data as reasonably indicative, particularly for the North West, then we have to look for an explanation in factors like female infanticide and foeticide.[3]

Foeticide and Sex Ratio at Birth

Female foeticide may indeed have been widespread in India even before the mid-1980s, when it began to occupy the limelight in scholarly and public discourse. One way to corroborate a high incidence of female foeticide, given the evidences of fatal discrimination of girl children at higher birth orders, is to see if the FMR at birth at higher birth orders becomes *more* adverse for females. Using SRS data for 1990-98, Mari Bhat (2002: 5256-5257) finds '... a clear indication of the FMR at birth falling with birth order' in the States of Punjab, Haryana and Himachal Pradesh. The author also finds indications to the effect that ' ... as a result of sex-selective abortions, the FMR at birth may have declined by 56 points in Punjab, 51 points in Haryana, 39 points in Himachal Pradesh, and about 18 points in Tamil Nadu and urban India as a whole' (Mari Bhat 2002b: 5256-5257).

For countries with relatively good registration records, the sex ratio at birth normally hovers between 103 and 107 males per 1000 females (Visaria 1971), which works out to 935 females per thousand males. In countries like Sweden, which have good registration systems, the sex ratio at birth has gradually become more masculine over time, evidently due to a decline in male foetal wastage. Males comprise a high proportion of stillbirths, so, when foetal wastage goes down, the incidence of male births goes up, as the registration data for Sweden attest. Improvements in the nutritional status of women, rise in the proportion of births attended by trained medical practitioners, declines in higher order births, have been identified in the literature as factors acting to reduce foetal wastage. In the Indian situation, declines in famines, improvements in per capita availability of food, and increase in antenatal care in rural areas are likely to have impacted on the nutritional status of women. At the same time, institutional deliveries and deliveries attended by a trained birth attendant have been increasing, and with fertility decline, the incidence of higher order births has gone down. We also have more direct evidence, from the SRS, of a fall in the stillbirth rate itself, by as much as 50%—from 18 per 1000 in 1971 to 9 per 1000 in 1998 (Mari Bhat 2002b: 5254).

In her analysis of census-based FMRs for 1981, 1991 and 2001 for India and six states (Himachal Pradesh, Haryana, Punjab, Rajasthan, Gujarat, Maharashtra and Kerala), Visaria (2007: 64-65) finds that while there was very little change in all-ages FMRs, child FMRs grew more masculine, particularly after 1991. Notably, the 1991-2001 decade was a time when female child mortality declined 'somewhat faster' than male child mortality. Hence, we should have expected the child FMRs to have grown *less* adverse for females, which is contrary to what we find. The answer to the seeming conundrum lies in the averting of female births through abortion, facilitated by new technology that made it possible to identify the sex of the unborn child (Visaria 2007: 63-65, 74). With the passing of the MTP (Medical Termination of Pregnancy) Act of 1971, abortion became legal under certain conditions—in the case of pregnancies that were unplanned or resulted from rape, constituted a grave threat to health of the mother, or were likely to result in a child born with physical or mental defects. Abortions could be carried out only by trained doctors, and the kinds of facilities that were required to be available were also stipulated by the Act. However, technologies (such as amniocentesis and sonography) that could be used to identify deformities in a foetus also facilitated the identification of the sex of an unborn child at no extra cost. In fact, these technologies were explicitly used to identify and abort female foetuses. It was in this context that the PNDT (Pre Natal Diagnostic Techniques) Act of 1994, which prohibited sex-determination tests, was passed. The PNDT law has however, been extensively violated. A high demand for sex determination has led to a number of service providers competing for a share of the market, which has acted to reduced costs of these tests (Visaria 2007: 69-71). While Visaria's study shows how foeticide has contributed to the growing masculinity of the FMR after 1991, child mortality too has been a contributory factor, according to a study by Sagar (2007). In the 1990s, while female child mortality declined at a faster rate than male child mortality, as of 1999, *it continued to be higher*, both in the first year of life as well as the first four years of life, thus suggesting that, apart from foeticide, girl foetuses that survive are vulnerable later in life as well. Data in fact show, that while girls are biologically stronger than boys, they are more susceptible to major communicable diseases. The incidence of anaemia is also higher for girls, which suggests that discriminatory nutritional and health factors come into play to push up the mortality of the girl child (Sagar 2007: 180-182).

We are able to get some indication also of the relative contribution of child mortality and foeticide to increasingly masculine FMRs from a study by Sudha and Rajan (2003), who use the 'Reverse Survival Technique' to compute district level SRB for males and females for 1981 and 1991. They find, looking at the SRB for 1981, that the values range from 91 to 112 (males per 100 females). Values greater than 107 are taken to be abnormal, and indicative either of foeticide or under-reporting of female births, both of which indicate '... varying forms of bias against girls, denying them physical or social existence' (Sudha and Rajan 2003: 4364-4365). In 1981, 29 districts in the country had SRBs that were greater than 107, as many as 10 in Punjab, and another 5 in Haryana. 'These are areas with among the greatest historical gender bias, and the most evidence of prenatal sex selection technology in 1981'. By 1991, the number of districts with abnormally high SRBs increased to 117, 'blanketing most of Punjab and Haryana, and also more than before in Rajasthan and Gujarat, Western UP, MP, Himachal Pradesh and Maharashtra'. Notably, some districts of south India too had distorted SRBs; 'We also see traces of this phenomenon in southern India' (Sudha and Rajan 2003: 4365). The authors go on to compute sex ratios of child mortality risk for the districts of India, which, as of 1981, were found to range from 67 to 128. Female disadvantage districts (with values of less than 100) '... are mostly concentrated in north India, stretching from the western boundary states through UP, MP, Bihar, to West Bengal (with traces in the north east and the peninsula)'. The corresponding figures for 1991 show that the range of values has broadened, from 58 to 165. Values below 100 continue to prevail in the northern areas, and also make an appearance in the south. Maps comparing these data with data on the SRBs show that '... the same areas in north / north west India show masculine estimated SRB concurrent with excess female child mortality. That is, *gender bias in birth and death patterns appear to operate simultaneously in these areas*' (emphasis added). Bivariate analysis carried out by the authors suggests that '... districts with higher deficits in births have greater female excess in deaths ...'. Sudha and Rajan also find, through multivariate analysis that in the northwest region, gender bias in child-mortality had gone down, which suggests a substitution of pre-natal for postnatal methods (Sudha and Rajan 2003: 4365-4367).

Fertility Decline and the FMR

We have seen how parity is an important factor fueling daughter dislike. There are two types of parity-related effects. First, as the literature cited so far suggests, higher mortality among *female* infants / children gets concentrated among the offspring of mothers who are at *higher* parities, for, as we have seen, there is far less tolerance for a subsequent girl child in the family. Hence, when higher parity female births are averted (due to fertility decline), excess female child mortality will get reduced (Das Gutpa and Mari Bhat 1997: 307). Since the SRB (Sex Ratio at Birth) is more masculine at higher parities (Das Gutpa and Mari Bhat 1997:312), when the proportion of high parity births declines, the average SRB, that is, the SRB aggregated for all parities, should become more *feminine*. However, declining fertility can also make FMRs more *masculine*, because ' ... during fertility decline, the total number of children desired falls more rapidly than the total number of sons desired. The difference in speed of these two trajectories narrows the space left for daughters, and leads to a greater pressure to remove girls' (Das Gupta and Mari Bhat 1997: 307). This *intensification effect* is believed to have been in evidence in India also; ' ... during the 1980s, the Total Fertility Rate fell by 20 per cent ... whilst the number of sons desired by women with no sons fell by only 7.4 per cent ... (which) suggests that the tolerance for daughters has decreased during this period of fertility decline' (Das Gupta and Mari Bhat 1997: 307). An example from China and Korea is also cited to bring out how the SRB is determined by parity and the intensification effects. Drawing on 1989 data for these two countries, the authors note that the sex ratios after the second birth were far higher in South Korea than in China. But, fertility was much lower in South

Korea as compared to China, so, the proportion of high birth-order births was less in South Korea. Consequently, China had a higher SRB (Sex Ratio at Birth) than Korea (Das Gupta and Mari Bhat 1997:309).

Retrospective Data

In this paper, we draw upon a hitherto untapped data source for the study of parity and intensification effects. The data are on the number of children by sex born to mothers in various age groups, that is, 15-19, 20-24, 25-29 etc. When we consider data for 1991, then, mothers in the age group 55-59 would have entered their reproductive careers in 1956, and those aged 15-19 in 1991. The data on children born to these women also provide an indication of their fertility levels, as shown by the Child Woman Ratio. As expected, older women were at higher levels of fertility. It is thus possible to compare the offspring FMRs of mothers who entered the reproductive ages at different points of time, over the course of a period of time when fertility was declining. The data on the children are of two types—children ever born, and children surviving. The FMR on children ever form approximates the sex ratio at birth, and the FMR on children surviving shows us the FMR among surviving offspring.

We need to note also that the retrospective data differ from the enumeration data in another fundamental way. The retrospective data are for different cohorts of mothers—the cohort of mothers who entered the reproductive ages in 1956, the cohort of mothers who entered the reproductive ages in 1961, and so on. So, they give a comparative picture of different such cohorts. The enumeration data, on the other hand, show data for the entire population at different points of time.

As we have noted in the discussion on data sources at an earlier point in this chapter, there are good reasons for considering a data source other than population enumeration data. Enumeration data are suspect, in the light of Mari Bhat's analysis to the effect that improvements in age reporting are likely to inject a spurious element in the interpretation of enumeration data (Mari Bhat 2002a and Mari Bhat 2002b). There is another reason why juvenile FMRs are problematic, namely, that excess female child mortality may not have fully manifested in the juvenile ages. In other words, the effect of excess female child mortality would be seen only after a sufficient ageing of a cohort of children has occurred. Composite variables like 'under five mortality' are prone to this sort of problem (Agnihotri 2000:29, 38, 95-96), and we can extend the argument to juvenile FMRs as well. It is noteworthy that the data on CEB and CS are not susceptible to the kinds of age-reporting errors in that they do not distinguish the children of women by age; the data only indicate how many children women of different ages have had. The retrospective data used in this paper show the numbers of children different cohorts of mothers have had over the course of their reproductive careers, and in the case of those with completed or near completed fertility, the data are not plagued by such problems. Yet, the retrospective data can be prone to error in the case of the younger cohorts of mothers, who have not completed their fertility careers, and whose children may not all have had a chance to grow through the juvenile ages. In interpreting the data, this has been kept in mind.

As we have seen, as in the case of other data sources, the retrospective data used in this chapter too has its share of limitations. These data on children ever born (CEB) and children surviving (CS) are as reported by mothers who were asked by census enumerators to provide details of their reproductive history. The data are about past events (births and deaths), and so they are called 'retrospective data'. Since these data are based on mothers' recollection of their own reproductive histories, they are susceptible to recall errors, and their accuracy may leave much to be desired. Through mathematical modeling, data of this kind have been used to estimate the overall child mortality rates when other more reliable sources of data are not available. In this paper, precise estimates are not the objective. The data are drawn upon to *roughly* gauge patterns and trends, and to look for underlying causes, rather than to attempt precise measurements.

In sum, though retrospective data has its limitations, so does the enumeration data of the census. In this chapter, we have drawn on the retrospective data to throw light on the broad issues. The analysis in this chapter is mainly for rural areas, though, in the case of the 2001 data, urban data and all areas data also have been briefly considered. We note, finally, that notwithstanding the limitations of the data, the findings, cross-checked with findings based on other types of data, do indicate a rather good degree of correspondence.

Findings

- Figure 1 shows the offspring FMRs for the States of India for mothers between the ages of 15-19 up to 50-54. Mothers aged 50-54 entered their reproductive careers in 1956, when they were in the 15-19 years age group. Similarly, mothers aged 45-49, 40-44, 35-39, 30-34, 25-29, and 20-24, and 15-19 entered the 15-19 age group in 1961, 1966, 1971, 1976, 1981, 1986, and 1991 respectively. So, what Figure 1 shows are the FMRs of the children for different cohorts of mothers, starting from the cohort that began its reproductive career in 1956, and up to the cohort that began its reproductive career in 1991. In this paper, while considering the 1991 retrospective data, we will refer to these as the 1956 cohort, the 1961 cohort, the 1966 cohort etc. We note also that in the case of the cohorts of mothers that entered their reproductive span before 1981, we are talking of women who have completed or near-completed their fertility, while the case of the 1981 and

1991 cohorts of mothers, this is not the case. So, we should not normally compare the two. It is however possible to arrive at tentative conclusions, as we will argue.

- In Figure 1, we see two types of offspring FMRs—that is, FMRs among Children Ever Born (CEB) and FMRs among Children Surviving (CS). 943 females per thousand males have been taken as the FMR at birth, and is shown by the horizontal line. Offspring FMRs below this value are taken to be abnormal, and to show discrimination against females. In the case of the FMRs for children ever born, as noted earlier, they are taken to approximate the sex ratio at birth. The FMRs among children surviving of course will be affected by the sex ratio at birth, but Figure 1 shows that the FMRs for surviving children in many instances are even more masculine than the FMR for Children Ever Born, indicating that discrimination against females is taking place *after* they are born.

(a) Offspring FMRs, 1956-1981

- In States from across the spectrum of regions of the country—Bihar, Uttar Pradesh, Madhya Pradesh, Maharashtra, Haryana, Punjab, Rajasthan, West Bengal, Orissa, Delhi, Tamil Nadu, Andhra Pradesh and Karnataka, we find that, when we consider the 1956, 1961, 1966, 1971, 1976, and 1981 cohorts of mothers, that is, the cohorts of mothers aged 50-54, 45-49, 40-44, 35-39, 30-34, and 25-29, it is the *younger cohorts of mothers* whose children have more gender-balanced *offspring FMRs*—that is, FMRs among children ever born and children surviving. The data show also, that invariably, older cohort women, on the average, have higher fertility (Figure 2).[4] Given this context of fertility decline, the fact that the curves slope upwards from right to left (Figure 1) suggests that the parity effect has operated to determine the slope of these curves. That is to say, given that the FMR is more masculine at higher birth orders, and since fertility decline involves, at an aggregate level, a decrease in children of higher birth orders, plausibly, fertility decline has led to a feminisation of the offspring FMRs. It is difficult to interpret this any other way, as will be argued presently. If it was the intensification effect that was at work, then the curves should have sloped *upward* from left to right, and not the other way around. Up to 1981, the curves are sloping *downward* from left to right, in most cases (Figure 1).
- We see also that by 1981, a vast amount of gender bias at birth has disappeared, plausibly due to the parity effect. Thus, in States like Uttar Pradesh, Delhi and Bihar, the gender bias at birth has greatly attenuated for the 1981 cohort of mothers, i.e., the cohort of mothers aged 25-29, as compared to the 1956 cohort of mothers, that is, mothers aged 50-54 in 1991 (Figure 1). Though between 1981 and 1991, these States have seen a

revival of gender bias at birth, which has caused a great deal of alarm, its magnitude appears to be small compared to what was traditionally the case.

- Indications are that the parity effect operates *more strongly* in States which display *steeper* parity related curves. *The data thus suggest that the parity effect was stronger in those parts of the country where discrimination against daughters was worse* (Figure 1).
- In States like Uttar Pradesh, Bihar, Haryana, Delhi, Punjab and Rajasthan, elimination of girls at birth *by traditional methods seems to have been quite extensive*, as is suggested by the adverse FMRs among the CEB (Children Ever Born) for the older cohort women, whose reproductive careers preceded the introduction of the amniocentesis-type new technologies (Figure 1). The normal sex ratio at birth has been taken as 946 females per 1000 males. Normally, the FMR among Children Ever Born should be at this level. The fact that it is far below this level suggests extensive female infanticide. We *do* find corroboration for abnormally high FMRs among Children Ever Born among the older cohorts of mothers. Thus, SRS (Sample Registration System) statistics show that even in 1968-69 (roughly corresponding to the cohort of mothers aged 35-39), the FMR at birth was highly adverse (less than 890) in Haryana, Punjab and Rajasthan, and 912 in Uttar Pradesh, which suggests a high incidence of female foeticide in these States even at that early date (Mari Bhat 2002b: 5256). Though these SRS data are for all areas (rural and urban combined), Figure 1 shows that the rural FMRs among Children Ever Born in the age group 35-39 roughly correspond to the SRS data. At the same time, Figure 1 also shows also that in the case of the older cohorts of mothers—mothers in the age groups above 35-39, the CEB FMRs were even more masculine. In Bihar, Delhi and UP, for the cohorts of mothers aged 45-49 and 50-54, it was about 850 or below. In Punjab, Haryana and Rajasthan, it was between 850 and 900 for these two cohorts. In Andhra Pradesh and Karnataka, it was around 900, while in Maharashtra and Karnataka, it was around 925 (Figure 1). The FMRs for children surviving were even worse than those for Children Ever Born. After all, it is the masculine FMRs for CEB that set the benchmark. Figure 1 suggests that mortality of surviving girl children had worsened after birth, with the result that the FMR for children surviving tended to dip below that of the FMR for Children Ever Born.
- We have seen how in the northern States, the FMRs among Children Ever Born was very masculine, as compared to the other States. We also find, between 1981 and 1991, in States like Uttar Pradesh, Bihar, Rajasthan and Delhi, not only were the FMRs becoming adverse for children ever born, they were even worse for children surviving, which suggests that not only was infanticide pronounced in these regions, subsequent and fatal neglect

of female children was pronounced also. Figure 1 suggests that, taking all cohorts of mothers into account—mothers aged 15-19 up to 50-54, this is the aggregate picture that would emerge. It is a pattern that chimes in with the findings of Sudha and Rajan (2003).

- Between 1981 and 1991, when the revival of gender discrimination at birth occurred, we see this pattern notably for Bihar, Uttar Pradesh and Gujarat, where both the FMR for children ever born and children surviving deteriorated.

(b) Offspring FMRs, 1981-1991

- By 1981, the parity effect seems to have exhausted itself in many north Indian States. It appears also that after 1986, the intensification effect started to operate. Thus, in Bihar, Punjab, Rajasthan, Uttar Pradesh, and Gujarat, we find some evidence of it in the case of young mothers, with the curve sloping *upward* from left to right in the younger ages. Taking Bihar as a case in point for purposes of illustration, we see in Figure 1 that the cohort of mothers aged 20-24 had *more masculine* offspring FMR than the older cohort of mothers aged 25-29. Likewise, the cohort of mothers aged 15-19 had a more masculine offspring FMR as compared to the cohort of mothers aged 20-24. We note here that the cohorts of mothers in the ages 15-19 and 20-24 cannot, strictly speaking, be compared with the 25-29 years cohort of mothers. (We make a working assumption to the effect that women in the 25-29 years cohort are those who have completed or near-completed their fertility careers. Hence, this cohort can be compared with cohorts of mothers aged 30-34 and above, but not with the cohort of younger mothers aged 15-19). However, if we take it that the cohort of mothers aged 15-19 has not completed its fertility, then, *cetirus paribus*, higher birth order children have yet to be born to the extent that they have been born to mothers in the 25-29 age group. So, on this count, the lower age groups should, on an average, have *less masculine* offspring FMRs. The fact that this is *not* the case is particularly conspicuous for the cohort of mothers aged 15-19. However, it may also be that the young mothers have not yet completed their fertility careers, and their completion of their fertility careers would change the sex composition of their children. We will return to this point when we look at the 2001 retrospective data.
- We see also from Figure 1 in Bihar, Punjab, Rajasthan, Uttar Pradesh, and Gujarat that in States like Bihar and Gujarat, though there has been a growing masculinity of the sex ratio at birth between the 1981 and 1991 cohorts of mothers, the FMR for children surviving too has become *more* masculine. We see this also to some extent in Uttar Pradesh. It is true that in the very young cohorts of mothers (15-19 and 20-24), the FMR for children surviving

could grow more feminine, once these cohorts of children age sufficiently or the young mothers have had more time to complete their fertility careers. We will look more closely at this when we examine the 2001 retrospective data. For the time being, we merely note, firstly, that the FMR for children ever born grow more masculine, due to either infanticide or sex selective abortion, aided by access to new technology that facilitated identification of the sex of the foetus. Also, the FMR for children surviving grew even more masculine, suggesting that those female foetuses who escaped the clutches of death suffered fatal discrimination later in their childhoods.

- Figure 1 shows that when we compare the 1986 cohort of mothers (the cohort aged 20 to 24) with the 1991 cohort (the cohort of mothers aged 15-19), the FMR for children ever born has fallen below that for children surviving in the case of Punjab. In Rajasthan and Haryana, we see that the FMR for children ever born is very close to that for children surviving, again indicating that there is practically no fatal discrimination at later stages of childhood after birth. In Punjab, throughout a half century, the FMR for Children Surviving is very close to the FMR for Children Ever Born—in other words, we see a tendency for female infanticide / foeticide to be the main operative factor, while in States like Uttar Pradesh, Bihar and Rajasthan, fatal discrimination of girls later in childhood is much more in evidence (Figure 1).
- The census *enumeration* data for Bihar for 1991 are likely to be plagued by under enumeration of females (Mari Bhat 2002b: 5245-5246), but the data we are looking at here are *not* population enumeration data. They are a different kind of data—retrospective data, and, in the absence of credible enumeration data for Bihar, these retrospective data are of special interest. The intensification effect, we see, occurs most sharply in the case of Bihar. This is substantially due to the deterioration of the sex ratio at birth, suggesting female infanticide, but the FMR for children surviving is also very masculine. At the same time, in Bihar, the parity effect over a longer period seems to have been as strongly at work as in a northern State like Uttar Pradesh.
- Overall, the intensification effect has been rather small compared the parity effect. Thus, it is the parity effect that has overwhelmingly been at work, *if one considers the entire period from 1956 to 1991.* We see some corroboration for this finding from a study by Guilmoto (2005) which shows, through a cross-sectional district-level analysis, that higher fertility varies positively with the child sex ratio (males per thousand females). Guilmoto arrives at this finding from multivariate analysis using district level data for India, separately for 1981,1991, and 2001 (Guilmoto 2005: 409).
- The intensification effect had not occurred significantly in the South Indian

States up to 1991, except mildly in Tamil Nadu. In the northern States—Uttar Pradesh, Rajasthan, and in the North East, in Bihar, the intensification effect is quite strong.

- It has been argued that the growing masculinity of the sex ratio at birth could be due to improvements in health conditions and midwifery practices, which favour male infants. In stillbirths, the proportion of boys is higher than that of girls. Consequently, when foetal wastage declines, one could expect an increase in the proportion of *male* births. The stillbirth rate can go down due to an improvement in the proportion of births attended by trained medical practitioners. It can also go down when there is a decline in higher birth orders. Both have been factors at work in India. The nutritional status of women is another factor. This could have been improving with increases in per capita availability of food and declines in absolute poverty. Moreover, the increase in antenatal care in rural areas could be expected to have an impact on the health status of women (Mari Bhat 2002b: 5254). However, it is unlikely that our evidence of masculinsation of the FMR among Children Ever Born can be explained away by these factors alone. We see in Figure 1 that, as of 1991, the intensification effect has been confined to States in the North, the North West, and Bihar in the North East. It seems unlikely that improvements in the health conditions of women and in midwifery practices were confined to these regions alone.

(c) Offspring FMRs and Mother's Education

- We have interpreted the curves in Figure 1 in terms of parity and intensification effects. We have argued that the slope of the curve for the major part of the past half-century preceding 1991 suggests the parity effect had been at work, due to which each successive cohort of women had more feminine FMRs. But could the slope have been determined by factors other than the parity effect? Findings from empirical studies show that female literacy, which we know from census data has been increasing since Independence acts to reduce excess female mortality (Bhattacharya 2006; Murthi *et al* 1995). Could it not then be that successive cohorts of women have more feminine FMRs merely because *more* of them are literate, rather than because they have lower fertility? Fortunately, the data permit us to examine this issue, to some extent. To do so, let us turn to Figure 3, which shows cohort fertility separately for educated mothers and for illiterate mothers.[5] It needs to be reiterated here, that the offspring fertility for women who have completed or near completed fertility (women aged 25-29 and higher cohorts), would, strictly speaking, not be comparable with younger women. So, we may consider only women with completed or near completed fertility. Figure 2 shows that fertility decline has occurred for mothers *regardless of their literacy status*. This jells with findings to that effect from a district level analysis of fertility in India (Guilmoto and Rajan 2001). It is noteworthy in this context that aspirations for children among the uneducated can be a factor in fertility decline (Bhat 2002 and McNay *et al.* 2003). Thus, we cannot dismiss the curve of the offspring FMR slope in Figure 1 as due to higher literacy in each successively younger cohort of mothers. We are therefore led to give due importance to the parity effect as an important factor determining the slope of the offspring FMRs from 1956 to 1981 in Figure 1. At the same time, we cannot dismiss the possibility altogether that in a parallel development. rising female literacy has acted in the direction of making the offspring FMRs more feminine. Such an investigation however is beyond the scope of this paper, in terms of the quantitative analysis that would need to be done—the thrust of this chapter is more explorative and tentative than conclusive or mathematically precise. At the same time, it is noteworthy, as the data in Sagar (2007: 181) indicates, the health circumstances of girl children was persistently poor as compared to male children. In this context, Dyson's (1987) argument that improvements in the FMR between 1971 and 1981 did not owe to improvements in the health conditions of children, but rather, to an increase of life sustaining resources, is salient. We will return to this issue later.

- We see from the shape of the offspring FMR curves in Figure 3 that, from the 1956 cohort of mothers up to the 1981 cohort, the parity effect was operating in the case of both educated and illiterate mothers. At the same time, educated mothers *did* tend to have more feminine FMRs than illiterate mothers in states like Tamil Nadu, Bihar, Punjab, Rajasthan, Uttar Pradesh, Madhya Pradesh, Delhi, West Bengal and Karnataka.
- It is noteworthy also that between 1981 and 1991, in Punjab, Uttar Pradesh, Delhi, Bihar, and Orissa, an intensification of daughter elimination occurred among educated mothers. Whereas in earlier decades, women's education tended to make the FMR more balanced, after the mid 1980s, there are indications that education no longer has been playing such a role (Figure 3). It is noteworthy also that in Punjab, Uttar Pradesh and Delhi, where the intensification effect has been very steep, the process has entailed worsening of the FMR among Children Ever Born (Figures 3 and 7). This suggests that educated mothers are practicing infanticide more than illiterate mothers. Of interest here is a study of villages in Punjab in which Das Gupta (1987) found that the desire for sons falls more slowly than the desire for daughters, and that this phenomenon is more pronounced among educated mothers because they want smaller families.
- We need also to consider one other factor which operates in the *same* direction as the intensification effect, namely, the process of 'sanskritisation'

or the emulation of upper caste lifestyles by the lower castes, which involves a withdrawal of women from the labour force as material conditions improve and it is no longer necessary for them to work. The 'effective co-operation' or partnership aspect of gender can, in this context, weaken (Dreze & Sen 1996: 155-159). The view that poverty reduction is likely to have been at the root of intensified female survival disadvantage is corroborated by cross sectional data for 296 districts, which show that higher levels of poverty go with more balanced FMRs, while, at the same time, female labour force participation makes the FMR more feminine (Dreze and Sen 1996: 157-163). In this context, we need also to consider Krishnaji's (1995) explanation for more balanced FMRs among working mothers, namely, that acute poverty makes it difficult for mothers to *fatally* discriminate in favour of their male children, since resources are at such a low level that children of both sexes are at high risk (Krishnaji 1995). What these explanations imply is that the evidence we have considered of the 'intensification effect' operating since the mid nineteen eighties could in fact be due to declines in female work force participation.

- We have already seen from Figure 1 that offspring FMRs became more masculine from the mid nineteen eighties in Rajasthan, Bihar, Punjab, Uttar Pradesh and Gujarat. Figure 8 shows us that in Bihar, Uttar Pradesh and Gujarat, offspring FMRs have worsened for both working mothers as well as non-working mothers. Moreover, in Punjab, Haryana, and Orissa, the offspring FMRs of working mothers deteriorated (Figure 8). Again, as in the case of literacy and the parity effect, we can't explain away the evidence of the intensification effect in terms of 'sanskritisation'.
- However, Figure 8 throws up the possibility of a fresh interpretation of the 'parity effect', namely, that, in part, pauperisation and the attendant increases in the incidence of working women, had acted in the direction of making the FMR more feminine. Again, this is beyond the scope of this chapter. Nonetheless, this interpretation would tend to reinforce Dyson's (1987) argument that FMR declines between 1971 and 1981 were *not* due to improvements in child health.

(d) Offspring FMRs Curves, 1981 and 1991

- The data not only show the parity and intensification effects, they also attest to the growing masculinity of the FMR over the decades. Let us take a closer look at the data, to see how they throw light on this aspect. We now turn to Figure 4 which shows offspring FMRs for 1981. If there had been no change in the values of these FMRs, then the *implied* curve for 1991 should be *above* the curve for 1981, as shown in Figure 5. Figure 6 shows what actually happened. In Tamil Nadu in the south, Gujarat in western

India, Bihar, and States in the northwest like Rajasthan and Delhi, and to a lesser extent, U.P, Punjab and Haryana, there has been a tendency for actual 1991 curve to shift *below* the 1981 curve. This effect is the most pronounced for Bihar (Figure 6). For States like Uttar Pradesh, Haryana, Punjab and Rajasthan, and Gujarat, this shift has involved only the younger cohorts of mothers. One can hypothesise, in the absence of data for earlier periods, that offspring FMR curves kept shifting downwards since the nineteen fifties, due to operation of mortality effects working across parities, to make the FMR more adverse.

- Rather than seeing the offspring FMR curve as a single curve, one may look at it in terms of just one among a *series* of curves. Entire curves at more and more recent points of time have kept 'shifting' downwards. We have data for two curves, for 1981 and 1991 (Figure 6), on the basis of which we postulate this phenomenon. In the absence of data for earlier time periods, we *postulate* rather than *demonstrate* the phenomenon as extending back in time. The fact that these curves are continually shifting downwards would account for the deteriorating (increasing masculinity) of FMRs in the population as a whole over the course of the century.
- Let us look at the phenomenon a little more minutely, taking the case of Bihar as an example of the right-to-left upward sloping curve (Figure 1). The offspring FMR for the 1956 cohort of mothers (the 50-54 cohort), we can see, is far more masculine than the offspring FMR a younger cohort of mothers, say, the cohort aged 20-24 (the 1986 cohort). On the face of it, this would appear to go counter to what we know about FMRs in the country, that is, that they have grown more masculine over time. *However, the 50-54 cohort of mothers does not represent the entire population of married women a particular point of time in the past.* In 1956, these women had entered their reproductive careers. In that year, i.e., in 1956, obviously, *there were women of other ages also in the population.* Thus, what we are comparing is the cohort of mothers that entered the reproductive ages of 15-19 in 1956, with other cohorts of mothers that entered the reproductive ages at different time points. On the one hand, due to the parity effect, we expect each younger cohort of mothers to have more balanced offspring FMRs, but on the other, there are indications that offspring FMRs deteriorate over time, due to the *continuing depredations of mortality*, as Mari Bhat (2002a:5108, 5112) has argued. However, excess female child mortality worsens less for the offspring of each successively younger cohort of mothers, because, due to fertility decline, each younger cohort of mothers has fewer higher parity girl children. Consequently, the parity effect, combined with continuing mortality depredation, operating in tandem, both preserve the slope of the curve and cause it 'shift downward', as we see

notably in the case of Bihar, in Figure 6. If we had data to construct curves for earlier census years, say, for 1951 and 1971, at which time, we know, mortality took a relatively high toll of females, making the FMR more masculine, we may have got more conspicuously outward shifting curves.

- In the period 1951-1991, as Bhat (2002b) shows, using population enumeration data from the census of India, the FMR in the 0-9 age group became more masculine. In the age group 10-19 also, there was a growing masculinity of the FRM, and, as in the case of the 0-9 group, this also was statistically significant (2002b: p.5108, table 3; p. 5112). In the first decades after independence, immunisation and disease control, and improvements in transport, allowing better access to urban areas, had made gender discriminatory practices more potent. Thus, as the younger children grew older, the girls continued to suffer higher mortality (Mari Bhat 2002b: 5252-5253). To apply this to the interpretation of our data, this happened to the children of every cohort of mothers. Consequently, *mortality acted on children within each cohort of mothers* to cause the offspring FMR curve to shift outwards. If data had been available, this should have been in evidence in census decade after census decade.
- When we come to the more recent period, from 1986 to 1991, as noted earlier, we see that the shape of the curve in Figure 1, again, taking Bihar as case in point, is now sloping upwards *from left to right*. This pattern had emerged *only after 1981*, as a perusal of Figures 5 and 6 shows. So, we are looking at a phenomenon that occurred between 1981 and 1991.

(e) Offspring FMRs, 2001

- Figure 9 shows rural offspring FMRs for selected States in 2001. We had seen from Figure 1 that in Rajasthan, Bihar, Punjab, Uttar Pradesh and Gujarat, offspring FMRs had worsened from the mid-eighties up to 1991. This was based on retrospective data for 1991. The offspring FMRs for rural areas from retrospective data for 2001 are shown in Figure 9. Figure 9 confirms the finding from Figure 1 to the effect that that there had been a worsening of offspring FMRs between the 1986 cohort of mothers (aged 30 to 34 in 2001) and the 1991 cohort of mothers (aged 25 to 29 in 2001). It will be recalled that we were not able to say this definitively from Figure 1, because of the possibility that as the children of young mothers grew older, or as young mothers proceeded on their fertility careers, it would change their offspring FMRs. Figure 9 confirms that in the case of Punjab and Gujarat, offspring FMRs did grow more masculine between 1986 and 1991, plausibly due to the intensification effect. The 2001 retrospective data for rural areas also attest to the intensification effect during this period (1986 to 1991) for Delhi, Haryana, Rajasthan and Himachal Pradesh, which the 1991 retrospective data for young mothers had not shown, plausibly because these young mothers had not completed their fertility careers and also because their children had not aged fully through the juvenile ages, allowing mortality to fully come into play.

- Subsequently, between 1991 and 2001, in these States, offspring FMRs actually began to grow more feminine, that is, the intensification effect got reversed. This resulted in inverted humps in the offspring FMR curves in these States (Figure 9). In the case of all areas data, we see inverted humps for Punjab, Haryana, Rajasthan and Gujarat (Figure 10). However, we need not take this seriously, at this point, since data showing the supposed reversal of the intensification effect was for young mothers, who have not completed their fertility careers, and whose children are unlikely to have completely or substantially aged through the juvenile ages. In other words, the data showing a reversal of the intensification effect are incomplete data. We will have to await the retrospective data of the 2011 census to really see what has happened in these States.
- Of the States which, as per 1991 retrospective data for rural areas, witnessed a worsening of juvenile FMRs between 1986 and 1991 (Rajasthan, Bihar, Punjab, Uttar Pradesh and Gujarat), we have seen that the 2001 retrospective data confirm this trend for Punjab and Gujarat (Table 9). What about rural areas in the other three States—Rajasthan, Bihar and Uttar Pradesh? In the case of Bihar and Uttar Pradesh, we do not see any such confirmation (Figure 9).
- In the case of Bihar after partition, that is, after Jharkhand was carved out of undivided Bihar, we see indications that between 1991 and 2001, in rural areas, the offspring FMRs have started to grow masculine for young mothers (aged 15 to 19). We see such a tendency also for Himachal Pradesh (Figure 9). We will have to await the retrospective data of the 2011 census to see if this persists even after the cohort of children of young mothers have had a chance to survive through to the higher ages.
- As far as the trend between 1991 and 2001 in rural areas is concerned, i.e., comparing the offspring FMRs for mothers aged 20-24 in 2001 and mothers aged 15-19 in 2001, in none of the States except Himachal Pradesh, Madhya Pradesh and Bihar (after Jharkhand was carved out of It), do we see indications that offspring FMRs have been worsening between 1991 and 2001 (Table 9). Again, these data are incomplete, as the young mothers of 2001 have yet to complete their fertility careers, and their children are as yet to have a chance to age completely through the juvenile years.
- Figure 11 presents offspring FMRs for Urban areas from the 2001 census. From this table, we see that between 1996 and 2001, in Bihar, Uttar Pradesh and, notably, Himachal Pradesh, there has been a worsening of offspring

FMRs for young mothers (aged 15-19). Of course, we will have to await the next census to see if this was a real or spurious trend, because, by 2011, the children of young mothers will have had an opportunity to age to older ages, and the mothers themselves would have had a chance to complete their fertility careers. Still, it is noteworthy that for Himachal Pradesh, the worsening of the offspring FMR for young mothers in urban areas has been very steep. Besides, the FMR for Children Ever Born has declined sharply in urban Himachal Pradesh between 1996 and 2001in the case of young mothers, suggesting a revival of infanticide (Figure 11).

(f) Offspring FMRs and Child Mortality

- We have argued that fertility decline, by preventing high birth order girls from being born, applied the brakes to the increasing masculinity of the FMR. Notably the nineteen seventies was a period of sharp fertility decline (Figure 2 and Jha 2008: 86—Figure 4.1), to which the averting of high birth-order female births are likely to have contributed. By 1981, this seemed to have neutralised gender discriminatory practices, which, as Mari Bhat (2002b: 5252-5253) points out, had been rendered highly potent by the new access to life-saving factors. The net effect was arguably at the root of the child mortality declines for females relative to males since 1971, which SRS data show (Mari Bhat 2002b: 5253). At the same time, as Figure 1 suggests, pre-natal discrimination also was getting greatly reduced during this decade. In the light of these developments, for States like Uttar Pradesh, Delhi, and Rajasthan, if we could construct surviving children FMR curves for 1971, we could expect them to be dramatically above the 1981 curves, in the same way as, in Figure 6, the FMR curve for surviving children for 1981 is above the curve for 1991.
- The feminisation of the offspring FMRs between 1971 and 1981 was especially steep for States like Uttar Pradesh, Delhi, Bihar, and Rajasthan, as per the retrospective data—we see this when we compare the child FMRs for the cohorts of mothers aged 35-39 (the 1971 cohort), 30-34 (the 1976 cohort) and 25-29 (the 1981 cohort). *Juvenile FMRs compiled from census enumeration data corroborate this pattern of growing feminisation of the FMR between 1971 and 1981, particularly for Uttar Pradesh, Delhi and Rajasthan.* These census figures, compiled by Premi (2001: 1877) are for *all areas*—that is, rural and urban areas combined. Since the relative falls in female mortality were greatest in rural areas (Mari Bhat 2002b: 5253), we can expect the rural FMRs to have grown even more feminine. Notably, data compiled for a longer time period (1971-1998) shows that the declines in relative child mortality were statistically significant and strong for Uttar Pradesh, Madhya Pradesh, Haryana, Punjab and Rajasthan (Mari Bhat

2002b: 5253).

- The Sample Registration System showed that over the nineteen seventies and the nineteen eighties, despite some discontinuities, child survival was improving more among females than among males (Mari Bhat 2002b: 5253). Over a longer time frame of three decades, from 1971 to 1998, we see this same pattern for most states, with the exception of Tamil Nadu, Andhra Pradesh and West Bengal. The greatest reductions in female child mortality were in the in the States of Uttar Pradesh, Haryana, Punjab, Rajasthan and Madhya Pradesh, where the coefficients are statistically significant (Mari Bhat 2002b: 5253-5254). When we consider the three-decade time frame (1971-1998) over which mortality falls took place, then, what we have to explain is how, despite declines in female mortality, juvenile FMRs became more masculine between 1981 and 1991 and 1991 and 2001. Obviously, to explain this, we would have to turn to the phenomenon of the elimination of females *before* birth. But when we consider a shorter span of time, say the 1970s, then, we see that the FMR grew more *feminine* in the country, from 1930 in 1971 to 934 in 1981, which was a break in the pattern of growing masculinity of the FMR since the beginning of the twentieth century (Premi 1991: 37).
- It is worth noting here that the improvement of the FMR from 930 to 934 between 1971 and 1981 have been interpreted as an artifact of changes in enumeration. The argument runs as follows: the decline in the FMR by 10 points between 1961 and 1971 (from 940 to 930) was due to a 10% increase in census undercount—the census undercount had increased from 8 persons per thousand in the 1961 census to 17 per thousand in the 1971 census. Assuming that it was mostly females that were undercounted, that would account for the worsening of the FMR between 1961 and 1971. Without the undercount, the FMR for 1971 may have been in the region of 937. Then, the FMR of 1981 (934) would fit in with the trend of increasing masculinity of the sex ratio (Premi 2001:1875). However, as noted, this explanation assumes that the undercount mainly affected females. For 1961 we have no sex wise break up of undercount, but we do have the figures for 1951, 1971, 1981 and 1991. In the 1951 census, the undercount for males and females was 8.6% and 11.2%. By 1971, the female undercount had increased to 18.3%, but the male undercount also increased to 15.3%. The relative index of undercount (females / males) of 1.30 for 1971 compares well with corresponding figure of 1.30 for 1951. In 1981, the male and female under enumerations stood at 17.1% and 18.9% respectively, and for 1991, the figures had changed marginally to 17.3% and 17.9% respectively. The relative index of undercount changed marginally for 1.11 in 1981 to 1.03 in 1991 (Premi 2001: 1877).

- We have argued that declines in female child mortality had contributed to making the FMRs more feminine between 1971 and 1981. But what was it that caused female child mortality to decline? Dyson (1987) argues that fertility decline in India allowed a greater share of resources in smaller families, and hence made for an improvement of the survival chances of female children. Thus, it was the fall in *demographically determined risk* that was at the root of falling female child mortality. Though more children were surviving, however, continued discrimination against them in terms of how well fed and cared for they were did not translate into higher mortality rates for female children—it acted, rather, to increase their frailty and susceptibility to morbidity (Dyson 1987). That the decline in female child mortality was not linked to improvements in the health circumstances of girl children is suggested also in cause of death statistics for India for 1980, 1990 and 1998. The data show that mortality due to anaemia was higher among girls than among boys, which indicates higher levels of malnutrition among girl children (Sagar 2007: 181).
- Figure 10 shows us the offspring FMRs for all areas (rural and urban) for 2001. Except noticeably in Himachal Pradesh, and also in the case of the new State of Bihar (which emerged after Jharkhand was carved out of it), there are no indications of the worsening FMRs for young mothers, aged 15-19 and 20-24. This is not as expected. Prior to 1986, in the course of the fertility transition, fertility decline meant that older cohorts of children—not just female children, but also male children—were not born. Since older cohorts of children have more masculine FMRs, on an aggregate level, it created a tendency for FMRs to grow more feminine. This applied the brakes to the worsening of the FMR, as we have argued. Post 1986, when it became possible to use technology to identify the sex of the unborn child, the births specifically of older birth-order *female* children could be averted. In this context, we expect the offspring FMRs for Children Ever Born to grow more masculine.
- On the face of it, there appears to be a hiatus between the retrospective data of 2001, on the one hand, and on the other, the census enumeration data for 1991 and 2001. Juvenile FMRs calculated from the enumeration data for 1991 and 2001 had sent alarm bells ringing across the country, by indicating a marked worsening of juvenile FMRs in many of the States. In accounting for this seeming hiatus, we need to note, first and foremost, that the retrospective data for young mothers—which indicate no worsening of the offspring FMRs in the decade of the 1990s—are incomplete. The children of these young mothers have not had a chance to age completely through the juvenile ages, and it may well be that when they have done so, their offspring FMRs will be found to have become more masculine. Moreover,

the young mothers are likely to have additional children, which again would change the composition of the offspring FMRs. Thus, we need not read too much into these data for young mothers. We will need to await the results of the 2011 census retrospective data for these young mothers to really see what has happened.

- We need to note also that the retrospective data differ from the enumeration data in another fundamental way. The retrospective data are for different cohorts of mothers—the cohort of mothers who entered the reproductive ages in 1956, the cohort of mothers who entered the reproductive ages in 1961, and so on. So, they give a comparative picture of different such cohorts. The enumeration data, on the other hand, show data for the entire population at different points of time.
- As we have noted in the discussion on data sources at an earlier point in this chapter, there are good reasons for considering a data source other than population enumeration data. Enumeration data are suspect, in the light of Mari Bhat's analysis to the effect that improvements in age reporting are likely to inject a spurious element in the interpretation of enumeration data (Mari Bhat 2002a and Mari Bhat 2002b). There is another reason why juvenile FMRs are problematic, namely, that excess female child mortality may not have fully manifested in the juvenile ages. In other words, the effect of excess female child mortality would be seen only after a sufficient ageing of a cohort of children has occurred. Composite variables like 'under five mortality' are prone to this sort of problem (Agnihotri 2000:29, 38, 95-96), and we can extend the argument to juvenile FMRs as well. It is noteworthy that the data on CEB and CS are not susceptible to the kinds of age-reporting errors in that they do not distinguish the children of women by age; the data only indicate how many children women of different ages have had. The retrospective data used in this paper show the numbers of children different cohorts of mothers have had over the course of their reproductive careers, and in the case of those with completed or near completed fertility, the data are not plagued by such problems. Yet, the retrospective data can be prone to error in the case of the younger cohorts of mothers, who have not completed their fertility careers, and whose children may not all have had a chance to grow through the juvenile ages. In interpreting the data, this has been kept in mind. In sum, though retrospective data has its limitations, so does the enumeration data of the census. So, taking this as the rationale, we have drawn on the retrospective data to throw light on the broad issues.

Summary and Discussion

Son preference, when family size goes down, it is argued, intensifies fatal discrimination against daughters (the 'intensification effect'). More specifically, higher birth order daughters, who impose additional burdens on parents in terms of dowry etc. are at grave risk. It does not appear, however, that in the Indian context, one can unequivocally infer a link between fertility decline and intensification of daughter discrimination. On the contrary, fertility decline in India seems to have put the brakes on a worsening of FMR, by having ensured that higher birth-order children, among whom girls are at greater risk of fatal discrimination, are not born. Since FMRs are more masculine among higher birth-order children, when fewer higher-birth order children are born, at an aggregate level, juvenile FMRs can be expected to become more feminine. This phenomenon—termed by Das Gupta and Mari Bhat (1997) as the 'parity effect', had applied the brakes on the growing masculinity of the FMR since 1956s up to 1986 in rural areas, the present study shows. (The analysis in this paper is mainly for rural areas, though, in the case of the 2001 data, urban data and all areas data also have been briefly considered).

Despite the parity effect, FMRs in India are known to have become more adverse over time, as attested by population enumeration data, due to a number of factors, including improvements in nutrition and health care, and better access to urban facilities due to improvements in transport, all of which gives new potency to gender discriminatory practices (Mari Bhat 2002b: 5252-5253). Concurrently, fertility decline, by preventing high birth order girls from being born, plausibly put the brakes on a worsening of the FMR, by acting to reduce both pre-natal and post-natal elimination of girls. As of 1991, that effect was strongest in Uttar Pradesh, Rajasthan, Delhi and Bihar.

We cannot entirely rule out other factors that acted parallel to the parity effect, such as increases in literacy of women, or increasing female labour force participation. Still, we do see indications of the parity effect operating.

'Retrospective data'—the type of data drawn upon in this chapter—are data on children ever born (CEB) and children surviving (CS) as reported by mothers who were asked by census enumerators to provide details of their reproductive history. The data are about past events (births and deaths), and so they are called 'retrospective data'. The data were collected for mothers in various age groups, that is, 15-19, 20-24, 25-29 etc. When we consider data for 1991, then, mothers in the age group 55-59 would have entered their reproductive careers in 1956, and those aged 15-19 in 1991. So, these data allow us to trace patterns of offspring FMRs over time. We need to note that the retrospective data differ from the enumeration data in another fundamental way. The retrospective data are for different cohorts of mothers—the cohort of mothers who entered the reproductive ages in 1956, the cohort of mothers who entered the reproductive ages in 1961, and so on. So, they give a comparative picture of different such cohorts. The enumeration data, on the

FIGURE 1: COHORT FMRs, Children Ever Born and Children Surviving, 1991, Rural Areas, Selected States of India

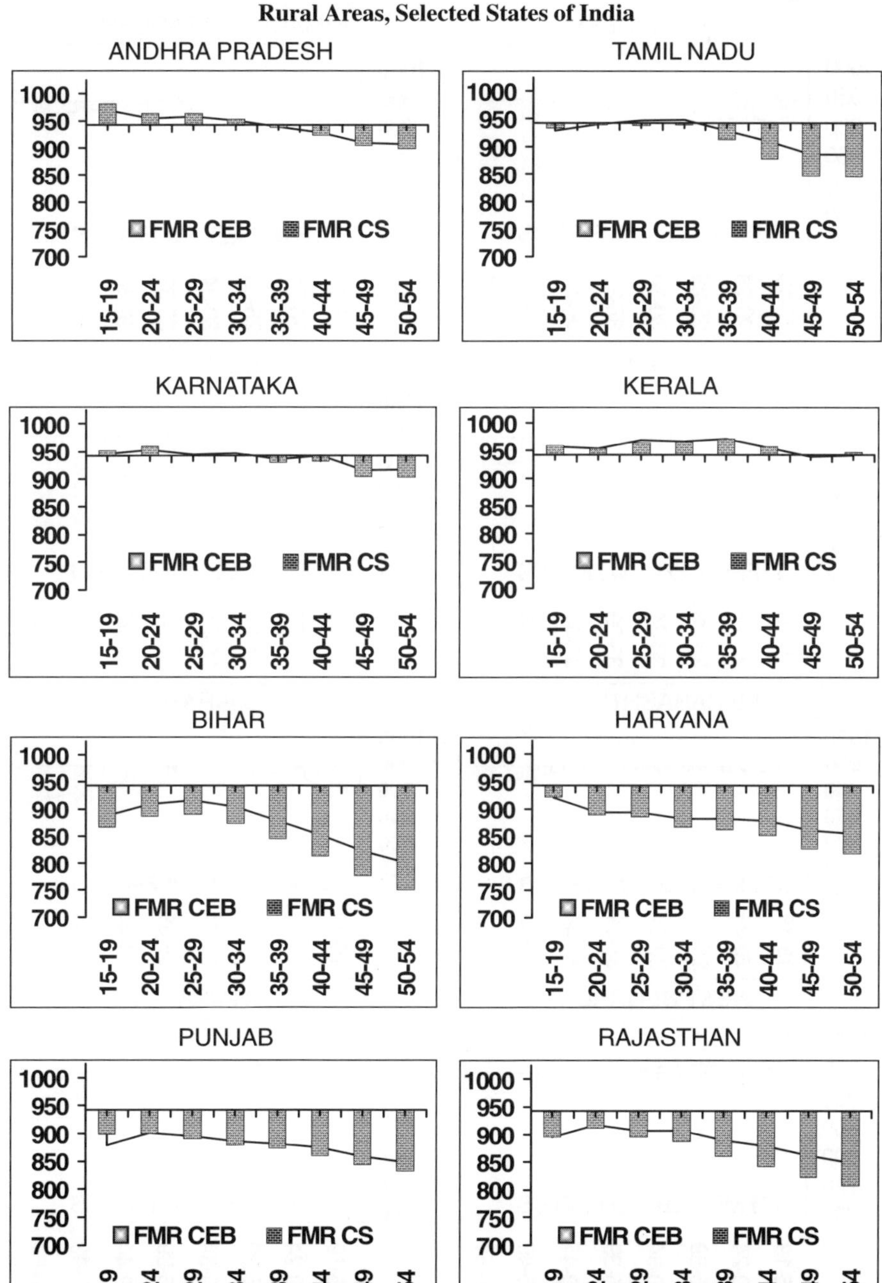

FIGURE 1 (*Contd*)

UTTAR PRADESH

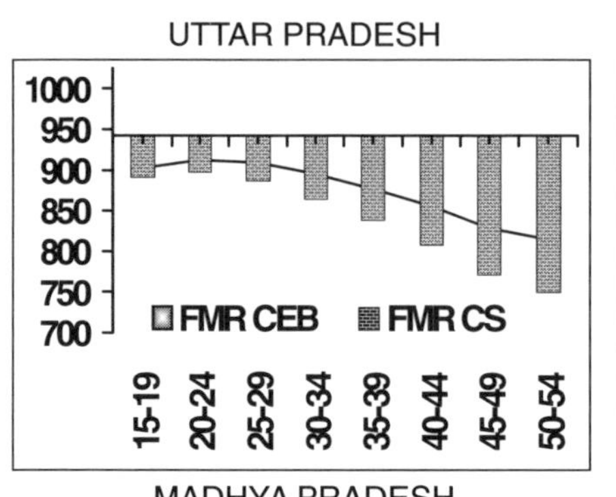

HIMACHAL PRADESH

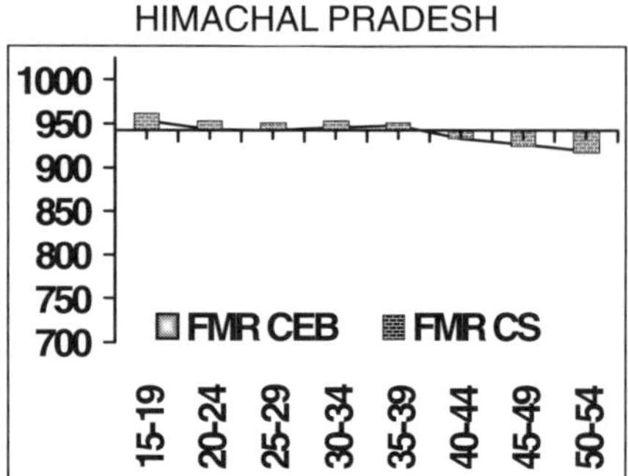

MADHYA PRADESH

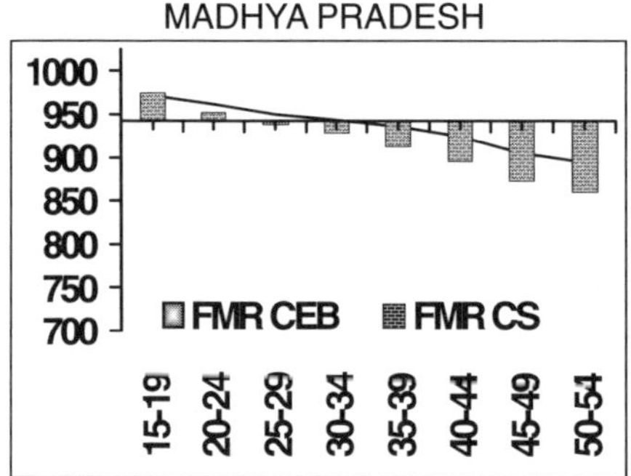

DELHI

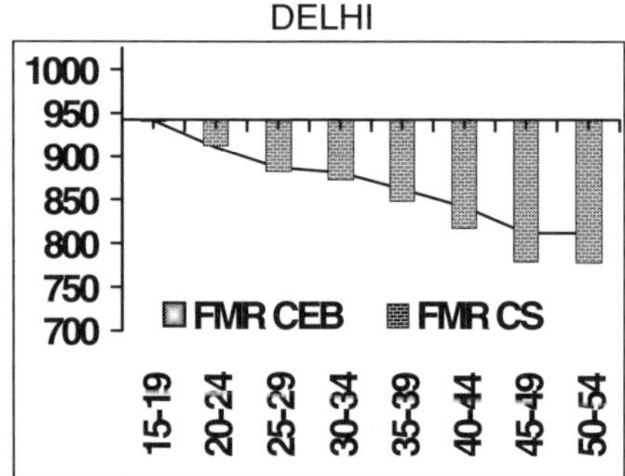

MAHARASHTRA

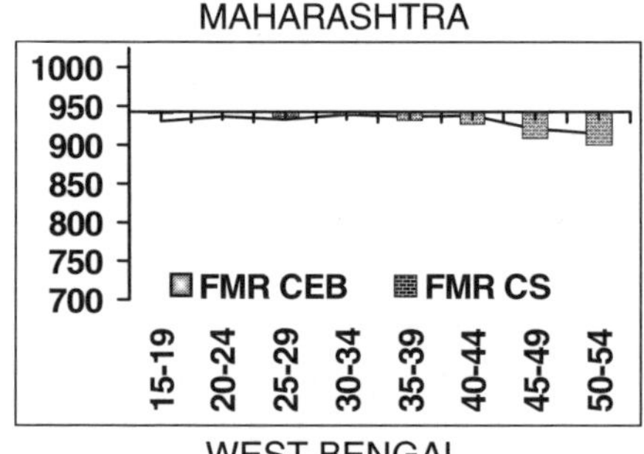

GUJARAT

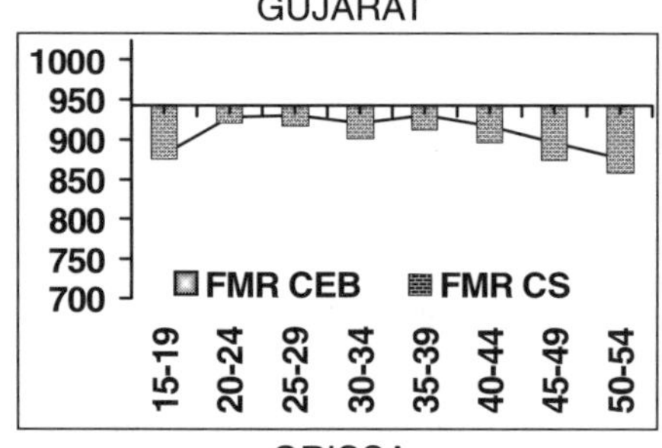

WEST BENGAL

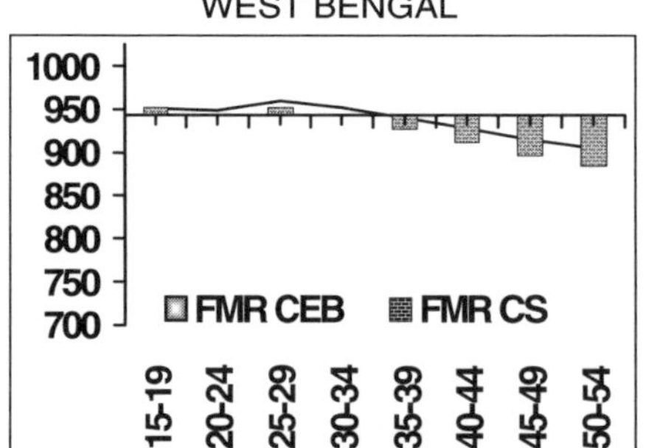

ORISSA

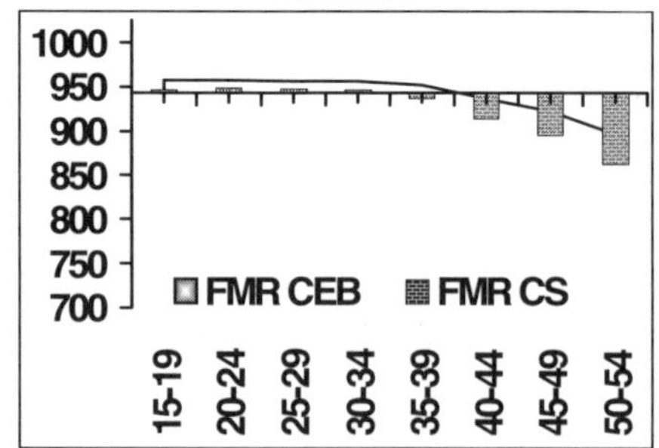

FIGURE 2 : Children even Born per Woman, Rural Areas, Selected States of India, 1991

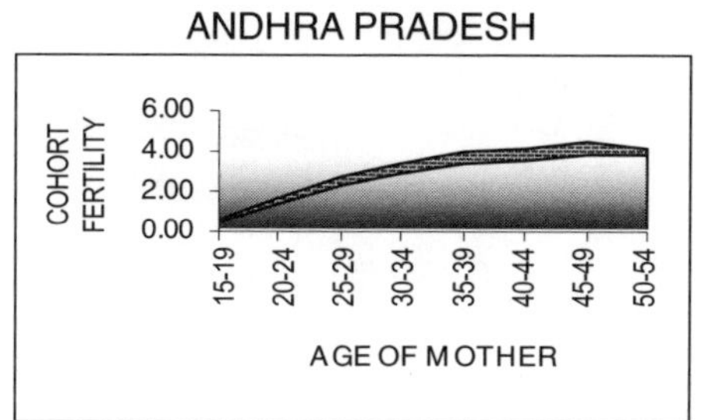

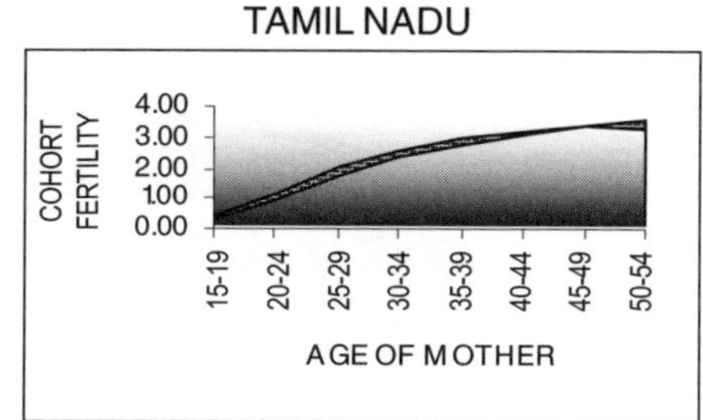

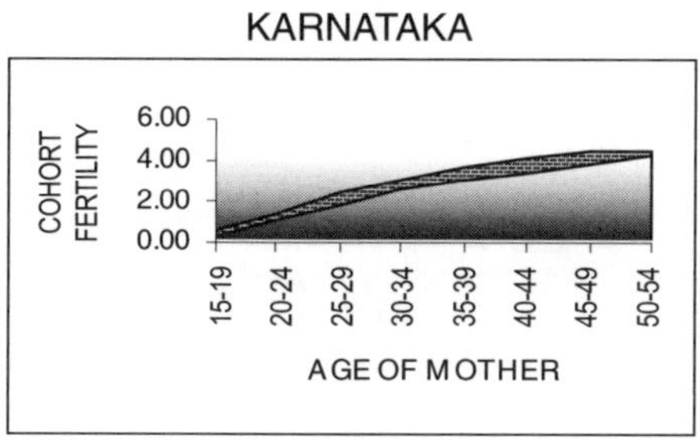

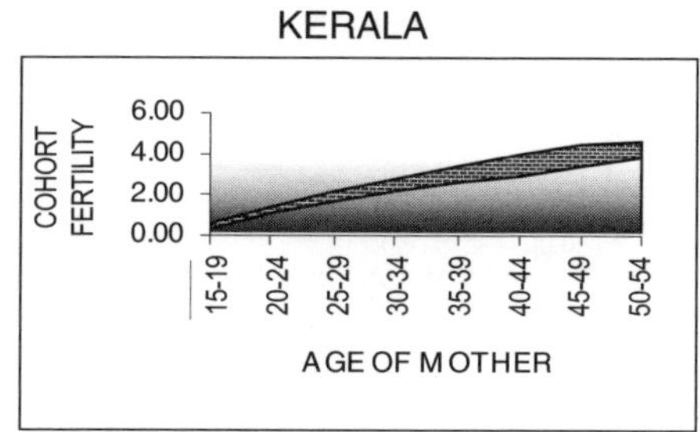

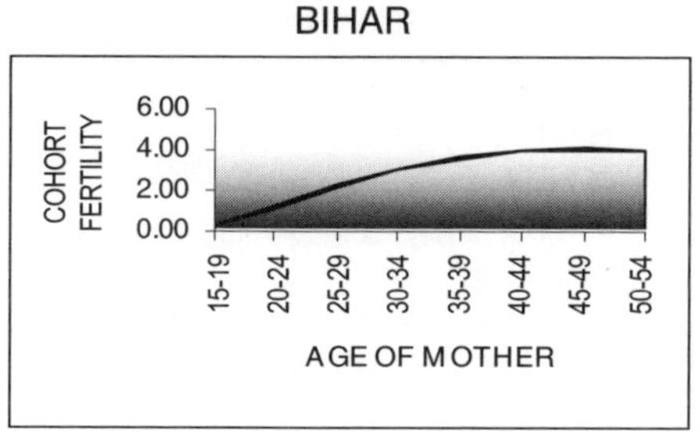

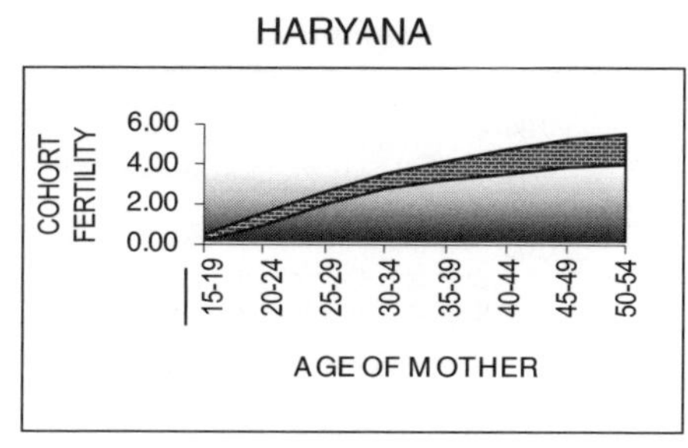

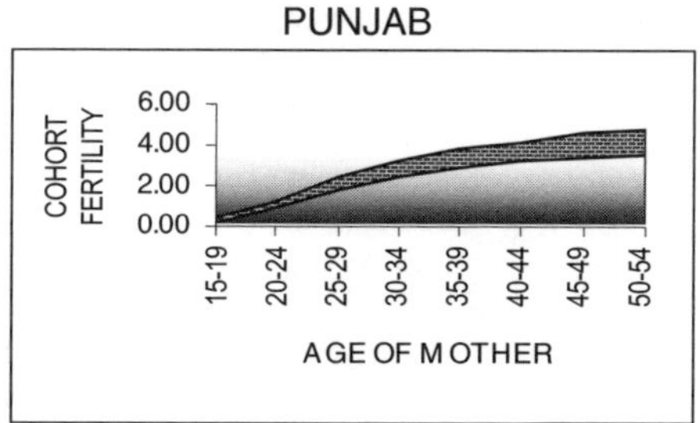

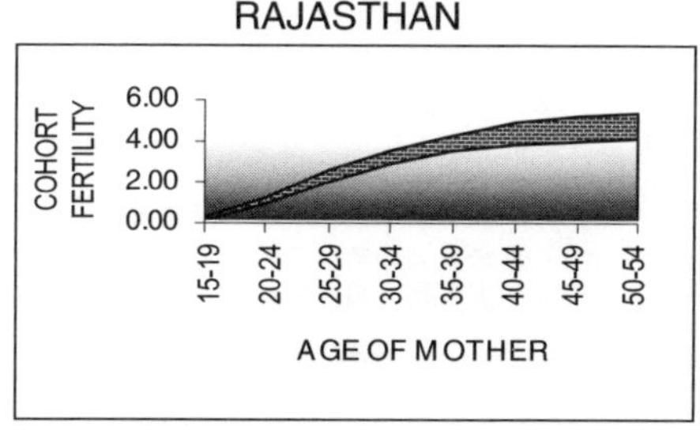

FIGURE 2 (*Contd.*)

UTTAR PRADESH

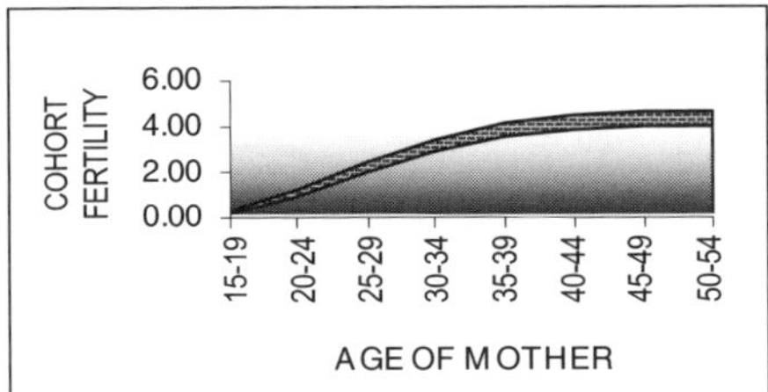

HIMACHAL PRADESH

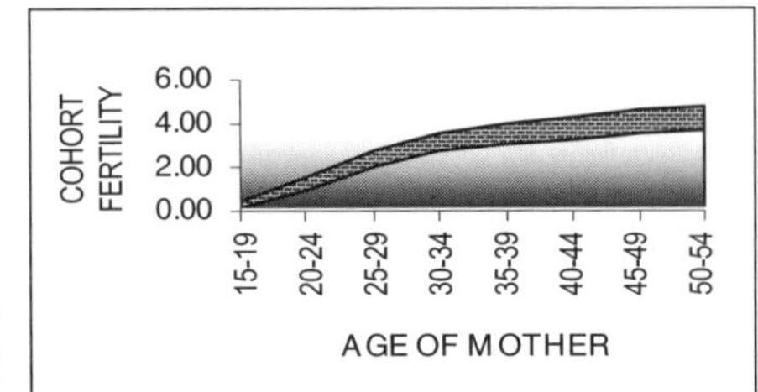

MADHYA PRADESH

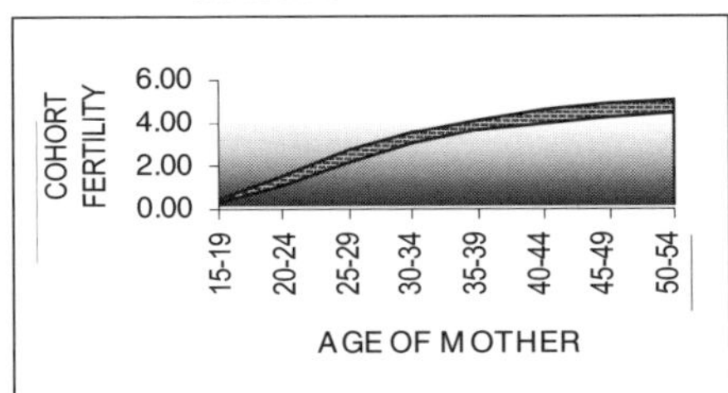

DELHI

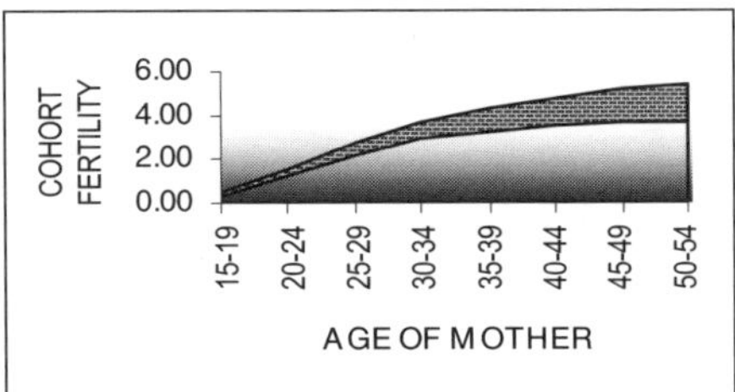

MAHARASHTRA

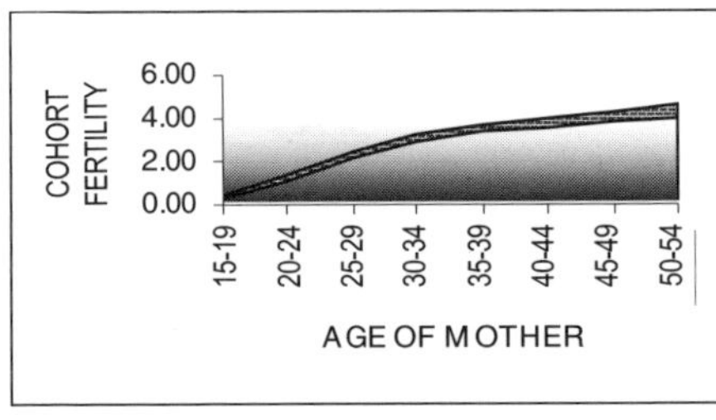

GUJARAT

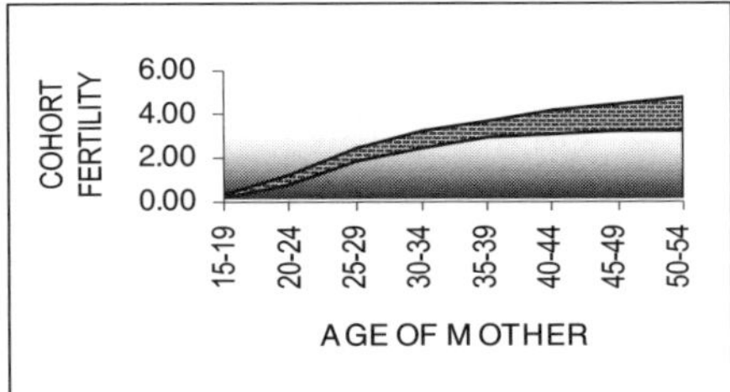

WEST BENGAL

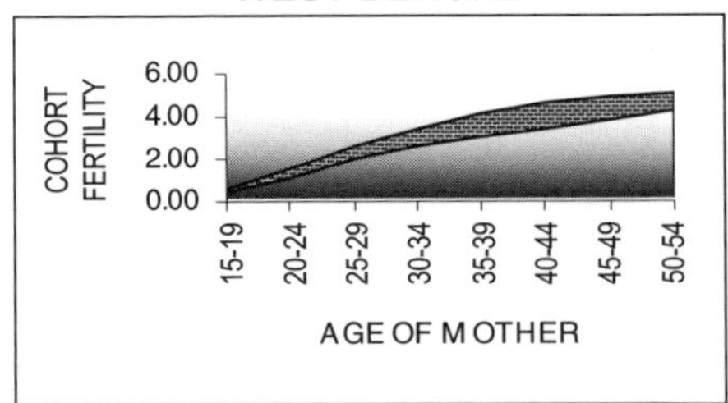

ORISSA

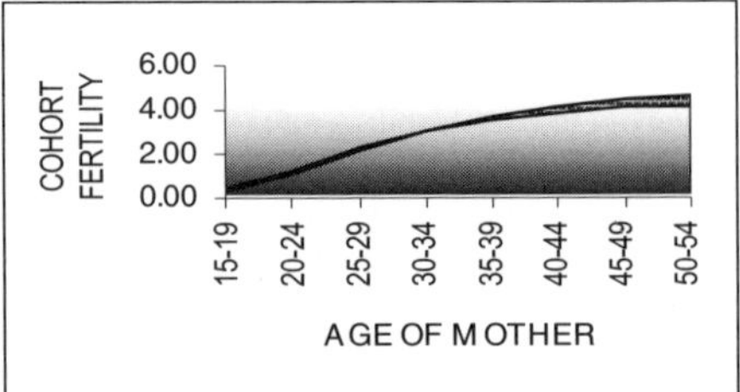

Note: Brick pattern shows the CEB for illiterate mothers. The shaded portion shows the CEB for educated mothers (mothers with a middle plus level of education).

FIGURE 3: FMRs, Children Surviving, Educated and Illiterate Mothers, 1991, Rural Areas, Selected States of India

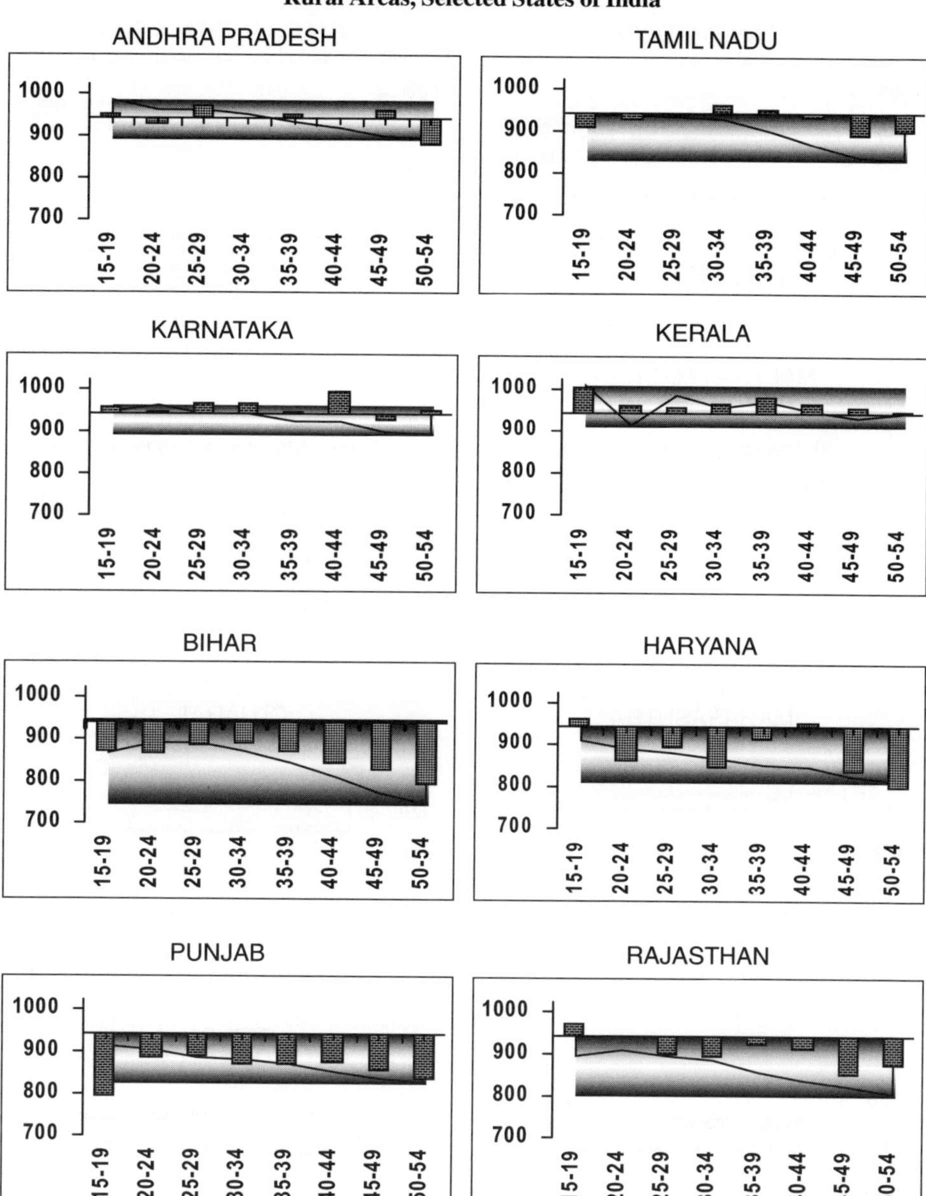

FIGURE 3: (Contd.)

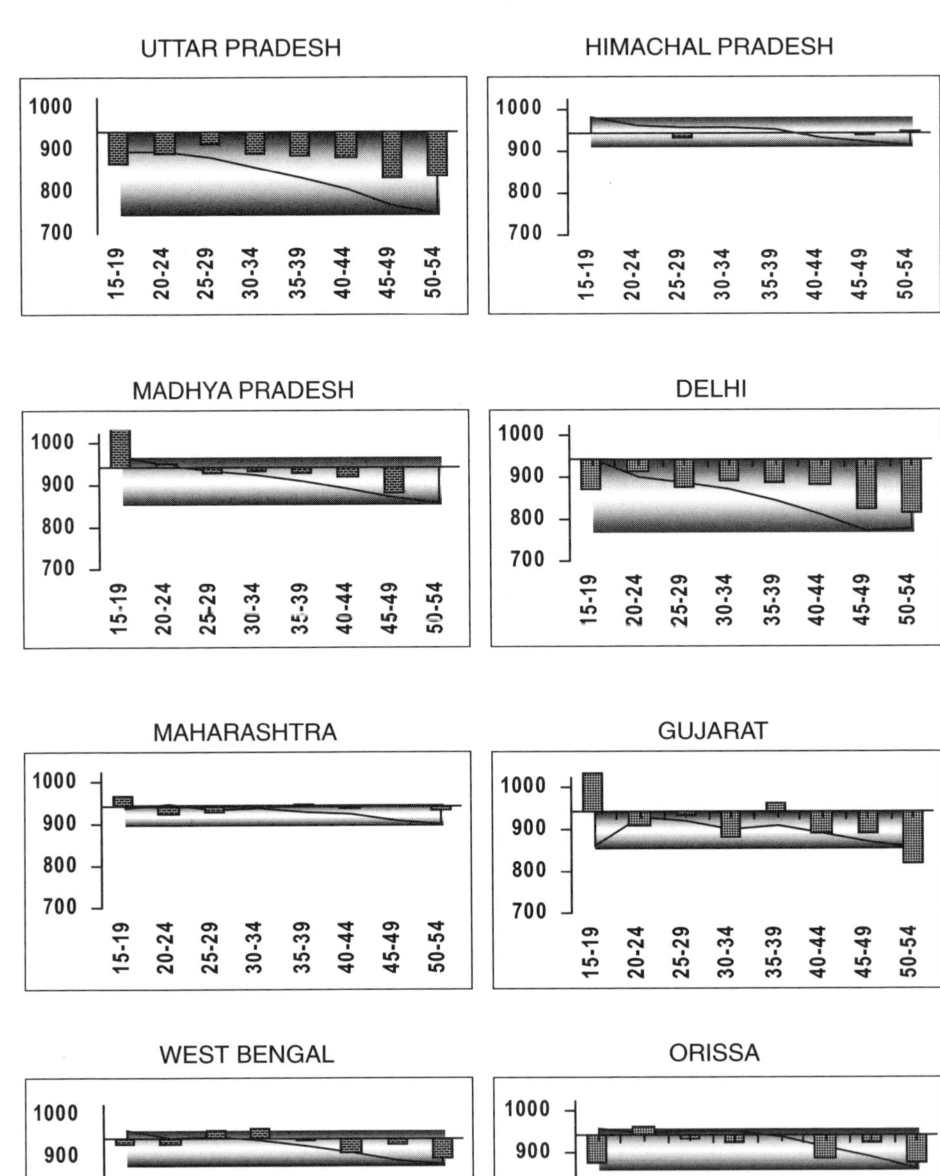

Note: Brick pattern shows the FMR for surviving children of educated mothers (middle plus level of education). Shaded portion shows FMR for surviving children of illiterate mothers.

FIGURE 4: Cohort FMRs, Rural Areas, Selected States of India, 1981

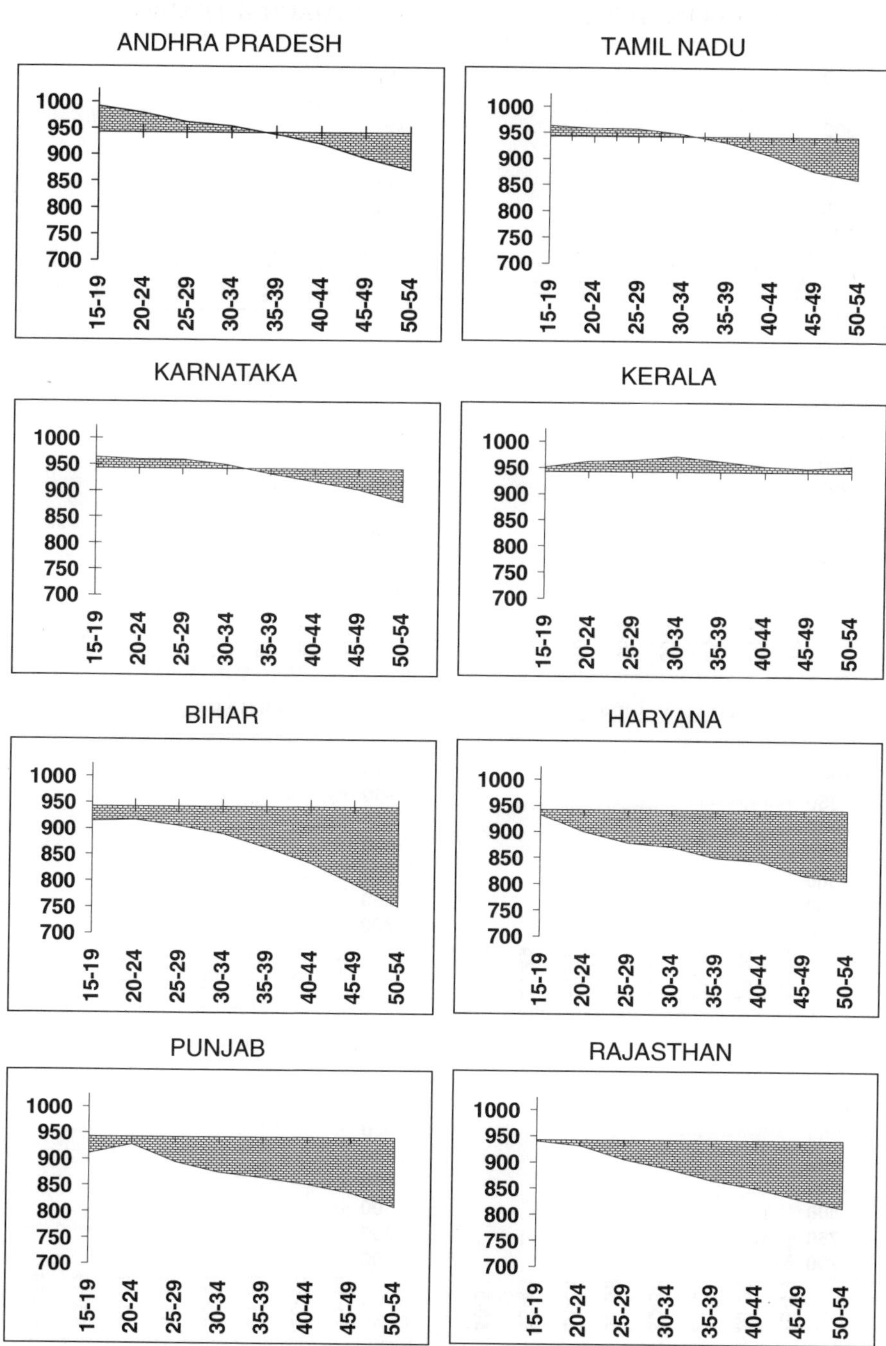

FIGURE 4: (*Contd.*)

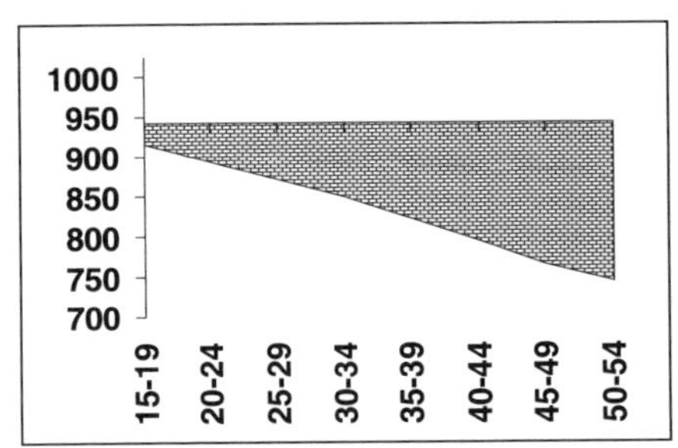

HIMACHAL PRADESH

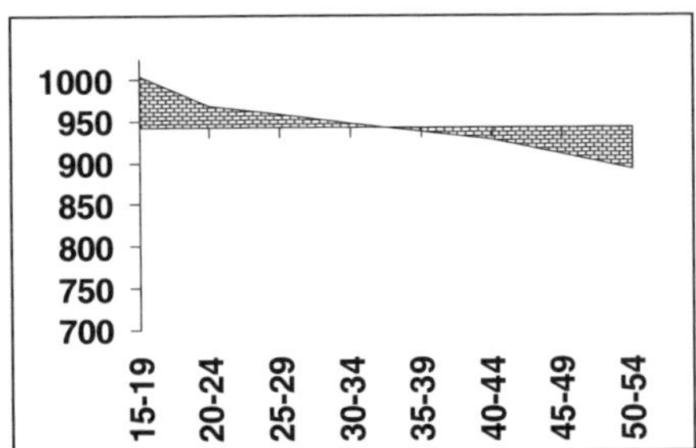

MADHYA PRADESH

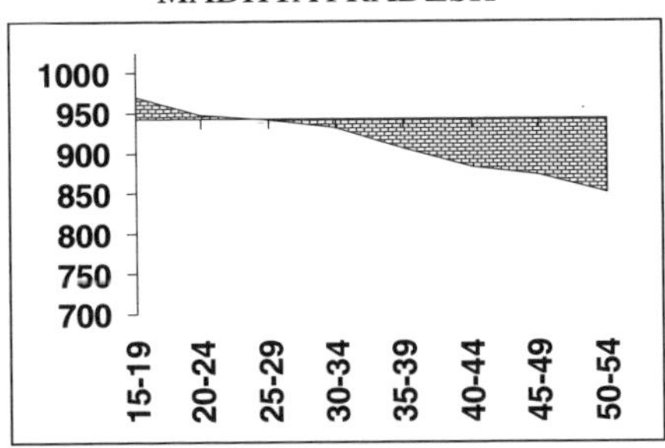

DELHI

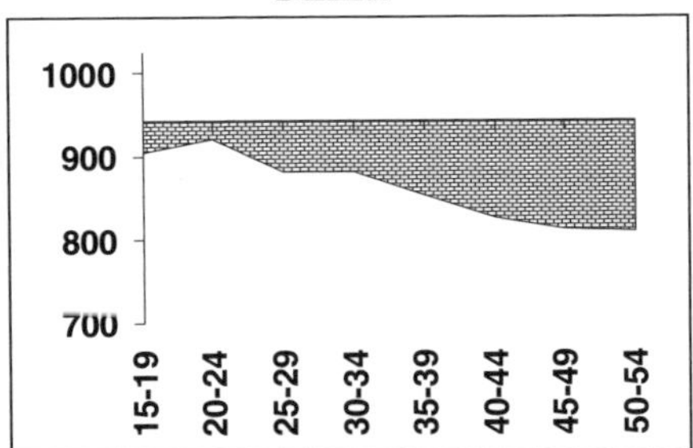

MAHARASHTRA

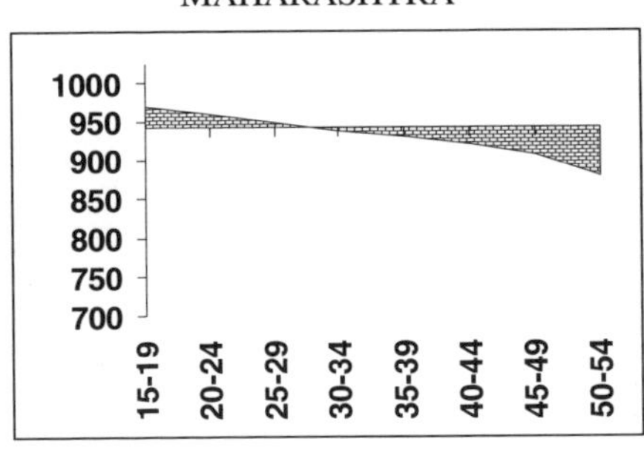

GUJARAT

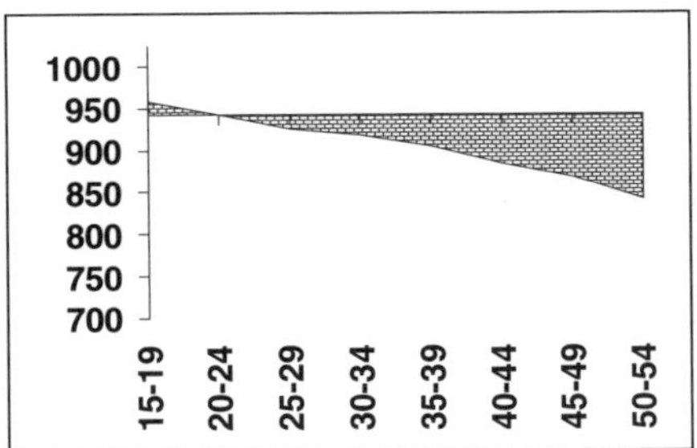

WEST BENGAL

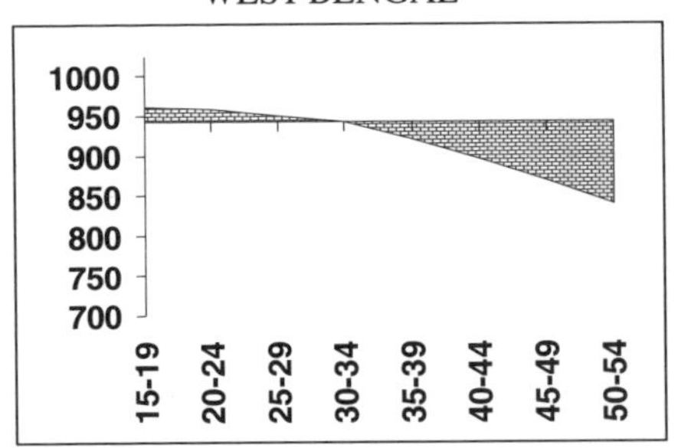

ORISSA

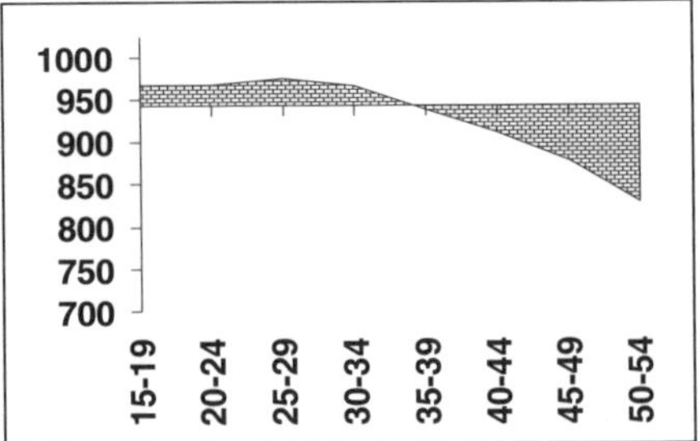

Figure 5: Cohort FMRs 1981 & Implied Cohort FMRs 1991, Rural Areas, Selected States of India

ANDHRA PRADESH

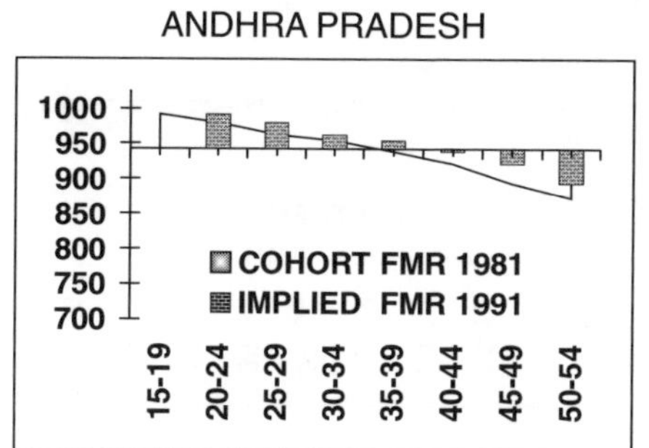

TAMIL NADU

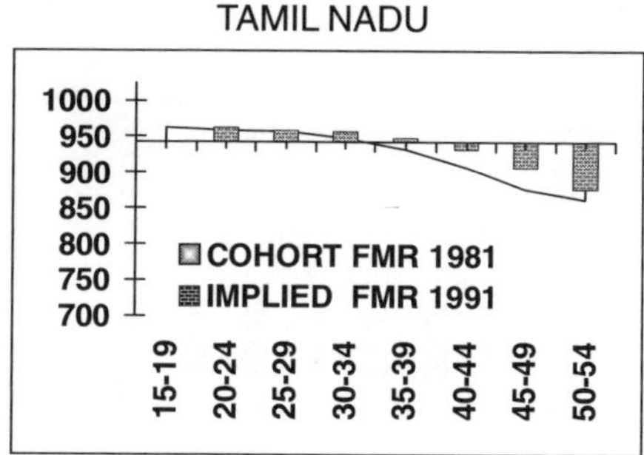

KARNATAKA

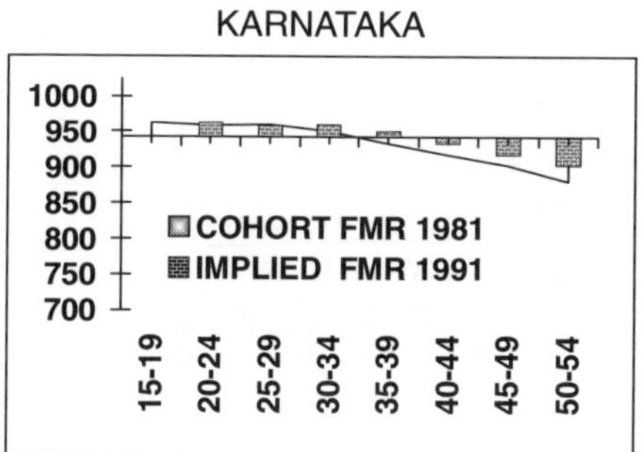

KERALA

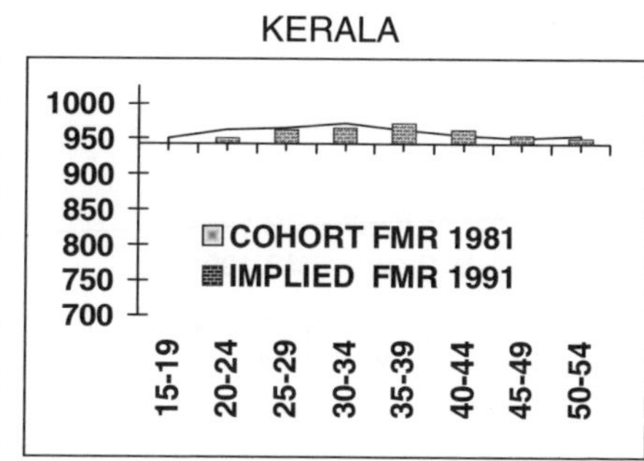

BIHAR

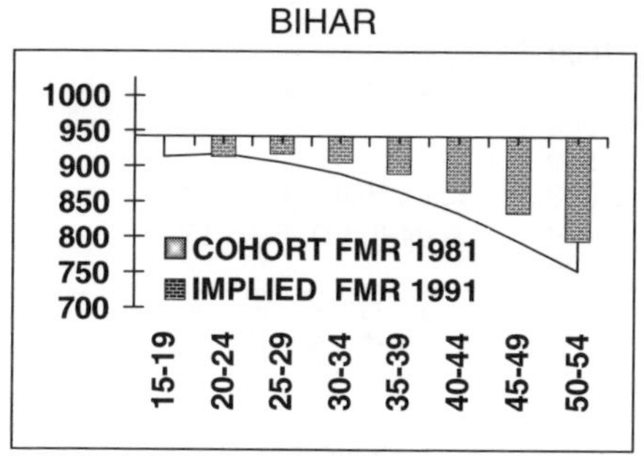

HARYANA

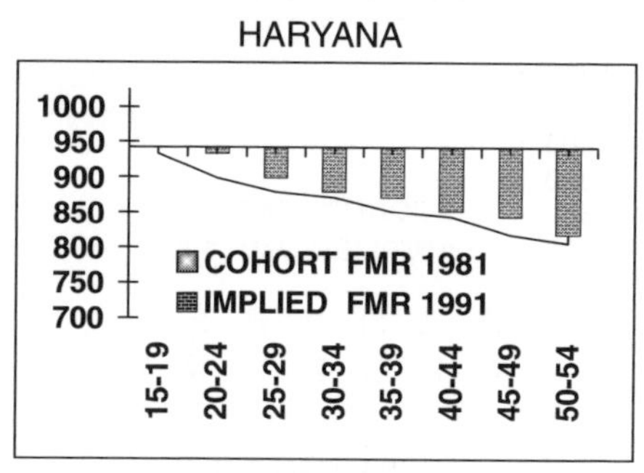

PUNJAB

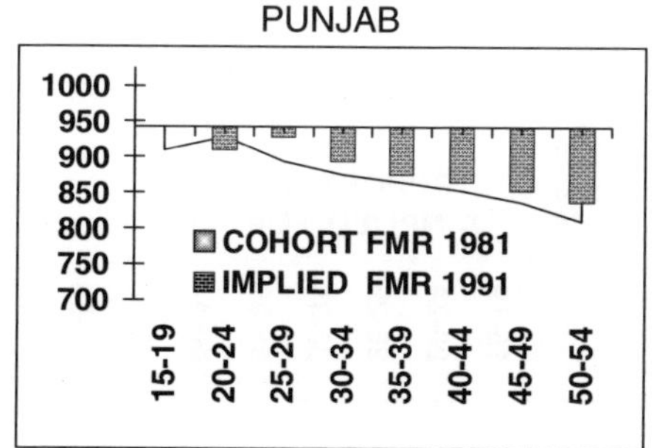

RAJASTHAN

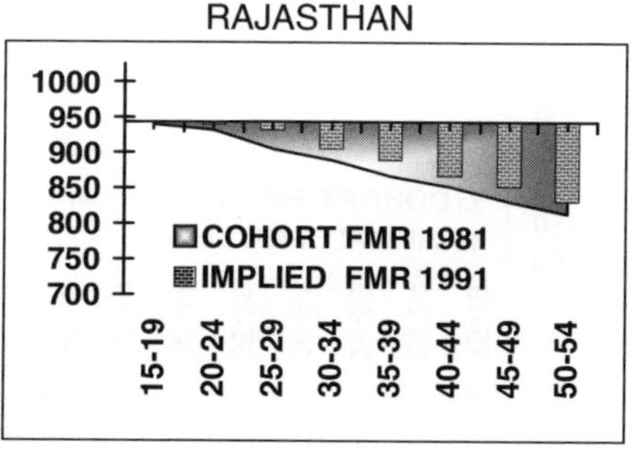

FIGURE 5: (*Contd.*)

UTTAR PRADESH

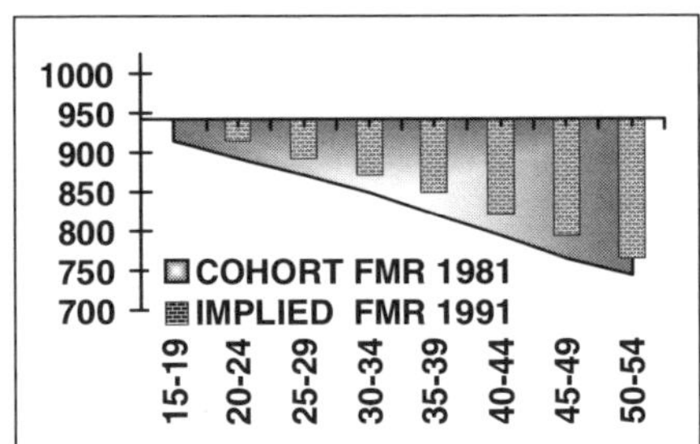

HIMACHAL PRADESH

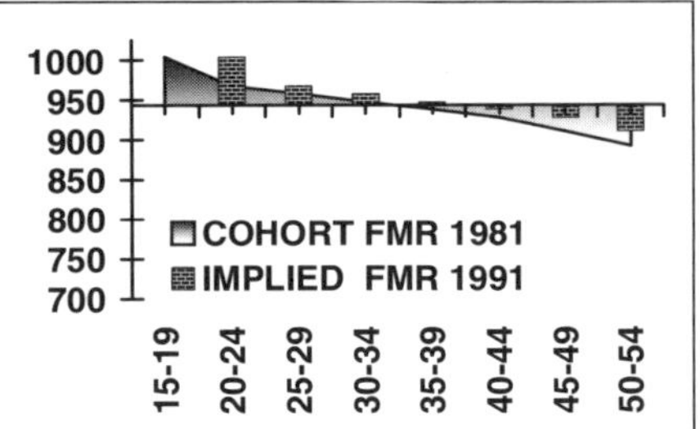

MADHYA PRADESH

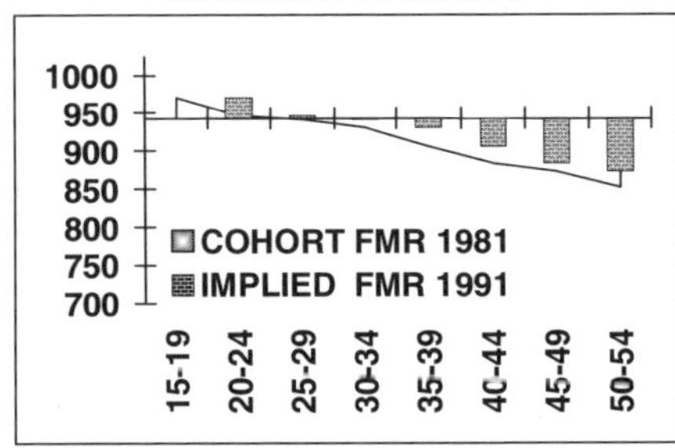

DELHI

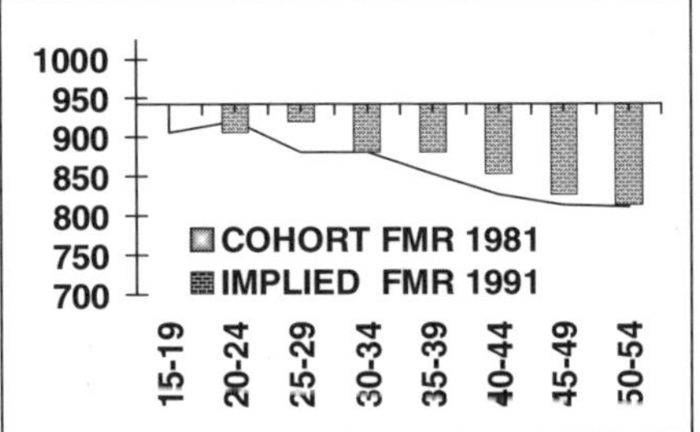

MAHARASHTRA

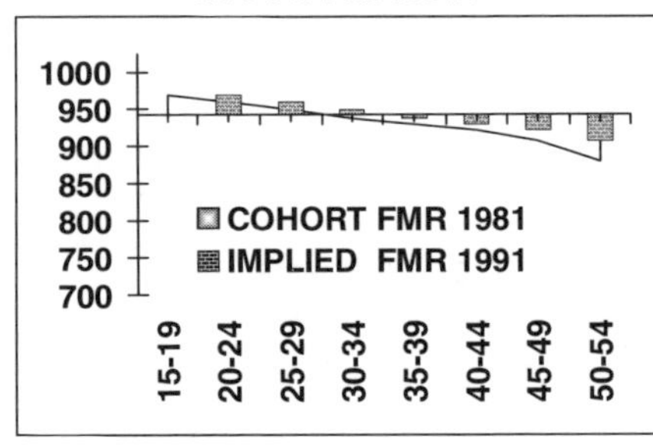

GUJARAT

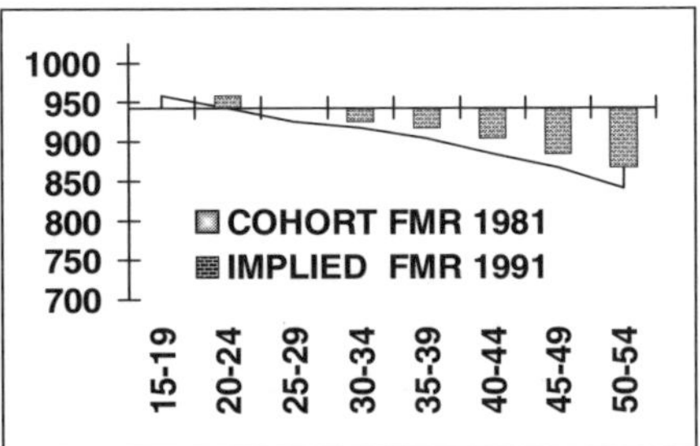

WEST BENGAL

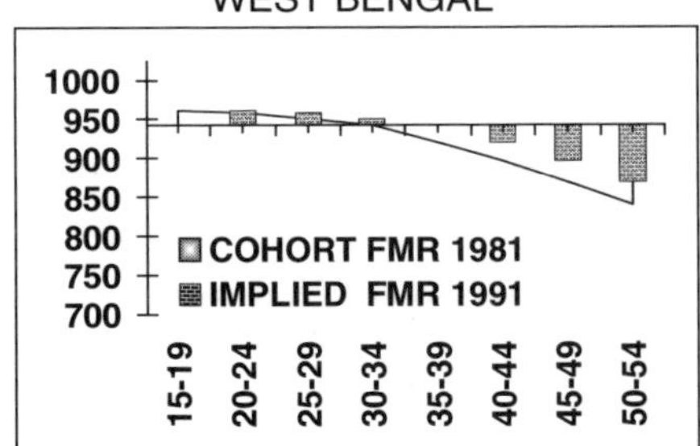

ORISSA

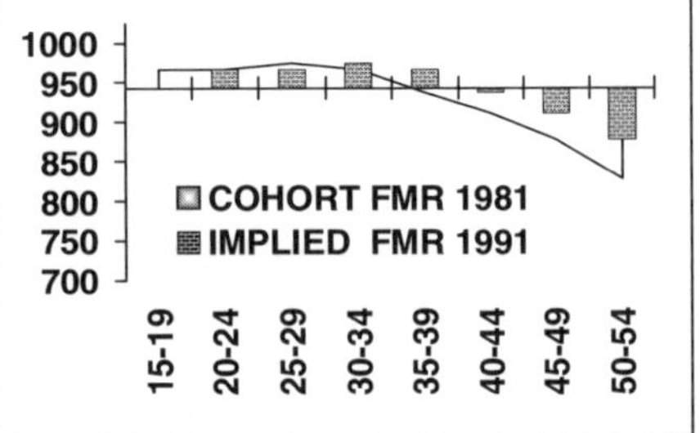

FIGURE 6: COHORT FMRs, 1981 & 1991, Rural Areas, States of India

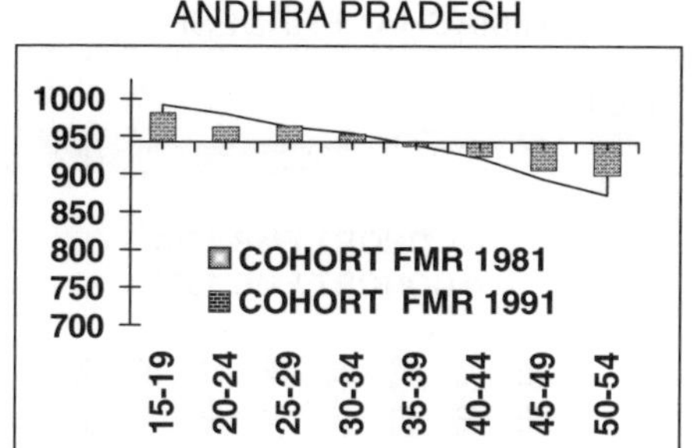

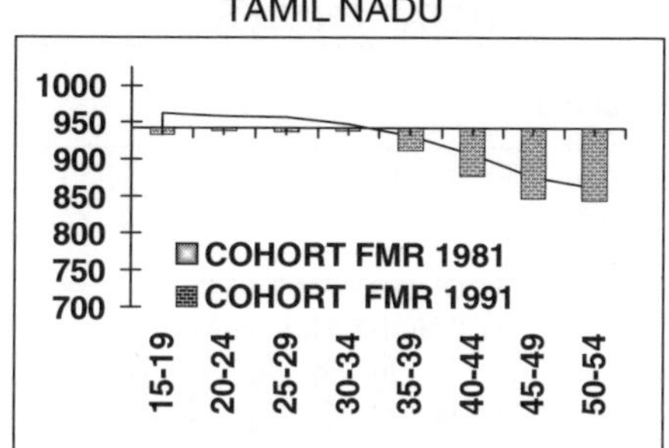

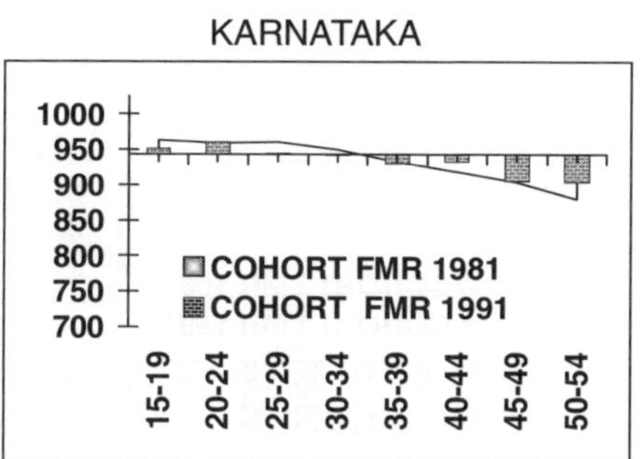

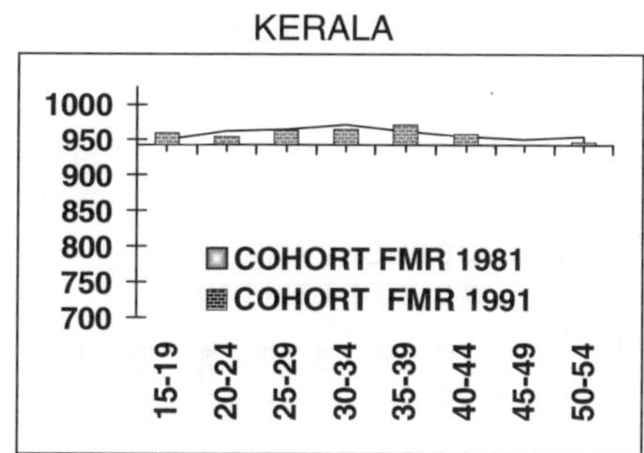

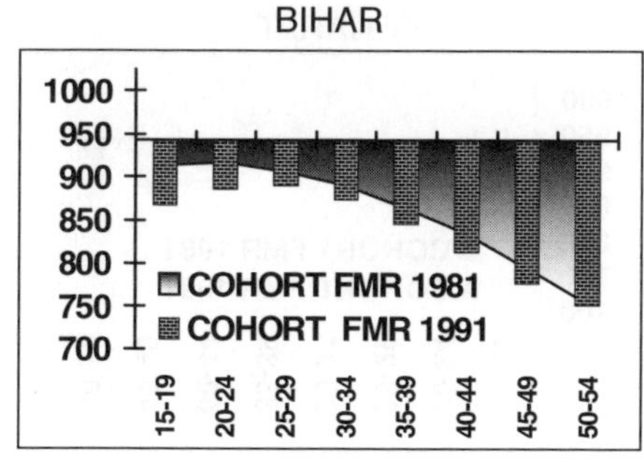

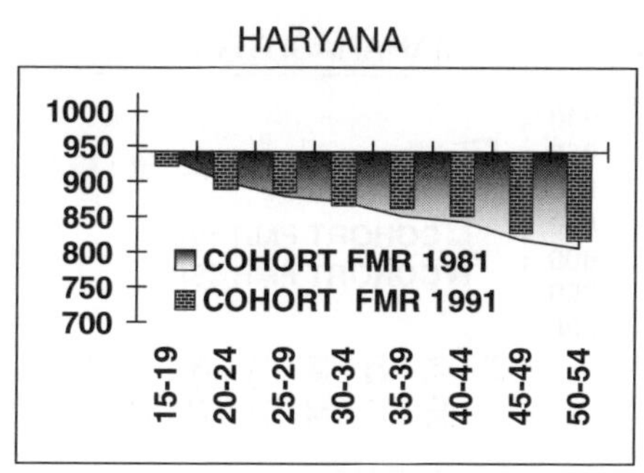

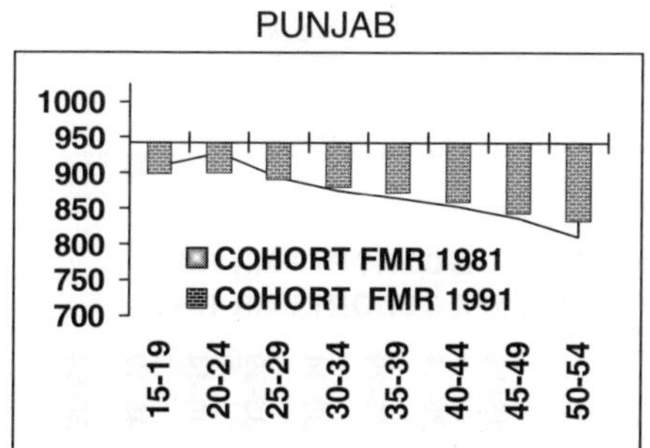

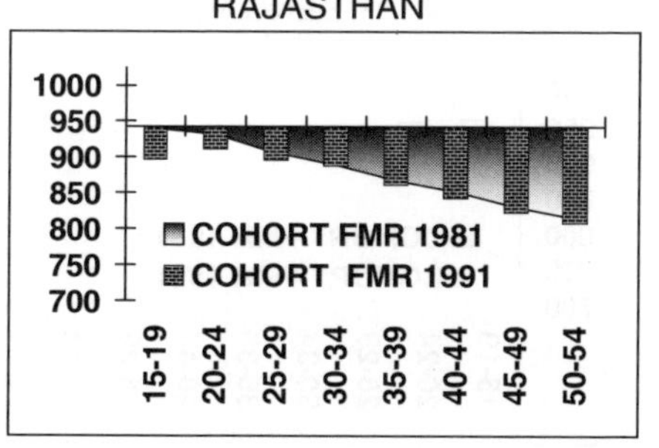

FIGURE 6: (*Contd.*)

UTTAR PRADESH

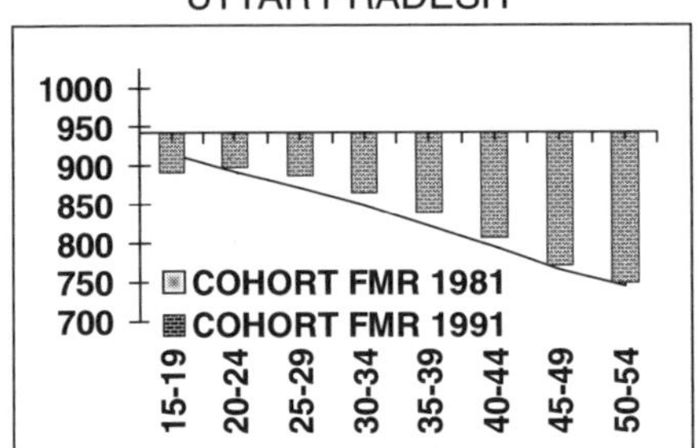

HIMACHAL PRADESH

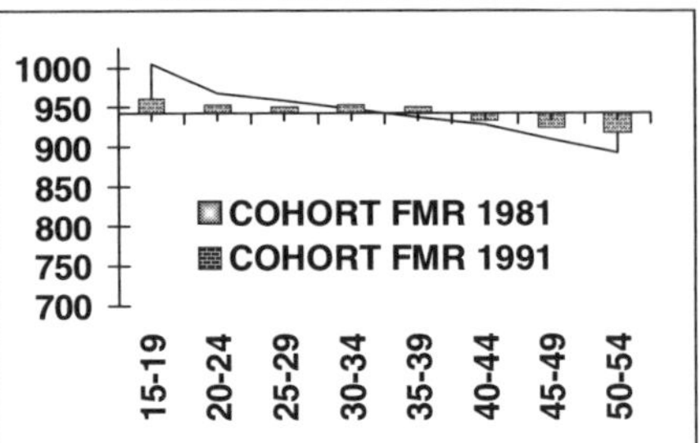

MADHYA PRADESH

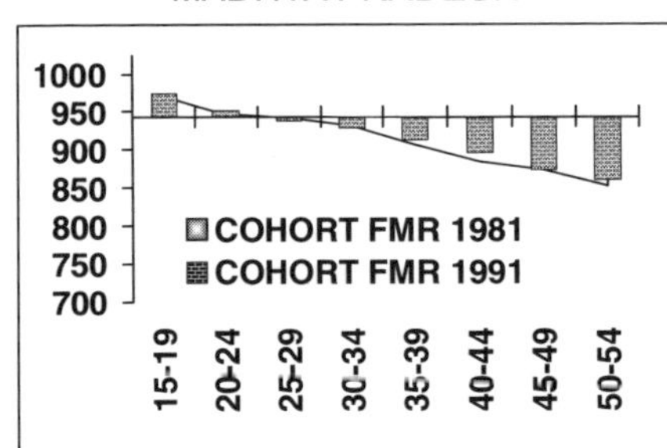

DELHI

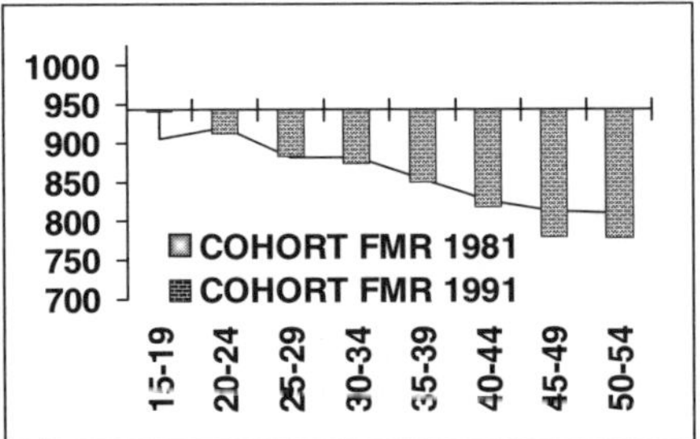

MAHARASHTRA

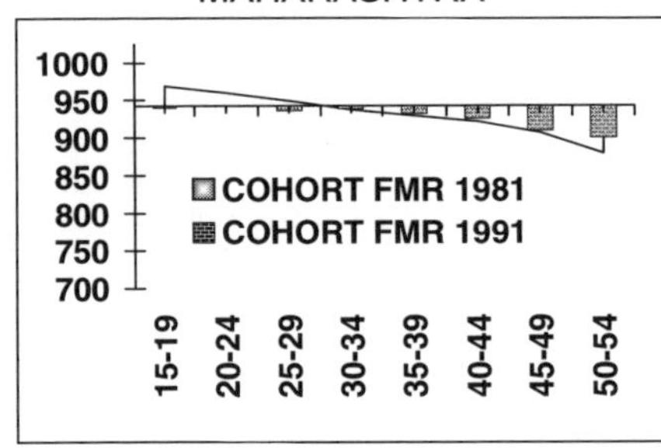

GUJARAT

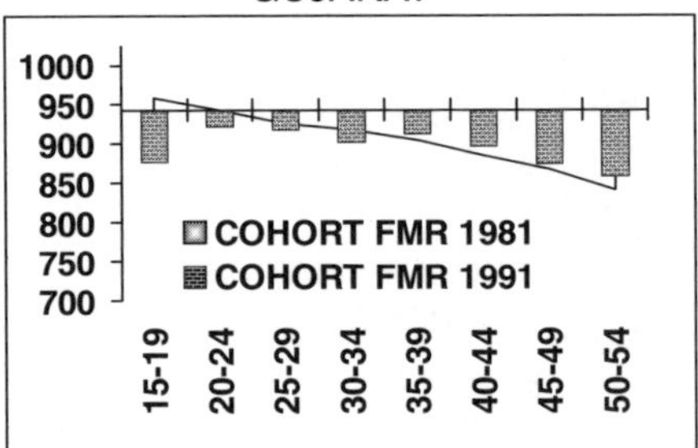

WEST BENGAL

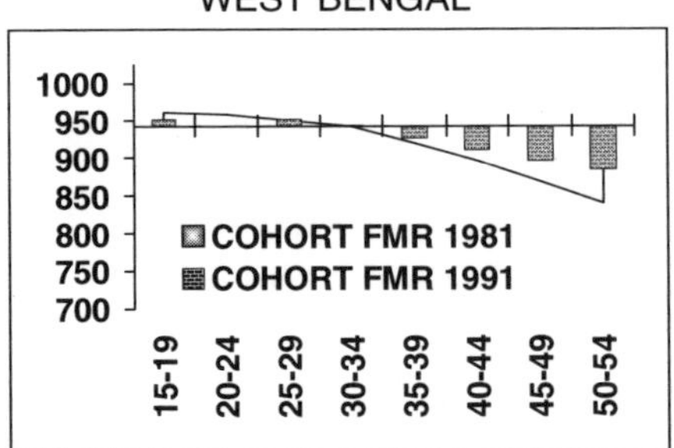

ORISSA

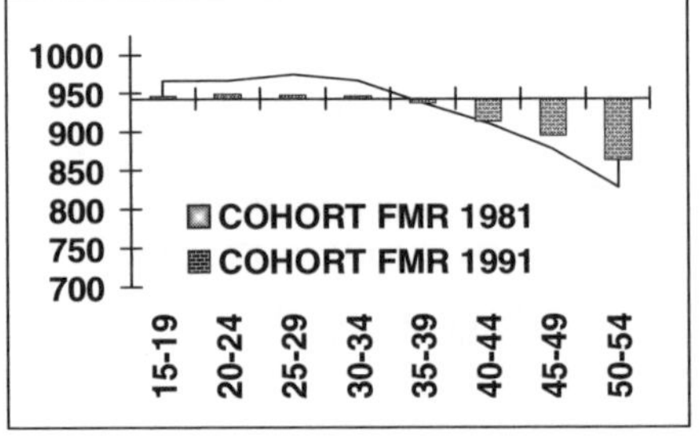

FIGURE 7: FMRs, Children Ever Born, Educated & Illiterate Mothers, 1991, Rural Areas, Selected States of India

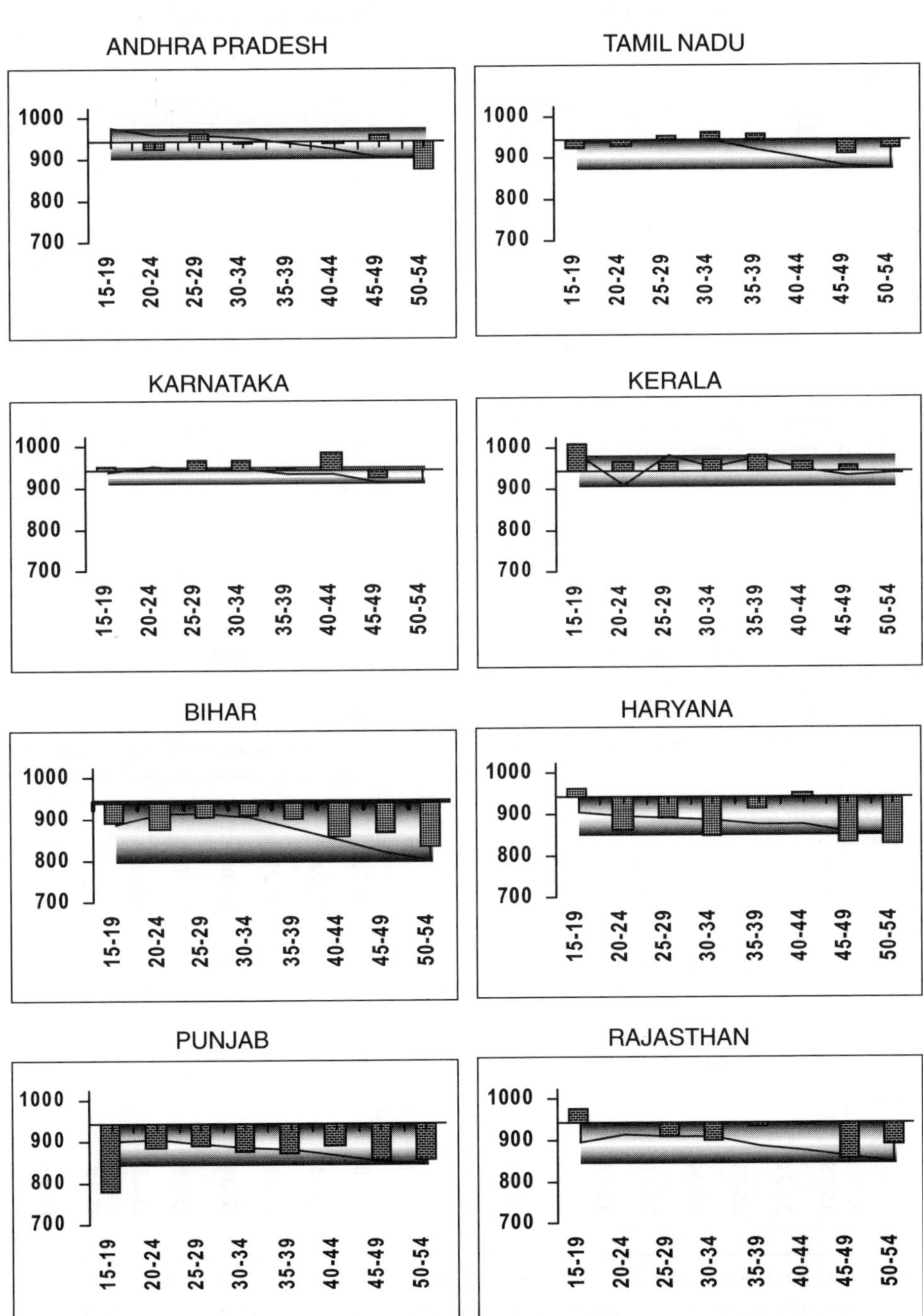

FIGURE 7: (*Contd.*)

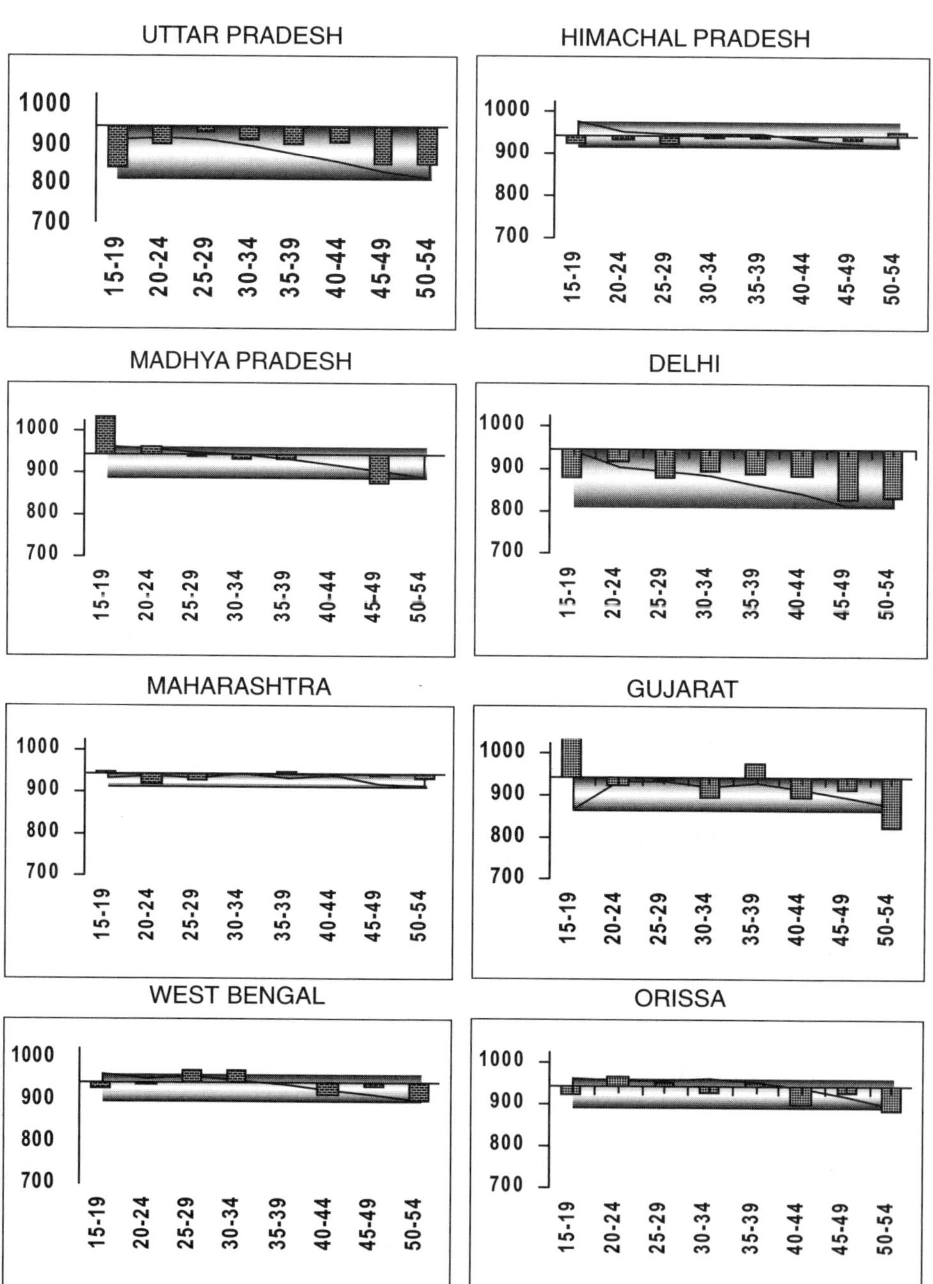

Note: The brick pattern shows the FMR for ever born children of educated mothers (middle plus level of education). The shaded portion shows FMR for ever born children of illiterate mothers.

FIGURE 8: FMRs, Children Surviving, Working and Non-Working Mothers, 1991, Rural Areas, States of India

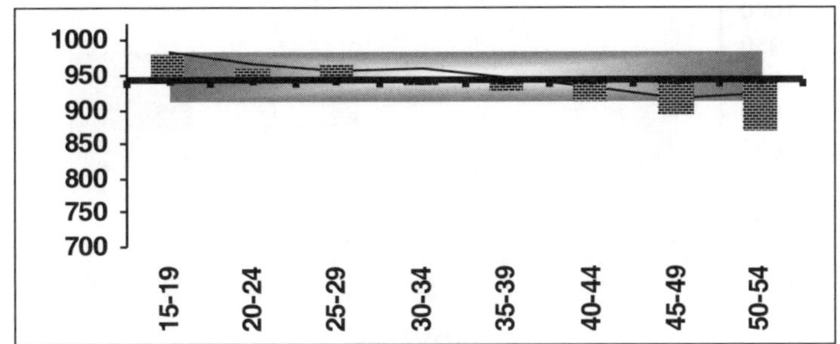

TAMIL NADU

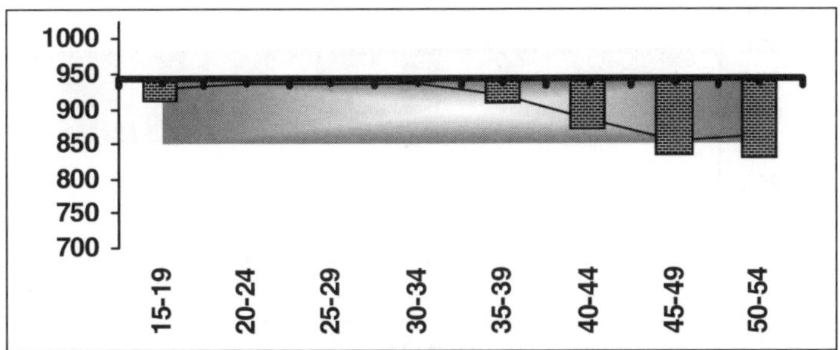

KARNATAKA

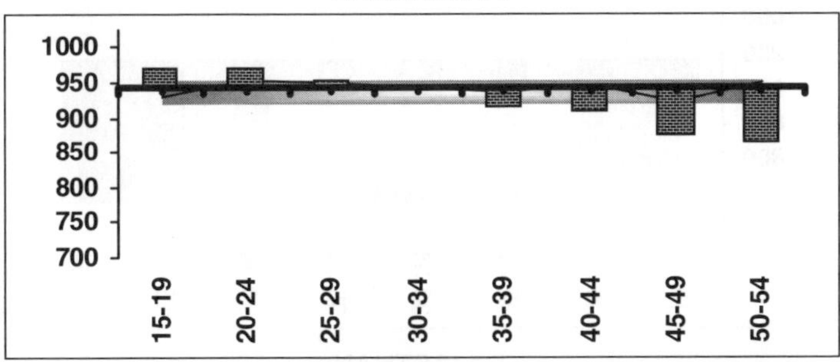

KERALA

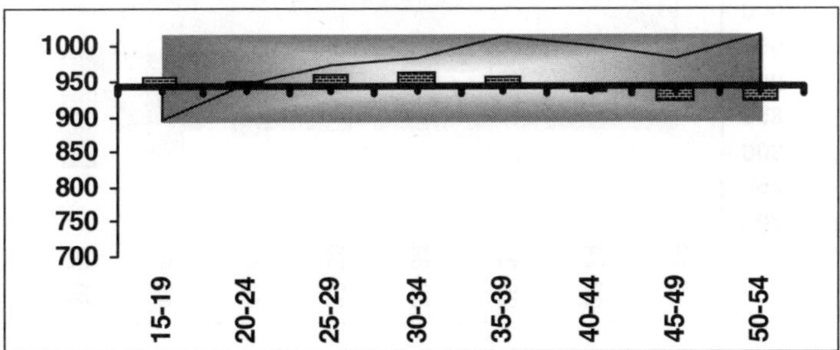

FIGURE 8: (*Contd.*)

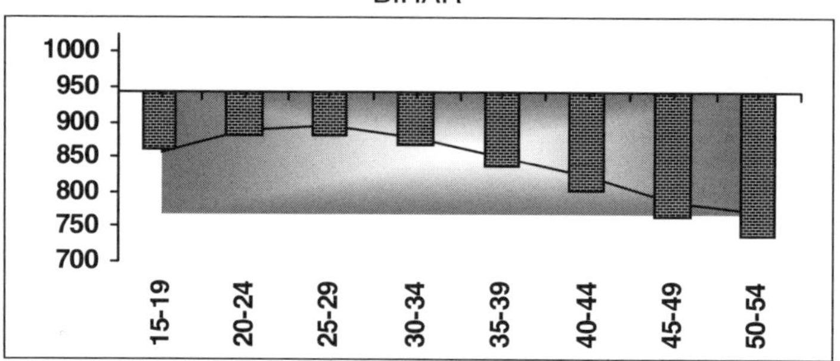

HARYANA

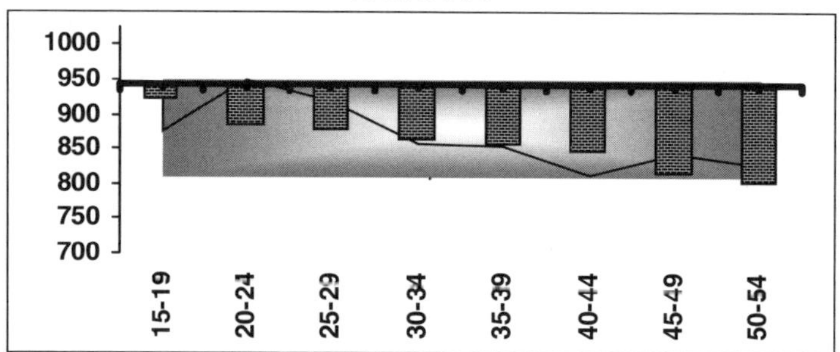

PUNJAB

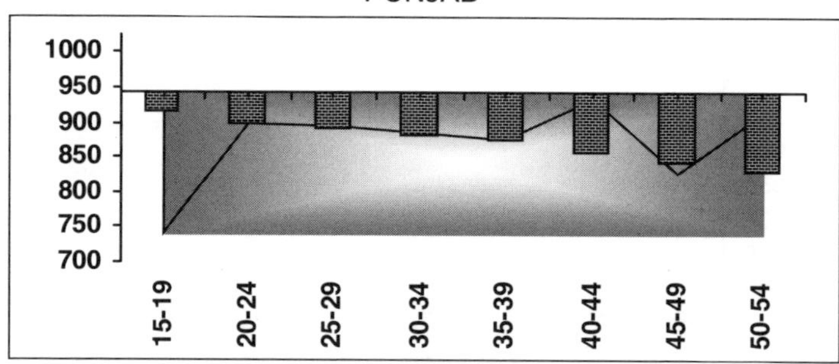

RAJASTHAN

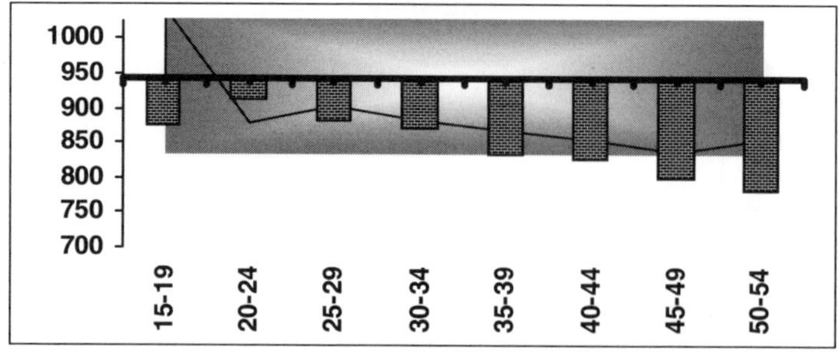

FIGURE 8: (*Contd.*)

UTTAR PRADESH

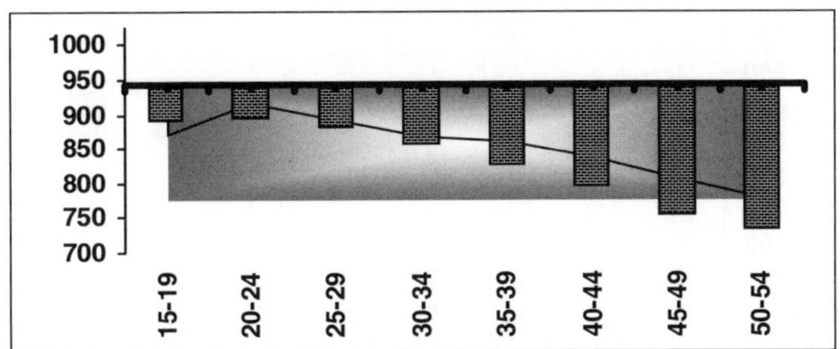

HIMACHAL PRADESH

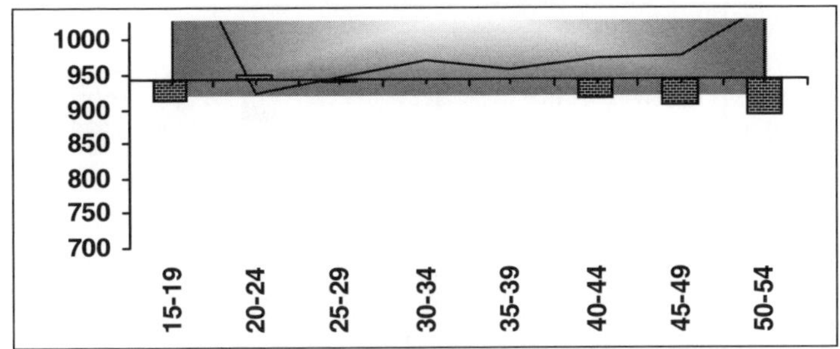

MADHYA PRADESH

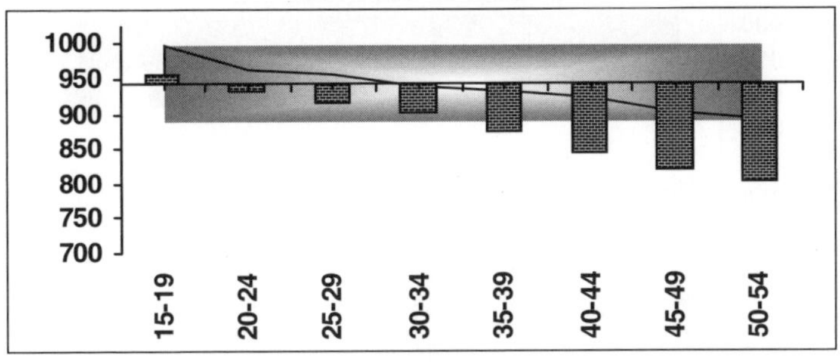

DELHI

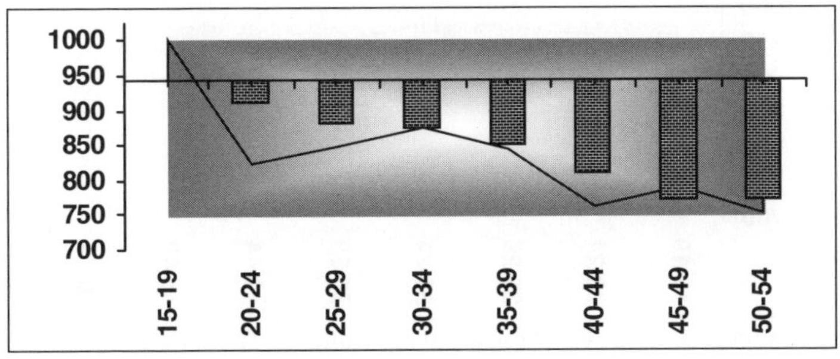

FIGURE 8: (*Contd.*)

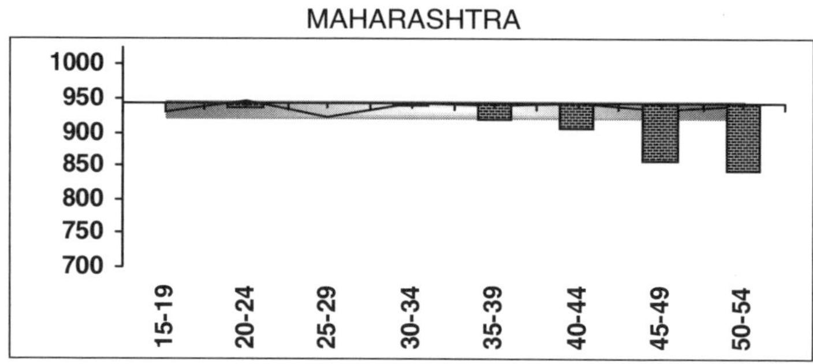

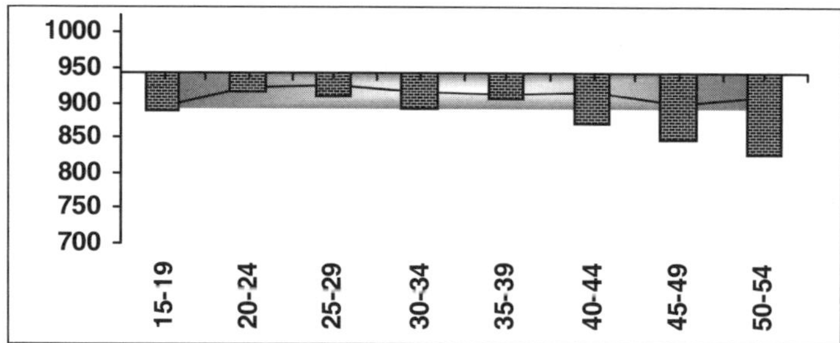

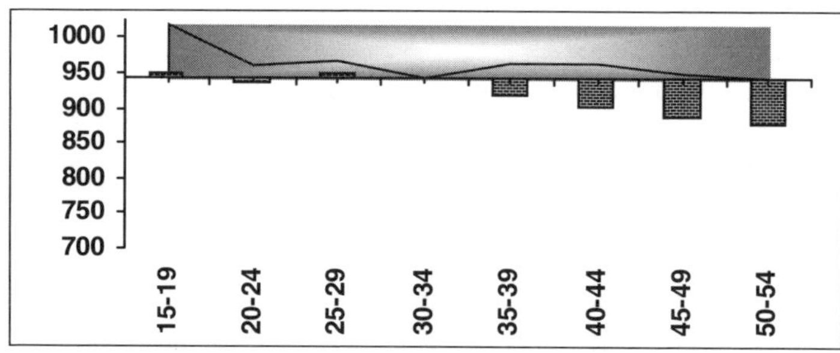

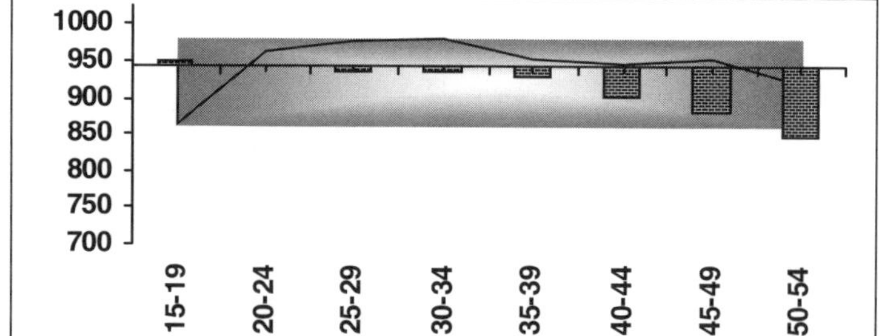

Note: Brick pattern shows the FMR for surviving children of non-working mothers. Shaded portion shows FMR for surviving children of working mothers.

FIGURE 9: FMRs, Children Ever Born and Children Surviving, 2001, Rural Areas, States of India

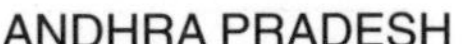

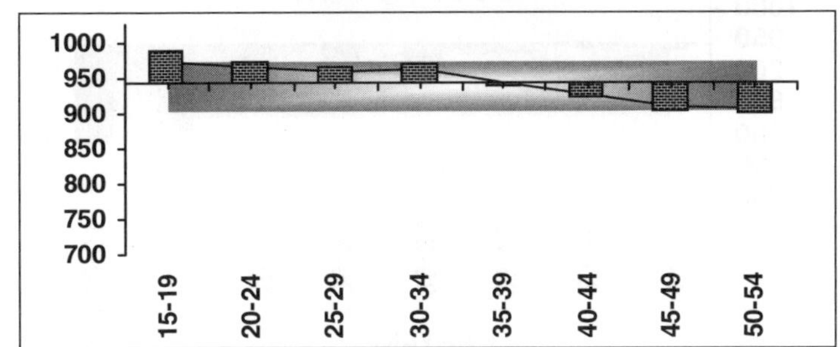

TAMIL NADU

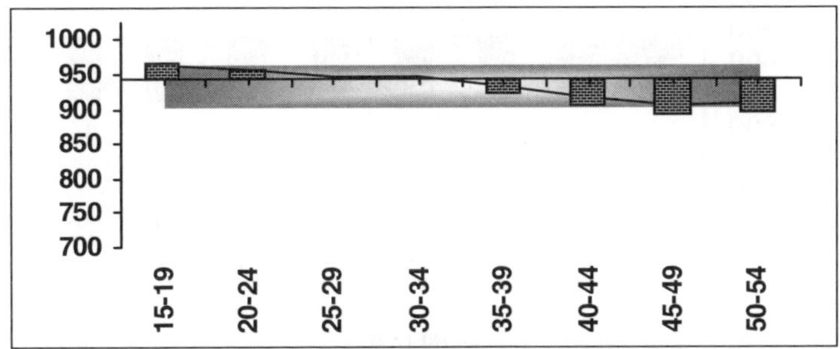

KARNATAKA

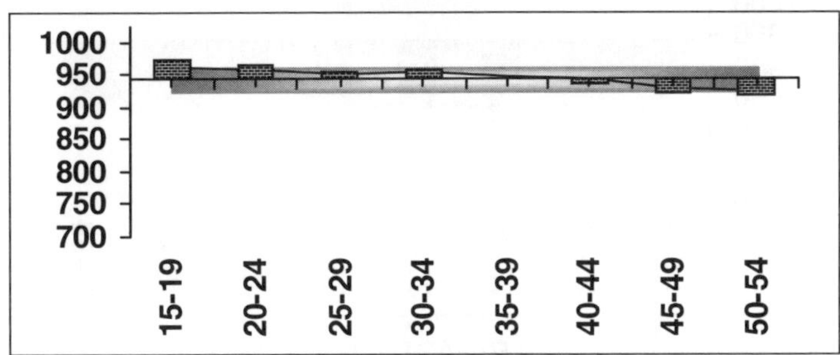

KERALA

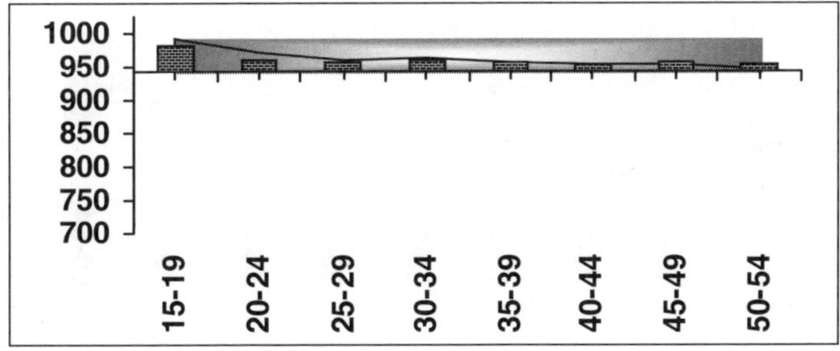

FIGURE 9: (*Contd.*)

UNDIVIDED BIHAR

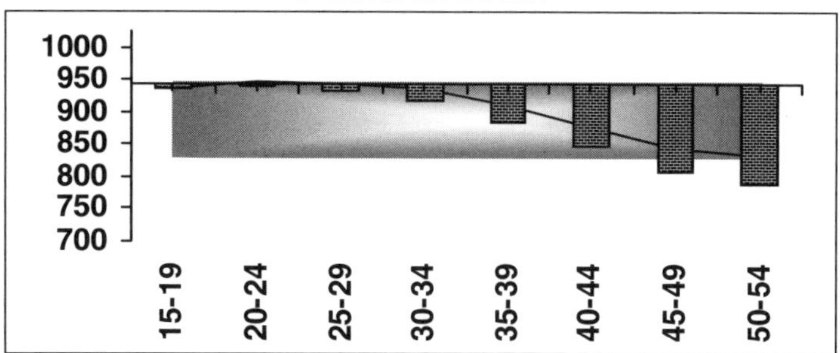

HARYANA

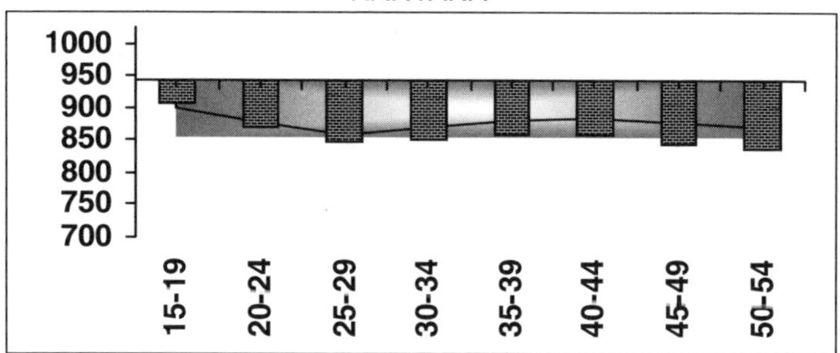

PUNJAB

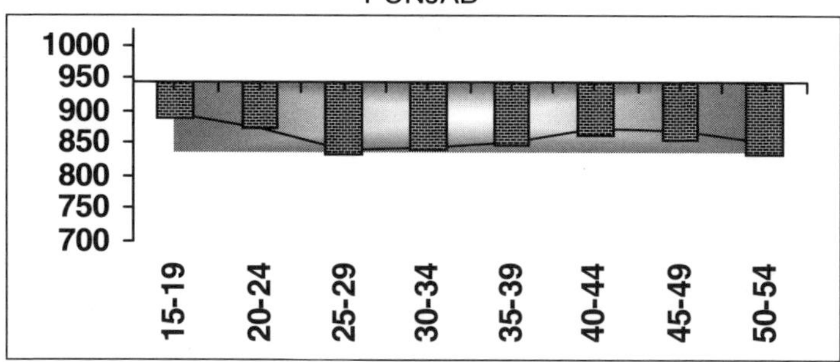

RAJASTHAN

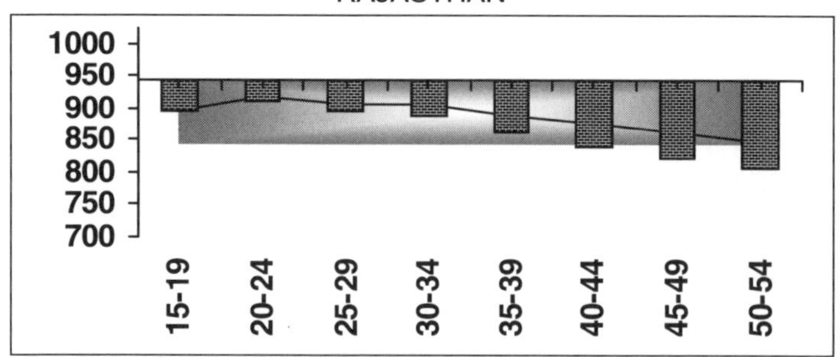

FIGURE 9: (*Contd.*)

UNDIVIDED UTTAR PRADESH

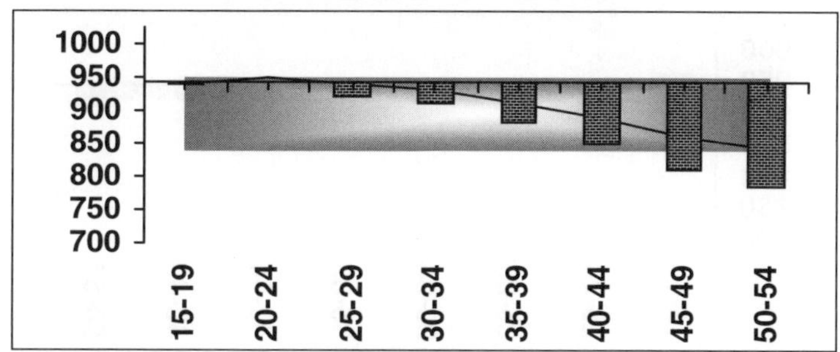

HIMACHAL PRADESH

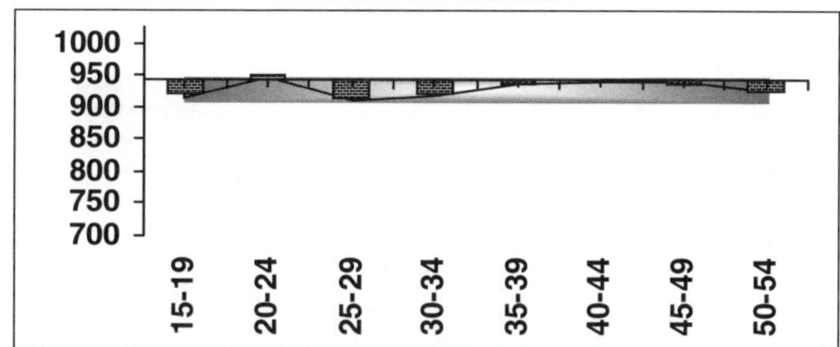

UNDIVIDED MADHYA PRADESH

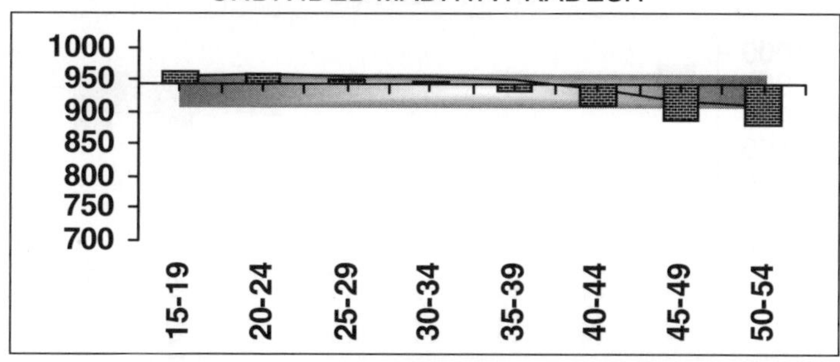

DELHI

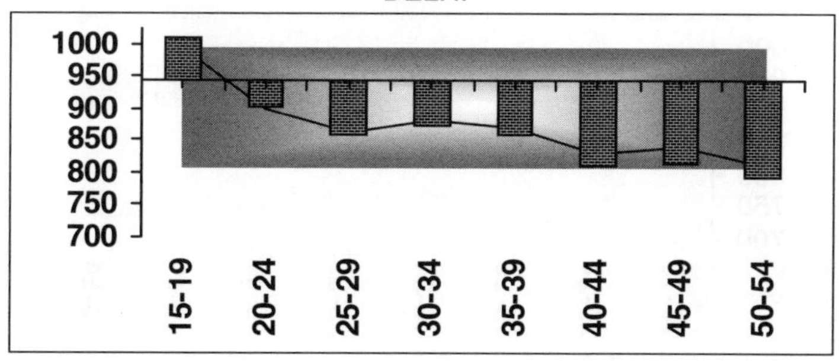

FIGURE 9: (*Contd.*)

MAHARASHTRA

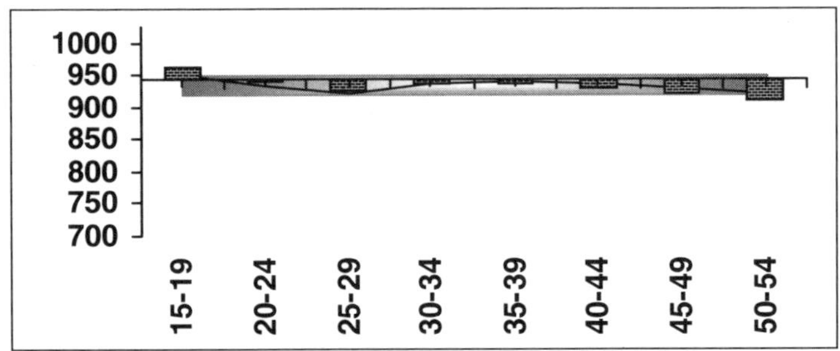

GUJARAT

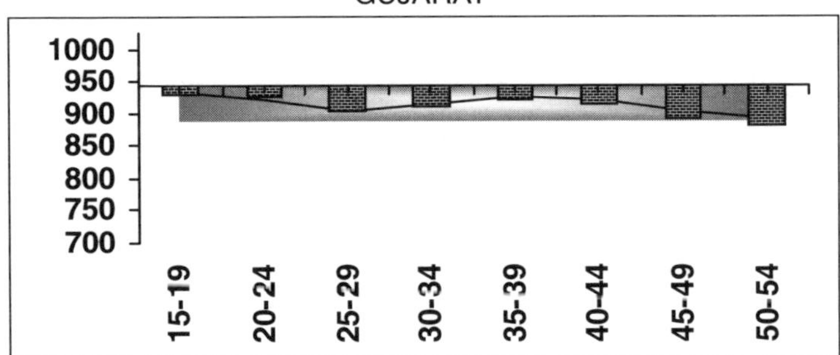

WEST BENGAL

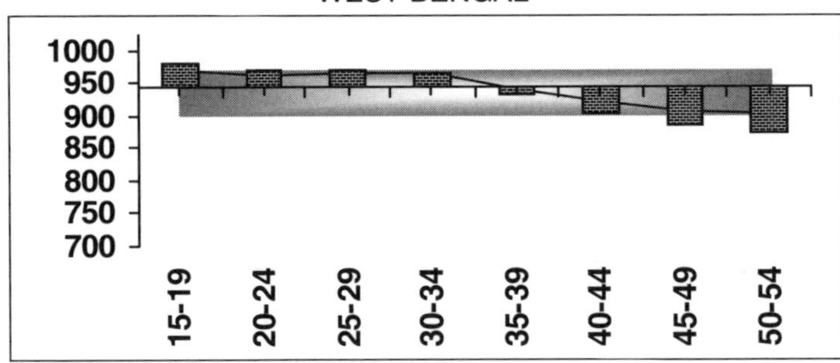

ORISSA

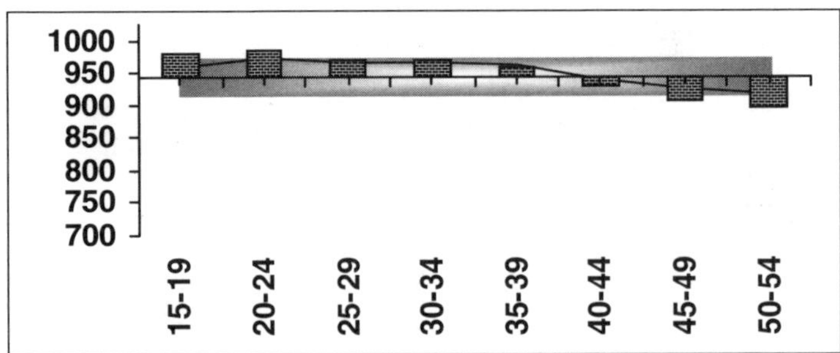

FIGURE 9: (*Contd.*)

UTTAR PRADESH

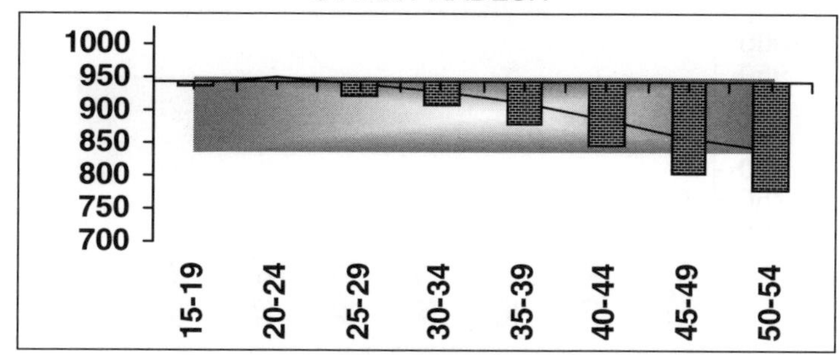

UTTARANCHAL

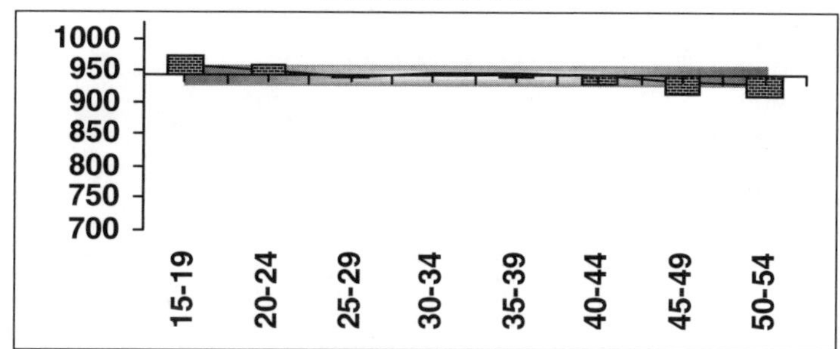

MADHYA PRADESH

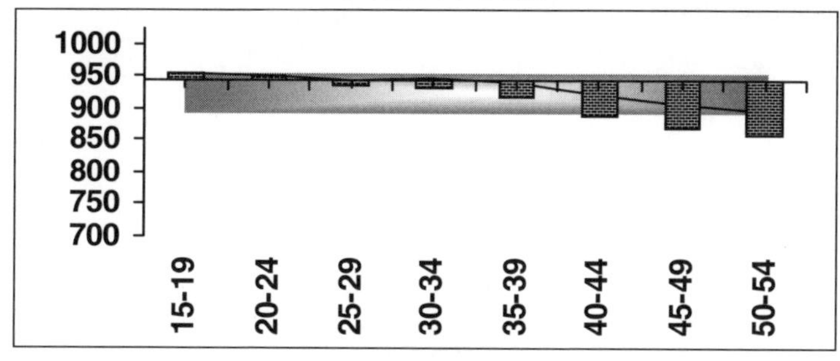

CHATTISTARH

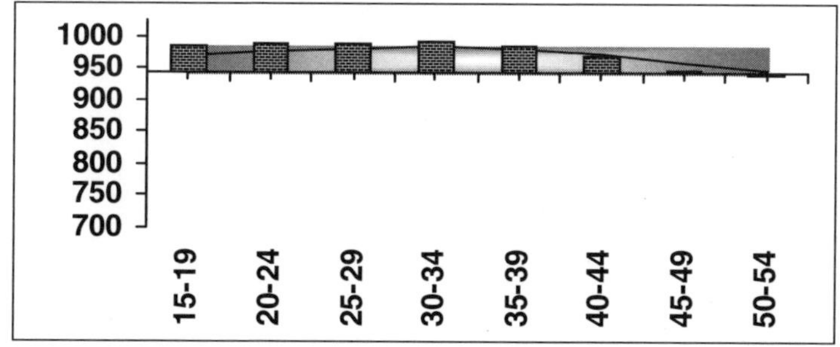

FIGURE 9: (*Contd.*)

BIHAR

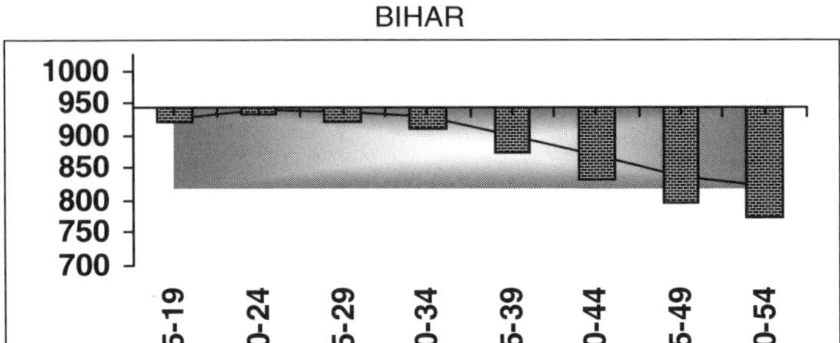

JHARKHAND

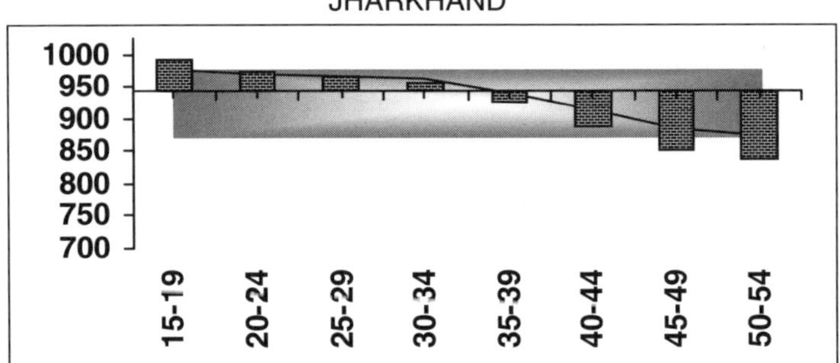

Note: Brick pattern shows the FMR for surviving children. Shaded portion shows FMR for Children Ever Born.

FIGURE 10: FMRs, Children Ever Born and Children Surviving, 2001, All Areas, States of India, 2001

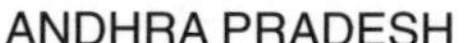

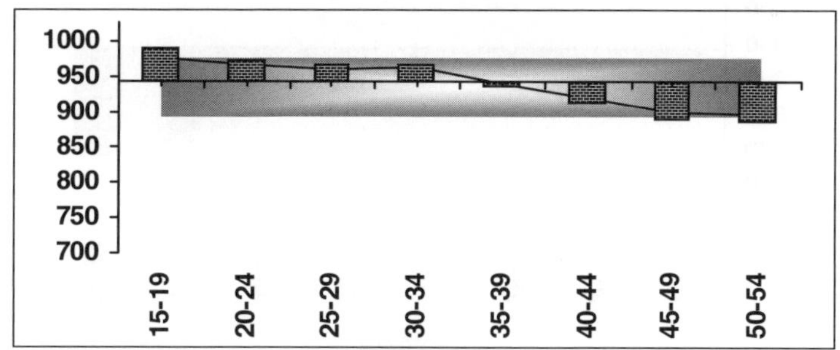

TAMIL NADU

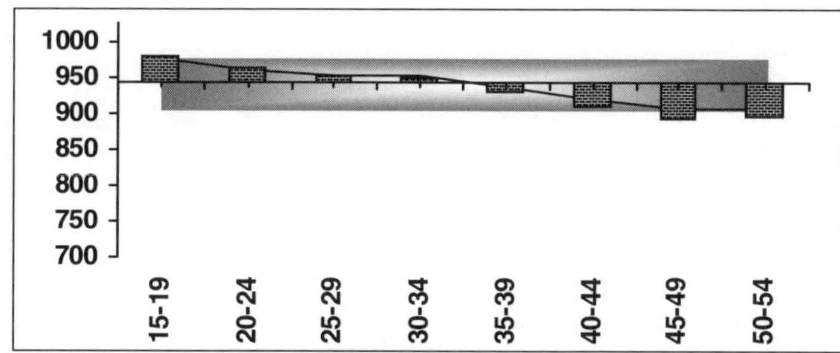

KARNATAKA

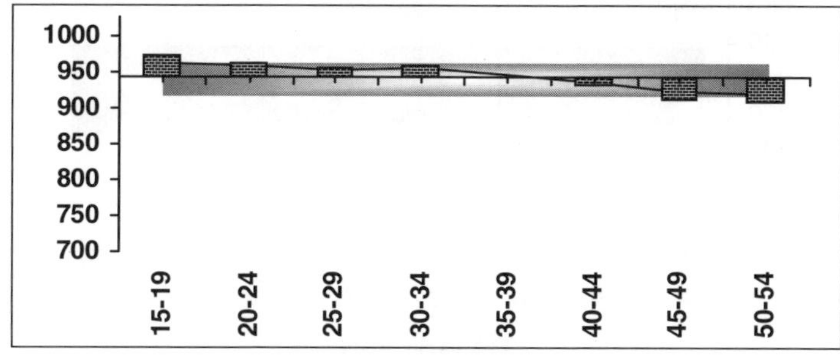

KERALA

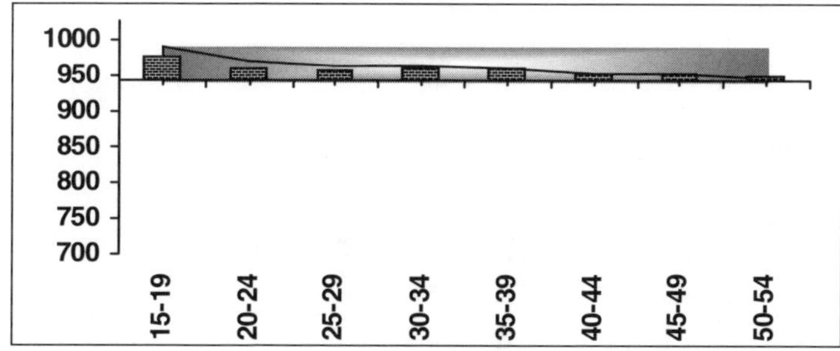

FIGURE 10: (*Contd.*)

UNDIVIDED BIHAR

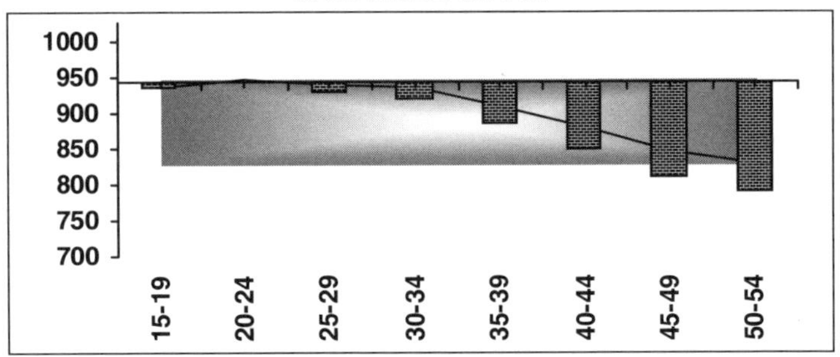

HARYANA

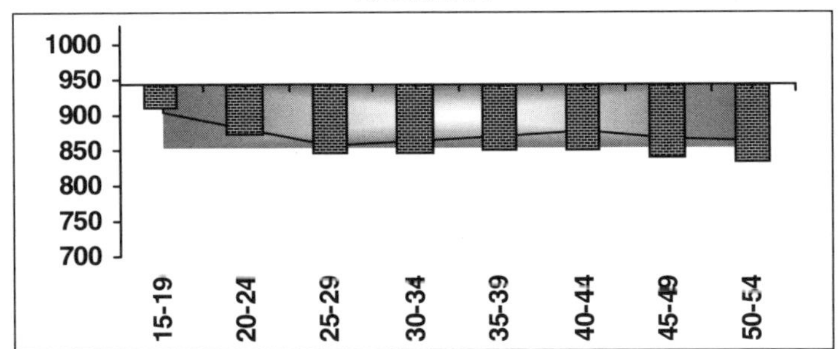

PUNJAB

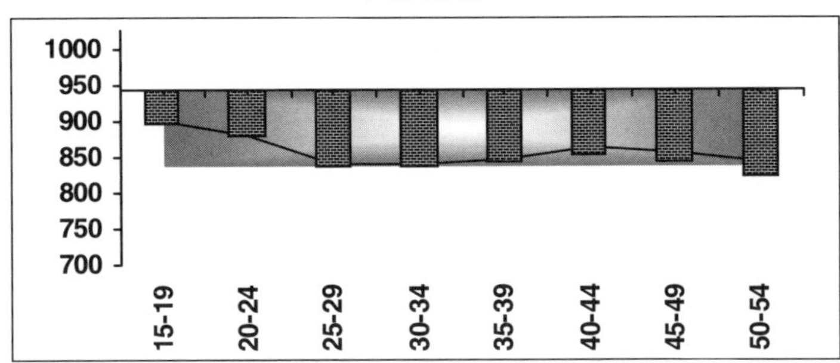

RAJASTHAN

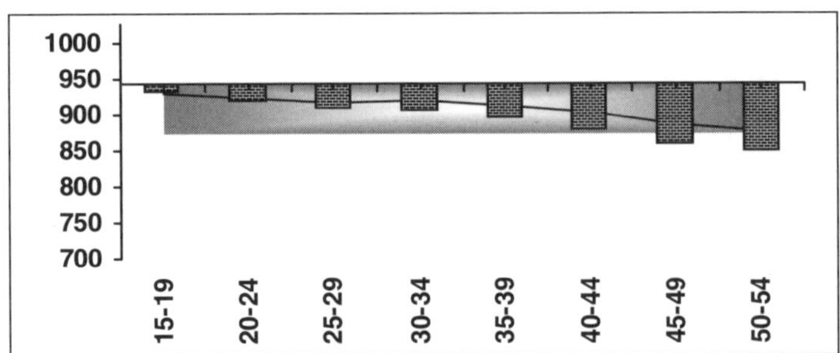

FIGURE 10: (*Contd.*)

UNDIVIDED UTTAR PRADESH

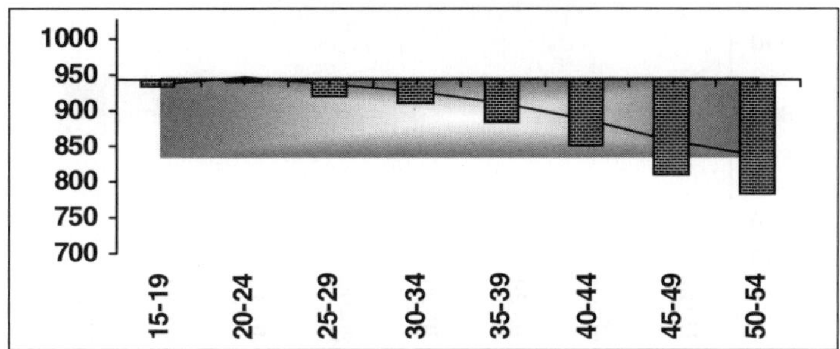

HIMACHAL PRADESH

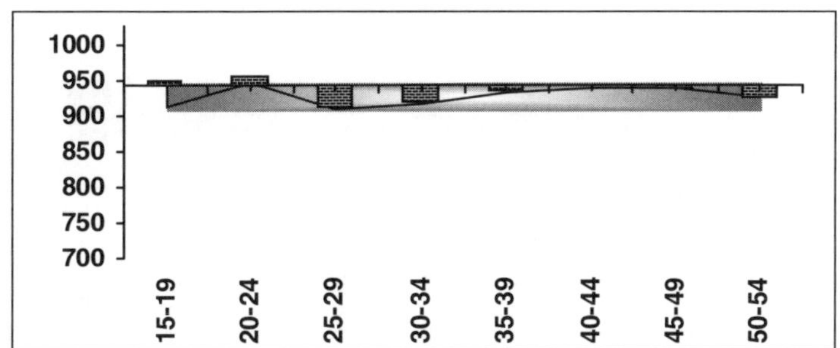

UNDIVIDED MADHYA PRADESH

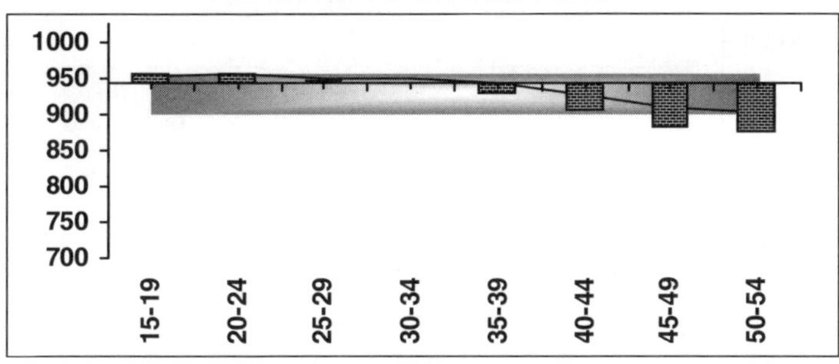

DELHI

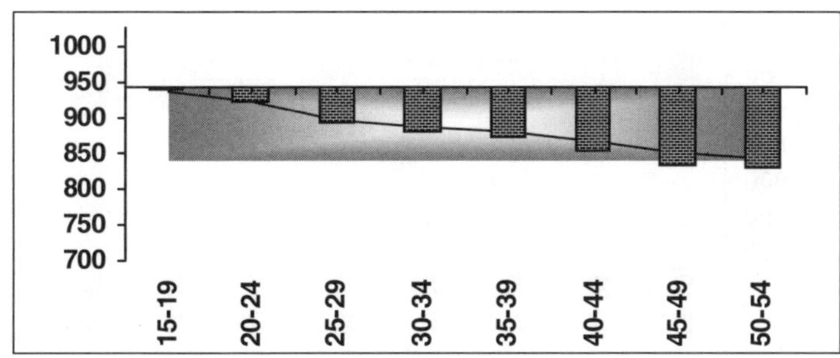

FIGURE 10: (*Contd.*)

MAHARASHTRA

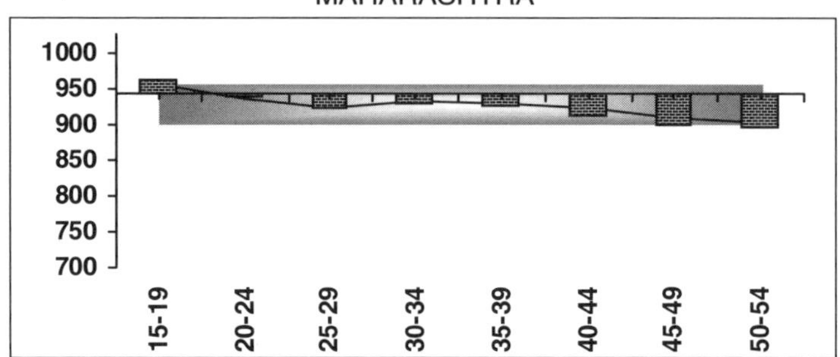

GUJARAT

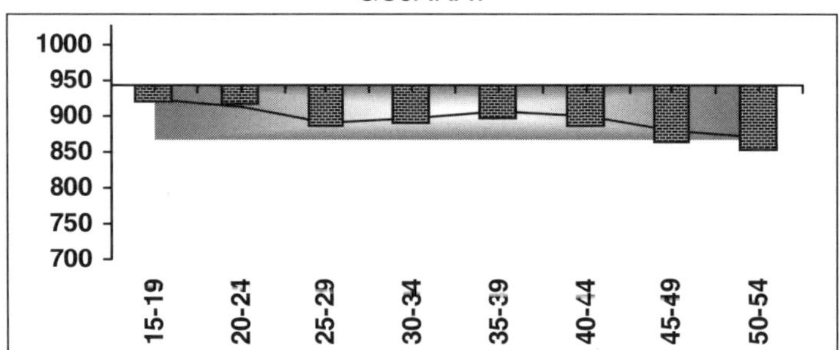

WEST BENGAL

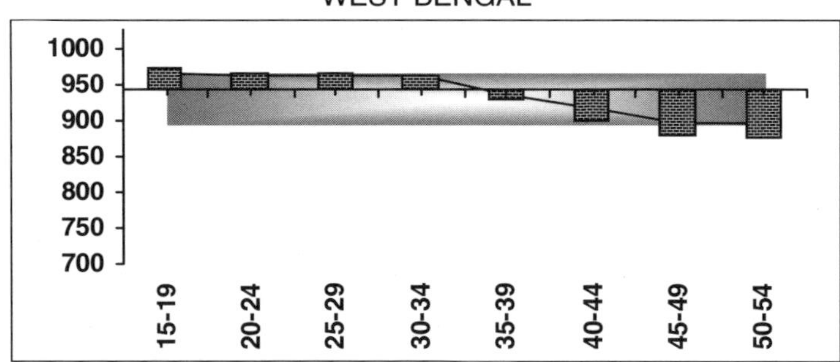

ORISSA

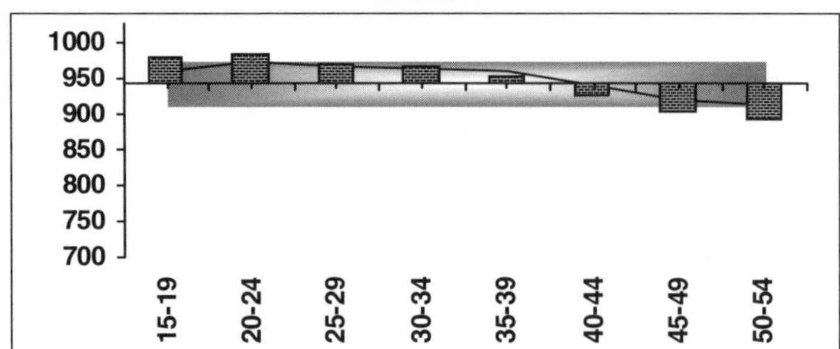

FIGURE 10: (*Contd.*)

UTTAR PRADESH

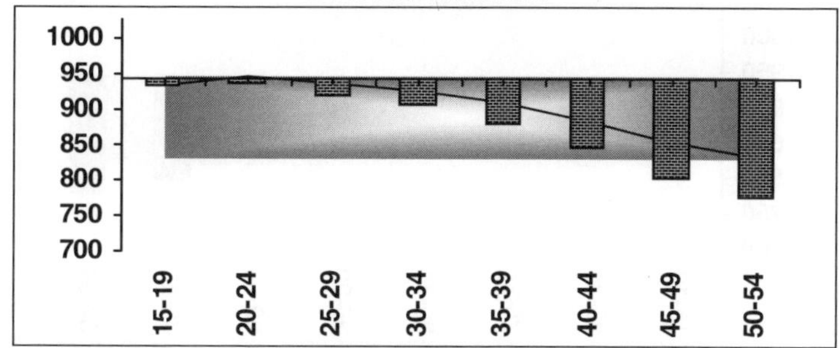

UTTARANCHAL

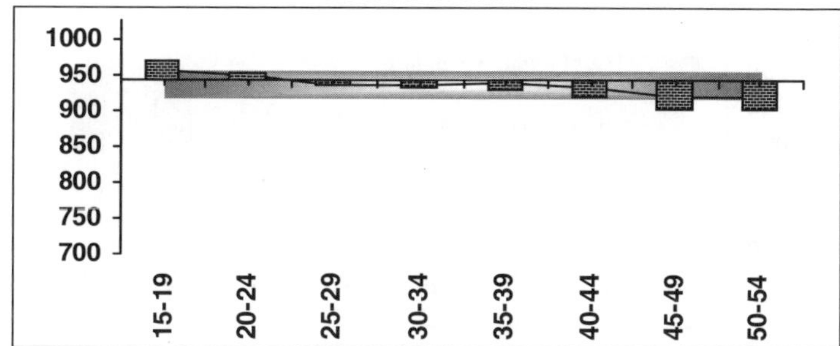

MADHYA PRADESH

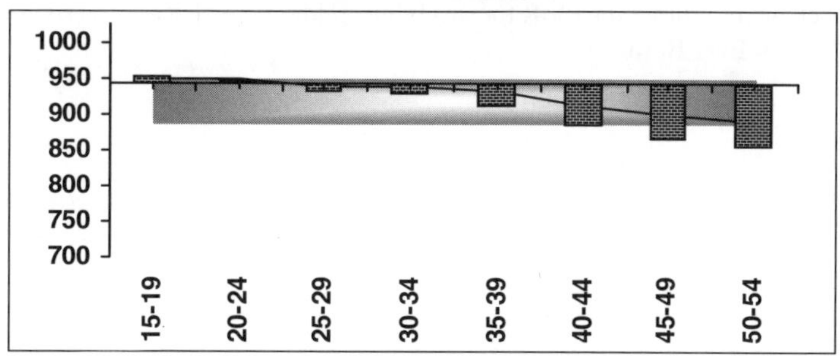

CHATTISTARH

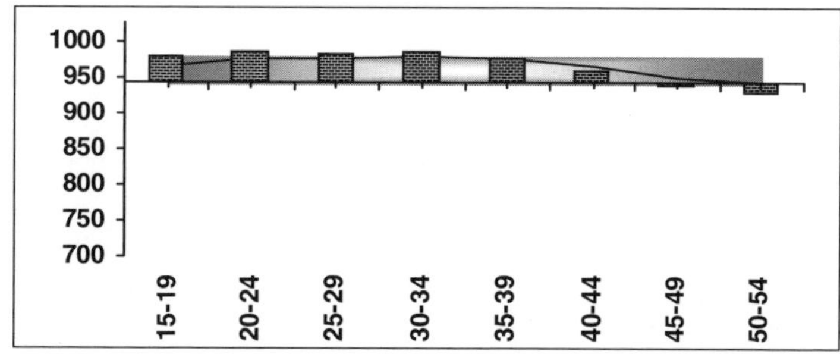

FIGURE 10: (*Contd.*)

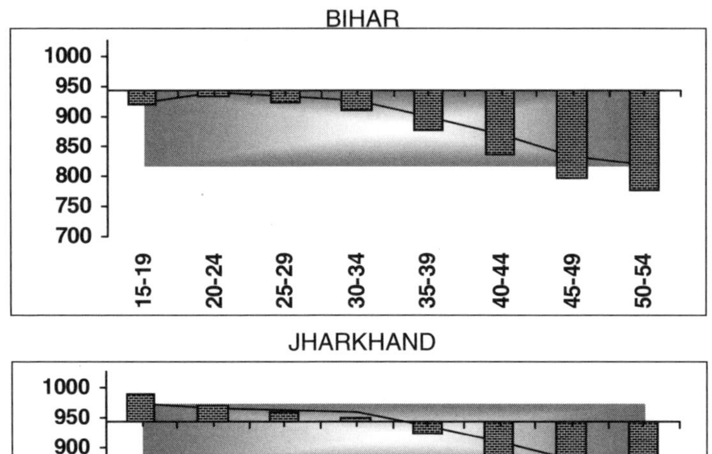

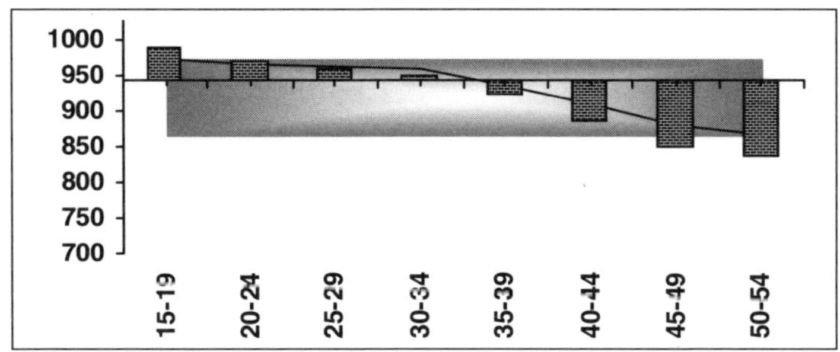

Note: Brick pattern shows the FMR for surviving children. Shaded portion shows FMR for Children Ever Born.

FIGURE 11: FMRs, Children Ever Born and Children Surviving, 2001, Urban Areas, States of India

ANDHRA PRADESH

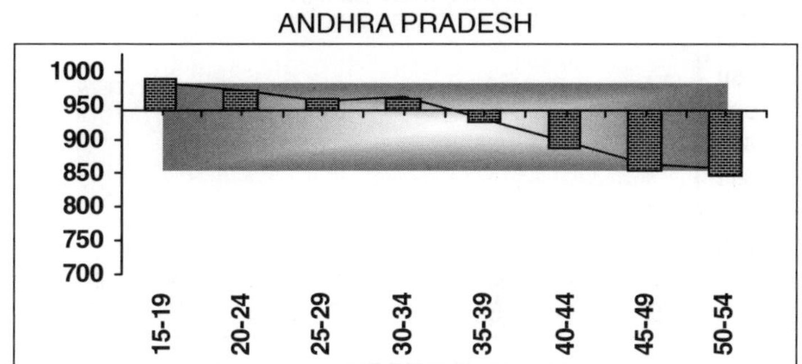

TAMIL NADU

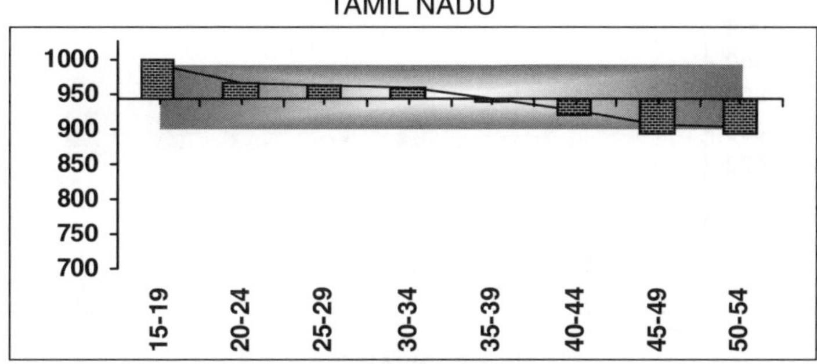

KARNATAKA

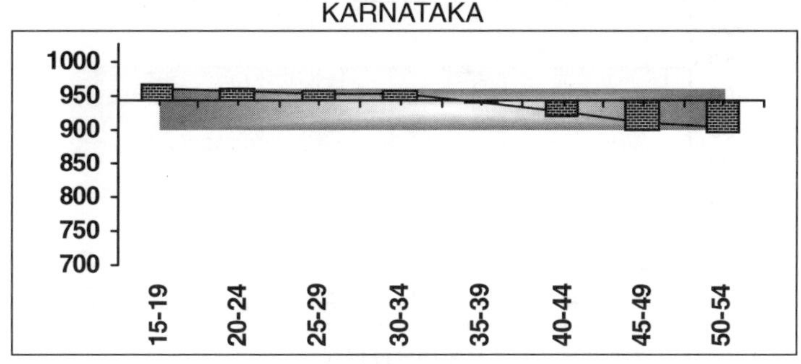

KERALA

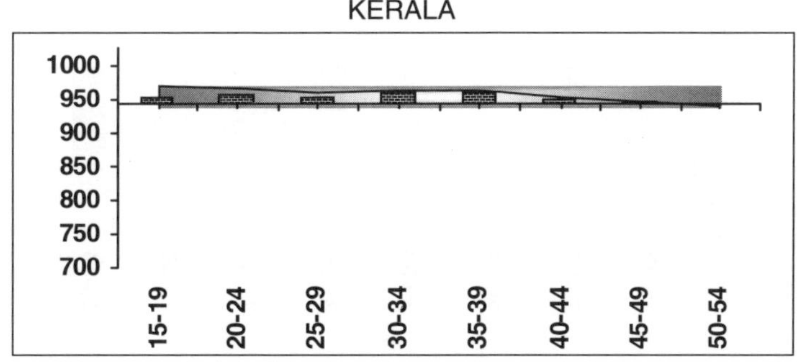

FIGURE 11: (*Contd.*)

UNDIVIDED BIHAR

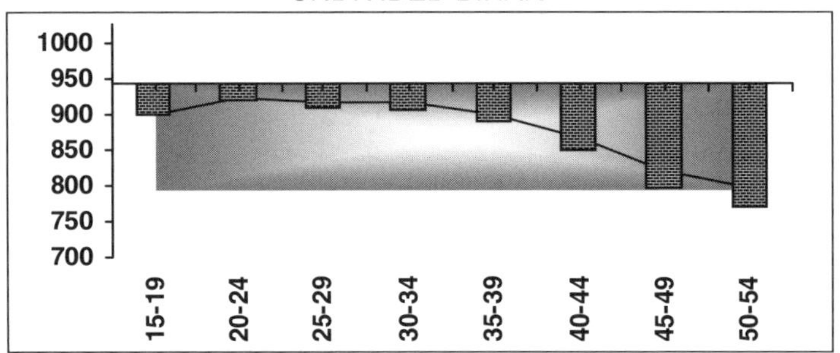

HARYANA

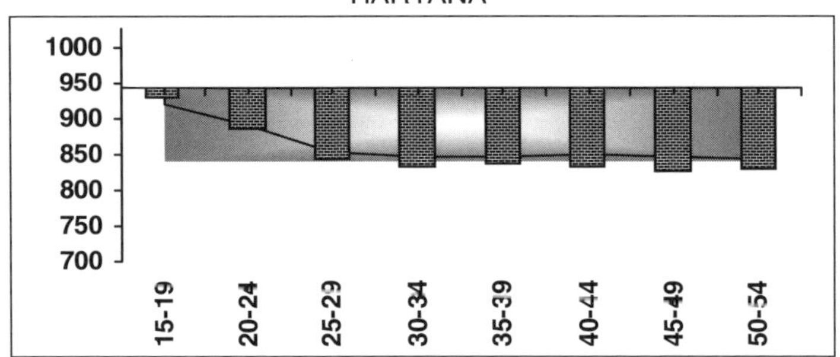

PUNJAB

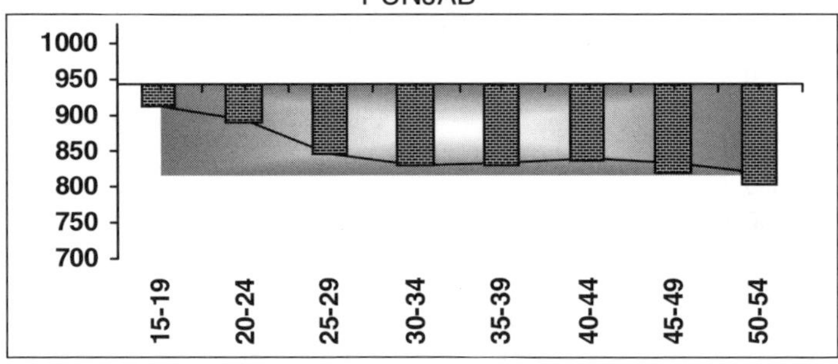

RAJASTHAN

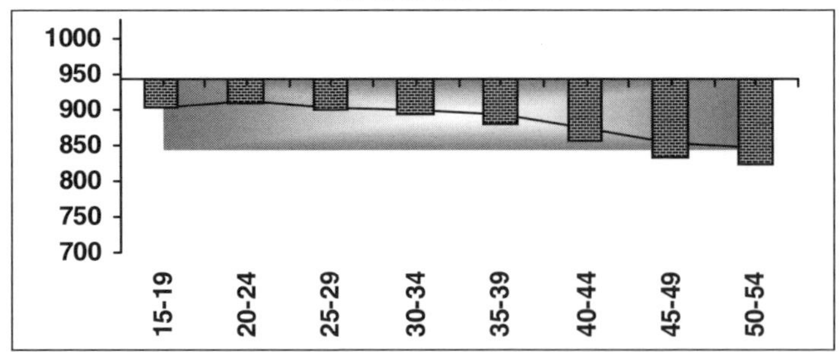

FIGURE 11: (*Contd.*)

UNDIVIDED UTTAR PRADESH

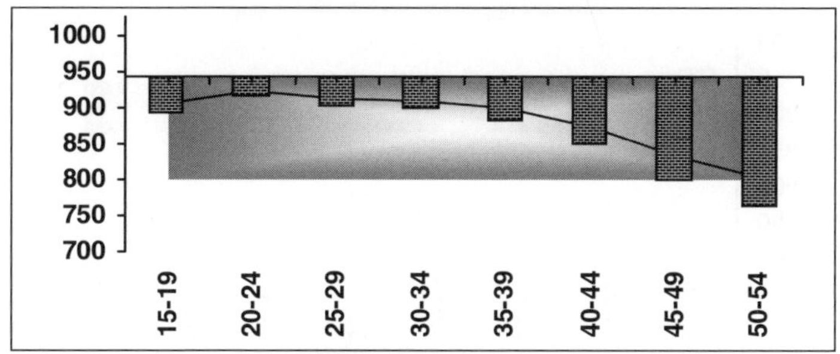

HIMACHAL PRADESH

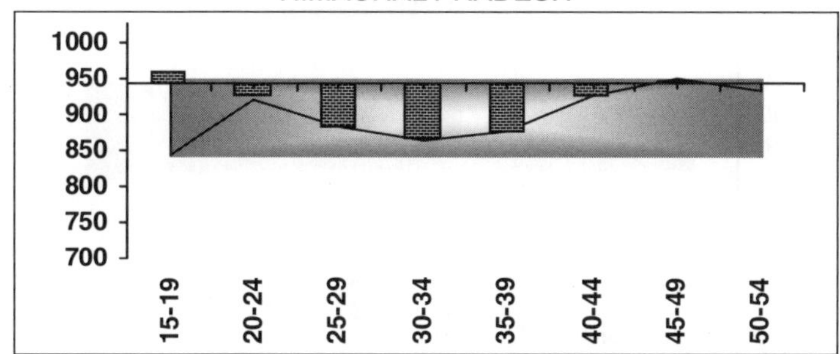

UNDIVIDED MADHYA PRADESH

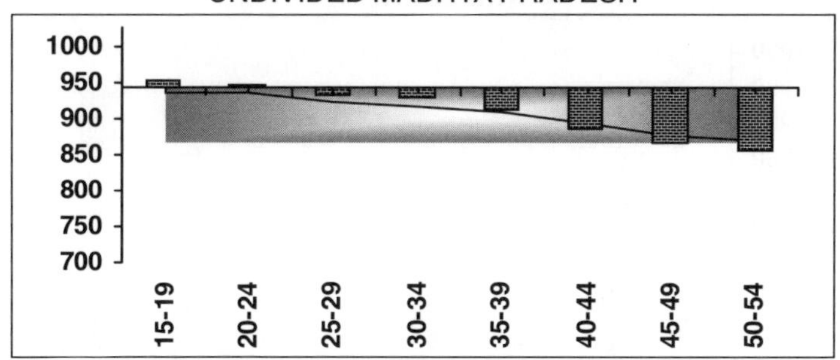

DELHI

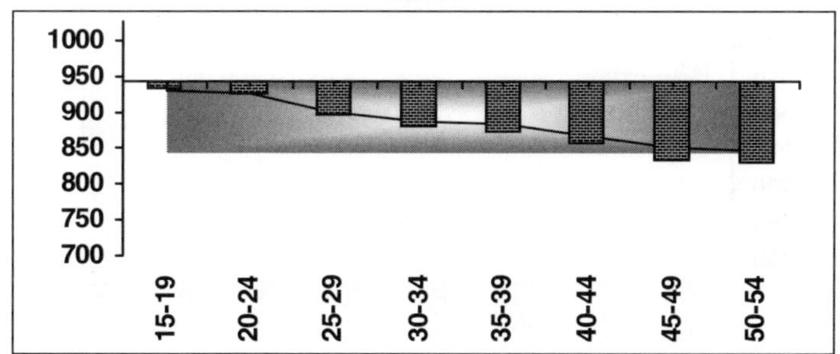

FIGURE 11: (*Contd.*)

MAHARASHTRA

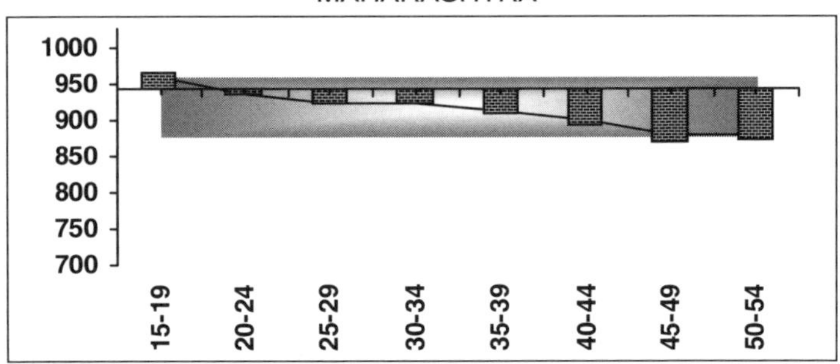

GUJARAT

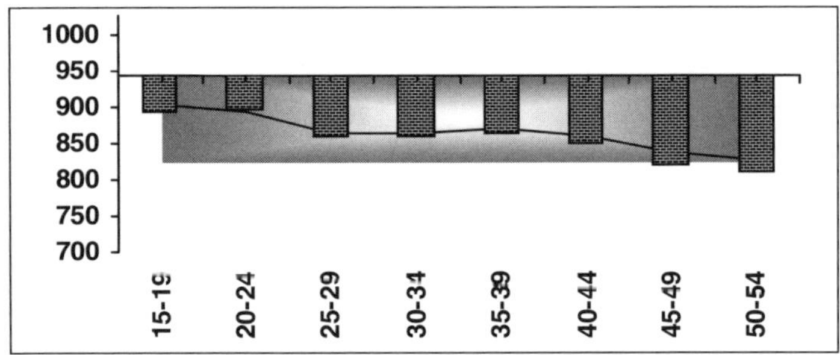

WEST BENGAL

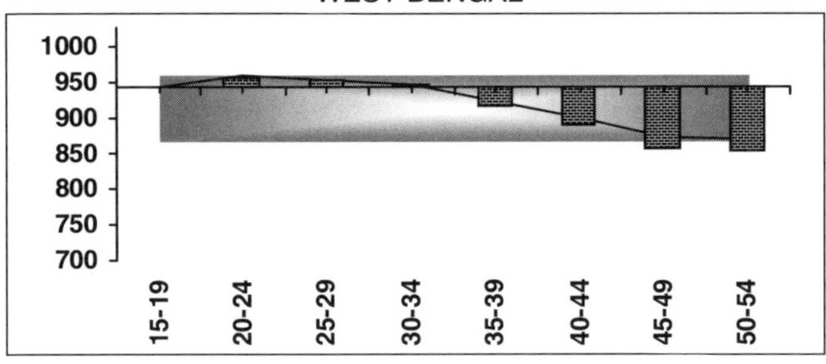

ORISSA

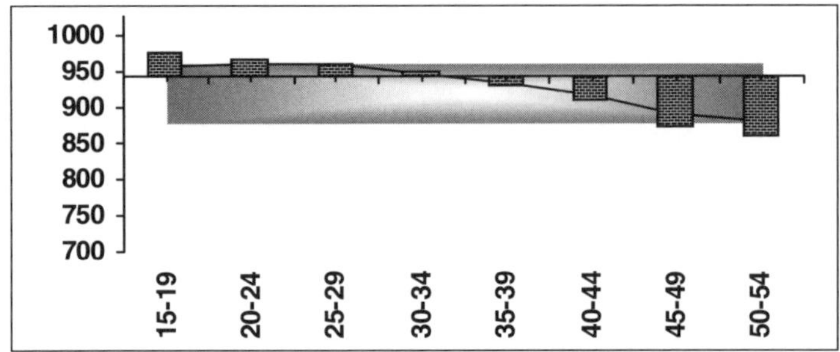

FIGURE 11: (*Contd.*)

UTTAR PRADESH

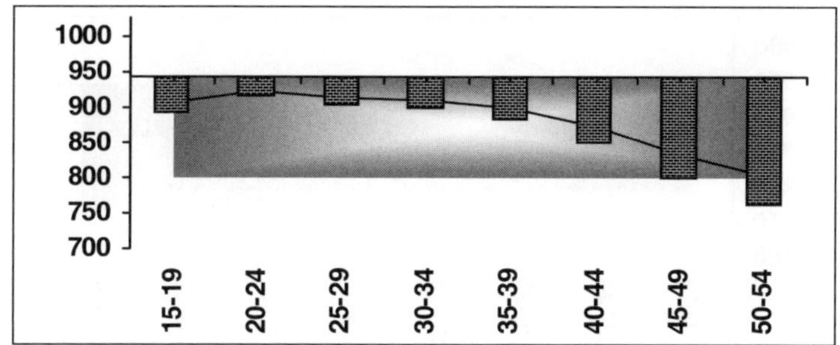

UTTARANCHAL

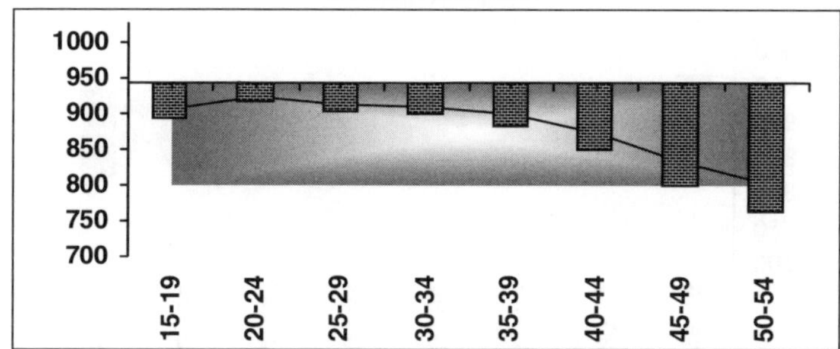

MADHYA PRADESH

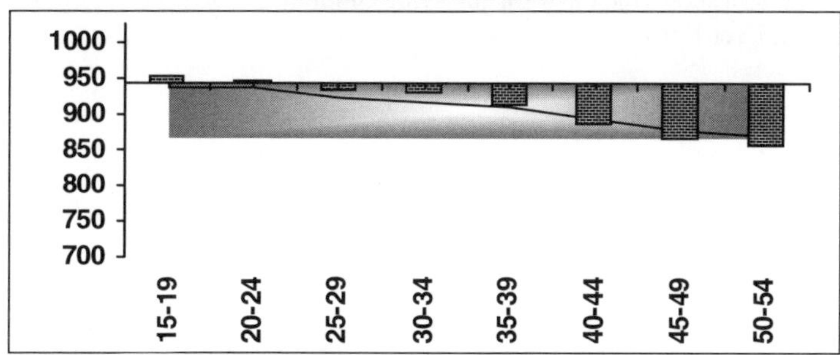

CHATTISTARH

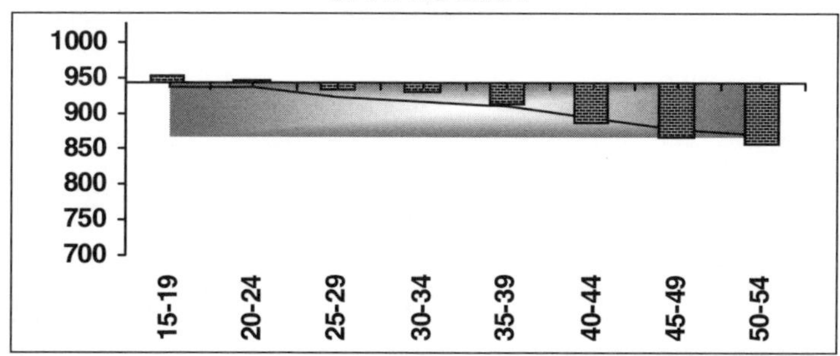

FIGURE 11: (*Contd.*)

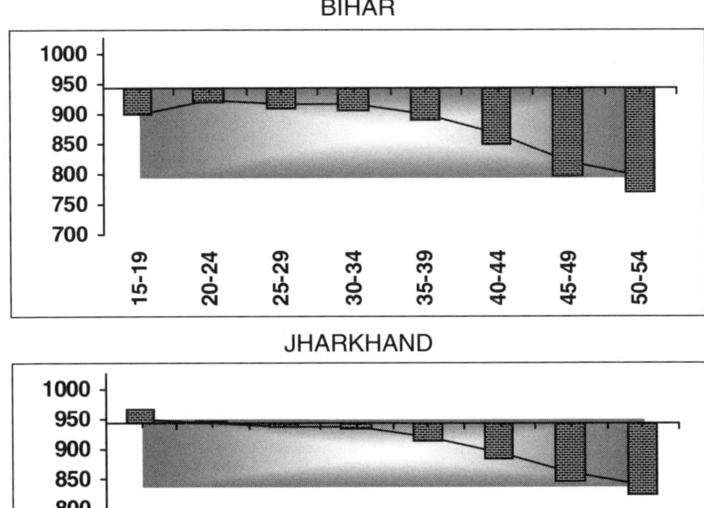

Note: Brick pattern shows the FMR for surviving children. Shaded portion shows FMR for Children Ever Born.

other hand, show data for the entire population at different points of time. Like all sources of data, the retrospective data have their limitations. Since these data are based on mothers' recollection of their own reproductive histories, they are susceptible to recall errors, and their accuracy may leave much to be desired. Through mathematical modeling, data of this kind have been used to estimate the overall child mortality rates when other more reliable sources of data are not available. In this paper, precise estimates are not the objective. The data are drawn upon to *roughly* gauge patterns and trends, and to look for underlying causes, rather than to attempt precise measurements.

The use of these retrospective data as an alternative to population enumeration data, has two major justifications. Firstly, the age reporting errors in the enumeration data pose a serious problem, as is suggested by Mari Bhat's analysis to the effect that improvements in age reporting were a critical factor in the worsening of juvenile FMRs based on population *enumeration data* (Mari Bhat 2002a and Mari Bhat 2002b). In the case of retrospective data, we are not concerned with the mother's reporting of the age of the child—the data are on the mothers' recollection of all the children she has had. The second reason why juvenile FMRs are problematic is that excess female child mortality may not have fully manifested in the juvenile ages—the effect of excess female child mortality would be seen only after a sufficient ageing of a cohort of children has occurred. Composite variables like 'under five mortality' are prone to this sort of problem (Agnihotri 2000:29, 38, 95-96), and we can extend the argument to juvenile FMRs as well. Thus, though retrospective data has its limitations, so does the enumeration data of the census.

Notably, the nineteen seventies was a period of sharp fertility decline (Figure 2; Jha 2008: 86—Figure 4.1), to which the averting of high birth-order female births are likely to have contributed. By 1981, this seemed to have neutralised gender discriminatory practices, which, as Mari Bhat (2002b: 5252-5253) points out, had been rendered highly potent by the new access to life-saving factors. The net effect was arguably at the root of the child mortality declines for females relative to males since 1971 shown by SRS data (Mari Bhat 2002b: 5253). The feminisation of rural offspring FMRs between 1971 and 1986, shown by the 1991 retrospective data for rural areas, was especially steep for States like Uttar Pradesh, Delhi, and Rajasthan. Juvenile FMRs compiled from census enumeration data corroborate this pattern of growing feminisation of the FMR between 1971 and 1981, particularly for Uttar Pradesh, Delhi and Rajasthan.

What was it that caused female relative to male child mortality to fall? Dyson (1987) argues that fertility decline in India allowed a greater share of resources in smaller families, and hence made for an improvement of the survival chances of female children. Thus, according to Dyson, it was the fall in *demographically determined risk* that was behind falling female child mortality. In this context, though more children were surviving, continued discrimination against them in terms of how well fed and cared for they are did not translate into higher mortality rates for female children—it acted, rather, to increase their frailty and susceptibility to morbidity (Dyson 1987). That the decline of relative female child mortality was not linked to improvements in the health circumstances of girl children is suggested also in cause of death statistics for India for 1980, 1990 and 1998. The data show that mortality due to anaemia was higher among girls than among boys, which indicates higher levels of malnutrition among girl children (Sagar 2007: 181). The averting of high birth-order female births had critically reduced socially determined risk so that girl children became less burdensome to a point where fatal discrimination against them was less likely. If discriminatory practices still continued, they were not so deadly as before, in part because there were fewer high birth order girls in the household, and partly because, the decline in demographically determined risk (due to fertility decline) had given the girl child a reprieve. (It was not however found possible to separately quantify demographically determined risk and sociologically determined risk.)

The intensification effect appears to be a relatively recent phenomenon, beginning in the mid 1980s. Between 1981 and 1991, the deterioration in rural offspring FMRs took place substantially through infanticide, though discrimination against surviving females was also in evidence. The aggregate picture in rural areas, taking all cohorts of mothers into account (the 1956 cohort up to the 1981 cohort), is that in States like Uttar Pradesh, Bihar, Rajasthan and Delhi, not only were the FMRs very adverse for children ever born, they were even worse for children surviving, which suggests that not only was pre-natal discrimination against females pronounced in these regions, fatal discrimination against female children was pronounced also. In the case of States like Punjab and Haryana, throughout a half century, we see a tendency for gender bias at birth to be the main operative factor, whereas in States like Uttar Pradesh, Bihar and Rajasthan, there is gender bias after birth also.

We need also to consider one other factor which operates in the *same* direction as the intensification effect, namely, the process of 'sanskritisation' or the emulation of upper caste lifestyles by the lower castes, which involves a withdrawal of women from the labour force as material conditions improve and it is no longer necessary for them to work. The 'effective co-operation' or partnership aspect of gender can, in this context, weaken (Dreze & Sen 1996: 155-159). The view that poverty reduction is likely to have been at the root of intensified female survival disadvantage is corroborated by cross sectional data for 296 districts, which show that higher levels of poverty go with more balanced FMRs, while, at the same time, female labour force participation makes the FMR more feminine (Dreze and Sen 1996: 157-163). In this context, we need also to consider Krishnaji's (1995) explanation for more balanced FMRs among working mothers, namely, that acute poverty makes it difficult for mothers to *fatally* discriminate in favour of their male children, since resources are at such a low level anyway that children of both sexes are at high risk (Krishnaji 1995). What these explanations imply is that the evidence we have considered of the 'intensification effect' operating since the mid nineteen eighties could in fact be due to declines in female work force participation. However, the retrospective data showed that in Bihar, Punjab, Uttar Pradesh and Gujarat, offspring FMRs have worsened for both working mothers as well as non-working mothers. Again, as in the case of literacy and the parity effect, we can't explain away the evidence of the intensification effect in terms of 'sanskritisation'.

It is noteworthy that after 1986, up to 1991, in Punjab, Uttar Pradesh, Delhi and Bihar, the intensification effect occurred both among literate as well as educated mothers. Thus, whereas in earlier decades, women's education had acted to make the FMR more balanced, after the mid 1980s, there are indications that education no longer has been playing such a role. In Punjab, Uttar Pradesh and Delhi, where the intensification effect has been very steep for educated mothers, the FMRs for educated mothers would have worsened for both Children Ever Born and Children Surviving. Would this have disappeared as the children of these young mothers aged 15-19 grew older? The 2001 census data available so far do not have offspring FMRs separately for educated and illiterate mothers—it is does not throw light on this issue. It is noteworthy however that the finding to the effect that female education intensifies gender bias is echoed by a study based in rural Punjab by Das Gupta (1987), who found that educated mothers, who desired fewer children, were more resistant to having fewer sons. It is noteworthy also that this is contrary to the findings of other studies, which show that female literacy acts to reduce excess female child mortality (Bhattacharya 2006; Murthi *et al* 1995). Chapter 12 however has a very different in focus from the studies by Bhattachrya (2006) and Murthi et al (1995). Several points can be made here. Firstly, this chapter shows elimination of daughters before birth among educated women, whereas the studies by Bhattacharya (2006) and Murthi *et al* (1995) find a relationship between female education and mortality differentials by sex among *living* children. Secondly, Bhattacharya (2006) and Murthi *et al* (1995) deal with aggregate district level data for the country as a whole (for 1981 and 1991), and do not profile particular regions. Thirdly, we see in chapter 12, that the evidence of the intensification of daughter discrimination among educated mothers begins to be seen only after 1986, whereas Murthi *et al* (1995) deal with the situation in 1981. Bhattacharya (2006) deals with the situation between 1981 and 1991. Fourthly, Bhattacharya (2006) and Murthi *et al* (1995) deal with 'all areas data', that is data for rural and urban areas combined, while here we are looking at data for rural areas only. As a final point, in both studies (Bhattacharya 2006; Murthi *et al* 1995), sex differentials in child mortality are studied using under 5 mortality data. This could potentially be a source of error—as Agnihotri (2000:29, 96) points out, when environmental conditions are harsh, male mortality tends to be high, and this can mask gender bias *in later years* when children have not had a chance to fully age through the 0-5 age group. This is not a reason to reject the findings of Bhattacharya (2006) and Murthi *et al* (1995)—it only suggests that their findings be treated with caution. Moreover, despite the differences in the focus of this chapter and that of the studies of Bhattacharya (2006) and Murthi *et al* (1995), we do see indications in Chapter 12 of educated mothers having more feminine offspring FMRs, taking into consideration the 25-29 cohort of mothers up to the 50-54 cohort, in States like Bihar, Rajasthan, Delhi, Uttar Pradesh, and Haryana. The greatest worsening of offspring FMRs are for the children of the younger cohorts of mothers—the 15-20 cohort of mothers, and notably in Punjab, Delhi and Uttar Pradesh, where daughter elimination has taken place before birth.

While the intensification effect gives cause for concern, female infanticide was far more acute a few decades earlier, before fertility decline set in. The magnitude of female infanticide from the mid 1980s appears to be small compared to what it was traditionally. It was found also that the intensification effect had not occurred in the South Indian States. Conversely, the parity effect was found to operate *more strongly* in the northern States, notably Rajasthan, Uttar Pradesh and Delhi, which display *steeper* parity related curves The data thus suggest that the parity effect was stronger in those parts of the country where discrimination against daughters was worse. Moreover, until 1986, the parity effect operated for both educated and illiterate mothers. Overall, while offspring FMRs were more feminine for educated mothers than for illiterate mothers, the parity effect operated for literate and for illiterate mothers both. After 1986, though, infanticide seemed to have increased among educated mothers in Punjab, Delhi and Uttar Pradesh.

Retrospective data for rural areas from the 2001 census corroborate the findings of the 1991 retrospective data for rural areas. They confirm that in the case of Punjab and Gujarat, offspring FMRs did grow more masculine between 1986 and 1991, plausibly due to the intensification effect. The 2001 retrospective data show this also for Delhi, Haryana and Himachal Pradesh, which the 1991 retrospective data for young mothers had not shown, plausibly because these young mothers had not completed their fertility careers and also because their children had not aged fully through the juvenile ages, allowing mortality to fully come into play. Notably, the 2001 rural areas retrospective data also confirm that the intensification effect had not occurred in the southern States up to 1991.

NOTES

1. The data on sex differences in mortality were for 1989-93. From this data, FMRs were computed for cumulated age segments, from 0-1 to 0-14, (assuming a sex ratio at birth of 945 females to 1000 males)
2. Literature as summarised by Mari Bhat (2002b: 5251), from the following sources: All India Census Report 1911, Dyson 1984, Natarajan 1972, Arnold 1989, Klein 1994.
3. It is noteworthy that data from the NFHS contradicts the SRS data in that it shows that between 1992-93 and 1998-99, child mortality declined more among boys than among girls (Mari Bhat 2002b: 5258).
4. Needless to say, caution should be exercised in interpreting figure 2, as the figures for women who have completed or near completed fertility (women aged 30+) would, strictly speaking, not be comparable with younger women. Still, in the critical years (women aged 30-35) to (women aged 40-45) we do see indications of fertility decline.
5. We have taken 'literate mothers' as mothers with a middle+ level of literacy. The data are from Census of India, 1991, Table F-8 PART B: EVER MARRIED WOMEN BY PRESENT AGE, PARITY, EDUCATIONAL LEVEL AND TOTAL CHILDREN EVER BORN BY SEX—RURAL. The educational levels for which these data are available are: 1. 'All Educational Levels', 2. 'Illiterate', 3. 'Literate but below middle' which includes figures for literates without educational level and educational level not stated, 4. 'Middle but below matric', 5. 'Matric but below graduate', and 6. graduate and above. We look only at women with a minimum educational level, and sow we aggregate the figures for 4,5 and 6. Below levels 4, 5 and 6., i.e., 1 and 3, contain either women without educational level or women with educational level not stated.

REFERENCES

Satish Agnihotri. 2000. *Sex Ratio Patterns in the Indian Population: A Fresh Exploration*. New Delhi: Sage Publications.

Satish Agnihotri, Richard Palmer-Jones and Ashok Parikh. 2002. 'Missing Women in Indian Districts: A Quantitative Analysis'. *Structural Change and Economic Dynamics*. 13: 285-314

David Arnold. 1989. 'Cholera mortality in British India, 1817-194', in Tim Dyson, ed. *India's Historical Demography: Studies in Famine, Disease and Society*. London: Curzon Press.

P.N. Mari Bhat. 2002a. 'On the Trail of "Missing" Indian Females. I: Search for Clues'. *Economic & Political Weekly*. 21 December 2002.

P.N. Mari Bhat. 2002b. 'On the Trail of "Missing" Indian Females. II – Illusion and Reality'. *Economic & Political Weekly*. December 28, 2002

Prabir C. Bhattacharya. 2006. 'Economic development, gender inequality, and demographic outcomes: Evidence from India'. *Population and Development Review*. 32 (2): 263-291.

Ashish Bose. 2007. 'Female Foeticide: A civilisational collapse', Tulsi Patel, Ed. *The Missing Girl Child.* New Delhi : Sage Publications, pp. 80-87.

Census of India, 2001. *Paper 1 of 2001: Provisional Population Totals*. Delhi: Controller of Publications.

A. Chahnazarian. 1988. 'Determinants of Sex Ratio at Birth: Review of Recent Literature'. *Social Biology*. 35 (3-4): 214-235.

Alice Clark. 1983. 'Limitations on female life chances in rural central Gujarat'. *Indian Economic & Social History Review*. 20(1): 1-25

Monica Das Gupta. 1987. 'Selective Discrimination against Female Children in Rural Punjab'. *Population and Development Review*. 13

Monica Das Gupta and P.N. Mari Bhat. 1997. 'Intensified Gender Bias in India: A Consequence of Fertility Decline'. *Population Studies*. 51 (3).

Kingsley Davis. 1951. *The Population of India and Pakistan*. Princeton: Princeton University Press.

Jean Dreze and Amartya Sen. 1996. India: Economic Development and Social Opportunity. Delhi: Oxford University Press.

Tim Dyson. 1984. 'Excess Male Mortality in India'. *Economic and Political Weekly*. 19 (10): 422-26.

Tim Dyson. 1987. 'Excess female mortality in India: Uncertain evidence on a narrowing differential', in K. Srinivasan and S. Mukherji Eds. *Dynamics of Population and Family Welfare*. Bombay: Himalaya.

Christophe Z. Guilmoto and S. Irudaya Rajan. 2001. 'Spatial patterns of fertility transition in Indian districts'. *Population & Development Review*. 27 (2): 713-738.

R. Jeffery & P. Jeffery. 1983. 'Female Infanticide and Amniocentesis'. *Economic & Political Weekly*. April 16 issue.

S.N. Jha. 2008. 'Population and Family Planning' (Chapter 4 of Rajiv Balakrishnan and Muchkund Dubey eds. *Social Development in India: Paths Tread and Road Ahead.* Delhi: Dorling Kindersley. 73-94).

S.N. Jha and Mamta Shree Ojha. 2008. 'Gender in Development' (Chapter 8 of Rajiv Balakrishnan and Muchkund Dubey eds. *Social Development in India: Paths Tread and Road Ahead.* Delhi : Dorling Kindersley. 203-230.

Irawati Karve. 1965. *Kinship Organisation in India*. Bombay: Popular Prakashan.

Klein, Ira. 1994. 'Imperialism, Ecology and Disease: Cholera in India, 1850-1950'. *The Indian Economic and Social History Review.* 31 (4): 491-518.

M.E Khan, Anker, R., Ghosh Dastidar, S.K. and Bairathi, S. 1989. 'Inequalities between Men and Women in Nutrition and Family Welfare Services: an In Depth Enquiry in an Indian Village', in J.C. Caldwell and G. Santow eds. *Selected Readings in the Cultural, Social and Behavioural Determinants of Health.* Health Transition Series No. 1. (Canberra: Health Transition Centre, Australian National University).

Ira Klein. 1994. 'Imperialism, Ecology and Disease: Cholera in India, 1850-1950'. *The Indian Economic and Social History Review.* 31 (4): 491-518.

N. Krishnaji. 1995. 'Working Mothers and Child Survival in Rural India: Insights from Spatial Patterns'. *Economic and Political Weekly*. November 4: 2803-2808.

Kristy Mc. Nay. 1995. 'Fertility and Frailty: Demographic Change and Health Status of Indian Women'. *Economic and Political Weekly.* October 28, pp WS-81-WS86.

Mamta Murthi, Anne-Catherine Guio and Jean Dreze. 1995. Mortality, fertility and gender bias in India. Discussion paper No. 61. Development Economics Research Programme. STICERD. London School of Economics.

D. Natarajan. 1972. Changes in Sex Ratio. Census Centenary Monograph no. 6. Census of India 1971. Delhi: Manager of Publications.

Tulsi Patel. 2007. 'The mindset behind eliminating the female foetus', in Tulsi Patel, Ed. *The Missing Girl Child.* New Delhi: Sage Publications, pp. 135-174

Mahendra K. Premi. 1991. *India's Population: Heading Towards a Billion.* New Delhi: B.R. Publishing Corporation.

Alpana D. Sagar. 2007. 'Between a Rock and a Hard Place', in Tulsi Patel, Ed. *The Missing Girl Child.* New Delhi: Sage Publications, pp. 175-202

S. Sudha and S. Irudaya Rajan. 1999. 'Female Demographic Disadvantage in India, 1981-1991: Sex Selective Abortions and Female Infanticide'. *Development and Change.* 30 (3).

Stephanie Vella. 2005. 'Low Fertility and Female Discrimination in South India: The Puzzle of Salem District', in Christophe Z. Guilmoto and S. Irudaya Rajan Eds. *Fertility Transition in South India.* New Delhi: Sage Publications.

Michael H. Teitelbaum. 1972. 'Factors Associated with the Sex Ratio in Human Populations', in G.A. Harrison and A.J. Boyce, eds. The Structure of Human Populations. Oxford: Clarendon Press.

Leela Visaria. 2007. 'Deficit of girls in India: Can it be attributed to female selective abortion?', in Tulsi Patel, Ed. *The Missing Girl Child.* New Delhi: Sage Publications pp. 61-79.

Pravin Visaria. 1971. *The Sex Ratio of the Population of India.* Monograph No. 10. Census of India 1961. Delhi : Manager of Publications.

Ingrid Waldron. 1998. 'Factors Determining the Sex Ratio at Birth', in United Nations. Too Young to Die? Genes or Gender? Population Division, Department of Economics and Social Affairs. New York. 53-63.

Part VII

GREYING IN THE LESS DEVELOPED WORLD

Chapter 13

Ageing in Kerala

S. Irudaya Rajan and *Sabu Aliyar*

The sharp increase in numbers of older people and their proportion in relation to the working age population is a worldwide phenomenon with vast economic and social implications. In India, the process is occurring much faster in the south, as compared to the northern States (Irudaya Rajan 2005). Among the South Indian States, Kerala is unique. It is demographically ahead of the rest of the country and is in the final stages of the demographic transition (to low fertility and mortality). A child born today in Kerala is expected to live to over 71 years of age. (The female child is expected to live 76 years, six more than her male counterpart). The younger age group, on the other hand, is shrinking. Thus, on an average, a woman in Kerala ends up producing just 1.6 children, which is a below replacement level of fertility. As a consequence of Kerala's increase in longevity and fall in fertility, its ageing scenario is much more prominent than in any other State in India (Zachariah and Irudaya Rajan 1997). The recently released 2001 census shows that Kerala has more than 10 percent of its population comprising of elderly.

In Kerala, as in other parts of the country, families have customarily supported elderly persons. With Kerala having undergone the demographic transition, however, the number of caregivers in families has been on the decline. Reduction in family size, national and international job-seeking out-migration flows, and a high work participation rate of women, have contributed to an attenuation of resources for the care of the elderly. At the same time, the increasing presence of older persons is making people of all ages more aware that we live in a diverse and multigenerational society. It is no longer possible to ignore ageing, regardless of whether one views it positively or negatively.

Even when families *can* support the older generation, they have greater difficulty in doing so because people above sixty years today live much longer than those of former generations and require care and medical treatment for many more years. Many older persons in Kerala who have worked in the formal sector and who have participated in pension or other income security schemes will be able to economically support themselves in varying degrees during their post retirement years. However, most elderly are not covered by any such schemes and earn their livelihood in the informal sector by working even at the age of 80 years. The majority of them are women. They have not been able, for one reason or another, to accumulate sufficient savings to ensure their well being in old age. It is vital that the social safety nets should be extended to cover all elderly persons.

Population Aging: Inter-State Analysis

As of 2001, India accommodated 77 million elderly people, a figure second only to the number of elderly in China. 29 million of India's elderly were above 70 years and 8 million were above 80. Uttar Pradesh led with the highest number of elderly (11 million) followed by Maharashtra (8.5 Million), West Bengal (5.7 million) and Tamil Nadu (5.5 Million). The smallest number of elderly was found in the union territory of Lakshadweep. In terms of the *proportion* of elderly in the population, the low fertility State of Kerala ranks number one, with 10.5% of its population comprising of elderly in 2001. Punjab and Himachal occupied the second largest position in terms of percentage of elderly, followed by the States of Tamil Nadu (8.9) and Maharashtra (8.7). Dadra and Nagar Haveli registered the lowest proportion (4). The percentage of elderly in the 80 years and above category is highest in Himachal Pradesh (1.3 Percent), followed by Kerala (1.2 Percent). (Table 1).

India is one of the few countries in the world where males outnumber females. However, among the elderly, female life chances are higher. Thus, at any age, there are more widows than widowers. Moreover, according to the 2001 census, the sex ratio among Indian elderly of 60 years and above is 1028 females for 1000 males. The trend is in favor of males in the age group of 70+ years, but then, again, it becomes favourable to females in the population of 80 years and above. Kerala has recorded the highest sex ratio—1247 females per 1000 males. The situation improves further to 1319 among elderly of 70+ years, and 1472 among elderly of 80 years and above (Table 2).

Table 3 shows various indices of population ageing in India. Kerala has registered the highest median age (27.9 years), indicating its status as a forerunner of demographic transition, followed by Goa (27.6 years), Tamil Nadu (27 years) and Pondicherry (26.5 years).

The index of ageing—the proportion of population aged 60+ to the population aged 0-14, a measure of the structure of dependency, is the highest for Kerala (40.2) followed by Goa (33.9), Tamil Nadu and Pondicherry. This is also true for median ageing and aged dependency ratio.

TABLE 1: Elderly in India, 2001

Rank	India / states	60+		70+		80+	
		Population	%	Population	%	Population	%
	India	**76826245**	**7.5**	**29376651**	**2.9**	**8060098**	**0.8**
01	**Kerala**	**3338428**	10.5	**1402678**	4.4	**389332**	1.2
02	Punjab	2200153	**9.0**	939859	**3.9**	299106	**1.2**
03	Himachal Pradesh	548890	**9.0**	245121	**4.0**	81152	**1.3**
04	Tamil Nadu	5545499	**8.9**	2097100	**3.4**	557029	**0.9**
05	Maharashtra	8464895	**8.7**	3094957	**3.2**	780039	**0.8**
06	Goa	112858	**8.4**	41928	**3.1**	10969	**0.8**
07	Pondicherry	81082	**8.3**	31939	**3.3**	8223	**0.8**
08	Orissa	3044221	**8.3**	1168791	**3.2**	293770	**0.8**
09	Uttaranchal	655726	**7.7**	258515	**3.0**	70331	**0.8**
10	Karnataka	4065985	**7.7**	1611495	**3.0**	457643	**0.9**
11	Andhra Pradesh	5798171	**7.6**	2082435	**2.7**	505185	**0.7**
12	Haryana	1590118	**7.5**	656182	**3.1**	184587	**0.9**
13	Tripura	232896	**7.3**	106606	**3.3**	35296	**1.1**
14	Chhattisgarh	1506393	**7.2**	534077	**2.6**	135486	**0.7**
15	West Bengal	5708014	**7.1**	2275599	**2.8**	670812	**0.8**
16	Madhya Pradesh	4292242	**7.1**	1609752	**2.7**	436919	**0.7**
17	Uttar Pradesh	11701369	**7.0**	4470314	**2.7**	1273057	**0.8**
18	Gujarat	3502295	**6.9**	1310502	**2.6**	374579	**0.7**
19	Rajasthan	3829791	**6.8**	1473636	**2.6**	394208	**0.7**
20	Manipur	145775	**6.7**	61569	**2.8**	17211	**0.8**
21	Jammu & Kashmir	678384	**6.7**	274603	**2.7**	82415	**0.8**
22	Bihar	5513117	**6.6**	2046843	**2.5**	566871	**0.7**
23	Lakshadweep	3732	**6.2**	1288	**2.1**	381	**0.6**
24	Jharkhand	1580601	**5.9**	553844	**2.1**	148144	**0.5**
25	Assam	1562062	**5.9**	601856	**2.3**	169824	**0.6**
26	Mizoram	49066	**5.5**	20108	**2.3**	5313	**0.6**
27	Sikkim	29144	**5.4**	11018	**2.0**	2716	**0.5**
28	Delhi	720743	**5.2**	269146	**1.9**	70929	**0.5**
29	Daman & Diu	8045	**5.1**	2930	**1.9**	811	**0.5**
30	Chandigarh	44977	**5.0**	18170	**2.0**	5216	**0.6**
31	Andaman & Nicobar Islands	17478	**4.9**	6222	**1.7**	1676	**0.5**
32	Meghalaya	105870	**4.6**	39790	**1.7**	11258	**0.5**
33	Arunachal Pradesh	49967	**4.6**	18063	**1.6**	5655	**0.5**
34	Nagaland	90540	**4.5**	37709	**1.9**	13644	**0.7**
35	Dadra & Nagar Haveli	8818	**4.0**	2618	**1.2**	611	**0.3**

Source: Based on the 2001 census.

TABLE 2: Sex Ratio among Elderly, 2001 Census

India / State	Sex Ratio (Females per 000 males)		
	60+	70+	80+
India	**1028**	**991**	**1051**
Andaman and Nicobar Islands	766	827	932
Sikkim	772	734	752
Nagaland	780	786	765
Jammu and Kashmir	846	820	837
Bihar	882	827	811
Uttar Pradesh	886	821	830
Arunachal Pradesh	889	892	900
Chandigarh	891	887	953
Assam	949	876	923
Meghalaya	957	991	1050
Delhi	963	925	996
Punjab	971	865	922
Mizorzm	977	1019	1184
Lakshadweep	979	1024	1177
Manipur	986	988	1033
Haryana	991	863	884
Utharanchal	1002	952	984
Jharkhand	1005	945	891
Tamilnadu	1013	977	1040
Himachal Pradesh	1021	997	1027
Orissa	1022	958	892
West Bengal	1047	1032	1093
Tripura	1064	1105	1230
Rajasthan	1084	1108	1261
Madhya Pradesh	1084	1112	1240
Andhra Pradesh	1099	1051	1215
Karnataka	1111	1137	1258
Gujarat	1148	1239	1410
Maharastra	1150	1063	1218
Chhattisgarh	1181	1182	1175
Pondicherry	1222	1239	1249
Daman & Diu	1239	1370	1886
Kerala	1247	1319	1472
Goa	1260	1424	1553
Dadra & Nagar Haveli	1270	1381	1406

TABLE 3: Indices of Ageing, 2001 Census

State	Median Age	Index of ageing	Age Dependency ratio
Jammu and Kashmir	21.6	18.7	11.6
Himachal Pradesh	24.5	29.1	15.1
Punjab	24.2	28.8	15.2
Chandigarh	24.6	17.2	7.6
Uttaranchal	21.5	21.2	13.8
Haryana	21.8	20.9	13.3
Delhi	23.5	16.0	8.4
Rajasthan	20.1	16.9	12.8
Uttar Pradesh	19.6	17.2	13.6
Bihar	19.5	15.8	13.0
Sikkim	21.6	15.4	9.0
Arunachal Pradesh	19.8	11.3	8.3
Nagaland	20.0	12.4	7.7
Manipur	23.1	20.6	11.1
Mizoram	21.7	15.6	9.3
Tripura	23.3	21.6	12.3
Meghalaya	18.1	10.8	8.6
Assam	21.6	15.7	10.3
West Bengal	24.1	21.4	11.9
Jharkhand	20.6	14.7	10.8
Orissa	24.1	24.9	14.1
Chattisgarh	22.3	19.6	13.0
Madhya Pradesh	21.1	18.4	13.1
Gujarat	23.6	21.0	11.5
Daman and Diu	23.7	18.6	7.5
Dadra and Nagar Haveli	22.3	11.3	6.6
Maharashtra	24.4	27.2	14.8
Andhra Pradesh	24.4	23.7	12.6
Karnataka	24.3	24.1	12.7
Goa	27.6	33.9	12.5
Lakshadweep	23.0	18.0	10.3
Kerala	27.9	40.2	16.5
Tamil Nadu	27.0	33.0	13.9
Pondicherry	26.5	30.8	12.6
Andaman and Nicobar Islands	24.5	16.7	7.5
All India	**22.7**	**21.1**	**13.1**

Aging in Kerala

According to the first census (1961 census) of Kerala State (Kerala State was formed as an independent State in 1956), the number of elderly aged 60 and above was just 10 lakhs. It increased to 26 lakh in 1991 (a 160 percent increase). According to the 2001 Census, Kerala had 33 lakh elderly persons representing around 10.5 percent of the total population. Their numbers are expected to increase to 57 lakhs in 2021 and 120 lakhs in 2061 and the proportion is likely to reach 40 per cent in 2061. While the Kerala population is growing at less than one percent, the growth of the elderly over the 1991-2001 decade was much faster, and the trend is likely to continue over next few decades. Over 1961-1991, the growth rate among the old old (aged 80+) hovered around 3 per cent. It is expected to register a growth rate of around 4 percent in the coming decades (Table 4).

TABLE 4: Demographic Profile of Elderly, 1961-2061

Year	Number of aged (millions)			Percentage Total			Growth rate (percent)		
	60+	70+	80+	60+	70+	80+	60+	70+	80+
1961	0.99	0.36	0.09	5.1	1.9	0.4	-	-	-
1971	1.33	0.50	0.13	6.2	2.3	0.6	3.47	3.66	4.71
1981	1.91	0.71	0.19	7.5	2.8	0.7	4.38	4.35	4.88
1991	2.57	1.00	0.29	8.9	3.4	1.0	3.48	4.06	5.59
2001	3.33	1.40	0.39	10.5	4.4	1.2	2.94	3.99	3.45
2011	4.20	1.94	0.54	12.2	5.6	1.6	2.61	3.86	3.85
2021	5.75	2.46	0.76	16.0	6.8	2.1	3.69	2.68	4.07
2031	7.78	3.52	1.01	21.3	9.7	2.7	3.53	4.31	3.29
2041	9.88	4.86	1.48	27.8	13.7	4.2	2.70	3.81	4.65
2051	11.48	6.22	2.11	34.4	18.6	6.3	1.62	2.80	4.26
2061	11.95	7.18	2.76	39.6	23.8	9.1	0.41	1.54	3.08

Note: Compiled by the authors for the periods 1961-2001 using the Indian censuses. The figures for the years from 2001 to 2061 are extracted from the population projections done by the authors.

The number of the oldest old (aged 80 and above) in Kerala was just 290000 in 1991. It is expected to increase to 8 lakh in 2021 and further to 27 lakh by 2061.The growth rates among the oldest old is higher than the young old and old old in Kerala over the last 40 years and it is expected to slow down in the coming decades. Age pyramids for Kerala are presented (2001 and 2061) to indicate the speed of ageing (Figure 2). Though the number of elderly in Kerala is much lower as compared to the populous states of India, Kerala leads with the highest proportion of elderly among Indian States and union territories, and has relatively more women as compared to male elderly than in any other

FIGURE 2: Age Pyramids, Kerala, 2001 and 2061

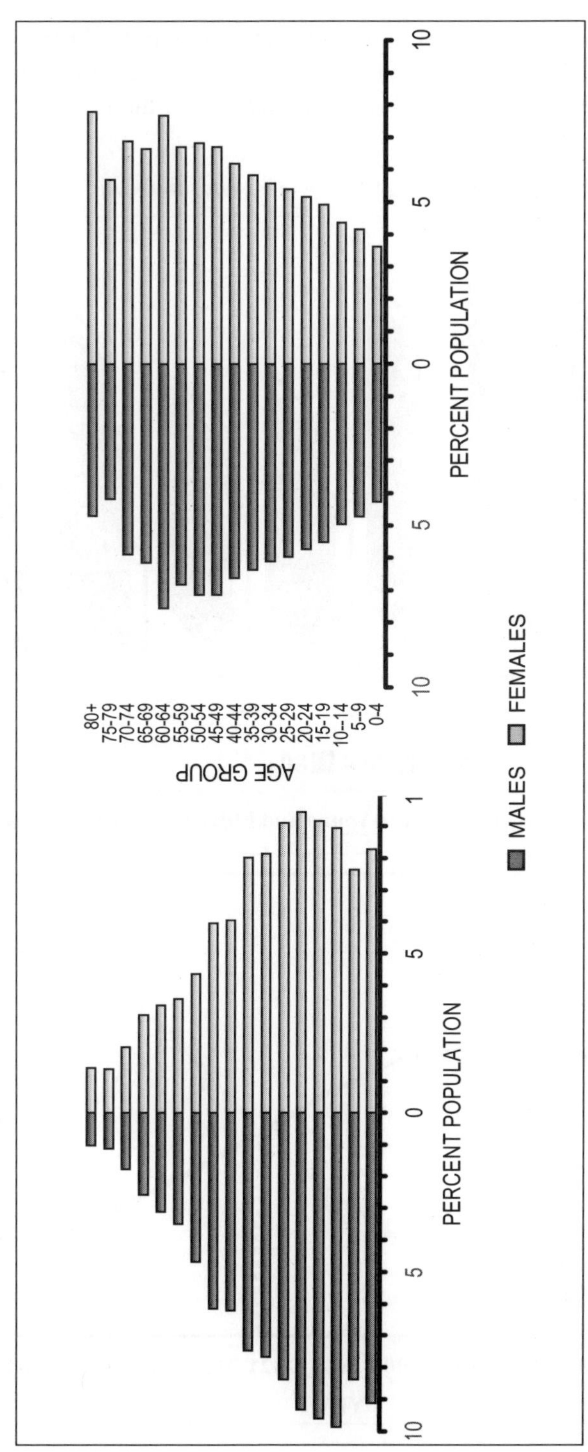

State of India. Kerala has the highest female expectation of life at birth and the gender gap was around 6 years in 2000. At age 60, a Malayali woman is expected to live 21 years, as against 19 years in the case of their male counter parts.

FIGURE 3: Sex Ratio Among Elderly in Kerala, 2001-2061

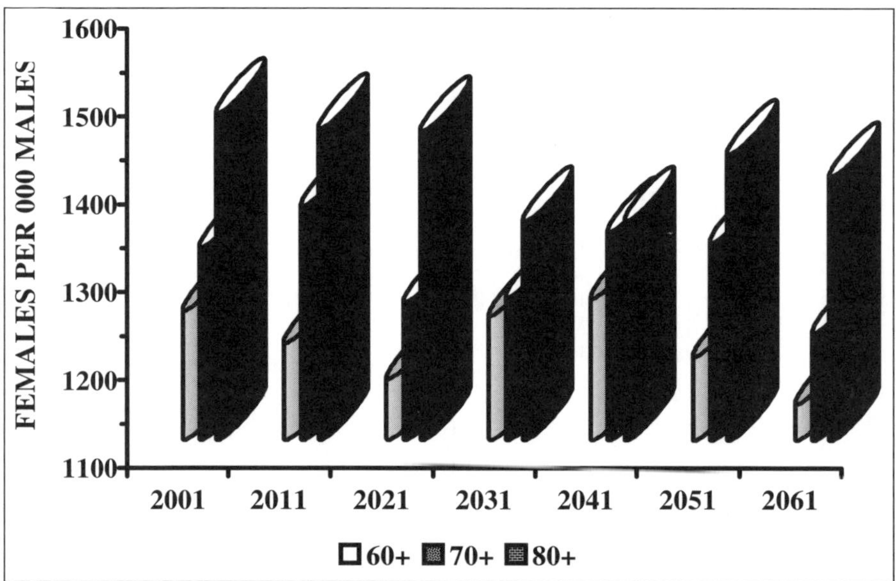

FIGURE 4: Expected Convergence between Young and Elderly Populations of Kerala

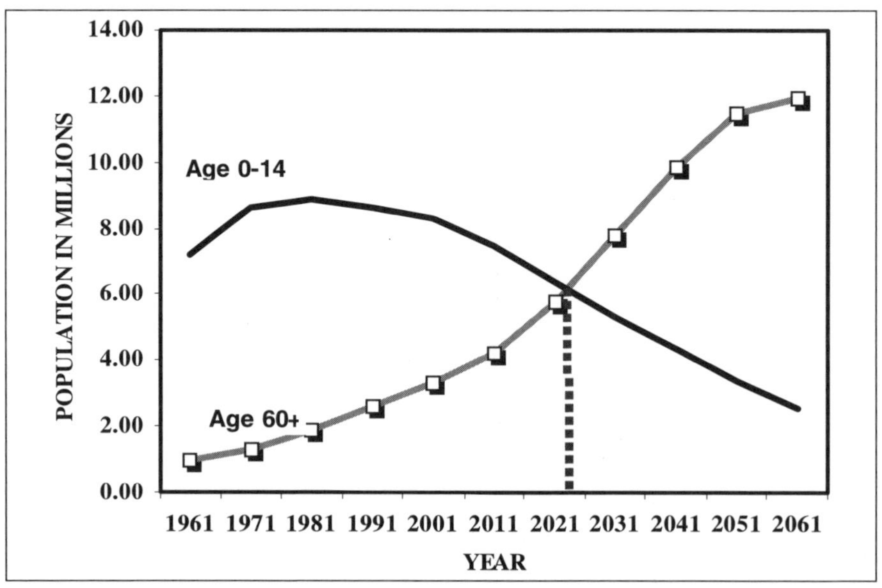

Dependency Ratios

The following ratios are presented for Kerala for the periods 1961 to 2061.

- *Young Dependency Ratio*: The number of persons aged 0-14 per 100 persons of intermediate age (working age 15-59)
- *Aged Dependency Ratio*: The number of persons aged 60 years and above per 100 persons of working age (15-59)
- *Total Dependency Ratio*: The number of persons in the non-working age group (0-14 and 60+) per 100 persons of working age (15-59)
- *Index of Ageing*: The proportion of the population aged sixty and above to the population aged 0-14.
- *Index of children*: The population aged 0-14 per 100 population aged 60 years and above.
- *Index of parents to children*: The population aged 60-74 per 100 population aged 40-44.
- *Index of oldest old to young old*: The population aged 80 years above per 100 population aged 60-64.

The Young Dependency Ratio, 82.7 in 1961, declined to 75.2 in 1971, 61.5 in 1981 and 49.9 in 1991, whereas the aged dependency ratio increased from 11.3 in 1961 to 11.6 in 1971, further to 13.2 in 1981 and 14.4 in 1991. The increase of the aged dependency ratio was by 3 points whereas the decrease in the child dependency ratio was by 33 points. At the present juncture, households in Kerala have gained in terms of reduced burden of dependents, having to take care of fewer children without having too much strain of having to care for elderly persons. Currently, every 100 persons in the working age group take care of 17 old people (Table 5).

The decline in fertility has reduced the overall dependency burden from 94.0 in 1961 to 64.3 in 1991. Though the aged dependency ratios are on the increase, the overall dependency ratio has shown a decline of 30 points during 1961-91.

The projected age dependency ratios for the period 2001-2061 are also shown in table 5. During this period, the young dependency ratios are expected to decline from 41 in 2001 to 16 in 2061. On the other hand, the aged dependency ratios are expected to increase from 17 in 2001 to 76 in 2061. The implications of these ratios for the future is that instead of every six working age persons there would be less than two working persons in 2061 who will have to share the responsibility of taking care of at least one aged person. Moreover, the probability of this aged person being a woman, who is a widow, less skilled, less educated and not working, non-recipient of social security allowance, unhealthy without health insurance, is also much higher.

TABLE 5: Dependency Rations, Aging Index and Familial Dependency Ratios for Kerala, 1961-2061

Year	Dependency ratio			Index of aging	Familial dependency ratio		
	Young	Old	Total		0-14 / 60+	60-74 / 40-44	80+ / 60-64
1961	82.7	11.3	94.0	13.7	731	105	23
1971	75.2	11.6	86.9	15.5	647	107	26
1981	61.5	13.2	74.7	21.6	466	134	27
1991	49.9	14.4	64.3	28.9	370	136	33
2001	41.1	16.5	57.6	40.1	250	130	38
2011	32.8	18.4	51.2	56.1	178	123	42
2021	26.6	24.0	50.6	90.4	111	148	44
2031	22.8	33.3	56.1	146.2	68	194	45
2041	20.3	46.3	66.6	228.2	44	255	55
2051	18.1	61.9	80.0	342.7	29	332	78
2061	16.0	76.1	92.0	476.1	21	377	109

Note: All ratios refer to 100.

The index of ageing, nearly 14 in 1961, increased to 15 in 1971 and 29 in 1991. We can also see from the table that the increase between 1961 and 1971 was by only 2 points, whereas this increase was 6 points between 1971 and 1981 and another 7 points between 1981 and 1991 indicating the acceleration of the ageing process in Kerala. Our projections indicate that the ageing index for the year 2041 will be 228, 5 times higher than 2001 value of 40. This simply means that in Kerala, the rate of increase among elderly persons will be much higher. In 2061, there is likely to be 476 elderly persons for every 100 children in Kerala.

Our household survey data show also that, in future, every household in Kerala has to take care of one child and an aged mother or father or both. The implications of this to the family would be quite substantial as the cost and care of an older person is different from that of a child.[1] For society, this shift in the dependency structure will mean a substantial change in the type of public sector expenditure. Furthermore, while the care of the child is the direct responsibility of the parents, the care of the extreme elderly has only a social obligation without any legal sanction.

Migration Surveys, 1999 and 2004

The Centre for Development Studies completed two migration surveys in Kerala in 1999 and 2004, covering 10,000 households throughout the State (Zachariah, Mathew and Irudaya Rajan, 2003; Zachariah and Irudaya Rajan, 2004). We have extensively tabulated raw data from this source for this paper so as to assess the various issues pertaining to the elderly.

In 1999, around 58 percent of households in Kerala did not have any elderly persons. The number declined further to 52 percent in 2004—a decline of six percentage points—indicating a changing household atmosphere, due to which the elderly do not stay with other members of the family. As almost half of the households in Kerala have no elderly persons to live with, they do not understand the advantages and disadvantages of elderly persons living with them. Another 33 percent of households in Kerala accommodate just one elderly —either a widow or widower of either from the husband's or wife's side. Two elderly living in the same households have gone up from 11 percent to 14 percent, indicating an increase in the life expectancy among elderly males and females. Almost one in six couples in Kerala live beyond sixty as couples without losing their partners. Households with more than three elderly formed less than one percent in 2004.

TABLE 6: Distribution of Households by the Number of Elderly, 1999 and 2004

No. of elderly	2004	1999
Nil	51.46	58.00
One	33.47	31.00
Two	14.19	10.50
Three	0.76	0.50
Four	0.12	0.00

Note: Special Tabulations from the Kerala Migration Survey and South Asian Migration Surveys.

To understand the district profile, we have tabulated the proportion of elderly in all districts of Kerala for the years 1999 and 2004, from the migration surveys. The results are presented in Table 7. Between 1999 and 2004, the proportion of elderly to the total population in Kerala has increased from 11 to 14 in the last five years. Among the districts of Kerala, in 2004, the highest proportion of elderly is found in Pathanamthitta followed by Kottayam. Ernakulam and Alappuzha and Thiruvananthapuram districts were above the State average. The lowest proportion was found in Wayanad. However, 12 out of 14 districts in Kerala have already crossed 10 percent mark, with Pathanamthitta district showing the maximum of 21 percent—double than the Malappuram figure. Districts which were the forerunners in the fertility and mortality transition, have reported higher proportion of elderly (Guilmoto and Irudaya Rajan 2001; 2002; 2005). In 2004, almost all the districts of Kerala have reported more proportion of female elderly in the population than males, except 3 districts of Kollam, Idukki and Malappuram. Hence, any social policy measures to enhance the welfare of the elderly should take note of this phenomenon.

TABLE 7: District-wise Proportion of Elderly Population in Kerala, 1999 and 2004

Districts	1999			2004		
	Male	Female	Total	Male	Female	Total
Thiruvananthapuram	10.60	11.10	10.90	13.62	13.92	13.77
Kollam	10.70	12.00	11.40	13.21	12.27	12.73
Pathanamthitta	17.50	13.60	15.50	20.48	21.21	20.86
Alappuzha	13.90	13.10	13.40	14.29	15.60	14.97
Kottayam	12.80	12.60	12.70	17.30	19.34	18.32
Idukki	8.90	6.10	7.60	11.43	9.47	10.47
Ernakulum	12.00	13.30	12.70	15.01	16.31	15.67
Thrissur	10.50	12.00	11.30	12.25	13.89	13.11
Palakkad	11.70	11.30	11.50	12.57	14.27	13.47
Malappuram	7.90	7.70	7.70	9.64	9.58	9.61
Kozhikode	10.00	11.00	10.50	13.15	13.07	13.11
Wayanad	7.40	7.60	7.50	8.57	10.14	9.38
Kannur	8.70	10.20	9.40	12.06	13.60	12.87
Kasargode	8.00	8.60	8.30	10.51	10.53	10.52
Kerala	10.70	11.00	10.90	13.17	13.85	13.52

Note: Special Tabulations from the Kerala Migration Survey and South Asian Migration Surveys.

Among the elderly in Kerala, close to 56 percent belong to young old (60-69 years). Another 31 percent are old old (70-79 years) and only 13 percent are oldest old (80 and above). Among the elderly, there are more females than males (Gulati and Irudaya Rajan, 1999). The sex ratio (males per 1000 females) of all the elderly age groups indicates the preponderance of women among elderly. In the age group 85 and above, there are 647 males for 1000 females. Most of the women lose their husbands in old age due to sex differentials in mortality and age differentials at the time of marriage. This is reflected among the sex ratios of the widowed. All these dimensions of widowhood among the aged should be considered very seriously when formulating economic and social security measures.

TABLE 8: Age Structure of Elderly in Kerala, 2004

Age	Male	Female	Total	Sex Ratio M/F*1000
60-64	30.44	31.02	30.75	869
65-69	25.24	25.86	25.57	865
70-74	19.45	17.67	18.50	975
75-79	12.60	12.13	12.35	921
80-84	7.86	7.29	7.56	956
85+	4.17	5.61	4.94	647

Note: Special Tabulations from the South Asian Migration Surveys.

The majority of the men (86 percent) were married; but among women, the majority (56 percent) came under the 'widowed' category. Similarly, close to 5 percent of women were reported as either single or divorced or separated as against 2.5 percent among men. Women require more social and economic attention in old age as most of them have no property or assets in their name. In an earlier study, around 60 percent of rural and urban elderly females and 30 percent of rural and urban males in India had no valuable assets in their name. Among the major States in India, Kerala ranks first in this regard, with 76 percent of its elderly women reporting no financial assets in their name (Irudaya Rajan 2004)

TABLE 9: Marital Status of the Elderly in Kerala 2004

Marital status	2004		
	Male	Female	Total
Single	2.0	3.1	2.6
Married	85.9	39.4	61.2
Widowed	11.5	55.9	35.1
Divorced/Separated	0.4	1.4	1.0

Note: Special Tabulations from the Kerala Migration Surveys.

We have also analysed the status of current co-residence arrangements among the Kerala elderly by sex as of 2004. Interestingly, in both Kerala and India, 2.5 percent of elderly live alone in their respective households (Irudaya Rajan and Sanjay Kumar, 2003). 4 percent of them are females and most likely, all of them are widows. Another 8 percent of elderly live with their spouses. Three-fourth of elderly males live with their spouses, children and grand children compared to 50 percent in the case of females. On the other hand, almost 40 percent of females live in Kerala without spouses but with their children and grand children as against just 11 percent in the case of males. Elderly living with strangers or non-relatives in a household is not common in Kerala. The number of old age homes in Kerala is 134, one-fifth of India's number. Currently, at least 5 old age homes are coming up every year. The number of inmates reported in the survey was 5076 persons, of which 60 percent are females (Irudaya Rajan 2002).

Social Security

Kerala has made remarkable progress in its demographic transition. The State has achieved below replacement level of fertility two decades ahead of the all-India target year of 2011. The TFR (Total Fertility Rate), which denotes the average number of children that would be born to a woman during her life time, if her passage through her child bearing years conforms to the current

TABLE 10: Living Arrangements among Elderly in Kerala, 2004

Living arrangement	Male	Female	Total
Living Alone	0.95	3.94	2.54
With Spouse Alone	10.56	5.07	7.65
With spouse, children and grand children	76.11	50.51	62.54
Without spouse but with children, grand children	11.42	38.47	25.76
Without spouse, but with relatives other than children and grand children	0.79	1.87	1.36
With non relatives	0.17	0.15	0.16
Total	100	100	100

Note: Special Tabulations from the Kerala Migration Surveys.

age specific fertility rates) declined from a high level of 5.6 in 1951-61 to about 1.7 in 1993, a level which is very much below the replacement level of 2.05. The population growth rate has declined to about 1 per cent per annum in 1995 from 2.3 per cent per year during 1961-71. Among all the States of India, longevity is highest in Kerala, for both men and women. (Zachariah and Irudaya Rajan 1997; Irudaya Rajan and Zachariah, 1998). While Kerala has the unique distinction of being the first State in India to complete the demographic transition, one of the immediate consequences has been population aging. In this context, let us briefly assess the social security programs in Kerala.

Successive governments in Kerala have introduced 35 social security and assistance schemes for the elderly, which are currently being implemented. Among the southern states, Kerala spends close to 3 percent of its budget for social security programs and the neighboring states of Tamil Nadu and Karnataka, the expenditure ranges between 2.3 and 2.5. Brief details about each scheme such as eligibility criteria, year of introduction, and annual expenditure incurred are given elsewhere (Irudaya Rajan, Mishra and Sarma, 1999). The schemes are classified into four categories and we shall list the programs meant for elderly.

A. Schemes which are Fully Financed by the State and Central Governments:

1 National Old Age Pension

B. Schemes which are Fully Financed by the State:

2 Kerala Destitute and Widow Pension Scheme
3 Kerala Agricultural Workers Pension Scheme
4 Special Pension Scheme for the physically handicapped and mentally retarded
5 Old age pension to craftsmen

6 Pension to sportsmen in Indigent Circumstances
7 Pension to Journalists in Indigent Circumstances
8 Pension to Cine Artists in indigent Circumstances
9 Pension to Freedom Fighters
10 Pension to Second World War Veterans

C. Major Schemes which are Financed with Partial State Support

11 Kerala Coir Workers' Welfare Fund
12 Kerala Construction Workers' Welfare Fund
13 Kerala Fishermen' Welfare Fund

D. Schemes which are Financed Outside the Budget and Operated by Respective Boards

14 Kerala Headload Workers' Welfare Fund
15 Kerala Abkari Workers' Welfare Fund Scheme
16 Kerala Toddy Workers' Welfare Fund
17 Kerala Agricultural Workers' Welfare Fund

Among the programs, the highest number of beneficiaries is reported for agricultural worker pension (5.3 lakh), followed by widow/destitute pension (2.1 lakh), pension for persons with disabilities (1.5 lakh) and national old age pensions (1.4 lakh) (details see Table 11). In total, close to 12 lakhs elderly persons are receiving some financial assistance from the Kerala government. Do they get the money regularly? Is it enough for sustaining the livelihood? We have to do more field level research on this subject. In this paper, we would like to document the agricultural worker pension scheme in detail.

TABLE 10: Social Assistance and Security Program Beneficiaries in Kerala, 2003

Schemes	Beneficiaries
National Old Age pension	134600
Agricultural Workers	527647
Widow/Destitute Pension Scheme	208445
Special pension for persons with disabilities	148553
Building and construction workers	37969
Second World War Veterans	5690
Handloom workers	7407
Tailoring workers	5450
Pension to Journalists	398
Pension to Toddy Workers	14929
Coir Workers	67000
Fishermen	28190
Ration Dealers	252

(Contd.)

Abkari Workers	97
Cine artists	146
Khadi workers	17
Freedom fighters	8888
Kerala	1195678

Source: Compiled from the latest economic review published from the state planning board, Government of Kerala, Thiruvananthapuram.

The district level profiles of beneficiaries for the three major pension schemes are presented in Table 11. The highest number of agricultural pension beneficiaries is reported for Thiruvananthapuram, followed by Alappuzha and Kozhikode. On the other hand, Malappuram leads with the highest number of widow/destitute pension beneficiaries, followed by Kollam and Kozhikode. In terms of national old age pension schemes, Palakkad leads with the highest, followed by Kollam and Malappuram. Is there any link between the number of elderly persons and the number of beneficiaries? It calls for further investigation.

TABLE 11: Major Pension Scheme Beneficiaries in Kerala by Districts, 2003

District	Agricultural workers	Widow/destitute pension	National old age pension
Thiruvananthapuram	91024	26484	9292
Kollam	33077	28133	15971
Pathanamthitta	17933	6636	3641
Alappuzha	68500	13969	7569
Kottayam	33560	10770	8890
Idukki	7979	2792	3930
Ernakulum	33870	16426	13994
Thrissur	50650	19143	11708
Palakkad	57154	19593	18748
Malappuram	52846	29345	15175
Kozhikode	62085	27290	9454
Wayanad	11843	4475	1448
Kannur	42908	15195	9171
Kasargode	15635	10131	5609
Kerala	527647	208445	134600

Agricultural Workers Pension Scheme

One of the major social assistance schemes implemented in Kerala is the Kerala Agricultural Workers Pension Scheme which came into existence in 1980 (for more details, see Gulati, 1990; Irudaya Rajan, 1999). The pension amount was originally fixed at Rs.45; it was raised to Rs.60 in 1987, to Rs.70 in 1991 and again to Rs.100 in 1996. According to the provisions of the scheme, the beneficiaries should be agricultural workers above the age of 60 and whose annual income does not exceed Rs.11000 (State Planning Board, 2004). An agricultural worker is defined as workers, other than those covered by plantation labour Act, depending principally on agricultural wages for livelihood and residing within the state for a continuous period of at least 10 years, immediately preceding the date of application. Agricultural workers with physical infirmity are also eligible for pension. The State Labour Commissioner is the administrator of the scheme. The amount is payable once in three months, in January, April, July and October by money order.

In 1999, 3.1 lakh persons had benefited by the scheme, of which, 58 per cent were women. Kerala had 19.47 lakh agricultural labourers and the scheme covered 16 per cent of them. The expenditure on this pension scheme increased sharply from Rs.1615 lakhs in 1986-87 to Rs.2690 lakhs in 1991 and to Rs. 3720 lakhs in 1999 (Table 12). The increase was due to increases in the coverage of workers and the upward revision of the rates effected in 1988 and 1991.

TABLE 12: Expenditure and the Number of Beneficiaries, Agricultural Workers Pension Scheme, 1980-81 to 1999-2000

Year	Beneficiaries	Expenditure (in Lakhs)
1980-81	293778	1092.3
1981-82	172376	744.2
1982-83	139817	446.0
1983-84	217659	1188.0
1984-85	250116	1132.0
1985-86	277821	1801.0
1986-87	261584	1615.0
1987-88	286733	1469.5
1988-89	299758	1925.7
1989-90	308346	2197.1
1990-91	316509	3062.3
1991-92	344301	2515.8
1992-93	340776	2690.3
1993-94	345650	3551.0
1994-95	344946	2000.0
1995-96	312944	3457.3
1996-97	312944	3457.3
1997-98	300784	4301.0
1998-99	304638	3720.0
99-2000	436452	NA

Source: Various (annual) issues of Economic Review, the State Planning Board, Government of Kerala, Thiruvananthapuram.

Concluding Observations

Can Kerala afford to provide social security or assistance or financial security for the growing number of elderly? Let us assess it with facts and figures. According to the 2001 census, the number of elderly in Kerala in 2001 was 33 lakhs. Kerala has approximately 4 lakh pensioners (retired from the Kerala government services plus retired from other state governments outside Kerala and returned to Kerala after retirement plus the military, railways, post and telegraph pensioners). In other words, close to 15 percent of the elderly in Kerala are the creamy layers of the senior citizens. They are not looking for any assistance from the Kerala government.

The work participation rates among elderly based on the NSS 1999-2000 round was around 50 percent for elderly in Kerala. One has to view these trends in work participation rates in the context of widespread of poverty and inadequate social security system. In Kerala, even at the age of 80, 10 percent of elderly continue to work. As long as they work, theoretically, they do not look for free money from the Government.

Two other important observations also can be made in this context. The absolute number of children has come down in Kerala and it has already led the Kerala government to close uneconomic schools. It simply means that the government can divert some money from primary education to social security.

According to the latest economic review, around 12 lakhs elderly are beneficiaries of various social security and assistance schemes in Kerala. They account for 40 percent of the elderly population. Not even a single systematic study exists in Kerala to assess the real beneficiaries.

If the government can implement all the schemes very seriously and provide assistance to the real needy among elderly (the senior author filed observations indicate starvation among Kerala elderly), Kerala can continue to run the social assistance schemes without much financial constraints. The budget for social welfare can be increased by diverting money from family planning and primary education. We hope that the government thorough panchayat level institutions will be able not only to identify the needy (real) beneficiaries but also enhance the financial assistance from the current level of Rs. 110 to Rs. 300 per month (Incidentally, West Bengal pays Rs. 300 as old age pension). For this, a bold step in the right direction is needed.

NOTE

1. In a recent discussion with a group of elderly in an institutional set up, an elderly couple remarked to the senior author: 'We want to stay with our children and grandchildren but they are not interested in us, hence we stay alone, and ourselves manage our day to day affairs'.

REFERENCES

Christophe Z Guilmoto and S Irudaya Rajan. 2001 Spatial Patterns of Fertility Transition in Indian Districts. *Population and Development Review*, Volume 27, No 4, pp.713-138.

Christophe Z Guilmoto and S Irudaya Rajan. 2005. *Fertility Transition in South India*. Sage Publications, New Delhi.

Gulati Leela,1990. Agricultural Worker's Pension In Kerala: An Experiment In Social Assistance. *Economic & Political Weekly*, Vol. XXV, No 6, pp. 339-344.

Irudaya Rajan, S and K C Zachariah. 1998. Long Term Implications of Low Fertility in Kerala. *Asia-Pacific Population Journal*, Volume 13, No 4, PP; 41-66.

Irudaya Rajan, S and Sabu Aliyar. 2004. Demographic Change in Kerala in the 1990s and Beyond In B. A. Prakash. Ed. Kerala's Economic Development: Performance and Problems in the Post-Liberalization Period. Sage Publications, New Delhi.

Irudaya Rajan, S. and Sabu Aliyar. 2004. Gender, Ageing and Social Security. SAMYUKTA. *Journal of women's studies*, Volume. IV Number.2 July 2004.

Irudaya Rajan, S and Sabu Aliyar. 2005. Fertility Change in Kerala. In Christophe Z Guilmoto and S Irudaya Rajan. Eds. *Fertility Transition in South India*. Sage Publications, New Delhi.

Irudaya Rajan, S, U S Mishra and P S Sarma. 1995. An Agenda for National Policies on Aging in India. *Research and Development Journal*, Journal of Helpage India. Volume.1, No.2. Pp. 38-53.

Irudaya Rajan, S, U S Mishra and P S Sarma. 1999. India's *Elderly: Burden or Challenge?* Sage Publications. New Delhi/Thousand Oaks/London.

Irudaya Rajan, S. 1989. Aging in Kerala: One More Population Problem? *Asia-Pacific Population Journal.* Volume 4, No. 2. June pp.19-48.

Irudaya Rajan, S. 2002. Home Away from Home: A Survey of Old Age Homes and Inmates from Kerala, India. *Journal of Housing for the Elderly*, Volume 16, No.1 and 2, Pp. 125-150.

Irudaya Rajan, S. 2002. Social Security for the Unorganized Sector in South Asia. *International Social Security Review*, Volume 55, No 4, Pp. 143-156.

Irudaya Rajan, S. 2004. Chronic Poverty among Indian Elderly. Chronic Poverty Research Centre and Indian Institute of Public Administration Working Paper 17, Indian Institute of Public Administration, New Delhi. 2004.

Irudaya Rajan S and Sanjay Kumar. 2003. Living Arrangements among the Indian Elderly: New Evidence from the National Family Health Survey. *Economic and Political Weekly*, Volume XXXVIII, No.1, January 4, pp. 75-80.

Irudaya Rajan, S 2001. Social Assistance for Poor Elderly: How Effective? *Economic and Political Weekly*, Volume XXXVI, No 8, February 24, Pp. 613-617.

Jhabvala Renana and R K A Subrahmanya Eds. 2000. *The Unorganized Sector: Work Security and Social Protection.* Sage Publications, New Delhi.

Leela Gulati and S Irudaya Rajan. 1999. The Added Years: Elderly in India and Kerala *Economic and Political Weekly*, Volume XXXIV, No 44, WS-46-51.

Phoebe S Liebig and S Irudaya Rajan. Eds. 2003. *An Aging India: Perspectives, Prospects, and Policies.* The Haworth Press Inc, New York. United States of America.

Robert J. Palacios and S. Irudaya Rajan. 2004. *Safety Nets for the Elderly in Poor Countries:* The Case of Nepal. World Bank Pension Primer Working Paper No. 44.

State Planning Board, Trivandrum. 1996. *Social Security Initiatives in Kerala*. Report of the Expert Committee. Government of Kerala.

Zachariah, K C and S Irudaya Rajan. Eds. 1997. *Kerala's Demographic Transition: Determinants and Consequences*. Sage Publications. New Delhi/Thousand Oaks/ London.

Zachariah, K C and S Irudaya Rajan. 2004a *Gulf Revisited. Economic Consequences of Emigration from Kerala – Emigration and Unemployment*. Centre for Development Studies, Thiruvananthapuram.

Zachariah, K C and S Irudaya Rajan. 2004b. Malayali Emigration Moving in to a Higher Orbit. *Passline*. Volume 8, No.7.

Zachariah, K C, E T Mathew and S Irudaya Rajan. 2003. *Dynamics of Migration in Kerala: Determinants, Differentials and Consequences*. Orient Longman Private Limited.

Chapter 14

The Family in South India: Past, Present and Future

John C. Caldwell, P.H. Reddy and *Pat Caldwell*

This chapter identifies changes that have taken place in family structure; analyses marriage patterns; assesses the situation of the old in the family; and speculates on the future. It draws heavily on a study of nine villages in the south Indian state of Karnataka, between 1979 and 1983 by all three authors, and by one of them, P.H. Reddy, in 1995. What comes through is that demographic, social and economic forces are interacting in transforming many, but by no means all, aspects of the family.

Family Structure

The study of the family bristles with definitional problems. Scholars like Kapadia (1966); Rao, Kulkarni and Rayappa (1986), Ramu (1991), and Wilson and Dyson (1992) have identified two broad family types, namely, nuclear, and joint or extended. Others (Caldwell et al. 1972; Reddy 1978, 1991; Caldwell, Reddy and Caldwell, 1988) have classified families into nuclear, stem, joint, joint-stem and other. We would, therefore, prefer to preface our paper with definitions of types of the family. The following classification is a slightly revised version suggested by Caldwell and his associates (1972: 2b,9).

1. *Nuclear.* Husband/wife and any unmarried children with or without one or more unmarried relatives of husband/wife.
2. *Stem.* In addition to the muclear family, includes one or more parents/ grandparents of the husband/wife.
3. *Joint.* In addition to nuclear family, consists of at least one related

ever married person of the same generation as that of husband/wife.

4. *Joint-stem.* Combines the features of both the stem and joint families. That is, these families must consist of a nuclear family[1] and at least one parent/grandparent of husband/wife and at least one related ever married person of the same generation as that of husband/wife.
5. *Others.* All the other families which cannot be classified into any of the four types mentioned above.

Indian and foreign scholars' tales abound on how the joint family system dominated the lives of the Indians. But it appears that the joint families always accounted for a lower proportion than did the nuclear families. For example, Gore (1968:235) says, "the fraternal or collateral joint family was never the most common form". Goode (1968:viii) asserts that the large joint family was not common at any time in India perhaps because of the great forces of fission, initially between daughters-in-law and later between brothers. Some studies conducted in both rural and urban areas have revealed a higher proportion of nuclear than joint families. For example, a study of 5,200 households in both rural and urban areas of five (now six) districts in the state of Karnataka, conducted in 1975 by the Bangalore Population Centre, revealed the percentage of different types of household as follows: nuclear 57.3, stem 30.8, joint 4.7 and joint-stem 3.4 (Reddy, 1978). In a study of three villages located in three different districts in Karnataka state, two-thirds of the families were nuclear and the rest were different forms of joint family (Rao, Kulkarni and Rayappa, 1986: 41). In another study of nine villages in southern Karnataka, 59 per cent of the households were nuclear and the remainder were stem, joint, joint-stem and other type of families (Caldwell, Reddy and Caldwell, 1988: 114). Of the 163 households studied in a city in southern Karnataka, over 68 per cent were nuclear and the remainder belonged to other types (Ramu, 1991).[1] Why, then, was so much made of the joint family system in India? Perhaps because the proportion of the joint families was higher in India than in other countries, especially in the developed world.

The disadvantages of the joint family system are often noted. But its advantages are not as often recognised. The joint family provides social, economic and emotional security to its members. Nobody in the village can dare attack a member of a joint family in which three or four grown-up brothers live with their parents and wives. The joint family is a symbol of unity and solidarity. The size of landholding of a joint family is economically viable. The joint family provides economic security to its members at times of need. When a brother or daughter-in-law falls sick, they do not have to worry about the work in the field or in the house; other members of the joint family attend to it. Similarly, they do not have to worry about their next meal; the joint family provides it. The relationship between parents and their grown-up sons and between brothers is warm and affectionate. But the same cannot be said about the relationship between mother-in-law and daughters-in-law and between daughters-in-law themselves who come from different families. In fact, the ultimate reason for the break up of the joint family is the friction between mother-in-law and daughters-in-law and between daughters-in-law themselves. When the joint family breaks, its members, especially male members, experience trauma. It is a clear proof of lack of unity and solidarity in the joint family. In fact, it is a "disgrace" in the public eye.

The Family in Rural Karnataka, around 1980

The family in rural southern Karnataka was the central focus of a study of demographic change carried out in nine villages 125 kilometres west of Bangalore in 1979-83 (Caldwell, Reddy and Caldwell, 1988). For most of the population the stem family, consisting of old parents, one married son and his wife and children was still the ideal. Inevitably, this meant that a large minority of families, namely those of the other married sons, were nuclear in residence. In addition, there were also joint families, largely among the larger landowners, especially Brahmins.

Perhaps the greatest change—certainly the most quantifiable one—has been the changing age of female marriage. South Indian women and men always married after puberty. There was no equivalent of the infant marriages of North India. Nevertheless, female marriage usually took place immediately after menarche, around 15 years of age, in the first quarter of the twentieth century. In Karnataka the average age of female marriage had risen to 18 years by 1971 and has continued since then to rise by a further year each decade. Even in rural areas, the new daughters-in-law who come into the households of their parents-in-law are no longer girls but young women. This, plus the fact that most now have some schooling, is already altering the intergenerational relationship.

Male age at marriage has risen very little in Karnataka, from an average of 24.3 years early this century to just under 25 years now. The spousal age gap remains the largest in India and is a force in restricting companionate marriage and in encouraging the son to side in disputes with his parents rather than his wife. Nevertheless, it is now around five years, instead of nearly twice as much at the beginning of the century, and this new situation, together with the education of the wives, is forcing change in marital relations.

Another very significant change has occurred in rural Karnataka over the last half century. At Independence, bridewealth was universally paid even by the higher castes. Now dowry is paid everywhere except by the Scheduled Castes and even some of their members are beginning to do so. Some of the explanation for the change is a marriage squeeze brought about by the rapid rate of population growth, which makes each age group larger than those older than it. In a situation where bridegrooms are considerably older than brides, this translates into a surplus of marriageable females. Competitive 'bidding' for scarce bridegrooms then results in a growing incidence of dowry. But the main reason for the rise of dowry is that educated men with the chance of a town job are preferred over farmers and this has resulted in a kind of marriage auction with a bidding up of the value of husbands.

South India, in contrast to North India and most other parts of the non-Muslim world, has been characterised by consanguineous marriages, that is, marriages between previously related brides and bridegrooms. This situation is rapidly changing. Even in 1980, 30 per cent of husbands and wives were close enough in previous relationship for that relationship to be exactly defined. But the fact that this was true in only 20 per cent of cases where the wife was under 30 years of age shows the rate of change and the very high levels of consanguineous marriage that must have existed before the present century. One-third of all Hindu marriages were consanguineous in 1981 and one-quarter of Muslim marriages. The ideal marriage is between a man and his sister's daughter, but, as there is often no suitable niece available, the most common are cross-cousin marriages, although, among Muslims, there are also parallel cousin marriages.

There are a number of reasons for the decline in consanguineous marriages. The most important is the spread of education and the decline of the "little tradition" in the face of the "great tradition" flowing from the urban areas and from the North. Awareness of the central northern Hindu tradition and imported ideas about risks to child health when parents are related are fusing to yield a feeling that such marriages are somewhat improper and probably unsafe. These reasons are sometimes used as an excuse for achieving more practical ends. In an age of soaring dowries and in a situation where dowry is half or less when relatives marry, there are good reasons for looking outside the family. Furthermore, it may be necessary to look afar in an increasingly heterogeneous population if one is trying to find a suitable match for an educated child or one with other qualities such as urban experience in childhood.

In rural Karnataka, marriage is still nearly universally arranged. In several years, among 5,000 people, we heard of only one elopement. In the past, the search for a marriageable young woman has been much more an effort to find the best daughter-in-law and recruit to the women of the household than it has been to obtain a wife desired by the son. This is still to a large extent true, although the situation has slowly been eroding. Sons, now increasingly educated, are usually consulted in the choice of a bride. Furthermore, the growth of non-farming jobs and the possibility of migrating to the towns has weakened patriarchal control. Even daughters are increasingly consulted in matters of marriage, though the virtuous ones are not expected to deviate from their parents' wishes.

Nevertheless, and in contrast with nearby Sri Lanka, the arrangement of marriages is not yielding to love marriages. The main reason is fear that any weakening might encourage cross-caste marriage. Elopement is identified with cross-caste marriage and the only elopement during the research period was to achieve this end. Not only are marriages arranged solely between members of the same caste but also only between persons belonging to the same sub-caste. The latter restriction is beginning to weaken among some of the better educated migrants to the towns but there is little sign as yet of it doing so in the rural areas.

The main changes to marriage are probably not quantifiable. Education and the availability of jobs beyond the extended family farm has led to a softening of patriarchal control, a strengthening of spousal bonds, and some crystallisation out, at least emotionally, of the beginning of the nuclear family.

A stem family residential system means a balance between stem and nuclear residential families. All are subject to change. The stem family may become nuclear when the older generation dies, and the nuclear families will become stem and joint ones as the younger generation marries. In 1980 the long decline of mortality meant that more sons were surviving to adulthood and hence, the proportion of nuclear households was rising. At the present time, the fertility decline of the last quarter of a century is beginning to affect the numbers in the newly married generation and this will in time lead to a decline in the proportion of nuclear families. What is not changing is the situation where the older couple live with the married son, and consequently, when most families have only one son—as will inevitably happen as the fertility decline continues—most families will be stem ones. At present, the oldest son is the first to marry and he and his wife reside with his parents. When the next son marries, they all live together for a while as a joint-stem family before one married son—usually the eldest—moves out with his wife and children.

It is not these arrivals into and departures from the family household that cause fundamental change. That kind of change occurs when the household and its lands are divided. This division fundamentally changes relationships. It is a recognised and public event, facilitated in adjudication of a fair division not only by relatives but by important village persons who are known for their fair-minded and judicious approach. In legal theory, in modern India, this division of property, which really decides the inheritance, should have equal participation by both daughters and sons. In fact, in the divisions occurring in the research area around 1980, only seven per cent gave any land to daughters.

There is tremendous variation in the timing of partition. In the research area just over two-fifths of these divisions occurred when the father was still alive. In every case of this type the home remained with the son who was living with his parents and caring for them.

Many different events can lead to the division of the property. In the research area, one-third were simple life cycle events, usually the death of the father but sometimes the number and needs of married sons. Another quarter arose from the need to differentiate between migrating sons and those staying to farm. But fully 40 per cent arose from family problems, mostly incompatibility within the larger family. Among those investigated by the research project, three-eighths arose either from discord between brothers or between sons and fathers. The majority were blamed on incompatible daughters-in-law. It is true that younger wives have much to gain by becoming household heads. Most argue that it also economically benefits their husbands but the evidence seemed to be that the farming of undivided land was more efficient than that of divided land. The sons, it should be noted, had little distinction made between them, and their allocations of land were similar in amount.

The major potential for family change lies in the fertility transition. At the time of the research, one-third of married couples where the wife was of reproductive age were employing contraception, mainly female sterilization. The proportion is probably now around a half and today's young married coupies are likely not to have the traditional family of six children but rather three. Their children will probably have two. This has been achieved by a persistent government family planning program and by changes in social and economic circumstances which create a demand for family limitation.

The family planning program itself, at least in South India, is a force for change. Its workers approach the younger couple for decisions about family planning. It was the traditional role of the older couple to press for grandchildren, but, because the Indian government and establishment have taken a position on family planning, they have largely abdicated this role and have not interfered in the negotiations between family planning workers and their daughters-in-law. This in turn inevitably changes the nature of the family in terms of both intergenerational and interspousal relationships. The achievement of a small family, with a heightened concern that the children should survive and succeed, alters the relationships between children and their parents and between husbands and wives.

The reasons for fertility control also evidence changes in both family and society. Parents increasingly want their children to stay at school with the aim of eventually securing a non-farming job, preferably in the modern sector. They know they would benefit most if they had a large number of children succeeding in this way but they also know that they cannot keep several children at school at once. Their greatest hope of successfully educating any children to the point of employment in the modern sector is to restrict their number. It may be a dream but it does make acceptance of sterilization more likely.

Changes in the Family

A basic question that has often been asked is whether the joint or extended family in developing countries like India is breaking up resulting in the nuclear or conjugal family. Before answering the question, it would be helpful to examine briefly the changes in population, number of households and household size in the nine villages in southern Karnataka, which were studied in 1979-83 and 1995.

The total population of the nine villages was 4,773 in 1980 and 6,706 in 1995. Thus, population in the nine villages increased by about 41 per cent over the 15 years. But there is a difference in the rate of growth of population in the large village and the eight smaller villages. The growth rate was about 34 per cent in the former and 48 per cent in the latter. There are two possible explanations for the difference in the rate of growth of population. One is that a greater proportion of males from the large village than from the smaller villages migrated to urban centres, including Bangalore city. This explanation is supported by a higher growth rate of female population than male population in both the large village and the eight smaller villages. In the large village, the growth rate was about 30 per cent in the male population and 38 per cent in the female population. In the eight smaller villages, the growth rate was 47 per cent in the male population and 49 per cent in the female population. The other possible explanation is that a greater proportion of couples in the large village than in the eight smaller villages controlled their fertility. The large village is almost like a town. It is axiomatic that a greater proportion of couples in towns than in villages adopt contraception and control their fertility.

The total number of households in the nine villages increased from 786 in 1980 to 1,374 in 1995, registering a growth rate of about 75 per cent. The rate of growth of households, too, differed between the large village and the eight smaller villages. The growth rate was 72 per cent in the large village and 78 per cent in the eight smaller villages.

There is a perceptible decline in the average household size in both the large and smaller villages. The average household size in the nine villages was 6.1 in 1980 and 4.9 in 1995. The average household size declined from 6.2 to 4.8 in the large village and from 5.9 to 4.9 in the smaller villages over the 15 years. Out-migration, fertility control and nuclearisation of households appear to be three possible reasons for the decline in the average household size.

The large village was one of the villages covered by the Economic Survey of Mysore carried out as part of the 1941 Census program by the Government of Mysore. The population increased by 87 per cent between 1941 and 1980 and by 34 per cent between 1980 and 1995. The population increase between 1941 and 1980 can be explained by declining mortality and that between 1980 and 1995, in terms of declining fertility.

Between 1941 and 1980, the number of households increased (by 65 per cent), while average household size also grew (from 5.4 to 6.2). Therefore, no argument can be advanced that nuclearisation of households occurred during 1941-80. But between 1980 and 1995, the number of households increased (by 72 per cent) even as average household size dwindled (from 6.2 to 4.8). This gives strong support for the claim that fairly rapid nuclearisation of households occurred during the 15-year period from 1980 to 1995.

The proportions of different types of family in all the nine villages in 1980 and 1995 also lend support for the argument that nuclearisation of families has been taking place. The proportions of nuclear families were 59 per cent in 1980 and 64 per cent in 1995. Stem families accounted for 30 per cent in 1980 and 25 per cent in 1995. Joint families constituted five per cent in both 1980 and 1995. Joint-stem families accounted for five per cent in 1980 and four per cent in 1995. Thus, nuclearisation of families is certainly under way.

The Situation of the Old

A study of the elderly, that is, those who were 60 years and above, and living in the nine villages in the state of Karnataka was undertaken in early 1995 with the main objective of identifying cultural, social and behavioural determinants of their health status. These were the same nine villages in which the causes of demographic changes were studied over a period of five years from 1979 to 1983 (Caldwell, Reddy and Caldwell, 1988). This section presents the situation in which the elderly find themselves.

The total number of the elderly in the nine villages was 417. They accounted for 6.2 per cent of the total population. This is in the expected direction. Of the 417 elderly, 405 could be studied—208, or 51 per cent, were males and 197, or 49 per cent, were females. The age reporting by the elderly was surprisingly good. Those aged 65 and above accounted for four per cent, those aged 70 and above for 2.7 per cent and those aged 80 and above for 0.6 per cent.

The religious and caste composition of the elderly was not exactly the same as that of the population. The differences perhaps reflect differences in mortality conditions among different religious and caste groupings. Among the 405 elderly, Hindus accounted for 86 per cent, Muslims for 11 per cent, and Jains for three per cent. In the total population of the nine villages, Hindus constituted 77 per cent, Muslims 20 per cent, Jains three per cent and others one per cent. Of the Hindu elderly, nine per cent were Brahmins; five per cent were Lingayats; 38 per cent were Vokkaligas; 18 per cent belonged to Scheduled Castes; 10 per cent belonged to Scheduled Tribes; and 21 per cent belonged to other castes. In the total Hindu population of the nine villages, four per cent were Brahmins; six per cent were Lingayats; 27 per cent were Vokkaligas; 17 per cent belonged to Scheduled Castes; 8 per cent belonged to Scheduled Tribes and 38 per cent belonged to other castes.

The differences in the proportions widowed among the male and female elderly are striking. As high as 78 per cent of the female elderly and only 18 per cent of the male elderly were widowed. Of the subjects of a study in northern Karnataka, the proportions widowed were 78 per cent among the female elderly and 19 per cent among the male elderly (Nair, 1989:65). The differences are due to the wide age gap between spouses. In Karnataka, men are older by 8-10 years than their wives (Caldwell, Reddy and Caldwell, 1988: 168). What is also striking is that only three per cent of the male elderly, as compared with none of the female elderly, were never married; one per cent of the male elderly and two per cent of the female elderly were separated; and only one per cent of the female elderly were divorced. These findings show that marriage is universal and separations and divorces are rare.

As high as 73 per cent of the elderly were illiterate. But the proportions illiterate were 88 per cent among females and 58 per cent among males.

The elderly were not without assets. About 17 per cent of the male elderly and six per cent of the female elderly reported owning money and/or gold, while as many as 73 per cent of the male elderly and only 35 per cent of the female elderly reported owning the house in which they were living. Also, about two-thirds of the male elderly and one-third of the female elderly reported owning some agricultural land. These assets enable the elderly to live with their adult children and seek care from them.

In India in general and in rural India in particular, children, especially sons, are also an asset because they provide care for the elderly. About nine per cent of the male elderly and 16 per cent of the female elderly did not have living children. Their condition may be said to be critical if they did not have assets like money, gold, house and agricultural land.

About 10 per cent of the female elderly, as compared with four per cent of the male elderly, were living alone. About 71 per cent of the male elderly and 20 per cent of the female elderly were living with their spouses. The difference is due to the higher incidence of widowhood among females than among males. The proportions of males and females living with sons, both unmarried and married, were much higher than those living with daughters, both unmarried and married. Only when old parents do not have at least one living son can they live with married daughters. In so far as unmarried daughters are concerned, they live with parents rather than the contrary.

Although many old parents own property, especially house and agriculture land, they depend on their grown-up sons for the management of the property and all types of support, including economic support. About 45 per cent of the male elderly and only eight per cent of the female elderly were not economically dependent on others. The rest were either partially or fully dependent. It is said that women in India are economically dependent on men throughout their life: on fathers when they are young, on husbands when they are adults and on sons when they are old.

When asked whether youngsters of today have less respect for the elderly, about 63 per cent of the male elderly and 59 per cent of the female elderly answered in the affirmative. But about 71 per cent of the male elderly and 67 per cent of the female elderly expected sons to provide care for aged parents. None of them expected government to provide care for the old. A vast majority of both the male and female elderly thought that old parents should live with their sons. Onlv 16 per cent of males and 10 per cent of females thought that spouses are the best people to live with in old age.

About 53 per cent of males and 62 per cent of females attributed the standard of their living that they had managed to maintain either entirely or partially to help from their children. About 31 per cent of the male elderly and only 21 per cent of the female elderly attributed their standard of living to the assets they possessed.

When asked about their living conditions, about 61 pet cent of males and 47 per cent of females described them as comfortable, and about 36 per cent of the former arid 45 per cent of the latter as less than comfortable but not destitute. Only a little over two per cent of males and six per cent of females described their living conditions as destitute. (The proportions describing their living conditions as destitute however appear to be underestimates).

It is rather surprising that about 81 per cent of the male elderly and 46 per cent of the female elderly described themselves as heads of the households. Many of them might be *de jure* heads, while their sons acted as *de facto* heads.

The respondents were asked whether they were being treated by their children as they expected. About 71 per cent of the male elderly and 61 per cent of the female elderly answered in the affirmative. In fact, 18 per cent of males and 21 per cent of females reported that they were being treated by their children better than they expected. However, about 10 per cent of both males and females reported that they were being treated by their children worse than they expected. Thus, the recent apprehensions that there is a decline in the traditional filial piety appear to be unfounded. The family continues to provide care for the elderly. "India—at least, rural south India—has little in the way of crisis arising from aging" (Caldwell, Reddy and Caldwell 1988: 193).

The Future

Some changes in the family are inevitable either as a result of continuing demographic change or because sufficient momentum has already been established. Demographic change will lead to the rise in the proportion of residential stem families. Social momentum will lead to ever fewer marriages between relatives, especially those between uncles and nieces.

Some changes will not occur in the near future. Caste will remain important in rural India and cross-caste marriages are unlikely to become common. As long as it is felt necessary to avoid them, a very considerable degree of parental influence over marriage is likely to remain.

The most significant transformation is likely to be in the relationships between young husbands and wives and between young parents and their children. In the short run, the latter may easily be the greatest. Parents will inevitably worry more about two children than six, will be more determined to educate them and will look more to them for affection. This concentration on children must bring husbands and wives into a more companionate relationship. This will inevitably be facilitated by a spousal gap of five instead often years.

There are Constitutional, legal and social provisions to provide care for the elderly in India. Article 41 of the Constitution enjoins on the State to make effective provision within the limits of its economic capacity and development for public assistance in case of unemployment, old-age, sickness, disablement, etc. But this is more true in theory than in practice. Many State governments provide a meagre monthly old-age pension ranging from Rs. 50 to Rs.75 to each of the destitute aged, maintain a few old-age homes for the destitute aged and provide grant-in-aid to voluntary organisations which maintain such homes.

Section 125(d) of the Criminal Procedure Code (1973) makes it incumbent on a person having sufficient means to maintain his father and mother who are unable to maintain themselves, and on getting proof of any neglect or refusal, a first class magistrate may order such person to make a monthly allowance of Rs. 500 per parent. In recent years, court judgments have interpreted the provision to include daughters. The Hindu Adoption and Maintenance Act, 1956, also recognises the obligation of a person to maintain his or her aged or disabled parents (Sec. 30(3)). So far very few old parents have invoked these legal provisions for their maintenance by their adult children, perhaps because there was no necessity.

The high proportion of stem families in India reflects the persistence of traditional filial obligation to parents. Customarily, old parents live with the eldest son. In the stem families, it is the eldest son's wife who provides care for her parents-in-law if they are in need of it. In spite of recent apprehensions that there is a decline in the traditional filial piety, the family continues to provide care for its elderly members. It is, therefore, wise for the Central and State governments to maintain the elderly at home by providing a relief in taxation (Raina, 1988: 169) or a sufficient monthly allowance to those who support their elderly parents or relatives.

NOTE

1. Although nuclear families accounted for the majority of the total families, the population living in them accounted for less than half of the total population. For example, in the nine villages studied in southern Karnataka, although nuclear households accounted for 59 per cent, only 40 per cent of the population at any given time were found living in them (Caldwell, Reddy and Caldwell, 1988: 187). The reasons are not far to seek: by definition, a nuclear family comprised fewer members than a stem or joint or joint-stem family.

REFERENCES

Caldwell, John C. *et al.* (1972). *Manual for Surveys of Fertility and Family Planning: Knowledge, Attitudes and Practices.* New York: The Population Council.

Caldwell, John C. and Caldwell, Pat. (1992). 'Family Systems: Their Viability and Vulnerability', in Eliza Berquo and Peter Xenos, eds., *Family Systems and Cultural Change* (pp. 46-66). Oxford: Clarendon Press.

Caldwell, John C, Reddy, P.H. and Caldwell, Pat. (1988). *The Causes of Demographic Change: Experimental Research in South India.* Madison: University of Wisconsin Press.

Gait, E.A. (1913). *Census of India.* Calcutta: Superintendent of Government Printing.

Goode, William J. (1968). Foreword. In M.S. Gore, *Urbanization and Family Change.* Bombay: Popular Prakashan.

Gore, M.S. (1968). *Urbanization and Family Change.* Bombay: Popular Prakashan.

Kapadia, K.M. (1966). *Marriage and Family in India.* Third edn. Bombay: Oxford University Press.

Nair, P.S. (1989). The Aged in Rural India: A Study of the Socio-economic and Health Profile. In S.N. Singh, M.K. Premi, P.S. Bhatia and A. Bose, (Eds.), *Population Transition in India.* New Delhi: B.R. Publishing Corporation, pp. 63-70.

Raina, B.L. (1988). *Population Policy.* New Delhi: B.R. Publishing Corporation.

Ramu, G.N. (1991). 'Changing Family Structure and Fertility Patterns: an Indian Case' *Journal of Asian and African Studies.* 26 (3-4): 189-206.

Rao, N. Baskara, Kulkarni, P.M. and Rayappa, P. Hanumantha. (1986). *Determinants of Fertility Decline: A Study of Rural Karnataka.* New Delhi: South Asia Publishers.

Reddy, P.H. (1978). 'Family Structure and Fertility', *Social Change.* 8(1), 24-32.

Reddy, P.H. (1991). 'Family Structure and Age at Marriage: Evidence from a South Indian Village'. *Journal of Asian and African Studies.* 26 (3-4): 253-266.

Wilson, Chris and Dyson, Tim. (1992). 'Family Systems and Cultural Change: Perspectives from Past and Present', in Eliza Berquo and Peter Xenos, eds, *Family Systems and Cultural Change.* Oxford: Clarendon Press, pp. 31-45.

Chapter 15

Family Care for Rural Elderly in the Midst of Rapid Social Change: The Case of Thailand

John Knodel and *Chanpen Saengtienchal*

Throughout Asia, as indeed in most of the developing world, the family has been the traditional social institution for the care and support of its elderly members. This informal system of support, with little or no governmental assistance and minimal market involvement, continues to be the primary system in operation today (World Bank 1994). Besides spouses, the elderly's children and children-in-law typically play central support and care-giving roles within a family. Indeed, elderly generally live and work with their children throughout Asia (Knodel and Debavalya 1992; Mason 1992; Knodel 1995). This arrangement also permits the elderly themselves to contribute in a variety of important ways to the maintenance and functioning of the household.[1] Under current conditions, probably no other aspect of the familial support system facilities intergenerational exchanges better or meets the wide range of the needs of the elderly more fully than coresidential living arrangements.

Rapid social, economic and demographic changes under way have profound implications for the circumstances under which the future elderly will live. A number of forces associated with socioeconomic development processes are generally seen as contributing to a weakening of family support for elderly members. These include urbanisation and the associated exodus of young adults from rural areas, expanding employment of women outside the home, and increasing exposure of the younger generation to westernised values, especially through the mass media and educational systems (Cowgill 1986; Mason 1992; Tout 1989). Moreover, reduced fertility and prolonged longevity are viewed as further undermining the family's ability to adequately cope with the needs of the elderly generation. Meanwhile, Asian and other societies of the developing world are facing unprecedented increases in the absolute numbers of older persons and, in many cases, unprecedented increases in their relative population share (Jones 1994).

Many policy makers and scholars alike believe it is in the government's as well the future elderly's interest to preserve this familial system of care and support and to assist in its adaptation to the on going process of socioeconomic and demographic change. They thus view with alarm the potential erosion of familial care and support as a likely consequence of strains emanating from the processes of social, economic and demographic change currently underway (Kosberg and Garcia 1991; Tout 1989). Most of the concerns expressed, however, have been based largely on impressions and theoretical preconceptions about the effects of socioeconomic development rather than systematic evidence about the actual impact. Indeed, some scholars are beginning to question whether the traditional support system is in fact as vulnerable as is commonly believed (Hashimoto, Kendig and Coppard 1992).

Despite its potential importance, research on the elderly and their support systems in developing countries has only recently begun. Quantitative documentation of the current baseline situation is now beginning to accumulate but systematic qualitative research into the situation is rare. Our analysis examines the situation in Thailand, focusing primarily on the rural elderly. In particular, it assesses the extent to which the substantial socioeconomic development that has characterised Thailand over several decades has affected the familial system of support there, especially the central feature of intergenerational coresidence.

Sources of Data

Thailand is fortunate in having a substantial amount of data available for assessing the social situation of the elderly. In our study, a variety of data sources are utilised to examine the family support system. Quantitative information on living arrangements is derived from the two most recent censuses (taken in 1980 and 1990), two general surveys of the elderly, and an tally of living arrangements based on an intensive study of several local rural communities. The first survey, known as SECAPT (Socioeconomic Consequences of the Aging Population in Thailand), was national in coverage and interviewed over 3000 elderly in 1986 (Chayovan, Wongsith, and Saengtienchai 1988). The second survey, conducted in 1990, interviewed approximately 1200 persons aged 60 and over, and was quasi-national in scope, covering one province in each of the four regions of Thailand. We refer to it as the WHO survey, since it was sponsored by the World Health Organization as part of a five country study of Aging in South East Asia (Andrews, no date).

Additional quantitative data on living arrangements comes from an intensive study we conducted in 1994 of support arrangements in four rural communities in two provinces, one in the Central Region (Kanchanaburi) and one in the Northeast (Surin).[2] One of the four communities studied was purposively selected because it was featured in a 1992 newspaper article focusing on the desertion of the rural elderly resulting from rural out-migration of young adults (Charasdamrong 1992) In each of the four communities, detailed information was collected for all resident elderly using household registration forms, key informants, and interviews with some of the elderly themselves. Extensive cross checking was done between these sources in order to gain as accurate a picture as possible of actual living arrangements. In addition, approximately 40 elderly were interviewed in-depth on matters of their support and living arrangements, so that this data source yielded a combination of quantitative and qualitative information on the elderly in these communities.

Qualitative data on attitudes, opinions and perceived behaviour pertaining to the care and support of elderly are provided by a series of focus group discussions conducted during 1990 and 1991 with Thai elderly and their adult children throughout Thailand.[3] The discussions were recorded and fully transcribed in the original Thai language. In addition, the complete set of transcripts was translated into English. Both Thai and English transcripts were formatted for use with the Ethnograph software program, to expedite our systematic review of the content (see Knodel 1993). In presenting the findings, illustrative verbatim quotations from the focus groups are included. In each quotation, the location and type of group or respondent from which it is drawn is indicated.

Results

A. Quantitative Data on Living Arrangements

Evidence presented in Table 1 from the censuses and surveys described above indicate that, despite the remarkable social and economic development that has engulfed Thailand over recent decades, a crucial aspect of familial care of the elderly in Thailand, namely coresidence with their children, is still very much the rule. Moreover, a comparison of the Thai census results for 1980 and 1990 provide an unusual opportunity to test whether living arrangements of the elderly are in fact changing over time. The census results are limited to elderly women because the information on which the results shown are based was collected in connection with fertility data and hence not for men.[4] Few other countries in Asia, or elsewhere in the developing world, actually have such truly comparable data on intergenerational coresidence for two points in time.

If all elderly women are considered (including those with no living children), 77% lived with a child in 1990 compared to 76% a decade earlier. If only women with living children are considered, the percentage coresident with a child increases to 82 percent for both 198Q and 1990.[5] Thus the census results make clear that coresidence of elderly women with their children remained stable during the decade of the 1980s. The fact that during this very same decade, social and economic development was particularly rapid and pervasive in Thailand adds particular significance to this finding within the context of the debate about the deleterious impact of such forces on familial care systems for the elderly (Kulick and Wilson 1992).

The levels of coresidence shown by the census are almost identical to those found by the two special surveys of the elderly during the same time period. Both the 1986 SECAPT survey and the 1990 WHO survey found that 77% of elderly overall coresided with one or more of their children. Although not shown in Table 1, both surveys indicated similar levels of coresidence for elderly men and women. In the case of the 1986 survey, 77% of each sex were coresident while for the 1990 survey, coresidence was slightly higher for elderly men than women (78% versus 76%). Hence even though the census results refer only to women, there is little reason to suspect that the experience of elderly men is any different with respect to the stability in the extent of coresidence. The two surveys also indicate levels of coresidence similar to the census when consideration is limited to elderly with living children. All of the data sets are consistent in showing that at least four out of five elderly Thais who have living children live with at least one of them. Table 1 also shows coresidence by type of area of residence. In both the censuses and the surveys, there is little rural-urban difference in the levels of coresidence among elderly. These results are contrary to the common assumption that urban life styles undermine filial piety and family care of the elderly.

As high as the levels of co-residence revealed by the censuses and surveys are, they understate the true level of the phenomenon. This is due to the narrow definition of co-residence necessitated by use of such data. One limitation of household surveys and censuses in Thailand is the general convention of treating dwelling units with separate addresses (house numbers) as separate households in accordance with the government's household registration system. As a result, coresidence in the same household is of necessity defined rather narrowly to mean living together in the same dwelling unit. Situations where elderly parents and children live in separate dwellings but belong to a common cluster of houses that are interdependent clearly occur in Thailand, especially in rural areas. In most respects, such arrangements can serve the same functional purposes as more narrowly defined coresidence for meeting the needs of the elderly (Cowgill 1972; Tuchrello 1989). Thus defining coresidence as living together within the same officially designated household (i.e. dwelling unit) understates the extent to which the living arrangements of elderly and their families are intertwined.

Both the 1986 SECAPT and 1990 WHO surveys of elderly provide indirect information from questions on frequency of contact with children that gives insight into this phenomenon. In cases of non coresident elderly, daily contact no doubt reflects a close proximity of residences and affords the adult child the opportunity to provide a variety of services to the elderly parent (and vice versa). In many cases, it probably reflects the fact that the elderly and their children live in related dwelling units that in some sense form a type broader multiple household in which various responsibilities are shared. It is not uncommon in villages, for example, for neighboring adult children to bring cooked food to their elderly parents on a routine basis.

As Table 1 shows, 88 percent of all elderly in the SECAPT survey and 84 percent in the WHO survey either live together with a child or are in daily contact with at least one child. If consideration is restricted to elderly with at least one child, both surveys indicate that 91 percent of elderly are in this situation. In some respects this is probably a more valid estimate of coresidence since in many cases there may be little qualitative difference in the nature of support received from children by elderly parents who coreside in the same dwelling unit and elderly who appear to live in separate households but are in daily contact with one or more adult children. Interestingly, this combined measure of coresidence and/or daily contact is slightly higher for rural than urban elderly in both surveys. In the case of the SECAPT survey, these results are the reverse of the slightly more common narrowly defined coresidence among urban elderly. Hence the higher percent of urban elderly that are literally coresident is more than compensated for by the higher percentage of rural elderly who, although not literally coresident, have daily contact with their children. These findings probably reflect differences in land availability and housing styles between urban and rural areas. Having separate dwelling units either within the same compound or nearby is more feasible in rural villages than in towns or cities where land and housing prices make such arrangements prohibitive for many.

Since the SECAPT survey included a listing of all members of each sample household, including information on relationship to head, it is possible to examine the living arrangements of those elderly who were not coresiding with one of their own children. One complication in determining the household composition, however, arises from the fact that the same Thai word (laan) is used to refer to a grandchild, nephew or niece, thus making it difficult to distinguish between them. Moreover, the term is sometimes used generically for younger relatives and thus on occasion encompasses more distant relatives

TABLE 1. Indicators of intergenerational coresidence, Thailand

	Total			Elderly with living children		
	Total	Rural	Urban	Total	Rural	Urban
% of Women 60+Who coreside with child						
1980 census	76	76	78	82	81	86
1990 census	77	77	76	82	82	84
%of elderly who coreside with child						
1986 SECAPT Survey	77	77	77	80	79	82
1990 WHO Survey	77	79	75	83	85	81
% of elderly who coreside and/or see child daily						
1986 SECAPT Survey	88	89	82	91	92	88
1990 WHO Survey	84	86	82	91	93	89

Sources: Knodel, Chayovan and Siriboon, 1992; Knodel, Chayovan and Saengtienchai, 1994; Knodel, Saengtienchai and Obiero.

of the younger generation. Despite this limitation, information on age and occupation that was also included in the household listing can be used roughly to distinguish cases where a younger generation relative was likely a dependent in the household from cases where he or she was able to contribute economically to the household and/or provide care-giving services for the elderly members.

Several indicators of living arrangements of non coresident elderly are presented in Table 2. The results make clear that elderly who do not live with their own children live in a diverse set of household situations. Slightly less than a fifth (18.8%) live in solitary (i.e. one person) households. Just over half of non coresident elderly live with a spouse, although in many cases the couple is living by themselves. If the almost 30% who live only with a spouse is combined with elderly in solitary households, we see that just under half of Thai elderly who do not coreside with a child live on their own while slightly more than half live with other household members. Overall, almost half of non coresident Thai elderly live with either a laan or child-in-law, primarily the former. Thus in the vast majority of cases where other household members are present, at least one is a younger generation relative. In some of these cases the younger relative is either economically active or an adult or both, while in others he/she may be a dependent, often a grandchild being cared for on a long term basis by the elderly person or couple.[6]

Results in Table 2 also indicate some differences between the living arrangements of childless elderly and those of non-coresident elderly parents. Childless elderly are less likely to live in solitary households and much less likely to live with a spouse (reflecting the substantial proportion among the childless who never married or whose marriage ended prematurely) but are much more likely to live with persons other than younger generation relatives (e.g. siblings). Moreover, childless elderly are not only more likely than non coresident elderly parents to live with a younger generation relative but when they do, the younger generation relative is much more likely to be an adult or to be economically active.

The impression that the family takes care of childless elderly merits some qualification in light of the fact that the SECAPT survey excluded elderly in collective households and that childless elderly are likely disproportionately represented among collective households. Results from the 1980 census indicates that only 1.7 percent of the Thai population aged 60 and over live in such households, primarily in temples where presumably they are Buddhist monks or nuns (Chayovan, Knodel and Siriboon 1990). Virtually no elderly reside in nursing homes or special homes for the elderly (Pichyangkura and Singhajend 1991).

TABLE 2: Thai Elderly not Coresiding with a Child by Living Arrangements and whether Childless

Living arrangement	Total	Childless	Has a child
% Live alone	18.8	13.4	19.8
% Live with spouse	52.1	28.8	56.3
% Live with spouse only	29.5	19.8	31.3
% Live with child-in-law	1.6	1.0	1.7
% live with 'Laan'	46.0	53.1	44.7
% Live with economically active 'Laan'	25.4	42.7	22.3
% Live with 'Laan' age 18+	24.7	47.6	20.6
% Live with any other person	21.8	54.0	16.0
No. of cases (Unweighted)	753	120	633

Note: Except for 'live alone' and 'live with spouse only' the categories shown are not mutually exclusive and thus the percentages do not add to 100.
Source: Siriboon and Knodel, 1994 (from the 1986 SECAPT Survey).

The living arrangements of the elderly in the four rural communities selected for intensive study are shown in Table 3 in some detail. Consistent with the more general survey results discussed above, very few elderly reside alone or only with their spouse. Overall, over 80 percent live with at least one child. As indicated above, one of the four communities, Community C, was purposely selected because it was featured in a newspaper article as exemplifying desertion of rural elderly due to out-migration to cities. Thus it is understandable that, of the four communities studied, Community C is characterised by the highest percentage (14%) of elderly who either live alone or only with spouse and the lowest percentage (75%) who coreside with a child. Nevertheless, even in this purposively selected community, the large majority still live with a child and almost half of the rest are in some living arrangement in which there is someone else in the household. Moreover, as discussed below, in only a few of the cases where elderly live alone or as a solitary couple do they appear actually to be deserted by their children or relatives.

TABLE 3: Living Arrangements of Elderly in Four Rural Communities

Living arrangement	Central Province		Northeast Province		Total
	Community A	Community B	Community C	Community D	
Couple alone	5.3	2.2	8.8	4.5	4.4
All alone	1.8	2.6	4.9	1.5	2.7
With ever-married child*	57.0	45.5	62.7	55.2	52.3
With single child only	32.5	38.4	11.8	31.3	31.4
Other arrangement	3.5	11.2	11.8	7.5	9.3
Total percent	100	100	100	100	100
Total N	114	268	102	67	551

* Includes some with one or more coresident single children.

Overall, less than 3% or only 15 of the 551 elderly in the four communities live alone. Among these, 7 live next to at least one married child and thus for most practical purposes have almost the same opportunity to participate in support exchanges with children as elderly who are literally coresident with a child. In 3 other cases the elderly live next to relatives and thus are not isolated from the family network of interaction and exchanges of assistance. In one more case, the elderly widow has only one son who lives in Bangkok but who provides some support and comes back to visit occasionally. In another case, a widow has an only son who stays with her on an occasional basis but, according to informants, drinks heavily, provides little assistance, and is more of a burden than a help to his elderly mother. The remaining 3 cases of elderly living alone appear to be truly deserted by their children and live off begging or offerings from their neighbors. For them the prevailing system of family support has failed. Two of these cases are in the purposively selected community as is the previously described case of the woman with the occasionally present but irresponsible son. One of the two case had been featured in the newspaper article.[7]

In addition to the elderly who lived alone, others lived only with their spouse. Overall, just over 4% or 24 of the 551 elderly were in this situation in the four intensively studied communities. These 24 individuals made up a total of 13 different households (11 elderly couples and 2 elderly with non-elderly spouses, i.e. below age 60). Again, some of these cases (5 out of the 13 households) actually lived next to married children and in another case a married child lived just a few houses away. In another case, the husband had a government pension from his time working in Bangkok and moved back with his wife, but no children, to a rural area where they have many family connections. Since the pension provided an adequate source of support for their modest lifestyle and they interacted frequently with neighboring relatives they were quite satisfied with their situation and did not perceive themselves as being deserted by their children.

In the remaining 6 households of elderly living only with a spouse, contact with children seems to be at best occasional and support modest or absent. In at least one case the couple appears clearly to have been deserted by their children. Nevertheless, even for some of these 6 cases, their lack of coresident or neighboring children may not be permanent and may reflect an assessment by those involved that, for the time being, the couple is able to fend for themselves. At some later pointy if the elderly's health fails or one of the spouses dies, children may return or take in parents. This of course can only be a matter of conjecture but the possibility needs to be borne in mind before all these cases can be said to represent failures of on the part of their children to care for their elderly parents. Other research indicates that the living arrangements of Thai parents as they age are closely linked to the life course of stages the couple and their children (Knodel, Chayovan and Siriboon 1991).

As the above analysis implies, in a number of the cases where elderly appear to live alone or only with spouse in a literal accounting of their living arrangements, they were in fact in situations consistent with the normatively sanctioned family support system. The intensive study of the four rural communities, however, also revealed the reverse situation. In some cases where the literal pattern of coresidence existed, the situation was nevertheless not one in which the needs of the elderly are being met by the younger generation in the normatively prescribed manner. For example, in at least 5 cases, the coresident child was handicapped, retarded or blind and had to be cared for by the elderly rather than the reverse. In at least another 5 cases, the elderly coresided with grand children who were minors and in their charge, sometimes with minimal or no support from the children's parents. Finally in at least 2 cases, the coresident child was clearly irresponsible leaving the elderly parents to fend for themselves, through begging or other efforts to support themselves.

All in all, the general picture of rural elderly provided by the intensive study of the four rural communities revealed a family system of support for the elderly that continues to function in the vast majority of cases. While cases exist in which children have deserted their elderly parents, they are rare. In most cases where children do not coreside or live next to the elderly, other relatives are available, either in the household of nearby. The persistence of a family support system, however, does not mean that the material well being of the elderly is adequate, however, as rural poverty is indeed pervasive and debilitating for many families affecting both older and younger members. For some families the poverty is partially ameliorated by contributions and remittances from members who have gone to the city for work. In these cases, the rural to urban migration of children can contribute to rather than detract from the elderly parent's well being.

B. Qualitative Data: Evidence from Focus Groups

As is increasing recognised by researchers examining aging issues in any depth on a cross-national basis, understanding the impact of socioeconomic structural change cannot be divorced from the cultural context in which the changes are occurring (Hashimoto 1991). In the case of Thailand, the persistence of coresidence during a period of major social and economic transformation, can be best accounted for by the strongly ingrained sense of obligations and gratitude of children to parents that are firmly grounded in the cultural values. The focus group discussions with Thai elderly and their adult children conducted during 1990 and 1991 make clear that care and support by adult children for elderly parents involves a strong sense of moral obligation that provides the normative basis for the prevailing pattern of living arrangements. Participants in groups in all regions spontaneously mentioned that parents deserve to be taken care of in their old age by their children as a form of repayment for bearing and raising the children. Moreover, this sense of moral obligation is shared by both older and younger generations and transcends economic status as well as rural-urban residence.

This shared value of parent repayment includes an understanding that at least one child should live with the elderly parents and thus underlies the current pattern of living arrangements. Although, repaying parents is viewed as a continual obligation that starts when the children are old enough to provide meaningful help, it is the care and support provided by children when their parents are too old to take care of themselves which is viewed as the culmination of this process of repayment. The following quotes from focus group participants, reveal the sentiment of most Thais.

Mr. Pui: Parents are supreme since they gave birth to us. We have to take care of them until death do us part.

[Central region, elderly, low socioeconomic status]

Mr. Khummee: We raised them. If we can't work anymore, it is their duty to the care of us.

Mr. Chanha: Since we have children, we live with them... They have to care for us since we are their parents and brought them up. They must be grateful...

[Northeast, elderly, high socioeconomic status]

Mr. Triam: Parents cared for children since they were babies so children must care for parents in return...

[Northeast, adult children, Low socioeconomic status]

The strong normative expectation of children taking care of parents in their old age revealed in the focus groups is also borne out by survey data. For example in a national survey of persons aged 15-44 conducted in 1986, 96% of respondent indicated that in general, elderly should live with children and 87% indicated that they themselves expected to live with their children (Chayovan, 1992). In Thailand, the ideal living arrangement for elderly is the stem family in which one adult child remains with his or her spouse to live together with the parents. This stem family arrangement, however, is the eventual form that emerges over time in the course of a dynamic process of household change as parents age (Foster, 1975). Single children may move out to find work outside of the home community, children who many may move out to form their own household and others may return to the parental household after some time away. Generally the goal of the elderly is to have one child remain as the designated care giver but this final stem family arrangement often does not emerge until the elderly are at more advanced ages. Many parents begin their elderly years with several children coresident. Over time, however, children move out until only one is typically left. Once this child marries and has children, a stem family structure results with the elderly parents, a married adult child with spouse and the grandchildren living together. This is reflected in comments by focus group participants as well as in the SECAPT survey results indicating that over 90 percent of coresident elderly whose children have all married live with only one of their adult children.

Mr. Loar: If there are many children, each goes to live separately but one of them must remain with the parents. It could be anyone. Usually the youngest daughter stays.

[Central, elderly, mixed socioeconomic status]

Mr. Paitoon: Either with many or few (children), there must be one left to care for parents... It doesn't matter how many children you have since only one will be left to care for the parents. Its the one lives with or nearby the parents.

[Northeast; adult children, high socioeconomic status]

A vast majority of both the elderly and the adult focus group participants believed that, in a family, one child will remain to coreside with the parents when other children have left home to establish their own family in a separate household or to move elsewhere to work. Out-migration by young adult children from rural villages for the purpose of seeking jobs and/or higher education is viewed as common and many villagers understand that it often results in permanent departures. The participants recognise that increasingly nowadays not only are economic opportunities for young adults generally concentrated in the cities but that this is particularly the case for those who receive secondary or higher education. Nevertheless focus group participants, especially the elderly ones, do not necessarily view the situation with alarm.

Choen: Some children move their families away from their native home. They move away and parents want them to stay here (in the home village). If parents can give them the land, they'll stay close to parents.

Moderator: If there are many children, with whom do parents want to be?

Niem: It's doesn't matter. Whoever is still home, parents are with that one... The one with me is the youngest. She is still with me now after getting married and other children moved out. [South, elderly, higher socioeconomic status]

Concerns about having no one to take care of the elderly as a result of out migration of children differ somewhat between the elderly and the adult children participants. For the elderly who are already in need of assistance, few fear that the process of out-migration of adult children will lead to their desertion since they are already in an arrangement that they do not imagine as altering, in which they live with or next to at least one child. They view the fact that at some point children will move out to have their own family as a normal phase of the family life cycle but they also view the fact that at least one child will stay behind with the parents as an equally normal circumstance. For these elderly, there is no doubt that their security and well being depends on the presence of the coresident child or the one who lives nearby. Indeed it is exactly for this reason that they view it as unlikely that their caretaker will leave the village, at least without some making some alternative arrangement for their care. It would be too serious a breech of the normatively mandated responsibility of the children for this to happen except in the most unusual of circumstances.

For the adult participants, the situation in old age is less certain. First of all, they have not yet reached the stage in their life in which assistance is currently needed from children of the type required by dependent elderly. At the same time they are well aware of the social and economic changes taking place that potentially threaten the way of life that up until the present served as the context for the family based care system that traditionally has provided security in old age. Virtually all Thai villages have witnessed the exodus of a large number of young people to work in cities and or to seek higher education, generally not to return except for visits. Some adults participants also complained that the current way of life has widened the distance between the parents and children.

It is thus understandable why some adult participants fear that the extent and nature of care that children provide elderly parents in the future may change for the worse. Nevertheless, most of the adult children participants believed that in their old age there will be a child to live with or live nearby as it used to be in their parents' generation. They see it as unlikely to have all children out-migrate without anyone staying behind or at least eventually returning to take care of the parents in their old age.

M: Do you think you will receive the same kind of support as you are giving to your parents?

Kane: We will receive less support. People tend to go away from home to earn their living.

Bunkwang: Yes, they go away to work.

Anonymous: They tend to be away from the parents.

Noolom: Most children nowadays hardly stay home when they finish school.

Sa-iem: They go to Bangkok to earn their living.

M: Do you think that the tendency will affect the support parents will be given?

Swangchit: They dare not leave us. They will have to care for us the same way we cared for our parents since they dare not to desert us.

Udom: Even with fewer children, there must be one to care for parents. [Northeast, adult children, high socioeconomic status]

There is no doubt that large numbers of rural young adults leave their home communities for work elsewhere, particularly in the cities. Assumptions that this will lead to a serious erosion of coresidence because no children will be left in the home community, however, have been premature because they ignore the fact that migration decisions are unlikely to be made independent of the children's concern for the care of parents. Thus it is very likely that in many families, out-migration of young adults is contingent on at least one child being left with the parents, especially at the stage where the parents are elderly and in need of assistance. The fact that parents often maintain some control over the property and that the coresident care taker in a stem family arrangement is usually rewarded with an extra share probably helps reinforce the system. However, it appears that this operates in the a more general normative context in which children are willing to accept responsibility for their elderly parents' welfare primarily out of a sense of affection and moral obligation (Knodel, Saengtienchai and Sittitrai 1995).

Conclusions

Is Thailand an exception to a more general third world trend towards the erosion of family care for societies elderly members? Without more solid data based on nationally representative sources that directly bear on the issues of concern, it is too soon to make any definitive judgement. There are some relatively reliable indications of declines in coresidence patterns in Korea and Taiwan, but given the extraordinary extent of economic and social development that has occurred in these two societies and indeed that has virtually moved them into the ranks of the world's industrialised economies, the reductions in coresidence seem remarkably modest (Veinstein *et al.*, 1990; Lee, Lin, and Chang, 1993; Kim and Choe 1992). Moreover, without additional information, it would be premature to assume these changes imply abdication of family responsibility by offspring (Suh 1992).

In settings such as Taiwan and Korea, sharply rising family incomes could result in the purchase of privacy by the better off who nevertheless remain physically and emotionally close to their children. Likewise, the maintenance of coresidence, such as in Thailand, does not guarantee that the quality of care-giving remains the same. Again, more in-depth systematic research is required before conclusions can be drawn. What is clear, however, is that allegations of the declining strength and deterioration of familial support and care systems in the third world await more solid and systematic documentation before they can be assumed to be a reality. Thailand's experience to date suggests that cultural constraints may well prevent the impending disaster that those raising alarms foresee.

NOTES

1. See special issue of *Journal of Cross Cultural Gerontology* (vol 10, nos 1 and 2, April 1995) on Focus Group Research on the Living Arrangements of the Elderly in Asia.
2. The two authors of this paper carried out the intensive survey as part of a collaborative arrangement between the University of Michigan and the Institute of Population Studies, Chulalongkorn University, to conduct research on ageing under the project 'Rapid Demographic Change and the Welfare of the Elderly'.
3. A total of 26 focus groups were conducted in Bangkok and in rural areas of all four regions of Thailand by the Institute of Population Studies in 1990 and 1991 in connection with a project coordinated by the University of Michigan on 'Comparative Study of Elderly in Four Asian Countries'.
4. The 1980 and 1990 Thai censuses are somewhat unusual in that they included direct questions about the number of a woman's children who live in the same household as she, the number who live elsewhere, and the number who died. Although this information was collected for the purpose of estimating fertility and mortality, it can also easily be used to examine coresidence with children. This information was solicited only for women who had ever been married. In the present analysis, women who never married are assumed to have no living children, a quite reasonable assumption in the context of Thailand.
5. In some cases, the number of own children living in the woman's household, or the number living outside the household, or both, are unknown. (Note that the census respondent can be any responsible member of the household and is not necessarily the woman herself). Women for whom the number of own children inside the household is unknown are excluded from analysis. This represents 7.3 per cent of women in 1980 and 3.0 per cent in 1990. However, women for whom the number of children living with the woman is reported (even if reported as 0) but for whom the number of living outside the household is unknown, are included. This represents 11.8 per cent of women

in 1980 and 6.6 per cent in 1990. In effect, this results in slightly underestimating the percentage coresident for women with at least one living child as all women with 0 given as the number of children inside the household and an unknown number of children outside the household are included in the denominator even though in some cases they may have no living children. Excluding such women from this calculation would increase coresidence from 82 per cent to 83 per cent for both censuses.

6. The situation where the elderly take care of a dependent grandchild whose parents are absent is sometimes referred to as the 'skip generation' pattern (Hashimoto 1991). Qualitative evidence from focus group discussions in Thailand with both elderly and adult children confirm that this pattern is well recognised among Thais (Knodel, Saengtienchai and Sittitrai 1995). Modifications of the skip generation pattern can also occur among coresident elderly when some of the grandchildren present are children of absent siblings rather than of the coresident child of the elderly.
7. According to villagers, the newspaper team spent only a few hours in the community taking photos and briefly talking with a few of them. Apparently, the reporter, having already decided on the main theme of the article, namely that rural elderly are being deserted by children who are forced off the land by poverty and drawn to the city by work, went looking for such examples. Our intensive systematic approach to studying the elderly in the village, which took about a week, reveals that while such cases do exist, they are quite exceptional.

REFERENCES

Andrews, Gary (Ed.) (Undated). 'Ageing in South East Asia: A Five Country Study'. The Centre for Ageing studies, The Flinders University of South Australia.

Charasdamrong, Prasong. (1992). 'The Misery of Those Left Behind'. *Bangkok Post,* 10 May 1992.

Chayovan, Napaporn. (1992). 'Support of Parents and Attitudes towards the Elderly among Adults in Thailand'. Report 195/35. Bangkok: Institute of Population Studies (in Thai).

Chayovan, Napapom, Malinee Wongsith, and Chanpen Saengtienchai. (1988). 'Socio-Economic Consequences of the Ageing of the Population in Thailand: Survey Findings'. Bangkok: Institute of Population Studies, Chulalongkorn University.

Chayovan, Napaporn, John Knodel and Siriwan Siriboon. (1990). 'Thailand's Elderly Population: A Demographic and Social Profile Based on Official Statistical Sources'. Comparative Study of the Elderly in Asia, Research Report No. 90-2, Population Studies Center, University of Michigan.

Cowgill, Donald O. (1972). The Role and Status of the Aged in Thailand. Pp 91-101 in D.O. Cowgill and L.D. Holmes *eds., Aging and Modernisation.* New York: Appleton-Century-Crofts.

Foster, B. (1975). Continuity and Change in Rural Thai Family Structure. *Journal of Anthropological Research.* 31:34-50.

Hashimoto, Akiko. (1991). Living Arrangements of the Aged in Seven Developing Countries: A Preliminary Analysis. *Journal of Crass-Cultural Gerontology.* 6 ; 359-381.

Hashimoto, Akiko, Hal Kendig and Larry C. Coppard. (1992). Family Support to the Elderly in International Perspective. In Kendig, Hal L. Akiko Hashimoto and Larry C. Coppard, *Family Support for the Elderly: The International Experience,* 293-308 New York: Oxford University Press.

Jones, Gavin W. (1993). Consequences of Rapid Fertility Decline for Old Age Security in

Asia. Chapter 14 in Richard Leete and Iqbal Alam., eds., *Revolution in Asian Fertility: Dimensions, Causes and Implications.* Oxford: Clarendon Press.

Kirn, Ik-Ki and Ehn Hyun Choe. (1992). Support Exchange Patterns of the Elderly in the Republic of Korea. *Asia-Pacific Population Journal.* 7(3): 89-104.

Knodel, John. (1993). The Design and Analysis of Focus Group Studies in Social Science Research, (in) David Morgan, ed., *Successful Focus Groups: Advancing the State of the Art.* Newbury Park, Ca: Sage, pp. 35-50.

Knodel, John. (1995). Introduction. *Journal of Cross-Cultural Gerontology.* 10(1-2): 1-6

Knodel, John and Nibhon Debavalya. (1992). Social and Economic Support Systems for the Elderly in Asia: An Introduction. *Asia-Pacific Population Journal* 7(3): 5-12.

Knodel, John, Napaporn Chayovan and Siriwan Siriboon. (1991). *Familial Support and the Life Course of Thai Elderly and Their Children.* Comparative Study of the Elderly in Asia; Research Report No. 91-12, Population Studies Center, University of Michigan.

Knodel, John, Napaporn Chayovan and Siriwan Siriboon. (1992). 'The Familial Support System of Thai Elderly: An Overview'. *Asia-Pacific Population Journal.* 7(3): 105-126.

Knodel, John, Napaporn Chayovan and Chanpen Saengtienchai. (1994). 'Are Thais Deserting Their Elderly Parents? New Evidence from the 1990 Census'. *BOLD.* 4(3) 7-12.

Knodel, John, Chanpen Saengtienchai and Werasit Sittitrai. (1995). 'The Living Arrangements of Elderly in Thailand: Views of the Populace'. *Journal of Cross-Cultural Gerontology.* 10(1-2): 79-111.

Knodel, John, Chanpen Saengtienchai and Walter Obiero. 'Do Small Families Jeopardise Old Age Security ? Evidence from Thailand'. *BOLD.*

Kosberg, Jordan I. and Juanita L. Garcia. (1991). 'Social Changes Affecting Family Care of the Elderly'. *BOLD.* 1(2): 2-5.

Kulick, Elliott and Dick Wilson. (1992). *Thailand's Turn: Profile of a New Dragon.* New York: St. Martin's Press.

Lee, Mei-jin, Hui-sheng, Ming-cheng Chang. (1993) *Living Arrangements of the Elderly in Taiwan: Qualitative Evidence. Comparative Study of the Elderly in Asia.* Research Report No. 93-26, Population Studies Center, University of Michigan, Dec. 1993.

Mason, Karen Oppenheim. (1992). 'Family Change and Support of the Elderly: What Do We Know'. *Asia-Pacific Population Journal* 7(3): 13-32.

Pichyangkura, Chart and Morakut Singhajend. (1991). 'Thailand National Review on the Elderly'. Paper presented at the Workshop on Population Aging, ESCAP, Bangkok, Thailand, 15-22 July 1991.

Siriboon, Siriwan and John Knodel. (1994). 'Thai Elderly Who Do Not Coreside with their Children'. *Journal of Cross-Cultural Gerontology.* 9 (1): 21-38.

Suh, Mee Kyung. (1992). 'The Elderly Population in Korea: Their Health Status and Kin-Based Social Support'; *Korea Journal of Population and Development.* 21 (2): 175-196.

Tout, Kj (1989). *Aging in Developing Countries.* Oxford: Oxford University Press.

Tuchrello, William P. (1989). 'The Society and Its Environment'. Chapter 2 in Barbara Leitch LePoer, ed., *Thailand: A Country Study,* Sixth Edition (Area Handbook Series), pp. 55-120. Washington: U.S. Government Printing Office.

Weinstein, Maxine, Te-Hsiung Sun, Ming-cheng Chang, and Ronald Freedman. (1990). Household Composition, Extended Kinship, and Reproduction in Taiwan. *Population Studies.* 44:217-239.

World Bank. (1994). *Averting the Old Age Crisis.* New York: Oxford University Press.

Chapter 16

Demographic Transition and Ageing in India and China

Rajagopal Dhar Chakraborti

Both India and China are now close to an 'agequake' (Wallace 1999); the proportions of people aged 60 plus have started rising in both countries and are projected to grow rapidly over the next 50 years. The two countries share many other similarities as well. Both are ageing at a relatively low level of development, and hence, resource availability for elderly care. True, China surpasses India by a significant margin on most indicators of economic development,[1] but vast tracts of the Chinese economy and society still maintain features very close to that of the predominant Indian socio-economic scenario. Second, in both India and China, family structure is still very traditional, with built-in mechanisms in both countries to ensure respect of the elderly. In Chinese society, the famous Confucian concept of 'Filial Piety'[2] governs the principle of care of the elderly by their children; and Indians have deep rooted religious and social convictions vis a vis care of elderly. Third, both are very populous countries, sheltering 33.9% of world's elderly populations. It is of interest to note also that more than half of developing countries' elderly (55.3%) and 64% of Asia's elderly live in India and China.

Data and Sources

In profiling the various facets of ageing in India and China, this paper taps various data sources. The major emphasis however has been on the data generated by two national reports on the ageing populations of India and China. For India, we draw on *The Aged in India: A socio-economic Profile*, brought out by the National Sample Survey Organisation (NSSO), Ministry of Planning and Programme Implementation, Government of India. This document reports on data from the Fifty-Second Round of the National Sample Survey (NSS), carried out in 1998. For China, we draw on data from a national survey conducted in late 2000 and reported upon in the government-controlled China Research Centre on Ageing (CRCA) in its publication *Situation of the Chinese Elderly (SCE).*

Ageing Dynamics in India and China

Ageing is spreading very rapidly both in India and China. Some of the major characteristics in the growth of ageing in these two countries are:

a. The number of elderly has more than tripled over the last fifty years. In India, the number of the aged rose by three and a half times from 20.1 million in 1950 to 72.6 million in 2000. China had 41.6 million aged in 1950. Their elderly population rose 128.9 million in 2000.
b. In the next fifty years, the numbers will triple further. In India the number of elderly will rise by almost four and a half times to 324.3 million in 2050; while in China, the figure will rise by little over 3 times to 437 million.
c. In both countries, the proportion of the elderly in the total population has grown steadily between 1950 and 2000. In the next fifty years, the growth is likely to be more rapid. In China, the proportion rose from 7.5 in 1950 to 10.1 in 2000, and is projected to rise to 29.9 in 2050. In India, the corresponding figures are 5.6, 7.6 and 20.6.
d. In the hundred years from 1950, the proportions of children (0-14), youth (15-24), and working age population will decline, while that of the elderly will rise.

Public Support for the Elderly

Through public policy documents, both India and China recognise the needs of the elderly and entrust the State with the responsibility of making effective provisions for public assistance in old age.[3] Provision for direct public support for old age is meagre in India and China, both in terms of networking as well as quantum of support. Here again, there prevails a notion of divided citizenship between the formal and informal sector, with regard to old age pensions. In both countries, whereas the urban formal sector provides a generous system of old-age pensions introduced early in the 1950s and surpassing the usual standards of developing countries, there are no public provisions for old age in rural areas, except marginal social assistance.

In India, only the retired employees of the public sector enjoy old age social security. At the end of March 1996, there were 19.43 million public sector employees (comprising 3.37 million in the Central government, 7.41 million in the State governments and another 6.46 million in the quasi-government organisations). The combined coverage in these schemes is less than 10 percent of the total labour force. This is a low figure, but fairly typical of countries at a similar income level (Palacios and Pallares 2000). As in other poor countries, low coverage is due to a very large agricultural population as well as an informal sector that bypasses taxes and social insurance contributions.

In China, before the 1980s, most urban workers were employed by State-owned enterprises and were hence provided with many benefits, including old age pensions (Croll 2000). By the late 1980s, however, economic and social reform had altered many of the Maoist institutions. Collective agriculture was replaced by the functional equivalent of family farms. Newly organised private businesses and factories created jobs in which the young could advance their careers without depending on their parents or the State. Thus, by the 1990s, due to extensive privatisation of the economy, only about a quarter of the urban work force was protected by State-provided benefits. It's estimated that the rest of the work force is 'employed outside state-owned enterprises' and 'not covered by any form of social insurance'.

In the countryside (home to 70 per cent of the population at the end of the twentieth century), a State-provided safety net is even less in evidence. Even before the 1980s, care of the elderly was mainly the responsibility of families and collective farms. At the very least, government and the collectives provided 'Five Guarantees'—food, clothing, medical care, housing, and burial expenses—to childless people and the infirm elderly (Du and Zhi-gang 2000). When collective farming was abolished in 1983 under Deng Xiaoping's 'Four Modernisations', the family became the sole caregiver for the elderly. Both the Chinese Constitution and the Chinese government have made it abundantly clear that care of the aged in China is primarily a family responsibility, an unavoidable part of a contract between generations. In this respect, neither the Communist Revolution nor the post-1978 reforms represents any significant break from what the Chinese have always regarded as the surest route to a secure old age, namely, that 'rearing a son for old age is like storing grain for a famine'. For centuries, filial piety was extolled as the highest virtue and caring for elderly parents was regarded as the key form of its expression (Ikels 1993).

In India, there are schemes for needy and destitute elderly; these are some kind of means-tested pension to older citizens. However, eligibility rules are often complicated and benefit levels vary significantly across States. While in Kerala, around 20 per cent of the aged have access to some kinds of pension (Dev 1994) in other States, only 10 to 15% of elderly do so. Pension levels vary across States, from 55 to 300 rupees per month, with the average in the range of 75 rupees. Since 1995, the central government has supplemented this with the NOAPS—National Old Age Pension Scheme (Government of India 1995). This program pays 75 rupees per month to destitute persons aged 65 and above. One estimate suggests that only 10 per cent of the elderly population in India is served by this scheme (Rajan 2001). Another scheme, introduced by the government in March 1999, an in-kind assistance programme called Annapurna, aims to provide 10 kilograms of rice or wheat per month to elderly who are destitute. In its maiden appearance, the programme supported 0.66 million people. It intended to reach out to larger destitute elderly in the successive years. In addition to such central government spending, each State spends on social assistance programs for the elderly out of its own budget. However, the sum total of these expenses leaves much to be desired. Combining the Central and State level programmes, a World Bank Report estimates that only 0.08 percent of GDP is spent on old age security (World Bank 2001). In addition, the Ministry of Welfare of the central government supports 'day activity centers', managed by private voluntary agencies for the elderly. Some elderly secure assistances from charitable nongovernmental organisations (NGOs), which, along with many religious groups, operate old age homes. However, not much information exists on either benefits or beneficiaries of such charitable old age schemes.

In China, the origin of an organised pension scheme goes back to 1991, when the Ministry of Civil Affairs introduced a public pension scheme in rural areas. This was not, however, a social assistance scheme; it was, rather, a scheme that tried to mobilise people's own savings for their old age. In 1997, 8.3 million people subscribed to the scheme at about 3 Yuan per month to provide for pensions of about 573.6 Yuan per annum to over half a million pensioners (Asian Development Bank. 2002). There has not been any further progress yet, as the party and the State Council have both recognised that the rural sector has not been ripe for commercial social security (Asian Development Bank 2002).

For India, National Sample Survey Data indicate that 79% of elderly (who ere ever engaged in wage / salaried job or as casual labour) in rural areas and 35% in the urban areas did not receive any benefits after retirement. In rural areas, every sixth aged person who retired from some employment received pension, whereas in urban areas, every second person was fortunate to receive pension (Table 1).

The elderly in China are not happy with the economic support received from social security institutions. With structural adjustment programmes and economic reform measures marginalising the role of government in the economy, things are going to be tougher for the elderly in future. Older persons' lives in China have been affected greatly by the social and economic transformations and demographic shifts that have occurred since the 1970s.

TABLE 1: Percentage Distribution of Aged Persons (who were ever Engaged in Wage/Salaried Job or as Casual Labour) by Category Oof Retirement Benefits, India, 1996

Region	Type of scheme	Coverage		
		Male	Female	Total
RURAL	Pension only	9.9	2.6	6.7
	Pension with other benefits	15.7	1.8	9.3
	No pension, but other benefits	6.9	2.8	5.0
	No benefits	67.5	92.8	79.0
URBAN	Pension only	17.1	0.5	15.1
	Pension with other benefits	37.2	15.3	32.8
	No pension, but other benefits	18.9	9.8	17.1
	No benefits	26.8	67.4	35.0

Source: *The Aged In India: A socio-economic Profile*, NNS Fifty-second Round July 1995-June 1996. NSSO, Department of Statistics, Ministry of Planning & Programme Implementation, Government of India, Calcutta, 1998.

Recent socio-economic reform seems to have had an unexpected negative impact on the foundations of the original safety net for the aged. Inflation continues to devalue pensions' purchasing power. Moreover, under the medical reform that began in the mid-1980s, people in urban areas are no longer guaranteed free medical care but are subject to sharing in some part of the payments. In rural areas, the basic collective security for the elderly has been greatly weakened. Table 2 shows that an overwhelming majority of elderly populations say 'no' when asked about supports from government and collective agencies.

TABLE 2: Percentage Distribution of Aged Persons' Response to Question whether they are Financially Supported by Different Category of Public Supports in China

Type of assistance	Response	Total	Male	Female
Government Relief	No	95.7	97.0	94.3
	Yes	3.3	2.2	4.5
	Can't Say	1.0	0.9	1.1
Collective Relief	No	97.3	98.1	96.5
	Yes	1.7	1.1	2.4
	Can't Say	1.0	0.9	1.1
Social Security Fund	No	87.0	84.3	89.8
	Yes	11.9	14.7	9.0
	Can't Say	1.1	0.9	1.2
Enterprise Support Relief	No	93.2	93.0	93.4
	Yes	5.6	6.1	5.5
	Can't Say	0.9	0.9	1.1

Source: Analysis of data from the Sample Survey of the Aged Population in China, China Research Chnteronag, 2002.

Old Age Homes

State support in the provision of institutions for older people is also grossly inadequate. At the end of 2001, China had only 8,665 urban elderly welfare units, with 282,494 beds and 200,067 occupants. The rural elderly welfare units numbered 26,650 with 684,202 beds and 489,236 occupants. In addition, there were 1343 homes for disabled veterans, endowed with 45,448 beds and housing 31,404 occupants. 90% of social welfare institutions in China are in the collective sectors, though private sector ownership has been encouraged in recent years (China Statistical Yearbook 2002). In India, while there are 728 Old Age Homes, only 547 among them seem active. Out of these, 325 homes are free of cost while 95 old age homes are on a pay and stay basis, and 116 homes have both free as well as pay & stay facilities. (For 11 homes, we have no information). A total of 278 old age homes all over the country are available for the sick and 101 are exclusively for women. Kerala has 124 old age homes, the maximum in any State (Help Age India 1998). Elderly living as inmates of old-age homes constitute 0.8 to 0.9 per cent of total elderly in India. In China too, not many elderly stay in old age homes.

The Chinese survey shows that on an average, 62.2% of the elderly do not have any information on senior homes and welfare homes. The lack of information is more with females (65.1%) than with males (59.8%); it is also more with urban residents (66.3%) than with the rural populace (58.0%). The survey states that 81.3% of Chinese elderly are unwilling to stay in such homes. Among those who are willing, the overwhelming majority of 78.9%, want to stay in old age homes for a long time. There is a slightly higher preference among the rural elderly for long time stay in homes. The general impression of the elderly toward such homes is also not very optimistic. Only 35.5% of elderly considers senior homes to be 'good'. A Survey on the aged on Old Age Homes in Calcutta city of India by the current investigator show that an overwhelming 88% of elderly do not have any knowledge of a nearby old age home. That there could be such homes as alternatives to problematic old age living conditions was not known to over fifty percent of the elderly interviewed. Elderly who were parents of a single child and those who held good jobs indicated a high preference for staying in old age homes.

Family Supports

In developing countries, the family is a vital institution for the well being of its older members. Co residence with other generations of family is both inevitable and desirable for the old. In the final years of life, individuals often experience reductions in physical functioning, and tend to acquire physical ailments and disabilities that make it difficult for them to carry out the activities of daily living. They become essentially dependent on others for physical and emotional supports. The household serves as a very satisfactory agency for these supports to the older members (Thornon, Chnag and Sun 1984). In many cultural settings, the family sets norms for the reciprocal relationship between the young and the old (Martin 1990). The family allocates roles for its members, maintaining a balance between different age groups such that they all reflect and contribute to the fundamental structure of the society as a whole (Casterline et. al. 1991). Sharing of accommodation within the extended family is an important source of emotional, physical and financial supports for the elderly in many developing countries, while State supports in industrial countries provide the aged with the ability to live independently.

Both the Indian and the Chinese survey data confirm that the extended, multi-generational family is a resilient feature of both Indian and Chinese society. The picture is almost the same in other Asian societies, except Japan and South Korea. The percentage of elderly living with children ranged from 67% in Indonesia to 85% in Singapore, barring Japan and South Korea, where the percentages have fallen below 50. But these proportions were still much higher than the multigenerational living arrangements in many developed countries (Chakraborti 2004).

Living with Spouse and Children

While living alone is one of the indicators of low status for elderly, living with spouse and children is an index of their care and support in old age. Table 3 summarises the living arrangements by elderly in India and China with their spouses and children. Almost three-fifths of the aged in China live with their children. Females are more likely to live with their children than males, particularly at older ages. Relatively few of the aged live with people other than their children, indicating that it is only within the immediate family that living arrangements are shared.

Although on an average, today's elderly in China have six grand children and four children and equal number of children and grandchildren-in laws, very few of them stay with them (Table 4). With children and grandchildren, most elderly stay in households with more than 3 members. The average household size rises slightly with the age of the older person, somewhat more so for women than men, reflecting the greater longevity of women.

The Indian data bring out a number of facets of elderly living arrangements.

- Around 58% of the elderly are currently married and almost all of them stay with their spouses. Older males are more likely than older females to live with a spouse. In rural areas, over 60% of elderly males stay with spouses *and* other family members, but only one third of elderly females did so. The male-female gap in living arrangements with spouse and other members are higher in urban areas. This gender

TABLE 3: Percentage of Co-residence of Elderly Aged 60 and over on China, 2000, and India, 1995-96

Living arrangement	Total			Rural			Urban		
	M	F	T	M	F	T	M	F	T
China									
With spouse only	33.9	21.4	28.0	29.8	19.9	25.3	38.3	22.8	30.7
With spouse & children	57.5	64.7	60.9	60.1	67.8	63.6	54.7	61.9	58.2
With others	3.5	4.5	4.0	3.6	3.4	3.5	3.4	5.6	4.4
India									
With spouse only				13.7	7.7	10.7	10.3	5.7	8.0
With spouse & children				75.0	39.0	56.9	75.1	35.4	54.9
				(45.1)	(25.1)	(37.0)	(44.9)	(21.5)	(35.3)
With children only				17.0	48.1	33.1	17.8	51.2	34.9
				(36.8)	(66.0)	(48.6)	(39.6)	(67.3)	(51.0)
With others				3.8	5.9	4.8	3.5	6.5	5.1
				(5.7)	(7.4)	(6.2)	(5.6)	(10.0)	(7.4)

Note: The figures in brackets indicates the findings of the NSS 42nd Round, 1986-87

Source: Analysis of data from the Sample Survey of the Aged Population in China, China Research, Chnteronag, 2002.

The Aged In India: A socio-economic Profile, NNS Fifty-second Round July 1995-June 1996, NSSO, Department of Statistics, Ministry of Planning & Programme Implementation, Government of India, Calcutta, 1998.

TABLE 4: Average Number of Children, Children-in-Laws and Grand Children and Grand Children-in-Laws and Average Number of those Staying with them in China, 2000

Total / male / female	Children		Children- in laws		Grand children and grand children in-laws	
	Average Number co-residing	Average Number co-residing	Average Number co-residing	Average Number co-residing	Average Number co-residing	Average Number co-residing
Total	4.0	0.7	3.7	0.5	5.8	0.8
Male	3.9	0.7	3.6	0.4	5.3	0.7
Female	4.1	0.7	3.9	0.5	6.3	0.8

Source: Analysis of data from the Sample Survey of the Aged Population in China, China Research Chnteronag, 2002.

differential is primarily because of the higher incidence of widowhood among elderly females than among elderly males.

- Around 10% of aged people stay with their spouses only. The percentage is lower in urban than in rural areas. About 5% of elderly live with friends and relations.

- Around 4% of elderly live alone.
- The proportion of aged who lived with their spouses also goes up significantly from 37% to the current 57% in rural areas from 1986/87 to 1995/96 and from 35% to 55% in urban areas.
- While 94% of the aged have children, only 33 to 34% lived with children only in 1995-96. In the 1986-87 survey periods, 49 to 51% were living with their children.
- The 1995-96 NSS survey shows that 94% of the elderly had at least one surviving child. The rural-urban differences are negligible with regard to the proportion of elderly living with surviving children.
- Between 42nd and 52nd Rounds, there have been some improvements in regard to the proportion of aged persons having their children alive. The improvement is prominent for males while the proportion remained the same for females.

Interestingly, proportions of elderly living with children are falling everywhere in Asia (United Nations Population Division, 1998). A study of rural China for a longer time period shows that in 1930's, there were no elderly living in simple conjugal units but in 1995, thirty percent of them were living in such households. The proportions of elderly living in multigenerational households dropped from 86% to 60% between the same time period (Benjamin and Rozelle 2000). In 1996, only 15 percent of elderly men and women in Japan mentioned children as a source of income, down from 30% in 1981 (Ogawa and Rutherford1997).

It has been stated that levels of parent-child co-residence are inversely related to socioeconomic development (Asis, Domingo, Knodel and Mehta 1995). Today, in Asian conditions, parent-child co-residence is mutually beneficial. Older adults receive the social, financial, and health support they require from the younger generation, and in turn, take care of young children or look after the home when the young adults are away. The house very often belongs to the elderly parents, and expensive living costs may not allow children to stay in alternative accommodation. However, expectations and preferences of today's working-age adults suggest that the economics of multi-generational living will not be a likely proposition in future. In the Philippines, where the actual proportion of elderly living with their children has not gone down much, fewer working-age adults wish to live with their children in the future (Natividad and Cruz 1997). In 1997, in South Korea, a mere 8% women of childbearing age indicated that they wished to live with their children when they grow old (Lee 1998).

Most of Indian society is patrilineal and patriarchal. Males dominate ownership of resources and preside over family decision-making. Women leave their parental home and move to their husband's house after marriage. Older adults generally live with the family of a married son. If they do not have a son, they prefer to move to some relative's house, when conditions so warrant, but, as a rule, they will not stay in the family of the daughters' marital homes. The Chinese system appears to be very similar. In contrast, in some of the Southeast Asian countries like Cambodia (Zachary and Kim 2002) and Thailand, elderly couples prefer to stay with unmarried daughters. In Thailand, there is a preference for living with the youngest daughter who is not likely to be married (Knodel, Chayovan and Siriboon 1992). Although the pattern of co-residence should have bearing on the nature and level of support provided to older adults, comparative analysis of the implications of the two systems is not yet available.

Bongaarts and Zimmer, in their reconstruction of demographic data on living arrangements of the elderly in 43 developing countries, including eleven Asian countries that participated in the DHS program between 1990 and 1998 (Bongaarts and Zimmer 2001) come out with findings that corroborate the Indian and other countries data. More specifically, the study shows that most older adults tend to live in large households, and are likely to be living with an adult child, who is more likely to be male than female. It also finds that on average, nearly one in ten older adults lives alone, and that the probability of living alone is greater for older women than older men. Women are much less likely to live with a spouse in the household, while a slightly greater proportion of older women than men live with adult children. It also noted a weakening of extended family links in conjunction with socioeconomic development.

We find also an inverse relation between elderly educational attainment and living arrangements with adult children: where levels of education are higher, older adults live in smaller households, with fewer children and other adults, and are more likely to be alone. The reasons are that: (a) older adults with higher levels of schooling, have higher skill formation, and therefore, are generally better able to care for themselves; (b) the better-educated older adults have a stronger preference for privacy than the poor and least educated. Conversely, where education is lower, older adults own fewer resources. They are therefore more dependent on adult children, especially on male offspring. Male children are more likely to control household resources than their sisters who, in general, move to another house after marriage, and are also likely to be restrained by cultural taboos from their sons' residence.

Economic Supports from the Family

In India, recent data (Table 5) show, many as 70 per cent of the aged had to depend on others for their bread and butter. The situation is worse for elderly females. Over 85% were found to depend on others, partially or fully. Elderly males are little better off – 49 to 52% of them *not* dependent on others. While the situation is slightly better in urban areas than the national average, the *rural* elderly are virtually dependents. Among elderly rural males, 48.5% claimed that they were not dependent, 18% were partially dependent and 31.3% were fully dependent. In the case of elderly rural females, 70.6% were fully dependent on others, 14.6% were partially dependent and only 12.1% said that they were not dependent on others. In urban areas, 51.5% of the elderly males claimed that they were not dependent on others, 29.7% were fully dependent and 16.9% were partially dependent. In the case of urban females, 75.7% were fully dependent on others, 11% were partially dependent and 11.5% were not dependent on others (Table 5).

In West Bengal, over 88.3% of the rural females and 85.1% of the urban females were fully dependent on others. These figures are the highest among the State level figures. Regrettably, in Kerala, which has the highest proportion of elderly in India and has several social security schemes, 73.6% of the rural females and 76% of the urban females are fully dependent. Even economically impoverished states of Bihar and Uttar Pradesh seem to have better status for the elderly as per NSS data.

TABLE 5: Percentage Distribution of Elderly Persons by State of Economic Independence for Each Sex in India, 1995/96

Sex	Rural				Urban			
	Not dependent on others	Partially dependent on others	Fully dependent on others	Total	Not dependent on others	Partially dependent on others	Fully dependent on others	Total
M	48.5	18.0	31.3	100.0	51.5	16.9	29.7	100.0
F	12.1	14.6	70.6	100.0	11.5	11.0	75.7	100.0
T	30.1	16.3	51.1	100.0	31.1	13.9	53.2	100.0

Source: The Aged In India: A socio-economic Profile, NNS Fifty-second Round July 1995-June 1996, NSSO, Department of Statistics, Ministry of Planning & Programme Implementation, Government of India, Calcutta, 1998.

NSS data provide details of the category of persons who support economically dependent elderly – children, grandchildren, spouse and others. In India as a whole, over 70% of the economically dependent elderly are supported by their children and grandchildren. This does indicate the almost total reliance on the family in the case of the elderly who are not economically independent. To be specific, children support 71.1% of the rural persons and 70.8% of the urban persons. Grandchildren support 5.0% of the rural persons and 5.4% of the urban persons. The share of spouse was 13.8% in rural and 15.2% in urban areas. The share of 'others', which includes the government among many others, is only 5.9% in urban and 6.9% in rural areas. Table 6 summarises these findings.

TABLE 6: Percentage Distribution of Economically Dependent Aged Persons by Category of Persons Providing Support, India, 1995-96

Sex	Rural				Urban			
	Spouse	Own children	Grand children	Others	Spouse	Own children	Grand children	Others
Male	11.3	76.6	5.0	7.1	10.5	79.2	5.4	4.9
Female	15.9	71.7	5.2	7.2	18.2	72.3	5.6	6.7
Total	14.2	73.5	5.2	7.1	15.6	72.8	5.5	6.1

Source: The Aged In India: A socio-economic Profile, NNS Fifty-second Round July 1995-June 1996, NSSO, Department of Statistics, Ministry of Planning & Programme Implementation, Government of India, Calcutta, 1998.

In China too, despite a much superior social safety network in place, elderly are still dependent on children for support. Two-thirds of elderly in the survey stated that they depend on children's economic support as first choice. Of those who were not primarily dependent on children's support, one fourth needed them as second choice. In rural China, more elder parents are dependent on children's income than their urban counterparts. More female are dependent on children's income than males (Tables 7, 8 and 9).

TABLE 7: Percentage Distribution of Elderly Persons by Economic Dependence on their Children for each Sex in China, 2000

Sex	Order of choice				
	1st	2nd	3rd	4th	Total
Total	64.5	22.9	7.9	4.7	100.0
Male	60.2	25.3	9.2	5.2	100.0
Female	69.2	20.3	6.5	4.0	100.0

Source: Analysis of data from the Sample Survey of the Aged Population in China, China Research Chnteronag, 2002.

TABLE 8: Percentage Distribution of Elderly Persons by Economic Dependence on their Children as First Choice for each Sex in Rural and Urban China, 2000

Urban			Rural		
Total	Male	Female	Total	Male	Female
44.6	41.4	56.9	79.1	76.8	82.0

Source: Analysis of data from the Sample Survey of the Aged Population in China, China Research Chnteronag, 2002.

TABLE 9: Percentage Distribution of Aged Persons by their Response on Category of Persons Providing Financial Support, China, 2000

Response	Children			Grandchildren			Relatives			Others		
	Total	Male	Female	Total	Male	Female	Total	Male	Female	Total	Male	Female
No	61.3	70.1	52.2	94.9	96.5	93.1	95.8	96.6	95.0	97.5	97.3	97.3
Yes	38.0	29.2	47.2	4.1	2.5	5.8	3.2	2.5	3.9	1.5	1.9	1.6
Can't say	0.7	0.7	0.6	1.0	0.9	1.1	1.0	0.9	1.1	1.0	0.9	1.1

Source: Analysis of data from the Sample Survey of the Aged Population in China, China Research Chnteronag, 2002.

To a great extent, the tables appear to be Indian replica. Where there is no adequate elder social security, the aged are bound to be dependent on children. In comparison to China, in Taiwan, only 37% of elderly are dependent on children as the major source of income. On the other hand, in Singapore where there is an almost universal pension scheme through CPF, 77% of elderly depend on the support from children as the major source of income. While it is true that pension supports often are not adequate for a decent living consistent with family's consumption growth, in another scenario, in the Philippines, where social security is much less spread than in Taiwan and Singapore, only 31% of elderly are reported to be dependent on children support (Hermalin 2002).

While families continue to support the elderly, certain groups among the elderly are particularly vulnerable, especially widows (Dreze and Srinivasan 1997). Informal safety nets are not always dependable and by no means adequate, even under the best of circumstances. The poor are especially vulnerable since their main source of income during old age, their children, are also likely to be poor and thus unable to provide more than limited support. There are reasons to believe that family support systems will come under increasing strain as life expectancy rises, especially in urban areas. As fewer children must support parents for longer periods of time, the per capita cost of parent caring rises at a steep rate. The tremendous jump in health care costs unaccompanied by suitable development of health insurance schemes multiples the burden on children.

Regulatory Role of the Government

While direct public support systems are not adequate for an honourable living in old age, public policies have increasingly been directed towards regulatory functions over family institutions. With modernisation, community control has become weak and the mechanisms for enforcing social contracts not always very effective. Governments have come forward with legislation, making child support to elderly mandatory. Penal laws, both in India and China, make it obligatory for a person having sufficient means to support his father and / or mother unable to maintain himself or herself.[4] Singapore passed a law to this effect in 1982. Following that, an amendment was made in the Chinese penal code, by which children can be imprisoned for neglecting their parents. In 1996, a new law on Protection of the Rights and Interests of the Elderly stipulated that families are to be the main providers of care for aged parents. In India, in 1996, the Himachal Pradesh Assembly passed a Parents Maintenance Bill wherein a simple procedure was introduced for parents who are ignored by their children to be given maintenance. In addition to making care of their parents obligatory for the errant wards, the bill aims at simplifying the procedure by authorising the sub-divisional officer (civil) to fix maintenance, with the Additional Commissioner as the appellate authority, so that the decision can be taken and cases disposed of promptly, bringing relief to older persons without loss of time. The Bill is waiting ascent of the President of India. The Government of Maharashtra has prepared a Bill on similar lines. The Government of Goa also proposes to initiate action towards introduction of a Parents Maintenance Bill.

Self Supports by the Elderly

Today, more and more elderly are trying to depend on themselves for present and future supports. In India, over 30% of elderly, both in urban and rural areas, are not dependent on others for economic supports. Almost fifty percent of elderly males are not dependent. One-seventh of economic supports of the aged come from spouses. In China, 25.7% of urban elderly (30.9% of males) depend on bank savings as means of support. 42.4% of elderly feels that savings are enough for old age. 48.6% of urban aged feel that they can manage their old age with current savings. Urban males are more optimistic; 53.4% of them feel that they have accumulated enough savings for old age.

However, participation in voluntary insurance-linked savings schemes is very limited, both in China and India. Many households at the bottom of the income distribution in India are too poor to save for old age. Available resources are needed for survival demands. Even those with some surplus resources, are unwilling to subscribe to savings instruments that require a commitment of several decades. Instead, these people prefer to use the surplus resources for self-insurance against emergencies or perhaps in short-term investments that increase their own productivity or the productivity of their children. People with comfortable surplus resources prefer to keep their money in banks and other short-term savings instruments. Very few Chinese are dependent on any voluntary commercial insurance for old age. Only 2.0% of elderly depend on commercial insurance as means of old age support. Only 0.8% of them bought medical insurance and even lesser (0.3%) bought accident insurance. A little over one per cent of elderly contributed to property insurance. All these forms of insurance are much less popular in rural than in urban areas. In China as well as in India, the insurance market, outside life insurance, has not yet developed much, and elderly apathy is a mere reflection of that. The reluctance to join old age insurance schemes is due to high transaction costs, poor service of insurance agencies, and rates of return that do not compensate for the loss of liquidity. Also, there is a general lack of awareness of the need to insure the risks of survivorship and longevity.

In China, the overwhelming majority of urban elderly own a house, while in rural areas, they are more dependent on children. In rural areas, 70% of housing structures are mud houses and such structures built by elderly in their prime time crumble when they grow old. Most elderly are unable to build houses again and are therefore dependent on children and others for shelter (Table 10).

TABLE 10: Ownership of Present Housing of Elderly by Sex and Rural-Urban Category in China

Owner	Urban			Rural		
	Total	Male	Female	Total	Male	Female
Self or spouse	62.7	69.7	55.4	41.4	48.6	32.7
Children	15.7	10.8	20.8	55.4	48.0	64.4
Others	15.5	14.2	16.9	2.7	2.8	2.6
Don't know	6.1	5.3	7.0	0.5	0.5	0.4

Source: Analysis of data from the Sample Survey of the Aged Population in China, China Research Chnteronag, 2002.

Indians too have planned their lifetime income in such a way that a majority of them own physical and financial property in old age. Over 80 per cent of the rural and 70.4% of rural aged owned some property. Again, around 70% of elderly males, both in urban and rural areas had some kind of financial assets. However, because of inheritance complications and old age mobility problems, many elderly have passed on the responsibility of management of such property to the younger members of the family. In some cases, children might have forced the parents to vest the management rights with them. While such intricate details are not available, table 11 provides a broad idea of the ownership and management of self-property and other assets by the elderly.

The ageing survey in China asked questions on whether elderly have skills and capital to do business. An overpowering majority have no such skills or capital (Table 12). In fact, only 3% of elderly reported that they were doing business. This is quite natural when around 90% of them have not done business

TABLE 11: Percent of Aged Persons with Financial Assets/Property in India, 1995-96

Sex	Rural				Urban			
	Owning financial assets	Having and managing financial assets	Owning financial assets	Having and managing financial assets	Owning financial assets	Having and managing financial assets	Owning financial assets	Having and managing financial assets
Male	69.5	56.9	80.4	65.1	70.2	58.1	74.2	60.5
Female	39.1	17.7	45.6	20.6	37.6	18.15	42.0	20.6
Total	54.2	37.2	62.9	42.7	53.5	37.9	57.8	40.1

Source: The Aged In India: A socio-economic Profile, NNS Fifty-second Round July 1995-June 1996, NSSO, Department of Statistics, Ministry of Planning & Programme Implementation, Government of India, Calcutta, 1998.

ventures when in the prime of their lives. Most of China's elderly grew up during the period of a radical socialistic structure of the economy where private business ventures were not encouraged. However, as the Chinese are being encouraged to move back to business activities on which they have had time tested skills for generations, property owning ventures and economic dependence of future elderly should see a sea change.

TABLE 12: Chinese Elderly with Skills and Capital for Business

Response	Elderly having skills						Elderly having capital for business					
	Urban			Rural			Urban			Rural		
	Total	Male	Female	Total	Male	Female	Total	Male	Female	Total	Male	Female
No	78.4	69.2	88.1	92.0	88.1	96.7	93.5	92.0	95.1	95.8	94.6	97.4
Yes	21.3	30.7	11.5	7.7	11.5	3.0	6.1	7.7	4.5	3.9	5.2	2.2
Can't say	0.3	0.1	0.4	0.4	0.3	0.4	0.4	0.3	0.4	0.3	0.3	0.4

Source: Analysis of data from the Sample Survey of the Aged Population in China, China Research Chnteronag, 2002.

Elderly Workers

Those elderly who could not accumulate sufficient asset income, are for obvious reasons, dependent on labour income even during old age. At a time when there is a trend towards early exit from the labour market in most countries with universal social security during old age, a large number of elderly are unable to exit the labour market. According to the 1991 Census of India, there were 22.2 million elderly workers in India. Of these, 17.8 million were males and 4.4 million females. This implies that 39.1% of the total elderly population were workers as against the figure of 37.5 percent for the total worker population. The elderly workforce participation rate was 60.5%. It was 16.1% for females, as compared to 51.6% for males. In rural areas, elderly work participation rate is larger than the all ages' population. The urban elderly, however, participate in the work force a little less than the general population. The female work participation is everywhere lower for the aged category than the all ages' population. In India, even people in the age group 80+ participate in the work force. Around 19% of them still work at age 80 and above. Every third male aged 80 and above is required to work for a living in India. Table 16 presents the statistics (Table 13).

TABLE 13: Work Participation Rate for the Elderly and General Population, India, 1991

Category	Total			Rural			Urban		
	Total	Male	Female	Total	Male	Female	Total	Male	Female
All Elderly	39.1	60.5	16.1	43.1	65.4	19.0	25.0	42.9	6.3
General	37.5	51.6	22.3	40.0	52.5	26.7	30.2	48.9	9.2
60-69 Age category	46.9	71.4	20.8	51.7	77.1	24.4	30.0	50.7	8.0
70-79 Age category	28.8	47.0	9.2	31.9	51.2	10.8	17.8	31.3	3.7
80+ Age category	19.3	31.7	5.7	20.9	33.5	6.7	13.4	24.7	2.6

Source: Census of India, 1991.

78 per cent of the elderly work force is engaged in agricultural activities. In the case of female workers, the figure is over 84%. As there is no age limit in self-employed agriculture, people continue to work in their farm and allied enterprises even after the age of 60 years. Most of the elderly workers (92.6%) were main workers and not marginal workers. In urban areas, elderly are generally engaged in work requiring considerable use of manual strength and physical hazard. Being uneducated and not adequately skilled, they have to be satisfied with low wages, insecurity of work and unhealthy working conditions.

The China 2000 ageing survey indicates that elderly are not required to work for living as much as they do in India. Only 0.8% of urban elderly have been found 'still on job' category. However, in rural areas, 39.7% of aged population were still engaged in farming activities. The average age at retirement in urban areas was found to be 56.1 years, and the average age of rural elderly to stop farm work is 60.7 years. The report however seems at variance with UN data which shows that 39% of males and 14% of females in the elderly age groups are in the work force (United Nations 2002). It is true,

China has much better social security system than India but this cannot explain the low rate of elderly work force in the urban areas, as evidenced by the ageing survey. In the more developed regions of the world with almost universal social security system, 21% of males and 10% of females are required to work (United Nations 2002).

Living Alone

Elderly living alone is growing phenomenon everywhere. It is an index of paucity of public and family supports; it is also an index of self-supporting survival mechanisms during old age. Nearly one in ten older adults in developing countries lives alone (Bongaarts and Zimmer 2001). In China, around 7% of its elderly do so. The figure is slightly less, at around 4% in India. More females are likely to live alone in old age than men. Women live longer than men, and are much less likely to live with a spouse in the household. Besides, in traditional Asian societies, women marry men older than them. The incidence of elderly living alone because of divorce, marital separation and never married status are very low in both India and China. The prevalence of widowhood among elderly females is very high in both countries. The Chinese data indicates that a widowed elderly woman spends on an average 13.5 years without her spouse. Such solitary living rises with age; widowed women in the age group spends 24.9 years without the husband. However, with the projected decline in mortality, the risk of widowhood will be lower in future.

TABLE 14: Elderly Living Alone in India and China

Country	Total			Rural			Urban		
	Total	Male	Female	Total	Male	Female	Total	Male	Female
China	5.1	9.4	7.1	6.5	8.9	7.6	3.6	9.8	6.6
India				2.5 (12.4)	6.1 (1.4)	4.3 (8.0)	3.0 (9.5)	6.0 (0.8)	4.5 (5.9)

Note: The figures in brackets indicates the findings of the NSS 42nd Round, 1986-87
Source: Data Analysis of the Sampling of Survey of the Aged Population in China, China Research Chnteronag, 2002.
The Aged In India: A socio-economic Profile, NNS Fifty-second Round July 1995-June 1996, NSSO, Department of Statistics, Ministry of Planning & Programme Implementation, Government of India, Calcutta, 1998.

The proportions of elderly living alone are higher in rural areas. A large number of people come from rural hinterland to urban areas for jobs and many of them stay there temporarily during the whole period of their work. A great majority of them return to their villages on retirement. As a result of crowded accommodation and rising living costs in urban areas, the elderly had been forced to live in rural areas away from their families, experiencing loneliness, boredom and neglect. The absence in the house of children and other household members, the absence or death of a spouse, and inadequate visits by relatives compound their loneliness and boredom. The Chinese data as well as the 42nd Round NSS survey data on single elderly confirm our hypothesis.[5]

NSS survey indicates that only 0.4% of elderly female are divorced or separated in India. The figure is over 2% in China. With a high proportion of marriages now ending in divorce, a large number of future elderly women will have the divorced / separated marital status. Divorced elderly women, unlike widowed women have no claim on their late husbands' pension rights. If divorce takes place at later ages, they may not be able to earn enough to make provisions for their old age. This places divorced women in a worse position than the widowed, who at least hold the pension rights of their late husbands.

TABLE 15: Divorced/Separated, Widowed and never Married Indian and Chinese Elderly

Marital status	Total			Rural			Urban		
	Total	Male	Female	Total	Male	Female	Total	Male	Female
China									
Never married	1.3	0.1	0.7	2.1	0.1	1.2	0.4	0.1	0.3
Divorced / separated	2.7	2.0	2.3	3.0	1.6	2.3	2.5	2.2	2.4
Widowed	19.3	53.8	35.5	25.9	58.6	40.6	12.3	49.3	30.4
India									
Never married				1.8	1.1	1.5	2.2	1.3	1.8
Divorced / separated				0.3	0.4	0.3	0.5	0.4	0.4
Widowed				20.9	40.8	39.8	17.8	60.9	39.8
				(20.7)	(61.6)	(42.4)	(18.4)	(64.9)	(42.4)

Note: The figures in brackets indicates the findings of the NSS 50th Round, 1986-87.

Source: Source: Analysis of data from the Sample Survey of the Aged Population in China, China Research Chnteronag, 2002.

The Aged In India: A socio-economic Profile, NNS Fifty-second Round July 1995-June 1996, NSSO, Department of Statistics, Ministry of Planning & Programme Implementation, Government of India, Calcutta, 1998.

The Future of the Support System

With modernisation, urbanisation and industrialisation in a society, family supports fall during old age (Cowgirl and Holmes 1972). In the developed, industrialised societies, the process has been very rapid, among other reasons, because of the public support itself which made the children shy of supporting parents. There is some evidence from other countries that public transfers are partially offset by reductions in private transfers. Cox and Jimenez find that for every dollar in public transfers to the elderly in Peru, private transfers are reduced by 37 cents (Cox and Jimenez 1992). The aged in the developed countries suffered temporarily because elderly well being transition, wonderfully summed up by Palmore and Manton (1974) :'early stages of economic development correspond to the relative decrement of resources held by the aged, but in economically advanced nations, entitlements such as pension plans begin to redress the previous losses incurred'. In such ageing, there is only a transition from high levels of well being based on family support systems to high levels of well being in which institutional supports are a major component.

The same transition does not hold for India and China. The family support system, despite its erosion, cannot break down because of time honoured Confucian values and religious sentiments. The long traditions of celebrating festivals within family networking, both in India and China, provide enough safety valves for intergenerational dependence on the family to continue. At the same time, there are very little possibilities for the further growth of public supports. The future of the aged in India and China essentially depends on the self-supporting programs by the aged themselves. The government can at the most play a regulatory role.

NOTES

1. As indicated by the World Bank's World Development Reports for different years.
2. 'Filial piety' or *xiao* is closely identified with 'Confucianism'. 'Filial' means of or due from a son or daughter. Filial piety reflects a social system based on the extended family. It was rooted in Chinese traditions extent before the fall of the last imperial dynasty in 1911. The system encouraged the accumulation of property and wealth and therefore made sons less inclined to go off on their own and set up new family units. This multigenerational extended family was the basic foundation for both production and distribution in agriculture and outside farm too.
3. The Indian Constitution in its Article 41 recognises the role of the State in providing old age supports.
4. In India the Code of Criminal Procedure 1973 [Section 125 (1) (d)] specifies such responsibility on the children along with section 20 (1) of the Hindu Adoption and Maintenance Act, 1956. In China under the Penal Code of 1980, children can be imprisoned for neglecting their parents.
5. There appears to be some reporting errors in the 52nd Round. It is difficult to explain how the proportion of single rural male elderly dropped from 12.4 to 2.5 in ten years.

REFERENCES

M.M.B. Asis, D. Domingo, J. Knodel, and K. Mehta. 1995. 'Living arrangements in four Asian countries: A comparative perspective'. *Journal of Cross-Cultural Gerontology* 10: 145–162.

Asian Development Bank. 2002. 'People's Republic of China Old-Age Pensions for the Rural Areas: From Land Reform to Globalization'.

John Bongaarts and Zachary Zimmer. 2001. 'Living Arrangements of Older Adults in the Developing World: An Analysis of DHS Household Surveys'. Working Papers No. 148. NewYork: Population Council.

D.L. Brandt Benjamin and Scott Rozelle. 2000. 'Ageing, Well-being and Social Security in Rural Northern China', in C Y Cyrus Chu and Ronald Lee Eds. *Population and Economic Change in East Asia*. (A supplement to *Population and Development Review*, Vol. 26).

John B Casterline et al. 1991. 'Differences in living arrangements in four Asian countries: The interplay of constraints and preferences'. *Comparative Study of the Elderly in Asia, Research Report No. 91-10*. Ann Arbor: Population Studies Center, University of Michigan, 1991

D.O. Cowgirl and L.D. Holmes (eds.). 1972. *Ageing and Modernisation*. New York : Appleton-Century-Crofts.

Rajagopal Dhar Chakraborti. 2004. 'The Greying of India; Population Ageing in the context of Asia'. New Delhi: Sage Publications.

China Statistical Yearbook 2002. Bejing: National Bureau of Statistics of China, China Statistics Press, Beijing, 2002

D. Cox and E. Jimenez. 1992. 'Social Security and Private Transfers in Developing Countries: the Case of Peru'. *World Bank Economic Review* 6 (1): 155-70.

Elizabeth Croll. 2000. "Social Welfare Reform: Trends and Tensions." In Richard Louis Edmonds (ed.). *The People's Republic of China after Fifty Years*. Oxford: Oxford University Press. 2000

S.M. Dev. 1994. 'Social Security in the Unorganised Sector: Lessons from the Experiences of Kerala and Tamil Nadu States'. *Indian Journal of Labour Economics*. Vol. 37, No. 4.

J. Dreze and P.V. Srinivasan. 1997. 'Widowhood and poverty in rural India: Some inferences from household survey data'. *Journal of Development Economics*. 54:. 217-234.

Peng Du and Guo Zhi-gang. 2000. 'Population and Ageing in China', in David R. Philips, ed. *Ageing in the Asia-Pacific Region*. London: Routledge.

Government of India. 1995. National Social Assistance Programme (NSAP): Guidelines. Delhi: Ministry of Rural Areas and Employment, Department of Rural Development.

HelpAge India, 1998. *Directory of Old Age Homes in India*.

A.I. Hermalin, Ed. 2002. 'The Well-Being of the Elderly in Asia: A Four Country Comparative Study'. Michigan: University of Michigan Press.

Charlotte Ikels. 1993. 'Settling Accounts: The Intergenerational Contract in an Age of Reform', in Deborah Davis and Stevan Harrell, eds. Chinese Families in the Post-Mao Era. Berkeley: University of California Press.

John Knodel, Napaporn Chayovan, and Siriwan Siriboon. 1992. 'Family support and living arrangements of Thai elderly'. *Asia-Pacific Population Journal* 12(4):51-68.

Hung-Tak Lee. 1998. 'Family welfare and reproductive health: The Korean experience'. Paper presented at KIHASA/UNFPA Seminar on Population and Development Policies in Low Fertility Countries. Seoul: Korea Institute for Health and Social Affairs (KIHASA).

L.G. Martin. 1990. 'The status of South Asia's growing elderly population'. *Journal Of Cross-Cultural Gerontology*. 5: 93–117.

Josena N. Natividad, and Grace T. Cruz. Patterns in living arrangements and familial support for the elderly in the Philippines. Asia-Pacific Population Journal 12(4): 17–34. 1997.

Naohiro Ogawa and Robert D. Rutherford.1997. 'Shifting costs of caring for the elderly back to families in Japan'. *Population and Development Review* 23(1): 59–74.

E. Palmore and K. Manton. 1974. 'Modernisation and the Status of the Aged: International Correlation'. *Journal of Gerontology*. 29:205-210.

R. Palacios and M. Pallares. 2000. International Patterns of Pension Provision. World Bank: Pension Reform Primer Working Paper Series.

S.I. Rajan. 2001. 'Social Assistance for Poor Elderly: How effective?' *Economic and Political Weekly*. February 24, 2001.

Arland Thornon, Ming-Cheng Chnag, and Te-Hsiung Sun. 1984. 'Social and economic change, intergenerational relationships, and family formation in Taiwan'. *Demography* 21(4): 475-499.

Paul Wallace. 1989. *Agequake: Riding the Demographic Rollercoaster Shaking Business and Our World.* London: Nicolas Brearly Publishing.

United Nations. 2002. Population Ageing 2002 Wall Chart. United Nations: Department of Economic and Social Affairs.

World Bank. 2001. Finance and Private Sector Development. India: The Challenge of Old Age Income Security. Mimeo, April 5, 2001.

Zimmer Zachary and Sovan Kiry Kim. 2002. 'Living Arrangements and Socio-Demographic Conditions of Older Adults in Cambodia'. Working Papers No. 157. New York: Population Council.

Chapter 17

Old Age Security: Families vs Governments or Families and Governments?

Mussaddeq Chowdhury and *Jeffrey Nugent*

Formal and informal programmes of old age security usually coexist in developing countries. Generally speaking, the relative importance of formal programmes rises with the level of development. Whereas many argue that developing countries must expand their formal programmes as soon as possible to fill the gaps in and substitute for crumbling informal programmes, this paper emphasises the need for going slow and maximising the complementarity between formal and informal programmes. Otherwise, neither type of programme may be sustainable.

Formal and Informal Schemes

Formal schemes refer to those which are set in place by legal/legislative methods or by employer-employee contract.[1] The social security scheme in the United States is one example of a formal scheme. Originally, this scheme was similar to a private insurance scheme where individuals deposited some portion of their salaries into a fund which would accumulate interest. Upon retirement, benefits would be paid out of the principal and accrued interest. In 1939, the system was converted into a pay-as-you-go basis whereby each generation of retirees is supported by the current generation of workers. Thus, this scheme may be viewed as a legally binding mechanism of intergenerational transfer. In India and several other former British colonies, there are Provident Fund schemes, more akin to the pre 1939 system in the U.S.

Informal schemes, on the other hand, refer to the provision of support by family and non family sources, although it is the former that is predominant. This is the major—often only—source of old age support in the LDCs. It is important to note that since normally there are no legal sanctions involved,[2] such support may rely crucially on the existing norms and belief systems of society. It should be further noted that such schemes may be successful but also fragile in evolutionary terms.[3]

Characteristics of Informal Schemes

At their most basic, informal systems are characterised by children taking care of their elderly parents; there are however many other informal mechanisms, such as local communities, informal clubs, kinship groups, patron-client relationships, and religious and other non governmental organisations. Even family support displays considerable diversity across time and space. Sometimes, support comes from family members within households and at other times from family members living in other households, often at considerable geographical distance. Support may come also from younger siblings, as in the case of a brother caring for a sister or the *mutual* support of two widows, or from much younger spouses married specifically for this reason.

Even in the more common case in which support for the elderly comes from younger family members, there are many instances where the care is provided by grandchildren rather than children and could take the form of providing companionship, help with housework or fetching water. Perhaps more importantly, in some societies like India and Bangladesh, it is primarily sons, and often the eldest sons (and their wives) who are responsible for their parents' care. In other societies like the U.S., it is primarily daughters caring for mothers and in still other cases, the responsibilities may be divided.

Likely Future of Informal Schemes

The likely dimensions of the problem of old age care in the LDCs appear staggering. Tracy (1991) quotes estimates[4] showing that in 2025, 71 per cent of the world's elderly population of 1.2 billion will live in the LDCs and the age dependency ratio[5] will have risen from 7 per cent in 1950 to 12 per cent. According to another source,[6] as fertility declines and life expectancy increases in the LDCs, the older population is expected to grow markedly—those 60 years and older, 70 years and older and 80 years and older are estimated to grow between 1985 and 2000 by 57 per cent, 63 per cent and 82 per cent respectively. It is noteworthy that the highest growth is projected to occur among the very oldest. Furthermore, Treas and Logue (1986) estimate that the life expectancy differences at age 60 between developed countries (DCs) and LDCs is only 2.4 years and 4.6 years for men and women respectively.[7] What this means is that, for persons who survive to age 60, societies and / or families may have to provide old age support for about the same number of years, regardless of the levels of *social and economic development.*[9]

Market Failure or Government Failure?

In the light of the above discussion, it seems reasonable to conclude that there will be a tremendous surge in the demand for old age care. But can one expect the supply *of formal* support mechanisms to grow rapidly in LDCs ? To attempt to answer this crucial question, it is necessary to examine the existing and foreseeable social, political and economic conditions.

Paucity of Formal Schemes

First, LDC governments often lack the capacity to collect taxes and dispense benefits and the proportion of the population engaged in full time wage employment is often insufficient to support programmes of social insurance. Second, the painful adjustments and cutbacks that DCs are presently having to make in their formal programmes offer sobering demonstrations of over extension and cost escalation. Not surprisingly, there is considerable reluctance in LDCs to institute similar schemes, given that the resource constraints there are even more severe. Third, there is a concern in LCDs for the perceived unwanted effects of formal old age security schemes. The picture of an elderly parent being sent out to a retirement home until (s)he dies is often viewed in LDCs as someone sentenced to death waiting in death row.

Fourth, many LDC scholars believe that the current (and changed) DC goal of redistributing the responsibility of the care of the elderly to families and communities while maintaining minimal government intervention is something the LDCs already have and are in danger of loosing if DC type schemes are introduced. Finally, only in few LDCs do the elderly have the type of organised political clout they enjoy in the DCs. Lacking the type of institutions[9] where numbers of voters may be important and political parties and lobbies may facilitate the exercise of political pressure to advance the cause of the weak and vulnerable groups like the elderly, most allocation decisions are undertaken on the basis of political patronage disadvantaging the elderly.

These reasons probably led Tracy (1991) to conclude that the dilemma faced by LDCs is '...how to offer support through federal and state programs without destroying the traditional responsibility of families to care for their elderly members'. The challenge is thus to ensure that the governmental schemes be small in size[10] and act *as complements* to, rather than substitutes of, informal schemes.

Reasons for Market Failure

The problem of access to old age support may be viewed as the non existence of markets for insurance. People do not know at what age they will be unable to work or at what age they will die. This means that, even if they could save for their old age, they would not know how much to put aside. What is required is a mechanism to provide insurance. But different people will die and be unable to work at different ages and a profit maximising insurance company should charge different premiums for different people. This gives rise to an information asymmetry because the (different) individual characteristics—family health history, dietary habits, lifestyle etc.—are known to the person concerned but not to the insurer.

Information asymmetry causes an adverse selection problem whereby only individuals with risks above those that can be covered by the premium would voluntarily chose to be insured. The result is that, in the long run, such a scheme would not continue to be available because the provider would be incurring losses. There is the related, but conceptually independent problem of moral hazard.[11] In this situation, the insured has an incentive to make fraudulent claims of old age support and—due to information asymmetry— the company will find it difficult to distinguish between legitimate and false claims. Even if the claim is legitimate, the company would, in most cases, be unable to determine whether the cause of the condition was due to an accident or whether it was negligence.

Traditional family based old age support systems can reduce, if not eliminate, many of these problems. People in such societies use informal risk pooling within multigenerational families or kinship groups to insure against the risks of old age dependency, of which two are especially important: the risk of becoming unproductive due to ill health and the risk of living long and having insufficient income.

The family's size and heterogeneity make possible the realisation of economies of scale and risk pooling within a diverse group, while substantially reducing the informational costs and asymmetries of formal systems. Within a family, there is little or no choice to opt in or out; thus the problem of adverse selection is reduced. Furthermore, the knowledge and monitoring of relatives—some or many of whom live nearby—can mitigate the problem of moral hazard. The cost of old age support in informal systems can also be held down because of the many useful activities the old can perform—cooking, taking care of small children, and cleaning or repairing the house. In addition, care of the old takes place within the household and so the care givers can engage in other activities, thus reducing the opportunity cost of care. In contrast to formal schemes which spell out every contingency and may lead to unexpected outcomes in a dynamic setting, family based systems are more flexible and can adjust more quickly to changing circumstances.

One problem faced by traditional systems is insufficient scope for diversification and risk pooling. This occurs, for example, if the entire family lives in the same village and cultivates the same plot of land; in such as situation, the risks are correlated and the gains from risk pooling are small. Extended families may attempt to reduce this problem by spreading risk beyond the village: a satellite family unit may be se up in an urban area or a son or daughter may be married into a geographically distant village.[12]

The upshot of this discussion is that private markets for insurance are not likely to develop in the face of information asymmetries. If we consider additional factors like the absence of stock and bond markets and clear and enforceable property rights (especially with respect to land ownership), the avenues open to those seeking to provide for their old age appear fairly limited.

Reasons for Government Failure

In the light of the private market failure discussed above, it is pertinent to examine whether the government can provide the optimum level of old age support. On purely theoretical grounds, the problem of information asymmetry would appear to be of the same magnitude for a govemment bureaucrat as it is for an insurance company. And thus—factoring in adverse selection and moral hazard—it is unlikely that a government scheme based on *voluntary* participation could be self sustaining.

One alternative that may appear attractive is an insurance scheme that is *compulsory* for every citizen. Such a scheme would appear to provide a mechanism for risk pooling[13] and enable the provider to charge an actuarial fair premium.[14] In addition to the likelihood of the persistence—and indeed, increase—of the moral hazard problem[15] that may render such a scheme unworkable, there is the logistic problem of collecting premiums from people in LDCs most of whom do not work in the formal sector.

The dilemma faced by LDCs is this: the informal system has some holes in it, such as widows without surviving children or with children too poor or too distant to be of help, which need to be filled or supplemented. Due to increasing life expectancy and earlier retirement, in the foreseeable future, the demand for old age support is almost certain to increase dramatically in LDCs, especially in rural areas. At the same time, however, the supply is likely to fall due to the declining numbers of children and the changes that accompany the process of modernisation.[16] The government, faced with severe budgetary constraints, is not likely to be able to do what is required on it own. What is called for is a carefully crafted set of policies ensuring that any government programme does not supplant an existing informal mechanism.[17]

Crowding Out or Crowding in?

'Crowding out' occurs when a government or other formal activity limits or constrains, that is, 'crowds out', some private or informal activity. Similarly, 'crowding in' occurs when a government or other formal activity facilitates some private or informal activity.

What is the motive for private transfers between people, usually members of a family? One group led by Becker (1974) argues that the motive is altruism, that is, selfless and genuine concern of the one for the welfare of the other.[18] If this group is correct, they the government would necessarily 'crowd out' private transfers. Another group, led by Kotlikoff and Spivak (1981) and Bernheim, Shleifer and Summers (1985) claim that the motive is one of inter temporal exchange. Since a public transfer does not necessarily undermine the private donor's desire or need to provide the transfer, crowding out may not occur.[19] When the motives are mixed, partial crowding out may occur.

Is it possible for a formal scheme to 'crowd in' the private sector ? It is obvious that this would be the case if there were complementarity among different types of support. A private donor may realise that the time and money spent would not be useful unless the elderly has access to a free or subsidised government clinic.[20] If receipt of public transfer increases the elderly's respect or bargaining power, crowding in may also result.

The empirical evidence of the relative importance of crowding out and crowding in is scarce. The reason for this is not difficult to understand. Few DCs have pervasive informal care giving and few LDCs have formal systems and thus data for estimating 'crowding out' and 'crowding in' are not easy to find. Latin American countries are something of an exception in that they have fairly comprehensive formal social security schemes but also apparently substantial private transfers. A study of Peru by Cox and Jimenez (1991) shows that public transfers crowd out private transfers but only partially.

Conclusions and Policy Recommendations

The above discussion may be summarised thus: (i) informal schemes of old age support, while not perfect, generally have substantial advantages over formal schemes in LDCs, (ii) formal schemes are unlikely to be instituted in the near future, at least in rural areas, (iii) even if formal schemes are initiated, they may merely 'crowd out' private donors and the excess demand may persist. The logical conclusion therefore, is to undertake formal schemes only to the extent that they complement informal ones. It would make sense to phase in such schemes gradually as and when informal schemes appear deficient. Simultaneously—and perhaps most importantly—all efforts should be made to strengthen the existing informal systems by providing proper incentives.[21]

Specific Policy Suggestions

(i) One of the most important factors contributing to the break up of social norms like providing old age care for parents is increased mobility. If children migrate to cities, not only are they less able to care for their parents physically, they are also less likely to provide monetary help.[22] Furthermore, these new emigrants may never qualify for formal support even though they may spend most of their working lives in urban areas.[23] Given the fact that urban in migration is almost certain to occur, the relevant policy choice is to mitigate its effects. In this connection, the role of bequests is important; the parent should be able to use his / her bequest in a strategic manner to induce old age care from children.[24] To increase the likelihood of old age care both for the rural out migrants upon retirement and for the elderly left behind in villages, communication links like bus services should be improved between urban and rural areas. This would induce support and assure the migrants of informal support in their communities of origin upon their retirement.

(ii) In most LDCs, there is what may be termed the 'urban bias'. This refers to distortions favouring the modern sectors (usually located in urban areas) and includes protective tariffs and quotas and/or the subsidisation of inputs like foreign exchange, credit and electricity. These policies siphon resources away from the rural to the urban areas and probably contribute significantly to rural out migration. Removal of these distortionary policies would discourage rural out migration and help preserve the traditional support means based on frequent contact and close proximity.

(iii) In order to 'crowd in' informal support, formal schemes should provide only those goods and services that complement rather than substitute those provided by the informal system. Community provided clinics, out patient health facilities and social amenities may make it more feasible for families to provide care within their homes or to periodically enquire after the welfare of the elderly.[25]

(iv) Crowding out may be minimised by limiting the amount of formal support. Small stipends or in kind support are unlikely to cause the children to shirk caring for elderly parents. On the contrary, public notice of the elderly receiving *some* support from other sources may raise their respect and increase both the livelihood and amount of informal support.

(v) Another option is to limit formal support only to those without family members able to provide care. This type of conditionality has several drawbacks. First, the transaction costs of introducing such conditionality maybe too high. Second, to be effective, there must be a mechanism whereby family members *able* to provide support actually *do* so. Third, those who have demand for old age care may not have children.

(vi) Special attention needs to be paid to the condition of widows, who are more vulnerable to not receiving care than married people. Long periods of widowhood are fairly common in LDCs and are the result of large age differentials between husband and wife at first marriage, higher life expectancy for females, lower remarriage and labour force participation rates for females and discriminatory policies against women with regard to inheritance and property ownership. Policy options would include the removal of discrimination and the encouragement of widow remarriage.

NOTES

1. In LDCs, governmental schemes of social security are generally confined to professionals working in the military, bureaucracy or large and especially foreign or government owned enterprises. Hence, only a relatively small segment of the population working in the formal sector has access to employer provided pension schemes. As such, these schemes are highly inequitable since they exclude the poorest segment of the population, that is, those working in the informal sector.
2. Even in cases where filial loyalty is backed up by formal sanctions as in China, 'where children who have come of age have the duty to support and assist their parents', according to the country's constitution, in practice such sanctions are very infrequently administered.
3. See Basu (1991) where he discusses how norms can change in a manner analogous to the evolutionary process. He compares the disappearance of norms with the disappearance of the white moth after the Industrial Revolution in England. The black moth was better able to blend into the soot laden air and thus be protected from predators.
4. Economic and Social Council. 1989. *Second Review and Appraisal of the Implementation of the International Plan of Action on Aging.* Report of the Secretary General (E/1989/13).
5. This is defined as the population aged 65 and above divided by the population aged 15 to 64.
6. United Nations Fund for Population Activities. 1985. *Population Perspectives: Statements by World Leaders*
7. Note, however, that there is substantial variation both *between* as well as *within* LDCs with respect to life expectancy.
8. An important offset in many LDCs, however, is a falling child dependency ratio due to declining birth rates.
9. Examples include political parties and lobbies.
10. Due to the resources constraints and the sociopolitical conditions of the LDCs discussed above.
11. This refers to the situation where insured people are negligent in protecting themselves from undesirable consequences once they are insured. If, for example, one's car is fully insured, one is less likely to install an auto alarm even if one lives in an area where auto theft is common.
12. For further details, see Rosenzweig (1988) and World Bank (1994)
13. This is because people who are less likely to be sick are now required to participate in the programme. Note that, while this may reduce adverse selection, the moral hazard problem is not alleviated by a government programme. On the contrary, to the extent

that a bureaucrat's incentive to monitor negligence and fraud may be less than that of a private insurance company employee, the moral hazard problem may well be worse. One can easily visualise a scenario where any gains made by reducing adverse selection may be wiped out by increased moral hazard problems, thus rendering the government scheme a failure.

14. In other words, the premium where the (expected) profit to the provider is zero.
15. Note that while a compulsory scheme may alleviate the problem of adverse selection, it does not help solve the moral hazard problem. People who are insured continue to have little or no incentive to protect themselves. In the likely event that a government bureaucrat is less likely to monitor fraud and negligence than a private insurer, the moral hazard problem may be worse.
16. As children migrate to cities, there are fewer sources of supply of old age care for elderly parents.
17. It is the view of many economists, for example, that the social security scheme of the U.S. has reduced the incentive to save for retirement.
18. One cares for one's elderly parent because one is concerned about his/her welfare. This concern is likely to be the greatest when the parent has not alternative means of support and is likely to decrease when such alternatives become available.
19. One may care for one's parents because one recognises the sacrifices the parent has made when one was young and, perhaps more importantly, one wants to instill in one's own children the norm of caring for elderly parents. In this connection, see Basil's (1991) concept of common teachings', which he calls social science's counterpart of the gene in biology in evolutionary terms. If a norm like caring for elderly parents serves to fulfill a useful social function, it tends to be perpetuated by common teachings where one generation acts to teach the next about the usefulness of the norm.
20. This would especially be the case if the donor realises that s(he) is unable to meet the entire expenses on his/her own. Note that the result may be the same regardless of whether the donor is acting due to motives of altruism or inter temporal exchange.
21. For details, see Nugent (1990).
22. Note that there are two offsetting factors at work here. A better job far away may make one *more* able to provide monetary help to one's elderly parents but the distance may also make it *less* likely that one would do so.
23. Work in the huge informal sector in urban areas of LDCs does not in general entitle one to a pension scheme.
24. For details see Nugent (1990).
25. Institutionalisation is a formal scheme that would crowd out informal support systems. For strong indictments against this, see Tout (1989) and Tracy (1991).

REFERENCES

Basu, Kaushik. (1991). 'Civil Norms and Evolution'. (Unpublished paper)

Becker, Gary. (1974). 'A Theory of Social Interactions'. *Journal of Political Economy* 82: 1063-1093.

Bernheim, B. Douglas, Andrei Schleifer and Lawrence H. Summers. (1985). 'The Strategic Bequest Motive'. *Journal of Political Economy.* 93 (December): 1045-1076.

Cox, Donald and Emmanuel Jimenez. (1991). 'Achieving Social Objectives through Private Transfers'. *World Bank Observer.* 5 (July): 205-218.

Kotlikoff, Laurence J. and Avia Spivak (1981). 'The Family as an Incomplete Annuities

Market'. *Journal of Political Economy.* 89 (April) 372-491.

Nugent, Jeffrey B. (1990). 'Old Age Security and the Defense of Social Norms'. *Journal of Cross Cultural Gerontology.* 5: 243-254.

Rosenzweig, Mark R. (1988). 'Risk, Implicit Contracts and the Family in Rural Areas of Low Income Countries'. *Economic Journal.* December.

Tout, Ken J. (1989). *Aging in Developing Countries.*

Tracy, Martin B. (1991). *Social Policies for the Elderly in the Third World.* New York: Greenwood Press.

Treas, Judith and Barbara Logue. (1986). 'Economic Development and the Older Population'. *Population and Development Review.*

World Bank. (1994). *Averting the Old Age Crisis: Policies to Protect the Old and Promote Growth.* Washington D.C.

Chapter 18

The Hospice as an Agency for Elderly Care: Field Perspectives from the Indian State of Kerala

Thulasibai, P.

The World Conference on Ageing in Vienna in 1984 first highlighted the demographic ageing taking place in developing countries. As in the case of the developed countries in the past, the developing countries of today are undergoing a demographic transition from high birth and death rates to low birth and death rates. One notable difference between longevity increases in the west and in the developing countries today, as the World Bank Report 1980 points out, is that while the economic changes that resulted from the agricultural and industrial revolutions led to the increase in nutrient intake, improvement in sanitation, water supply and better housing, due to which mortality levels went down and longevity increased, the success of medical science, especially in controlling infectious disease has weakened the link between income/GNP and health/life expectancy. On account of longevity increases and, at the same time, decreases in the young-age population due to falls in fertility, the proportion of elderly has been on the rise in the developing world.

It is noteworthy also that even though the share of elderly in the LDC populations is low compared to what it is in the developed countries, the LDCs contribute substantially to the world's elderly population, because of the sheer size of national populations in the less developed world. To illustrate, while India's age composition is typical of underdeveloped countries, with a relatively high young age population, the sheer size of the country's population being what it is, the UN had projected that by the year 2001, one in seven elderly persons above the age of 60 would to be from India (UN Report 1991). From only 12 million persons above the age of 60 in 1901, the number of elderly in India crossed 20 million in 1951 and went up to 57 million in 1991. It is expected that the 100 million mark will be reached in 2013. Sixty-three percent (36 million) of the elderly population in 1991 was in the age group of 60-69 years while 11 percent (6 million) were in the age group of 80 years and above. In 2016, the numbers are expected to be 69 million in the case of elderly people above the age of 60 and 11 million in the case of elderly people above the age of 80 years (Government of India 1999).

Of all the States of India, Kerala is most advanced in the demographic transition. The birth rate in Kerala is 17.2, where as the national level is 24.7. In Thrissur is still lower i.e. 16.5. The efficient primary health care system, the high literacy rate, especially female education, and good health awareness have contributed to the lower birth rate in Kerala, resulting in a smaller young population, while the lower mortality rate has in turn resulted in longer life expectancy. Thus, while expectancy of life is 70 years for males and 73 for females in Kerala, in India it is 64 for males and 65.6 for females.

Of all the States in India, Kerala has the highest proportion of elderly persons above the age of 60. While the overall figure for India is 7.9 per cent, in Kerala, the proportion is 10.2 per cent. The proportion of elderly women is 11.5 percent and elderly men, 8.9 per cent (Census of India 2001). According to the 1991 census, there were 25.5 lakh elderly persons in the State, who formed 8.8 percent of the total population. The number of elderly in the year 2001, estimated at 10.9%, is projected to touch 25 percent by the year 2031. The elderly population in Kerala is growing at about two times faster than the total population of the State. Due to the longer life expectancy and increase in the aging population, Kerala acquired the epithet 'the state of old people'. This in turn owes much to Kerala's special health scenario, which is often considered at par with those of many industrialised countries. Certain factors need special mention in this context. The most important among them is the high degree of health promotion by the rulers even from the day of the Princely State of Tranvancore, and the activities of Christian missionaries in the spheres of health and education, especially female education. Moreover, investments in health and education by all elected government in Kerala helped to set a foundation of a well organised primary health care system.

Combined with increased longevity, owing to the decreased fertility rate, there is a rise in the dependence burden.[1] The dependency ratio, i.e., the number of people above the age of 60 divided by the number of people between the age of 15 and 59, is expected to rise from 12 percent in 1981 to 20 per cent in 2020. Dependency is relatively more for female elderly. More aged people are residing in rural areas than in urban areas, and economic dependency is also more in rural areas. As per the study by the National Sample Survey Organisations, 78 percent of the elderly are residing in rural areas and 22 percent are in urban areas.

Coping with Ageing

Coping with aging becomes difficult when traditional community support systems disintegrate. In societies where extended family systems are prevalent, the elderly are able to continue to perform useful and valued functions, and they enjoy high status.[2] This tends to be lower in societies, which favour nuclear families. Changes in family systems have also arrived in India, where a strong joint family system once existed. Traditionally, the community forms an important external force that reinforces the ability of the family to offer a caring environment for the aged. Thus the elderly in the traditional societies such as those in India enjoyed an unparalleled sense of honour and authority in the family or community. They also participated in decision-making responsibilities in the economic and political activities of the family and were treated as repositories of experience and wisdom.

With a decline of the traditional way of life, these props have attenuated. Today the western way of life is considered to be 'modern'. As with food, housing style and education, retirement homes and old age homes are now considered to reflect the 'wave of the future'. Among the states of India, Kerala has the highest number of retirement homes. What do we know about this way of living, from the experience of the west? The western world has witnessed many hard sell retirement communities. These systems came into being on the belief that they are the answer to the loneliness and isolation of older people. Studies done in such places revealed that these retirement enclaves seemed to promote an 'aged subculture but of retreats type'. Those preferring to interact only with the aged turned out, on the average to be less active, lonelier, less confident and less satisfied with life and also less healthy than those who preferred interacting with all ages in the larger community.

Sadly, in Kerala, ageing is still not recognised as a social problem. Barring some stray initiatives at the official and Non Governmental Organisation levels, Kerala society is yet to evolve a genuine care strategy sensitive to the predicaments of its aged generation. At best, ageing is seen as a problem within the family, very often heaping guilt in the minds of children who themselves must live life by the second and have little time to spare for the elderly back home. Even fairly large amounts of money can do little to compensate the loneliness and absence of love that the elderly experience. In a manner of speaking, it is the price that a society is paying for the longevity it has achieved without creating the support system so necessary to offer quality life to those who now live into their 70s and 80s and beyond.

The longevity and the low birth rate that the State achieved as part of the much-debated 'Kerala Model' of development has unleashed many 'second generation' problems, the socio-economic impact of the graying population being one among them. While the proportion of the aged in the national population would cross only the 10 per cent mark in 2020, Kerala would cross the 20 percent mark by then. At the national level, persistence of poverty and poor access to health care facilities are major factors that hamper longevity, particularly among tribals and dalits.

Old Age Homes

Kerala has around 95 old age homes. Around 80 of them are in the private sector. The government has set apart Rs. 5 lakhs each for 40 panchayats for setting up old age homes and another Rs. 42 crores is proposed to be spent on upgradation of existing old age homes under the Modernisation Government Programme (MGP). But there is no provision for assessment or vertical and horizontal integration of the schemes. Moreover, old age homes still carry a stigma in Kerala society. Even elderly persons who go to old age homes on their own want to go back to their kith and kin when they fall ill.

There are at least two reasons why old age homes have become a necessity in Kerala. The first is the migration of youngsters to the Gulf and other destinations for employment and the second, the difficulties that care givers within homes face, particularly in the care of the very old with multiple organ impairment. In the case of the poor, it is all the more important that the State steps in to facilitate care of the elderly who would otherwise be left to die a slow death without proper medial care and support.

The total lack of a strategy to tap the potential of elderly retired persons is another issue. Most of the employed in the State retire at the age of 55 and all their capabilities and the expertise they acquire from the service go to waste once they are out of service. It is very important that there be a concerted effort to utilise the capabilities of the elderly. That will also keep them engaged. It is a good sign that retired teachers are now leading most of the private medical colleges. Even at the lower level, retired hands can be posted in some jobs like those of curators, library assistants, and the like.

Care of Elderly

Since most of the elderly persons studied were living either as couple or with close relatives, they were getting some kind of care. Among males, about two-thirds were getting care from their wives and in the remaining cases, the caregivers were children or close relatives. In the case of women, nearly two-thirds were taken care of by their children or by close relatives.

The fact that there is a caregiver does not however necessarily mean that the elderly get *adequate* care. From close observation and interaction with them, it was found that care received was adequate only in the case of 60 percent of the respondents. For the remaining 40 percent, care giving was thoroughly inadequate or lacking. There are a few cases in which the relation with the caregiver is strained. In most of the cases the relation is found to be good or somehow the elderly people cope with the situation.

Social Interaction

With advancement in age, social relations also tend to weaken, for various reasons. Participation in social, cultural and religious activities begin to diminish. Only about one-third of the elderly maintain close relationship with their friends and frequently meet them, and these are mostly men. About one-third of the men and more than half of the women in the sample reported that they had no close friends and that they rarely go out. Only about 40 per cent of the elderly participated in outside activities and that too is mainly in religious activities and social function like marriages, or family gatherings. Elderly persons who come to live with their children often faced restrictions in their movements and contact. When other members of the family went out, they were made to sit alone behind closed doors or even locked homes. Also, they were not allowed to mix freely with neighbours. In many cases, the condition of the elderly was really very bad in their houses.

The Hospice

When care of the elder members of the family becomes difficult, the younger household members may want to send them to old age homes for professional care. But in most of the old age homes, these people are not getting the proper care they need. This brings us to the issue of the hospice. Hospice and hospice care are terms some times used to describe in-patient palliative care units. It actually refers to a philosophy of care, rather than a specific building or service, and may encompass a programme of care and array of skills useful in wide range of settings. The hospice is a concept derived from medieval times, symbolising a place where travelers, pilgrims, the sick, the wounded, or the dying can find rest and comfort. An ideal contemporary hospice offers a comprehensive care programme for patients facing life-threatening or terminal illnesses, which includes comfort to their families. Home care is a significant part of the hospice concept. Terminal care is an important part of palliative care and usually refers to the management of patients during their last few days or weeks or months of life. Home care is a significant part of the hospice concept. Those who are not well enough to come to the clinic are helped by the home care system. Trained volunteers go to the homes of the patients and nurse them, periodically and whenever needed. Indian philosophy affirms life and regards dying as a natural process that should be neither hastened nor prolonged, and which can be met with richness of spirit. Palliative care and hospice services make it possible for patients to live and die with dignity.

In sum, the hospice can provide critical medical and nursing care, as well as psychological and spiritual support for the ailing elderly, augment the family support structure, help the elderly be independent and productive, and provide comfort and sophisticated symptom relief to the dying so as to help them die a peaceful, calm and dignified death. These aspects are illustrated with case study material compiled by the present author, who is a retired civil surgeon running a hospice—the Santhitheeram Charitable Trust, in the rural suburbs of Thrissur city in Kerala. Santhitheeram Charitable Trust was established on 27th February 2001 to cater to those unfortunate elderly persons who are left alone in their homes. Our target is to provide medical and nursing care as well as emotional and spiritual support for totally bed-ridden patients, and provide them with a painless and peaceful life till their end.

Aged people need medical help as well as a compassionate approach, for most of them are bed-ridden and uncared for. To that end, as a primary step for the establishment of a hospice, I, along with some other doctor friends, had given medical training to a few lady volunteers who were willing to work for the sick and aged. After the successful completion of their training, they were sent to the homes where the aged people stay.

Nature of Care

The main diseases which affected the bedridden elderly were of three types: post stroke paralysis, post operative disabilities, and other debilitating disease like cancer, dementia, malnutrition, and arthritis. When I made a systematic follow up study of 25 cases of totally bedridden patients in their houses, I got very encouraging and satisfactory results. Out of the 25 cases, 9 patients recovered when they were given timely and proper care. In five cases we could intervene only in the last stages. Still we could make them comfortable and peaceful during their last days. In another six cases the family members did not co-operate and we could not do much as the patients were also in irrecoverable stages. Some of them suffered from dehydration, hypoglycemia, hypoproteinemia, anaemia etc. and had a miserable end to their life. Others were continuing with care and were improving. Cooperation from relatives is very important in home care service. The absence of responsible persons in the home is one of the main problems we faced in giving proper care for the sick elderly at home. In most of the houses, a widower or a widow or both, sick and old, were living without any support from the younger generation. When they become bedridden, a home nurse or care-giver alone will not be able to look after them at home. Hence they will have to be institutionalised. Therefore we feel that in addition to home care, institutionalised care also should be provided to those elderly sick who have nobody to care for them at home. In home care services, since the involvement and co-operation of the family members is so very important and since the absence of young family members is a recurrent feature in the modern nuclear family set up, both in the urban and the rural areas in Kerala, institutionalised care has become imperative.

In two cases of post stroke paralysis, we were very late in getting the information and the patients were in a very miserable condition, due to lack of proper care. They died within a week. The others, being cared for, were recovering. We sent trained care-givers to their homes regularly to give them food and medicine on time, to clean them up, bathe them, to make them do exercises etc. These care-givers give instructions to the family members on how to take care of the bed-ridden patients. In some cases, doctors visit the patients in their homes when needed. Day and night help is rendered by the care-givers as per the request of the relatives. We have many testimonials from family members appreciating the timely help and service given by the doctors and the care givers in bringing their relatives back to normal life.

We know that the type of care now given is not at all adequate to solve the problems of the sick elderly in Kerala, as so many are suffering silently, unnoticed and uncared for, in their homes. With proper care, love and affection, their suffering can be relieved and many of them can be brought back to their independent life again. They require medical and nursing care, and emotional, psychological and spiritual support from qualified professionals.

This is the ultimate aim of Santhitheeram. Santhitheeram provides continuous medical and nursing care, as well as emotional and spiritual support to take care of the sick and suffering elderly with affection and love, so that their twilight days may be painless and peaceful. Santhitheeram is trying its best to direct its activities towards the awareness programme also. But we are very sorry to say that we find it very difficult to get support from any governmental or non-governmental organisations engaged in this field. In Kerala though the awareness programmes in all other fields are being conducted very actively and effectively, the awareness in the care of old and sick is almost nil among the public. The government as well as non-governmental organisations should come forward to do effective awareness programmes in this field.

Domiciliary Service Scheme

In some cases, I observed that aged people are abandoned by their relatives, for they think that there is no hope of recovery. But I know, from my personal experience that with proper and timely care, we can more or less successfully treat at least some victims of stroke, brain injury, partial paralysis or even a state of coma. So we actually demonstrate to the relatives how to deal with such cases and help them to recuperate. I have personal satisfaction that I could manage some cases with remarkable success through our domiciliary care schemes. A few case studies are given here to give some insight into the kind of service rendered by the home-care system. (Names are changed to protect the identity of the patients).

Seventy-year old John came to my clinic one day, with a bleeding ulcer on his foot. When the dressing was removed, there was profuse bleeding with bubbles, and a severe foul smell from a deep ulcer under his toes. The ulcer was full of maggots and the tissues were all eaten away by them. One of the toes was almost detached from the foot. The tip of his middle toe was gangrenous. I told his 12-year-old grandson who had accompanied him about the seriousness of the situation and asked him to tell his parents to admit his grandfather immediately in a hospital. The next day also John came in an auto with the boy, complaining that his sons and daughters had not time to take him to the hospital or bring him to my clinic. So I instructed one of my volunteers to go to his home and take care of him. She went to his house and cleaned and dressed his wound, and gave him proper medication. When I visited his hut, I found the floor smeared with cow dung, from which flies infested the wound and produced the maggots. I advised the household not to use cow-dung any more. With one full month's proper care, nursing and medication the wound healed completely. When the foul smell stopped and the wound started healing, one day, John's son came to his father's home and told our care giver that he would have sent his father 'somewhere else' where 'some other people' could do this kind of dressing and activities! Anyhow, John has resumed his routine work on his farm now, growing vegetables. Now he goes to the market everyday to sell areca nuts and coconuts, all grown by him, and leads an independent life.

Another son was in a dilemma as to how to look after his mother as well as ensure the welfare of his family. When Shankran called me for help, his mother Parvathy Amma was totally bed-ridden. Shankaran and his wife were employed, but had taken leave on loss of pay for about six months, in order to give the mother total care and attention. But his mother's condition did not improve. I sent our volunteer Sathy there. She was given the duty of complete care of the patient, from morning to evening, till Shankaran came back from his office. Sathy helped the patient to get up from the bed, and made her do the routine exercises. She even made her walk slowly to the bathroom. (It is a natural happening that organs go into a state of inactivity, if not in use for a certain period. With the aid of proper physiotherapy and regular exercises, we can rejuvenate the cells and help these organs to recuperate from degenerative changes). After two months Parvathy Amma was able to do all her personal activities independently. Their son's letter of gratitude and appreciation, for our service, tells me how happy he is now with the recovery of his mother, which he had not in the least expected.

Similar was the case of Raghavan Nair, a 75-year-old retired teacher. He was also totally bed-ridden after an operation. He had TUR (TransUrethral Resection) for enlarged prostate. When I examined him I understood that he had no physical ailments at all. He had been bedridden after his surgery. But even after the prescribed rest period, he was afraid to get up from the bed. His relatives restricted his movements and dissuaded him from getting up for fear of an accidental fall. He was confined to his bed and was using a bed-pan. Whenever I visited him, I spent some time with him, giving him repeated assurances, and made the family members aware that only if they made him get up and walk would he become independent as before. I sent my volunteer Mary to the patient's house just for two days. The reassurance and self-confidence imparted by her made him free of his needless fears. Necessary instructions were given to the family also for the support of the patient. After one month Raghavan Nair came to see me, walking about one kilometer. He is back on track now.

Then there is the case of an eminent doctor in a very pathetic condition in his own son-in-law's nursing home. Following a minor surgery on the tongue, for biopsy, he was not taking any food, and he was not talking or getting up from the bed. When I entered his room he was curled up in the bed closing his eyes. The railings of the cot were raised. When I called to him he opened his eyes. Then I asked him, 'Why are you sleeping in the day time?' He said, 'Because I have nothing else to do'. His relatives, nurses and other staff of the nursing home, ready to do anything, surrounded him. I asked him why the railings of the cot were raised. He said it was done to prevent him from falling from the bed. I assured him that he would never fall down, and that all the people near him would support him even if he was in danger of falling. Then I lowered all the railings. I started talking to him about his younger days. He became very much interested and slowly he recovered from his depression. After a week, I could make him walk and come out of the room. After two weeks he started going to his daughter's home in the afternoons. His daughters and sisters were spellbound at his recovery, which was not at all expected. He went back to his house after a few months. I get news of him regularly through his sister, who is a friend of mine.

Bidding a Warm Adieu

Once, I had to witness the very tragic and miserable end of an eminent lady professor. One afternoon, I got a call from an old man asking me to come and see his sister, who was very sick and bedridden. On my way, I asked about the patient. I learnt that she was not staying with her brother. She was staying in an old age home. She had been sent out from her own house by her only daughter and son in law, when she had a fall and fractured femur, about three or four years ago. I was shocked to learn that she was an eminent professor who taught in a famous college in Palghat. She had taught a lot of eminent personalities, including a cabinet minister. I had heard of her in my childhood, as she had taught my elder brothers too. I had to witness her end, which happened within a few minutes of my visit. It was miserable. She did not have proper food, clothes, or medicines, not even a cot or a good bed. The old age home was only a portion of a house, run by a young couple for their livelihood. I had to perform her last rites, even though I had seen her for the first time. This event, I can never forget in my life.

Sadly, though some people are ready to look after their aged parents, the lack of medical awareness and knowledge about nursing care discourages them from carrying out their responsibilities. This makes the life of the aged miserable. The case of Santhamma, aged 83, is a case in point. She was totally bed-ridden with catheter in situ. When I visited her, her condition was pathetic. She was almost like a skeleton with her wrinkled skin. Her limbs were bent, incapable of movement. She was attended by a home-nurse, who was incompetent. When the patient had diarrhoea a few days before, she was not given any food, or any liquid for fear of increasing the diarrhoea. As a result, she was totally dehydrated. Without proper, periodical cleaning or removal, the catheter was blocked, and urine was leaking out of the catheter. With the help of our nursing assistant Lakshmikutty, I changed the catheter and gave the patient a bladder wash. We asked the family members to give her plenty of liquid to correct dehydration, instead of fearing a bed-wetting. Lakshmikutty visited her regularly for a week. It was a week of peace and painlessness for Santhammaa, which helped her to leave this world comfortably, without any suffering.

Another case, of 84-year-old Janaki Amma, was an encouraging one for my professional career and its primary goal. After an accidental fall, she was admitted to the hospital with a fractured hip. She has a daughter and a son, but both were settled in USA. They came and entrusted the care of their mother to their cousins in the neighbourhood and flew back. After her discharge from the hospital she was brought home, with Ryles tube for feeding and with a urinary catheter. She was diabetic and was in a semi-coma. Two home nurses were appointed to attend on her but they were indifferent to and incapable of looking after the bed-ridden patient. I sent our volunteers Lakshmikutty and Mary to her and they gave her proper care, like regular cleaning, physiotherapy, and feeding. After two weeks the lady was able to get up from the bed, sit on a chair and watch the TV. She started talking cheerfully, and shared jokes with our volunteers. After a month she expired one morning, without suffering any chronic symptoms.

My experience as a medial practitioner in rural areas brought home to me the fact that no one is ready to take over the responsibility of the helpless aged ones, who had once worked for their prosperity. This tendency is a moral flaw, which has badly affected our culture. Or is it a fall out of the rash modernisation of our social set-up? Sometimes it seems like it is indifference caused by the widening generation gap. Whatever it may be, the elderly have to suffer unnecessarily. Our hospice opens its doors to shores of peace. It aims at helping the sick and aged to go through their twilight years peacefully and comfortably, until they depart this world.

NOTES

1. Another factor is that due to the increase in the migration of younger people to other states and foreign countries for employment, there is a rapid decrease in the young supporting group.
2. In Kerala, the 60th year of life has been taken as point of turning old and we the Keralites celebrate it as a tradition, *Shashti Poorthi*. Traditionally, the aged had a respected position in the families earlier. They were the decision makers and the main pillar of the household. However, the State government employees here retire at the age of 55, which is the lowest retiring age in central and other state government services.

Index